The Color of America Has Changed

The Color of America Has Changed

How Racial Diversity Shaped
Civil Rights Reform in California,
1941–1978

Mark Brilliant

OXFORD
UNIVERSITY PRESS
2010

OXFORD

UNIVERSITY PRESS

Oxford University Press, Inc., publishes works that further
Oxford University's objective of excellence
in research, scholarship, and education.

Oxford   New York
Auckland   Cape Town   Dar es Salaam   Hong Kong   Karachi
Kuala Lumpur   Madrid   Melbourne   Mexico City   Nairobi
New Delhi   Shanghai   Taipei   Toronto

With offices in
Argentina   Austria   Brazil   Chile   Czech Republic   France   Greece
Guatemala   Hungary   Italy   Japan   Poland   Portugal   Singapore
South Korea   Switzerland   Thailand   Turkey   Ukraine   Vietnam

Published by Oxford University Press, Inc.
198 Madison Avenue, New York, New York 10016

www.oup.com

Oxford is a registered trademark of Oxford University Press

Library of Congress Cataloging-in-Publication Data
Brilliant, Mark.
The color of America has changed : how racial diversity shaped
civil rights reform in California, 1941–1978 / Mark Brilliant.
p. cm.
Includes bibliographical references and index.
ISBN 978-0-19-516050-5
1. California—Race relations—History—20th century. 2. Civil rights
movements—California—
History—20th century. 3. Minorities—California—History—20th century.
4. California—Ethnic
relations—History—20th century. 5. California—Social conditions—20th century. I. Title.
F870.A1B75   2010
305.89009794'09045—dc22   2009053907

1 3 5 7 9 8 6 4 2

Printed in the United States of America
on acid-free paper

Acknowledgments

In a better world, a book's acknowledgments would encompass as many pages as the book that those being acknowledged did so much to make possible. In the meantime, the length of this book, if not the length of these acknowledgments, is but a footnote next to the depth of my gratitude to the people without whom I would not have completed it.

Professors Ed Beiser, Tom James, Ted Sizer, and Alan Zuckerman of Brown University inspired me to throw myself into the class struggle (of sorts). "Why not walk some of that undergraduate idealism you talk," they each, in their own way, cajoled me, as they each, in their own way, tried to coax my trajectory into public high school teaching upon graduation.

With their prodding, I headed to Brooklyn. At Lafayette High School, I spent four of the most challenging and rewarding years of my life. It is there where the idea that evolved into this book began to emerge. As the multicultural curricular culture wars of the day raged, I wondered what shape a multicultural civil rights history of the United States might take, one that better reflected the diversity of the students I taught. For pointing me down this path and teaching me far more than I ever taught them, I am forever indebted to my many determined Lafayette students. I am equally indebted to the friendship, support, and lessons about history and how to teach it that I learned from the dedicated Lafayette teachers who took me under their wings, especially Pat Compton, Bruce Gleitman, Shelly Hyman, Rick Mangone, Tony Ruggiero, Phil Scroggins, and Al Teutonico.

Reading, researching, and writing *about* class (and race) struggles, which I undertook as a graduate student at Stanford University, is a far cry from being *in* them, as my Lafayette experience has never stopped reminding me. Though I sometimes felt guilty and often felt hypocritical about studying what I was studying where I was studying it—like I was spewing forth from a soap box perched beneath a palm tree—I always felt extraordinarily privileged to have the opportunity that Stanford's School of Education, where I first matriculated, and Department of History, to which I later transferred, gave me.

Beginning with my dissertation committee, David M. Kennedy, my principal adviser, embodies the very best of what it means to be a history professor—as a teacher, scholar, writer, and mentor. I will forever strive to achieve the stratospherically high standards he set and count myself lucky if I ever manage to arrive even a fraction of the way there. David Tyack was also an extraordinary graduate adviser and role model. His book on the history of urban education, which I read as an urban educator, inspired me to apply to graduate school, and his warmth and generosity kept me there when I contemplated leaving. Finally, Richard White, who arrived toward the end of my time at Stanford, disseminated trenchant insights at critical junctures in the final stages of my dissertation, as well as a stirring, albeit daunting, example of breadth and depth as an historian.

Beyond my dissertation committee, Al Camarillo believed in my work enough to support it for two wonderful years at Stanford's innovative Center for Comparative Studies in Race and Ethnicity, which he was so instrumental in creating. Many years later he did me the enormous favor of reading a near final draft of the book manuscript that the dissertation he supported in its formative years became. His assurance that I could and should finally let it go was instrumental in me doing so. William Nelson sponsored me for an extraordinary year as a Golieb Fellow in Legal History at New York University School of Law. There, he and the members of the lively colloquium he ran contributed immensely to burnishing the legal aspects of my work. Gordon Chang encouraged me early on to cast my historical net wider than San Francisco and assisted me with chapters as I heeded his wise counsel. Other faculty members who helped shape my dissertation in one way or another include Bart Bernstein, Larry Cuban, George Fredrickson, and Estelle Freedman.

After completing my doctorate, Yale University's Howard Lamar Center for the Study of Frontiers and Borders took me aboard as a postdoctoral fellow. There, Jay Gitlin, John Mack Faragher, Howard Lamar, George Miles, and Steve Pitti presented me with the gift of time, space, and critical feedback to begin the long haul of revising my dissertation into a book. They also introduced me to their talented group of graduate student "westerners," many of whom are now professors. Gerry Cadava, Ben Madley, Christian McMillen, Bob Morrissey, Dara Orenstein, Aaron Sachs, Ashley Sousa, Melissa Stuckey, and Julie Weise, among others, warmly welcomed me into their weekly "westerners" lunch, drafted me on to their department's softball team, and engaged me in instructive conversations about my work. Ben and I later reconnected at Berkeley. As my manuscript neared completion, he did me the enormous favor of meticulously editing and insightfully commenting on a draft of the entire thing, transporting it to a better place that it would not have reached without him.

Following my year at the Lamar Center, Jon Butler, who was then chair of Yale's Department of History, hired me as lecturer, offering me my first taste of life as a professor. During that rewarding year, I struck up friendships with fellow lecturer Andy Jewett and his wife, Healan Gaston, both of whom provided incisive input on chapters under revision. So, too, did Robert Johnston, whose vibrant family welcomed me into their home for many memorable evenings.

Other people who made my two years at Yale memorable included Seth Fein, Christiane Noakels, and Remo Fabrri.

As my time in New Haven wound down, the Department of History and Program in American Studies at the University of California, Berkeley afforded me the incredible opportunity to join their ranks as an assistant professor. From my rigorous job talk Q&A forward, my Berkeley colleagues pressed me to produce a book, as opposed to a revised dissertation. More importantly, they devoted long hours to help me realize their charge. Robin Einhorn, Paula Fass, Kerwin Klein, David Henkin, David Hollinger, Leon Litwack, Waldo Martin, Kathleen Moran, and Christine Rosen have each read more than one draft of my entire manuscript and more than that many drafts of particular chapters. They have also provided copious and critical written and oral feedback. David Hollinger has been especially generous with his time and input, which he first began providing when I solicited his advice as a graduate student.

Other Berkeley colleagues to whom I am grateful for sharing their precious time and valuable suggestions include Richie Abrams, Brian DeLay, Prachi Deshpande, John Efron, Victoria Frede, Jon Gjerde, Paul Groth, Jeff Hadler, Richard Hutson, Larry Levine, Robin Li, Goodwin Liu, Margaretta Lovell, Rebecca McLennan, Don McQuade, Martin Meeker, Tom and Barbara Metcalf, David Montejano, Dan Perlstein, Mark Peterson, Harry Scheiber, Andy Shanken, Richard Cándida Smith, Yuri Slezkine, Dick Walker, Wen-Hsin Yeh, and Peter Zinoman.

I also received tremendous input from the detailed reports generated by the "mid-career" review committees convened on my behalf by Beth Berry, chair of the Department of History, and Christine Rosen and Kathleen Moran, director and associate director of the Program in American Studies. Those reports, in turn, generated equally detailed and useful reports from the faculty meetings held to discuss them, which Beth, Christine, and Kathleen so helpfully distilled and shared with me. I only wish that the reports were not redacted, so I could do more here than extend a generic expression of gratitude to the numerous colleagues whose guiding voices are contained in them.

More than anything else, the friendships I forged with Jennifer Spear and Mark Healey have highlighted my time at Berkeley. Through countless conversations over, among other things, long walks with our water-loving dogs (in Jen's case) and long runs and bike rides (in Mark's case), Jen and Mark have contributed in inestimable ways to this book and even more to my life beyond it.

Beyond the individuals at the institutions where I have been formally affiliated, I received scrupulous and shrewd input on an early version of this book from David Gutiérrez and Henry Yu, as well as important contributions on one or more chapters from Louis Anthes, Rachel Bernard, Gareth Davies, Mike Engh, Neil Foley, Ruben Flores, Paul Frymer, Risa Goluboff, Tom Guglielmo, Daniel HoSang, Kevin Keenan, Mary Lui, Donna Murch, Dara Orenstein, Peggy Pascoe, Sam Roberts, Greg Robinson, Daniel Rodgers, Marc Rodriguez, Robert Self, Deedee Sullivan, Scott Tang, John Witt, and Chuck Wollenberg.

The bulk of this book's research took place in four repositories: Berkeley's Bancroft Library, the California State Archives in Sacramento, and Stanford's Special Collections and Hoover Institution. In addition, I visited—or received materials upon request from—numerous other places listed in the archival abbreviations. In response to my many requests for guidance, access, and, of course, copies, I never failed to receive anything but the most knowledgeable, skillful, and courteous assistance from, among others, Polly Armstrong, Brooke Black, Peter Blodgett, Jeff Crawford, Bill Frank, Michael Hironymous, Linda Johnson, Peter Kraus, David Kessler, Carol Leadenham, Jennifer Mandel, Steven Mandeville-Gamble, Karl Matsushita, Theresa Salazar, Wayne Silka, Susan Synder, and Genevieve Troka.

Interviews (either in person, over the phone, or through mail or e-mail) supplemented some of the archival work I conducted. For so generously sharing their time and recollections with me, I thank Stephen DeLapp, Quentin Kopp, Gigi (Marcus) Lane, Jacques Levy, Melissa Marcus, Sylvia Méndez, Fred Oyama, Phyllis Oyama, Ed Steinman, and Alice (Oyama) Yano.

The exceptional administrative and staff support I have received over the years has afforded me the luxury of being able to devote so much of my work time to my scholarship and teaching. For that I thank, among others, Christine Capper, Marianne Bartholomew-Couts, Marcia Condon, Alexis Cox, Jean Delaney, Amy Duncan, Yadira Figueroa, Leah Flanagan, Sabina Junega Garcia, Jill Gerstenberger, Molly Goetz, Barbara Hayashida, Margarita Ibarra, Linda Finch Hicks, Deborah Kerlegon, Mabel Lee, Ruth Lowy, Greg Martin, Lisa Mihajlovic, Philippa McFarlane, Hilja New, Gertrud Pacheco, Kristina Perkins, Lupe Ramirez, Margo Richardson, Teresa Rodriguez, Victor Rotenberg, Paul Schwochow, Tami Taisler, Darril Tighe, Monica Wheeler, and Catherine Woolf.

At Oxford University Press, Susan Ferber championed my book before it was even a done dissertation. Her rapid-fire responsiveness, indefatigable support (especially when I despaired of ever finishing), and, above all, expert editing, beginning even before OUP placed me under contract and continuing to the very end, proved indispensable. So, too, did the extensive and instructive comments Susan solicited from four readers. If this book is, like Swiss cheese, more than the sum of its absences, then Susan deserves enormous credit for that.

A remarkable circle of friends surrounds me. From the beginning of graduate school, Rob Reich has set a standard of fierce intellect and loyal friendship against which I measure myself and inevitably fall short. Now an associate professor in the Department of Political Science at Stanford, Rob has read practically every page of everything I have written, right down to an entire version of this book's penultimate draft. He has always helped me find the analytic "so what" amidst all of the narrative "what," while he and his dynamic partner, Heather Kirkpatrick, have always helped remind me of the far more important "so what" beyond the job.

Gina Marie Pitti was also there from the beginning of graduate school. A gifted historian whose own work has done much to shape my historical thinking, Gina, more than anyone else, accompanied me on the long and (because of her, much less) lonely march to the dissertation mountaintop. Not only did she carefully read all of my dissertation chapters (some more than once), but she always managed to steer me down the best path and away from all the others I would have foolishly followed without her.

I met David Greenberg during my Golieb Fellowship year in New York. We quickly became friends and started exchanging chapters shortly thereafter. I felt like a minor league ball player getting his first taste of the majors, as I read David's exquisitely crafted prose and received his meticulous line edits and extensive overall comments. That David went to such lengths on my behalf after we had only just met speaks volumes to the mensch that he is.

Matt Dallek introduced me to David. He also introduced me to genuine scholarly collaboration. In a gesture of uncommon decency, Matt shared with me binders full of materials he had culled from collections in the Bancroft Library, saving me weeks of time and scores of dollars. Matt's writing and scholarship have been inspirations, and his contributions to my writing and scholarship have been manifold.

Joe Crespino's father once ribbed him about his dissertation, "Son, when ya gonna finish that big ole' book report of yours?" Joe's friendship and feedback went a long way to helping me finish that "big ole' book report" of mine.

Other friends from graduate school whose contributions are embedded in this book in one way or another include Steve Andrews, Shana Bernstein, Rob Blecher, Liz and Kurt Borgwardt, Jana Bruns, Roberta Chavez, Joby Gardner and Martha Mabie Gardner, William Howell, Bill Koski, Akiba Lerner, Sameer Pandya, Nate Persily, Danny and Vered Porat, Jon Schoenwald, Joe Tringe, and Martín Valadez

Beyond Stanford, Andy, Kathy, Samantha, and Bradley Barish have been my family away from my family. My oldest and best friend, Andy has accompanied (and often bankrolled) me in the pursuit of our favorite pastime—chasing those elusive little rainbows (as in trout), which made chasing the even more elusive Clio a lot easier when I returned. My many years now in California have been enriched beyond measure by the wonderful Barish bunch with whom I have marked almost every major turn in our lives' wheels.

Wendy Rosov has been my alter ego from the time we met in graduate school through the time we became neighbors in Berkeley. One of my staunchest supporters and best sounding boards, Wendy's belief in me has pulled me through countless times that I did not share her faith. Her loyalty and generosity know no bounds. Thanks, too, to Peg Sandel (and Talya and Gaby) for enriching Wendy's life and embracing me and my family into the family that she and Wendy have begun to build together.

Ever since we didn't like each other when we first met at swimming practice in our first year as undergraduates, Steven Goode has been one of my closest friends. Goodey has always taken a keen interest in my scholarly as well as not-so scholarly pursuits. He not only read many of this book's chapters in their earliest and messiest incarnations, but he did so with a sharp eye and unsparing tongue for academic-ese. If the final product passes Goodey's muster, then I'll know I've done good. Thanks, too, to Nyla Goode for making Goodey better and being so good to me and my family.

Sean Kelly, another college friend and teammate, was a philosophy graduate student at Berkeley when I arrived at Stanford. As we rekindled our friendship, Sean often provided a crucial outside-the-discipline-but-still-in-the-academy perspective to assist me. Harvard's Department of Philosophy could not have a brighter or nicer chair.

Pat Murphy, still another college friend and teammate, and Julie Baker, introduced me to the exhilaration of rock climbing in Yosemite. Thanks to them for taking me away and, above all, not letting go when I was on belay.

During my Golieb Fellowship year in New York, I spent quality time with old friends from my high school teaching years. Richard Rivera and Cyndi Centeno honored me by asking me to be the (honorary Jewish) godfather to their beautiful daughter, Indira, who has only grown more so in every way in the years since. Always interested in my historical work, Richard peppered me with queries and pushed me to sharpen my ideas. Through Richard, I met Wendy Cortes with whom I spent much cherished time. Michael Buckley put me up and put up with me for a most memorable summer. Nelson Iocolano pressed me with his always kennly insightful points of view. Together, Richard, Mike, and Nelson have taught me a life's worth of lessons in loyalty.

Other friends—and dear family friends—who contributed to the completion of this book in one way or another include Judd and Anjali Brandeis, Sue, Julia, and David Goldberg, Colin Schmidt, Marvin and Joyce Stein, and James Wyatt.

Finally, my family . . .

During the years that it took me to produce this book, my cousins Susan, Paul, and Ellen Sugarman showered me with kindness—not to mention great fishing and fish—in Boston and Cape Cod. Cousins Shirley and Al Sokol took me into their wonderful home, family, and world in Brooklyn. Aunt Ronit and Uncle Jack Zimmerman took me on an unforgettable vacation in France, which did so much to jumpstart my graduate studies. They have been in my corner ever since. Uncle Jack Kalman, Purple Heart and all, always made me beam with pride with his stories from the World War II Pacific. Uncle Joe and Aunt Betty Kestenbaum bequeathed to me from a very young age a passion for history and Democratic politics, supplemented with clippings after clippings that arrived in the mail. Well into his nineties, Uncle Joe loved nothing better than walking me through his old Lower East Side stomping grounds, singing FDR's and Give 'Em Hell Harry's praises, while denouncing (and detailing) "the corruption in every Republican administration since Warren G. Harding."

My small but growing family in Israel—Unlcle Tal and Aunt Tirtza Brody; Kareen (Brody) Azrieli and Yoav, Hilah, Eden, and Yonatan Azrieli; Ron, Lena, Maya, and Noa Brody—has always made every effort to be as close to me as they can be despite all the distance between us. Their calls, e-mails, and pictures, coupled with the time we've managed to find together, have always served to spur me on to the finish line with the hope that after I reach it there will be more time for all of us to be together.

No one values education more than my Grandma Shirley Brody. Over the course of her now 102 years, she has done everything in her power to insure that her children, grandchildren, and great grandchildren receive the best possible formal education, which she herself never had. She is a gift and inspiration.

My brother Jon has long been a source of inspiration and pride for me. If I had a fraction of his resilience, courage, and perseverance, I'd have finished this book years ago. My sister Ellen has been no less a source of inspiration, as well as admiration. She has long lived the type of activist's life about which folks like me only write. Scott Ingvoldstad was as lucky to find her as I am lucky to have him as my brother-in-law, and their son, Baschen, as a nephew.

Lisa Frydman has been better than the woman of my dreams from the moment she entered my life. She has lived through every word in these pages, each of which has her love and legal eagle influence etched upon it. Many "public interest" lawyers figure favorably in this book. Lisa equals them all in my mind in terms of her skill and dedication and exceeds them all when it comes to the profound lack of self-righteousness with which she pursues her profoundly righteous work. My respect for her could not reach higher, and my love for her could not run deeper.

Lisa is also an equally extraordinary parent, thanks in larger part to the example of her own extraordinary parents, Ami and Rita. Fortunately for me, the Frydman's are a package deal—the familial equivalent of the gift that never stops giving. For giving so much to me, even when I was too often too consumed by work to respond in kind, I thank Ami and Rita, Dahlia and Bryan Weiss, Dan Frydman and Anita Trush, and Juliana, Jake, Jonathan, Joey, and Cid. I am especially grateful to Rita for the weeks she spent in Berkeley to help out as I struggled to finish up—and to Ami for supporting me by parting with her for that long.

When Ezra Max Brilliant was born in August 2008, I discovered that the house of myself that I thought I knew so well after so many years had another room, and in that room there was a closet, and in that closet there was a shoe-box, and in that shoebox I could fit the house that I knew before Ezra. He is the joy of the world, and I look forward to enjoying him all the more now that this book is done. That I was able to enjoy him as much as I did during his first year without risking my career owes in good measure to the architects of the UC Faculty Family Friendly Edge program. They designed enlightened policies that children of all working parents should receive, as Ezra did and for which I am forever grateful.

Lastly, my parents, Marvin and Renee Brilliant. More than anyone and anything else, their boundless love and tireless labors of love (of one kind) made this finally ending labor of love (of another kind) possible. To you, Mom and Dad, I dedicate this book.

Contents

Abbreviations of Organizations

ACLU	American Civil Liberties Union
ACRR	American Council on Race Relations
CIC-LA	Catholic Interracial Council of Los Angeles
CCFP	California Committee for Fair Practices
CCFEP	California Committee for Fair Employment Practices
CFCU	California Federation for Civic Unity
CREA	California Real Estate Association
CSO	Community Service Organization
FEPC	Fair Employment Practices Commission
FWA	Farm Workers Association
JACL	Japanese American Citizens League
MALDEF	Mexican American Legal Defense and Educational Fund
MAPA	Mexican American Political Association
NAACP	National Association for the Advancement of Colored People
NAACP-WC	National Association for the Advancement of Colored People, West Coast Regional Office
NFLU	National Farm Labor Union
SRRC	State Reconstruction and Reemployment Commission
UFW	United Farm Workers

The Color of America Has Changed

INTRODUCTION: CALIFORNIA AND THE WIDE CIVIL RIGHTS MOVEMENT

"What Americans must realize, what they can no longer afford to ignore," declared Carey McWilliams in 1943, "is the simple and obvious fact that the color of America has changed."[1] McWilliams's pronouncement, published in his *Brothers Under the Skin*, was as prescient as it was anomalous. Presciently, it anticipated by half a century a chorus of similar statements made by journalists, scholars, and policy makers.[2] Anomalously, it cut against the prevailing binary view of the "race problem" in the 1940s. "To most Americans," wrote a reviewer of *Brothers Under the Skin* in the *Nation*, "the race problem means only the Negro problem, and few even know that the term 'colored people' applies to any races other than the Negro."[3]

No book published in the 1940s did more to reinforce the predominant understanding of the "race problem" as the "Negro problem" than Gunnar Myrdal's 1,500 page opus, *An American Dilemma: The Negro Problem and Modern Democracy*.[4] Myrdal's path to *An American Dilemma* stretched from Sweden, where he was an internationally recognized economist, to the American South, where he conducted his research. Viewed from the former Confederacy, it made perfect sense to maintain, as Myrdal did, that the plight of African Americans differed in kind, rather than degree, from that of all other racial groups.[5] Although Myrdal acknowledged "other problems of race relations," he paid little attention to them.[6] Explaining their omission, Myrdal reasoned, "There is a quantitative difference between . . . the discrimination against the Negro," on the one hand, and other "'racial' minorities," on the other hand, which "is so great that it becomes qualitative." For Myrdal, the "Negro problem" stood alone as "America's greatest and most conspicuous scandal."[7]

McWilliams thought differently. Unlike Myrdal, who approached the "race problem" from the South, McWilliams's route to *Brothers Under the Skin* ran from the Colorado Rockies through southern California. Viewed from America's "racial frontier," as McWilliams referred to the West, in general, and the Pacific coast, in particular, McWilliams maintained, "We have . . . overemphasized the Negro and failed to correlate the Negro problem . . . with the Chinese problem, the Mexican problem, the Filipino problem."[8] This premise expressed itself in the structure of his book about "colored minorities."[9] Only the book's penultimate chapter addressed "the Negro Problem." The preceding chapters presented histories of Americans of Native, Chinese, Mexican, Japanese, Hawaiian, Puerto Rican, and Filipino descent. *Brothers Under the Skin* thus painted a very different picture than *An American Dilemma*: a country crisscrossed by color lines, riven with multiple "race problems," rather than bisected by the lone color line of the "Negro problem."[10]

At the time of its publication, no state reflected this pluralization of the "race problem" better than California, as McWilliams captured in an unpublished essay on the "strange shiftings and changes in our minority racial groups" wrought by World War II. As rural farm workers headed to urban airplane factories and shipyards or joined the armed services, tens of thousands of Mexican braceros (imported Mexican agricultural workers on short-term contracts) replaced them, causing "some friction between [the] importees and [the] . . . resident Mexican population," the latter of whom comprised 7.2 percent (758,400) of the state population by 1950. Meanwhile, hundreds of thousands of African Americans flocked to California's cities from beyond the state's borders, increasing their percentage of the population to 4.4 percent (462,172) by 1950 from 1.8 percent (124,306) in 1940. Their arrival, McWilliams asserted, introduced "an entirely new problem." African Americans were neither "aliens" nor "foreigners," and they brought with them the "backing of important national . . . organizations," as well as a "strong press [and] church." None of these advantages, however, precluded them from being barred from vast segments of the housing market by racially restrictive covenants. As a result, they had little choice but to take up residence in places vacated by the tens of thousands of Californians of Japanese descent (1.4 percent of the state's population, or 93,717, in 1940, and 0.8 percent of the state's population, or 84,956, in 1950)—both American-born citizens and Japanese-born immigrants deemed by courts and Congress ineligible to become citizens through naturalization—who were torn from their Little Tokyos (and elsewhere) and forcibly relocated to internment camps. By contrast, Californians of Chinese descent (0.6 percent of the state's population, or 39,556, in 1940, and 0.6 percent of the state's population, or, 58,324, in 1950) experienced job opportunities previously denied to them. In addition, they witnessed the repeal of the Chinese Exclusion Act in 1943, which had barred both Chinese immigration and naturalization (prohibitions that would remain in effect for Japanese immigrants for nearly another decade). Taken together, these developments highlighted the complex contours of race on America's "racial frontier"—a much more variegated milieu than Myrdal or most Americans knew. They also pointed to California's equally complex civil rights era, during which a plethora of precedent-setting developments would illuminate the non-binary (neither white/black, nor white/nonwhite) nature of civil rights making in multiracial settings.[11]

The Color of America Has Changed examines the civil rights consequences of California's racial diversity—how America's "racial frontier" became America's civil rights frontier. Focusing on a wide range of legal and legislative initiatives pursued by a diverse group of reformers—racial liberal lawyers, lawmakers, and leaders in statewide civil rights organizations—it begins with the cases that challenged California's multiracial forms of legalized segregation in the 1940s and concludes with a brief discussion of the conundrum created by the multiracial affirmative action program at issue in the United States Supreme Court's 1978 *Regents of the University of California v. Bakke* decision. From World War II through *Bakke*, California's multiple "race problems" shaped and complicated the multifaceted efforts of civil rights reformers to resolve them. In the process, the Golden State emerged as a civil rights vanguard for the nation.

This cutting edge status owed in part to the numerous civil rights firsts or near-firsts that occurred in California. To begin with, the cases that dismantled the state's legalized segregation in the second half of the 1940s included the first United States Supreme Court decisions against laws targeting Japanese immigrants deemed "aliens ineligible to citizenship," including, most notoriously, the Alien Land Law; the first federal court rulings against the particular application of school segregation to students of Mexican descent; and the first cases, in either federal or state courts, to strike down judicial enforcement of racially restrictive housing covenants, as well as a state law prohibiting interracial marriage.[12]

As California's civil rights struggles moved beyond legalized segregation, the state was at the forefront of fair housing litigation and legislation. Fair housing, along with fair employment, were the top civil rights priorities for African Americans across the country outside the South, where toppling Jim Crow was the focus.[13] During the 1950s, California-based NAACP attorneys spearheaded the nation's first courtroom victories against segregation in both public housing and private housing tract developments supported by government backed mortgages.[14]

This momentum began to carry into the legislative arena in the late 1950s. Under Democratic governor Edmund G. (Pat) Brown, California enacted some of the country's first state civil rights laws covering employment, businesses, and housing. Brown's active support of these measures earned him and his state a reputation as a national civil rights leader. Brown proved far less supportive of a host of agricultural labor-related proposals. Nevertheless, California was an epicenter of Mexican American civil rights advocacy, much of which made agricultural labor rights synonymous with civil rights. In this realm, the campaigns led by César Chávez resonated nationally.[15]

Moving from the fields to the classrooms, California was also the site of precedent-setting educational civil rights litigation in the 1970s. This included cases involving de facto segregation in school districts whose student bodies encompassed more than black and white students; bilingual education for non-English-speaking Chinese immigrant students; and affirmative action in higher education admissions for African Americans, Asian Americans, Latinos, and Native Americans. The bilingual education and affirmative action cases reached the United States Supreme Court in 1974 and 1978, respectively.[16]

Just as California was a national bellwether for civil rights action, so, too, was it a harbinger of national civil rights reaction. In 1964, state voters resoundingly rejected a 1963 fair housing law, which, in turn, anticipated the 1966 eclipse of Pat Brown by Ronald Reagan. This shifting of the state's ideological center of gravity would be reprised in the presidential election of 1968. As gubernatorial candidate in 1966 and 1970 and governor from 1966 to 1974, Reagan patented a "Southwestern strategy." A complement to his party's much better known and infamous "Southern strategy," Reagan's Southwestern strategy grew out of his recognition of growing Mexican American disaffection with Brown, for devoting too much attention to African American civil rights and too little attention to Mexican American civil rights. As part of this strategy, Reagan courted Mexican American voters by pitting bilingual education (which he supported) against school desegregation through busing (which he opposed). GOP leaders from Richard Nixon to George W. Bush would later adopt versions of Reagan's Southwestern strategy.[17]

Although these many separate, precedent-setting threads of California's civil rights history provide a powerful basis for viewing the state as a national civil rights vanguard, the tapestry they create when stitched together provides an even more compelling claim. It reveals the unique challenges and disparate shapes of civil rights making in multiracial places. In the large swaths of the United States where the "race problem" was synonymous with the "Negro problem," civil rights reformers concentrated their attention on that fight. Their efforts made resolving the "Negro problem" synonymous with the civil rights movement. In California, however, the presence of multiple "race problems," each of which tended to attach itself to the state's different racial groups in different ways or degrees, militated against the making of a single civil rights movement. Instead, the state witnessed a diverse, and mostly divergent, set of civil rights struggles. Put another way, the bulk of California's civil rights litigation and legislation action took place in the wide space between the poles of cooperative interracial coalitions and contentious conflicts between potential coalition members.

This was not due to an absence of attempts to come together; on the contrary, from the 1940s forward, civil rights reformers issued frequent calls and engaged in fleeting efforts, to join forces. Nor was it due to disagreement over ultimate goals. Like their counterparts across the country, California's civil rights reformers espoused the basic tenets of racial liberalism, which grew out of New Deal liberalism. If the safety net the New Deal unfurled offered what Franklin Roosevelt described as "greater security for the average man than he has ever known in the history of America," then racial liberalism sought to stretch that net.[18] It endeavored to help deliver the nation's not-so-chosen people, increasingly referred to as "minorities" or "colored minorities" in the 1940s, to Roosevelt's promised land, which had proven far more welcoming to whites.[19] "While we have moved away from *laissez faire* doctrines in economics," Carey McWilliams wrote about the changes wrought by New Deal liberalism, "we still anachronistically pursue *laissez faire* theories in population matters." Racial liberalism proposed to correct that anachronism, which McWilliams attributed to a misplaced aversion to harnessing state power for "democratic objectives."[20] It represented what he referred to elsewhere as a "movement to outlaw racial discrimination by direct legislation," as well as litigation.[21]

To this end, what *security* was to New Deal liberalism, *nondiscrimination* and *equal opportunity* were to racial liberalism.[22] These were the terms that figured most prominently in the racial liberals' lexicon and best encapsulated their aspirations. In their pursuit of this goal, racial liberals were strategic and pragmatic in their civil rights decision-making rather than wedded to a fixed ideological agenda. Seeking to leverage change through the legal and political systems meant prioritizing litigation and legislation choices based on a tactical sense of what was possible in particular times and venues. As cases were won, and bills were passed, and times changed, racial liberals pursued new variations on racial liberalism's protean and capacious antidiscrimination theme, some of which had previously been dismissed as impossible.[23]

Though hardly a panacea for redressing the deep-seated, structural nature of racial inequalities, racial liberalism was more than a feebly focused attempt to achieve mere formal legal equality through the dismantling of legalized segregation, as some critics charge.[24] According to these critics, when World War II ended, the liberal/labor/left civil rights coalition that had been forged in the 1930s and solidified in the 1940s pushed for an expanded and permanent version of the wartime Fair Employment Practices Commission (FEPC) established by Roosevelt's Executive Order 8802 in 1941 to combat racial discrimination in defense industries. After the war, however, as the iron curtain fell abroad and the anticommunist chill set in at home, a coalition of northern business interests and southern segregationists portrayed the wartime FEPC as a communist plot, quashing the realization of anything like it until the enactment of the 1964 Civil Right Act.[25] With hopes for a permanent FEPC dashed, civil rights activism retreated to politically safer and substantively narrower ground. The NAACP, as historian Jacquelyn Dowd Hall writes, "abandoned both economic issues and the battle against segregation in the North and devoted its considerable resources to clear-cut cases of de jure segregation in the South." In so doing, she continues, "the link between race and class" which FEPC had embodied, "weaken[ed]."[26] Historian Robert Korstad offers a similar assessment. "The black challenge of the 1950s and 1960s," he writes, "marginalize[d] economic concerns" and privileged instead "a single-issue attack on Jim Crow."[27] The "opportunities found" during World War II, Korstad and Nelson Lichtenstein lament, were "lost" thereafter.[28]

This declensionist interpretation of the early civil rights era certainly reflects developments in the South and in Congress, where a permanent FEPC was, indeed, a dream deferred while dismantling Jim Crow became the focus of so much attention. A markedly different history, however, unfolded in California.[29] With litigation campaigns against legalized segregation over before the Cold War had barely begun, the state's racial liberals pursued precisely the kinds of antidiscrimination measures that were off the table in the South and Congress.[30] Viewed from California, then, dispersion, rather than declension, describes the trajectory (or, more accurately, trajectories) of racial liberalism from World War II forward. Viewed from California, too, the challenge to racial liberalism was as much internal as external—as much about how to forge a movement out of the multiplicity of "race problems" confronted by the diversity of "colored minorities" as about how to sustain a civil rights reform agenda during the Cold War that reached beyond the pursuit of mere formal legal equality through litigation against legalized segregation.

To rise to this challenge and secure their overarching objective of equality of opportunity through antidiscrimination litigation and legislation, California's civil rights reformers often analogized the plights of different minority groups. They accentuated the discrimination in general that each group faced in order to help facilitate coalition building across groups on behalf of particular antidiscrimination litigation and legislation goals. "Discrimination or unfair treatment against any minority," declared attorneys for the Japanese American Citizens League (JACL) in 1947, "redounds to the detriment of all minorities."[31] What was in the civil rights interests of one minority, in other words, was also in the civil rights interests of other minorities. Such analogical proximity provided the basis for a common front, at least in theory.

In practice, the analogy and its presumption of a harmony of civil rights interests between racial groups and, in turn, a natural alliance between them could only be pressed so far. As those same JACL attorneys acknowledged, each of the state's "racial groups" confronted "problems" that were "necessarily varied and different" from one another.[32] Although California civil rights reformers might have been united behind the ultimate aim of racial liberalism, they often found themselves divided over the specific antidiscrimination measures they prioritized in their litigation and legislation agendas. Herein lay the challenge of racial diversity to racial liberalism: the tension over how to reconcile a sameness (or universalism) with respect to ends with a difference (or particularism) with respect to means.

During the 1940s, for example, civil rights lawyers sought to dismantle the state's multiracial segregation statutes that "applied to all non-Caucasian groups" with mere "minor variations" between them, as McWilliams wrote in 1947.[33] Those minor differences, however, proved major enough to force the litigation down separate tracks, reflecting how legalized segregation affected African Americans, Japanese Americans, and Mexican Americans differently. Distinctions without much of a difference on the diagnostic side—variations on a general theme of racial discrimination—proved to be distinctions with a difference on the prescriptive side. Distinct civil rights priorities reflected distinct racialized experiences.[34] Different axes of discrimination demanded different avenues of redress.[35]

The institutional imperatives of litigation and legislation only exacerbated the challenge of racial diversity to racial liberalism. Initiating a court case or introducing a legislative bill required abstract general principles to be pressed into and pursued down discrete channels. In this way, the processes of litigation and legislation operated like a prism on light. They refracted the ostensibly singular phenomenon of racial discrimination into a spectrum of antidiscrimination cases and bills, further militating against the making of a multiracial civil rights movement despite the hopes of California racial liberals to forge one. For this reason, too, though the separate streams of California's civil rights struggles occasionally crossed, they never converged into a civil rights movement river.

This lack of confluence, however, did not preclude the realization of consequential civil rights reforms; indeed, though they were less cohesive than the movement in the American South, California's civil rights struggles were, considered as a whole, more robust in terms of their legal and legislative reform agendas and accomplishments. Nor did this lack of confluence owe to lack of trying to build interracial coalitions in order to forge a multiracial civil rights movement. In fact, this book begins with one such effort.

Chapter 1 focuses on the founding and foundering of the California Federation for Civic Unity (CFCU) at the end of World War II, one of dozens of California racial liberal organizations launched during the 1940s. Distinguished by its combined statewide and interracial focus, the CFCU struggled from its inception to find common ground—a "united front of all the minority groups," as one San Francisco NAACP and CFCU leader put it—in the face of the wide range of "race problems" those groups faced.[36]

While the CFCU groped for common ground, lawyers representing Japanese Americans, Mexican Americans, and African Americans, respectively, spearheaded a series of separate cases against California's various forms of legalized segregation during the second half of the 1940s. Chapter 2 examines the challenge to the Alien Land Law brought by the Japanese American Citizens League (JACL)—*Oyama v. California*—which reached the United States Supreme Court in 1948. Chapter 3 focuses on the challenge to the segregation of Mexican American students in California's public schools. *Mendez v. Westminster School District of Orange County*, which culminated in the Ninth Circuit Court of Appeals in 1947, took aim at the claim that most (though not all) students of Mexican descent possessed inadequate proficiency in English to attend non-"Mexican" schools. Chapter 4 considers the fair employment legislation and fair housing litigation priorities pursued by the West Coast Regional Office of the NAACP (NAACP-WC) during the second half of the 1940s, after having opened in San Francisco in 1944. It pays particular attention to the legal campaign against racially restrictive housing covenants, whose victims were overwhelmingly African American. California was the nation's epicenter for this litigation, which earned the NAACP-WC-affiliated attorney most associated with it a prominent place alongside the national NAACP's leading litigators in the United States Supreme Court case that ruled against the constitutionality of judicial enforcement of racially restrictive housing covenants in 1948. That same year, as Chapter 4 also discusses, the California Supreme Court delivered the nation's first decision against a state interracial marriage ban similar to those on the statute books in thirty other states at the time.

Individually, the cases examined in Chapters 2–4 marked the first major victories in California's post-World War II civil rights struggles. Collectively they toppled the state's matrix of legalized segregation, compressing into a few years what would not begin in the South until 1954 with *Brown v. Board of Education* and would not end until 1967 with *Loving v. Virginia*. Collectively, too, they demonstrated how a common problem—state-sanctioned segregation—did not lend itself to a common solution, namely, a coordinated litigation campaign.

The divergent trajectories reflected in the diverse challenges to legalized segregation in the 1940s continued into the 1950s, as racial liberalism in California ventured down antidiscrimination legislation and litigation roads that began where legalized segregation ended. During the 1950s, which is the chronological focus of Chapter 5, the NAACP-WC supplanted the CFCU, which disbanded in 1956. As the most prominent statewide civil rights organization, the NAACP-WC continued to pursue the fair employment legislation and fair housing litigation agenda it had articulated in the 1940s. These priorities, NAACP-WC leaders believed, were of equal importance to all "colored minority persons throughout the region," as the organization's regional director put it. However, advocacy organizations for Californians of Mexican and Japanese descent belied the NAACP-WC's reasoning by analogy in their pursuit of other forms of antidiscrimination legislation. Most notably, as Chapter 5 discusses, the burgeoning Mexican American Community Service Organization (CSO), out of which César Chávez would emerge, campaigned for a state law to provide old-age pensions for long-term resident noncitizens, a preponderance of whom were born in Mexico.

That none of the NAACP-WC's or CSO's legislative goals were enacted until the end of the 1950s attests to how legislating antidiscrimination posed a far more formidable challenge to civil rights reformers than litigating legalized segregation. The latter, according to McWilliams, "was accepted throughout the state with scarcely a murmur of audible protest," while the former spawned stiff and insurmountable resistance.[37] This resistance began to crack (though hardly disappeared) as a result of the election of 1958, as Chapter 6 documents. Upon assuming office, Governor Pat Brown made civil rights—or, more specifically, the NAACP-WC's civil rights agenda—a top priority. He threw himself behind legislation for fair employment in 1959 and fair housing in 1963. In the process, he reasoned by analogy from the plight of African Americans to that of other nonwhite groups, positing a harmony of civil rights interests among them. Meanwhile, leaders representing organizations from the largest one of those groups—Mexican Americans—pursued an agenda focusing on other issues, including old-age pensions for long-term resident noncitizens, stemming the tide of Mexican-immigrant agricultural laborers, and securing a minimum wage, unemployment insurance, and collective bargaining rights for domestic farm workers. Only on the first of these Mexican American civil rights priorities did Brown deliver.

Civil rights issues contributed to the demise of Brown and the rise of his successor, Ronald Reagan, as Chapter 7 demonstrates. Though a Brown speechwriter would remember the years 1959 to 1963 as a time when "liberalism was . . . rolling," it was not rolling in the direction that Chávez and an increasing number of Mexican American leaders desired.[38] Moreover, with the hard-fought passage of fair housing legislation in 1963, it would soon be rolling off a cliff. Reagan's trouncing of Brown in November 1966 was due, in no small part, to his vocal opposition to fair housing. While Reagan campaigned against fair housing, he also courted the growing number of Mexican American voters whom the Brown administration had disappointed. Reagan's resounding success with white laborers and moderate (though, for a Republican, unprecedented) success with Mexican Americans underscored the fragility of the coalition of Democrats with labor and minority groups that a Brown adviser predicted in 1960 would endure for years.

By the late 1960s and early 1970s, California's largely separate civil rights struggles collided, as Chapter 8 details. During Reagan's first term, school desegregation decisions in Los Angeles in 1970 and San Francisco in 1971 made "forced busing," as its opponents decried it, the wedge issue that "forced housing" had been in the 1960s. Burgeoning bilingual education initiatives added fuel to the "forced busing" fire. Leaders in the Mexican American Legal Defense and Educational Fund (MALDEF) recognized a tension between desegregation and bilingual education, while Reagan exploited it in his 1970 re-election bid. Busing for desegregation, he maintained, would come at the expense of bilingual education programs. The conflict between these two educational civil rights policies manifested itself most dramatically in San Francisco in the early 1970s. There a desegregation suit brought by the NAACP ran into opposition from San Franciscans of Mexican and, especially, Chinese descent. Concurrently, a bilingual education case on behalf of non-English-speaking Chinese immigrant students, with input from MALDEF on behalf of Spanish-speaking students, wended its way to the United States Supreme Court, where it scored a major victory in 1974. Thereafter, as schools across the country grappled with how to reconcile desegregation with bilingual education, Americans increasingly encountered the challenge of multiracial civil rights making, with which Californians had been grappling for decades.

Carey McWilliams's pluralization of the "race problem" in *Brothers Under the Skin* is among the reasons his contemporary admirers have annointed him an "American prophet."[39] His reformist aspirations, however, obscured his foresight. Though rightfully hailed as "one of the earliest U.S. figures to see race through California eyes," McWilliams neglected to follow the logic of his multipronged diagnosis through to multipronged policy prescriptions.[40] Instead, he concluded *Brothers Under the Skin* with a call for a sweeping, one-size-fits-all "national policy against discrimination." This "Fair Racial Practice Act" would encompass "all colored minority groups."[41] It stemmed from his conviction that the differences he identified in the discrimination experienced by "colored minorities" paled in comparison to their overarching similarity and could be addressed in one fell policy swoop. Anticipating the reasoning by analogy that so many California civil rights reformers would adopt, McWilliams presented the "Negro problem" as of a piece with the other "race problems," as if racism afflicted "colored minorities" in more or less the same way. Similar problems, in turn, would lend themselves to similar solutions. This presumption made good sense when considered from the perspective of someone hoping to construct multiracial coalitions around common policy goals. However, it stood in uneasy tension with the particularities of the "race problems" it sought to analogize— particularities the legal and legislative processes only accentuated. Commencing almost on cue with the publication of *Brothers Under the Skin*, California's post–World War II civil rights struggles would quickly expose the limits of McWilliams's prophetic vision. They would also compel a rethinking of America's civil rights era history, such as the one this book offers.

For very good and obvious reasons, civil rights historians have long set their sights on the South.[42] More recently, they have turned their attention to the North and advanced a "long civil rights movement" interpretation. Chronologically, this interpretation locates the civil rights movement's origins during the New Deal and acceleration during World War II, rather than in the mid-1950s with *Brown v. Board of Education* and the Montgomery Bus Boycott. Substantively, it emphasizes how the movement's reform aspirations were broader than the attainment of formal legal racial equality through the dismantling of Jim Crow laws (at least initially, before the Cold War banished the movement's radical members and with them their more radical agenda). Geographically, it highlights the breadth and depth of civil rights struggles in various northern locales occurring contemporaneously with, rather than subsequently to, those in the South.[43]

As important as these revisions have been, they remain incomplete, especially when considered in light of California's role as a civil rights vanguard for the nation. In particular, the efforts of "long civil rights movement" historians to direct "our attention northward" have either left the West out or simply conflated it with the North, defined as anything outside the South.[44] Yet, if racism and the attempts to combat it manifested themselves in different ways on either side of the Mason-Dixon line, as historian Thomas Sugrue notes, they took even more variegated shapes in those places west of the one hundredth meridian, like California, where the "race problem" was never singular, never simply synonymous with, nor reducible by analogy to, the "Negro problem."[45]

Of course, leading historians of the American West have long recognized racial diversity as one of the region's defining attributes. Richard White has called attention to the West's "peculiar pattern of race relations," and Elliott West to its "interactions" and "conflicts" among "many racial/ethnic groups."[46]

John Mack Faragher has urged scholars to tell "the story of the many disparate groups that make up the modern West." Doing so promises to remodel "'the black/white binary' (or the practice of defining race relations as, primarily, the interactions of whites and African Americans)," as Patricia Nelson Limerick has described it—to write "a history that matches our census," as West has urged.[47] These observations and exhortations, however, have not suggested what shape such a remodeling might take—or, more specifically, what analytic difference the West's demographic differences might make for understanding its civil rights history in comparison with and contrast to that of the South and North.[48]

Nor, for that matter, have the burgeoning number of scholars who have answered the call to examine race relations through the comparative, multiracial lens of California and other places in the West.[49] Much of this new scholarship concentrates on cities and the degree to which conflict or cooperation or some combination of both captures the dynamics of "multiracial relations."[50] While the state-level account presented here addresses instances of conflict and cooperation, it concentrates on the space between them—the separate tracks of civil rights along which the preponderance of civil rights action in California unfolded. More importantly, this book advances a conceptual framework— different axes of discrimination, different avenues of redress—to capture the contours and point to the consequences of civil rights making in multiracial settings.[51]

Ultimately, *The Color of America Has Changed* calls for rethinking the civil rights era as not only "long" but also "wide"—wide geographically, wide demographically, and most importantly, wide substantively in terms of the range of "race problems" and responses to them. Only through such a widened lens can this momentous period in United States history be apprehended as the national phenomenon that it was.[52] Moreover, only through such a widened lens does a multiracial civil rights past that illuminates America's increasingly multiracial civil rights present and future come into view.

CHAPTER 1

"AN INTEGRATED . . . PROGRAM FOR RACIAL JUSTICE"

Joseph James was a baritone before he became a boilermaker. Trained at Boston University's College of Music, James came to San Francisco in 1939 as part of a Federal Theatre Project troupe to perform in the 1939 Golden Gate International Exposition. When the exposition ended, James remained. The World War II economy afforded him the opportunity to pursue a second career as a welder in the yards of the Marinship Corporation in Sausalito, just north of San Francisco.[1]

Marinship had an agreement with the International Brotherhood of Boilermakers, Iron Shipbuilders, and Helpers of America to employ only union members. For African Americans, however, the Boilermakers, made an exception, at least for the first year or so of Marinship's operation. Local No. 6, which had jurisdiction at the shipyard, barred them from membership, but cleared them to work. Then, on August 14, 1943, Local No. 6 chartered Auxiliary A-41, a separate and unequal union lodge, whose members were required to pay same and equal dues. All African American Marinship workers, Local No. 6 decreed, needed to join Auxiliary A-41 in order to receive union work clearance.[2]

James refused to be relegated to what he denounced as a "Jim Crow fake union." He mounted a campaign to eliminate Auxiliary A-41 and integrate Local No. 6. Until that happened, James and his supporters withheld payment of their union dues. In response, the company, at the union's behest, refused to employ them.[3]

Thurgood Marshall, head of the NAACP Legal Defense and Educational Fund, flew from New York to San Francisco to represent James. Over the course of the next year, Marshall remained closely involved in the case as it wended its way through federal and state courts. During that time, James became president of the San Francisco chapter of the NAACP. As James's case unfolded, the budding local labor and NAACP leader began to harbor bigger organizational dreams for his adopted city. "I have long visualized a united front of all the minority groups," he wrote Marshall.[4]

James's vision began to take shape at the statewide level in 1945 in what would soon become known as the California Federation for Civic Unity (CFCU).

The CFCU, on whose first board of directors James served, was one of scores of organizations that sprouted across the country during the 1940s "to promote better race relations," as Fisk University's *Monthly Summary of Events and Trends in Race Relations* described them in late 1943.[5] One of these new groups was the Chicago-based American Council on Race Relations (ACRR), which helped launch the CFCU. Shortly after its formation, an ACRR leader told an audience at the annual convention of the NAACP, "Now interest in the whole realm of race relations is surging with a vigor and scope undreamed of when the NAACP was organized, that would not have been thought possible even ten or five years ago."[6] Two years later, another ACRR leader counted approximately three hundred "race relations committees" across the country.[7] In California alone, James identified nearly sixty organizations "known variously as 'Councils for Civil Unity' [and] inter-racial committees."[8]

The proliferation of these groups, which represented an organizational expression of the rise of racial liberalism during World War II, lent credence to a prediction that Carey McWilliams ventured in October 1944. Having long been in the "vanguard of aggression" against "racial minorities," California would, in the postwar period, "lead the nation" in the opposite direction and "establish a new pattern of race relationships . . . that would have national and even international importance."[9] The state that journalist John Gunther would describe on the first page of his *Inside U.S.A.* in 1947 as the nation's "most sophisticated and most bigoted" would see, in McWilliams's vision of the future, the forces of sophistication triumph over the forces of bigotry.[10]

McWilliams joined James in helping to establish the CFCU, serving on its first advisory council.[11] The CFCU stood apart from California's other racial liberal groups owing to its combined statewide, rather than local, and interracial, rather than intraracial, focus.[12] Like McWilliams, the CFCU recognized a wide range of "race problems." Like McWilliams, the CFCU viewed these "race problems" as sharing much in common with one another—as "not entirely distinct."[13] Like McWilliams, the CFCU called for legislation and litigation to replace the state's "laissez-faire" approach to "majority-minority relations."[14] Finally, like McWilliams, the CFCU believed that "an integrated . . . program for racial justice" could be developed.[15]

This belief, however, existed in uneasy tension with the CFCU's recognition of the "real distinctions" between the problems in California, and elsewhere in the West, as opposed to those in other regions of the country.[16] How to forge "an integrated . . . program for racial justice" out of a plurality of "race problems"? The CFCU wrestled with this question—and the tension it embodied—from its inception. Unable to arrive at a satisfactory answer, the CFCU foundered from its founding. Its fate reflected in microcosm the challenge that racial diversity posed for racial liberals throughout California's civil rights era to forge a multi-racial civil rights movement.

The legal fight that Joseph James initiated culminated in a California Supreme Court decision on December 30, 1944. The Boilermakers, the state's highest tribunal ruled, had to admit "Negroes . . . to membership under the same terms and conditions applicable to non-Negroes" in order to retain their "closed [union] shop" at Marinship.[17] Though the NAACP hailed the verdict as "one of the great blows struck by the courts of our land in the battle for human rights," Herbert Resner, one of James's attorneys, worried that the victory would prove pyrrhic if the work that brought James and his fellow plaintiffs to Marinship disappeared altogether.[18] "The real problem of the day," Resner wrote Marshall, "is the question of the future employment of Negro workers—in fact, of all workers."[19] James struck an even more ominous chord. "May this seething mass of variegated color stay busy now that the war is over," he brooded forebodingly in November 1945.[20]

California lawmakers also harbored grave concerns about postwar employment. In August 1943, the state legislature created the State Reconstruction and Reemployment Commission (SRRC) to advise on postwar planning. The SRRC's formation coincided with the peak of civilian employment in World War II California, reaching nearly 3.5 million, up from nearly 2.5 million in April 1940. This forty percent spike in civilian workers over the course of three years outstripped the state's rate of overall population growth—from 6.9 million in April 1940 to 8.5 million in January 1944—by nearly twofold.[21]

The SRRC responded to the exploding number of workers across California by preparing for the inevitable unemployment of so many of them. "No State in the Union," warned the SRRC's chair in March 1944, faced "weightier postwar problems."[22] Unemployment was the weightiest. As Governor Earl Warren told the first joint meeting of the SRRC and its accompanying Citizens Advisory Committees in March 1944, "Hundreds of thousands of war workers . . . recognize that their present jobs must terminate with military victory." He, therefore, charged the SRRC with the task of making plans in order to prevent California from becoming a "casualty of the war" in its aftermath.[23]

Initially, the SRRC described its charge in quotidian terms: to make plans to reconvert the economy from wartime to peacetime and, in the process, reemploy laid off war workers and returning veterans.[24] As the war's end drew closer, the SRRC grew shriller. Its first *Report and Recommendations*, issued in January 1945, warned, "California will soon face the greatest employment crisis in its history." Aircraft and shipbuilding—the industries that provided the lion's share of California's wartime employment boom—confronted the bleakest future, with at least eighty-five percent of their employees expected to lose their jobs.[25]

Job losses would be accompanied by housing shortages, both of which would be exacerbated by continued population growth. Together, *Fortune* magazine warned in 1945, these developments portended "serious social instability and increased problems of law enforcement." California faced a "detour through purgatory," even if the best preparations were made for the "dark days ahead," and an even worse fate if they were not.[26]

Such dire predictions soon began to come to fruition. By the end of 1945, overall civilian employment had dropped to 3.25 million from 3.5 million at its peak in the summer of 1943. Manufacturing employment hemorrhaged at a greater rate—from 1.15 million at its height to 600,000 in November 1945.[27] Despite plummeting jobs, the population continued to climb. The total number of state residents would soon eclipse the SRRC's 1945 prediction of 8.5 to 9 million for 1950, ultimately stretching to 10.5 million by decade's end. This growth would catapult California past Pennsylvania, Ohio, and Illinois to become the nation's second most populous state after New York. More people, of course, required more housing of which there was an "intolerably distressing" shortage, as Governor Warren bemoaned in December 1945.[28] Some 625,000 new homes needed to be built over the next five years. What had been a "prewar problem," noted the second SRRC *Report and Recommendations*, had now become a "crisis."[29]

Early in 1945, Warren drew a connection between the impending "war letdowns" and the "upsurges of racial prejudices" they threatened to trigger.[30] Though "war letdowns" were indeed a concern of the SRRC, racial prejudices were not what it had in mind when it warned of the impending "serious social instability."[31] When Elam Anderson, president of the University of Redlands, expressed concern about the "increasing tide of intolerance toward minority groups" in 1944 and demanded "intelligent postwar planning . . . to build dikes against this possible flood," SRRC director Alexander Heron replied that such problems were "local rather than statewide concerns."[32] Later in the year, Heron attributed the SRRC's failure to produce "studies dealing with minority groups" to its focus on employment. "As long as there are jobs enough for all workers," Heron maintained, "prejudice and resentment against groups is less likely to become serious."[33] Heron did not say what would be done if those jobs disappeared, as his SRRC was anticipating.

The closest the SRRC came to addressing the issue that Anderson raised was a recommendation from one of its many citizens advisory committees in October 1945, which called for the California legislature to enact a "fair employment practices" law. This proposed measure would "guarantee equal rights to live and earn a living to all . . . citizens regardless of race, color, or creed."[34] Paul Scharrenberg, chair of the Citizens Advisory Committee on Social and Industrial Welfare and director of the California Department of Industrial Relations, explained the reasoning behind the recommendation. In 1937, the state created a Committee on Race Relations in California whose charge was to disseminate "educational material" to promote "voluntary acceptance of the anti-discrimination principle." This voluntaristic educational approach, however, had "not kept pace with the movement of minorities into the industrial cities." Singling out the World War II influx of African Americans and noting that the United States was "the most important prop of a United Nations which contains all the races of the world," Scharrenberg insisted, "It is high time that education be supported by legislation and discrimination abolished once and for all."[35]

Scharrengberg's call to supplement education with legislation to curb racial discrimination spoke to a nationwide tendency that was undergoing transformation. As of 1945, according to the Social Science Institute at Fisk University, nearly seventy percent of 163 organizations it surveyed, which were dedicated to improving racial relations, pursued their work through various forms of "public education." These included mass meetings, lectures, radio programs, publications, and mobile exhibits.[36] Increasingly, though, legislation and litigation were either supplanting or supplementing education. Writing in 1951, sociologist John Burma noted the shift away from antidiscrimination initiatives that emphasized "understanding, proper education, co-operation, and good will," and toward "more direct action of legislation and the courts." As evidence, Burma cited the proliferation of antidiscrimination bills in state legislatures. He noted how "the word 'prejudice'" infrequently appeared in these measures and attributed that omission to the primacy that the bills' sponsors placed on "action" over controlling "feeling." Though only a small percentage of these bills managed to pass into laws, and though those laws were overshadowed by existing laws sanctioning discrimination, Burma nevertheless viewed the 1940s as a watershed. "Never," he wrote, has there "been a time in United States history in which so much emphasis has been placed on antidiscrimination legislation."[37] Antidiscrimination legislation and litigation, rather than anti-prejudice education, were becoming the weapons of choice in the racial liberal arsenal.

In the midst of this transition, the SRRC deliberated the fair employment practices recommendation of its Citizens Advisory Committee on Social and Industrial Welfare. During the hearing, Heron observed that the absence of such a law meant that any employer in the state could notify prospective employees that "he will not employ negroes, or Jews," among others. Preventing such discrimination, Scharrenberg explained, was the purpose of the fair employment practices recommendation. "An oriental or colored man would have an equal chance with you and me," he told the SRRC. "No discrimination against race or color. That is all it does."[38] The recommendation passed. However, it would be almost fifteen years before California lawmakers would heed it and enact a fair employment practices law.

Buried alongside a litany of other proposals—which began with a call for a "basic topographic mapping program" and concluded with a call for a "reforestation survey"—the fair employment practices recommendation was hardly a call to action.[39] "The Commission has done nothing directly on the minority issue," charged former SRRC staffer Miriam Roher in the *New Republic* in January 1946. She attributed this inaction to either a "realization that there is no sense treating symptoms when there are causes to be eradicated," or a "reluctance to expose dirty linen in public."[40] Whatever the reason, Roher's observation was borne out by the almost complete silence on the "minority issue" in the nearly sixty reports, studies, and pamphlets generated over the course of three years by the over six hundred people who served on the SRRC and its various Citizens Advisory Committees. Among the dozens of recommendations made in areas where the SRRC concentrated its attention—agriculture; aviation; education; highways, hospital, and public works; housing; natural resources; ports and harbors; recreation; social security and industrial relations (which included employment); veteran's affairs—only the fair employment practices recommendation addressed the prospect that "during reconversion minority groups may again be discriminated against." This inattention worried Roher. In her view, postwar unemployment sowed "the seeds of a nasty conflict," made even nastier by the "fact that so many of the recent arrivals have skins with pigmentation different from that of most Californians." The state's "melting pot is boiling faster than ever," Roher cautioned, and "it is safe to predict some very stormy times."[41]

Roher's ominous forecast echoed Governor Warren's warning from the previous year. Despite his concerns, however, Warren did not press the legislature to address them. Instead, he opened the 1945 legislative session with a call for a Commission on Political and Economic Equality (CPEE). Like the SRRC, the CPEE, if approved by the legislature, would be advisory only. It would conduct research into and make recommendations for how best to enforce the state's limited existing antidiscrimination statutes, while proposing additional related legislation.[42] A more robust fair employment practices bill was also introduced in the 1945 legislative session by Los Angeles assemblyman Augustus Hawkins, California's lone African American assembly member. Warren, however, chose not to endorse it, despite coaxing from his legislative secretary to do so "in view of the publicity that has been given the enactment of such legislation in New York"—the nation's first state fair employment practices law.[43] For Carey McWilliams, Warren's proposed CPEE represented an effort to "artfully sabotage" the prospects for fair employment practices "by urging a committee to 'study the problem'" instead.[44] In the end, Warren's alternative to fair employment practices suffered the same fate in the California legislature as fair employment practices. Both bills died in legislative committees.[45]

While he publicly called for a CPEE, Warren privately requested a list of all existing state antidiscrimination statutes.[46] A memorandum on "Statutes prohibiting discrimination re Negroes, etc." soon arrived on his desk. It listed five statutes, including the Civil Rights sections of the Civil Code of California, enacted in 1905 and amended in subsequent years to prohibit discrimination in places of public accommodation, as well as laws from the Labor Code and Civil Service Act, enacted in 1939 and 1941, respectively, that prohibited discrimination in public works contracting and civil service employment. Curiously, the list also included provisions from the School Code permitting school districts to create "separate schools" for children of "[American] Indian . . . Chinese, Japanese or Mongolian parentage." Apparently, the omission of "Negroes" from the school segregation statutes earned it a place on the list of state antidiscrimination laws that Warren requested.[47]

That omission aside, public education was one of several instances of legalized segregation in California. Indeed, had Warren asked for a list of his state's discriminatory laws to accompany the list of antidiscrimination laws he requested, it would have been the longer of the two. Besides permitting segregation of students within its schools, California outlawed "all marriages of white persons with negroes, Mongolians, members of the Malay race," denied land ownership and commercial fishing licenses to "aliens ineligible for citizenship" (which targeted Japanese immigrants who were legally barred from becoming naturalized citizens), and mandated segregation for African Americans within the state's National Guard.[48] In addition, California judges routinely enforced racially restrictive housing covenants, which represented a form of judicially supported, if not legislatively imposed, segregation.

That neither Warren nor the SRRC contemplated the dismantling of legalized segregation, while the state legislature rejected bills for both fair employment practices and a CPEE, corroborated Carey McWilliams's claim from two years earlier about the transition that had yet to take place from New Deal liberalism to racial liberalism. "While we have moved away from *laissez faire* doctrines in economics," McWilliams wrote in 1943, "we still anachronistically pursue *laissez faire* theories in population matters."[49] This, no doubt, suited the overwhelming majority of Californians. In response to a 1947 poll about the "biggest problems" facing the state, a mere two percent cited racial troubles, which was half the response that traffic received. The following year, not even one percent of Californians polled cited racial troubles. For both years, adequate housing was the top concern, receiving thirty-seven and forty percent, respectively.[50]

The California Federation for Civic Unity (CFCU) hoped to spark the change for which McWilliams implicitly called. Initially named the California Council for Civic Unity, the CFCU, emerged out of two 1945 conferences. The Pacific Coast Committee on American Principles and Fair Play, which had been formed in 1943 and focused its attention on the exiled and interned Japanese Americans, organized these conferences. Their original purpose was to tackle the "problems of the returning Japanese Americans." Conference attendees, however, pushed for more.[51] After all, they reasoned, the "problems facing the Japanese Americans were not entirely distinct from those facing other racial minority groups." Moreover, the anticipated postwar downturn in employment threatened to make matters worse. In response, conference participants called for a coalition-based attack on "all forms of racial discrimination."[52] To spearhead this effort, they proposed an organization that would provide "some kind of *integration* of all groups working on problems related to racial tensions"[53] The CFCU was born.

A federation of dozens of "community organizations and agencies . . . devoted to the improvement of interracial and intercultural relations," the CFCU sought to lead a "state-wide movement for improvement of interracial and intercultural relations."[54] Echoing McWilliams, the CFCU called for "planning and scientific method" as a response to the state's laissez-faire approach to majority-minority relations. More specifically, the CFCU aimed to apply pressure on the state government and its agencies to secure "equal opportunity . . . for all persons" in the areas of employment and housing, as well as desegregation in a variety of public and private settings, including schools.[55] Through the "ongoing collaboration" of existing groups—most of them local and minority group-specific—the CFCU aspired to "support . . . the rights of all racial minorities."[56] It would do so by developing "*a coordinated program* of inter-racial and inter-cultural groups on the West Coast."[57] Years later, Josephine Duveneck, one of the CFCU's founding members and first president, recalled, "What soon became evident was that these small, detached groups needed to compare notes with each other." Guided by the CFCU, they then needed to identify and pursue a "common goal."[58]

Shifting from local organizing and programming to "a state organization with a state-wide program," CFCU leaders maintained, signaled an important new direction.[59] In "do[ing] for the entire state what each local organization does for its city or town," as Joseph James described the CFCU's function, the CFCU was unique both to California and the country.[60] With the CFCU, a 1946 American Council on Race Relations (ACRR) report observed, "California becomes the first state . . . to establish a statewide voluntary organization in the field of racial and intercultural relations."[61] The CFCU thus represented a novel and notable alternative to the prevailing approach, which, according to noted African American sociologist Charles Johnson, was for "each minority group [to have] its own organizations dedicated to the advancement of the particular group . . . [with] little or no effective organization or program working to bring together these various minorities for a concerted effort."[62] Instead, the CFCU reflected what the ACRR's executive director characterized as a growing appreciation for "the interrelationship between the various minority problems." That appreciation, in turn, highlighted the importance of "minority groups to band together for common objectives."[63]

Implicit in this characterization was a tension between group-specific problems and multigroup solutions. On the one hand, CFCU leaders recognized "real distinctions between the characteristic [race] problems" in places like California in comparison to elsewhere, as Laurence Hewes, Jr. of the ACRR's regional office in San Francisco observed. Besides "problems of Negro-white relations and of anti-Semitism" in California, which had parallels across the country, there were "very specific issues" confronting Californians of Japanese, Chinese, and Mexican descent, among others.[64] On the other hand, CFCU leaders believed that "field work" could "develop cooperative understanding" among the different groups, which would in turn yield "a total program" suitable to all.[65] A multiplicity of minority problems, in other words, need not preclude a coalition of minority groups and their white allies in pursuit of a common ground agenda.

In theory, this made practical political sense. Given the little interest that the SRRC, governor, state legislature, and state residents evinced in the issues that concerned the CFCU, joining forces offered the best chance for the organizations under the CFCU umbrella to pressure state lawmakers. "Local organizations," insisted one CFCU leader, "are weak without a strong state organization for united effort on major policy questions." So, too, were "intra-group" organizations, even those with a statewide reach such as the NAACP or Japanese American Citizens League (JACL), which operated in "almost complete isolation" from one another, according to another CFCU leader. Instead, "success is far more likely" through a statewide, "inter-group" organization, which the CFCU represented. This kind of approach would render "it unnecessary for any one group to fight its battle alone."[66] There was, as Duveneck put it, "strength and prestige" in the kind of coalition that the CFCU sought to create.[67]

In practice, however, the challenge of arriving at a singular avenue of address from a plurality of axes of discrimination confounded the CFCU's ambitions from the outset. For example, as one of the 1945 conferences that gave rise to the CFCU unfolded, Henry Taketa of the JACL drew attention to what he deemed to be the uniquely urgent plight of Japanese Americans. "Ordinarily," he maintained, "our community problems would be much like those of the Negroes and Spanish-speaking minorities." These, however, were no ordinary times. In Taketa's estimation, Japanese Americans' "problems [were] very distinct, very pressing, very acute and very discouraging." Above all, Japanese Americans returning from wartime exile lacked places to which they could return. "Our homes are sold and lost. . . . We have to start all over again."[68]

In response, Joseph James attempted to reassure Taketa. He acknowledged that the "evacuee," unlike everyone else, "has to strike roots all over again." Simultaneously, he sought to draw Taketa's attention to what he saw as the parallels between Japanese American and African American experiences. "The problem of these evacuees," James observed, "is part and parcel of the problems we negroes have been facing for 300-odd years." Moreover, James explained, "we have developed certain techniques" for combating racial discrimination. These "we offer freely to members of the Japanese-American group . . . and invite them to join forces with us to see what we can do about correcting some of these abuses."[69]

The conference report did not record Taketa's response. Did he bristle at James's apparent failure to recognize that Taketa's JACL, like James's NAACP, had also "developed certain techniques" for fighting racial discrimination? Did he recoil at James's effort to equate the plights of African Americans and Japanese Americans, after Taketa had called attention to some of their current differences? Did he question the depth of commitment in James's offer, given how little attention the NAACP had paid to internment and the legal cases challenging internment during the war?[70] Was he worried about the potential conflict of interest between the NAACP and JACL's concerns over housing in light of the fact—not mentioned by either but surely recognized by both—that African Americans were in many cases now the occupants of places where Japanese Americans had resided before being interned?[71]

Following James's extension of "an outstretched hand" on behalf of the NAACP to Japanese Americans, a leader of the Sacramento Council for Civic Unity noted, "The returning evacuees are learning the importance of working with the Caucasians." This, however, was not the case for other groups. Chinese Americans, he complained, were "less ready to work with" with his organization, which was "not getting cooperation . . . from the Mexicans and Filipinos," as well.[72]

As the conference deliberations exposed the challenge to fulfilling the CFCU's coalition vision, Duveneck reminded participants, "It is one of our functions not to develop antagonisms." Rather, the goal was to find "common ground," and then "go on to the next step" which would never be taken "if you go bang up against" each other. "We all have some common ground."[73] Duveneck proved to be only half right. On the one hand, conference attendees, and subsequently members of the CFCU, agreed upon racial liberalism's overarching goal as well as the means to achieve it: equal opportunity through antidiscrimination litigation and legislation. This was, in the words of one CFCU leader, the "basic principle which binds everyone together," the foundation for "united group" action, rather than the divided pursuit of "'justice for Negroes,' for Japanese, or for Italians, or Jews or Catholics."[74] On the other hand, agreement in general principle did not necessarily translate to agreement over specific paths to pursue the overarching goal that bound the CFCU's constituent groups together. Well over two years after her call for common ground, Duveneck observed that one of the difficulties facing the fledgling CFCU was the inability to reach a "cooperative understanding" for a "total program." Instead, Duveneck observed, the different groups the CFCU sought to unite demonstrated an inclination "to evaluate total programs in terms of the specific problems of each."[75] Whatever vision of ultimate destination might have bound CFCU members together, they remained divided over different roads to get there.

This division, which Duveneck believed could be transcended through the work of the CFCU, persisted. In 1950, Richard Dettering, the CFCU's executive director, emphasized what he took to be the organization's unique contribution to forging a "new human rights movement" in California. The CFCU, in Dettering's view, represented the "only organization even pretending" to cultivate a "statewide framework" for "inter-group" action. These efforts, however, were bearing little fruit. As Dettering lamented, "there is still a notable lack of solidarity" among the various "intra-group organizations" the CFCU hoped to cohere into a coalition that was a prerequisite for the movement the CFCU desired. Instead, intragroup rather than intergroup efforts predominated, with each minority group having "one or more formal organizations representing their interests on the local, regional and state levels." Like the CFCU, these organizations, which included the NAACP, JACL, League of United Latin American Citizens, Community Service Organization, and Chinese American Citizens Alliance, targeted "problems of tension and discrimination." Unlike the CFCU, however, they concentrated "on their own groups." Though Dettering acknowledged this as "a necessary step before inter-group organization can be effective," he insisted that it had "inherent limitations" when it came to building a statewide movement. Only the CFCU's intergroup approach, Dettering maintained, could provide "particular minority" groups with a "wider and more sympathetic community audience, bringing them closer into the mainstream of civic life." There was, simply put, political power in numbers. This was especially critical in a state whose "human relations" problems had not "progressed to the legislative stage, but remain[ed] in a condition of laissez-faire," as

Dettering told attendees at the CFCU annual convention in December 1949. "There are 2,000,000 Californians subject to racial and religious discrimination," Dettering continued. Their voices needed to be heard at every level of governance in the state, "but only on the state level does that figure of 2,000,000 add up to 2,000,000."[76]

As the 1940s ended, however, that addition remained far from fruition. In 1944, Carey McWilliams proclaimed sociologist Robert Park's description of California as "a congeries of culturally insulated communities" to be the best "characterization of the state [that] has ever been made."[77] That characterization remained apt at the decade's end. Despite the CFCU's efforts to promote a "new human rights movement" grounded in "common interests and causes," there was "almost complete isolation between the various racial and cultural groups" in the state, as Dettering observed.[78] After nearly five years of trying, the CFCU had failed to find the common ground it sought.

Joseph James's concern that California's "seething mass of variegated colors stay busy" as war time work disappeared trumped his hope for a "united front of all the minority groups," which was gathering little momentum in the second half of the 1940s. In 1946, Marinship closed its Sausalito yard. James's courtroom triumph from the previous year could not secure his union job. Without that work, he was forced to relinquish his dream of helping to build a multiracial coalition to fight for civil rights in California, and he headed back East to pursue his singing career in New York.[79]

James's CFCU colleague, Duveneck, did not leave California. Nor did she leave the CFCU, staying with the organization she helped found until it folded in the mid-1950s. Years later, Duveneck reflected on her CFCU experience. She noted fondly how the CFCU brought together the state's "best people, that is people with the deepest sense of democracy and the most sincere desire for racial brotherhood." At the same time, she suggested why those good intentions never gathered more momentum than they did. "'Minority groups,'" she wrote, did not constitute "a mass of homogeneous particles." As much as "they all encounter the prejudices of the dominant group in greater or lesser degree," those prejudices manifested themselves in different ways. As a result, the "problems of adjustment . . . differ widely."[80]

Duveneck's retrospective observation was borne out by the campaigns against legalized segregation in California that unfolded alongside the founding and foundering of the CFCU during the second half of the 1940s. Collectively, these cases captured what Carey McWilliams described as the "spectrum of segregation" that "applied to all non-Caucasian groups" across the country. Individually, however, they demonstrated the difficulty of translating the CFCU's overarching goal of equality of opportunity through antidiscrimination litigation and legislation into a coordinated campaign. A common denominator problem—legalized segregation—did not yield a common front response. What McWilliams deemed to be minor "variations" on a segregationist theme, in fact, proved major enough to force the litigation down separate paths, reflecting how legalized segregation affected African Americans, Japanese Americans, and Mexican Americans in different ways.[81] These cases marked the first major battles in California's post-World War II civil rights history and produced precedent-setting victories with nationwide implications. They also reflected the largely separate civil rights trajectories that characterized California's civil rights era, despite the best intentions of the CFCU to find common ground.

When Larry Tajiri invoked the term "Jap Crow" in 1944, he meant to convey what he took to be the parallel plights of Japanese Americans and African Americans.[1] A journalist, born and raised in Los Angeles, Tajiri served as editor of the *Pacific Citizen*, the newspaper of the Japanese American Citizens League (JACL). During the war, Tajiri worked from Salt Lake City, where both the *Pacific Citizen* and JACL headquarters had been forced to relocate from San Francisco in 1942.[2] Like some 120,000 of the roughly 127,000 people of Japanese descent (Nikkei) residing in the continental United States in 1940, Tajiri and the JACL leaders who came to Utah from California had been exiled from their homes.[3] Unlike the vast majority of Nikkei, Tajiri and his JACL counterparts avoided internment, in what President Franklin Roosevelt himself called "concentration camps," by heading east during the brief window of "voluntary evacuation" time in March 1942.[4] Banished, if not behind barbed wire, Tajiri decried the "racial nature of [the] evacuation," how "Japanese American *citizens* were evacuated [but] white 'enemy aliens' were not." In this crucible of "segregation," Tajiri observed, a "common color consciousness . . . with other colored groups" was slowly emerging. With it, Tajiri hoped, would come a commitment to mount a collective campaign to complete "the unfinished racial business of democracy." "Jap Crow," Tajiri believed, resembled "Jim Crow," and the "ultimate solution" to both necessitated "correlation" with other "problems of color and race in America today."[5]

To this end, Tajiri endorsed Carey McWilliams's proposal in *Brothers Under the Skin* from the year before for a sweeping federal antidiscrimination law, a "Fair Racial Practice Act" that would encompass "all colored minority groups."[6] The effort to enact this legislation, Tajiri believed, would foster the kind of "co-ordinated action by America's 'minorities'" Tajiri favored. Such coordination, however, required "a groundswell of support from the discriminated groups," and that, Tajiri acknowledged, had yet to gather momentum. "Many Japanese Americans," Tajiri believed, "accepted . . . prejudices against Filipinos, Mexicans, Negroes, and Jews." Consequently, Tajiri conceded, "our group has far to go along the road to the actual co-ordination of our desire for integration with the mass hopes of all 'minorities.'"[7]

Joseph James, president of the San Francisco chapter of the NAACP, also hoped to effect the "co-ordination" of which Tajiri spoke by joining the causes and constituencies of the NAACP, JACL, and kindred organizations. Speaking at one of the 1945 conferences that launched what would become the California Federation for Civic Unity (CFCU), James linked the recent plight of the Japanese American evacuees with the three-century-old plight of African Americans.[8] In so doing, James implied that Tajiri's Jap Crow did indeed correlate with Jim Crow.[9]

Or did it? Just a few months later, James alluded to a salient difference in the experiences of African Americans and Asian Americans that complicated the prospects for the interracial coalition building that he, like Tajiri, endorsed. "The Negro is unquestionably a citizen," James wrote, and "thoroughly American." This thoroughgoing American-ness, James continued, accounted for why "the Negro has been able to establish alliances with sections of the Caucasian society where the Orientals"—who were, by James's implicit contrast, less "thoroughly American" and less "unquestionably" citizens—"could not."[10] It also explained why James believed that the JACL would benefit from "join[ing] forces" with the NAACP, as he invited his JACL counterparts in California to do.[11]

In distinguishing between degrees of African American and Japanese American American-ness, James unwittingly echoed Supreme Court Justice John Marshall Harlan's famous lone dissent in the 1896 *Plessy v. Ferguson* case that upheld state sanctioned segregation laws provided that the segregated facilities were equal. In their legal campaign to overturn *Plessy*, James's NAACP colleagues would draw upon Harlan's denouncement of "the arbitrary separation of citizens on the basis of race" and his insistence that "our Constitution is color-blind and neither knows nor tolerates classes among citizens." Yet, Harlan's willingness to strike down legalized discrimination as applied to black *citizens* did not extend to Chinese *noncitizens*. Harlan proclaimed the "unconditional recognition by our government . . . of the equality before the law of all citizens of the United States, without regard to race." He then asserted, "There is a race so different from our own that we do not permit those belonging to it to become citizens of the United States." What scandalized Harlan was how the segregation statute at stake in *Plessy* allowed "a Chinaman" to travel in the same train car as "white citizens," while "citizens of the black race" could not. The "color-blind" Constitution whose praises Harlan sung in solo against his Supreme Court brethren's chorus of "separate but equal" might not "know nor tolerate classes among citizens."[12] However, distinctions between citizens and immigrants (e.g., African Americans versus Chinese immigrants), as well as between immigrants themselves (e.g., Europeans who could immigrate and naturalize versus

Chinese, and later other Asians, who could not), posed an entirely different question. Simply put, Harlan's brand of "color-blind" constitutionalism ended where Chinese (and, by subsequent extension, other Asian) ineligibility to immigrate and naturalize began.[13]

As Harlan's dissent made clear, legalized discrimination in the United States did not simply encompass citizens. Noncitizens, too, or, more precisely, immigrants who were racially ineligible to become citizens through the naturalization process were the targets of a species of discriminatory federal and state laws. The most pervasive and pernicious of these at the state level were the so-called Alien Land Laws, which barred "aliens ineligible for citizenship" from being able to own land. As of 1947, one noted legal scholar counted eleven states with "anti-Japanese land laws."[14] The JACL's *Pacific Citizen* described these laws, in general, as "the keystone of discriminatory legislation against persons of Japanese ancestry," and the *Open Forum* of the American Civil Liberties Union's (ACLU) Southern California Branch referred to the California Alien Land Law, in particular, as "easily the most disgraceful and internationally harmful piece of legislation in California's history."[15] To strike it from the statute books, lawyers affiliated with the JACL and ACLU mounted a challenge in 1944 that reached the United States Supreme Court three years later.

Oyama v. California marked the "most important" of several "test cases" in which the JACL was involved in the immediate aftermath of World War II, according to Saburo Kido, a lawyer who participated in these cases and served as JACL president from 1940 to 1946.[16] As *Oyama* unfolded, it demonstrated how "Jap Crow" diverged from Jim Crow. *Oyama* reflected what the JACL referred to as "problems and adjustments which are peculiar to Americans of Japanese ancestry."[17] It became, in the words of one of its supporting attorneys, "*the* case for the Japanese community."[18] As Tajiri remarked in 1952 in a statement that alluded to the limits of the Jap Crow /Jim Crow analogy he drew in 1944, the Alien Land Law represented "the backbone of discriminatory activity against the Japanese in California and . . . their citizen children."[19] To break that "backbone," the legal campaign against the California Alien Land Law proceeded down a separate track from the contemporaneous court challenges to other forms of legalized segregation in California that disproportionately targeted other groups. In the process, *Oyama* underscored the difficulty of developing the "co-ordinated action by America's 'minorities'" that Tajiri called for in the same year that the case began.

While visiting JACL headquarters in Salt Lake City in 1944, attorney Abraham Lincoln Wirin proposed a legal challenge to the California Alien Land Law.[20] His timing could hardly have been worse. With the United States locked in with Japan, with Americans of Japanese descent locked in Supreme Court sanctioned internment camps, and with a 1944 poll of Los Angeles residents revealing that sixty-five percent of respondents favored a "constitutional amendment . . . for the deportation of all Japanese from this country and forbidding further immigration," the prospects for a sympathetic hearing in a case against the Alien Land Law appeared worse than slim.[21] Wirin, however, was no stranger to long legal odds. He specialized in representing underdogs such as Harry Bridges, a Congress of Industrial Organizations (CIO) leader whom the Roosevelt administration tried to deport to his native Australia in the late 1930s and early 1940s for his alleged Communist Party membership. Yet, Wirin's 1942 decision to defend Americans of Japanese descent—the ultimate underdog litigants of the day—against internment proved too much for even Bridges to bear. He accused Wirin of "representing the enemy" and severed ties with him. Bridges's CIO followed suit.[22]

Born to a poor Jewish family in Russia in 1900, Wirin moved to Boston in 1908. His parents changed his first name to Abraham and middle name to Lincoln. Young Abraham Lincoln—who later went by either A.L. or Al—worked his way through high school and Harvard, where he earned his bachelor's degree with honors in three years. He then pursued a law degree at Boston University, after which he took a job in the national office of the ACLU in New York. In 1931, Wirin moved to Los Angeles. Following a stint as a commercial and bankruptcy lawyer, which he detested, Wirin became counsel for the ACLU of Southern California. A few years later, he received a brutal introduction into his new legal career. Shortly after arriving in California's Imperial Valley with a court injunction against local authorities and citizens attempting to prevent the meetings of striking vegetable workers, Wirin was abducted, beaten, and abandoned in the desert by opponents of his legal work. By the early 1940s, Wirin had become counsel for the JACL, in addition to remaining counsel for the ACLU. From this position, Wirin persuaded the JACL to join him in submitting an amicus curiae— or, friend of the court—brief to the Supreme Court in the case of Gordon Hirabayashi, who challenged the government's curfew order, which was the prelude to internment. In addition, Wirin participated in the oral arguments before the Supreme Court in two of the internment-related cases.[23] The JACL's entry into these cases marked a shift away from the accommodationist stance the organization had assumed in the face of the government's round-up of Japanese Americans and Japanese immigrants who were ineligible for citizenship at the outset of World War II. This more confrontational JACL posture would continue with the active role the organization played in the Wirin-led case against the Alien Land Law.[24]

That case would soon involve the family of Kajiro and Kohide Oyama. Born in 1899, Kajiro immigrated to the United States in 1914. The oldest of three brothers, Kajiro left his family's small farm in a small Japanese coastal town at the behest of his father who had come to California in 1905. On his father's advice, Kajiro purchased a first-class ticket in order to minimize his chances of being detained at the Angel Island immigration station in the San Francisco Bay. On his teacher's advice, he brought his flawless report card and a dream to attend the California Institute of Technology. Kajiro's father, who was then living and working for a salt company just south of San Francisco, had other plans for his son. Shortly after Kajiro arrived, his father presented him with a pair of overalls and took him to Orange County. There, he began to work on a farm leased by one of his two uncles who lived in the area. Kajiro's father then returned to northern California, where he died the following year.[25]

Much later in life, Kajiro would describe himself as having been "determined to become a successful farmer." This determination manifested itself in his indefatigable work ethic and insatiable thirst for learning about how to farm. While making the rounds from farm to farm during a stint as a truck driver, Kajiro would trade his help with packing and loading produce for lessons in how to cultivate it. "I wanted to learn how they farmed," he recalled years later. "If I helped them they were willing to teach me. I was still a young boy and I asked them to teach me everything." Those lessons, most likely, included instruction in how to circumvent the Alien Land Law. In 1923, he purchased six acres of farmland in Chula Vista in San Diego County and placed title to the property in the name of Arthur Glower. A bookkeeper at a local market, Glower had taken a paternalistic interest in Kajiro, sometimes referring to him as his son. The attachment was mutual. Oyama turned to Glower for advice for the rest of his life.[26]

As Oyama's farming hopes flourished, he returned to his hometown in Japan to get married. His new wife, Kohide, joined him on his newly purchased farm in 1923. During the next decade, Kohide gave birth to five children. In 1934, Kajiro transferred title of the six acres to his oldest son, Fred, who was six years old. At the time, Kajiro's U.S.-born cousin, Yonezo (Dick) Oyama, held the title, having assumed it from Arthur Glower. Court records indicate that Kajiro and Kohide paid Dick $4,000 for the property and recorded the title in Fred's name. Three years later, Kajiro and Kohide, engaged in a similar transaction for an adjoining two acres, this time from their U.S.-born niece. By 1937, then, Fred held title to eight acres. In between the two purchases, Kajiro successfully petitioned the San Diego County Superior Court to become legal guardian of Fred's property in order to serve as its caretaker.[27]

To expand his farming business, Kajiro moved his family to much larger tracts of leased land in Orange County in the late 1930s. The Chula Vista property, however, remained in Fred's name. Meanwhile, his mother's brother and his family lived there until early 1942 when implementation of President Roosevelt's Executive Order 9066 culminated in the evacuation and incarceration of "all persons of Japanese ancestry," as per the subsequent exclusion orders. During the brief period of "voluntary evacuation," a traveling seed salesman with whom Kajiro did business presented the Oyamas with the chance to avoid incarceration by leasing farmland in Utah. Kajiro seized the opportunity and brought four other Nikkei families with him in what one of his daughters, Alice Oyama Yano, would later describe as a *Grapes of Wrath* migration in reverse.[28]

Two-and-a-half years later, as the summer of 1944 drew to a close, Fred was sitting on a tractor preparing to go to work on the family's forty-acre farm in Payson, Utah. A law enforcement official approached and served Fred with legal papers addressed to him and his father. California prosecutors, Fred was informed, had initiated steps to seize the two adjoining parcels of Chula Vista land that were in his name. Filed on August 28, 1944 by a San Diego County deputy district attorney on behalf of both the county's district attorney and state attorney general, the "Petition to Declare an Escheat to the State of California" began by referring to the Oyamas as a whole as members of the "Japanese Race" and the Oyama parents—Kajiro and Kohide—as "natives of the Empire of Japan" and therefore ineligible for citizenship in the United States. It then charged Kajiro and Kohide with perpetrating a "fraud upon the People of the State of California" for the "subterfuge and cover" of deeding the property they purchased to Fred "willfully, knowingly and with the intent to violate the Alien Land Law."[29]

Fred's reaction to the news he received that fateful summer morning in 1944 was a combination of "stunned silence" and shattered dreams, as he recalled years later. Seventeen at the time, Fred was approaching the age when he would have the chance to fulfill his wish to honor his country by serving in its armed forces. Somehow, he had managed to cling to that aspiration amidst his family's exile and the internment imposed upon his fellow Nikkei. Though he would recover from his "stunned silence," he would never reclaim his broken dream. He invoked his asthma to get classified as ineligible for military service. Instead, upon graduating high school in Utah, Fred worked briefly in a defense plant in Chicago at the tail end of the war.[30]

Meanwhile, California's action against the Oyamas came to the attention of JACL president and attorney Saburo Kido. Kido asked Kajiro to travel from Payson to JACL headquarters in Salt Lake City. Upon his arrival, Kido told Kajiro that he wanted to use his case to test the Alien Land Law. That the Oyamas had not lived on that land for years before World War II made it a "sure winner," Kajiro recalled Kido telling him. (Presumably, the state would have a harder time proving the "subterfuge and cover" it charged, since Kajiro was clearly not profiting from the land he had previously purchased and placed in Fred's name.) At first, Kajiro refused, telling Kido that the property's limited acreage rendered it "not worth his time and effort." Kido persisted, and Kajiro consented after Kido vowed to "collect donations" so that Kajiro would not have to "spend even a penny." Through Kido, then, Al Wirin now had the Alien Land Law legal challenge he sought.[31]

Drafted by state Senator Francis J. Heney and state Attorney General Ulysses S. Webb, the California Alien Land Law, as it was officially known, passed the California legislature with overwhelming support in 1913. The law drew a critical distinction between two classes of "aliens"—those "eligible to citizenship" and "all aliens other than those" who were "eligible to citizenship." Unlike aliens eligible for citizenship, aliens ineligible for citizenship could neither "acquire, possess, enjoy and transfer real property" nor "lease lands for agricultural purposes" for more than three years.[32] One year after the law's passage, fifteen-year-old Kajiro Oyama arrived in Japan and began working in the fields.

In distinguishing between immigrants based on their eligibility for citizenship, the architects of the Alien Land Law exploited the language of the federal naturalization law. Initially restricting naturalization to "free white person[s]" in 1790, Congress revised the statute in 1870 to also include "aliens of African nativity, and . . . persons of African descent." Beginning in 1878, courts across the country confronted the issue of whether immigrants who were neither "free white" nor of "African nativity . . . [or] descent" could become naturalized citizens. The first of these racial prerequisite cases involved a Chinese immigrant to California. The court ruled that "a native of China, of the Mongolian race, is not a white person within the meaning" of the federal naturalization statute and was therefore not eligible for naturalized citizenship. Other courts extended this reasoning to other immigrants from Asia.[33]

In theory, the California Alien Land Law encompassed all aliens ineligible for naturalized citizenship. In practice, it targeted Japanese immigrants.[34] Not only had their numbers spiked in the wake of the 1882 Chinese Exclusion Act (from 1,147 in 1890 to 41,356 in 1910, which represented 1.7 percent of the total state population), when Japanese immigrants replaced Chinese immigrants as California's major source of agricultural labor, but so, too, had the number of farms they operated (from 37 in 1900 to 1,816 in 1910) and number of acres they owned (from 2,442 in 1905 to 26,707 in 1913) and leased or contracted (from 59,416 in 1905 to 254,980 in 1913).[35] These demographic and economic changes, in turn, fueled the passage of the Alien Land Law. As Webb explained in 1913, "[The alien land law] seeks to limit their [i.e., the Japanese] presence by curtailing their privileges which they may enjoy here; for they will not come in large numbers and long abide with us if they may not acquire land."[36] Because only the federal government had the power to restrict immigration, the Alien Land Law represented California's effort to curtail Japanese immigration by other means.[37]

Despite Webb's best efforts and aspirations, the Nikkei population nearly doubled between 1910 and 1920 (from 41,356 to 71,952), while the number of farms they operated nearly tripled (from 1,816 to 5,152).[38] Similarly, between 1913 and 1920, the number of acres they owned also nearly tripled (from 26,707 to 74,769), while the number of acres they leased or contracted grew by over half (from 254,980 to 383,287).[39] Issei (Japanese immigrants) farmers had found ways of circumventing the law. One of the most common strategies—which Kajiro Oyama would eventually adopt—was to transfer land ownership from Issei parents deemed ineligible for citizenship (like Kajiro Oyama) to their Nisei children who were citizens by virtue of their birth in the United States (like Fred Oyama).[40]

California's anti-Japanese forces bristled at the Alien Land Law's ineffectual enforcement, even though the total amount of land either owned, leased, or contracted by Californians of Japanese descent amounted to just over two percent of the 29.3 million acres of agricultural land in the state in 1920.[41] To close loopholes in the law, the nativist Joint Immigration Committee—a coalition that included the Native Sons of the Golden West, American Legion of California, State Federation of Labor, and California State Grange—placed an initiative on the 1920 ballot. Most notably, the measure, which passed by an overwhelming three-to-one margin, established the legal presumption that any land purchased by an ineligible alien and then transferred to a citizen or eligible alien represented an attempt to evade the Alien Land Law.[42]

The federal government aided California's anti-Japanese forces in the early 1920s. In 1922, the Supreme Court ruled that Takao Ozawa—a Japanese-born, American-raised, Berkeley-educated, English-speaking Christian—was neither Caucasian nor, consequently, eligible for naturalized citizenship, though he was otherwise "well qualified by character and education."[43] By extension, all Japanese immigrants were ineligible for citizenship. One year later, the Supreme Court upheld the constitutionality of California's Alien Land Law in a series of cases.[44] These decisions, as well as subsequent ones in 1925 and 1934, gave unequivocal Supreme Court sanction to race-based discrimination between groups of immigrants—those eligible for naturalized citizenship versus those ineligible—when it came to the right to own or lease land.[45]

Buoyed by victories in both the United States Supreme Court and the California court of public opinion, California's Joint Immigration Committee lobbied both the California legislature and the United States Congress for even greater restrictions. Both acceded to these demands. California tightened its Alien Land Law yet again in 1923, and Congress passed the Johnson-Reed

Immigration Act of 1924.[46] This law adopted the "aliens ineligible for citizenship" language based on California's Alien Land Law, stipulating that "no alien ineligible for citizenship shall be admitted to the United States."[47] As with the Alien Land Law, so, too, with the Immigration Act of 1924: what appeared to be a race neutral formulation—applying to all "aliens ineligible for citizenship"—was in fact directed at Japanese immigrants.[48]

The revisions to both the Alien Land Law and United States immigration law, along with the rulings in the United States Supreme Court, had at least some of the impact their proponents desired. Between 1920 and 1930, the Japanese-descent population in California grew more slowly than in previous decades and then declined overall from 1930 to 1940 (from 71, 952 in 1920 to 97,456 in 1930 to 93,717 in 1940).[49] At the same time, the number of farms operated by Californians of Japanese descent fell from 5,152 in 1920 to 3,956 in 1930, and the total number of acres they farmed, as either owners, lessees, or contractors plummeted from 458,056 in 1920 to 288,000 in 1930.[50] As a result, by 1934—the same year that Kajiro Oyama purchased the land whose title he placed in his son's name—one observer described the Alien Land Law as a dead letter law.[51] A San Joaquin Valley newspaper attributed the law's lax enforcement in the decade before World War II to the profit motive. "It has never been conscientiously enforced," the *Selma Enterprise* explained, "because it interfered with business transactions that were profitable to landowners, lawyers, and others."[52] To this explanation, a *Business Week* article added the "diplomatic risk" that more stringent enforcement would have entailed.[53]

Pearl Harbor, however, resuscitated the Alien Land Law. In January 1942, California Attorney General Earl Warren noted "the revival of interest in the enforcement of the Alien Land law." This included a California Senate resolution calling for prosecutors to investigate violations. To this end, Warren convened a meeting in San Francisco in February 1942 of district attorneys and sheriffs to discuss what he called the "innumerable violations" of the Alien Land Law.[54] At that meeting, as well as in a memorandum, Warren linked enforcement of the law to national security. "Great caution," he warned, needed to be taken to prevent California land from slipping "into the hands of enemy aliens who will use [the land] as a starting wedge to undermine our entire system of government." Lest there be any confusion over the "enemy aliens" who were the law's target, Warren singled out the "all too harmless-looking Japanese farmers [who] carry on their activities in close proximity to some point of military importance," serving as "the eyes and ears of our enemy," and standing "ready to pull our house down at a moment's notice."[55] Warren reinforced this assertion of treason by proximity in testimony to a congressional committee later in the month. He identified aircraft manufacturing plants "surrounded entirely" by land occupied by Californians of Japanese descent. The "absence of sabotage" in these places up until that point, he charged, was the "most ominous sign" of its imminence. To thwart it, he advocated immediate action, including more vigorous Alien Land Law enforcement, was needed.[56] Shortly thereafter, in March 1942, the Kern County prosecutors filed what the *Los Angeles Times* described as the "first alien-land law case" of World War II.[57]

When Warren became governor in November 1942, Robert Kenny succeeded him as attorney general. At the time of his election, Kenny was president of the National Lawyers Guild (NLG), the lone nationwide organization of politically progressive attorneys founded in 1937. Though the NLG had often allied itself with the ACLU, it did not do so over the Nikkei incarceration, which the Guild supported.[58] As attorney general, Kenny threw his office behind Alien Land Law prosecutions with unprecedented vigor. In 1943, the same year he blasted the "insane barriers that separate man from man" and praised "Negroes . . . [as] among our country's most desirable citizens," Kenny implored district attorneys across the state to prosecute Alien Land Law violations. His exhortation to his counterparts at the local level represented the logical extension of the briefs his office filed that same year in support of the federal government's position in the curfew and evacuation cases then wending their way to the United States Supreme Court. As Kenny explained in a press release, "Persons of Japanese ancestry" were "largely unassimilated . . . and possessed strong religious, ideological, and family ties with Japan." Because many of them also resided close to strategic sites, such beaches and military bases, government officials needed to take "prompt action."[59] In 1944, the same year Kenny disparaged racism as "America's most distinctive weakness . . . and . . . prominent evil" at a dinner in honor of Carey McWilliams, he also denounced the "Japanese, as a race" for "the cunning and defiant schemes" they employed to evade the Alien Land Law. These included purchasing land "just under the wire" in 1913 when the Alien Land Law was first enacted, using American-born Japanese "decoys," and exploiting the diplomatic concerns of the United States vis-à-vis Japan to undermine enforcement.[60]

To enforce the law, Kenny accelerated his predecessor's efforts to appropriate "all Japanese farm land to the state," as the Native Sons of the Golden West applauded him for doing.[61] This amounted to 226,094 acres spread over 5,135 farms valued at just under $66 million in 1940.[62] Though Californians of Japanese descent operated only 0.7 percent of farm acreage in the state, which corresponded to half of their 1.4 percent representation of the overall population, they managed to secure a forty-two percent share of the commercial truck crops across the state.[63] This included a fifty to ninety percent market share for a variety of crops—such as celery, peppers, strawberries, cucumbers, artichokes, cauliflower, spinach, and tomatoes—with an annual value of $35 million.[64] Alien Land Law enforcement thus threatened to destroy the niche in the agricultural market that Californians of Japanese descent had managed to carve out for themselves.

Though the Alien Land Law had been on the books since 1913, California authorities had initiated only fourteen escheat proceedings through 1943. Of these, seven occurred during the years 1920 and 1921, four in 1942 and 1943, and all but three targeted Japanese aliens ineligible for citizenship. Over the course of 1944 and 1945, however, the number of Alien Land Law prosecutions quadrupled that of the preceding thirty years, in what the JACL's Tajiri described as "one of the biggest land grabs in history" perpetrated against the state's "weakest citizens."[65] Of these prosecutions, all fifty-five targeted Japanese aliens ineligible for citizenship.[66]

The state senate's Donnelly Committee on Japanese Resettlement spurred on this spike in cases. At his committee's first hearing in Fresno in August 1943, Senator Hugh P. Donnelly criticized the "laxity" of Alien Land Law enforcement. The consequence of this, Donnelly warned, echoing Warren and Kenny, was "exposing the country to espionage."[67] Two year's later the committee's final report reiterated its chair's indictment. "The Alien Land Law has not been properly enforced . . . since its adoption," the report charged, though state law enforcement officials had at least recently stepped up their prosecutions.[68] The overwhelming majority of the fifty-five cases they launched during the war's final two years involved land purchased by Japanese immigrant parents in the name of their American-born children, some of whom were serving in the military.[69] Kenny described property acquired in this way as being "owned and controlled by subjects of the Japanese empire" and, therefore, a "fraud upon the people of California" by the "alien Japanese" who used their "American born Japanese" children as a "mere subterfuge and cover" for their illegal activity.[70] The San Diego County district attorney's office adopted Kenny's language verbatim on August 28, 1944 when it initiated its escheat action against Fred Oyama's eight acres.[71]

California's Alien Land Law prosecutions sent shock waves well beyond the fifty-five cases brought in 1944 and 1945. Some forty-five percent of California Issei and forty percent of California Nisei worked in agriculture.[72] Many of these Issei faced the threat of being charged with violating the Alien Land Law or the reality of paying steep fees to avoid being charged, while many of these Nisei grappled with the possibility that the property for which they held title might be seized by the state.[73] In addition, Nisei property owners could not secure title insurance on property purchased with money earned by Issei family or friends, while prospective Nisei property owners needed to provide proof that the money they were using to purchase property was not earned by an alien ineligible for citizenship.[74] Simply put, the proliferation of Alien Land Law prosecutions, according to the ACLU, "cast a cloud over the validity of the titles held by Japanese Americans in California" and, consequently, complicated "any transactions involving such property."[75] For these reasons, the Alien Land Law in California and elsewhere, according to one critic, loomed as "the most serious legal impediments to resettlement" of the Nikkei.[76]

As the Oyama's case headed for trial in San Diego County Superior Court, the Department of War rescinded its nearly three-year-old exclusion order effective January 2, 1945. Shortly thereafter, Kenny delivered a speech to a state-wide sheriffs' meeting. He called for restoring and safeguarding the rights of returning evacuees.[77] Despite this call, Californians of Japanese descent came home to what the *Pacific Citizen* described as "a virtual reign of terror," victims of "more than 100 separate cases of arson, intimidation and attempted murder" from 1945 through the first half of 1946.[78]

These incidents prompted a steady stream of letters to Governor Warren, including one from Eleanor Roosevelt. Warren's reply to Roosevelt acknowledged the "tyranny of the Caucasian," the "good many instances perpetrated by hoodlums who usually operate under the cover of darkness." At the same time, Warren insisted, "our people are not disposed to make the lives of Japanese-Americans or the Japanese more difficult."[79] More typically, Warren's office issued a stock reply, claiming that the governor was doing his utmost to cultivate a "tolerant public opinion in connection with the problem," that there were limits to what he could do given the localistic nature of law enforcement, but that within those limits he would continue to do everything in his power "to see that the Japanese-Americans have their constitutional rights protected."[80]

Not surprisingly, the governor's office made no mention of the "law enforcement" being meted out by the state against the returning evacuees in the form of the Alien Land Law prosecutions. Nor did they address the role that Warren himself played in promoting these efforts as World War II drew to a close. On July 9, 1945, he signed into law a bill designed to tighten the Alien Land Law and promote its enforcement. Passed unanimously by the state legislature and backed by Kenny, the measure, which the *Open Forum* described as "conceived in a fit of racism," appropriated $200,000 for Alien Land Law prosecutions and freed the law's escheat provisions from statute of limitations requirements.[81] Most importantly, the law provided financial incentives (namely, the splitting of proceeds from the sale of escheated property between state and local governments) for local district attorneys who, as one governor's aide put it, were previously "loath to undertake proceedings under the act, since the investigation and prosecution of violations are expensive."[82] The San Diego County district attorney, whose office was about to go to trial in the case it launched the year before against the Oyamas, was particularly keen on the financial inducement. Because local governments bore the brunt of the costs involved in Alien Land Law prosecutions, he wrote Warren, they should "benefit from the sale of the escheated lands."[83] Warren's legislative secretary offered the same reasoning in recommending the governor sign the bill, adding that its would facilitate "more effective enforcement."[84]

Almost on cue, San Diego County Superior Court Judge Joe Shell handed down his ruling in the case brought by California prosecutors against the Oyamas. At the time, the family, which had returned from Utah, was sharecropping land elsewhere in San Diego County, after the "supposed friend" to whom they entrusted the land they were leasing prior to fleeing to Utah refused to return it to them. "He made so much money during the war years," recalled Fred Oyama, that "he conveniently forgot about his promise."[85] As for the land the family owned in Chula Vista, Judge Shell ruled in September 1945 that it "did escheat to and become and remain the property of the state of California." No member of the Oyama family had "any right, title, or interest" to the land purchased by the parents and then deeded to their son.[86] "Coming at the time when the evacuees were trying to resettle and rehabilitate themselves economically," Shell's verdict dealt a "terrific blow," as one JACL account put it.[87]

To muffle that blow, Al Wirin wasted little time appealing directly to the California Supreme Court, which agreed to hear the case and thereby circumvent the normal legal process. Saburo Kido, who would join Wirin as co-counsel, urged the state's highest tribunal to take this atypical procedural step given the "growing constitutional injunction against racial discrimination." The Alien Land Law, he added without explicating, "indirectly affect[ed] all minority groups."[88] Similar requests arrived from the Catholic Interracial Council of Los Angeles, as well as the Los Angeles chapter of the National Lawyers Guild.[89]

An attempt by Wirin to get Los Angeles-based NAACP-affiliated attorney Loren Miller to draft a "statement . . . for filing with the [California] Supreme Court in [Oyama] in behalf of the N.A.A.C.P.," however, came to naught.[90] Though the Open Forum indicated that it "expected" the NAACP to join the ACLU, Catholic Interracial Council, and National Lawyers Guild in filing its own amicus brief, the NAACP never followed through.[91] At the time, Miller was consumed with racially restrictive housing covenant cases, the overwhelming number of which involved African Americans.[92]

As Oyama headed for the California Supreme Court, JACL leaders convened in Stockton in December 1945 to devise a response to the "alarming increase of escheat cases [that] imperils the civil rights of all Japanese Americans." Conference attendees, including Wirin and Kido, addressed the prohibitive costs that individual defendants were forced to bear. In response, they launched the Civil Rights Defense Union of Northern California (CRDU).[93] This was part of a broader JACL effort to "begin to carry the burden of protecting our rights in the courts" by assuming "major responsibility" from the ACLU.[94] The CRDU would concentrate on "cases involving the rights of persons of Japanese ancestry," beginning with *Oyama*, which reached the California Supreme Court on June 13, 1946.[95]

As it did, the *Open Forum* hoped that "history" would be "made for democracy."[96] On Halloween 1946, the California Supreme Court dashed that hope, upholding the trial court's ruling in favor of escheating the Oyamas' Chula Vista land to the state. "The property in question passed to the State of California by reason of deficiencies existing in the ineligible alien [Kajiro Oyama], and not in the citizen [Fred] Oyama," declared Justice Douglas Edmonds. "The citizen is not denied any constitutional guarantees because an ineligible alien, for the purpose of evading the Alien Land Law, attempted to pass title to him." In other words, the Alien Land Law barred Fred's father from purchasing land. Passing title of land he purchased to his citizen son did not render the initial purchase any less illegal. Rather, it represented a "subterfuge for the purpose of evading the Alien Land Law." State authorities thus acted within the law when they petitioned to escheat the land. "Property which the citizen never had," proclaimed the majority opinion in a fit of legal legerdemain, "he could not lose." Consequently, "he acquired nothing by the conveyance and the Alien Land Law took nothing from him." The Chula Vista land first purchased by Kajiro in 1923, deeded to Fred in 1934, and cultivated by the entire family were in fact never theirs to begin with—or so the logic of the California Supreme Court went. Not a single justice dissented.[97]

The only silver lining for Wirin and his clients could be found in the terse concurring opinion of Justice Roger Traynor. In a single sentence, Traynor implied his moral opposition to the ruling, but conceded his legal obligation to abide by it. "I concur in the judgment on the ground that the decisions of the United States Supreme Court [upholding the Alien Land Law] cited in the main opinion are controlling," Traynor wrote, "until such time as they are reexamined and modified by the Court."[98] Traynor's concurrence, Wirin hoped, sent a signal to the nation's highest tribunal to hear the case.[99] This had been Wirin's preferred destination from the outset. As he explained to Judge Shell at the beginning of the trial on August 21, 1945, "The matter . . . is one of considerable consequence . . . [and] will call for a decision by the higher courts."[100] Whether Traynor's signal would have the effect Wirin hoped it would remained to be seen.

In the meantime, the *Pacific Citizen* denounced both the substance of the California Supreme Court's decision as well as its "unfortunate timing," just days before Californians were set to vote on Proposition 15.[101] Introduced by state senators Jack Tenney and Hugh Burns in 1945, Proposition 15 sought to etch the Alien Land Law into the California Constitution. Proponents of Proposition 15 portrayed it as a moderate, technical measure—"merely validat[ing] statutes . . . heretofore enacted by the Legislature and now in full force."[102] Opponents of Proposition 15, however, found nothing modest about it. They knew, for example, that Tenney backed a failed attempt earlier in the year to secure passage of a joint resolution to Congress from the California legislature requesting deportation of the entire Nikkei population and prohibition of any future Japanese immigration to California.[103] They knew, too, that Tenney chaired and Burns served on the state legislature's Joint Fact-Finding Committee on Un-American Activities in California, whose 1945 report declared the "great majority" of Issei to be "loyal to Japan," while "many" Nisei remained "disloyal to the United States."[104] Not surprisingly, then, Proposition 15's opponents, such as Daniel Marshall of the Catholic Interracial Council of Los Angeles, blasted the measure as "a crude restatement of the fundamental principle of Hitler's . . . racist doctrine."[105]

To prevent its passage, the JACL's Mike Masaoka, who had served with four of his brothers in the famous Japanese American 442nd Regimental Combat Team, spearheaded a statewide campaign against Proposition 15.[106] Drawing on over $100,000 in contributions, the Masaoka-led effort denounced Proposition 15 for seeking to "make race discrimination constitutional," while touting the loyalty of the Nikkei, in general, and the 25,000 Nisei GI's, in particular, whose "outstanding war record . . . has earned the right to fair play and decent treatment."[107] They had, as General Joseph Stilwell put it, purchased "an awful big hunk of America with their blood and lives" on the battlefields of World War II, which supporters of Proposition 15 were bent on seizing.[108]

Anti-Proposition 15 pamphlets reprinted an October 1946 letter to the *Los Angeles Times* from Akira Iwamura, a former sergeant in a Nisei intelligence unit that served in the South Pacific. After being honorably discharged, Iwamura returned home to Fresno County to face an Alien Land Law prosecution against his family's farm. "Why," he asked, "does California with its Alien Land Law and Proposition 15 keep kicking us in the teeth?"[109] Iwamura's story prompted a letter to Governor Warren from an elderly woman, among others, urging him to take action against the "injustice rampant . . . in our beloved state."[110] In response, Warren's legislative secretary deferred responsibility to the state's voters. Only they had the power to repeal the Alien Land Law—or, alternatively, if they so chose, constitutionalize it by passing Proposition 15.[111] Coming on the heels of the California Supreme Court's *Oyama* ruling, Masaoka feared that the state's voters would "automatically conclude that Proposition 15 should be affirmed."[112]

A majority of Californians, however, drew no such conclusions. On November 5, 1946, they rejected Proposition 15 by a vote of 1,143,780 to 797,067. Though decisive, the defeat carried little legal significance. The Alien Land Law, after all, remained on the books, even if it was not in the state constitution. Moreover, the state's Alien Land Law prosecutions persisted.[113] As an act of political symbolism, however, and as a barometer of public opinion, Proposition 15's defeat was hardly inconsequential. The *Pacific Citizen* hailed it "an event of major significance . . . the end of four decades of political scapegoatism directed against the state's residents of Japanese ancestry."[114] Kido was equally effusive. He attributed the outcome to "the contributions of the alien Japanese towards the war," which, in turn, demonstrated how "Americanism is not a matter of race or blood, but of the heart and mind." The defeat of Proposition 15, he continued, marked "a new chapter in the attitude towards the persons of Japanese ancestry in California," adding, "since California has been the standard bearer for anti-Oriental legislation," the outcome would reverberate nationwide.[115] Masaoka echoed Kido. In his estimation, the vanquishing of Propostion 15 "presage[d] a new era which will be free of discriminatory legislation for persons of Japanese ancestry." Moreover, it signaled a political coming of age for Japanese Americans, "the first time Nisei citizens organized, financed and carried an important political fight in California."[116] The people of California had spoken, pronounced the ACLU's *Open Forum*. "Elections," they declared, "do not follow court decisions!" In so doing, "They kept a 'constitutional law' out of the constitution."[117] The task remained to render that law unconstitutional.

To this end, Wirin and his legal team promptly filed a petition for rehearing with the California Supreme Court. Among other points, the petition claimed that the Proposition 15 vote dramatically altered the political and legal context within which the California Supreme Court had ruled in *Oyama*. If the purpose of Proposition 15 was to win popular validation for the Alien Land Law, and if the voters refused to grant such validation, then the law must be considered invalid. The Court "accentuated the racist features of the Alien Land Law," concluded the petition, "at a time when the people of California by the rejection of Proposition No. 15 have indicated that they do not approve the shabby practice of racial intolerance." It therefore needed to catch up with the "shifting sands of time" and reverse its recent ruling.[118] The justices, however, disagreed and rejected the petition.

Wirin and his allies, including Kido and lawyers for the Civil Rights Defense Union of Northern California, now turned to their final recourse, requesting an audience with the United States Supreme Court on February 25, 1947.[119] Their request received additional support—in the form of amici curiae briefs—from the national ACLU, National Lawyers Guild, and American Jewish Congress. As he had done when *Oyama* was before the California Supreme Court, Wirin solicited NAACP support, this time in a letter to Thurgood Marshall.[120] Once again, though, Wirin's overture to the NAACP failed to generate the brief he sought.

Opponents of the Alien Land Law recognized, as Masaoka put it, that "the purely legalistic precedents" might have militated against their appeal to the United States Supreme Court. However, they hoped that "the historical and sociological background of the enactment of California's present Alien Land Law" and its "present-day discriminatory enforcement" would prevail upon the justices' "social consciousness."[121] Meanwhile, California prosecutors continued their Alien Land Law enforcement efforts, and California elected officials continued to help fund them. Though JACL lobbying contributed to the defeat of a 1947 bill that proposed another $200,000 appropriation to enforce what a JACL letter sent to all members of the California legislature described as an "obsolete law" that "victimizes American veterans of Japanese ancestry," it could not prevent the legislature from appropriating $75,000.[122] Nor could JACL efforts prevail upon Governor Warren to strike the appropriation from the budget. This left overturning the law in court as the JACL's only remaining option. The United States Supreme Court made that possible on April 7, 1947 when it agreed to hear *Oyama*.[123]

With oral arguments set for October, Wirin and his legal team drew on lessons from their state court losses and shifted the focus of their legal attack.[124] In both the San Diego County Superior Court and California Supreme Court, Wirin had mounted a broad-gauged challenge to the constitutionality of the Alien Land Law as applied to both aliens ineligible for citizenship and their citizen children. His pretrial response to the charges levied against the Oyamas, for example, insisted that the Alien Land Law "discriminates against persons [i.e., both aliens ineligible for citizenship and their citizen children] solely because of race."[125] Having failed to persuade the California courts with this line of argument, Wirin and the lawyers who joined him on the briefs he submitted to the United States Supreme Court advanced an argument that parsed the racial discrimination meted out by the Alien Land Law into two groups (i.e., aliens ineligible for citizenship and their citizen children) and led off with the law's impact on the second one of those groups: "The Alien Land Law . . . deprives Fred Oyama, a citizen, of the equal protection of the laws and of the privileges and immunities of a citizen." Elaborating on how "the statute sanctions . . . patently discriminatory treatment of American citizens on racist grounds," they explained. "A gift by a parent to child," which is what Kajiro and Kohide Oyama and their attorneys maintained that their purchase of the eight acres of Chula Vista land was for their son, Fred, "is a normal, usual and expectable occurrence. In the case of an American citizen child whose parents are British aliens, no burden is cast upon citizens to prove his gift." However, the same gift by parents who were Japanese aliens ineligible for citizenship to their Japanese American citizen child could be denied unless the child could demonstrate that the parents acted without intending to circumvent the Alien Land Law. This unequal treatment between two "different classes of citizens"—those whose parents could naturalize and those whose parents could not "based solely on racial origin"—was unconstitutional. It denied Fred Oyama "one of the privileges inhering in every other citizen except those whose parents happen to be Japanese—the privilege of the unlimited bounty of the parents eager, as are all parents, to advance [their child's or children's] welfare as best they can."[126]

The *JACL Reporter* commented on the tactical thinking that drove the shift in Wirin's legal strategy as *Oyama* went from the California courts to the nation's court of last resort. "Everyone knows how much [Wirin] wanted to have a sweeping decision on the basic point" of the constitutionality of the Alien Land Law itself. He did not relinquish that aspiration. However, he did subordinate it, recognizing that the "first thing was to have the Oyama case reversed," and then, "if possible," to go for more.[127] Given the precedents on behalf of the Alien Land Law, it was a daunting enough challenge to secure a ruling against the law's applicability to the citizen children of aliens ineligible for citizenship. If doing so allowed for the possibility that the Supreme Court could leave the law's applicability to their parents in place, that was a chance that Wirin and his legal team were now willing to take. Better a partial victory than a total defeat.

The pursuit of that victory soon received an enormous eleventh-hour boost. Wirin and Kido, who was now one of Wirin's law partners, had been hoping to secure the services of a more high-profile attorney to accompany Wirin in oral arguments.[128] To this end, Charles Horsky, a Washington, D.C. based attorney who joined Wirin and Kido on their appeal to be heard by the Supreme Court, brought the case to the attention of Dean Acheson with whom Horsky was in practice.[129] No doubt Acheson, a former undersecretary of state and future secretary of state, recognized *Oyama*'s foreign policy implications. Wirin had stressed this dimension of the case elsewhere in an effort to win government support. On April 9, 1947, for example, just two days after the Supreme Court agreed to hear *Oyama*, Wirin urged Roger Baldwin, National Director of the ACLU, to "take up with General MacArthur . . . the matter of the government, through the Department of Justice, filing a . . . brief . . . amicus urging the Supreme Court to hold California's Alien Land Law unconstitutional." Such action, Wirin believed, would "further" America's "democratic program in Japan."[130] Wirin likely struck a similar chord when he, Kido, and Masaoka met with Acheson to persuade him to join them. Their efforts succeeded, with Acheson agreeing to take the case *pro bono*.[131]

Oral arguments in *Oyama* began at noon on October 22, 1947. Over two hundred people packed the Supreme Court chambers. Wirin led off, seeking to persuade the Court to rule against the constitutionality of the entire Alien Land Law, which had been his aspiration from the outset. One JACL eyewitness described Wirin as "confident and convincing . . . a real expert who made his living fighting California's discriminatory statutes." After a half hour, Acheson approached the bench. The *Pacific Citizen* described him as "the most distinguished lawyer ever to plead the cause of the Japanese."[132] As he opened his case, "The black-robed justices straightened up and looked at him with a noticeable air of respect. The busy page boys paused in their errands. The spectators craned their necks. There were excited whispers." In contrast to Wirin, Acheson plotted the more moderate legal course that had been the emphasis of pretrial strategizing. Rather than challenging the constitutionality of the entire Alien Land Law, Acheson confined his attack to the law's violation of the rights of the American citizen children of Japanese immigrants ineligible for citizenship.[133]

Attorneys for the state of California followed Wirin and Acheson. They received a much less sympathetic hearing. The assistant attorney general from San Diego County who went first exceeded his allotted time, in part because the justices "literally bombarded" him with questions that he had "a very uncomfortable time" answering. Kido took this as a good omen.[134] So did Masaoka. "I think we're going to win this one. . . . I hope. I hope," he wrote, though he doubted the Court would go beyond "uphold[ing] the rights of citizen Oyama" and strike down the Alien Land Law in its entirety.[135]

On January 19, 1948, the Supreme Court fulfilled Masaoka's tempered hopes. From a legal standpoint, the victory for opponents of the Alien Land Law was a partial one. The majority of six justices did not invalidate the entire statute, only its applicability to American citizens of Japanese descent like Fred Oyama. In the words of Chief Justice Fred Vinson, who wrote the opinion, "The California law points in one direction for minor citizens like Fred Oyama, whose parents cannot be naturalized, and in another for all other children—for minor citizens whose parents are either citizens or eligible aliens, and even for minors who are themselves aliens though eligible for naturalization." Such a double standard— "the only basis" for which was that "[Fred's] father was Japanese and not American, Russian, Chinese, or English"—could not be maintained absent a "compelling justification," which the state failed to provide. As for the Alien Land Law's discrimination against Fred's father and other aliens ineligible for citizenship (as opposed to all other aliens), the majority opinion avoided it. The "first contention" of Wirin and his co-counsel—which, for strategic reasons now borne out by the verdict, had emphasized the law's discrimination against Fred and other citizen children of aliens ineligible for citizenship—sufficed to reverse the California Supreme Court's decision. Beyond that, the majority of the United States Supreme Court refused to venture.[136]

The concurring opinions, however, displayed no such inhibitions. Justice Hugo Black (joined by Justice William Douglas) expressed his preference to "reverse the judgment" of the California Supreme Court in *Oyama* and "overrule the previous decisions of this Court that sustained" California's Alien Land Law, as well as similar measures in other states. "The effect and purpose of the [California] law is to discriminate against Japanese because they are Japanese," which thereby ran afoul of the equal protection clause of the Fourteenth Amendment.[137] Justice Frank Murphy (joined by Justice Wiley Rutledge) drafted the second concurring opinion. He delivered a detailed history of California's "anti-Oriental virus," which "infected" many Californians and "spawned" the Alien Land Law. Like Black, Murphy viewed as utterly specious the claim advanced by the law's defenders that the race-neutral formulation of the Alien Land Law somehow rendered it nonracist. Any such legalistic defense of it, not only ran counter to the United States Constitution and United Nations Charter, but was also tantamount to support for Nazism. "In origin, purpose, administration and effect, the Alien Land Law does violence to the high ideals of the Constitution of the United States and Charter of the United Nations," he concluded, "It is an unhappy facsimile, a disheartening reminder, of the racial policy pursued by those forces of evil whose destruction recently necessitated a devastating war. It is racism in one of its most malignant forms."[138] For Wirin, Justice Murphy's opinion was "particularly . . . noteworthy."[139] The *Open Forum* explained why, calling it "the best brief summary of California's 'yellow peril' hysteria . . . a gem on racism."[140]

Even the dissenting opinions in *Oyama* had little to offer in defense of the Alien Land Law. For Justice Stanley Reed (joined by Justice Harold Burton) in one dissent and Justice Robert Jackson in another, the problem with the majority opinion was its failure to address head-on the constitutionality of the Alien Land Law as a whole. Reed's concurrence insisted that "unless the California Land Laws are to be held unconstitutional," then the steps the state took to enforce the law "must be accepted as legal." Jackson agreed, but went further than Reed and Burton in insinuating his disdain for the law. While acknowledging the "unnecessary severity by which the Oyama's lose both land and investment," Jackson nevertheless insisted upon the constitutionality of California's action until such a time that the Court struck down the entire Alien Land Law.[141]

Initial reaction to *Oyama* reflected the ambivalence to be expected from a partial legal victory. On the one hand, the lead *Pacific Citizen* headline declared, "Oyama Case Decision Upholds Nisei Rights." On the other hand, the headline just below read, "U.S. Supreme Court Majority Avoids Ruling on Validity of California Alien Land Statute."[142] Mainstream newspapers registered similar reservations, reflecting what the *JACL Reporter* described as "a tendency to belittle the decision" immediately after it was handed down for dodging "the issue of the constitutionality of the Alien Land Law."[143] The *Los Angeles Times*, for example, noted the Court's preference to issue rulings "only so far as is necessary to decide" the matter at hand "left doubts and an area of evasion and litigation." The *Washington Post* pronounced the verdict a victory for "the great majority of citizens . . . who are devoted to constitutional democracy." Nevertheless, the *Post* lamented, "It is difficult to imagine a more unsatisfactory decision" than the "halfway" one the Supreme Court delivered."[144]

Mixed reactions, however, soon gave way to more favorable ones, as the practical, rather than legal, upshot became apparent. Though legally the Alien Land Law remained on the books, its enforceability had been dealt a crippling blow. At the time of the decision, approximately ninety percent of the pending escheat cases involved transfers of land from Japanese parents, who were ineligible for citizenship, to their citizen children.[145] *Oyama* provided the precedent to close these cases. On January 27, 1948, less than two weeks after the Supreme Court rendered its decision, California Attorney General Fred Howser, who succeeded Robert Kenny in November 1946, wrote Wirin, "There is little if anything left of our alien land law." Consequently, he saw no other option besides dismissing pending cases.[146]

Howser's sweeping decision came as a pleasant surprise to Wirin. "I must confess," he confided to Masaoka, "that when I first began to talk to Howser, I didn't dream that he would be willing to dismiss *all* the cases," just "the parent-child cases."[147] Howser's action, in fact, reflected "a more liberal and friendly view as to the effect of the [*Oyama*] decision" than even Wirin himself took.[148] This was an especially unexpected surprise coming from a man whose office had not only defended the Alien Land Law but who himself had just four years before, as Los Angeles district attorney, referred to the impending return to California of the Nikkei evacuees as a "second attack on Pearl Harbor."[149] Shortly after Howser informed Wirin of his intention to drop the remaining Alien Land Law cases, Warren's office announced that the governor's proposed budget for the 1948–1949 fiscal year would contain no appropriation for the law's enforcement.[150] *Oyama*, proclaimed the *New Republic*, "virtually brings to an end California's longest-standing piece of anti-Japanese legislation." Still, the Alien Land Law's continued presence in the state's statutes remained a "blot on Americanism," as the *Open Forum* put it, and an embarrassing impediment to the United States in international affairs.[151] For this reason, the fight against the remnants of the Alien Land Law would continue into the 1950s.

In the meantime, the JACL focused its litigation attention on another California-based, Wirin-led, and Acheson-supported case. Like *Oyama, Tarao Takahashi v. Fish and Game Commission* involved a statute based on the aliens-ineligible-for-citizenship classification, which one commentator of the day described as "the prime root of discrimination against the Japanese in this country."[152] More specifically, *Takahashi* involved a Japanese immigrant who had resided in Los Angeles since 1907 and received a license from the California Fish and Game Commission to earn a living as a commercial fisherman every year from 1915 until he was interned in 1942. The following year, while Takahashi's two sons and two sons-in-law were serving in the U.S. armed forces, the California legislature amended Section 990 of the state's Fish and Game Code to prohibit the granting of commercial fishing licenses to "alien Japanese."[153] (Prior to then, the Fish and Game Commission issued commercial fishing licenses to qualified applicants without regard to citizenship status, despite nearly thirty legislative attempts between 1919 and 1943 to restrict such licenses to either citizens or aliens eligible for citizenship.[154])

The blatant racial discrimination of the new law worried the state senate's Donnelly Committee on Japanese Resettlement, which called for a revised letter of the law to maintain its old anti-Japanese spirit. "There is danger," the committee noted, "of the present statute being declared unconstitutional, on the grounds of discrimination, since it is directed against alien Japanese." To avert that possibility, the committee recommended making the law "apply to any alien who is ineligible to citizenship."[155] In 1945, the California legislature passed such a measure, Senate Bill (SB) 413.

The *Open Forum* described the new law as designed to "discourage evacuees from returning to California . . . and costly to a group of about 500 industrious, America loving aliens who are ineligible to citizenship through no fault of their own."[156] By contrast, a representative from the state attorney general's office viewed SB 413 as "a step in the right direction, constitutionally speaking, because it deletes specific reference to alien Japanese and substitutes all persons . . . ineligible to citizenship."[157] On May 2, 1945, Warren signed the bill into law.

One year later, following Takhashi's return to Los Angeles from Manzanar in October 1945, Wirin sued the Fish and Game Commission to compel it to issue a commercial fishing license to Takahashi.[158] On June 13, 1946, Los Angeles County Superior Court judge Henry M. Willis ruled in Takahashi's favor. In response, Attorney General Kenny appealed directly to the California Supreme Court.[159] On October 17, 1947, just five days before oral arguments in the United

States Supreme Court for *Oyama* were slated to begin, California's highest court overturned Judge Willis's ruling on Takahashi's behalf. As in *Oyama*, Justice Douglas Edmonds wrote the majority opinion, which supported the legal reasoning the state attorney general's office offered in support of SB 413. Whereas Judge Willis had viewed the substitution of "person ineligible to citizenship" for "alien Japanese" in SB 413 as a "thin veil" employed to "eliminate Japanese aliens from the right to a commercial fishing license," Justice Edmonds insisted, "Takahashi has not established with any certainty that the legislature intended to discriminate against the Japanese by enacting the 1945 amendment."[160] After all, as Edmonds continued, "All of the races ineligible to citizenship are included and no one group in particular is singled out"—not only Japanese, but "Hindus and Malayans," as well, at the time of the law's passage. By not isolating "one group in particular," the law managed to pass constitutional muster with the majority of the California Supreme Court.[161]

Justice Roger Traynor had tried to thwart this line of argument. He requested that Wirin provide data to corroborate Judge Willis's claim that "it was commonly known to the legislature of 1945 that Japanese were the only aliens ineligible to citizenship who engaged in commercial fishing in ocean waters bordering on California." In response, however, Wirin presented no specific numbers. Instead, he wrote in a letter to the California Supreme Court justices, "Aliens ineligible to citizenship, other than Japanese who have applied for commercial fishing licenses, have been so small, so nominal and so inconsequential in number, that it appears clear that the 1945 Amendment was aimed almost entirely, if not exclusively, against persons of Japanese ancestry."[162] Absent the numerical data Traynor requested, the dissenting opinion, written by Justice Jesse Carter and joined by Traynor and Chief Justice Phil Gibson, found "highly persuasive," but not conclusive, that the law in question was "aimed solely at Japanese . . . in spite of the fact that race is not mentioned by name in the statute." Instead, the dissenters rejected the law's constitutionality on the grounds that it deprived aliens ineligible for citizenship who were commercial fishermen "the means of making a livelihood."[163] The *Open Forum* alluded to this line of argument when it summarized the California Supreme Court's ruling in *Takahashi* with the headline, "Let Aliens Die."[164]

As in *Oyama*, Wirin, joined by Acheson and Kido among others, appealed *Takahashi* to the United States Supreme Court on January 16, 1948. Three days later, they received what the JACL's Samuel Ishikawa described in a letter to the ACLU's Baldwin as a "considerable moral boost" when the Supreme Court delivered its *Oyama* decision. Nevertheless, Ishikawa continued, *Oyama* still left open "the question of whether the classification 'ineligible to citizenship'" could be employed to "veil [racist] legislation." For Ishikawa and his JACL counterparts, "The constitutionality of this question . . . [was] more clearly defined in the Takahashi case."[165] *Takahashi*, Ishikawa explained in a letter to the NAACP's Marian Wynn Perry, involved a "clearer case of discrimination" against aliens ineligible for citizenship than *Oyama*, which Masaoka believed made the law at issue in *Takahashi* "so much more vicious and undefensible than even the alien land law."[166] The switch in statutory language from "alien Japanese" in 1943 to "person ineligible to citizenship" in 1945 exposed the latter formulation for what it was—"a convenient circumlocution by which to evade constitutional limitations," as the appeal for a hearing to the United States Supreme Court by Wirin and his co-counsel contended.[167] For this reason, Ishikawa hoped to persuade the NAACP to do what it had not done in *Oyama* and file an amicus brief in *Takahashi*.

Coming at a time when NAACP lawyers were for tactical reasons focusing their litigation on cases where race could be isolated as a doctrinal variable, Ishikawa's distinguishing of *Takahashi* from *Oyama* on grounds that *Takahashi* involved a "clearer case of discrimination" than *Oyama* was a shrewd move.[168] Less than a month later, the NAACP joined the CIO and United States Department of Justice in filing briefs in support of the petition for certiorari, which the Supreme Court granted on March 15, 1948.[169] Thereafter, as *Takahashi* headed for oral arguments, the NAACP filed another amicus brief, this time in conjunction with the National Lawyers Guild. Other amici curiae briefs came from the JACL, ACLU, American Jewish Congress, American Veterans Committee, and the United States Department of Justice. According to the *Open Forum*, the Department of Justice's contribution marked "the first time in history the Attorney General of the United States has filed a brief amicus curiae in behalf of Californians of Japanese birth."[170]

As he had done in *Oyama*, Acheson joined Wirin when *Takahashi* reached the United States Supreme Court for oral arguments in April 1948. This time, though, their efforts contributed to a much less equivocal, though still circumscribed, ruling. Writing for a seven-justice majority, Justice Black delivered the decision he had wanted the Supreme Court to issue in *Oyama*, namely, a wholesale rejection of the law in question. However, Black avoided grappling with the contention of Wirin and his allies that "racial antagonism directed solely against the Japanese" drove the passage of SB 413. "We find it unnecessary," Black wrote, "to resolve this controversy concerning the motives that prompted enactment of the legislation." Instead, he took a page out of the dissenting opinion in the California Supreme Court's *Takahashi* decision and struck down the law on the grounds that it precluded "lawfully admitted aliens," whose ranks included aliens ineligible for citizenship, "from earning a living in the same way that other state inhabitants earn their living." State laws could target "alien inhabitants," in some cases, such as the Alien Land Law whose applicability to aliens ineligible for citizenship had been sustained in *Oyama*. However, the majority opinion in *Takahashi* held, such targeting must be "confined within narrow limits." SB 413 overstepped those boundaries.[171]

The majority's effort to distinguish *Takahashi* from *Oyama* did not sit well with either the concurring or dissenting justices. For Justice Murphy (joined by Justice Rutledge). who wrote the concurring opinion, SB 413, like the Alien Land Law, was just "one more manifestation" of California's long-running "anti-Japanese fever." The Court "should not blink," as the majority opinion did, at how SB 413, like the Alien Land Law, "is a discriminatory piece of legislation" and should be rejected for violating the equal protection clause on that basis alone. As for the dissenting opinion written by Justice Reed (and joined by Justice Jackson), the majority opinion's effort to parse the right to own property from the right to make a living was a distinction without a difference. The latter, as embodied in "the right to fish" at issue in *Takahashi* was "analogous" to the former, which was at issue in *Oyama*.[172] If *Oyama* let stand the Alien Land Law's constitutionality as applied to aliens ineligible for citizenship, then *Takahashi* needed to do the same when it came to the state's refusal to grant commercial fishing licenses to aliens ineligible for citizenship.

Both the majority and dissenting opinions in *Takahashi* took for granted the constitutionality of the aliens-ineligible-for-citizenship classification, which derived from federal immigration and naturalization law. They differed only over what exactly constituted the "narrow limits" that states possessed for enacting legislation that targeted aliens ineligible for citizenship. To press those limits with respect to what remained of the Alien Land Law after *Oyama*, the Masaoka brothers, represented by Wirin, launched one of two test cases that reached the California Supreme Court in 1952. Using money from the GI death benefits of their one brother who died in World War II (among the four, of five, brothers who served), they contracted to buy land in Pasadena. Upon it, they proposed to build a house and deed it to their mother who was born in Japan and hence ineligible for citizenship.[173] This plan purposely ran afoul of the Alien Land Law's reach in the wake of *Oyama*, ironically inverting the transaction that Kajiro Oyama engaged in when he placed title of the land he purchased in the 1930s in the name of his citizen son in order to circumvent the Alien Land Law. The other test case involved the purchase of property by Sei Fujii, a Japanese born, American raised, University of Southern California educated attorney who owned and published a Japanese/English newspaper. Fuji and the Masaoka brothers had the same motive, which Fujii's attorney conveyed to the Los Angeles County Superior Court in 1949, "We wanted to get this case to a higher court to find out what is left of the alien land act."[174]

Three years later, a divided California Supreme Court ruled that there was in fact nothing left. "Constitutional principles declared in recent years" by the United States Supreme Court in *Oyama* and *Takahashi*, among other cases, wrote California Chief Justice Phil Gibson in the majority opinion, "are irreconcilable with the reasoning of the earlier cases" that upheld the Alien Land Law. The Alien Land Law as a whole "is invalid as in violation of the Fourteenth Amendment."[175]

California Attorney General—and future Governor—Pat Brown refused to appeal the case to the country's court of last resort. California, he declared, would no longer adhere "to a philosophy of a 'super race,' nor insist upon being a vindictive outpost of racial discrimination."[176] After nearly four decades, the law that the *Pacific Citizen* described as "the most discriminatory and harmful piece of anti-Japanese legislation" was now not only inapplicable to the citizen children of aliens ineligible for citizenship, as *Oyama* ruled, but to aliens ineligible for citizenship themselves.[177] "California's Alien Land Act," declared Kido, "is dead."[178]

Long dead before the death of the Alien Land Law were the lemon trees on the eight acres of Chula Vista land that reverted back to the Oyamas following the resolution of their case. In addition, the house where the family lived from 1923 to 1937 was in such disrepair by the time they could reclaim it that the state condemned it. Nevertheless, the Oyamas needed to pay back taxes plus interest on the property. Deeming the old farm bad luck, Kohide insisted that Kajiro sell it, which he did. By then, the industrious and resilient couple already owned a sixty-acre farm in Palm City, which they purchased following a stint as sharecroppers upon their return to California in 1945. In 1949, Fred left the family farming business to pursue his college education at San Diego State, while his brother served in the United States Army occupying Japan. The Supreme Court ruling in the case that bore Fred's name combined with a United States history class he took in college helped restore the faith in his country that had been shatterd on that late summer day in 1944 when he received word that California prosecutors intended to escheat his family's land. Able to recite the Pledge of Allegiance again, he pursued a career as a middle school math teacher. In that capacity, he not only recited the Pledge every school day but also insisted that his students do the same—"in correct fashion" and with "earnestness." Anything less required repetition.[179]

In a speech delivered at the JACL's national convention in December 1944 shortly after he launched his legal campaign against the Alien Land Law, Al Wirin exhorted his audience to think of "the fight for the restoration of your rights [as] . . . a fight you are also carrying on for the Chinese in the United States, the Negroes in the United States, for the Jews in the United States, and for all minority groups."[180] Wirin's sentiments expanded upon those of Larry Tajiri from earlier in the year when the *Pacific Citizen* editor highlighted what he saw as the parallels between "Jap Crow" and "Jim Crow."[181] They also anticipated an exchange Wirin had with Thurgood Marshall following oral arguments before the Supreme Court in *Oyama* in 1947. "This case," Wirin recalled Marshall explaining his attendance, "will tell the Negroes what we're going to get out of this court." Marshall's intuition jibed with Wirin's. "The Japanese cases," Wirin believed, "had to be decided favorably before the Supreme Court was ready to decide the Negro cases." For Wirin, *Oyama* involved a variation on the same legalized segregation theme that the NAACP was attacking in its cases that culminated with *Brown*. The former simply involved "small[er] segregation" than the latter.[182]

Yet *Oyama* also involved *different* segregation than *Brown*, as Wirin and Marshall no doubt recognized. When it came to crafting legal arguments, Alien Land Laws that sanctioned discrimination between two classes of citizen children (those whose parents were or were not eligible for naturalized citizenship) as well as between two classes of non-citizen parents (those who were or were not eligible for naturalized citizenship) raised distinct legal questions from those involving school segregation laws that did not involve issues of citizenship status. Most specifically, "the question of whether the classification 'ineligible to citizenship'" could be employed to "veil [racist] legislation," as the JACL's Samuel Ishikawa had written the ACLU's Roger Baldwin in January 1948, figured into *Oyama* in ways that were altogether absent from *Brown*.[183] This question and the litigation involved to answer it pointed to the limits of just how far Wirin's claim about the parallels between the fights for "Japanese rights" and "for all minority groups" could be pressed.

So, too, did the formation of the JACL Legal Defense Fund in late 1946. Modeled after the NAACP's Legal Defense and Educational Fund, the JACL's counterpart proposed to "protect the civil and property rights of persons of Japanese ancestry in the United States and . . . participate in litigation involving the civil liberties of other racial minorities." These aims—on behalf of people of Japanese descent and on behalf of "other racial minorities"—were not necessarily one and the same.[184] As Masaoka explained before a 1947 hearing of President Truman's Committee on Civil Rights, "We persons of Japanese ancestry, citizens and aliens alike, have many problems in common with other minority and racial groups in the United States. At the same time, we have several that are peculiarly and exclusively our own."[185] To the extent that these "problems" did not overlap, a 1948 report from the JACL National Planning Committee chaired by Kido endorsed the JACL's "emphasis at all times . . . on problems pertaining to the welfare and interest of persons of Japanese ancestry."[186]

Of course, privileging "the welfare and interest of persons of Japanese ancestry" did not preclude paying attention to "other minority and racial groups." As a January 1947 JACL "Statement of Policy" noted, "We believe that as we work for the solution to the problems peculiar to our own minority group, we are helping . . . to solve the total problems of all minorities."[187] To this end of assisting with "problems" not "peculiar" to people of Japanese descent in order to help "solve the total problems of all minorities," the JACL submitted an amicus brief in a California school desegregation case involving Mexican Americans on appeal to the Ninth Circuit in 1946, as well as one in the racially restrictive housing covenant cases on appeal to the United States Supreme Court in 1947.[188]

These instances of multiracial cooperation, however, remained the exception rather than the rule. They neither reflected nor foreshadowed the emergence of a multiracial civil rights movement in California. Rather, they revealed how the state's multiple civil rights struggles occasionally crossed but never coalesced into something enduring. In the case of the JACL, in the aftermath of *Oyama*, its priorities remained predominantly group specific given the "problems" it continued to identify as unique to "the welfare and interest of persons of Japanese ancestry."

As a matter of litigation, this focus was reflected in *Takahashi*, as well as the cases that challenged what remained of the Alien Land Law. As a matter of legislation, Joe Grant Masaoka, regional director of the JACL in Northern California, spelled out the "unfinished business on erasing discrimination toward Japanese Americans" at the annual convention of the California Federation for Civic Unity in San Francisco in November 1948. Under "state laws," he placed at the top of the list compensation for "settlements paid by Nisei defendants to abate alien land law proceedings" in light of *Oyama*'s vindication of "rights of citizens in their properties."[189] For Wirin, recovering these "unjust settlements" was of "even greater importance" than the legal challenge to the post-*Oyama* remnants of the Alien Land Law.[190] Two years later, California-based JACL activists created a state JACL-Anti-Discrimination Committee to lobby Sacramento for "legislation of interest and welfare to persons of Japanese ancestry," of which securing old-age pensions for Japanese immigrants who remained ineligible for naturalized citizenship in 1951 was given first priority.[191]

Of course, the necessity of such a measure would be eliminated if Congress dispensed with the category of aliens ineligible for citizenship. As a report by the JACL National Committee on Legislative Matters explained in September 1948, "Since most state and local discrimination against persons of Japanese ancestry is based upon 'ineligibility to naturalization,' this Committee feels that the enactment of appropriate federal legislation will nullify and void these statutes."[192]

For this reason, the JACL's "National Legislative Program" for 1949 prioritized "a bill to secure equality in immigration and naturalization" for "Japanese, Koreans, and other people of Asia and the Pacific Islands." It would be modeled after the "Chinese formula" from 1943, in which Congress rescinded Chinese immigration exclusion and removed the prohibition on naturalization for Chinese immigrants already residing in the United States. Thereafter, the JACL national legislative agenda included securing compensation for evacuee property that had been lost or damaged while being held by the government during the war, returning property to "law-abiding aliens," extending the Soldier Brides' Act for two more years, admitting children of Soldier Brides' Act marriages, granting statehood to Hawaii, and, finally, more "general civil rights legislation," such as federal laws for a permanent FEPC and against lynching and poll taxes.[193]

To secure "Issei naturalization rights," which Masaoka described in November 1946 as "the only real and permanent solution to the whole problems of legalized discrimination and persecution" against all people of Japanese descent, the JACL joined forces with the Committee for Equality in Naturalization.[194] In 1949, Robert Cullum, a leading figure in the Committee for Equality in Naturalization, which was an outgrowth of the Citizens Committee to Repeal Chinese Exclusion and Place Immigration on a Quota Basis from earlier in the decade, offered a "Japanese American Audit" in the pages of *Common Ground*. He noted how 1948 marked the year when "the group status of Japanese Americans has moved ahead with greater strides than in any single year since the turn of the century." Yet, "the most fundamental liability" still remained: racial barriers in immigration and naturalization laws.[195]

In the meantime, though "Jap Crow" in California had yet to be vanquished completely as the 1940s drew to a close, it was certainly reeling. *Oyama* had broken what Tajiri described as "the backbone" of discrimination against Californians of Japanese descent.[196] It, along with the defeat of Proposition 15 and *Takahashi*, prompted Joe Grant Masaoka to marvel in late 1948 at the "truly remarkable" demise of "discriminatory practices directed against Japanese Americans" over the course of the previous three years.[197] The *Pacific Citizen* waxed even more whiggish. The once potent anti-Japanese forces in California, it exclaimed, had lost their punch and now numbered just "a few assorted crackpots [on] the lunatic fringe of racism."[198]

In 1952, Congress passed the Immigration and Naturalization Act (also known as the McCarran-Walter Act). The law eliminated the racial barrier to naturalization and with it the category of aliens ineligible for citizenship.[199] Following its enactment, Kajiro and Kohide Oyama wasted no time acquiring the citizenship they had long been denied. Kajiro quickly developed an affinity for politics. He became a regular voter and devoted Republican. His favorite politician would prove to be Ronald Reagan, with whom Kajiro shared an antipathy for César Chávez's efforts to organize farm workers. During Reagan's successful 1980 presidential bid, Kajiro's contributions earned him an invitation to the White House with other big donors to celebrate Reagan's victory. He declined. At eighty-one, he was still too immersed in work—this time in the garden of the house he and Kohide retired to in Lemon Grove, California—to justify time away for such frivolity.[200]

CHAPTER 3

"THE PROBLEM OF SEGREGATION AS APPLIED TO MEXICAN-AMERICANS"

Fred Ross attended an integrated Los Angeles elementary school, at least until his mother realized it. When she did, she confronted the principal. "That's not the way my boy's been raised," she insisted, as the principal tried to tout the virtues of integrated education by pointing to black and white pupils walking together. "I've brought him up to stay with his own [white] kind and that's the way it's going to be."[1] She could not have been more wrong about her son's future.

During the second half of the 1940s, Ross attracted Carey McWilliams's attention as an "extremely talented grass-roots organizer." McWilliams singled out Ross's role in launching the Bell Town Improvement League, which mobilized a group of African American and Mexican American parents in Riverside County in opposition to the school segregation of their children.[2] Ross's work in Bell Town was part of a broader initiative he spearheaded to establish local, interracial organizations throughout southern California communities. These Unity Leagues, as Ross referred to them, aimed to do at the local level what the California Federation for Civic Unity (CFCU), for which Ross would later serve as executive director, sought to do at the state level. They would, as Ross put it, identify "some of the most severe" problems that "minority people" confronted in common and mount a collective response to them.[3] Ross explained the reasoning behind his Unity Leagues in a letter to Lawrence Hewes, Pacific Coast Regional Director of the American Council of Race Relations (ACRR), which initially sponsored Ross's work and supported the formation of the CFCU. "Through joint effort," he wrote in 1947, the prospectus for success would be substantially improved "because of the pooling of energies . . . and . . . common front presented against attempts by the opposition to divide and alienate them."[4]

Bell Town was just one of at least a dozen southern California communities, by McWilliams's count, that were embroiled in school desegregation battles in the mid-1940s.[5] The most precedent-setting of these—*Mendez v. Westminster School District*—pitted four Orange County school districts against approximately 5,000 students "of Mexican and Latin descent and extraction."[6] Ross helped organize some of the parents who brought the case, which attorney David C. Marcus filed in federal district court on March 2, 1945.[7] As *Mendez* unfolded, the Bell Town Improvement League enlisted Marcus's legal support. Their case, Marcus exclaimed in 1946, promised to be "the first . . . involving both MA [Mexican American] and Negro segregation in the annals of California jurisprudence!"[8] Meanwhile, something comparable to that collaboration had developed in *Mendez*, which Marcus was then preparing for the Ninth Circuit Court of Appeals. Though the students in *Mendez* were all Latino (and overwhelmingly Mexican American), the organizations that filed amicus briefs on their behalf—NAACP, JACL in conjunction with the ACLU, and American Jewish Congress (AJC)—lent *Mendez* a multiracial coalition dimension of its own.

If the Bell Town Improvement League and *Mendez* were any indication, then, fighting school segregation, it appeared, was giving rise to the kind of coalition building that Ross envisioned for his Unity Leagues—interracial action against multiracial discrimination with roots in southern California but branches that stretched to the American South. After all, as McWilliams saw it, *Mendez* reflected "a fairly consistent pattern" between school segregation of Mexican Americans in southern California and the Southwest, more generally, and African Americans in the South.[9] The NAACP's Robert Carter agreed. *Mendez*, he wrote in 1947, involved "basically . . . the same problem" as the NAACP's school desegregation litigation that would be decided by the United States Supreme Court in 1954 in *Brown v. Board of Education*.[10] Numerous academic and journalistic treatments of *Mendez* have echoed Carter, highlighting how the parallels between the two cases helped the former (*Mendez*) "set a precedent" or "pave the way" for the latter (*Brown*).[11]

Focusing on the obvious convergences between *Mendez* and *Brown*, however, obscures the less obvious, but ultimately more significant, underlying divergences. To be sure, the Orange County school districts sued in *Mendez*, like their counterparts in *Brown*, viewed the students they segregated through racist lenses. "An attitude of racial superiority such as that of Hitler" rooted in a belief that "Mexicans" were an "inferior people," as Marcus charged, drove the school districts' segregationist practices.[12] This attitude, Marcus maintained, was "the evil we are attempting to reach and the cancer we seek to eradicate." The racist motivations driving the segregation at issue in *Mendez* and *Brown*, in other words, were quite similar. The legal and administrative methods for justifying the segregation, however, were quite distinct. In *Mendez*, unlike in *Brown*, the school districts on trial lacked a clear statutory basis, as well as United States Supreme Court sanction, for their actions. Mexican Americans, both sides in *Mendez* agreed, were "white," and California's school segregation statutes did not sanction the separation of white students from one another. For these reasons, the Orange County school districts on trial in *Mendez* needed to employ what Marcus assailed as "varied and devious excuses to justify the practice of segregation."[13] The most common of these excuses, which shaped *Mendez* in ways that were also altogether absent in *Brown*, was that Mexican American students lacked adequate English-language proficiency to attend "English-speaking" schools. As a matter of litigation, then, Marcus needed to demonstrate that this, and the other purportedly pedagogical justifications for segregation it subsumed, lacked merit. Proving what Marcus recognized as the "real reason" for the segregation of the students he represented—that is, racism—required first disproving the school districts' claim that English-language proficiency (or lack thereof) and other ostensibly educational rationales justified their actions.

Ultimately, *Brown* confronted the question of whether "separate [but otherwise equal] educational facilities" for black and white students "solely on the basis of race" were "inherently unequal," as United States Supreme Court Chief Justice Earl Warren put it.[14] By contrast, *Mendez*, which was decided on Warren's watch as California governor, addressed the legality of separate but otherwise equal schools for most (but not all) legally white students of Mexican descent owing to their purported "English language deficiencies" (and other related pedagogical pretexts).[15] These aspects of the case helped render it "sui generis," according to the federal district court judge who heard *Mendez*, and ultimately circumscribed the case's court rulings.[16] Though both *Mendez* and *Brown* struck historic blows against de jure school segregation, *Brown* overturned the infamous "separate but equal" doctrine upheld by the Supreme Court in *Plessy v. Ferguson* in 1896. By contrast, *Mendez* left *Plessy*, as well as California's school segregation provisions, in place, which perhaps helps explain the absence of any reference to *Mendez* in *Brown*. Since California law did not specify students of Mexican descent, the courts could and did rule against their segregation without having to rule against the state's school segregation laws. Beyond that, the courts also accepted the principle of language-based segregation, provided that students segregated for their supposedly insufficient English were properly tested. This caveat would figure into subsequent cases in California and elsewhere in the Southwest involving Mexican American students, further underscoring the important differences between Mexican American and African American school segregation and desegregation that *Mendez* revealed.[17]

For these reasons, *Mendez* was not simply reducible to essentially the "same problem" that the NAACP confronted in the cases that culminated in *Brown*. Distinguishing between the two cases does not undermine the importance of *Mendez*. Nor does it diminish the pervasiveness and perniciousness of the segregation at issue in the case. Rather, *Mendez* was unique and important on its own terms. Making *Brown* the lodestar for and measure of *Mendez*'s place in United States civil rights history runs the risk of missing what makes *Mendez* historic in its own right—as a case that tackled what former ACLU national director Roger Baldwin described in a 1955 letter to Thurgood Marshall as "the problem of segregation as applied to Mexican-Americans."[18]

Viewed from this vantage point, *Mendez* was to Mexican Americans in California what *Oyama* was to Japanese Americans. It exposed axes of discrimination and avenues of redress that Mexican Americans, in particular, confronted. It also foreshadowed a post-*Mendez* trajectory that would, in many ways, be similarly (if not exclusively) group-specific. Consequently, to the extent that opposition to school segregation in California in the 1940s gave rise to a multiracial coalition to combat it, that coalition proved to be thin and fleeting rather than thick and enduring. Indeed, rather than building upon the limited collaboration forged during the *Mendez* litigation—which would have been the natural extension of his Unity Leagues work—Ross began focusing his attention in 1947, when *Mendez* was ultimately decided by the Ninth Circuit Court of Appeals, on launching what he called "a Mexican NAACP . . . to help direct this minority group" down particular avenues of redress that flowed from particular axes of discrimination.[19]

Seima Munemitsu's tragedy presented Gonzalo Méndez with an opportunity. Incarcerated with his family at the Colorado River Relocation Center in Poston, Arizona, Munemitsu sought reliable tenants to lease his forty-acre farm in Westminster, California. Word of Munemitsu's aspiration made its way to Méndez through a banker with whom both men were friendly. At the time, the Mexico-born Méndez and his Puerto Rico-born wife, Felícitas, ran a small cantina in nearby Santa Ana. The children of migrant workers, who had themselves worked in the fields, the Méndezes seized the chance to run their own farm. Gonzalo signed a lease with Munemitsu, sold the cantina, and moved the family, which then included three children, to the Munemitsu's farm in 1943.[20]

Financially, the Méndezes thrived, cultivating asparagus with the help of fifteen workers. In addition, Gonzalo worked as a foreman at another farm of 120 acres, supervising 35–50 workers.[21] Educationally, however, the Méndez children met a different fate. The Westminster School District to which they moved in 1943 housed two elementary schools. A few blocks and a world separated them. Westminster school officials and residents referred to one, the Westminster School, as the "English-speaking" or "American" school and the other, the Hoover School, as the "Spanish-speaking" or "Mexican" school.[22] Prior to relocating to Westminster, the Méndez children attended a "Mexican" elementary school in Santa Ana. In Westminster, however, the Méndezes lived closest to "Belgians" and "Anglo-Saxon[s]," according to Gonzalo. The children of those families, he continued, all attended the Westminster School.[23] So, too, had the Munemitsu children, similar to other Japanese American children throughout southern California, including the Oyamas.[24] So, too, had Gonzalo during the 1920s (at least until fifth grade when he had to forsake school for work).[25] And so, too, Gonzalo and Felícitas resolved, would their children.

When the school year began in September 1943, Gonzalo's sister, Soledad Vidaurri, who had moved to Westminster from San Diego with her husband and children to live and work on the farm with the Méndezes, took her Méndez niece and two nephews, along with two of her own children, to the Westminster School. Upon their arrival, the teacher tasked with admitting students looked at the children and determined that only the lighter-skinned and less obviously Spanish-surnamed Vidaurris could stay. Their darker-skinned and more obviously Spanish-surnamed Méndez cousins would have to matriculate at the Hoover School. As Felícitas put it, "Mine were dark . . . and Méndez."[26] Outraged, Soledad gathered up all five children and stormed home.[27]

When Gonzalo and Felícitas heard what happened, they resolved to fight back. Initially, their resistance took the form of refusing to send their children to school. This prompted a home visit from the Westminster school superintendent, Richard Harris. "He went to my house on my ranch in 1943," Méndez testified in 1945, "to see why I didn't send my children to school. At the time I was a little sore . . . . I didn't want to send my children to the Hoover School." Harris, however, was unmoved. He instructed Méndez to return his children to the school where they had been placed, which Méndez eventually acquiesced to, rather than attempting to "make or coax [Harris] to take my children" into the Westminster School.[28]

At the same time, Méndez organized a "Father's Association." With an eye on the next school year, he sought to mobilize other parents to pressure Westminster school officials to "unite the schools." This effort helped persuade the school board to place a bond issue before Westminster voters to fund the consolidation of the town's two elementary schools. In August 1944, however, a majority of Westminster residents rejected the measure. That same month, Méndez, along with a handful of others he led, including Felícitas, Soledad, and members of the Santa Ana Latin-American League of Voters, met with Harris at the Westminster School. When Harris told the group "he couldn't do anything" to help them, Méndez inquired, "Suppose I bring my children . . . at the start of the school [year], to enroll . . . in this school. Will that be accepted?" It would not, Harris replied.[29]

The following month, as the school year began, the Méndezes, joined by other parents, kept up the pressure. They met with the superintendent of all

Orange County schools, as well as Harris. In these meetings, they delivered a letter denouncing Westminster School District's "racial discrimination" and demanding an end to "the segregation of American children of Mexican descent," some of whom had siblings who were "soldiers in the war." In response, the Orange County superintendent claimed he lacked the authority to act, while the Westminster superintendent claimed he lacked the money to act, pointing to the failed bond initiative.[30]

While his children continued to attend the Hoover School in 1944–1945, Méndez lobbied school officials to integrate Westminster's two schools. Finally, after a year-and-a-half of trying through mobilization and persuasion, Méndez turned to litigation. As he explained at a Westminster School Board meeting, "I said, 'If you was me, you wouldn't do it? Would you be satisfied to have your children segregated in a different school? 'Well,' [one of the board members] said, 'I don't think so.' 'Well, I said, that is all there is left for us to do.'"[31] Shortly thereafter, the Méndezes hired Los Angeles attorney David C. Marcus.

The son of Jewish immigrants from Eastern Europe, Marcus was born in Iowa in 1905.[32] After moving to New Mexico with his family, where he would briefly pursue an engineering degree at the University of New Mexico, Marcus headed to California. He earned his bachelor's degree from the University of California at Los Angeles and law degree from the University of Southern California. During the 1930s, the Mexican consulate in Los Angeles and San Diego hired Marcus to handle cases involving Mexican nationals. At a consulate-sponsored dance, Marcus, who was then divorced from his first wife, met Yrma Maria Davila. Davila's father had been a doctor to Mexico's President Álvaro Obregón, and her family fled from Mexico to the United States following Obregón's 1928 assassination. Davila's eventual marriage to Marcus likely added a personal punctuation to Marcus's *Mendez* litigation. That California's antimiscegenation law did not preclude their union, even as Orange County school districts were preventing the mixing of "white" and (most) "Mexican" students, accentuated one of the charges Marcus levied years after his marriage to Davila about the arbitrary and invidious nature of the school districts' segregationist practices.[33] So, too, had Marcus's own bouts with anti-Semitism from adolescence through law school.[34]

As Marcus's legal reputation grew among Los Angelinos of Mexican descent, Ignacio López, editor of the Spanish-language weekly *El Espectador*, hired him in 1943 to bring a desegregation suit against the city of San Bernardino on behalf of López and roughly 8,000 other Mexican Americans. Decided in a federal district court in February 1944, *Lopez v. Seccombe* ruled that the city's practice of barring its Mexican American residents from a variety of public recreational facilities, including a swimming pool, violated the Constitution's equal protection clause.[35] Marcus's *Lopez* victory caught the attention of Henry Rivera, who delivered the Méndez's produce to market in Los Angeles. When Rivera heard about the Méndez's resolve to challenge the Westminster School District, he told them about Marcus. Using money earned from their farming, the Méndezes hired Marcus. To expand his case and defray Marcus's fees, the bulk of which the Méndezes ultimately paid, Gonzalo sought legal allies and financial support from fellow Mexican Americans in nearby towns where Mexican American students were also segregated. He received assistance from Fred Ross, who was then organizing Unity Leagues across Orange County.[36]

On March 2, 1945, Gonzalo Méndez, along with his children Sylvia, Gonzalo, and Jerome, became the lead petitioners in a suit brought by Marcus on behalf of "some 5,000 other persons of Mexican and Latin descent and extraction all citizens of the United States" against four Orange County school districts. The named respondents included the superintendents and trustees of the Westminster School District, along with their counterparts in El Modena, Garden Grove, and Santa Ana.[37]

When *Mendez* was filed, California could count itself among twenty-two states plus the District of Columbia with school segregation laws.[38] California's statute had roots that ran to 1863 when the legislature forbid "Negroes, Mongolians, and Indians" admittance into public schools attended by white children.[39] Nearly a century later, in February 1946 as *Mendez* was unfolding, the JACL's *Pacific Citizen* observed, "The [school segregation] law [in California] has been used mainly to achieve the segregation of Mexican American children." This struck the paper as curious, for "nowhere in the law [was] the word *Mexican* used."[40] Instead, the statute— Section 8003 of the California Education Code— read, "The governing board of any school district may establish separate schools for Indian children . . . and for children of Chinese, Japanese, or Mongolian parentage." Thereafter, Section 8004 stipulated "when separate schools [were] established for Indian children or children of Chinese, Japanese, or Mongolian parentage," those students "shall not be admitted into any other school."[41]

Statutory specifics mattered little to school districts with sizable Mexican descent populations. As a California educator observed in 1920, "One of the first demands made from a community in which there is a large Mexican population is for a separate school."[42] These demands escalated during the 1920s, and especially after the 1924 Johnson-Reed Immigration Act. Though California nativists fought to include Mexicans in the restrictive quotas imposed by the 1924 law, California agricultural interests helped foil them.[43] Consequently, Mexican immigration surged, as other sources of foreign labor disappeared. In 1930, California's Mexican Fact-Finding Committee issued a report that estimated an over threefold increase in the number of Mexican immigrants residing in the state, from roughly 89,000 in 1920 to 234,000 in 1930.[44] This influx increased the total Mexican descent population from 121,000 in 1920 to 368,000 in 1930.[45]

The vast majority of the Mexican newcomers settled in southern California. As they did, racially restrictive housing covenants specifying them spiked.[46] So, too, did patterns of residential and social segregation in public swimming pools, movie theaters, and restaurants.[47] When residential segregation failed to translate to school segregation, local school authorities took action. They built new "Mexican schools" or redrew school attendance zone boundaries to achieve segregation.[48] As a result, by 1928, a survey of schools in eight southern California counties found 90–100 percent Mexican descent enrollment in sixty-four schools.[49] Another study, based on Orange County in the early 1930s, reported that seventy percent of the county's 4,000 Mexican descent students, who comprised twenty-five percent of the total student population, attended schools with one hundred percent Mexican descent enrollment.[50] This pattern of pervasive segregation persisted into the 1940s. As Marcus explained, "I only selected four" school districts, but "there are many more" in Orange County "where the segregation is practiced."[51] Carey McWilliams echoed Marcus. "Segregation [in schools]," he wrote in January 1947, "is the rule wherever Mexicans reside in sizable colonies."[52]

Despite what McWilliams described as a "fairly consistent pattern" between school segregation of Mexican Americans in southern California and the Southwest, more generally, and African Americans in the South, there were also revealing—and, as the *Mendez* litigation would demonstrate, legally significant—differences.[53] To begin with, California school segregation laws targeted multiple groups. Conspicuously absent among those specified, however, were "Negroes," who fought to remove themselves from the law's provisions in the late nineteenth century, and "Mexicans," the state's most segregated group.[54] Consequently, school districts that sought statutory justification for segregating students of Mexican descent sometimes resorted to conflating "Mexican" with "Indian," since "Indian," along with "Chinese," "Japanese," and "Mongolian," did appear in the statute.[55] California Attorney General Ulysses S. Webb supported this tactic in 1929 and 1930. He acknowledged that there existed "no authority" for establishing separate schools for "Mexicans" as a whole. However, "Indian" Mexicans—who comprised "the greater portion of the population of Mexico"— were "subject to the laws applicable to other Indians," which included school segregation.[56] Though a bill to revise the law to apply less ambiguously and more comprehensively to all students of Mexican descent was defeated in the California legislature in 1931, segregating "children of Mexican extraction, on the theory that many of them may have some Indian blood," as one leading opponent of this practice put it in 1945, persisted in some school districts.[57]

California's school segregation statutes also parted ways with their counter-parts in the South by being optional. Only "when separate schools [were] established for Indian children or children of Chinese, Japanese, or Mongolian parentage" did the law require those students to attend the segregated schools.[58] Moreover, the segregation of Mexican descent students was not monolithic. Though all four school districts Marcus sued contained one or more all "Mexican"/"Spanish-speaking" schools, all four districts had at least some students of Mexican descent enrolled in their "American"/"English-speaking" schools. As Claremont Graduate School professor W. Henry Cooke observed in 1948, "Few, if any, cases of segregation of Mexican-Americans have been absolute in nature."[59] For example, while Westminster's K-8 Hoover School had 152 students of Mexican descent, its K-8 Westminster School had fourteen students of Mexican descent sprinkled among its 642 students.[60] In El Modena School District, the one "Mexican" elementary school had 260 students, while the one "English-speaking" elementary school had 117 students, twenty-two of whom were of Mexican descent.[61] Garden Grove Elementary School District, according to trial testimony by one of its Mexican descent residents, also included a small number of Mexican students in at least one of its three "English-speaking" K-5 schools, though the district's superintendent claimed that they were "Spanish," not "Mexican."[62] Finally, Santa Ana's fourteen elementary schools contained three that were 90–100 percent "Mexican descent," eight that were 90–100 percent "English speaking," and three that were mixed with from 25–45 percent "Mexican descent."[63] *Mendez* focused on two of these schools, one that was "a wholly Mexican attended school" and another that had seventy-six "Spanish-speaking pupils" and 161 "English-speaking pupils."[64]

Such porousness (however limited) in the segregation of students of Mexican descent helps explain why the NAACP's Marshall and Carter excluded California from its list of seventeen states plus the District of Columbia where "segregation in education is a universal policy" in the amicus brief they would later file in *Mendez* during its appeal to the Ninth Circuit.[65] In some cases California's non-"universal" segregation of students of Mexican descent possessed a class-based distinction, as Fred Ross, for example, discovered while organizing in El Modena. "I'll tell you why I think they took them in," Ross recorded one man explaining about the few students "from the better [Mexican] families" admitted to the predominantly non-Mexican school in town. "Their dads are both foremen in the groves."[66] Similarly, Cooke noted how Mexican American parents with "sufficient influence could usually have an exception made for their children."[67] In other cases, segregation of students of Mexican descent had a color-based inflection, as evidenced by the willingness of the Westminster School to admit the lighter-skinned Vidaurris but not their darker-skinned Méndez cousins. In still other cases, students of Mexican descent could avoid segregation in their local "Mexican" school by claiming that they were of Spanish descent.[68] In all cases, segregation of students of Mexican descent ended by middle or high school, though, to be sure, only a small fraction of those students who started in elementary school made it that far and a smaller fraction still managed to graduate.[69] The rest had been driven away by an economy that afforded few opportunities to them beyond picking or packing produce, a regime of psychometric testing that deemed them intellectually and culturally deficient, and a curriculum that consigned them to vocational education.[70]

Though not all students of Mexican descent were segregated in the four districts Marcus sued, no students other than students of Mexican descent attended the segregated "Mexican" or "Spanish-speaking schools," including nonwhite students. The first witness Marcus called, a Mexican American mother who had a few years earlier sought for her children the "privilege" of attending one of Garden Grove's non-"Mexican" schools, noted how that school included not only some students of "Mexican ancestry" but also "Filipinos . . . Japanese and . . . Negroes" along with "white American children." Another witness whose children were denied admission to another non-"Mexican" Garden Grove school observed, there were "no Mexicans [at that school], but there is niggers," quickly changing the epithet to "Negroes," after Marcus prompted her. Still another witness from Garden Grove wanted to know why "Japanese . . . and Filipino boys attended" the school from which his Mexican American children were barred.[71] In Santa Ana, according to the superintendent, black students received permission to transfer out of their neighborhood school, leaving it "100 percent Mexican," and into a school whose population included 136 white students and twenty-five black students. He explained, "They are permitted to transfer to the school where they will find most of their own people," rather than be a "very small minority" in the "Mexican" school.[72] As for Westminster, Gonzalo Méndez commented on how the Japanese American children whose family's house the Méndezes were leasing had attended the very school to which the Méndez children were denied admission.[73]

More than anything else, language—or, more specifically, the school districts' claim that lack of English proficiency was the reason for the segregation they admitted practicing—presented the most salient distinction between segregation of students of Mexican descent in southern California (and elsewhere in the Southwest) and African Americans in the South. The "linguistic qualifications" of the segregated students was an "important feature" of the case, explained United States District Court Judge Paul J. McCormick for the Southern District of California in Los Angeles at a pretrial hearing in *Mendez v. Westminster* in June 1945. It also helped render this "very important" case, as Judge McCormick described it at the outset, "sui generis," unlike any other school segregation case to date.[74] Four years later, Carey McWilliams echoed McCormick. "The language issue in the schools," he wrote, sparked "more discussion and controversy" than any other issue in the "bundle of issues that is called 'the Mexican Problem.'"[75]

No one in the United States knew the "language issue in the schools" better than George I. Sánchez. In a 1955 letter to the NAACP's Thurgood Marshall, former ACLU national director Roger Baldwin described Sánchez as "the ablest man in the United States on the problem of segregation as applied to Mexican-Americans."[76] Sánchez spearheaded the fight against Mexican American school segregation in Texas in the 1940s, while keeping close tabs on *Mendez*. Born in Albuquerque in 1906, Sánchez finished high school at sixteen and began teaching in an impoverished rural school immediately thereafter. During his summers, he attended the University of New Mexico. Sánchez then pursued graduate work, earning a PhD in educational administration from the University of California at Berkeley. Thereafter, he took a position at the University of Texas at Austin. In 1941, the League of United Latin American Citizens, a Mexican American civil rights organization formed in 1929, elected Sánchez president.[77]

The following year Sánchez sought to enlist ACLU assistance in attacking the "problems related to the Spanish-speaking people of the Southwest—particularly those who are citizens."[78] In a letter to Baldwin, Sánchez suggested a legal challenge to the "so-called 'pedagogical' reasons for segregation" of students of Mexican descent.[79] School officials, Sánchez wrote Baldwin, claimed that students of Mexican descent "did not speak English" and, therefore, a "better educational situation [would] obtain" for them in a segregated setting.[80] Such reasoning was necessitated in Texas, as in California, Sánchez explained, because "Jim Crow legislation does not apply" to "the Spanish-speaking people."[81] As educationally specious as Sánchez deemed the "so-called 'pedagogical' reasons for segregation," he also knew that they were legally significant and needed to be explicitly addressed in any court challenge. Though Sánchez had indicated in September 1942 that this reasoning could be "easily refuted," nearly two-and-a-half years later he noted how "no one has demonstrated that the 'pedagogical reasons' for segregation are spurious."[82] Absent that, courts would "not go over the heads" of school officials when "they claim that it is educationally desirable to segregate Mexicans."[83] Rather, they would give them "wide latitude" for determining how best to run their schools.[84] Unlike a legal challenge to the differential treatment meted out to black students who spoke the same language as white students, the legal challenge Sánchez envisaged required judges to question educational decision-making with respect to what was the best pedagogical approach for students who supposedly possessed varying English-language skills. Courts loath to intercede thus had a ready-made rationale for inaction. The challenge, then, was to demonstrate "that actual facts give the lie to the 'pedagogical reasons' offered" and instead demonstrate "that segregation is inimical to good education." Until that happened, Sánchez wrote Baldwin in 1945, "I do not think that we will ever win . . . a school segregation case."[85] As "self-evident" and "trite" as it might seem to prove what Sánchez viewed as the irrefutable educational "unsoundness" of segregated schools, it was an undertaking that could not be avoided.[86]

For this reason, Sánchez would have likely harbored little hope for a successful resolution to *Mendez* had he seen Marcus's petition that launched the case on March 2, 1945. Whereas Sánchez believed that a "thorough-going analysis of school segregation" was an essential precondition to litigation—including "the gathering of statistics" and the collecting of affidavits from a variety of "experts" on the "pedagogical unsoundness of the various aspects of segregation"—Marcus's initial filing did not touch upon the school districts' purportedly pedagogical rationales for segregating the students he represented.[87] Instead, he stressed that the Orange County school districts he was suing segregated their "American Mexican" students, as he would describe them in a subsequent filing, "solely for the reason" that they "are of Mexican or Latin descent." This practice, in turn, constituted "discriminatory conduct" and violated the students' rights to "equal treatment with other persons and to equal protection of the laws."[88]

In response, lawyers for Orange County insisted that lack of English proficiency on the part of "a large number of children" from families of "Mexican or Latin descent," rather than the mere fact that those children were of "Mexican or Latin descent," drove the school districts' segregation. "That for the efficient instruction of pupils from said families," argued Deputy Counsel George F. Holden on behalf of County Counsel Joel E. Ogle, "the Westminster School District has found it desirable to instruct said pupils at different locations than are provided for the instruction of pupils who are familiar with the English language . . . during the period they are in the lower grades." Doing so served "the best interests" of both students of "Mexican descent" and their "English-speaking" counterparts "until they acquired some efficiency in the English language."[89] Holden and Ogle made identical claims in their initial answers to Marcus's charges on behalf of the other school districts, adding that Garden Grove also chose to reserve its "English-speaking" school for students who were "more advanced according to the American standards in personal hygiene."[90] What Marcus deemed arbitrary and discriminatory, Holden and Ogle deemed purposeful and pedagogical. Their defense lent credence to Sánchez's assertion to Baldwin, just days after Marcus filed *Mendez*, that any legal challenge to the segregation of Mexican American students would have to "dispute the pedagogical reasons under which school boards find it possible to maintain segregated schools."[91]

Judge McCormick agreed, as became evident in a pretrial hearing held on June 26, 1945, the purpose of which was to reach agreement on the specific issues to be addressed in the trial that was slated to begin the following week. For McCormick, the central question was not whether Marcus's clients had been segregated, but whether there was "discriminatory segregation." If they were "segregated solely and exclusively because of their ancestry or lineage," McCormick explained, paraphrasing Marcus's position, that would constitute illegal discrimination. If, however, they were segregated on the basis of their "linguistic qualifications"—that is, their "inability . . . to grasp instruction the same as children who are so-called English-speaking children"—that would be "within the proper scope of school authority." Under these circumstances, segregation was not synonymous with discrimination. The "mere fact" that there were all "Mexican" schools in each of the districts that Marcus sued "wouldn't necessarily establish . . . unjust discrimination." The school districts could have legitimate pedagogical reasons for the segregation they practiced "which would not impinge the constitutional right to equality of educational facilities in the public school systems."[92] The districts' attorneys would just need to demonstrate that legitimacy during the trial, while Marcus would have to refute it.

Marcus bore the heavier burden for at least two reasons. First, McCormick expressed his disinclination to insinuate himself into the decision-making of educational authorities, which is precisely the position Sánchez said courts would take in Mexican American school segregation case. "The Court, McCormick insisted, "couldn't set itself up as the standard of school management," nor could it be the arbiter of aptitudes of public school students. Second, the presence of some students of Mexican descent in the "English-speaking" schools undermined Marcus's claim that discrimination based on ancestry alone accounted for the segregation. In an exchange about El Modena School District, Marcus inquired, "Did I understand the Court to say that . . . the admission of 25 Spanish-speaking pupils in the Roosevelt School would . . . indicate that . . . there was no discrimination?" McCormick replied, "It would have the tendency to indicate that there wasn't any fixed line of demarcation between children of Mexican lineage and other children." What about El Modena's Lincoln School whose entire student body of 249 was "Spanish-speaking pupils," Marcus retorted. That, McCormick responded, could also be explained by "other factors" besides "race . . . ancestry . . . or . . . lineage," in particular, the "mental ability of the student[s]," which "wouldn't be an unjust or unreasonable discrimination." This was precisely the school districts' position—"that the segregation is based entirely on the language difficulty," which, in turn, rendered those students "unable to make the grade" in the "English-speaking" schools. They "can't keep up with the other students," Holden contended. "That," McCormick replied turning Holden's contention into a question, "narrows it down pretty well to the issue" to be determined during the trial.[93]

It also required Marcus to switch litigation gears. Though Marcus's initial petition did not broach what McCormick saw as the main issue, he wasted little time doing so once he realized just how central it was to both the districts' case and the judge's understanding of how to approach it. Early in the pretrial hearing, he objected to the characterization of his clients as "Spanish-speaking." The term suggested that they did not speak English, which Marcus would not concede, lest it reinforce the rationale for segregating them. Referring to his opposing counsel, Marcus implored McCormick, "When they recite the fact that there are Spanish-speaking pupils, it would leave the inference with the Court . . . that these pupils only speak Spanish. As a matter of fact, we are prepared to show that they speak English and spoke English prior to attending school, and that the only discrimination practiced is . . . because they are of Spanish descent." McCormick, however, did not share Marcus's reservations. The distinction was one of "degree . . . not kind," he replied. As a result, "English-speaking" versus "Spanish-speaking" continued to be employed throughout the trial despite its connotation, along with similarly loaded terms to describe the English abilities of the students in the "Mexican" schools, including "not efficient in English" and "handicapped by their deficiency in the English language."[94]

More importantly, during the trial itself, which was held over five days in early July 1945, Marcus pressed the school districts' superintendents over how exactly they ascertained the English abilities of the vast majority of students of Mexican descent in each district who were relegated to the "Mexican"/"Spanish-speaking" schools. Their answers proved critical in making Marcus's case. Garden Grove's superintendent said that either he or a principal administered an oral exam by talking to the students of Mexican descent who his district segregated.[95] Similarly, Westminster's superintendent testified that he had a "conversation with the children, asking for a response in other than yes or no" in order to determine the students' capacity "to carry on a conversation in the English language in an intelligible manner."[96] The other two districts on trial did not even bother testing. "The children that enroll[ed]" in El Modena's "Mexican"/"Spanish-speaking" school, according to its superintendent, received no tests whatsoever. After all, he explained, "It is highly impossible to test a child that can't speak the English language." As for Santa Ana, the students' Spanish surnames were all that the district officials needed to know. In response to a query from Marcus about whether Santa Ana "determined . . .

whether or not [students] were of Mexican descent by looking at their names," the superintendent responded, "Very largely, certainly."[97]

Many of the parents Marcus brought as witnesses reinforced the superintendents' incriminating testimony, indicating that their children received no English tests, not even in those school districts that claimed to administer them.[98] Moreover, all the parents who were asked by Marcus if their children spoke English insisted that they did.[99] A fourteen-year-old student from El Modena who had recently graduated from the town's "Mexican"/"Spanish-speaking" school drove home the parents' claim by testifying in flawless English. She also spoke about the "plenty of white children, Americans" who were her neighbors but not her classmates and noted a conversation she had with her school's principal about why "the American children and the Mexican children" were "separated." During that conversation, she said, she also complained about how the handful of "pupils of Mexican descent" at the "English-speaking"/"American school" came to consider themselves "superior . . . and sometimes they wouldn't even talk to us." When asked about this student's testimony, El Modena's superintendent dismissed her as an exception—"one of our best students" with an "I.Q. that is very high."[100]

While Marcus expected the parents and two students he called as witnesses to help make the case he brought on their behalf, he received inadvertent assistance from the school officials themselves. Their testimony, he observed after the trial, provided the "strangest type and quality of substantiation," coming as it did from the "sources" most "adverse" to his case. Taken together, it revealed what Marcus referred to as the "varied and devious excuses to justify the practice of segregation."[101]

Superintendent James L. Kent of Garden Grove proved to be the most revealing of the "true motive[s]" beyond the "supposed language handicap," as as an amicus brief written by Charles F. Christopher of the National Lawyers Guild of Los Angeles and A.L. (Al) Wirin of the ACLU of Southern California put it.[102] Kent's district had been the lone one to defend segregation on grounds beyond English proficiency in the initial responses to Marcus's filing of the suit, maintaining that the district also chose to reserve its "English-speaking" school for students who were "more advanced according to the American standards in personal hygiene."[103] During his testimony, Kent elaborated on this and other reasons for segregation. "Mexican children," Kent claimed, had "generally dirty hands, face, neck, and ears." They, therefore, required special instruction in "cleanliness," which Kent cited as a reason for segregating them, as well as "manners, which ordinarily do not come out of the home." They also needed instruction in "social habits," such as "cleanliness of the mind, mannerisms, dress, ability to get along with other people." These lessons, too, necessitated segregation, given that the students for whom they were geared possessed more "physical prowess" than "mental ability" and would consequently acquire a "feeling of inferiority" in a classroom that included "white child[ren]." Kent initially even testified, "I don't believe he [i.e., the Mexican] is of the white race," but he retracted that statement following a recess.[104]

Kent's testimony remained consistent and consistently racist right down to the very end of the trial when his own attorneys called him to mitigate the damage he had inflicted on their case. Coming from a bilingual home, Kent claimed, "handicapped" students of Mexican descent "throughout [their] school life." This assertion prompted Judge McCormick to intervene with a question that belied his initial predisposition against judicial meddling into school affairs. "Wouldn't his [i.e., the child of Mexican descent] assimilation efficiency be improved by putting him with children who speak English rather than with those who had the bilingual disqualification which you mention?" McCormick inquired. Kent's answer evaded the question. Moreover, he insisted, desegregation between schools would still produce segregation within one school. "The result would be about 90 percent of our low group, out of that mixing, would be the Mexican group."[105] In short, Kent viewed "Mexicans" as "an inferior people, and he clung to his superiority complex to the last," as Marcus summarized his testimony.[106]

So, too, albeit somewhat less explicitly, did Kent's counterparts, though they at least attempted to hew more closely to their districts' defense of segregation on pedagogical grounds. Unlike Kent, Superintendent Harold Hammarstan of El Modena denied that students of Mexican descent were "inferior in any way." Still, he maintained, "most of them" lacked a "basic understanding of the English language when they start first grade." Even in the case of the exceptional twenty-five students of Mexican descent in El Modena's "English-speaking" school, Hammarsten considered them to be "generally speaking of the whole group" on a "lower" level of "aptitude" than their schoolmates. Consequently, integrating El Modena's schools, as Marcus and his clients sought, would be educationally unsound. Given the differences in "ability," desegregation would "naturally throw all of the Mexican students into one group." The few exceptions to this rule would result in the deprivation of intellectual role models for the other students of Mexican descent.[107]

Superintendent Richard F. Harris of Westminster echoed Hammarsten. The students in the "Spanish-speaking" school were, he testified, "inferior only in so far as their ability to grasp English words and meanings and conceptions are concerned." This inferiority, however, had far-reaching educational implications. It meant that those students, by and large, lacked the "ability" and "background" of their counterparts who came from "English-speaking home[s]."

They matriculated in school, for example, without knowledge of "Mother Goose rhymes" and "stories of our American heroes, stories of our American frontier." Absent such ostensibly essential "cultural backgrounds," they were at an educational disadvantage and thus needed instruction in a segregated setting to overcome them. The segregation practiced in Westminster, Harris insisted, was "entirely on an ability basis." Among the students at the "Spanish-speaking" school, "nearly all" lacked the ability to attend the "English-speaking" school. As for the exceptional few, it was "from an educational standpoint, a good thing" to leave them where they were in order to be role models and leaders for their peers.[108]

Not content to let the superintendents' own testimony torpedo their defense, Marcus concluded the trial with two expert witnesses. Taking the districts' pedagogical defense of segregation at face value, they each testified that segregation did not serve the students' "best [educational] interests." Ralph Beals, chair of the Department of Anthropology and Sociology at the University of California at Los Angeles, insisted, "Segregation defeats the purpose of teaching English" and "slows up the process . . . of Americanization." In addition, segregated students "become hostile to the whole culture of the surrounding majority group."[109] Marie Hughes, a doctoral student at Stanford University with educational experience in New Mexico and Los Angeles, reiterated Beals on every point. According to McWilliams, Marcus's use of expert testimony marked "perhaps the first time in a test case" that such a strategy was employed.[110]

Following the trial, Judge McCormick asked the lawyers to submit answers to a series of questions he posed. In response, Marcus emphasized how Orange County's claim that "lack of knowledge of the English language by the children of Mexican ancestry was the principal reason for segregation" conflicted with the evidence adduced. None of the witnesses, Marcus stressed, "testified that any *genuine or definite test was used* to determine" the English proficiency of the students Marcus represented.[111] Instead, the testimony of the school officials, corroborated by that of the parents and students, revealed that the segregation Marcus challenged stemmed from a litany of "fictitious, trumped and false" beliefs in their inferiority—not only vis-à-vis students of "Anglo Saxon descent," but also vis-à-vis "Portuguese and Japs and Negroes."[112] Prejudice, not pedagogy, drove the school districts' segregation, though proving the former had required disproving the latter, as Marcus had discovered as *Mendez* unfolded.

If that was not enough to persuade the court to rule in their favor, the fact remained that "children of Mexican descent are white and Caucasians—not colored."[113] Marcus's invocation of Mexican Americans as white was a tactical move.[114] It grew out of a pretrial agreement between the lawyers on both sides of *Mendez* that "there is no question of race," as Judge McCormick put it.[115]

Instead, Marcus argued, his clients' were "denied the equal protection of the laws because . . . they are of Mexican ancestry." As a practical matter, Marcus saw little difference between race and ancestry discrimination. The school districts' "ism," he argued, "whatever it may be called, is at war with the American idea of equality." As a legal matter, however, characterizing his clients as "white" and the "ism" they faced as something other than "racism" allowed Marcus to present the judge (and, on appeal, judges) who heard his case with at least two paths of least resistance for ruling against the Orange County school districts without having to rule more broadly and boldly against California's segregation statutes or any legal precedents that upheld segregation. First, the state's school segregation statutes omitted any reference to students of Mexican descent among the groups it identified. There was, in other words, "no authority . . . to segregate children in attendance at Public Schools upon *any basis* except when expressly authorized by law."[116] In particular, California's school segregation laws, as Christopher and Wirin noted in their amicus brief, did not authorize "separate schools for persons who speak Spanish as distinguished from those who speak English, or separate schools for those of Mexican descent."[117] Second, moving from the statutes to the case law, although there existed numerous legal precedents for segregation between racial groups, those precedents did not address the legality of segregating one group of white students from another group of white students. When the school districts' attorneys leaned heavily on one such race-based school segregation precedent, Marcus deemed it inapplicable to *Mendez.* It involved "segregation of 'colored children'" and was, therefore, a "worthless" precedent to cite as "authority to segregate white children on the basis of descent."[118] That Marcus had previously secured a victory in a racially restrictive housing covenant case in which the court held that there was no such thing as a "Mexican race" no doubt reinforced his sense of the strategic sensibility of employing a similar line of argument in *Mendez.*[119] Likewise, Christopher and Wirin dismissed other cases the Orange County lawyers invoked because they dealt with "separate races."[120]

These claims about the unprecedented nature of *Mendez* echoed those of Judge McCormick. "I don't believe there is any case in the books that parallels this case," he commented during the pretrial hearing. [121] As the trial drew to a close, he elaborated, "Since there is no race question here . . . it means we have a novel situation." Taking his cue from McCormick, Marcus argued that he could find "no case which decides this question for or against petitioners contentions."[122] This novelty, in turn, afforded McCormick the opportunity to rule against the Orange County districts without having to overturn California's school segregation statutes or challenge the numerous legal precedents that upheld state-sanctioned segregation, most notably *Plessy v. Ferguson.*

McCormick seized that opportunity in the decision he delivered on February 18, 1946. Though unequivocally a victory for the students of Mexican descent that Marcus represented, it was much less an unequivocal victory against de jure school segregation. On the one hand, McCormick rejected the school districts' purportedly pedagogical justification for segregation. Their claim that students of Mexican descent possessed "English language deficiencies" was, McCormick ruled, little more than a pretext for "arbitrary discrimination." In El Modena, "No credible language test is given to the children of Mexican ancestry." Similarly, Santa Ana administered tests that McCormick deemed "hasty, superficial and not reliable." In some cases, Santa Ana school authorities simply segregated students according to the "Latinized or Mexican name of the child." To drive home his point, McCormick peppered his ruling with references to the "so-called Spanish-speaking pupils," the phrasing and repetition of which added a hint of sarcasm to his forceful opinion. On the other hand, McCormick left the door open for segregation based on English ability. "The only tenable ground upon which segregation practices in the defendant school districts can be defended," he wrote, "lies in the English language deficiencies of some of the children of Mexican ancestry as they enter elementary public school life." In other words, "English language deficiencies," if properly identified, could serve as a legitimate basis for school segregation.[123]

Just how legitimate, though, remained unclear. Even as McCormick acknowledged a crack in the door for the school districts to segregate their students according to their English proficiency, he expressed deep reservations about the educational and social merits of doing so. Educationally, he echoed the testimony of Marcus's expert witnesses and cited evidence that "clearly shows that Spanish-speaking children are retarded in learning English by lack of exposure to its use because of segregation." Socially, he viewed segregation as anathema to assimilation. The "commingling of the entire student body," he proclaimed, "instills and develops a common cultural attitude among the school children which is imperative for the perpetuation of American institutions and ideals." School segregation—whatever its rationale—breeds "antagonisms in the children and suggest[s] inferiority among them where none exists." Nevertheless, the crack remained, at least in theory. Language-based segregation, while perhaps educationally and socially unsound in McCormick's view, was not necessarily illegal.[124]

Having discounted the school districts' administration of what he described as their "only tenable ground" for segregation, McCormick cleared the way to strike at the school segregation as practiced in the Orange County districts before him. On first blush, he cut a wide legal swath. Separate, he announced, in ringing terms that foreshadowed Chief Justice Warren's words in *Brown*, can never be equal: "The equal protection of the laws' . . . is not provided by furnishing in separate schools the same technical facilities, text books and courses of instruction to children of Mexican ancestry that are available to the other public school children regardless of their ancestry. A paramount requisite is social equality. It must be open to all children by unified school association regardless of lineage." On second blush, however, McCormick's focus on "children of Mexican ancestry" and "lineage" allowed him to avoid grappling with the constitutionality of California's school segregation statutes beyond their inapplicability to students of Mexican descent. Those laws, McCormick wrote, applied to "specific situations"—meaning the specific groups identified in them—"not pertinent to this action." Since they were "not pertinent" to the case at hand, McCormick did not rule on them, though he did express his disdain for all "distinctions . . . based upon race or ancestry."[125] Instead, his final word on the matter called for the school districts charged in *Mendez*, and others similarly situated in the territory covered by McCormick's district court, to stop "segregating . . . pupils . . . of Latin or Mexican descent"—or, at least, devise a more appropriate language test upon which to base any continued segregation.[126]

Taking a cue from McCormick's ruling, the Texas Office of the Attorney General chose the latter course, adopting the narrow reading of *Mendez* that McCormick's opinion allowed as legal cover for the continued segregation of students of Mexican descent. It interpreted the case as proscribing segregation "based solely upon Latin American or Mexican descent," but permitting "separate classes or schools" in cases of "language deficiencies or other individual needs or aptitudes" through grade three, provided that "examinations, and other properly conducted tests, [were] equally applied to all pupils." To support this interpretation of *Mendez*, the Texas Office of the Attorney General quoted McCormick's assertion that "English language deficiencies," if properly tested for in the early grades, could serve as legitimate grounds for segregation.[127]

This also proved to be the path that El Modena School District took. When the new school year opened in September 1946, school officials began testing those students from the "Mexican" school who requested transfers. They promptly failed eight out of the first ten tested. This "thoroughly aroused" the town's Mexican descent residents, according to Fred Ross. With Ross's assistance, they organized the El Modena Unity League, circulated a petition denouncing the school board's action, forced an emergency meeting of the board and superintendent, and went to court to demand the implementation of the *Mendez* decision, which was granted to them.[128] This victory, however, proved to be Pyrrhic, at least in El Modena. Segregation within El Modena's two elementary schools replaced segregation between them. As one eyewitness account put it, "Well, after the order they put them all together in both schools—but it's like oil and water, I guess. . . . So now instead of two, they've got twenty-four segregated schools—twelve in each building!"[129] The sweep of Judge McCormick's decision—hailed by *La Opinión*, a Los Angeles-based Spanish-language daily, as a "brilliant judicial exposition," and by Marcus as "one of the greatest judicial decisions in favor of democratic practices granted since the emancipation of the slaves"—appeared to narrow in the face of the intransigence of El Modena's school officials.[130]

Their counterparts in Westminster, however, were more forthcoming. When the 1946–1947 school year began, they integrated the town's two elementary schools.[131] Meanwhile, in neighboring Riverside County, the threat of a Marcus-led lawsuit by the Bell Town Improvement League, proved to be enough to prevail upon school officials to desegregate.[132] "If there were as many as one segregated Mexican American pupil," Ross paraphrased the school superintendent as saying, "see to it that he gets unsegregated immediately." This "complete victory," as Ross described it, "marked the end of Ice Age educational policy in West Riverside."[133]

These victories for desegregation occurred while Orange County attorneys were engaged in appealing *Mendez* to the Ninth Circuit Court of Appeals. Carey McWilliams, who would later join one of the amicus briefs filed in the appeal, explained that the school districts' lawyers "elected to appeal on the judgment issue alone," meaning McCormick's order to desegregate Orange County's schools. Under these circumstances, McWilliams continued, McCormick's "finding as to the facts will have to be accepted."[134] These factual findings had demolished the school districts' claims, which were the centerpiece of their original defense, that "efficient instruction of pupils" from Mexican descent families made it educationally "desirable" to segregate them until they became more proficient in English.[135]

Consequently, the school districts' attorneys switched their litigation strategy from an emphasis on pedagogical reasons for segregation to a reliance on the infamous legal precedent of *Plessy v. Ferguson*. As per *Plessy*, they insisted that the segregation practiced in the districts Marcus sued was separate but equal. They cited McCormick's opinion on this point, which said that "the record before us shows without conflict that the technical facilities and physical conveniences offered in the schools housing entirely the segregated pupils, the efficiency of the teachers therein and the curricula are identical and in some respects superior to those in the other schools in the respective districts."[136] This boiled down the case on appeal to "one main issue": upholding McCormick's decision would "necessitate the overruling of *Plessy v. Ferguson*."[137] Would the Ninth Circuit be so bold as to take this momentous step? This was the implicit question and challenge posed by the Orange County school districts' lawyers.

Marcus tried to ratchet down the stakes, presenting the Ninth Circuit with the option of upholding McCormick's decision without having to strike down *Plessy*. To this end, Marcus disputed his opposing counsels' claim of separate but equal. Whatever equality McCormick noted in the "technical facilities," "physical conveniences," teacher "efficiency," and "identical . . . curriculum," the fact remained that "the segregation practiced retards Spanish-reading children in learning English, fosters antagonisms, and creates inferiority in the children." Separate was not—and could not—be equal. In addition, Marcus argued, the tests used to ascertain English proficiency were, as McCormick found, "hasty, superficial, and not reliable." More boldly, Marcus charged that "discrimination solely because of ancestry" violated the Fourteenth Amendment, even if "'equal facilities and equal instruction'" were provided. Though approaching an argument for the Ninth Circuit to rule against *Plessy*, Marcus made sure to reiterate how both sides had agreed at the outset of the trial that "race discrimination" was not at issue "since persons of Latin and Mexican extraction are members of the 'white' race." *Plessy* and its progeny, in other words, did not apply and could be avoided. Anticipating this argument, the school districts' attorneys insisted that if *Plessy* could support separate schools for "Negro" and "Chinese" children, then it could also support the practice of requiring "certain children of the white race to attend a school separate and apart from other members of the same race."[138]

Four amici curiae briefs supported Marcus's appeal. One came from the ACLU and National Lawyers Guild, who had previously joined together in the lone amicus brief filed in *Mendez* in the district court. This time, however, Saburo Kido, on behalf of the Japanese American Citizens League (JACL), joined them. The *Pacific Citizen* hailed the JACL's November 1946 filing as "the first instance of JACL action in a test case which did not involve persons of Japanese ancestry." JACL leader Mike Masaoka described the move as reflective of "a growing awareness on the part of the JACL leadership of the common interests of all racial minority groups."[139] Together, the brief's authors argued that the Fourteenth Amendment proscribed "discrimination because of ancestry or nationality" as much as it did discrimination based on race. Such discrimination, they maintained, was reflected in how the school districts' stated rationale for segregation—"the alleged unfamiliarity with the English language"—masked "the real reason for the segregation," which was "the un-scientific and un-American theory of the supposed inferiority of the children of Mexican descent as compared to others." If that was not enough, though, California's segregation statutes made no provision for separating Spanish-speaking students from English-speaking students, nor did it mention students of Mexican descent.[140] The implications of this statutory silence were reiterated in the amicus brief filed by California Attorney General Robert Kenny. It "remove[d] any doubt but that as to children of Mexican or Latin descent the State Legislature has directed the separate schools shall not be maintained." Beyond that, Kenny expressed support for the more sweeping challenges to segregation advanced in the other two amicus briefs submitted by the NAACP and American Jewish Congress (AJC), both of which took direct aim at *Plessy*'s separate but equal doctrine.[141]

Mendez had caught the NAACP's leading litigators by surprise. "We did not anticipate this case," wrote William Hastie to Thurgood Marshall, who had been Hastie's star pupil at Howard University law school in the early 1930s and was now head of the NAACP's Legal Defense and Educational Fund.[142] Indeed, though *Mendez* had been filed in federal district court in March 1945 and decided there in February 1946, it was not until April 1946 that Marshall first inquired about the case.[143] As Marshall and his colleagues learned about *Mendez*, they understood it as analogous to the Southern, African American school desegregation cases they were then litigating on the road to *Brown*. *Mendez*, Robert Carter wrote in 1947 shortly after he and Marshall filed their amicus brief, involved "basically . . . the same problem."[144]

Reflecting this assumption about the overlap between *Mendez* and the NAACP's other desegregation cases, the NAACP's amicus brief neglected the particularities of the case. Only the page-and-a-half introduction and a few paragraphs in the middle of the 31-page document offered any hint that *Mendez* was a case set in the West, rather than in the South, and involved Mexican American, rather than African American, students.[145] Even then, the differences paled in comparison to the overarching similarity: like segregation of African American students in the South, segregation of Mexican American students in southern California, according to the brief's lead argument, was a classification based on "race and color." Such "distinctions on racial grounds," the brief concluded, were "inimical to our best interests and contrary to our laws."[146] For the NAACP, then, *Mendez* was no more (or less) than another test case on the road to *Brown*. As Carter would recall years later, when he served as a judge in the United States District Court for the Southern District of New York, "The NAACP's amicus brief [in *Mendez*] was the forerunner of its brief in *Brown v. Board of Education* arguing that segregation *per se* violated due process and equal protection guarantees." It was here that "the all-out-attack position had been articulated."[147] It was here, too, that the organization first deployed social science to buttress that attack, as Marshall would later note.[148]

While the NAACP's contribution to *Mendez* would prove to be an important milestone on its road to *Brown*, it had no discernible impact on the Ninth Circuit's *Mendez* ruling. Nor, for that matter, did the AJC's brief, though it, unlike the NAACP's, at least addressed one of the major arguments the Orange County school districts made for the pedagogical benefits of separating students who do not speak English. Such separation, the AJC argued, was "inconsistent with that policy of rapid and full adjustment of immigrants upon which the federal naturalization law, with its short residential requirement is predicated."[149]

On December 9, 1946, all the Ninth Circuit judges, rather than the usual panel of three, convened in San Francisco to hear oral arguments in *Mendez*. They sat before an overflowing courtroom assembled to witness what the *San Francisco Chronicle* called "one of the most important [cases] ever to come under Federal jurisdiction in this area."[150] No doubt the judges knew that they were poised on the cusp of civil rights history. Four months later, on April 14, 1947, Judge Albert Lee Stephens delivered the Ninth Circuit's decision. He noted the "argument in two of the amicus curiae briefs"—the NAACP's and AJC's—for the court "to strike out independently on the whole question of segregation on the ground that recent world stirring events have set men to the reexamination of concepts considered fixed." He then scurried back to the safer ground that the briefs submitted by Marcus, the ACLU/JACL/NLG, and California Attorney General had identified as part of their arguments. Insisting that judges must be ever vigilant of abusing the enormous powers delegated to them—of "rationaliz[ing] outright legislation under the too free use of the power to interpret"—Stephens conceded, "We are not tempted by the siren who calls to us that the sometimes slow and tedious ways of democratic legislation is no longer respected in progressive society." Stephens then affirmed McCormick's district court ruling, but on the narrowest of grounds. "The segregation in this case," he wrote, "is without legislative support."[151]

The Ninth Circuit thus avoided not only a head-on confrontation with *Plessy* and the cases that upheld it, but also with California's school segregation statutes (as had McCormick, though less explicitly). The issue of whether or not the Fourteenth Amendment's equal protection clause rendered separate inherently unequal did not figure into the decision. Instead, the case turned on a statutory silence—"that the California law does not include the segregation of school children because of their Mexican blood." As for the law and its condoning of school segregation for "Indians under certain conditions and children of Chinese, Japanese or Mongolian parentage," the Ninth Circuit left it untouched. The state permitted segregation between "children of parents belonging to one of the great races of mankind" to which it referred, but not within one of those "great races," which subsumed both white non-Mexican and white Mexican students.[152] In addition, the ruling left open the possibility that legitimate English tests could be devised to segregate students, as McCormick had done.[153] For these reasons, the final court stop for *Mendez* spoke much more to what made the case unique to Mexican American students than it did to whatever similarities their segregation and the legal challenge to it bore to the African American students who would, seven years later, have their case addressed by the United States Supreme Court in *Brown.*

For these reasons, too, the *Open Forum* denounced the Ninth Circuit's ruling as a "cold legalistic decision."[154] The NAACP's Carter was a bit more upbeat, though still lukewarm. He noted how the Ninth Circuit had significantly narrowed the reach of the District Court's ruling. Still, Carter acknowledged, *Mendez* brought "the American courts closer to a decision on the whole question of segregation."[155] As for Sánchez, he considered the case "unquestionably good but only partially satisfactory." Though it declared "illegal" the segregation of "Mexicans as such," it still allowed "grouping for instructional purposes" through third grade."[156]

Well before the Ninth Circuit insisted that school desegregation was a legislative rather than judicial responsibility, Manuel Ruiz, Jr. had been pressuring California lawmakers to strike down the state's segregation statutes.[157] Born and raised in East Los Angeles, Ruiz received undergraduate and law degrees from the University of Southern California. After being rebuffed in his efforts to join a law firm, despite an almost straight A transcript, Ruiz went into private practice. While working as an attorney, Ruiz became an activist and leader in the Los Angeles Mexican American community, serving as co-chair of the Los Angeles Coordinating Council of Latin-American Youth, which he helped found in 1941, and which he later described as California's "first formally organized Mexican-American lobby."[158] In 1943, Ruiz was appointed to Governor Warren's Citizens Advisory Committee on Youth in Wartime. From this position, Ruiz spearheaded the committee's November 1944 recommendation to repeal the California's school segregation law.[159]

Assemblyman William Rosenthal proposed a bill that dropped "Indian" from the language of the school segregation law, but still left school districts free to segregate "children of Chinese, Japanese, or Mongolian parentage." In response, Ruiz scribbled in the margin "Rosenthal misunderstood—we want *no* separate schools."[160] He then wrote to Rosenthal, acknowledging the "technical" advantages to Rosenthal's approach, but bemoaning the inability to "carry on a crusade in its support."[161] As he carried out his personal crusade, Ruiz disputed the claims of school officials' claims that "language barriers" justified school segregation. "If immigrant Italian, French, or the children of some other national origin had been similarly segregated," he wrote, "the process of assimilation of the people into our national life would have been retarded several generations."[162] In addition, Ruiz highlighted the importance of school desegregation in California for United States policy abroad, especially in Latin America in order to demonstrate that "the Good Neighbor policy was not simply an ideal of our beloved Franklin Delano Roosevelt."[163] Ruiz's appeals, however, failed to persuade California legislators. Though a desegregation bill introduced by Rosenthal passed the assembly in 1945, it died in the senate.[164]

Undeterred, Ruiz appealed directly to the future author of the Supreme Court's *Brown* decision, Governor Earl Warren. Drawing Warren's attention to the statutory provision that "makes possible the segregation of persons of Mexican extraction in our public school system," he urged the governor to lean on the state legislature to repeal the measure in a special meeting of that body set for 1946.[165] Ruiz's note befuddled Warren's legislative secretary, Beach Vasey. Having "carefully read" the state's segregation law, Vasey replied, he "couldn't understand how it applies to persons of Mexican extraction," since they were not specified in the statute.[166] In response, Ruiz explained, "Those school districts which segregate children of Mexican extraction do so upon the theory that they have Indian blood in their veins."[167] In a follow up letter, Ruiz reminded Warren of a meeting they had the year before in which Warren "stated in strong terms that it was [his] belief that Section 8003 . . . ought to be repealed."[168] That reminder did not move Warren. The special session of the legislature the governor convened in 1946 did not take up the subject of the state's school segregation law.

One year later, however, and just four days after the Ninth Circuit's *Mendez* ruling, Warren struck a different chord. He urged California state Senator Herbert Slater, chair of the senate's Committee on Education, to vote for a desegregation bill similar to the one that failed to pass just two years earlier, and which Warren himself had neglected to support.[169] Warren's revised position echoed reasoning expressed in a letter he received from Ninth Circuit Judge William Denman, who wrote a concurring opinion in *Mendez*. California's school segregation law, Denman insisted, not only "does a grievous wrong to [the] thousands of our citizen children" of Mexican descent who found themselves victimized by it, but it also provides "justifiable ground to all the Latin American countries to consider whether our claimed respect for Latin American culture and desire for Latin American amity are sincere." Echoing Denman, Warren wrote Slater, "I personally do not see how we can carry out the spirit of the United Nations if we deny fundamental rights to our Latin American neighbors."[170]

Two months later, the bill that Denman and Warren wanted landed on the governor's desk. As it did, the Warren's legislative secretary, Vasey, reminded him about the Ninth Circuit's judgment in *Mendez*. Though the court had "definitely criticize[d] the practice of . . . segregating the Mexican children in Orange County," it nevertheless left the California school segregation law intact. The measure before Warren proposed to fix that—"to remove from the law the right given to the school districts to segregate children of Indian, Chinese, Japanese and Mongolian parentage." To uphold "democratic principles," Vasey urged Warren to follow the legislature's lead and reach beyond the Ninth Circuit's ruling in *Mendez*.[171] Warren heeded this advice. On June 14, 1947, he signed the bill into law. After nearly a century on the books, statutory school segregation in California was no more, though efforts to desegregate California's K-12 public schools through both litigation and legislation would continue for decades afterward.

As for Gonzalo and Felícitas Méndez, they did not wait for the California legislature or governor or Ninth Circuit to take action. In 1946 the Munemitsus returned to the farm they had leased to the Méndezes, and the Méndezes moved back to Santa Ana shortly thereafter. At the time, their case was pending in the Ninth Circuit, but Gonzalo Méndez decided, once again, to take matters into his own hands. He informed school officials in Santa Ana that he intended to enroll his children in one of the city's "white" schools. In response, Santa Ana school officials took a different approach to Méndez's request than their Westminster counterparts had taken just a few years before. They admitted the Méndez children.[172]

In a December 1946 response to an inquiry he received about *Mendez*, Thurgood Marshall confided "confidentially" that he had "serious doubt" about "the timing for an all-out attack on segregation per se in the present United States Supreme Court."[173] Though Marshall did not explain his reservations, years later Al Wirin, who participated in *Mendez* while leading the litigation in *Oyama*, did. "Had we taken on the business of Negro discrimination" at the time of *Mendez*, "we'd have lost, it was too early." *Mendez* was a "manageable legal and constitutional problem," in Wirin's estimation, "precisely because it wasn't negro, because it was Mexican."[174]

Mendez, however, was not simply different in demographic degree from the African American desegregation cases that the NAACP was handling, as Wirin suggested, but also in legal kind. George I. Sánchez captured this distinction in a 1948 exchange he had with Marshall following a federal district court decision in a Texas desegregation case in which Sánchez and Wirin had been involved. Like *Mendez*, the case of *Delgado v. Bastrop* permitted some English proficiency-based segregation provided that "scientifically standardized" tests were given to determine it.[175] On the heels of *Delgado*, Marshall contacted Sánchez on Wirin's recommendation to request the affidavits of the educational experts who testified in the case. Marshall believed that those materials would aid the NAACP in a case it was litigating elsewhere in Texas. Sánchez, however, did not think so. "I doubt very much that the affidavits which I have would be of any assistance to you," since they involved "denial of the pedagogical soundness of segregation that is based on the 'language handicap' excuse." This rendered Mexican American school segregation a very different legal matter than African American school segregation. Consequently, Sánchez, concluded, "my experts on this particular [Mexican American] case could not very well qualify as experts" in the African American case about which Marshall had approached him.[176]

Five years later, as the Supreme Court took up *Brown*, Sánchez held firm to this conviction. "There is no connection!" he exclaimed to Wirin in October 1953 between "the present segregation cases before the Supreme Court" and "the *Mendez* and *Delgado* decisions." As Sánchez saw it, "our cases really were on the 'due process' clause," by which he meant that the nonstatutory, language-based segregation of Mexican American students was "arbitrary [and] capricious." By contrast, *Brown* was rooted in "the equality ('discrimination') clause." Only a case that "attack[ed] Negro segregation where there is no law decreeing such segregation" would serve as a parallel case, and "only in such a case would we be concerned."[177]

Sánchez's concluding quip alluded to a reservation that Baldwin expressed to Wirin around the same time—and which Wirin sought to refute. If the segregation of students of Mexican descent was illegal simply because they were not specified in the state school segregation statutes, as the Ninth Circuit ruled in *Mendez*, that did not imply that the lawyers who made that argument, like Wirin and Marcus, were "content in merely making" the courts' "point that Mexicans are of the same race as Anglos." On the contrary, Wirin insisted, "The Mexican school segregation cases were broader in scope than merely protecting the rights of Mexicans. And certainly none of them has protected the rights of Mexicans at the expense of Negroes." Nevertheless, he noted, "The courts in the Mexican school segregation cases have virtually entirely ignored the 'separate but equal' doctrine."[178] The Ninth Circuit's ruling in *Mendez* illustrated Wirin's point, though he still deemed it an important victory.[179]

Wirin did not add, though he very well could have, that the Ninth Circuit's avoidance of *Plessy* in *Mendez* rendered it very different *Brown*. Perhaps for this reason *Mendez*, which Wirin referred to as "the pioneer case involving segregation of Mexican school children," did not receive even a footnote's mention in the Supreme Court's opinion in *Brown*, despite the fact that it was written by Chief Justice Earl Warren under whose watch as California governor *Mendez* had been decided and the state's school segregation statutes legislated away.[180] Nor did *Mendez*—either the case or any reference to it—appear in Warren's *Brown* files.[181]

These omissions do not diminish the importance of *Mendez*. On the contrary, *Mendez*'s importance owes in large degree to its distinctiveness. The particularities of Mexican American school segregation in California reflected particularities in the more general experiences with discrimination confronted by Californians of Mexican descent—just as the Alien Land Law at issue in *Oyama* did for Californians of Japanese descent. Focusing on *Mendez's* distinctiveness helps explain why Fred Ross, for example, did not emerge from the campaign against de jure school segregation in California, in which he participated as an organizer in Orange and Riverside counties, with a buoyed belief in the efficacy of the interracial organizing that had been his emphasis when he first began working in southern California for the American Council on Race Relations. Instead, despite the interracial collaboration and success achieved by the Bell Town Improvement League and reflected in the collection of organizations that filed amici curiae briefs in *Mendez*, Ross's efforts shifted away from interracial Unity Leagues and toward Mexican Americans. In the same year that the Ninth Circuit rendered its decision in *Mendez*, Ross helped launch the Community Service Organization (CSO) in Los Angeles, which he would describe in 1948 as "a Mexican NAACP."[182] Such an organization was imperative, he believed, since "every other minority . . . was organized and moving forward except the Mexican American." With the CSO, Ross resolved, to fill this organizational void for "by far the largest, [and] in many ways[,] the most kicked around group in the community."[183]

While Ross was nurturing the CSO, Ernesto Galarza was mounting the first substantial effort to organize California farm workers in the post-World War II era, a disproportionate number of whom were of Mexican descent. Galarza believed that what Ross was doing in Los Angeles, and later in California more generally, as the CSO spread, needed to be undertaken at the national level. "There should probably be a national body whose main concern is the Mexican American minority," he wrote in *Common Ground* in 1949. As models, Galarza pointed to the NAACP and JACL.[184]

Neither Galarza nor Ross eschewed interracial collaboration altogether. "I think it possible," Galarza wrote, "that joint committees of Mexican Americans and other minority groups can be organized locally for co-operation on issues which affect any or all members of those minorities."[185] Similarly, Ross and other CSO leaders participated in the California Federation for Civic Unity (CFCU).[186] Nevertheless, both Galarza and Ross offered qualifications to collaboration. For Galarza, "the fight for Negro rights is not wholly applicable" to Mexican Americans. The organization he envisioned "cannot be created by adopting ready-made patterns."[187] Similarly, Ross's agreement to become executive director of the CFCU in 1952 came with the understanding that "he would devote whatever time was available" to spreading the CSO into northern California. After all, in Ross's estimation, when he assumed his CFCU post, Californians of Mexican descent outside of Los Angeles remained "completely unorganized for civic action on its own issues," much less for "cooperation with other groups working on the same or similar problems."[188] From its inception, then, the CSO sought to advocate for California's most populous and "most disadvantaged minority," to address "their own problems" first, which were rooted in their own "peculiar economic, social, and political status," and to pursue "cooperation [with] other groups" second. In the conflict that Ross and Galarza posed between the particular ("their own problems") and the general ("issues which affect any or all . . . minorities"), priority needed to be given to the particular—in much the same way that JACL made the same choice in the face of the same conflict it confronted during and just after *Oyama.*

Among their own problems, Ross deemed the "most serious" to be the "general lack of citizenship" of Mexican immigrants, while Galarza believed the "most serious weakness" to be "lack of economic organization [i.e., unionization]," especially among Mexican descent agricultural workers. These problems subsumed other problems. Moreover, they were exacerbated in multiple ways by what Ross called the "language handicap" and Galarza called the "language barrier," as well as the proximity of the border, which, among other things, discouraged the pursuit of citizenship, according to Ross, because of the dreams that Mexican immigrants harbored about an "eventual return to Mexico."[189]

For Carey McWilliams, *Mendez* was "one of many current indications that the Mexican minority throughout the Southwest has begun to attain real social and political maturity."[190] If the work of Ross and Galarza in the immediate aftermath of *Mendez* was any indication, however, the "social and political maturity" did not take the shape that McWilliams had envisioned in the conclusion to *Brothers Under the Skin.* For McWilliams, an appreciation for and correlation of multiple "race problems" would, he hoped, lead to a unified push for a comprehensive antidiscrimination solution to them. For Ross and Galarza, however, Mexican immigrants and their United States born children confronted numerous issues particular to them. These group-specific problems did not readily lend themselves to "common front" solutions such as Ross hoped to find through the "joint effort" Unity Leagues organizing that had been his initial focus.

If *Mendez*, like *Oyama*, was any indication, then, finding common denominator issues for common front action was an elusive endeavor. Both cases involved a particular manifestation of de jure segregation that targeted a particular group and required a particular line of legal argumentation. In this way, *Mendez* reflected and foreshadowed the emergence of Mexican American-inflected civil rights struggles in California—just as *Oyama* did for Japanese Americans. Among these, the issue of English-language proficiency would resurface within the context of desegregation litigation brought by the NAACP in California and elsewhere in the Southwest. However, this time it would be advocates for students of Mexican (and Chinese) descent, rather than school district officials, who would make the case that language—or, more specifically, bilingual education—was an educational priority, which took precedence over desegregation.[191]

CHAPTER 4

"JIM CROW IS JUST ABOUT DEAD IN CALIFORNIA"

Like the majority of migrants who flocked to Los Angeles in the 1920s, Loren Miller came from the Midwest, having been born on a farm in Nebraska in 1903 and raised in Kansas. Unlike the majority of his fellow Midwestern transplants, Miller was African American (at least by the "one drop rule" standard of the day) and college educated. His father, according to Miller, was "probably born in slavery" from which he escaped with his parents around 1860. His mother was the descendant of Dutch and Irish immigrants who came to the United States in the eighteenth century.[1] Miller arrived in California in 1929 with a bachelor of laws degree from Washburn College in Topeka. He worked as a journalist for African American newspapers, including the *California Eagle*, which he purchased in 1951, and the *Los Angeles Sentinel*. From the beginning of his journalism career, Miller distinguished himself as a fierce critic of both white racism and the black middle-class leadership that, in his view, did not do enough to combat it. Not content to confine his criticism to newspapers, Miller passed the California bar exam in 1934 and, as the *Los Angeles Times* put it three decades later, embarked on a career of "trail-blazing triumphs, particularly in the field of housing discrimination," that made him "one of the nation's great . . . civil rights attorneys."[2]

Miller began to build his towering legal reputation in the 1940s, when, according to Carey McWilliams, he led the legal campaign against racially restrictive housing covenants in Los Angeles with "consummate skill."[3] In one of the many cases he handled, Miller submitted a lengthy brief to the California Supreme Court on behalf of a group of African American homeowners charged with violating covenants that limited "use or occupancy of property . . . to persons of the white or Caucasian race." In his brief, Miller asserted that the enforcement of such covenants represented an anomalous example of legalized segregation in California. "Segregation not only does not exist in California, in any other field than residence," Miller wrote, "but it is specifically forbidden by statute in places of public accommodation." To reinforce his point, Miller referred to California's public education system. "Separate schools," he claimed, "are forbidden and the law has been vigorously upheld by the courts of this state."[4] Had he specified the omission of African Americans from California's school segregation law or spoke in the future tense about it, Miller would have been right. Instead, Miller's claim appeared in a brief filed on February 8, 1946—ten days before United States District Court Judge Paul J. McCormick issued his decision in the case of *Mendez v. Westminster*, nearly a year and a half before the California legislature would pass and Governor Earl Warren would sign the bill striking down the state's school segregation law, and over two years before the United States Supreme Court would eviscerate the state's Alien Land Law and the California Supreme Court would strike down the state's antimiscegenation law.

Miller's oversight of the extant legalized segregation in California is as striking as it is revealing. It attests, in part, to the separateness of the various campaigns then being waged against the different manifestations of legalized segregation in California. It also attests to Miller's focus on one particular form of legalized segregation for which "Negroes," Miller wrote in 1947, were the "chief victims."[5] During the 1940s, Miller, by his own accounting, handled the "overwhelming majority" of cases in which African Americans were the targets of racially restrictive housing covenant enforcement in California courts.[6] So daunting was the challenge that Miller undertook that Prentice Thomas, assistant special counsel in the New York-based NAACP Legal Defense and Educational Fund, cautioned Thomas Griffith, president of the NAACP's Los Angeles chapter, against such litigation. It would, Thomas warned in January 1943, require "great expenditure of effort and money."[7] Miller, however, was undaunted. In his estimation, racially restrictive housing covenants represented "the most important single issue of civil liberties now facing this community and this nation."[8] The hurdles were high, but the stakes were higher.

The NAACP West Coast Regional Office (NAACP-WC), which opened in San Francisco in November 1944, shared Miller's concerns and kept close tabs on his efforts. "The over-all housing situation is bad enough," wrote NAACP-WC regional director Noah W. Griffin in 1945, "but . . . discriminatory practices make it even worse for Negroes."[9] Griffin's monthly reports to NAACP headquarters frequently included updates on the legal campaign against racially restrictive housing covenants. While those battles raged in California courtrooms, Griffin threw the NAACP-WC behind the fight to enact a state fair employment practices law. Though hardley a panacea, fair employment practices represented a response to what Griffin identified as the NAACP-WC's "paramount concern," namely, the threat of massive postwar job losses.[10]

During the 1940s, Miller's legal campaign and Griffin's legislative work experienced very different outcomes. On the one hand, the United States Supreme Court ruled in 1948 that judicial enforcement of racially restrictive housing covenants was unconstitutional. Though this case—*Shelley v. Kraemer*—did not emanate from California, Miller's path-breaking California litigation earned him a prominent role in both the preparation of briefs and the presentation of oral arguments. In addition, a few months later, in another case that did not include Miller or the NAACP-WC, the California Supreme Court issued the nation's first ruling against an interracial marriage prohibition similar to those on the statute books in thirty other states at the time. *Perez v. Sharp* involved a Mexican American woman, deemed to be "white" by the Los Angeles County Marriage License Bureau, who was prevented from marrying a "Negro" man. On the other hand, the California legislature repeatedly rebuffed fair employment practices bills, while California voters rejected a fair employment practices ballot proposition in November 1946.

Considered together, these countervailing developments captured both the significant accomplishments and profound limits of racial liberalism in California as the 1940s drew to a close. The dismantling of legalized segregation in courts—*Oyama, Takahashi, Mendez, Perez*, and the various California cases that paved the way for *Shelley*—was one thing; the enactment of antidiscrimination laws, beginning with one that covered workplaces was quite another. The former prompted the *Los Angeles Sentinel* to declare, "Jim Crow is just about dead in California in October 1948," while the latter demonstrated just how fraught and formidable would be the antidiscrimination road that began where legalized segregation ended.[11]

In March 1947, Loren Miller delivered a speech entitled, "The Coast Housing Problem and its Solutions." Miller's remarks catalogued many facets of the "housing problem" on the West Coast, in general, and California, in particular, for which his litigation against racially restrictive housing covenants represented a partial solution. "Even if all housing on the Pacific Coast were open to all groups," Miller explained, "Negroes would still be without sufficient housing due to in-migration. Racial restrictive covenants aggravate this situation. The West Coast, particularly California, has more of this problem, and more cases, than any other state."[12] There was not enough housing in California because of the state's World War II population boom, and not enough housing for African Americans, in particular, due to racially restrictive housing covenants.

While the state's total population increased by a little over fifty percent during the 1940s, from 6.9 million to 10.6 million, its African American population grew by nearly four hundred percent, from 124,306 in 1940 to 462,172 in 1950.[13] The vast majority of black newcomers settled in Los Angeles County or the Bay Area. As they searched for housing, they faced a Catch-22: either squeeze into the small swaths of the real estate market not covered by what Griffin referred to in July 1945 as the "continually widening . . . grasp" of racially restrictive housing covenants that forced African Americans into "an ever tightening noose," or seek out property owners who were willing to rent or sell to them in the large swaths of real estate market that were covered by such covenants.[14] The first option risked what Miller described as the "evil products" that accompanied residential segregation across the country, including overcrowding, crime, and disease.[15] The second option risked prosecution, eviction, and, in some cases, violent opposition.

As of mid-1946, Miller estimated that "eighty percent of the land occupied by Negroes in Los Angeles is covered by race restrictions."[16] This "wholesale violation" of the widespread covenants, Miller explained, triggered a "vigorous counter-attack." Defenders of racially restrictive housing covenants filed a "staggering number of lawsuits"—roughly two hundred between 1942 and 1946.[17] With "more suits filed in Los Angeles [against] Negroes" than there were "in the rest of the country," Los Angeles became, as Carey McWilliams wrote in 1949, "the proving ground where the arguments were tested and the legal ammunition accumulated" for the 1948 United States Supreme Court showdown over racially restrictive housing covenants.[18]

McWilliams's specification of "Negroes" was no oversight. He knew that the groups specified in racially restrictive housing covenants were not limited to "Negroes." As Miller observed, "It is a rare agreement indeed that does not frown upon use and occupancy by all persons included within the term 'non-Caucasian,' and of late years even that language has been improved upon and some of the more recent agreements forbid use and occupancy by any person whose blood is not entirely that of the white race." This capacious category, according to Miller, included "Negroes . . . persons of African descent . . . Armenians . . . Hindus . . . descendants or former residents of the Turkish Empire . . . Japanese . . . Chinese . . . and . . . Mexicans."[19] To Miller's list, a *Nation* article added, "Jews, Latin Americans . . . Indians . . . Greeks . . . Assyrians, Filipinos, Persians, Koreans, Arabs, Ethiopians . . . Hawaiians, Puerto Ricans, and 'non-Caucasians' in general."[20]

Yet, as inclusive as they were in print, in practice during the 1940s in California racially restrictive housing covenants were enforced overwhelmingly in courts against the state's newest wave of "non-Caucasian" arrivals. "Negroes," Miller maintained in May 1946, "have borne the brunt of the battle against race restrictive covenants."[21] The Japanese American Citizens League's (JACL) Larry Tajiri agreed. "The war and manpower needs on the Pacific coast resulted in the migration to the area of a large number of Negro workers and their families," Tajiri wrote in the *Pacific Citizen* in May 1946, "and it is against this group that the present campaign for restrictive covenants is aimed."[22] Indeed, as the JACL considered filing an amicus brief in a consolidated group of cases that Miller was preparing to try in the California Supreme Court in 1947, the organization could not locate a single pending case involving a person of Japanese descent in the 30–40 cases it counted as then before the state's highest tribunal.[23] In fact, in one of the few courtroom victories Miller secured prior to the United States Supreme Court's ruling on racially restrictive housing covenants in 1948, a Los Angeles County Superior Court judge cited the presence of "non-Caucasians, including Japanese" as rendering "void" the attempt to enforce the neighborhood covenant against Miller's client, an African American surgeon.[24] The distinction that the opponents of Miller's client drew between African Americans whose occupancy they opposed and Japanese Americans whose occupancy they accepted (at least enough not to bring suit) reinforced a claim that Miller made in a brief filed in another one of his cases on appeal to the California Supreme Court. The "sole object," he wrote, "is to bar Negroes from occupancy."[25] This in turn, Miller observed in another venue, meant "the problem of acquiring a decent home in a decent neighborhood is particularly acute for Negroes (more so than other minorities)."[26]

ACLU and JACL attorney Al Wirin noted that Mexican Americans experienced something similar to Japanese Americans when it came to enforcement of racially restrictive housing covenants. In October 1945, ACLU national director Roger Baldwin queried Wirin about bringing "a Mexican covenant case," on the heels of Wirin's participation in *Mendez*, which Wirin described as his "first Mexican American case." Wirin replied that "technically" such litigation was "ill-advised." The only way the case that Baldwin had in mind could be brought was reactively, rather than proactively. A signatory to a racially restrictive housing covenant would have to sue a person or persons of Mexican descent for violating it. As far as Wirin knew "no such case [was] pending in California."[27] Among the previously settled cases, Miller pointed to "at least two instances" in which state superior court judges "refused to enforce covenants proscribing Mexicans," unlike the vast majority of Miller's cases in which courts enforced covenants against African Americans. Explaining these rulings, Miller noted in 1947, "Courts, following census classifications are apt to rule that Mexicans, no matter how large their degree of Indian blood, are 'Caucasians,'" as *Mendez* demonstrated, "and are not proscribed by covenants barring non-Caucasians."[28] This conclusion echoed sobering advice that Miller passed along to one of his African American clients after she lost a racially restrictive housing covenant case her neighbors brought against her. Though the ruling meant that she had to move from the home she had purchased, she could, Miller explained, retain ownership and lease her property to "Mexican or white persons, but not to Negroes."[29]

Testimony from some of Miller's own cases also revealed how litigants who sought to enforce their neighborhood's racially restrictive covenants distinguished between African Americans and Mexican Americans. During one trial, for example, Miller asked a witness if he would object if an educated black judge or "George Washington Carver, the scientist" moved into the neighborhood on the grounds that they would drive down property values? "Yes," he replied. As for neighbors of Mexican descent, the witness felt differently, explaining, "I don't feel that [they] would depreciate the value of my property," unlike "non-Caucasian[s]."[30] During another trial, Miller posed a series of questions to a witness about the "Mexican occupancy" in her neighborhood. In response, the witness noted the "medium-dark" skin of members of the Chavez family, the "dark" skin of the Gonzales couple, and the "rather swarthy" skin of a Mrs. Garcia and her son. Implicit in Miller's line of questions about skin color was an argument he introduced at the trial's outset that "Mexicans are not persons of [the] Caucasian race" because they possessed "a large admixture of Indian blood." This, for the purposes of Miller's argument, meant that the covenant the witness sued to enforce had already been violated. Miller's opposing counsel objected. The neighborhood's residents of Mexican descent, he insisted, were "Caucasian." Whatever the shade of their skin, then, it was Miller's African American clients who marked the arrival of the "first colored people," as another witness testified, and triggered the case to enforce the neighborhood's racially restrictive housing covenant.[31]

In some instances, Miller even unearthed evidence of Mexicans (as well as Jews, among others) as signatories to, rather than targets of, racially restrictive housing covenants. "I am amazed every time I scan the list of signers of such documents," Miller wrote in May 1946. "Churches, banks, baseball parks, Whittier College (a Quaker institution in the suburbs of Los Angeles), Mexicans, the native born, the foreign born who must sign their names with an X, Catholics, Protestants, members of the Jewish faith have all succumbed to high pressure campaigns and helped to enrich cagey promoters who circulate such documents amid an atmosphere of race baiting."[32] In short, Miller viewed African Americans to be the "chief victims" of racially restrictive housing covenants, which he deemed to be "the most important single issue of civil liberties now facing this community and this nation."[33]

As Miller waged his legal campaign, he confronted a constitutional "stumbling block."[34] Although the Fourteenth Amendment forbade "any State" from "deny[ing] to any person within its jurisdiction the equal protection of the laws," the United States Supreme Court had ruled in 1926 that nothing in the Constitution "prohibited private individuals from entering into contracts respecting the control and disposition of their own property."[35] As agreements between private non-state actors, racially restrictive housing covenants and their court enforcement did not run afoul of the Fourteenth Amendment. As Miller explained, "The favorite argument of proponents of race restrictive agreements is that these covenants are merely private contracts with which the state is not concerned."[36] Moreover, they had a Supreme Court precedent on their side, which declared "covenants . . . perfectly legal."[37] Nearly twenty years after that decision, courts in nearly twenty states plus the District of Columbia had agreed.[38]

To surmount this formidable legal hurdle, Miller, drew on the recently published work of a University of California, Berkeley law professor and argued that judicial enforcement of private action—specifically, a court upholding a covenant—was in fact state action. In a brief he submitted to the California Supreme Court in February 1946, Miller spelled out what he referred to as the "Constitutional Question" in cases in which courts upheld racially restrictive housing covenants. "It would be strange indeed," Miller wrote, "if the state could escape responsibility for its acts where its courts had decreed discriminatory action against a particular class." No less than "law . . . made by legislators," law interpreted by judges represented "the voice of the state." For this reason, "judicial action *is* state action."[39]

This line of argument had received its first favorable hearing in a case that Miller argued before a California trial court just a few months earlier. In this case, Miller represented a select group of African Americans, including the actresses Hattie McDaniel and Louise Beavers along with numerous doctors, musicians, and businessmen, who had purchased homes in the upscale "Sugar Hill" (West Adams Heights) section of Los Angeles. Their case reached Judge Thurmond Clarke's courtroom on December 5, 1945. Though the *California Eagle* expected the trial to run for more than a month, Clarke disposed of it in a day.[40] Shortly thereafter, Miller wrote the NAACP's Thurgood Marshall about what had transpired. "We started trying the 'Sugar Hill' cases yesterday, and moved the Court to exclude all evidence on behalf of plaintiffs," who were a group of eight white families seeking to enforce their neighborhood's housing covenant.[41] Clarke upheld the motion. His decision, Miller explained in a subsequent letter to Marshall, had been based on the claim that judicial enforcement of racially restrictive housing covenants would "deny . . . defendants [i.e., those charged with violating the covenants] equal protection of the laws . . . and . . . would constitute a taking of defendants' property without due process or any process of law." In a brief, but forceful, opinion, whose brevity Miller attributed to Clarke's desire to "avoid . . . direct conflict" with precedents from the "revered" California Supreme Court, the judge pronounced, "The Negro race are accorded, without reservations and evasions, the full rights guaranteed them under the 14th Amendment of the Federal Constitution. Judges have been avoiding the real issue for too long. Certainly there was no discrimination against the Negro race when it came to calling upon its members to die on the battlefields in the defense of this country in the war just ended."[42]

NAACP executive secretary Walter White hailed the decision a "magnificent" and unprecedented triumph.[43] White's colleague, Marian Wynn Perry, noted how the case marked the only "favorable" one of its kind in the United States.[44] Miller, however, was more guarded. He viewed the outcome as the legal equivalent of "pulling a rabbit out of the hat"—"a rather neat trick" in light of the precedents he confronted. Moreover, he added, that the decision was only a lower court's, and task remained to "make it stick"—first in the California Supreme Court and then in "the holy of holies," the United States Supreme Court.[45]

Hoping to get there, Miller forged ahead with his many other cases and honed his other arguments against racially restrictive housing covenants. These included what Miller referred to as the "question of change" in neighborhoods covered by covenants drawn up before World War II that were contiguous with neighborhoods not covered by covenants whose African American populations had increased substantially with the demographic changes wrought by the war. As Miller described this process in one case, "Here we have a situation in which . . . a single isolated street [covered by a covenant] had been enveloped by areas of Negro occupancies—areas which had changed since the imposition of the covenant and in which Negro occupancy continued to increase."[46] The transformation in the non-covenanted area just beyond the covenanted area, Miller maintained, so altered the conditions under which the covenant had been signed as to render it inapplicable and unenforceable. "A neighborhood," he maintained in another case is "more than a group of homes located on certain streets" that might be covered by a racially restrictive housing covenant. It was also the stores, schools, and parks in the vicinity. A change in this broader neighborhood, which Miller referred to as "the neighborhood . . . in the true sense," should, in turn, allow for a change in the narrower neighborhood.[47] That the "change had occurred outside the immediate [covenanted] area is of no consequence, if such change affects property within the restricted area," which Miller insisted it did in still another case.[48]

The "question of public policy" also figured in Miller's arsenal of arguments. Racially restrictive housing covenants, he claimed, "contravene[d] public policy" by "compound[ing] segregation and nourish[ing] its evil products." These included "the high incidence of disease . . . crime and . . . juvenile delinquency" found in the overcrowded segregated neighborhoods. Though rendering racially restrictive covenants unenforceable in court (if not illegal) would not "dissolve Negro communities" owing to "ethnic solidarity [and] popular prejudice," it would at least remove the "artificial restraints" they imposed.[49]

In another case, Miller offered another "public policy" argument when he invoked Ashley Montagu, Ruth Benedict, and Gunnar Myrdal as some the "social scientists and anthropologists" whose work repudiated the racism reflected in racially restrictive housing covenants. Courts needed to follow these scholars' lead in order to "keep pace with the changing concepts of our times." They needed to jettison "as unsound and unscientific the complex of beliefs and superstitions regarding the inferiority of certain races out of which residential segregation by race grew" and over which the recently concluded war had been fought.[50]

In October 1947, Los Angeles County Superior Court Judge Stanley Mosk agreed. In a case that pit, among others, a disabled veteran of both World War I and World War II, represented by Miller, against the pastor of the Wilshire Presbyterian Church, who was described by the *Los Angeles Sentinel* as "one of the ring leaders in the effort to keep the area lily-white," Mosk issued a stinging rebuke to the pastor's efforts. In a letter to Thurgood Marshall, Miller conveyed Mosk's opinion, which read: "We read columns in the press each day about Un-American activities. This Court feels there is no more reprehensible un-American activity than to attempt to deprive persons of their own homes on a 'Master Race' theory. Our Nation just fought against the Nazi's race superiority theory. One of these defendants was in that war and is a Purple Heart veteran. This Court would indeed be callous to his constitutional rights if it were now to permit him to be ousted from his own home by using 'race' as the measure of his worth as a citizen and neighbor. The alleged Cause of Action here is thus inconsistent with the guarantees of the Fourteenth Amendment to the Constitution." Mosk's ruling, according to the *Los Angeles Sentinel*, marked only the second time that either a state or federal court found racially restrictive housing covenants to violate the Fourteenth Amendment. The first time had occurred two years earlier in Miller's "Sugar Hill" case. These victories boded well for the impending United States Supreme Court showdown, for which Miller was then preparing in conjunction with lawyers from NAACP headquarters, even as he was also readying numerous other cases for the California Supreme Court.[51]

Though Miller's briefs challenged notions of racial superiority and inferiority that racially restrictive housing covenants presumed, they did not challenge the concept of race itself as a way of parsing the human species. In court, however, Miller broached this subject. Querying a witness in the trial phase of one case in November 1944, Miller asked, "How do you tell [the difference] between black and white?" In response, the witness replied that he used "color" as his guide, but conceded that in "some cases you practically wouldn't be able to tell very well." Seizing the opportunity, Miller then asked, "Some white-colored people, aren't there?" The witness concurred: "There are some white that is negroes."[52]

In another case filed the following year and tried in February 1946, Miller questioned the categories of Caucasian and non-Caucasian after his opposing counsel insisted, and the judge agreed, that "Mexicans are a Caucasian race." Miller responded, "I don't know what a Caucasian is or a non-Caucasian, anthropologically. And I doubt whether anybody in this court room knows, because we are not anthropologists." That said, Miller continued, "I do know that Mexicans have a large admixture of Indian blood." They also "may have a large admixture of Caucasian blood," as do a "good many negroes." Why, then, Miller wanted to know, did the judge and opposing counsel draw a distinction between Mexican Americans, considered Caucasian, and African Americans, considered non-Caucasian? After all, "if Indian blood is not Caucasian and does not translate a person into a non-Caucasian," as in the case of Mexican Americans living in the covenanted neighborhood at issue, "then we are applying one rule to Indian blood and we are applying another rule to Negro blood. We are saying a drop of negro blood makes a person non-Caucasian, but a drop of Indian blood does not make a person non-Caucasian." As the case unfolded, Miller pressed this issue with a witness who objected to having black neighbors, in violation of the covenant, but not "Mexicans." Did they "appear to have an admixture of Indian blood," Miller asked? Were they "swarthy-skinned"? What about the color and texture of their hair? In pursuing this line of questioning, Miller endeavored to erode the Caucasian/non-Caucasian distinction inscribed into most racially restrictive housing covenants. Neither the witness, who objected to having African American, but not Mexican American, neighbors, nor her attorney, who insisted that "they [i.e., Mexican Americans] are of the Caucasian race," were persuaded. Nor, for that matter, was the trial court judge who ruled against Miller and upheld the covenant's bar against non-Caucasian, meaning African American, occupancy.[53]

In still another case, a defendant who Miller represented, befuddled the plaintiffs' attorney when he asserted, "I am not a Negro." Taken aback, the lawyer responded, "On what do you base that statement?" The witness replied, "My mother was pure white." As for his father, he had never seen him. In any event, he continued, "I'm not black. I'm what you see." What the lawyer saw, he asserted for the record, was a man with "dark skin," "kinky hair characteristic of negroes," and a nose in the shape of "many negro noses"—definitely not a "man of the pure white race." To settle the matter, the judge suggested that "expert testimony" might be required. This, however, was not something for which another one of the plaintiffs' attorneys said they anticipated, nor was it necessary. After all, what more evidence did the court need than that which was quite literally before it in the witness box? The legal precedents "show that the first way of determining whether or not a person is a Caucasian, whether they are Chinese, or whatever they are, is by observation." The judge concurred. While conceding that the defendant had some "characteristics" of "races . . . who are not negroes," his "relationships"—including his wife who said her mother was "full-blooded Indian" and father "part Negro" and son, who attended "principally . . . a negro school" for college—settled the matter. The defendant, the judge deemed, "is in the class of a non-Caucasian." Miller protested, "That brings us to the point as to what definition the Court is going to give to non-Caucasian," the discussion of which was then omitted from the record.[54]

That discussion, however, was not omitted in another racially restrictive housing covenant case that began in 1944 and would eventually be consolidated with a number of cases that Miller was handling on appeal to the California Supreme Court. In *Davis v. Carter*, attorneys led by Hugh E. Macbeth defended jazz musician Bennett (Benny) Carter and his wife Ynez, among others, against a racially restrictive housing covenant prosecution brought by Edythe Davis. The Carters had arrived in Los Angeles from Harlem in 1943. The following year they purchased a home whose owners had signed an agreement in 1928 that barred ownership or occupancy "by any person except one of the white or Caucasian race."[55] Edythe Davis, who testified that she had no problem with "colored people" as workers in her home but not as "social equals," sued the Carters. Her husband, lawyer LeCompte Davis, represented her. During the trial, a witness testified that Davis boasted that he would "have all the Negroes out of that whole district in four months."[56] Davis's opposing lead counsel, defendants' attorney Macbeth, was an African American Harvard Law School graduate who had been active in civil rights in Los Angeles since the early 1920s.[57]

Like Miller, Macbeth challenged the racism reflected in racially restrictive housing covenants. Macbeth's response to the original complaint filed against the Carters denounced the precedents cited against his clients for being "based upon policies existing before Adolph Hitler's 'Mein Kampf' war of conquest for so-called Aryan racial supremacy and conquest of the peoples of the world."[58] Unlike Miller, Macbeth devoted far more attention to repudiating the concept of race in order to undermine the edifice upon which racially restrictive housing covenants rested. Whereas Miller agreed to stipulations that his clients were "negroes, and not of the White or Caucasian race," Macbeth refused to do so.[59] As soon as the trial commenced in Los Angeles County Superior Court on June 29, 1945, Macbeth announced, "I will not stipulate" that the Carters were, as the judge put it, "of the Negro race." Macbeth continued, "I am challenging all this Negro business" and would only "stipulate that they are all members of the human race." To do otherwise, Macbeth maintained, would be to "stipulate myself out of court," given the precedents upholding racially restrictive covenants and the racial categories they took for granted. He added, "I am challenging a thing that you call a fact, that is different race." This "race business," he remarked later, "is a myth."[60]

To shore up his claim, Macbeth called University of California, Berkeley anthropologist Paul Radin as an expert witness. Asked by Macbeth, "How many races of human beings do the anthropologists indicate," Radin answered, "At the present time there is considerable doubt in the minds of most anthropologists whether it is possible to make any kind of an accurate and distinctive classification." Thereafter, Davis objected to Macbeth's queries to Radin about whether it was possible to discern race by physical appearance, in general, and with respect to the defendants, in particular. The judge sustained each objection. He then instructed Macbeth, "I shall find in this case . . . that each of the defendants . . . belong to the Negro race and do not belong to the Caucasian or white race." Macbeth persisted. Radin, he said, had examined the defendants and concluded, "Each of them are in the extreme range, dark range of the Caucasian race." Once again Macbeth's opposing counsel Davis objected. Radin's professional opinion, he contended, "has no bearing on the question of whether in the eyes of the law either of these defendants is a Negro or a white person and it is not the subject of expert testimony." He reiterated this point later in the trial. "It doesn't take an expert witness" to determine what "the mass of people regard as a black man."[61] How a person looked and with whom he or she associated were all that was required. The judge agreed, having already stated his opinion on the matter based on what his eyes had seen of the defendants' appearance and what his ears had heard of the defendants' associations.

Although the judge and plaintiff's attorney subscribed to a popular understanding of race, the defense repudiated it. "You and I are arguing about something that we as human beings do not know," namely, "what is white and what is black and what is negro and what is Caucasian," Macbeth's co-counsel, Eva Mack, insisted. By confounding the categories on which racially restrictive housing covenants were based, the defense hoped to render those covenants unenforceable. Put another way, if "race is a question of fact and it isn't a question of law," as Macbeth posited early in the trial, and if the fact of race could not withstand scrutiny, then neither could any covenant premised upon race.[62]

On the question of "what is white," then, when the judge pronounced the plaintiff's attorney Davis "a white man with a decidedly reddish complexion," Macbeth replied, "What do you mean, white, white as his collar? He wears a white collar, I will stipulate that, your Honor, but he is of a pinkish, brownish, reddish complexion, not white." Later in the trial, when an exasperated Davis blurted, "I am a white man," Macbeth retorted, "No sir, you are ruddy, you are pinkish, you aren't white." In fact, he continued, "none of us are white," adding, "off the record you are going to have a lot of fun on this race business."[63]

On the question of "what is black," Macbeth's clients insisted that whatever it was it was not them. "I am definitely not a black man," Benny Carter told Davis. Nor, for that matter, had he ever seen a black man. What then, Davis wanted to know, did Carter's marriage certificate, driver's license, and voting registration cards indicate in the boxes set aside for racial identification? Carter did not recollect filling out the first two and had yet to register to vote in California. Even if he had, Macbeth interjected, it was irrelevant. "These applications for licenses are made in a loose fashion," Macbeth maintained. "Nobody swears to them." As for those "poor colored people" who specified their "so-called racial group," Macbeth lamented, they did so "like they have to Heil Hitler in Germany to get by."[64]

Finally, on the question of "what is Caucasian," the defendants claimed that in fact they were. This, they conceded, was not a self-definition they would have used prior to the trial. However, during pretrial preparations their attorneys, led by Macbeth, demonstrated otherwise, drawing on definitions of Caucasian from the work of anthropologist Ashley Montagu, as well as the Webster's New International Dictionary that included North Africans among Caucasians. "What is a Caucasian?" the plaintiff's attorney asked Carter, who answered, "A mixed race of people."[65] Other defendants reiterated this definition of Caucasian in their testimony.

As the trial drew to a close, the frustrated plaintiff's attorney Davis, who had been repeatedly foiled in his attempts to obtain an admission from the defendants that they were black, negro, or non-Caucasian, nevertheless felt confident that he would be vindicated. Following an exchange with a defendant who claimed he was "brown" (not "black" like his "shoes") and belonged to the "mixed race of people [who] are Caucasians," Davis asserted, "I don't think there is any court but what will say he knows he is a black man." Perhaps, Macbeth replied, but "courts have a way of changing their minds."[66]

Three years later, the United States Supreme Court changed its mind. In April 1947, the NAACP filed a petition for certiorari in *Shelley v. Kraemer*—a case involving an African American couple from St. Louis who were sued to prevent them from occupying a house they had purchased in a neighborhood covered by a racially restrictive housing covenant. One month later, the NAACP also sought a Supreme Court audience for a similar case from Detroit, *McGhee v. Sipes*. On June 23, 1947, the Court agreed to hear *Shelley* and *McGhee*, and later added two other companion cases from Washington, D.C. For the first time in over two decades, the nation's highest tribunal would consider the constitutionality of racially restrictive housing covenants.[67] Though none of the many California cases that Miller was then appealing to the California Supreme Court were included, Miller, along with Thurgood Marshall, played an integral role in preparing the briefs and delivering the oral arguments in *McGhee*. So, too, did the federal Department of Justice, with Attorney General Tom Clark filing an amicus brief for the cases under consideration and Solicitor General Philip Perlman leading off the oral arguments, which took place on January 15 and 16, 1948.[68]

The JACL also sought to contribute to the Supreme Court's consideration of racially restrictive housing covenants. Eiji Tanabe, head of the JACL's southern California office, had broached the idea of a "joint effort" between the JACL and NAACP in a letter to Miller in May 1947.[69] Five months later, after that joint effort had failed to materialize, Fred Fertig, executive secretary of the JACL's Los Angeles chapter, followed Tanabe's lead. He asked Miller to recommend ways "organizations such as ours can cooperate with you in the prosecution of the cases."[70]

Around the same time, in late October 1947, Mike Masaoka issued a report in his capacity as head of the JACL's Anti-Discrimination Committee based in Washington, D.C. After detailing developments in the *Oyama* and *Takahashi* cases, which were then the JACL's primary legal concerns, Masaoka wrote, "I don't think we can afford not to be represented with our own brief in these cases," whose oral arguments were scheduled for January 1948. Masoka's reasoning was part substantive and part strategic. Substantively, Masaoka believed, the JACL could "offer a significant contribution . . . by pointing out the history of Japanese housing in urban areas on the west coast . . . and our present difficulties in finding housing, even though we are prepared to purchase better housing in so-called restrictive areas." Strategically, he believed, "a good strong brief will enhance our position among other minorities."[71]

A little over a month later, the JACL followed Masaoka's recommendation. The JACL's amicus brief, written by Al Wirin, Saburo Kido, and Fred Okrand, began by noting how the "problems" of Americans of Japanese descent, with which the JACL was "primarily concerned," were "necessarily varied and different from other racial groups." When it came to racially restrictive housing covenants, however, these divergent experiences converged, as Wirin, Kido, and Okrand argued by delineating numerous examples of how racially restrictive covenants "affected the American Japanese," both before and after World War II.[72] This convergence, however, had its limits. As the JACL's Larry Tajiri observed the year before, African Americans were the "group that the present campaign for restrictive covenants is aimed [at]."[73] A group of California attorneys, including future CFCU president Isaac Pacht, echoed Tajiri in their amicus brief. Though African Americans were not "alone," they were the "chief victims," as Miller himself had also said, and as the "great majority" of cases brought in Los Angeles County since 1943 underscored.[74]

Nevertheless, Wirin hoped to introduce what the ACLU of Southern California's *Open Forum* described as "new 'color'" to the racially restrictive housing covenant cases.[75] To this end, he, along with Miller and Okrand, petitioned the United States Supreme Court in November 1947 to hear two non–African American Los Angeles cases. One—*Amer v. Superior Court*—involved a Chinese American World War II Purple Heart recipient, Tom Amer. The other—*Kim v. Superior Court*—involved a Korean American dentist who was a World War II Bronze Star recipient, Yin Kim.[76] To be sure, *Amer* and *Kim* attested to the application of racially restrictive housing covenants to groups other than African Americans. Yet, they also spoke of the difficulty that the JACL had in locating a Japanese American case.[77] Indeed, the JACL's short amicus brief in support of *Amer* and *Kim* to be heard by the country's highest court made no mention of any Japanese American racially restrictive housing covenant cases. Instead, it described the JACL's "chief interest" to be "problems pertaining to persons of Japanese ancestry" and secondary interest to be "problems affecting anyone else." The "widespread growth of race restrictive covenants" fell into the latter category. It represented a "phenomenon" in which "a wrong done one group by reason of its race ultimately curtails the rights of other racial groups."[78]

To buttress his petition for certiorari, Wirin wrote Thurgood Marshall for NAACP assistance in drawing the Court's "attention . . . to the fact that housing restrictions affect racial groups in addition to Negroes."[79] He asked Miller to "back up" his request to Marshall.[80] Though Marshall believed that *Amer* and *Kim* provided the "basis for all of us to point out to the court in the pending cases the extent of the restrictive covenants to persons other than Negroes," the NAACP did not produce the amicus brief for certiorari Wirin requested.[81] Nor did the Court agree to hear *Amer* and *Kim* alongside the African American racially restrictive housing cases for which oral arguments took place in January 1948. This was just fine with Wirin's ACLU colleague, Clifford Forster, who wrote Marshall, "I don't know whether Al told you but I have consistently, for the past few months, informed him that we would in no way be responsible for these cases." Legally, *Amer* and *Kim* were "pending in the United States Supreme Court on extremely dubious procedural writs." Substantively, Forster continued, he had "no reason to think that the court does not know that restrictive covenants apply to persons other than Negroes." For that reason, Forster concluded, *Amer* and *Kim* were best left in California until after the Supreme Court reached its decision.[82]

On May 3, 1948, a unanimous United States Supreme Court delivered what Miller hailed as a "landmark in constitutional law."[83] The Court's single opinion in *Shelley* latched on to the "judicial action *is* state action" argument that Miller had been making in his extensive California litigation. The Fourteenth Amendment, the Court declared, forbade "state action"—"exertions of state power in all forms"—in the service of racial discrimination. Though "private conduct, however discriminatory or wrongful" was permissible, anything that "bears the clear and unmistakable imprimatur of the State" was not.[84] Court enforcement of racially restrictive housing covenants bore such an imprint, though racially restrictive housing covenants themselves did not. Put another way, private property owners could write as many racial restrictions into housing covenants as they wanted. They could not, however, seek judicial enforcement of them in the event that they were violated. In effect, the Supreme Court did to racially restrictive housing covenants what it had done to the Alien Land Law in *Oyama* just a few months earlier: defanging, if not altogether dismantling the discriminatory practice before it. For his role in the Supreme Court's decision, Los Angeles County Superior Court judge Stanley Mosk hailed Miller as "more than any other single person . . . responsible for this milestone on the path toward true democracy."[85]

On the same day that the Supreme Court promulgated its decision, NAACP-WC director Noah Griffin wrote Marshall about a racially restrictive housing covenant suit that had been filed against an African American couple in Sacramento.[86] An assistant to Marshall replied, "By this time you no doubt have read of the United States Supreme Court's decision . . . holding these covenants unenforceable. . . . This, of course, is our case and represents a complete justification of the Association's position over the past 31 years." After summarizing the gist of the decision, he suggested that Griffin do the same for the attorneys in Sacramento so that they would dismiss the case.[87]

Shortly thereafter, the California Supreme Court rid its docket of the numerous racially restrictive housing covenants that were pending. In one of these cases—which was the consolidation of seven cases, all handled by Miller—the Court wrote on May 18, 1948, "In the *Shelley* and *McGhee* cases, the plaintiffs sought the enforcement of racial covenants similar in essential aspects to those now before us. . . . It follows [in light of the United States Supreme Court's rulings] that the judgments here must be reversed."[88] The other cases were similarly dismissed.[89]

A footnote in *Shelley* noted the application of racially restrictive housing covenants to "Indians, Jews, Chinese, Japanese, Mexicans, Hawaiians, Puerto Ricans, and Filipinos, among others."[90] However, the Los Angeles Realty Board's response to the United States Supreme Court's ruling underscored just how much African Americans had become by the 1940s the primary targets of racially restrictive housing covenant enforcement. In an August 1948 letter to the National Association of Real Estate Boards in Washington, D.C., the president of the Los Angeles Real Estate Board wrote, "The experience has been uniform that whenever and wherever Negroes have occupied homes . . . [that] this has not only depreciated the value of the properties which they own, but has depreciated the values of all surrounding properties." To thwart the "threat of Negro occupancy," the Los Angeles Realty Board urged their parent organization to "sponsor the adoption of an amendment to the Constitution of the United States" to grant courts the power to enforce racially restrictive housing covenants, which, of course, *Shelley* had proscribed.[91]

The Los Angeles Realty Board did not have the popular singer Nat King Cole and his family in mind, but rather the "vast numbers of Negroes" who possessed the "purchasing power" to make "suffer most . . . the owners of comparatively modest homes."[92] That same month, however, Cole's new neighbors demonstrated that they, too, opposed "occupancy by Negroes," regardless of their fame or wealth. Shortly after Cole purchased a $75,000 home in Los Angeles's upscale Hancock Park, the Hancock Park Property Owners offered to buy it back from him for $100,000. Cole spurned the offer and was subsequently welcomed to his new home with the word "Nigger" burned into his lawn. The Coles, however, remained put.[93]

Though *Shelley* meant that the Coles could not be forced out by a racially restrictive housing covenant, it did not preclude a litany of other tactics and barriers that could serve similar ends. For that reason, Miller cautioned against "overestimat[ing] the immediate effect on residential segregation" that the Supreme Court's decision would have. "The last legal prop had been knocked from under the ghetto," but numerous other impediments remained.[94] An editorial in *The Crisis* captured some of these obstacles when it described the upshot of *Shelley*. "It means that if Negroes have the money and can find sellers, and are willing to take their chances in a hostile atmosphere, they can now buy and move in."[95] These were enormous caveats. They represented part of what *The Crisis* described as "the Goliath in [the] path away from ghetto evils of overcrowding, exploitation, crime, disease, and death" that remained in the aftermath of the dismantling of court enforcement of racially restrictive housing covenants. They represented, as well, the targets of subsequent battles in the war against housing discrimination, which Miller and the NAACP-WC would confront in the decades ahead.

A little over four months after the United States Supreme Court handed down its *Shelley* decision, the California Supreme Court issued its *Perez v. Sharp* ruling. *Perez* made California "the first state court to recognize that [anti]miscegenation statutes violate the Equal Protection Clause," as Chief Justice Earl Warren would put it in *Loving v. Virginia*, which struck down the antimiscegenation laws that remained in force in sixteen states nearly two decades later.[96]

Moreover, *Perez* completed what *Oyama, Takahashi, Mendez,* and *Miller's* myriad housing covenant cases had started in California earlier in the 1940s, namely, the dismantling of the state's multiracial system of legalized segregation.

Perez involved a Los Angeles-born-and-raised couple that met in 1942. At the time, Sylvester Scott Davis, Jr., later identified as "Negro" in his half of his application to the Los Angeles County Marriage License Bureau, was a nineteen-year-old assembly-line worker at Lockheed Aviation in Burbank, California whose parents had roots in Louisiana. Andrea Dena Pérez, later identified as "white" in her half of the application, was a twenty-year-old Lockheed Aviation employee whose parents came from Mexico. Pérez caught Davis's attention as she was being given a tour of the factory floor. Davis asked his boss if he could help train Pérez in her new position as an assembly-line worker. Job training quickly evolved into courtship. Interrupted when the Army drafted Davis to fight in France in 1944, their relationship resumed upon Davis's return from service, and an engagement soon followed.[97]

Two major obstacles stood between engagement and marriage. First was Pérez's father, who vehemently opposed his daughter's marriage to a black man.[98] Second, and more formidable, was California law. Ignominiously and tellingly sandwiched between Section 59 of the California Civil Code, which outlawed incest, and Section 61, which prohibited bigamy and polygamy, Section 60, which dated to the advent of California statehood, declared, "All marriages of white persons with negroes, Mongolians, members of the Malay race, or mulattoes are illegal and void."[99] Section 69 added, "no license may be issued authorizing the marriage of a white person with a Negro, mulatto, Mongolian or member of the Malay race."[100] As of 1947, California could count itself as one of thirty states that forbade marriages between whites and "Negroes" or "mulattoes," one of the fifteen states that forbade marriages between whites and "Orientals" or "Mongolians," and one of the six states that forbid marriages between whites and "Malays."[101] These laws—of which California's was, according to its supreme court, "more inclusive than most," though it did not single out "Indians" or "Hindus" as in other states—represented the raison d'être of legalized segregation.[102] As Gunnar Myrdal observed in *An American Dilemma,* "The whole system of segregation and discrimination . . . is defended as necessary to block 'social equality' which in turn is held necessary to prevent 'intermarriage.' . . . The ban on intermarriage . . . is the end for which the other restrictions are arranged as means."[103]

Knowing that California law precluded them from marrying, Pérez reached out to Dorothy Marshall, wife of attorney Daniel Marshall. Pérez knew the Marshalls through babysitting she had done for their children. Moreover, they knew Pérez's fiancé, Davis, through his mother, with whom the Marshalls attended the same Catholic church.[104] When Marshall learned of the plight of Pérez and Davis, he was president of the Catholic Interracial Council of Los Angeles (CIC-LA). Inspired and assisted by Father John LaFarge, a Harvard-educated Jesuit who helped found the nation's first Catholic Interracial Council in New York City in 1934, Marshall and a former college roommate, journalist Ted LeBerthon, launched the CIC-LA in 1944.[105] A mix of 40–50 people—"most whites and Negroes, but a few Chinese, Filipinos and Mexican[s] and even two converts from Judaism"—comprised the CIC-LA's initial membership.[106] One of the many racial liberal organizations springing up across World War II California, the CIC-LA drew its inspiration from Catholic social teachings. As its "Declaration of Principles" proclaimed, "The Catholic Interracial Council of Los Angeles rejects artificial inequalities due to racial myths . . . . The spiritual aspect of that rejection flows from the common membership of all races in the Mystical Body of Christ. It is premised upon the natural law that the rights of all races are identical in . . . sacredness to the rights of white persons. The God-given dignity and destiny of every human person must be fully recognized in laws, government, institutions and human conduct."[107]

To realize his vision, Marshall led the CIC-LA's two-year campaign to integrate the California Knights of Columbus, as well as Catholic schools and hospitals.[108] Reaching beyond Catholic circles, he also contributed to amicus briefs filed by the ACLU in *Oyama* and *Takahashi* and submitted his own amicus brief in one of the many racially restrictive housing covenant cases that would reach the California Supreme Court in 1948. According to LeBerthon, Marshall believed that "gradualism is intellectual dishonesty."[109] This was especially evident in his decision to take up the case that Pérez brought him. Indeed, more seasoned civil rights litigators of the day were loath to handle such cases. In 1945, for example, the NAACP's Thurgood Marshall declined to participate in the appeal of an Oklahoma antimiscegenation case, seeing "very little chance of success because of the precedents involved."[110] The legal scholar with whom Marshall consulted on the matter, Milton Konvitz, concurred. He deemed it "extremely hazardous at this time" to press the antimiscegenation issue.[111]

The California legislature, with Governor Warren's approval, lent credence to the concerns of Marshall and Konvitz. In the biennial legislative sessions of 1943 and 1945, the legislature amended Section 69 of the Civil Code, without touching the provision that prohibited issuing marriage licenses to "a white person with a Negro, mulatto, Mongolian or member of the Malay race."[112] Warren signed both bills into law. In neither case did he nor any of his staff comment on Section 69's antimiscegenation provision, though they were undoubtedly aware of it.[113] In September 1943, for example, Army Chaplain Eugene C. Noury, a Catholic priest, sent an "Open Letter to the Governor of California," which was published in the *Associated Filipino Press* in Los Angeles. Noury acted on behalf of the soldiers of the First Filipino Infantry to which he was assigned. Although they were granted American citizenship in mass ceremonies upon enlisting, the Filipino American GIs could not marry white women in California and a handful of other states. Noury urged Warren to support "the abrogation of the marriage law against the Filipinos." In response, Warren's press secretary wrote, "Any action to validate such marriages in this State would have to come through legislation," which, he did not add, was not forthcoming. Unsatisfied, Noury appeared before the California legislature and repeatedly sought an audience with Warren. His efforts yielded "some flag waving and tongue-chewing democracy," according to one account, "but no action."[114]

Beyond the prohibitive precedents and politics, antimiscegenation laws also ranked low on the list of priorities for the NAACP's constituency, at least according to Gunnar Myrdal's, *An American Dilemma*. Myrdal reported that whites deemed antimiscegenation laws the most important Jim Crow laws to maintain, and blacks deemed them the least important to challenge, preferring instead to focus on discrimination in employment, housing, voting, and education.[115] Little wonder, then, that the NAACP's Marshall told the ACLU's Roger Baldwin in 1944 that attacking statutory prohibitions against interracial marriage did "not constitute a practical issue."[116]

Catholic church leaders in Los Angeles took a much dimmer view of Dan Marshall's plans. Before launching *Perez*, Marshall and his CIC-LA had come to be seen as "crackpots, lunatic fringe, starry-eyed idealists" by the Los Angeles Chancery Office. Afterwards, Catholic leaders branded them pariahs and heretics.[117] On April 4, 1947, the CIC-LA issued a press release announcing, "Interracial Marriage Ban to be Attacked." Though it did not mention Pérez and Davis, the press release indicated that plans for the attack had already commenced. The strategy would be to challenge the California law on First Amendment grounds, as a "violation of the religious liberty of a Catholic interracial couple," presumably Pérez and Davis, "to participate in the full sacramental life of the religion of their choice."[118]

Though the CIC-LA's press release invoked no less than the Holy See himself in support of its campaign against California's antimiscegenation law, Los Angeles Auxiliary Bishop Joseph T. McGucken would have nothing whatsoever to do with the undertaking. He wasted little time in responding to a letter Marshall sent outlining his legal plan, sketching the Catholic teachings that supported it, and requesting that McGucken testify.[119] McGucken began by admonishing Marshall for misconstruing Catholic theology, although he did not elaborate on where and how. He then reproached Marshall for plotting a reckless legal course that would do more to foment social unrest than right racial and religious wrongs. "I cannot think of any point in existing race relationships that will stir up more passion and prejudice than the issue you are raising," McGucken warned. Finally, he adamantly refused Marshall's request that he testify in court. Though he could not stop Marshall from going forward, McGucken implored him "to consult with some older heads before attempting this issue, particularly since you are planning to involve the Church in it." Likening Marshall to "Don Quixote," McGucken concluded, "The problem you have so much at heart is not to be solved by any short-cuts."[120] How it would be solved otherwise, McGucken neglected to say.

Undeterred, Marshall forged ahead with his preparations. A few months later, on August 1, 1947, Pérez and Davis went to the Los Angeles County Marriage License Bureau to file their application. If the clerk who processed the application of Pérez and Davis was anything like Rosalind Rice, head of the Los Angeles County Marriage License Bureau in 1948, he or she no doubt took his or her job of patrolling the racial borders of California marriages quite seriously. As Rice explained to the *Los Angeles Sentinel*, "I don't just sit here and look at people and say, 'You're white,' or 'You're Negro.' I took time to study these things." Her studies, asserted this self-proclaimed "first white child" born on a Nebraska Indian reservation, yielded a "sixth sense." Just in case her "sixth sense" failed her, though, Rice was especially fond of the ency-clopedia as a back up—"as fine a reference as you can get," she insisted. Never-theless, Rice conceded occasional difficulties. "East Indians are the hardest race to detect," she confessed. "Some are of Negro, some of Mongolian, and some of Malay origin, and some are pure Aryan." Sometimes African Ameri-cans gave her trouble, too. For example, Rice once denied a license to a "light skinned lady who wanted to marry a person who was obviously a Negro," reported the *Los Angeles Sentinel*.[121] Whether Rice would have had similar trouble with Pérez and Davis is impossible to say. Certainly, the clerk who refused to issue the couple a marriage license did not appear to have any difficulty, which is just what Marshall anticipated. Indeed, no sooner had Pérez and Davis been rebuffed than Marshall sued the Los Angeles County Clerk's Office.[122]

As *Perez* unfolded, "most of the civil-rights organizations," according to Carey McWilliams, "failed or refused to participate in the case on the assump-tion that miscegenation statutes could not be successfully challenged in courts."[123] NAACP-WC regional director Noah Griffin just ignored the case, making no mention of it in the monthly reports he sent to NAACP headquarters until after the California Supreme Court decided it. Instead, Griffin's updates devoted far more attention to the efforts then afoot to litigate racially restrictive housing covenants and legislate fair employment practices.[124]

About *Perez*'s chances in the California Supreme Court, an attorney from ACLU headquarters in New York wrote Dan Marshall, "I presume that it will be lost."[125] On October 1, 1948, the California Supreme Court proved this prediction wrong. A one-vote majority of four agreed that California's antimiscegenation law was unconstitutional, though they disagreed over why. Justice Roger Traynor wrote the lead opinion, which Chief Justice Phil Gibson and Justice Jesse Carter signed. At the time, Traynor, who grew up in a mining town in Utah's Wasatch mountains and received his undergraduate and law degrees from University of California, Berkeley where he joined the law faculty in 1929, was nine years into what would eventually become a thirty-year tenure on California's highest court, during which he would earn a reputation as one of the nation's towering legal innovators and intellects.[126] Traynor began by affirming Marshall's primary contention, while adding to it. In his initial filing to the California Supreme Court, Marshall advanced a First Amendment (religious freedom) argument. California's antimiscegenation law denied Pérez and Davis the "right to participate fully in the sacramental life" of the Catholic Church to which they both belonged.[127] To this, Traynor added that marriage, too, was a fundamental right and any race-based restrictions on fundamental rights required the presence of "a clear and present peril arising out of an emergency" to withstand the test of constitutionality. Absent an emergency, "the state clearly cannot base a law impairing the fundamental rights of individuals on general assumptions as to traits of racial groups."[128] Interracial marriage posed no such emergency.

Traynor next took aim at the claim made by the law's chief defender in the case, Los Angeles Deputy Counsel Charles Stanley, Jr., that the antimiscegenation statute passed equal protection muster because it applied equally to all racial groups (i.e., blacks could not marry whites and whites could not marry blacks). "The decisive question," Traynor wrote, "is not whether different races, each considered as a group, are equally treated," since the right to marry is an individual, not group, one. Traynor elaborated upon this point as he answered the question of how to reconcile the legal case against California's Jim Crow marriage law with the slew of legal precedents that upheld Jim Crow laws in places like public schools and railroad cars. Here Traynor engaged in some deft legal parsing. "A holding that such segregation does not impair the right of an individual to ride on trains or to enjoy a legal education is clearly inapplicable to the right of an individual to marry," he asserted. In the former cases, the Supreme Court stipulated that separate facilities did not violate the "right of an individual to be treated without discrimination because of his race," provided that those separate facilities afforded "substantially equal treatment" to the individual members of the different racial groups. In the latter case, however, the state had no separate but equal option to which to retreat. A black student denied entry into a white school could at least attend a segregated black school. A black man, like Sylvester Davis, forbidden to marry a white woman, like Andrea Pérez, had no analogous alternative short of finding a nonwhite Andrea Pérez clone. Though socially and politically the impediments to interracial marriage were far greater than those to interracial education, legally, in Traynor's view, they were, ironically, easier to resolve. "Human beings," he asserted evocatively, "are bereft of worth and dignity by a doctrine that would make them as interchangeable as trains."[129]

Just as he found no emergency to justify the antimiscegenation law, Traynor also found the law lacking a "legitimate legislative objective," especially when considered in light of the "strong [legal] presumption" against any race-based legislation that was then emerging. Put another way, the most intense form of judicial scrutiny that applied to legal restrictions on fundamental rights, such as religious freedom and marriage, also applied to race-based legal restrictions. "Race restrictions," Traynor wrote, "must be viewed with great suspicion." Here, too, California's antimiscegenation law came up short.[130] To illustrate, Traynor tackled claims about the inherent physical and mental inferiority of non-"Caucasians," as well as the "deplorable results" wrought upon the children of such marriages, as providing a "legitimate legislative objective" for prohibiting interracial marriage. Stanley had taken this position when, for example, he referred to the "excellent evidence of loss of vitality and fertility" when whites married nonwhites, as well as the "definite showing . . . that the white race is superior physically and mentally to the black race."[131] In response, Traynor's opinion drew on a host of culturalist social scientists, such as Gunnar Myrdal and Ruth Benedict. With the weight of scholarly opinion behind him, Traynor observed, "The data on which Caucasian superiority is based have undergone considerable reevaluation by social and physical scientists in the past two decades." Whatever statistical evidence might be brought to support the claim of "Caucasian superiority" had nothing to do with race (nature) and everything to do with "environmental factors" (nurture). Simply put, there was "no scientific proof that one race is superior to another."[132]

Nor for that matter was there any sociological justification—or what Stanley described in oral arguments as the state's desire to avert "certain disharmonic conflicts." This line of argument had the advantage of avoiding the thorny question of innate racial characteristics, which placed the law's defenders in the company of eugenicists and Nazis. It required an empirically easier showing that "race tension" accompanied interracial marriages. Traynor recoiled at such claims. He replied, "It is no answer to say that race tension can be eradicated through the perpetuation by law of the prejudices that give rise to the tension." By such logic, "mixed religious unions" warranted prohibition as well.[133]

California's antimiscegenation statute was as arbitrary as it was unreasonable, Traynor hammered home. Taking, for the moment, the validity of the racial categories in the California antimiscegenation statute, he argued that the law in fact did little to prohibit interracial marriage per se but rather tolerated "extreme racial intermixture"—as Marshall had also argued. The law "does not prevent the mixing of 'white' and 'colored' blood. It permits marriages not only between Caucasians and others of darker pigmentation, such as Indians, Hindus, and Mexicans, but between persons of mixed ancestry, including white." For a law that purported to preclude "racial intermixture," it certainly tolerated an "extreme" amount of it.[134]

Finally, Traynor concluded with another social science-informed attack, this one on the coherence of the law's racial categories. Both sides in the case, Traynor observed, "have assumed that under the equal protection clause the state may classify individuals according to their race in legislation regulating their fundamental rights."[135] This assumption, however, was belied by a growing number of scholars who not only attacked notions of racial superiority and inferiority, but also the concept of race itself upon which race-based laws were premised and without which they lacked a foundation. Traynor had tipped his hand in this direction during oral arguments, offering what historian Peggy Pascoe has described as a "gift no lawyer had ever before received in a miscegenation case: judicial willingness to question the entire enterprise of race classification."[136] "What is a negro? . . . What is a mulatto? . . . If you can marry with 1/8, why not 1/16, 1/32, 1/64?," Traynor pressed Stanley. "We have not the benefit of any judicial interpretation," Stanley stammered in response between one of Traynor's volleys. Then, after another, "I agree that it would be better for the Legislature to lay down an exact amount of blood, but I do not think that the statute should be declared unconstitutional as indefinite on this ground." Why not, Traynor wanted to know. After all, "Anthropologists have not been able to furnish" the very proportional "blood"-based criteria that Stanley was recommending for legislators to adopt. In fact, Traynor continued, "[Anthropologists] say generally that there is no such thing as race." Stanley suggested that such claims were "sensational." Traynor, however, would have nothing of it. "The crucial question is how can a county clerk determine who are negroes and who are whites," he maintained. How, in other words, could marriage license clerks (and, for that matter, the legislators who passed the laws that the clerks were to administer) make the very racial determinations that academic experts deemed impossible?[137] Amplifying this point in his opinion, Traynor cited Franz Boas's claim that "the number of races distinguished by systems of classification 'varies from three or four to thirty-four.'" The uncertainty among experts over what exactly constituted a race rendered the state's antimiscegenation law "too vague and uncertain to be upheld as a valid regulation of the right to marry." It was yet another reason that the law must fall.[138]

In advancing this line of argument, Traynor ventured down a path that Loren Miller had broached and Hugh Macbeth explored during their racially restrictive housing covenant litigation prior to the commencement of *Perez*. The records of some of those cases, including the briefs and trial court testimony, were on file in the California Supreme Court on appeal well over a year before oral arguments in *Perez*. In one of those cases, for example, Macbeth refused to stipulate, as Marshall had in *Perez*, that the defendants he represented were, as the judge in the case put, "of the Negro race." Instead, Macbeth told the court, "When you talk about race you are talking about a myth or dealing with one of the phases of human lunacy," adding that his view was the legal equivalent of being the first person "who argued the world was round and not flat." To buttress his claim, Macbeth summoned University of California, Berkeley anthropologist, Paul Radin, as an expert witness. Radin's testimony prompted Miller to remark in January 1947, "In a recent California [racially restrictive housing covenant] case, a witness for the defendants was a distinguished anthropologist who testified that the terms 'Caucasian' and 'non-Caucasian' are almost meaningless and that, contrary to popular belief, neither skin color nor hair texture are infallible guides to racial identity."[139] As one of Macbeth's clients had put it, officials who oversaw applications for various kinds of official documents like marriage licenses "look at you and sometimes they just put down what they think you are. Heaven knows they don't know"—which was now Traynor's point with respect to the operation of California's antimiscegenation law.[140]

The fourth and final justice in the majority—the swing vote—wrote a separate concurring opinion. Justice Douglas Edmonds confined himself to the fundamental "right to marry" which was "protected by the constitutional guarantee of religious freedom," as Marshall had argued from the outset. For Edmonds, the First Amendment alone disposed of the matter.[141]

Lawyers for Los Angeles County initially sought to appeal *Perez* to the United States Supreme Court but ultimately decided against doing so.[142] In the meantime, reaction in newspapers, magazines, and law reviews ranged from rhapsodic to reserved. The *Nation* hailed Marshall's victory as "in some respects . . . the most important civil-rights victory that racial minorities have yet won in American courts."[143] The *Interracial Review*, voice of the national Catholic Interracial Council, declared the decision to be of "great significance," removing one of the nation's "major moral and legal scandals."[144] The *California Law Review* proclaimed *Perez* a "revolutionary decision."[145] By contrast, the *San Jose Mercury News* spoke in more measured tones, noting the "abstract victory" *Perez* represented, since "social forces" would preclude any more than an "exceptional few" from taking advantage of the opportunity the case's resolution afforded.[146] The African American *Los Angeles Sentinel* struck a similar chord. As much as the verdict "vindicated" democracy and "added dignity" to "personal freedom," no statutory scuttling could ease the gravitational pull of the "law" of social convention. As such, the *Sentinel's* editors observed, "We don't expect any large and concerted rush of whites and Negroes or of whites and Orientals to local marriage bureaus. The rigidity of the color-caste system is still such as to discourage all but the most venturesome as is proved in states where no such ban has ever existed."[147]

Little more than a month after the California Supreme Court's ruling, the first such "venturesome" couple—a Philippines-born woman and an Illinois-born Air Force sergeant—married in San Francisco.[148] A month later, on December 13, 1948, Andrea Pérez and Sylvester Davis submitted a second marriage license application to the Los Angeles County Marriage License Bureau.[149] This one was approved, and on May 7, 1949, nearly two years after their application had been rejected, Andrea Pérez and Sylvester Davis exchanged vows at St. Patrick's Church in Los Angeles. Though California law could no longer bar interracial marriages, Californians, including Pérez's father, Fermín, did not have to embrace them. Disapproving of his daughter's decision to marry a black man, neither Fermín nor any other members of the Pérez family attended the wedding.[150]

That same year, Governor Warren had the opportunity to remove the no-longer- enforceable antimiscegenation law from the state's Civil Code—just as he had done two years earlier with the state's school segregation provisions in the aftermath of *Mendez*. Though the president of the state County Clerk's Association urged Warren to take this step, Warren's legislative secretary advised his boss, "Retaining the present statutory prohibition against interracial marriages does no particular harm." Warren heeded this advice.[151] Despite its potent symbolism, Warren's decision did not undermine the powerful claim made by the editors of the *Los Angeles Sentinel* in October 1948. Reacting to the California Supreme Court's decision in *Perez*, and referring back to the United States Supreme Court's decision in *Shelley* and the Ninth Circuit's decision in *Mendez*, the *Sentinel* proclaimed, "Jim Crow is just about dead in California."[152] To reinforce its point, the *Sentinel* could—and should—have referenced *Oyama* and *Takahashi*. The toppling of statutory segregation that would not begin in the South until 1954 with *Brown v. Board of Education* and not end in until 1967 with *Loving v. Virginia* managed to be compressed in California into less than a decade during the 1940s.

Shortly after the California Supreme Court issued its *Perez* decision, Loren Miller sent a copy of the opinion to William Hastie. At the time, Hastie, the former Howard University Law School mentor to Thurgood Marshall, was governor of the United States Virgin Islands. In his reply to Miller, Hastie, wrote, "We are certainly developing a body of law which few dared hope for ten years ago."[153] California stood on the cusp of this hopeful development. Courtroom victories, Carey McWilliams commented in July 1949, had resulted in "less miscellaneous Jim Crow discrimination here [in California] than in any major region of the country." Amidst these triumphs against legalized segregation, however, were a string of defeats against efforts to enact fair employment practices during the 1940s, which was the top legislative priority of the NAACP-WC. This countervailing current to the trend that Hastie and McWilliams described indicated a limit to just how much racial liberalism a majority of California's legislators and voters would tolerate. Dismantling explicitly discriminatory laws, culminating with *Perez*, according to McWilliams "was accepted throughout the state with scarcely a murmur of audible protest." By contrast, erecting explicitly antidiscriminatory laws, beginning with fair employment practices, spawned stiff and insurmountable resistance, through the 1940s and into the late 1950s.[154]

During these years Assemblyman Augustus (Gus) Hawkins was the state legislature's leading proponent of fair employment practices. Born in Shreveport, Louisiana in 1907, Hawkins moved with his family to Los Angeles in 1920. In 1934, three years after earning his bachelor's degree in economics from UCLA, Hawkins, aided by his campaign manager Loren Miller, unseated the lone African American member of the California legislature to become the new lone African American member of the California legislature (until 1948).[155] In 1945, Hawkins introduced Assembly Bill (AB) 3—the California Fair Employment Practice Act—which called for the "prevention and elimination of practices of discrimination in employment . . . against persons because of race, creed, color, national origin, or ancestry" to be enforced by an appointed and compensated "State Commission on Fair Employment Practices."[156] In a letter he sent to Manuel Ruiz, Jr., head of the Los Angeles Coordinating Council of Latin-American Youth, Hawkins insisted, "discrimination because of race, religion, national origin and ancestry is the number one problem we now face."[157]

To tackle it in the workplace, Hawkins's bill sought to do at the state level something akin to what President Franklin Roosevelt's 1941 Executive Order 8802 (which barred discrimination in federally funded defense industries and established a Fair Employment Practices Committee to assure compliance) had done at the national level during the war. When Congress refused to legislate an extension to Executive Order 8802 into the postwar period, the "Fair Employment Practice Commission Movement," as one scholar described it in 1946, shifted to the states. In 1945, legislatures in twenty-one states introduced over fifty fair employment practices bills, with New York becoming the first state to pass one into law in March 1945.[158]

In California, AB 3 became the top legislative priority of the fledgling NAACP-WC and its regional director, Noah Griffin. "The support given this bill by our branches," observed Griffin in June 1945, "far exceeds anything heretofore done by them in an organized way."[159] Beyond the NAACP-WC, a Statewide Committee for a California FEPC emerged to back AB 3. Judge Isaac Pacht, who would eventually serve as president of the CFCU, chaired the committee's southern California wing and Dan Marshall served as vice chair. Northern California executive committee members included Griffin, Ruth Kingman (another future CFCU president) and California Attorney General Robert Kenny.[160]

As AB 3 shuffled from one assembly committee to another, Beach Vasey, Governor Warren's legislative secretary, noted that the bill's staunchest support came from organized labor and African Americans. On the latter, Vasey wrote Warren in February 1945, "Hawkins is making so much capital of his FEPC that he is solidifying the present Democratic swing among negro voters." To check this development, Vasey recommended that Warren endorse amending a related bill he supported, which called for a toothless advisory-only Commission on Political and Economic Equality, to include FEPC provisions.[161] Two weeks later, Vasey went further. Noting "the publicity that has been given the enactment of such legislation in New York," he asked if Warren would consider endorsing AB 3.[162] The governor took no steps in either direction, and the California assembly killed both Hawkins's bill and Warren's tepid alternative to it.[163]

Determined to "carry on this fight without slackening," as Kenny put it in July 1945, the Statewide Committee for a California FEPC convened separate meetings of its northern and southern wings in October 1945.[164] Attendees agreed that the prospect of passing fair employment practices in the state legislature was "remote." As an alternative, they called for what one of them described as a "great crusade" to secure the measure through the initiative process. That undertaking, which would eventually become Proposition 11, "must depend on knowing that all progressive groups are ready to concentrate their major attention on collecting signatures and raising funds for FEPC," declared David Hedley of the National Lawyers Guild at a meeting of the executive leadership of the Statewide Committee for a California FEPC. As for "all other measures on the 1946 ballot," Hedley continued, they "would receive secondary consideration."[165]

This privileging of fair employment practices legislation comported well with the NAACP-WC's agenda. As Griffin observed at the end of 1945, his organization's members not only sent the "largest delegation" to Sacramento to support the AB 3, but, after the bill's defeat, they were second only to the CIO in extending "their financial support as well as efforts to secure signatures for the [Proposition 11] initiative."[166] Thereafter, rallying NAACP-WC "branches behind the passage of a state FEPC," which Griffin described as his "most effective job of coordination" for 1945, remained his organization's paramount concern in 1946.[167] By contrast, the privileging of fair employment practices squared less well with the JACL's agenda. During 1946, the JACL spearheaded what Mike Masaoka described as "the first time Nisei citizens organized, financed and carried an important political fight in California."[168] That fight focused on Proposition 15, rather than Proposition 11, which sought to write the Alien Land Law and subsequent legislative revisions to it into the California Constitution.[169]

For the California Council of Civic Unity—which would soon be renamed the California Federation for Civic Unity (CFCU)—Propositions 11 and 15 were the "two measures on the November ballot of greatest interest."[170] "Greatest interest," however, did not necessarily translate to equal interest among the constituents that the CFCU hoped to unite into a statewide coalition of civil rights forces. As Fred Ross discovered while attempting to organize a Unity League in San Diego in 1946, "One of the Nisei leaders had attempted to get the backing of the Negroes in the distribution of literature on Proposition 15, to no avail." To secure "Negro support," Ross explained to the "Nisei involved," he "would have to produce on Proposition 11." More generally, Ross continued, "his [i.e., the Nisei's] group should team up with the Negroes and Mexican Americans in a common drive" for Proposition 11 and against Proposition 15.[171]

Beyond San Diego, the limits to the common drive that Ross sought were reflected in Griffin's monthly reports to NAACP national headquarters in New York. Though he frequently discussed developments in the fight for fair employment practices in 1945 and 1946, he made no mention of Proposition 15, *Oyama*, or *Takahashi*. Conversely, no JACL representative attended the northern or southern California meetings of the Statewide Committee for a California Fair Employment Practices Commission in October 1945. Nor did any JACL leader serve on the organization's executive committee, a reflection perhaps of the JACL's perception that FEPC addressed "problems other than those directly affecting persons of Japanese ancestry," as Mike Masaoka would comment about the push for a federal FEPC in 1947.[172] Finally, the best testament to the "common drive" that never materialized in favor of Proposition 11 and against Proposition 15 can be gleaned from their very different fates at the polls. On November 5, 1946, a decisive majority of California voters rejected Proposition 15. This outcome, according to the editors of the JACL's *Pacific Citizen*, represented the "repudiation of the principles involved in the Alien Land Law and similar legislation of a discriminatory nature."[173] At the same time, an even more decisive majority of California voters rejected Proposition 11. The *Pacific Citizen* attributed the vote to "the rising tide of reaction throughout the state and nation." Though the paper's editors expressed surprise at just how "completely" the electorate "repudiate[d] this proposal to guarantee equal work and employment opportunities for all people," they neither commented on, much less attempted account for, the divergent implications of the two propositions at the polls.[174]

A little over a month before the vote, Laurence Hewes, Jr., head of the American Council on Race Relations's regional office in San Francisco, suggested that the outcome of Proposition 11 would make it "possible to forecast modestly the outlines of race relations on the Pacific Coast."[175] Hewes did not mention Proposition 15. Taken together, however, the final disposition of the two measures provided, if not a "forecast . . . of race relations," then a radar image of the current conditions. On the one hand, the defeat of Proposition 15 indicated waning support for statutory segregation. As the editors of the *Pacific Citizen* remarked, though the Alien Land Law remained on the books, "the rejection of Proposition 15 by a plurality of more than 250,000 persons proves that these racist statutes no longer represent public policy."[176] This claim would be reinforced over the next couple of years with courtroom victories against legalized segregation's many guises in California in *Oyama, Takahashi, Mendez*, and *Perez*, as well as the California legislature's striking down of the state's school segregation law in the wake of *Mendez*. On the other hand, the defeat of Proposition 11 suggested a threshold for just how much racial liberalism a majority of the state's voters would accept. With the outcomes of Propositions 11 and 15, California found itself at a civil rights crossroads. Rejecting state-sanctioned discrimination was one thing; erecting state-sanctioned antidiscrimination was quite another—or so the majority of Californians who opposed both Propositions 11 and 15 suggested.

Opponents of Proposition 15 cast the measure as an effort to "make race discrimination constitutional," over and above the statutory legality it long possessed, as the JACL's Joe Grant Masaoka wrote in his case against Proposition 15 that appeared in the 1946 ballot. Proponents of Proposition 15 led by its sponsors, state Senators Jack Tenney and Hugh Burns, corroborated Masaoka's claim. "Japanese aliens," declared Tenney and Burns in their Proposition 15 ballot argument, engaged in "all manner of subterfuges . . . and other nefarious schemes and devices" in order to evade the Alien Land Law. In so doing, they threatened national security, as they had done during World War II, by acquiring "land adjacent to vital defense areas and industries prior to, and for a considerable time after, the sneak attack by the Imperial Japanese Government on Pearl Harbor." As recently as 1945, such arguments had worked to secure funding from the state legislature for Alien Land Law prosecutions. In November 1946, however, they failed to prevail upon the sizable majority of California voters who rejected

Proposition 15 and, in the process, according to the *Pacific Citizen*, demonstrated their "opposition . . . to race-baiting legislation."[177]

Unlike Proposition 15, Proposition 11 was not "race-baiting legislation." Supporters of Proposition 11, like opponents of Proposition 15, defended the measure in the quintessentially racial liberal terms of antidiscrimination and equality of opportunity. The Proposition 11 ballot argument, signed by Hawkins, Miller, and Marshall, among others, insisted that the measure "furthers the cause of American democracy which rests on equality of opportunity" by "extend[ing] as a civil right the privilege of employment without discrimination because of race, religion, ancestry or national origin." By contrast, like supporters of Proposition 15, opponents of Proposition 11, led by agribusiness and other big business interests, drew on both race- and red-baiting arguments. In their ballot argument, for example, they insisted that "religious, national or racial intolerance is a matter of individual conscience that can not be changed by legislative coercion." Efforts to do so, they continued, would only backfire. Casting fair employment as forced employment, they contended, "Any attempt to force employees to work with other employees whom they disliked will generate friction and intolerance rather than overcome it." As evidence they pointed to the "serious trouble" that fair employment practices would create for farmers who "usually found it necessary to confine the hiring to one group in order to avoid ill feeling and even violence between minorities." If that was not enough reason to vote against it, opponents of Proposition 11 charged that it was part of "the communistic plan of promoting discord in democratic countries."[178] In short, whereas proponents of Proposition 11 portrayed it as a small, logical next step along a civil rights continuum—from striking down laws that legalized discrimination to enacting laws that proscribed discrimination—opponents of Proposition 11 cast it as a giant step backward—a form of state sanctioned (reverse) discrimination against employers' right to hire, promote, and fire as they saw fit. Their arguments prevailed upon an even greater majority of Californians who voted against Proposition 15. Moreover, those same arguments would continue to help thwart the passage of a state fair employment practices law for the next thirteen years.

Rather than wait for voters and legislators to come around to supporting fair employment practices, a small band of Richmond, California activists decided to press the issue at the local level. Their efforts, which began one month after the defeat of Proposition 11, would reach the California Supreme Court in 1948 and the United States Supreme Court in 1950. Their efforts would also serve as a left-wing challenge to the NAACP-WC's push for fair employment practices in California and across the country, forcing the organization's leaders to clarify that their vision of fair employment practices meant equality of opportunity over equality of results (or, proportional representation in hiring).

In December 1946, members of the Richmond branches of the NAACP and Progressive Citizens of America (PCA) met with representatives from Lucky Stores, Inc., an Oakland-based supermarket chain. At the time, Lucky did not employ a single African American in its stores, including the five it operated in Richmond. In their meeting, the Richmond NAACP and PCA representatives, according to PCA leader John E. Hughes, "asked Lucky to consider the hiring of Negro clerks in proportion to Negro trade." Lucky refused. It did not want to anger its white employees nor alienate its white patrons who harbored "anti-Negro sentiment." Instead, Lucky agreed to "experiment" with the hiring of a single black clerk in a handful of their Richmond stores "before giving consideration to the hiring of more Negro clerks." Dissatisfied with this "token-hiring" and outraged by the violent apprehension of an alleged African American shoplifter by a Richmond police officer and Lucky clerk, Richmond NAACP and PCA representatives demanded another meeting with Lucky officials. Once again, they asked Lucky to "endeavor to hire Negro clerks until the proportion was roughly equal to that of the negro trade." Once again, Lucky refused.[179]

With no other recourse, such as an FEPC created by a fair employment practices law, a group of Richmond NAACP and PCA members, never numbering more than six, picketed a single Lucky's supermarket. To stop the picket, Lucky Stores filed for an injunction in Contra Costa County Superior Court, which they received in June 1947. Hughes and Louis Richardson of the Richmond NAACP, however, disregarded the court order, once again staging a picket with signs that read, "Lucky's Won't Hire Negro Clerks in Proportion to Negro Trade, Don't Patronize." Their efforts earned them a contempt of court citation, for which their punishment was to be two days in jail and a $20 fine each. Lawyers for Hughes and Richardson appealed, and what began as the case of *Lucky Stores vs. Progressive Citizens of America* turned into *Hughes v. Superior Court*.[180]

As it made its way up to the California and United States Supreme Courts over the course of the next several years, *Hughes* posed a difficult dilemma for the regional and national NAACP. On the one hand, both the regional and national NAACP steadfastly supported state and national efforts to enact fair employment practices laws. Richmond made a particularly compelling case for such measures. As the city hemorrhaged Kaiser shipyard jobs, a worried Walter White wrote Griffin in July 1945, "Some of the city officials, among whom I understand the Mayor is most active, are advocating sending newcomers 'back where they came from,' especially Negroes."[181] Four years later, the NAACP's amicus brief to the United States Supreme Court in *Hughes*, written by Thurgood Marshall and Robert Carter, noted how black unemployment in Richmond was "greatly disproportionate to unemployment among whites." The Richmond NAACP and PCA picketers were thus "motivated by the quite understandable desire to improve their economic lot." On the other hand, the regional and national NAACP rejected the means through which the Richmond NAACP and PCA sought to achieve the ends of "greater opportunity for employment to Negroes by abolishing discrimination based upon color in hiring practices." As Marshall and Carter explained, "We . . . oppose a proportional or quota system in hiring and feel that persons must be given job opportunities in accordance with ability rather than in accordance with race or color."[182]

Amicus briefs filed by the CIO and ACLU took similar views. They supported the right of the Richmond NAACP and PCA activists to picket for employment opportunity, but spurned their demand for hiring in proportion to patronage.[183] Even worse than the demand, from the perspective of the NAACP, were those doing the demanding. Among the NAACP branches that Griffin implicated in September 1944 as "greatly influenced by Communists," Richmond was the most notorious in Griffin's view.[184] It was, Griffin wrote in November 1947, "completely under the control and domination of a small Communist group," which included Hughes himself.[185] Such communist influence on branch activities violated the NAACP's anticommunism policy, which was spelled out in March 1947 at a West Coast Regional Conference in San Francisco attended by Griffin, Marshall, and Miller, among others. It also threatened to thwart the NAACP's overarching objective to "integrate the Negro completely within the framework of the United States Constitution."[186]

Whatever dilemma *Hughes* may have posed to the NAACP, it presented no such problem for the California and United States Supreme Courts. On November 1, 1948, one month after it ruled in *Perez*, the California Supreme Court upheld the injunction that the Contra Costa County Superior Court had issued against the demonstration of Hughes and Richardson. The picketers' demand for hiring in proportion to patronage, Justice B. Rey Schauer opined on behalf of the majority, was illegal. It called for "arbitrary discrimination upon the basis of race and color alone, rather than a choice based solely upon individual qual-ification for the work." If the picketers' prevailed, they would set a dangerous precedent—"other races, white, yellow, brown, and red, would have equal rights to demand discriminatory hiring on a racial basis." Since the picketers' demand was illegal, so, too, was their picket.[187]

A year and a half later, a unanimous United States Supreme Court agreed. For Justice Felix Frankfurter, who wrote the Court's opinion, the "broad question" posed by the case was, "Does the Fourteenth Amendment of the Constitution bar a State from use of the injunction to prohibit picketing of a place of business solely in order to secure compliance with a demand that its employees be in proportion to the racial origin of its then customers?" The answer was no. Nothing in the Fourteenth Amendment, nor for that matter the First Amendment, precluded the

Contra Costa County Superior Court from acting as it did, given the "mischief furthered" by the "evil of picketing to bring about proportional hiring." To rule otherwise would open a Pandora's Box of "community tensions and conflicts." Echoing the California Supreme Court's concerns, Frankfurter wrote, "To deny to California the right to ban picketing in the circumstances of this case would mean that there could be no prohibition of the pressure of picketing to secure proportional employment on ancestral grounds of Hungarians in Cleveland, of Poles in Buffalo, of Germans in Milwaukee, of Portuguese in New Bedford, of Mexicans in San Antonio, of the numerous minority groups in New York, and so on through the whole gamut of racial and religious concentrations in various cities."[188]

In his dissenting opinion in *Hughes* in 1948, California Supreme Court Justice Roger Traynor noted the absence of a state fair employment practices law, which both the California legislature and electorate in Proposition 11 had rebuffed. Without such a law, Traynor argued, there existed no prohibition against businesses such as Lucky Stores to discriminate in "favor or against Negroes." Lucky Stores, therefore, could very well, if it so chose, adopt a "policy of proportionate hiring" in favor of black job applicants in order to offset "the fact that everywhere [black job seekers] turn for jobs they are likely to encounter the barrier of discrimination." Though a state fair employment practices law that "prohibited consideration of the race of applicants for jobs . . . might" render "the demand for proportional hiring" illegal, "neither the Legislature nor the people have adopted such a statute."[189]

Nor were they in any hurry to do so. The Richmond City Council, however, did. In May 1949, it unanimously passed an ordinance barring discrimination based on "race, creed, color, national origin or ancestry" in both city employment and businesses receiving city contracts or franchises. Though limited in terms of its employment coverage and geographic reach, Richmond's fair employment practices ordinance was nevertheless the first fair employment practices law to be enacted by a city in California. Another decade would have to pass before the state legislature followed Richmond's lead.[190]

In July 1949, the NAACP held its annual national convention in Los Angeles. As part of the program, Carey McWilliams delivered a speech on "Minority Rights on the West Coast." He began by highlighting the multiracial nature of the "racial question" in California. He then sketched the state's "ugly record in the treatment of racial minorities" and turned to a discussion of the "remarkable change in opinion . . . in the last decade," especially the last five years. "California," he exclaimed, "has begun to repudiate the racism which has disgraced its prior history." For these reasons, compared to the rest of the United States, McWilliams concluded, California was proceeding "at a somewhat faster pace . . . and with greater ease and assurance" in "fight[ing] clear of the pattern of racial discrimination which has mocked [the country's] ideals for generations."[191]

Several months later, Richard Dettering, executive director of the CFCU, offered a less upbeat assessment than McWilliams. Speaking to the CFCU's annual convention in December 1949, Dettering lamented how "human relations" in California "has not yet progressed to the legislative stage, but remains in a condition of laissez-faire." Though litigation during the 1940s had dismantled legalized segregation in the state, legislation to "curb discrimination" had yet to be enacted. Referring to the recently completed session of the California legislature, Dettering noted, "Every bill which could have conceivably stepped on someone's toes," including the latest (and last) attempt of the decade to pass a state fair employment practices law, "was scuttled."[192] When it came to antidiscrimination legislation, as opposed to Jim Crow litigation, much work remained.

As of 1950, however, the prospects for venturing down the antidiscrimination legislation road that began where legalized segregation ended appeared dim. On the one hand, the Cold War political climate cast a pall of suspicion over both the means and ends of antidiscrimination activism. As the CFCU's Josephine Duveneck and Ruth Kingman observed in February 1948, "Unfortunately, it is becoming increasingly difficult to undertake any kind of activity in the area of civil rights of racial and/or religious minorities without being forced to face the charge of Communism."[193] On the other hand, the "state-wide organization" for "concerted action" which the CFCU sought to cultivate, and which was especially critical in light of the constraints imposed by the inhospitable political climate, had yet to coalesce.[194] As much as the CFCU endeavored to provide "a forum and a medium of action which makes it unnecessary for any one group to fight its battle alone"—to identify and pursue in tandem the "basic principle which binds everyone together"—Dettering found little evidence of such binding. "There is," he complained in June 1949, "almost complete isolation between various racial and cultural groups."[195]

The "isolation" Dettering lamented could be discerned in the various legal campaigns that McWilliams hailed for having produced in California over the course of the second half of the 1940s "less miscellaneous Jim Crow discrimination . . . than in any major region of the country."[196] Though the NAACP-WC's Griffin claimed in February 1946 that there was "a significant showing that minority groups recognize similar problems and realize the need for joining in the fight that involves civil rights," the separate track attacks on legalized segregation that were then afoot belied Griffin's claim.[197] (Griffin himself, for example, made no mention of *Mendez* in his monthly reports to NAACP headquarters until he referred to a case involving, as he put it, "Spanish children segregated in school" in December 1946.[198] Moreover, he was altogether silent on *Oyama* and *Takahashi*.) Instead, these cases reflected what the ACRR's Hewes described as some of the "very specific issues affecting" the West Coast's different "colored minority groups." They also pointed to the limits of the "makings" of an "integrated, regional program for racial justice" that Hewes, like Griffin, saw emerging in 1946, despite the evidence to the contrary.[199] The different trajectories reflected in the different challenges to legalized segregation in the 1940s would continue into the 1950s, as California's multiracial civil rights struggles ventured down antidiscrimination legislation and litigation roads that began where legalized segregation ended.

CHAPTER 5

"PROBLEMS AS DIVERSIFIED AS ITS POPULATION"

In February 1949, NAACP assistant secretary Roy Wilkins traveled from New York to San Francisco to attend a meeting with leaders of his organization's West Coast Regional Office. Led by California, the seven states encompassing the NAACP-WC confronted a daunting challenge and unprecedented opportunity, as Wilkins saw it. On the one hand, the NAACP-WC had seen its membership plummet from 24,618 in December 1945 to 9,530 in 1950.[1] Wilkins attributed this decline to a combination of postwar job losses and a Cold War political atmosphere that cast a cloud of communist suspicion over civil-rights-oriented organizations. On the other hand, Wilkins pointed to the "vast potential for new membership" created by the influx of African Americans, as well as what he took to be the less "fixed" and more "fluid" pattern of race relations in the region than in the "older territory in the East."[2] Few developments demonstrated this fluidity better than the cases waged over the preceding five years that dismantled California's alien land, school segregation, and antimiscegenation laws, as well as its court enforcement of racially restrictive housing covenants.

Into this milieu, Wilkins's office dispatched thirty-three-year-old Franklin Williams in September 1950 to replace Noah Griffin as the NAACP-WC regional director. A native of Queens, New York, and a veteran of World War II, Williams earned his law degree from Fordham University and then joined the NAACP Legal Defense and Educational Fund as an assistant to Thurgood Marshall.[3] Upon assuming the helm of the NAACP-WC five years later, Williams realized quickly just how fluid race relations in the West, and especially California, were. Indeed, they were much more fluid than Wilkins probably imagined when he described them as such the previous year.

In a 1951 report to NAACP headquarters, Williams reflected on his region's distinctiveness. The West Coast, in general, and California, in particular, possessed "problems . . . which are not duplicated in degree anywhere else in the United States." Foremost among these was the presence of "other minorities."[4] The region's racial diversity, Williams later claimed, echoing Carey McWilliams from the previous decade, made it the country's "New Frontier" in "race relations."[5] In this setting, the "race problem" was not synonymous with "the relationship between Negroes and white persons," but also included "descendants of almost any so-called colored nation, or even the 'original American himself.'" Reflecting on the implications California's racial diversity, Williams distinguished the "new 'problem' [of] the Negro" in the West from those of their other "colored" predecessors. Unlike Californians of Mexican, Chinese, and Japanese descent, for example, African Americans were not set apart by a "common language," "common culture," or set of "nationalistic ties except those with the very people who refused to accept [them] as an integral part of society." Darker skin might unite Californians of color in some ways, Williams seemed to suggest, but nativity, language, and culture divided them in others, and, in fact, did more to link African Americans with their white counterparts.[6]

Here, then, was another aspect of the West's fluid race relations, rooted not so much in the legal victories achieved in the 1940s, but rather in how those cases reflected what Williams described as California's "human relations problems as diversified as its population and as complex as its topography."[7] In the face of this fluidity, Williams could have concentrated on the specific task that brought him to California: re-building NAACP-WC membership by "re-stimulating local program and community interest" and "eliminating Communist influence."[8] Instead, he sought to transform the NAACP-WC into the leading statewide civil rights organization in California. To this end, he welcomed the "growing interest in civil rights" in California but lamented the proliferation of civil rights groups—he counted over fifty—that "have come into existence working for 'unity,' 'tolerance,' or just plain civil rights." These mostly upstart groups undermined support for the NAACP, as Williams saw it. Moreover, they served no purpose that the NAACP did not already serve. As Williams told attendees at the fifth annual convention of the California Federation for Civic Unity (CFCU), "There is little that has or can be accomplished by another . . . civil rights organization . . . in the state of California that could not have been accomplished under the aegis and banner of the NAACP."[9] Though Californians "interested in civil rights [did] not think in terms of Negroes alone" but also "Japanese, Chinese, Mexican, et al.," members of these groups, according to Williams did "not consider themselves 'colored.'"[10] Williams, however, did. His thinking, in turn, buttressed his belief that non-white Californians shared common problems, which, in turn, lent themselves to common solutions, the pursuit of which Williams wanted the NAACP-WC to lead.[11]

To this end, Williams, echoing McWilliams and the CFCU from the previous decade, called for a "general program to which we are all sincerely dedicated."[12] More specifically, he viewed the NAACP-WC's top priorities during the 1950s— the passage of fair employment practices legislation and pursuit of fair housing litigation—as responses to the "most pressing problems" for all "colored minority persons throughout the region."[13] Herein, he believed, resided the specific legislative and legal means for forging the "cooperation and unity" on behalf of the general "common goal" of "equality of opportunity for all people."[14]

As the 1950s unfolded, however, leaders and organizations representing some of those other "colored minority persons" belied Williams's reasoning by analogy in their prioritization and pursuit of other civil rights issues. For example, in 1953 when the NAACP-WC declared fair employment practices to be "the 'number one' legislative aim of the civil rights forces in California," the burgeoning Mexican American Community Service Organization (CSO), where a young César Chávez was cutting his activist's teeth, launched what would become a nearly decade-long campaign to legislate old-age pensions for long-term resident non-citizens, a disproportionate number of whom were born in Mexico.[15] Meanwhile, Ernesto Galarza, linked Mexican American civil rights with labor rights and sought to unionize farm workers through the National Farm Labor Union, a forerunner to Chávez's United Farm Workers. Finally, California Japanese American Citizens League leaders prioritized their own version of an old-age pensions for non-citizens bill, while also seeking reimbursement from the state for payments paid during the 1940s to settle Alien Land Law cases.

In the end, Williams's call for a civil rights coalition led by the NAACP-WC on behalf of fair employment practices legislation and fair housing litigation stood in uneasy tension with his recognition of the West, in general, and California, in particular, as the nation's new race relations frontier. Though the separate civil rights streams that comprised California's civil rights struggles would occasionally cross in the 1950s, they never converged into the river that Williams envisioned. Coalition building through reasoning by analogy from the plight and priorities of African Americans to other "colored minority persons," as Williams did, only went so far. The different civil rights paths reflected in the separate campaigns to dismantle the multiracial manifestations of legalized segregation in California in the 1940s continued into the 1950s, even as the state's civil rights struggles began to gain more traction in the legislative realm. Williams, as it turns out, was more right than he realized when he pronounced California's "human relations problems" to be "as diversified as its population and as complex as its topography."[16]

On December 3, 1951, the *San Francisco Chronicle* reported that California was poised to become "the testing ground for one of the most far-reaching and drastic legislative proposals affecting 'civil rights' that has ever been submitted to American Voters." An organization called "America Plus" had just announced plans to collect the requisite signatures to place a "so-called 'Freedom of Choice' Amendment" to the California Constitution on the November 1952 ballot.[17] The news startled Franklin Williams. He sent an urgent letter to Walter White, Roy Wilkins, and Thurgood Marshall, and others in the NAACP's national office, detailing the terms of the "Freedom of Choice" initiative, which, he added, was being spearheaded by "our leading witch-hunter" and national chairman of America Plus, state Senator Jack Tenney.[18] Barely a year into his job as regional director of the NAACP-WC, and in the midst of hatching plans to mount an offensive campaign for fair employment practices legislation, Williams found himself instead forced into waging a defensive battle against the "Freedom of Choice" initiative.

Though innocuously named, the "Freedom of Choice" initiative was insidiously aimed at undoing the civil rights past and foreclosing the civil rights future. The proposed amendment, Williams explained, "guarantees the right of all private owners, places of accommodation, etc., to choose their own guests, patrons and tenants—in other words, it would offset any civil rights statute and give legal support to racial and religious discrimination." It also sought to extend similar guarantees to employers vis-à-vis employees, thereby precluding the passage of fair employment practices laws. Finally, it endeavored to provide state constitutional cover for racially restrictive covenants among private homeowners. In light of Proposition 11's defeat in 1946, Williams believed that there was a strong chance that the initiative would pass. If it did, he feared, it would set a precedent for other states to duplicate and "destroy any hope of further civil rights advances for many years to come."[19] With the fight against the "Freedom of Choice" initiative, Williams officially launched the second front in a two-front war, the first against the "substantial inroads" made by the Communist Party within certain NAACP chapters and the second against the "un-American Fascist idea" reflected in the proposed amendment, in particular, and opposition to civil rights legislation, more generally.[20]

Williams was not alone. Josephine Duveneck, president of the CFCU, responded to the announcement of America Plus's plans by sending a letter to her organization's board and affiliates. The proposed amendment she wrote, represented a "travesty of social justice." She exhorted CFCU supporters to take steps to "defeat this most dangerous move against American democracy."[21] These steps included convening an emergency meeting—attended by Williams, among others—to strategize a response. Meeting attendees called for the formation of a "statewide citizens' committee" whose members were to be drawn from the "broadest possible basis," with the exception of "Communist, Communist-front, Fascist or other subversive groups or individuals."[22]

These initial steps squared with Walter White's suggested course of action. White recommended that Williams organize the "most impressive committee possible" led by "Jews and Negroes." However, he cautioned, the committee should not be too "heavily weighted" with members of those groups who stood to lose the most by the enactment of the "Freedom of Choice" amendment, lest it "play into the hands of Tenney and his crowd." Strategically, too, White urged Williams to "make some statement prior to the communists coming into it."[23]

As it turns out, the fight against the "Freedom of Choice" initiative never reached the ring. Its supporters failed to muster the requisite signatures to place the measure on the ballot in the face of some strong public opposition to it. The *San Francisco Chronicle*, for example, opined, "The 'freedom of choice' label is, of course, window dressing. What the measure seeks to sell to the people of California is freedom to discriminate."[24] State Attorney General—and future Governor—Pat Brown decried the measure for threatening to move "this country back hundreds of years to bigotry, discrimination and persecution."[25]

Having achieved a defensive victory against "Freedom of Choice," Williams turned the attention of NAACP-WC's attention back to the offensive battle for fair employment practices legislation that it had been waging since its founding in 1944. Efforts to add California to the list of states with fair employment practices laws—eleven by 1953—had failed in each of the biennial legislative sessions since 1943.[26] These repeated failures prompted the NAACP-WC's Tarea Hall Pittman, who would eventually succeed Williams as regional director, to describe California as "a state that was filled with Southerners and other people that were in sympathy with undemocratic forces."[27] However, the resounding defeat dealt to those "undemocratic forces" behind the "Freedom of Choice" initiative buoyed the hopes of fair employment practices supporters. In December 1952, the NAACP-WC announced its plans to press for fair employment practices in the upcoming legislative session. A press release indicated that "an NAACP-sponsored" bill would soon be introduced in the legislature and called for a "state-wide mobilization" to support.[28] Lest any "subversive organizations or individuals" think that the NAACP-WC meant to include them in fair employment practices legislation rally, a subsequent press release stressed "non-Communist groups and organizations only would be welcome at the mobilization."[29]

When the legislative session began in January 1953, Williams mailed letters to each member of the California legislature alerting them to the impending introduction of the NAACP sponsored fair employment practices bill by Assemblymen Augustus (Gus) Hawkins of Los Angeles and William (Byron) Rumford of Berkeley, the state legislature's only African American members. It urged the state's lawmakers to support fair employment practices, which, it added, would be modeled after the first such law in the country passed in New York in 1945.[30] Accompanying Williams's letter was a questionnaire. Of the forty California legislators who responded, the vast majority expressed opposition to fair employment practices legislation.[31] Their constituents, by and large, shared their recalcitrance. According to a September 1952 California Poll, only sixteen percent of respondents voiced support for such a law.[32]

Undaunted, the NAACP-WC forged ahead. It convened a meeting in San Francisco at the end of January, which adopted a fair employment practices resolution as its first order of business. The resolution made it the "policy" of the NAACP-WC and its branches to "campaign uncompromisingly for the passage of state and local FEP legislation containing specific provisions for . . . enforcement."[33] The next day, the organization sponsored a meeting with other groups interested in the enactment of a state fair employment practices. Representatives from the CFCU, CSO, JACL, ACLU, CIO, and Jewish Labor Committee, among other organizations, attended. The "movement" for fair employment practices, according to one leading NAACP-WC participant, was "officially accepted and launched."[34]

If this was a "movement," however, its NAACP-WC leaders did not appear to be especially concerned with attracting followers. As the minutes of the meeting reveal, the NAACP-WC's principal concern seemed to be wresting control of statewide leadership for fair employment practices legislation from other groups, in particular the CFCU, which had led the lobbying for fair employment practices in 1949 and 1951. "In many efforts made in this state," the minutes recorded, "the NAACP has not been in the vanguard." That, the message implied, needed to change. For those who wanted to fall in line with the change, fine. For those who did not, no matter. As the minutes continued, "We intend to move ahead in California whether you come along or not. This is not to exclude you but we are going to put up a solid front in promoting mobilization for FEP." As for why the NAACP-WC felt compelled to assume this "vanguard" role, the answer was simple: it was their constituency that needed the legislation the most. "We are perfectly aware that Negroes are the last hired and first fired."[35]

One week later, at a meeting in Fresno, the California Committee for Fair Employment Practices (CCFEP) was born. With the CCFEP, according to Williams, the NAACP-WC "took the leadership in spearheading the . . . state-wide fair employment practices campaign." The new organization's chosen name—CCFEP rather than NAACP-WC—represented an attempt to mollify vigorous criticism from "several of the Civic Unity and Jewish agencies" about the NAACP-WC's assumption of "direct organizational leadership of FEP." Williams considered the criticism "unjustified" and conceded little to it besides the CCFEP's non-NAACP title. Beyond that, though, the CCFEP, Williams indicated, was little more than an extension of the NAACP-WC. As Williams's described the CCFEP's leadership, "We had our regional chairman, C.L. Dellums, elected as overall chairman of the Committee and Nathaniel Colley, president of our Central Area, elected as one of the 6 co-chairmen. William Becker, of the Jewish Labor Committee, a staunch supporter of the Association in this region, was selected upon our insistence as the secretary for the Committee."[36] Reflecting on the CCFEP years later, Becker corroborated Williams's claim about the NAACP-WC dominance of the CCFEP: "the major factor in determining the priorities and the content of [fair employment practices] . . . was the NAACP, represented by Franklin Williams."[37]

This influence exacted a cost. It threatened to alienate potential supporters of fair employment practices, or so CCFEP executive secretary Edward Howden cautioned the NAACP-WC's Pittman. Howden, an Oakland-born and Berkeley-educated World War II veteran, became active in fighting for civil rights after returning to the Bay Area from military service. By the early 1950s, he had carved out a notable niche for himself within California's civil rights circles. In addition to his positions as executive director of the San Francisco Council for Civic Unity and executive secretary of the CCFEP, Howden hosted a weekly fifteen-minute radio program, *Dateline Freedom*, which reported on civil rights issues.[38] In his letter to Pittman, Howden acknowledged that the NAACP-WC "has assumed responsibility for the campaign," but he questioned whether the organization was taking the necessary steps to "involve all available and capable organizational resources in the crucial remaining part of the fight." He cited the JACL as an example, which had contributed money "to the drive *prior to* the mobilization and in response simply to form mailings," but was nevertheless "not consulted concerning the campaign nor its aid requested except financially and in terms of general attendance at the mobilization." As if that was not impolitic enough, the JACL's "regional director was greeted in Sacramento by a mobilization leader with an accusing inquiry as to why JACL was not more fully represented there; and no subsequent contact of any kind has been made." The NAACP's leadership style, Howden concluded, ran the risk of driving away organizations like the JACL and with them many "potentially effective chapters in various parts of the State." A less domineering approach to directing the CCFEP, Howden implied, would have drawn greater participation by the JACL and its members in the fight for fair employment practices. "What, in short, is desired of us," Howden asked on behalf of the non-NAACP-WC organizations like the JACL, when it came to contributing to the NAACP-WC led CCFEP?[39]

Howden's letter suggested that a change in organizational approach might help expand the CCFEP's reach beyond the NAACP-WC and into a broader coalition. JACL leaders themselves, however, suggested otherwise when they articulated and pursued their legislative priorities over the course of the late 1940s and early 1950s. In the late 1940s, for example, Mike Masaoka described the campaign for a permanent federal FEPC as addressing "problems other than those directly affecting persons of Japanese ancestry."[40] A few years later, the newly created JACL Anti-Discrimination Committee (JACL-ADC) in California, which was a state level counterpart to Masaoka's Washington DC-based national JACL-ADC, placed "FEPC bills" at the bottom of the legislative priorities it categorized as of "indirect concern to persons of Japanese ancestry." By contrast, the bills of direct concern, which were to be given "priority consideration," included one that would grant old-age pensions to Japanese immigrants who were, at the time, still ineligible to naturalized citizenship, and another that would provide compensation for settlements paid for Alien Land Law escheat prosecutions by California authorities during the 1940s.[41]

In lobbying the California legislature for the first of these bills in May 1951, Senate Bill (SB) 734, the JACL-ADC of California wrote the state senate's Social Welfare Committee that its passage would help alleviate some of the "undue hardships peculiar to no other group" that Californians of Japanese descent had experienced in recent years. In particular, the proposed legislation would provide "qualified aliens," namely, those who were ineligible to naturalized citizenship, to receive state old-age pensions on par with citizens. The JACL-ADC of California estimated that roughly 2,000 of the 20,000 Issei in California fell into this category. Their ranks included former agriculture and domestic workers who were uncovered by federal Social Security.[42] As for the second JACL priority bill, Toru Ikeda of the JACL-ADC wrote Governor Warren that Assembly Bill (AB) 2611 would allow for the recovery of money ceded to the state as a result of the World War II era enforcement of the Alien Land Law.[43] "Some Nisei had made compromise payments to the State to save their properties," while other Nisei "who were still in relocation camps lost their homes and lands altogether," wrote Joe Grant Masaoka and June Fugita to Warren.[44] This "legalized blackmail," explained Tats Kushida, another JACL-ADC member, to Warren, "resulted in more than $400,000 extorted from Japanese American landowners."[45] While SB 734 went down to defeat in 1951, AB 2611 passed by an overwhelming margin, and Warren signed it into law. Looking ahead, a JACL "California Legislative Report" from January 1952 reiterated the centrality of a bill granting "old age pensions for Issei." This was the JACL's top legislative priority, and it belied the NAACP-WC's assertion at the end of 1952 that fair employment practices legislation was not just "the 'key issue' confronting" the NAACP but all "the people of California."[46]

Like the JACL, the burgeoning CSO supported fair employment practices, but did not accord it the top priority status that the NAACP-WC did. Launched by Fred Ross in Los Angeles in 1947, the CSO, according to Ross, aspired to be a "Mexican NAACP."[47] As Ross saw it, "Every other minority . . . was organized and moving forward except the Mexican American." Yet, they were "by far the largest, [and] in many ways[,] the most kicked around group in the community."[48] Improving the plight of Mexican descent Californians, Ross believed, began with harnessing their untapped political potential. As Ross explained, "What appeared to be needed, in order effectively to level the road-blocks . . . was an organization designed to unify and activate the actual and potential political power that existed in the Colonia," or, "just traditional American democracy, with a special Colonia flavor."[49] The CSO marked "the first time in their organizational history [that] the M.A.'s [Mexican Americans] of L.A. were being offered what the Negroes and Jews had for years," Ross wrote Saul Alinsky, whose Industrial Areas Foundation (IAF) placed Ross on the payroll in August 1947.[50]

Ross's IAF organizing began in the East Los Angeles neighborhood of Boyle Heights. With only approximately 4,000 of 25,000 potential Mexican American voters in Boyle Heights registered, the CSO aimed to achieve "effective bargaining power through a thorough-going program of voter education based upon precinct-by-precinct door-to-door registration." Increasing the number of Mexican Americans on the voting rolls would pave the way to electing a Mexican American. In a labor-intensive grassroots campaign, Ross spent the fall of 1947 recruiting. Wearing cowboy boots and speaking little Spanish, Ross, accompanied by one of the five original CSO members, devoted weeknights from 6:30 until midnight knocking on doors and visiting with families—an average of two per night.[51] By 1949 Ross reported that CSO membership stood at nearly 1,000 active and semi-active members, with sixty-five deputy registrars who had registered some 15,000 Mexican American voters.[52] That same year those newly registered voters helped catapult Boyle Heights's own Edward Roybal onto the Los Angeles City Council, the first Mexican American to hold such a position since 1881. Only two years earlier, Roybal, then a thirty-year-old UCLA graduate, World War II veteran, and social worker, had finished a distant third in his bid for a council seat, with fifteen percent of the vote. If Roybal's election was any indication, the grassroots seeds sown by Fred Ross and the CSO were starting to sprout.[53]

In June 1952, the CSO expanded to northern California. Following a lecture that Ross delivered to a San Jose State sociology class, a group of students, including Herman Gallegos and Alicia Hernández, approached Ross and invited him to visit the heavily Mexican descent East San Jose. With Ross's instruction in grass roots organizing, Gallegos and Hernandez opened the state's second CSO chapter in the state's second largest Mexican descent community, where fewer than ten percent of eligible Mexican Americans—1,600 out of 21,000— were registered to vote. A young César Chávez soon joined.[54]

As the CSO spread, Ross wrote an enthusiastic letter to Alinsky. Long considered "'unorganizable,'" Mexican Americans were experiencing success in "building solid foundations of voting strength as underpinnings for its social action programs . . . CSO has met the acid test; it works!" Ross tempered his enthusiasm with a realistic assessment of the task ahead. Except for a few pockets of Los Angeles and San Jose, "the Mexican American population of California (over 800,000) . . . continues to be the largest, least civically active, least organized minority in the region." For that reason, he called for launching CSO chapters in at least forty other places across the state where Californians of Mexican descent were concentrated.[55]

Though Ross's vision of the road ahead for the CSO in 1953 did not conflict with the NAACP-WC campaign for fair employment practices legislation that emerged that same year, it did not complement it. The state's "sleeping giant," as Roybal described Mexican Americans in 1954, had barely begun to stir.[56] Rousing it from its slumber required, first and foremost, an organizational campaign such as the one on which the CSO had embarked. Ross and other CSO leaders recognized this. On numerous occasions in the early to mid-1950s, they emphasized that voter registration stood at the top of the CSO priority list. As Ross declared in 1954, "The CSO has found an answer . . . register and vote!"[57]

Nine months later, Roybal echoed Ross's sentiment at the CFCU's annual convention. Addressing an audience whose members were a who's who of the state's present and future civil rights leaders—including Loren Miller, Tarea Hall Pittman, and Nathaniel Colley of the NAACP; Herman Gallegos, César Chávez, and Fred Ross of the CSO; William Becker of the San Francisco Jewish Labor Council; Edward Howden of the San Francisco Council for Civic Unity— Roybal insisted, "The greatest need in California today [for Mexican Americans] is *organization*." Once organized, Roybal stressed, Mexican Americans could then elect local leaders who would, in turn, devote themselves to local issues, such as neighborhood improvement. Citing East Los Angeles as an example, Roybal explained, "Seven years ago, the Mexican community was ignored. . . . Today there are sidewalks and streetlights, and C.S.O. is an important and respected community organization." Of course, Roybal did not believe that the Mexican American leaders swept into office by a wave of CSO-registered voters would or should confine themselves exclusively to streetlights, sidewalks, sewage, sanitation, and the like. Eventually, they would take stands on "issues such as FEPC, public housing, urban redevelopment, and other vital needs of the people of the state." For the moment, though, organization and voter registration was essential.[58]

Significant steps were already being taken in these directions. According to Ross, the organization had registered over 92,000 voters between 1949 and 1954, including 30,000 in 1954 alone. In addition, it had enrolled 5,000 others in CSO-sponsored citizenship classes. Much work, however, remained. To this end, Ross criss-crossed the state—routinely logging over 2,000 miles per month in his car—to help organize local CSO chapters. Once established, these chapters would pour themselves into the door-to-door campaign on behalf of the 252,518 Spanish-speaking citizens in twenty-one California counties who had yet to register as of March 1956.[59]

In 1953 the CSO began lobbying for a state law providing old-age pensions for long-term resident non-citizens, the preponderance of whom were born in Mexico. On the heels of the formation of the CCFEP, Ross urged CSO president Anthony Rios to launch a letter writing campaign in support of such a measure, Assembly Bill (AB) 2059. The letters, Ross instructed, should stress "the service" that the bill's proposed beneficiaries "have given to industry and agriculture in California during the last 40 years since they first came over from Mexico." In addition, they should highlight the military service of so many of the American citizen children of those Mexican descent Californians whose non-citizenship status, despite years of residence, left them without any old-age assistance. Finally, Ross added, the letters on behalf of AB 2059 should emphasize that the proposed beneficiaries of the measure had paid their fair share of taxes over the years and thus merited the benefit that the bill's passage would provide.[60] Ross urged Chávez and the San Jose CSO chapter to take similar action. As Chávez recalled many years later, "Fred talked to us about old age pensions for non-citizens. He said it would be a great issue, help a lot of old timers who had no money or pensions and relieve a lot of pressure on their kids." Though Ross cautioned that this campaign would be grueling, he encouraged the CSO to undertake it.[61]

The CSO's pursuit of old-age pensions for non-citizens differed from the JACL's. As a December 1954 letter on "JACL Legislative Priorities" explained, "Ours would be . . . concerned with aliens who were ineligible for citizenship prior to the McCarran-Walter Act [1952], where the C.S.O. hopes to extend old-age assistance to all aliens." The former group was small and composed almost exclusively of Issei. The latter group was large and composed disproportionately of Mexican immigrants. For this reason, the JACL bill stood a much better chance of success. For this reason, too, presumably, the JACL did not propose a joint JACL/CSO lobbying effort on behalf of the two different bills.[62]

Despite these differences, the separate JACL and CSO pursuits of old-age pensions for non-citizens bore one overarching similarity. They both reflected axes of discrimination and consequently avenues of redress that were rooted in legal distinctions drawn between citizens and non-citizens (as had been the case with the Alien Land Law). In Ross's estimation, "lack of citizenship" posed "the most serious obstacle to self-organization and group advancement" for Californians of Mexican descent. It left them politically powerless, "unable to command the respect and attention of public officials," and owed to a number of reasons. First and foremost, Mexican immigrants faced "never-ending discrimination," not simply because they were "dark-skinned," but also because they were "foreign" and "laborers." This "unfair treatment," in turn dissuaded them from pursuing citizenship. So, too, did California's proximity to Mexico, to which many Mexican immigrants dreamed of returning. As a result, they "mentally assumed the status of temporary visitors in a foreign country" and "lost interest in the betterment of their immediate surroundings." Other inhibiting factors included the challenges of "proving legal entry, due to the laxity of Border officials in the early days," the "intimidation and insulting treatment" of immigration officials, and the "difficulties in producing evidence of continuous residence in this country due to the migratory nature" of the work in which so many Mexican non-citizens engaged.[63]

Whatever the reason, citizenship (or lack thereof), according to CSO leaders in the 1950s, was the root cause of many problems confronting Californians of Mexican descent. As a result, citizenship classes, voter registration drives, and securing old-age pensions for long-term resident non-citizens were the priorities pursued by the CSO. This, of course, did not translate to opposition to the contemporaneous campaign for fair employment practices legislation. It did, however, belie the claim of the NAACP-WC in late 1953 that fair employment practices was "the 'number one' legislative aim of the civil rights forces in California."[64] As Gallegos, one of the founding members of the CSO's San Jose chapter, recalled years later, many Mexican Americans perceived fair employment practices to be "primarily aimed at blacks."[65]

This perception echoed the distinction the JACL drew between legislation of "direct concern to persons of Japanese ancestry" versus legislation of "indirect concern to persons of Japanese ancestry," which included fair employment practices.[66] It also helps explain the NAACP-WC's 1953 insistence that it "intend[ed] to move ahead" on fair employment practices "whether you [i.e., other civil rights groups] come along or not."[67] Finally, it found support in the pages of "The Case for Fair Employment Practices Legislation in California," which the CCFEP compiled in support of the fair employment practices bill (AB 900) introduced in January 1953 by Assemblymen Hawkins and Rumford. On the one hand, the CCFEP's publication suggested that employment discrimination targeted "millions of persons in racial, religious, and ethnic minority groups" in California in more or less equal measure. It read, "462,000 Negroes, 85,000 Japanese-Americans, 58,000 Chinese-Americans, 800,000 Mexican-Americans, 985,000 foreign-born, 2,135,000 Catholics, 400,000 Jews are frustrated in their aspirations, deprived of their inalienable rights to full enjoyment of democracy, equal opportunity, and the pursuit of happiness. They are victims of discrimination in employment." On the other hand, the vast majority of examples of employment discrimination cited in "The Case for Fair Employment Practices Legislation in California" involved African Americans. For example:

A check of 312 banks in the greater Los Angeles area reveals that only five branches employ Negroes in any white collar capacities.

Of the seven major petroleum companies operating in California, only one employs Negroes above the custodial level in either shop or office departments.

Of the big four companies in the aircraft industry in the Los Angeles area, only two employ Negro girls in office-clerical positions.

With but two exceptions, the 16 major insurance companies studied in the Los Angeles area employ Negroes only in custodial jobs.[68]

Under these circumstances, it is not surprising that NAACP-WC regional director Williams would single out "the Negro job-seeker" as "always at a disadvantage in a time of declining employment," in a 1954 report. "He," Williams continued, "needs the protection of fair employment legislation and orders."[69] Under these circumstances, it is also not surprising that the CCFEP's William Becker described fair employment practices for the West Coast Regional Office of the NAACP as "their priority." And since they were the "major factor in determining the priorities and the content of the bill," they made sure that the CCFEP did not get "hurt by being drawn into other things." The CCFEP "maintained a very disciplined approach," Becker recalled. "We weren't getting into side issues," which meant avoiding the central priorities of the JACL and CSO for whom fair employment practices was peripheral.[70]

Not surprisingly, then, when the CCFEP held its rally for AB 900 in Sacramento in March 1953, more than half of the 503 delegates who attended, according to the NAACP-WC, were NAACP members. The rest came from a smattering of religious, civic, and labor groups, among others. Assemblyman Hawkins kicked off the event with a keynote address attended by over one thousand people. Less than a month later, however, AB 900 met the fate of Hawkins's previous fair employment practices bills, dying in an assembly committee. The closeness of the vote, however, and the organizational structure that had been established in the campaign for AB 900 boded well for the future. "Definite groundwork had been laid," declared Pittman.[71]

The NAACP-WC built upon that groundwork. At the end of 1953, the organization's annual report reiterated the call for all branches of the NAACP in the region to "campaign uncompromisingly" for fair employment practices.[72] In 1954, it dispatched representatives to a CFCU-sponsored conference on civil rights legislation for the upcoming legislative session. There, Pittman declared fair employment practices to be the NAACP-WC's "first priority." Becker, representing the AFL and Jewish Labor Council, as well as John Despol of the CIO-California Industrial Union Council, agreed.[73]

Haruo Ishimaru of the JACL and Tony Rios of the CSO, however, articulated different "major concerns." For the JACL, a ballot proposition to remove the language of the unconstitutional Alien Land Law from the California Constitution received top billing followed by the JACL's failed old-age pensions bill from the previous legislative session. The CSO, meanwhile, pressed for its version of an old-age pensions bill, which encompassed a much broader group than the JACL's. Though the CSO, unlike the JACL, included fair employment practices legislation as a "major concern," the NAACP made no mention of either the JACL's or CSO's old-age pension proposals in its enumeration of legislative priorities. The conference, as a whole, however, did not omit the issue. Although attendees "unanimously agreed" that "the major and common concern of all groups present" was to exert "all possible effort" to mount another "coordinated statewide movement" for fair employment practices, they also "felt that the bill for old-age pensions for non-citizens was one deserving high priority support from all civil rights organizations."[74]

This dual-pronged approach, however, failed to materialize. In November 1954, many of the same people who attended the conference on civil rights legislation earlier in the year reconvened and revived the CCFEP. As per the organization's title, fair employment practices alone was the group's focus.[75] The next month the CFCU followed the CCFEP's lead. Fair employment practices, it announced, was "The Legislative Objective for California—1955." At the same time, the CFCU acknowledged, it needed to sell fair employment practices to some of its affiliated organizations who represented non-African Americans. To this end, the CFCU proposed a forum for addressing the "Interest and Significance for Non-Negro Minority Groups of F.E.P.C. Legislative Campaigns."[76] Implicit in the CFCU's proposal was a recognition that fair employment practices was not resonating with "Non-Negro Minority Groups" in the same way that it was with African Americans. Williams appeared to concede as much when he identified the principal wellsprings of support for fair employment practices. "From 1953 to the present," Williams reported in April 1955, "much ground work was laid [for fair employment practices] by the Association in developing a close rapport with the A.F. of L."[77] Years later, CCFEP chair Dellums, offered a similar assessment, based on who provided financial support. "Labor and NAACP branches," he recollected, "supplied over ninety percent of the money" for the fair employment practices campaigns in the 1950s, with the "additional money" coming from unspecified "individuals."[78]

As the NAACP-led CCFEP waxed in the 1950s, the CFCU waned. In February 1955, as the CCFEP prepared for the 1955 legislative session, the CFCU's Ruth Kaiser, who helped launch the organization a decade earlier, expressed concerns over its future. Reflecting the CFCU's original aspiration to find common ground, Kaiser recommended a convention where organizations, including the NAACP, CSO, and JACL, "could conduct their own business in separate sessions." Afterwards, however, "Their members [would] come together in workshops on housing, employment and other issues of common concern."[79] A few months later, in May 1955, CFCU president Irving Rosenblatt, who was also a co-chair of the CCFEP, sent an "urgent message" to organizations and individuals affiliated with the CFCU. "No other organization," in Rosenblatt's view, was attempting to "meet common needs of all groups" across the state involved in "the field of human relations." To salvage his foundering organization, Rosenblatt recommended a "minimum program," including the continuation of the CFCU's role as a statewide "inter-organization liaison" and convener of "statewide conferences."[80] Josephine Duveneck, another founding member of the CFCU, doubted this would make a difference. "Few organizations could be counted on to increase their financial help to [the] CFCU," Duveneck observed. For that reason, she conceded, "possibly [the] CFCU should close up."[81] One year later, it did. At its final board meeting, Rosenblatt noted, "There has been more infighting in the field of civil rights recently than ever before, and therefore a great need for a coordinating organization." Duveneck agreed about the need. However, she added, "CFCU is not it." Instead, a "new coordinating agency will evolve from a felt need on the part of various groups throughout the state."[82] In the meantime, the NAACP-WC-led CCFEP was about the closest thing there would be.

Under the CCFEP's leadership, fair employment practices inched closer to passage in the legislative sessions of 1955 and 1957. In 1955, in what Williams described as "an historic milestone," a fair employment practices bill (AB 971) passed through the assembly by a vote of forty-eight to twenty-one, only to die in a senate committee.[83] Afterwards, Becker wrote CCFEP supporters, praising them for the "tremendous job" they performed "at the grassroots level." He then exhorted them to redouble their efforts in 1957. Noting that Michigan had become the fourteenth state to enact a fair employment practices law, he told CCFEP supporters that they now had "two years to develop the interest and understanding of your State Senator" so that California would follow suit.[84] Two years later, under the "leadership" of the NAACP-WC, as Williams described his organization's role, a fair employment practices bill (AB 2000) emerged from the assembly with an even greater margin (sixty-one to fifteen) than it received in 1955.[85] As in 1955, though, the measure failed in the senate.

In response, some frustrated fair employment practices supporters broached the possibility of a statewide ballot proposition. The NAACP-WC, however, torpedoed the suggestion, insisting, "the serious question of extending equal job opportunities to all Californians would become submerged, distorted, and perverted in the slogans and propaganda directed at the general public in a referendum campaign."[86] A majority of Californians, in the NAACP-WC's estimation, were no more willing to enact fair employment practices through the initiative process in the late 1950s than had been willing to do so in 1946 when they dealt Proposition 11 an overwhelming defeat. As a matter of strategic politics, then, it made more sense to keep applying political pressure through the CCFEP on the state's elected representatives, while limiting the popular vote to replacing fair employment practices opponents with supporters.

The most prominent of these elected representatives was Republican governor Goodwin Knight. In 1953, Knight succeeded Earl Warren when President Eisenhower appointed Warren chief justice of the United States Supreme Court. In Knight's estimation, "strained race relations . . . most certainly [did] not exist" to warrant a fair employment practices law, which neither Knight nor Warren before him supported.[87] Following the defeat of fair employment practices in 1955, Williams and Dellums wrote Knight, urging him to rally Republican support behind fair employment practices.[88] Knight did not respond, even though he had been urged by his campaign directors in 1954 not to "concede to the Democratic group . . . a potential of four hundred thousand colored voters in California."[89] During his 1958 re-election campaign, Knight proved little more amenable to another fair employment practices appeal from Williams. "This is a problem . . . [of] individual bias," Knight wrote Williams. For that reason, "It will only end only when a majority of our citizens are ready and willing, with true understanding, to terminate such personal bias." As for a "State FEPC," Knight was noncommittal, eschewing "blame for something which the State Legislature has failed to do."[90]

In 1953, the same year that the NAACP-WC assumed the lead of the newly formed CCFEP, Franklin Williams declared housing discrimination to be "the number ONE concern of the NAACP on the NEW FRONTIER." Unless dealt with immediately, Williams warned, "the tremendous influx of Negroes and the pattern of segregation which is being foisted upon them" threatened to generate "large sprawling ghettos reminiscent of Harlem and South Chicago." As he did with fair employment practices, Williams linked the plights of all Californians of color, declaring "residential segregation" to be "the West's number ONE problem for minorities."[91] This reasoning by analogy, however, was belied by the NAACP-WC's litigation against housing discrimination during the 1950s, which focused exclusively on African Americans, who, as in the 1940s, were the "chief victims," as Loren Miller put it in 1947.[92]

The NAACP-WC's litigation against housing discrimination proceeded alongside its efforts to legislate fair employment practices. Unlike the fair employment practices campaign, however, in which the NAACP-WC led other organizations and individuals under the auspices of the CCFEP, the NAACP-WC's pursuit of fair housing was largely a solo effort. The decision to fight housing discrimination through litigation, rather than legislation, reflected a tactical calculation. When some attendees at the February 1953 meeting that gave rise to the CCFEP suggested expanding the organization's focus beyond fair employment practices, Assemblyman Hawkins disagreed. A broader-gauged antidiscrimination bill that encompassed more than just employment, Hawkins claimed, would "give some individuals an excuse to vote against the [fair employment practices] bill." Instead, he suggested doing "one thing at a time."[93] The following year, NAACP-WC representatives reaffirmed fair employment practices as their "first priority." As for fair housing, they acknowledged, "Agitation for legislation in the field at this time [would meet] with likely defeat." The "judicial rather than the legislative process," therefore, represented the most propitious route at the time for fair housing.[94]

To this end, the NAACP-WC sought to build upon the Loren Miller's legal victories against racially restrictive housing covenants that had culminated in the United States Supreme Court in 1948. In May 1952, NAACP-WC regional director Williams convened a meeting of NAACP-affiliated lawyers to strategize "a region-wide legal attack on racially segregated public housing."[95] Housing discrimination and the residential segregation it bred, Williams wrote in his 1954 annual report, pervaded the West. "Obscured as long as the Negro population was small in our Region," the "great migration" of African Americans during World War II drew increasing attention to the problem. "All manner of evils trail in the wake of residential segregation," the report continued, including "crime, juvenile delinquency, disease" and school segregation.[96]

Miller of Los Angeles and Nathaniel Colley of Sacramento became co-chairs of the Regional Legal Redress Committee that emerged out of the May 1952 meeting. Eighteen years Miller's junior, Colley was the youngest of six children born to a widowed mother in Snow Hill, Alabama in 1919. As a child in the cotton fields, Colley never picked his weight in cotton, in part because of allergies, but also because of a penchant to steal away from the fields and immerse himself in the poetry of Tennyson, Browning, and Longfellow. After graduating as high school valedictorian, Colley attended Alabama's Tuskeegee Institute, where he worked as a lab assistant for George Washington Carver and took a degree in chemistry. He served as an officer during World War II in the Pacific. Upon completing his service, Colley attended Yale Law School because his application to the segregated University of Alabama was rejected. He graduated with honors, earning the prize for the best essay written by a third-year law student. In 1948, Colley headed for Sacramento, the hometown of his college sweetheart and wife, Jerlean. He promptly sought information about a state exam he needed to take in order to begin his practice, only to be turned away by "the lady at the counter," who, in Colley's recollection, "told me that [information brochures] were only given to those who had *already* graduated from law school." Colley assured her that he had. She replied, " 'I mean an accredited law school,' " at which point Colley presented his "Yale degree, with honors, written in Latin." The clerk capitulated. Colley took the exam and earned the highest score. Despite being at the top of the statewide list, Colley recalled years later how "no state agency would have me. He turned to private practice, hanging his shingle in Sacramento in 1949. Though he described himself as a "pretty effective capitalist" as a private practitioner, Sacramento city officials suspected Colley to be a Communist operative for bringing cases against police brutality and employment discrimination. By 1952, when he joined Miller as the co-chair of the Regional Legal Redress Committee, the thirty-three-year-old Colley had earned a reputation as a rising legal star, and he would play a leading role in the NAACP-WC for years to come.[97]

At the meeting that gave rise to the NAACP-WC's Regional Legal Redress Committee, attendees predicted that courts in California would "not tolerate racial segregation in public housing."[98] Less than six months later, in the committee's first test case, a California court vindicated this prediction. In the case of *Banks v. Housing Authority of the City and County of San Francisco*, Mattie Banks, a single mother of two children, was refused a spot in an all-white (except for one man of Chinese descent) project. The Regional Legal Redress Committee took the case on behalf of Banks and a group of 679 San Francisco African Americans also denied apartments in six of the city's seven low rent developments.[99] Citing the need to preserve local "customs and traditions" and to maintain "peace and order," the city Housing Authority refused to disrupt the existing racial composition of the various neighborhoods where public housing was located. "In the selection of tenants for the projects of this Authority," declared a 1942 Housing Authority resolution, "this Authority shall not insofar as possible enforce the commingling of races, but shall insofar as possible maintain and preserve the same racial composition which exists in the neighborhood where a project is located."[100] In accordance with its "neighborhood pattern" policy, the city set aside only one of its seven low-rent housing developments for blacks. (Of the other six, one was reserved for Chinese Americans and the remainder for whites.) During cross-examination, a NAACP attorney asked the executive director of the San Francisco Housing Authority, "If you had a Negro family with the best of qualifications for housing . . . would you admit him to any one of the five housing projects now reserved for whites under the neighborhood pattern?" "No," replied the housing authority chief. The accommodations offered to African Americans might indeed be separate, he insisted, but they were equal, and in proportion to their representation in the city as a whole.[101]

NAACP attorneys bore into the Housing Authority's reasoning. The city, they insisted, operated a race-based quota system that violated the Fourteenth Amendment. "The right to equal protection of the law under the 14th Amendment is an individual right," explained Miller to a *San Francisco Chronicle* reporter as he awaited the superior court's decision. "A Negro has a right to be judged as eligible as an individual, not as a member of a race."[102]

Superior Court judge Melvin Cronin agreed. The Housing Authority's claim to be nondiscriminatory through its separate-but-equal "neighborhood pattern" policy rested on outmoded legal arguments. In particular, Judge Cronin relied upon the United States Supreme Court's ruling in the racially restrictive housing covenant cases from 1948 (*Shelley*), which outlawed any judicial enforcement of housing covenants (although not the covenants themselves). "By extension of the logic and reason of these cases," he opined, "it is apparent that the doctrine should not apply to a public housing project, financed by public funds and supervised by a public agency."[103]

Judge Cronin's opinion drew anonymous hate mail; one postcard denounced him as "a traitor to our white race" who "shall be killed to give other traitors their lesson."[104] More importantly, Cronin's verdict also withstood an appeal. As a state appellate court explained, "The Constitution speaks of the individual, not of the racial or other group to which he may belong." Inasmuch as the Housing Authority's "neighborhood pattern" selection criteria rested on racial group distinctions as the basis for determining public housing placements, the Housing Authority violated the Fourteenth Amendment.[105] The United States Supreme Court subsequently refused to hear *Banks*. The lower court rulings stood firm, and the Regional Legal Redress Committee could celebrate its first legal victory and the "first victory on the appellate level in the United States on the question of public housing."[106]

Having dealt a mortal blow to racial discrimination in public housing, the Regional Legal Redress Committee turned its attention to private housing. It sought a test case involving a tract developer "who refuse[d] to sell houses to Negroes," as Colley had called for in 1952.[107] This particular form of housing discrimination covered a much broader swath of the housing market than de jure segregation in public housing. In the Bay Area alone, for example, Williams noted in September 1952 that fewer than 600 of 100,000 building permits issued for the construction of family homes between 1946 and 1951 "were available to Negro families."[108]

One such family was that of Oliver Ming, a McClellan Air Force Base employee and World War II veteran. On January 15, 1954, Ming sought to purchase a new home in a Sacramento subdivision where eligible prospective buyers could avail themselves of Federal Housing Authority (FHA) and Veteran's Authority (VA) financing. Though Ming met the financial requirements, real estate agents working for the subdivision refused to sell to him or any other African Americans.[109] Ming's plight soon came to the attention of Miller, Colley, and Williams. Fresh from their victory in *Banks*, the NAACP-WC's Legal Redress Committee lawyers took up Ming's case—"the first such legal challenge to the pattern of private discrimination" practiced by contractors of new tract developments, which was an "almost universal" pattern in the West.[110]

Ming represented the next step in the legal campaign against housing discrimination. Miller described it as an "extension, rather than an application, of settled principles . . . a new problem in governmental activity for which there are no exact precedents." Unlike *Banks*, which involved public housing and clearly implicated the state in racial discrimination, *Ming* involved a more attenuated relationship between the government and builder where "their dealing with one another in respect of the Negro buyer are tenuous and tortuous." As Miller posed the question at stake in the case, "May a private citizen" who benefits from federally-backed guarantees on mortgages, such as the builders Ming sued, "exclude, on racial grounds," individuals like Ming "who would otherwise be eligible for the benefits intended by Congress?"[111]

The defendants in *Ming*—the subdivision developers—insisted that they could. They invoked what they took to be their fundamental and unfettered right to contract—"to sell to whomever they choose . . . to decline to sell to any person they choose," as the judge in *Ming* paraphrased their claim.[112] No mere government mortgage guarantees, the developers contended, could circumscribe this right.

The NAACP lawyers, of course, disagreed. It was precisely because of the government mortgage guarantees, they retorted, that the defendants were obliged to sell to financially qualified African Americans. The legal logic applied here flowed out of the United States Supreme Court's racially restrictive housing covenant ruling from 1948, which forbade "state action" in the service of racial discrimination.[113] As Colley put it, "When one dips one's hand into the Federal Treasury," as did the defendants in *Ming* through the government backed mortgages from which they benefitted, "a little democracy necessarily clings to whatever is withdrawn."[114]

In June 1958, a Sacramento County Superior Court judge concurred. He described the case as "a situation where plaintiff's right not to be discriminated against in acquiring housing collides with defendants' right to contract with whomever they choose." What ultimately tipped the balance of this rights conflict in Ming's favor was "the utilization of federal administrative process, the gaining of federal assistance in attracting buyers by advertising F.H.A. and V.A. financing . . . and ultimately mortgage guaranties of loans" by the builder. "Those who operate under that law and seek and gain advantage it confers," the judge concluded, are no less implicated in state action and, therefore, no less precluded from engaging in racial discrimination than would be a court upholding a racially restrictive housing covenant.[115]

The *San Francisco Chronicle* hailed *Ming* as "highly significant and long-awaited."[116] Yet, nothing better demonstrated just how far the fight for fair housing still had to go than the ordeal of Willie Mays, which began the year before *Ming* concluded. In the fall of 1957, the twenty-six-year-old Mays was in the prime of his hall-of-fame career when his New York Giants played their final baseball game in the Big Apple's Polo Grounds. In anticipation of the team's upcoming move to San Francisco, Mays and his wife took a house-hunting trip in November 1957. The young couple soon discovered a place to their liking. They bid $37,500, and the owner accepted, but reneged shortly thereafter. The neighbors, he exclaimed, made him do it. "I'm just a union working man," cried William Gnesdiloff, a construction worker, "and I'd never get another job if I sold this house to that baseball player. I feel sorry for him, and if the neighbors say it would be okay, I'd do it." If San Franciscans eagerly awaited the arrival of their new team, some of them were much less eager to have the team's star player and his wife as neighbors.[117]

"That is no place for colored people to live," explained Guy Paratore, cousin of one of Gnesdiloff's employers. Another neighbor concurred and elaborated. "Certainly I objected," he declared, "I happen to have quite a few pieces of property in that area and I stand to lose a lot if colored people move in. But I didn't force Gnesdiloff to do anything. I told him to use his conscience, but that he'd get a bad name if he went through with this. I certainly wouldn't like to have a colored family near me." Martin Gaewhiler, the most vocal opponent of the sale, agreed, though he clarified just whom he meant by "colored." Gaewhiler, according to a report drafted by Edward Howden of the San Francisco Council for Civic Unity, "was quite direct in his deprecation of 'colored people' generally." Their entry into the neighborhood, he believed, would send property values plummeting and cause "grievous financial loss." When Howden pointed out that "at least one Chinese and one Filipino family were already in the area," Gaewhiler "drew a sharp distinction between these and the allegedly undesirable Negro." Gawhiler's opposition to African American neighbors, but not Chinese or Filipino ones, underscored how housing discrimination was not so much "the number ONE problem for minorities," in general, as Williams had asserted, but rather for African Americans, in particular.

The incident shocked Mays. He had "never been through this kind of stuff before," he claimed, in the "mixed neighborhood" in Manhattan where he lived. Eschewing anger—"I'm not even mad about it now"—the Korean War veteran struck a cautionary Cold War chord instead. "Talk about a thing like this goes all over the world, and it sure looks bad for our country." Mays's wife, Mae, was less diplomatic. "Down in Alabama where we come from, you know your place and that's something, at least. But up here it's a lot of camouflage. They grin in your face and then deceive you."

San Francisco Mayor George Christopher insisted that the incident was an aberration. He expressed a "deep feeling of regret at this most unfortunate occurrence," extended the "warmest invitation" to Mays and his wife to be guests in the Christopher home "until you find suitable housing," and assured the couple that "San Francisco is a very understanding city and it's not our practice to preclude anyone's living where he wants to, regardless of race." San Francisco NAACP president John Adams, Jr. knew otherwise. "The case of Willie Mays seeking a home," he lamented, "is dramatically enacted daily by hapless Negro families whose lack of prominence does not command the attention of the press and official San Francisco. Segregated islands of residency are springing up all over this city due to practices and policies of real estate groups." If it could happen to Willie Mays of all people and in San Francisco of all places, Adams suggested, then it was all the more likely to happen to less notable African Americans in ostensibly less cosmopolitan places.

Public pressure and private mediation ultimately secured Mays and his wife the house they wanted. Nevertheless, the incident, according to one of the national NAACP's housing discrimination specialists, dramatized "the necessity for a law covering private housing." This, in fact, had already been identified as a top priority—alongside fair employment practices—by NAACP leaders in California. Although they had scored a couple of significant legal victories in the 1950s, they had made no legislative headway. Instead, they chose to prioritize the pursuit of fair housing legislation over fair employment practices legislation, though that would soon change.

While the NAACP-WC and CSO spent part of their time battling one kind of infiltration in their ranks—Communists—as they pursued their civil rights priorities during the Cold War, Ernesto Galarza fought another kind of infiltration, namely, temporary and undocumented agricultural workers from Mexico. A precursor to César Chávez and the United Farm Workers, Galarza and the National Farm Labor Union (NFLU) spearheaded the first substantial post-World War II efforts to organize farm workers in California, a disproportionate number of whom were of Mexican descent. Born in Mexico in 1905, raised in Sacramento, and educated at Occidental, Stanford, and Columbia, Galarza joined the NFLU, which was the successor to the Southern Tenant Farmers Union, as director of research and education shortly after receiving his doctorate in economics in 1947. H.L. Mitchell, president of the NFLU, quickly dispatched Galarza to Arvin, California, just south of Bakersfield in the San Joaquin Valley, to help organize Local 218 at the DiGiorgio Farms.[118]

When a strike ensued in October 1947, DiGiorgio, whose revenues exceeded $18 million the year before, responded with a variety of tactics: evicting striking workers who lived on company property, arresting picketers on trumped up charges, smearing the union as "Communist-inspired" and thus prompting hearings before Jack Tenney's State Senate Committee on Un-American Affairs, and hiring undocumented Mexicans and braceros as replacements. By November 1949, not a single member of the NFLU local remained on the DiGiorgio payroll.[119]

That same year, Galarza called for a "national body whose main concern is the Mexican American minority," similar to the NAACP for African Americans and the JACL for Japanese Americans.[120] In Galarza's estimation, the "most serious weakness" to be addressed by the Mexican American organization he envisioned was "lack of economic organization"—unionization—among agricultural workers.[121] To remedy this, Galarza received funding from the ACLU affiliated Robert Marshall Trust, as well as the American Federation of Labor (AFL). With this financial aid, ACLU national director Roger Baldwin explained to George Sánchez in July 1948, "Ernesto Galarza has been employed by the National Farm Labor Union to tackle" the issue of "establishing among the Mexicans themselves, a civil rights organization."[122]

For Galarza, civil rights and labor rights were inextricably bound. As Mitchell explained to Baldwin in July 1951, Galarza "found that the main problems [confronting Mexican Americans] were economic," especially among "the vast majority [who] were employed as migratory workers on large-scale farms in the southwestern United States."[123] Baldwin, however, disagreed, viewing civil rights as a separate matter from labor rights and, therefore, Galarza's use of the money as a misappropriation. "While I have no question as to the usefulness of organizing Mexican-American farm laborers, nor any lack of faith in Ernesto's intentions and abilities," Baldwin retorted to Mitchell, "the fact remains that the funds were not used for the purposes for which they were given—namely, to build a national civil rights defense organization among the Mexican-Americans similar to the defense agencies of the Negroes and the Japanese-Americans."[124] Baldwin registered a similar complaint to Sánchez, criticizing Galarza for getting "side-tracked in the California strikes" and achieving "practically nothing along the lines of our intention."[125]

Nor did Galarza manage to accomplish much of what he intended. He described the challenge he faced as tantamount to undertaking "an elephant hunt . . . with a pop gun," and, he could have added, without much of a hunting party to accompany him.[126] Though Franklin Williams wrote Galarza in October 1951 that he was "most anxious to establish a closer rapport between the NFLU and NAACP as the economic problems with which you are struggling are clearly of great concern to the Negro worker in California," nearly seven years later Williams's anxiety and the source of it remained, suggesting little had changed.[127] As he told an NAACP leader in California's Central Valley in March 1958, "I am very anxious that we get something going on the migrant workers' situation."[128] Galarza's linkages to the CSO were hardly more substantial.[129] Not until 1957, for example, did CSO president Anthony Rios call for "a program and the appointment of a permanent committee approved by the Board," chaired by Galarza, to tackle the problems of farm workers.[130] Though Galarza applauded the "possibility of immediate action by the CSO . . . to cooperate in the area of improving living standards for food growing and processing workers," his union would not survive the decade to reap the benefits of that proposed cooperation.[131]

Even if the NAACP-WC and CSO had contributed more to Galarza's efforts in the 1950s, they still would have only a "pop gun" between them to conduct their "elephant hunt." Leaving aside the lack of resources that the NFLU had relative to agribusiness and the Cold War climate that rendered unionization even more suspect to red-baiting than non-unionization civil rights issues like fair employment practices, the nation's labor law provided little ammunition for farm workers, relegating them to second-class legal status in comparison to industrial workers. A dozen years before Galarza came to California, the historic National Labor Relations Act had granted "employees . . . the right to self-organization, to form, join, or assist labor organizations, to bargain collectively through representatives of their own choosing, and to engage in other concerted activities for the purpose of collective bargaining or other mutual aid or protection." By Congress's definition, however, the word *employee* did "not include any individual employed as an agricultural laborer." Though agricultural workers could attempt to organize, they lacked the statutory support necessary to translate their "right" to unionize into reality. Unlike industrial workers, then, farm workers could not legally compel their employers to recognize their union, nor could they submit their dispute to the National Labor Relations Board for resolution.[132] Such "right-to-work voluntary unionism," as Galarza described it, would prove to be "the 8 ball behind which" farm workers and their organizers would have to operate, wreaking "disastrous effects" on the "organization, civil rights, economic betterment and general welfare of farm labor in California."[133]

If no law existed to force agricultural employers to negotiate with agricultural unions, no law enforcement existed to prevent those same employers from tapping what Sánchez described in a 1948 letter to Galarza as the "reservoir of cheap labor" in Mexico. "The alien worker," Sánchez complained, "becomes, in effect, a strike-breaker or 'scab.' "[134] During the post-World War II era, "alien"— or non-domestic—agricultural workers included, above all, braceros and undocumented immigrants (or "wetbacks," as they were almost universally called). For Galarza, "Braceros and 'wets' [were] two sides of the same phony coin." Their presence served "to cut down the wages of farm labor, to break strikes and to prevent [union] organization; to run American citizens off farm jobs, especially on corporation ranches."[135]

Launched in the summer of 1942, the Bracero Program was initially conceived as a wartime measure that provided for the recruitment and importation of Mexican field hands on short-term contracts. Advocates of the program—mostly large-scale growers—insisted that there was a shortage of domestic agricultural labor.[136] Detractors, led by organized labor, claimed that there were plenty of American workers to fill the jobs—unemployment in 1940 was, after all, still hovering around fifteen percent—and that foreign workers would drive down wages.[137] Prior to 1942, President Roosevelt sided with the opponents. However, as the draft depleted the domestic labor force and war industries drew workers from fields to factories, Roosevelt changed his mind and negotiated an agreement with Mexico. By 1947, 219,546 braceros had crossed the border.[138]

Though the number of braceros declined in the late 1940s, the Korean War prompted agribusiness to clamor for a new and improved Bracero Program. Congress obliged, passing Public Law (PL) 78 in July 1951, which paid little heed to Mexico's demands that the United States establish a system of domestic recruitment and institute penalties for growers who hired undocumented Mexicans. President Truman signed the measure into law against the advice of his Department of Labor. Over the next thirteen years, PL 78 would be repeatedly renewed, remaining in effect until the end of 1964.[139] During the span of its twenty-two years, the Bracero Program recruited 4.6 million Mexican workers, the lion's share of whom went to work on a tiny fraction (two percent) of commercial farms, nearly sixty percent of which were in California.[140] Between 1952 and 1962, braceros in California averaged thirty-one percent of the temporary agricultural labor force.[141] They were accompanied by another source of Mexican labor—"green carders." Under a provision in the 1952 McCarran-Walter Act (PL 414), Mexicans issued "green cards" by the INS at the request of employers could either reside in the United States for up to three years, or they could live in Mexico and commute across the border.[142]

In theory, braceros and green carders could not displace domestic workers. In theory, braceros and green carders could not be used as strike breakers. In theory, braceros and green carders had to be paid the prevailing wage in the area for the work they performed. And in theory, the Border Patrol existed to repel undocumented immigrants, no matter how much agribusiness might prefer them to domestic workers. In practice, the law and law enforcement operated otherwise. According to report prepared by Galarza and delivered to the United States Senate Subcommittee on Labor and Management Relations in February 1952, "The assurance that Mexican nationals will not 'bump' domestic farm workers is one of the cornerstones . . . of the alien labor recruiting program. Nevertheless, the record is convincing that such displacement has been going on systematically for a number of years." The presence of so many Mexican workers, in turn, exerted downward pressure on the "prevailing wage," which became "the basement to which domestic wages were lowered, thus accomplishing the reverse of what Congress had promised the American people."[143]

Galarza's testimony was part of what he described in 1952 as the union's "two-pronged campaign," with one prong directed against "nationals" (i.e., braceros and green carders) and the other prong directed against "wetbacks," whose numbers, according to the 1951 *Report of the President's Commission on Migratory Labor* had swelled to some 400,000 of the nation's one million migratory workers.[144] As part of this campaign, Galarza and the NFLU called for laws that provided farm labor with the same New Deal protections accorded industrial labor: collective bargaining guarantees, minimum wage, and social security.[145] They passed resolutions at union conventions urging Congress and the president to end the Bracero Program—and the "exploitation of both the American and Mexican farm workers" that it caused—and to do more to stem the undocumented immigrant traffic.[146] They agitated for legislation "to make it a felony to transport, harbor, conceal, or employ an alien who is in this country illegally."[147] They publicized instances of growers refusing to hire domestic workers while employing thousands of braceros, or, even worse, firing domestic workers in order to hire non-domestic ones.[148] They recorded numerous instances of braceros and undocumented Mexicans being used to replace striking domestic workers, as well as the Border Patrol teaming up with immigration officials and the Mexican consul on behalf of growers to "openly process acknowledged illegals in violation of the international agreement."[149]

If the Border Patrol was not going to do its job, the NFLU would do it for them.[150] In March 1951, the union led by Galarza dispatched a "flying squad" to Westmoreland, California, thirty miles north of the Mexican border. When three grower-chartered buses took aboard over one hundred undocumented Mexican workers, the union members followed the bus to the border town Calexico where immigration officials initiated proceedings to "legalize" them. "Halfway through the proceedings," according to Galarza, "union representatives called the Mexican consul and demanded the men be deported." They also "filed charges of violation of the Mexican agreement," which were subsequently "substantiated by the fact that officials agreed to deport them."[151] The incident, Galarza told a *New York Times* reporter, offered "proof positive—if any more is needed—of the tacit or active collaboration that goes on between ranchers and the Immigration Department and other federal branches to circumvent the requirements that labor shall be imported in an orderly way only on specific certifications of need."[152] Repeatedly foiled, a frustrated Galarza vowed to "stop all trucks [carrying Mexicans] that the Border Patrol leaves unmolested" and to "beat the hell out of a few" of those who crossed union picket lines.[153]

Such harsh sentiments and draconian tactics reflected Galarza's pro-union, rather than anti-immigrant, politics. Galarza knew full well that Mexican workers who came to the United States were the victims of economic and political forces beyond their control. Reflecting this recognition, Galarza and the NFLU called on the United States to help Mexico "offer a far larger degree of economic security to its people" and to root out policies that undermined Mexican prosperity. They advocated amendments to immigration laws to target employers who hired undocumented immigrants, thereby placing "the burden of responsibility . . . where it belongs—on those who profit from the poverty and need that drives the wetbacks into exile."[154] They defended the rights of braceros by detailing the yawning chasm separating the provisions of the Bracero Program from the practices of braceroism. As Galarza wrote in his 1956 *Strangers in Our Fields*, "Loose enforcement of the law" translated to "shameful neglect of the legal rights of Mexican nationals."[155] Above all, the NFLU opened its doors to *all* farm workers, not just domestic ones. "Our view was not to exclude the wetbacks," Galarza explained.[156] Nor, for that matter, did the NFLU exclude braceros or green carders. As Galarza wrote in a 1952 letter to H.L. Mitchell, "many of our members have them," referring to "border passes," or green cards.[157]

That said, the NFLU's open door policy had limits. As fraught with risk as the decision to join a union was for domestic farm workers, it was even more dangerous for non-domestic ones. "The Mexicans," Galarza wrote in 1948, "are in no position to bargain for wages with corporations. They do not speak English. They are completely ignorant of any legal obligations that employers may have. They cannot file claims. . . . They are, in short, perfect strike breakers."[158] Similarly, four years later, Galarza explained to Mitchell, "They [green carders] are afraid of being mixed up in strikes because the growers might also ask for the cancellation of their passes." Thus, though Galarza understood the plight of Mexican farm workers and the larger political economic forces that gave rise to it, his unionization efforts could not accommodate it. "They cannot free ride on our work," he insisted. Either they join and take their chances with the growers, or not join and have the union "work for elimination of the border pass system." The same logic applied to braceros and undocumented Mexicans as well.[159]

By default, then, not by design, the NFLU's tactics drove a wedge between those farm workers born in, or legally immigrated to, the United States and those who arrived in the country, often as strikebreakers, as braceros, "wetbacks," and "green carders."[160] For this reason, Carey McWilliams's July 1951 description of the United States / Mexico border as "one of the most unreal borders in the world [for] it unites rather than separates the two peoples" would have struck Galarza as only half right.[161] For growers who counted on the border's government-managed permeability for a steady stream of Mexican workers anytime they wanted, especially during strikes, the border was little more than a line in the desert. For Mexican descent unionists, however, the unreal border did at least as much to divide as to unite.

Though Galarza continued to view "braceros and 'wets' [as] two sides of the same phony coin," after 1954 he focused more of his attention on the bracero side of the coin. As Frank L. Noakes, chairman of the U.S. Section of the Joint U.S.-Mexico Trade Union Committee, explained in the foreword to Galarza's *Strangers in Our Fields*, "Because of an aroused public opinion leading to better law enforcement, the number of wetbacks has been greatly reduced."[162] That better law enforcement included, above all, Operation Wetback. Launched in June 1954—just one month after the Supreme Court issued its ruling in *Brown v. Board of Education*—Operation Wetback dispatched a beefed up Border Patrol, assisted by 750 immigration officers as well as local law enforcement agencies, across agricultural regions in the Southwest.[163] The round-up quickly exceeded the U.S. Commissioner of Immigration's goal of 1,000 apprehensions per day, ballooning to just under 1.1 million by year's end, according to the Immigration and Naturalization Service (INS).[164]

While the number of undocumented Mexicans in the United States declined in the wake of Operation Wetback, the number of braceros replacing them soared. This prompted Galarza to observe in 1955, "While one agency of the United States government rounded up the illegal aliens and deported them to Mexico . . . [an]other government agency was busily engaged in recruiting workers in Mexico to return them to U.S. farms."[165] What one arm of the federal government (the INS) did with Operation Wetback, another arm of the federal government (the Department of Agriculture) undid by increasing the flow of braceros. In 1955, the number of bracero contracts issued nearly tripled from the year before—from 153,975 to 398,703—and would reach 444,408 in 1959.[166]

In 1956, Galarza published *Strangers in Our Fields*. In it, he distinguished between "Wetbacks who cross the border on their own to bootleg their labor at cut-rate prices" and "citizens of Mexico who enter the United States legally" as braceros. Given his obvious scorn for the wetbacks, the "strangers" that Galarza referred to were the braceros. Galarza documented and decried the chasm between the legal provisions of the Bracero Agreement and the everyday practices of the Bracero Program—"the loose enforcement of the law" and, consequently, the "shameful neglect of the legal rights" of braceros.[167] In so doing, he offered two implicit policy prescriptions: either close the gap between the program in theory and in practice or shut it down.

Neither option appealed to the California State Board of Agriculture, which adopted a resolution in September 1956 denouncing *Strangers in Our Fields* for its "derogatory statements regarding the use of contract Mexican Nationals which have been proved to be contrary to fact, misrepresentations of fact, or which are otherwise false or misleading."[168] Governor Goodwin Knight, who appointed the State Board of Agriculture's members, proved no more sympathetic. In 1957, as bracero employment peaked at 34 percent of the average seasonal work force in agriculture, Galarza urged Knight to "receive a delegation of domestic workers." He wanted the governor to "learn directly from them what has been going on in California agriculture," which Galarza deemed "one of the major problems facing the state."[169] Knight, however, stonewalled. While he acknowledged "some violations on the part of some growers, he nevertheless insisted, "it is the firm policy of my administration that our citizens shall be given the opportunity in preference to the Nationals of any other country." Galarza persisted, albeit to no avail.[170] In April 1958, he wrote Knight, "A large number of domestic farm labor families are today on relief because their job opportunities and earning capacity were cut back last fall and winter by reason of preference given Mexican Nationals."[171]

Four months later, a young CSO organizer discovered the problem with which Galarza had been wrestling for over a decade. In August 1958, César

Chávez went to Oxnard, California, to organize a CSO chapter. He brought plans similar to those he had used to launch CSO chapters throughout the state, including house meetings, voter registration drives, and citizenship classes. He anticipated the "biggest issue" to be a dangerous railroad crossing in the Mexican part of town that had once contributed to the death of one of his friends. He was mistaken. In house meeting after house meeting, Chávez recalled, "They hit me with the bracero problem." The issue caught Chávez by surprise. He "didn't fathom how big that problem was." At first, he sought to avoid it. Soon, however, he came to see it as a "vicious racket of the grossest order" and began "fighting to get those jobs from the braceros."[172]

For thirteen months the Oxnard struggle included picketing growers who used braceros, signing up for jobs at the local Farm Placement Bureau, and, once registered, going to the fields to demand that Mexican Americans and legal Mexican immigrants replace Mexican braceros, as per the Bracero Program's provisions. Eventually, the local growers' association capitulated. They agreed to hire CSO members at the CSO office. "That was a most beautiful victory," Chávez exclaimed. "We became a hiring hall. We had them!" From then on, when Oxnard farm workers came to the CSO for help finding work, Chávez would tell them, "'You want to drive a tractor? Okay. You go find me a bracero on a tractor, and you've got a job.'" This approach "worked like magic." Not only did it send Oxnard farm workers "all over the valley" in search of braceros, but it also led to an explosion in attendance at CSO meetings. The experience, according to Chávez, awakened him to "the potential of organizing the Union."[173] Beyond that, when considered alongside the contemporaneous fights for fair employment practices and fair housing led by the NAACP-WC, it also highlighted the separate streams of civil rights advocacy unfolding in California during the 1950s.

While Chávez joined Galarza in the fight to improve the plight of California farm workers, the election of 1958 witnessed a fight over a ballot proposition that threatened to extend to all workers what had heretofore been one of the major causes of the farm workers' plight. Proposition 18 sought to add a new section (1-A) to Article I of the California Constitution, declaring, "All men should be free to elect voluntarily whether to join or not join a labor organization."[174] Galarza recognized Proposition 18 for what it was: an attempt to relegate industrial labor to the "right to work"/"voluntary unionism" status of agricultural labor, which was the law in eighteen states at the time. When proponents of the measure offered a $10,000 reward to the "first person who can prove that voluntary unionism as provided under Prop. 18" would redound to the disfavor of workers, Galarza responded by pointing to the predicament of agricultural workers. "The members of my organization have functioned under voluntary unionism since 1936," he wrote. "We do not need a crystal ball to predict what will happen to industrial labor unions" if Proposition 18 passed. "All we have to do is look at the 8 ball behind which we have been for 20 years."[175]

Galarza also seized the opportunity presented by Proposition 18 to press fellow opponents of the measure about whether they would follow the logic of their opposition from the factory to the field. To C.J. Haggerty, secretary-treasurer of the California State Federation of Labor, Galarza suggested forging an alliance of both agricultural and non-agricultural workers to combat Proposition 18 and local ordinances like it. "Perhaps what we are doing and plan to do in the fields could contribute to discourage the current general anti-labor campaign," Galarza wrote in 1957.[176] To Democratic gubernatorial candidate Pat Brown, Galarza commented, "Agricultural workers in California have been subjected to right to work system since Associated Farmers publicly announced it more than twenty years ago." He then inquired, "whether the Democratic party in California proposes to extend and now express its opposition to right to work controls now operating in agriculture?"[177] Though Brown did not respond, he did make opposition to Proposition 18 the centerpiece of his campaign—just as his opponent Senator William Knowland made support of Proposition 18 the centerpiece of his.

Knowland's decision to embrace Proposition 18 presented the Democrats, in general, and their gubernatorial candidate Brown, in particular, with more political fodder. Even the Republican incumbent Knight, for example, refused to endorse Knowland, insisting that the senator and aspiring governor "introduced an 'un-Republican' issue to the campaign by sponsoring the 'right-to-work' initiative."[178] Rather than gravitate toward the center, Knowland dug in his heels as the campaign progressed. He allowed his wife to dash off a blistering letter to two hundred California Republican leaders in which she charged Knight with threatening to allow California to become "another satellite of Walter Reuther's labor-political empire." Only under Knowland's leadership could California remain the "last hope of saving our country from the piggy-back-labor-socialist monster which has latched on to the Democratic Party and to some Republicans as well, 'poor Goodie' being a perfect example."[179]

With Knowland as its standard-bearer, the California Republican Party abandoned what had been its traditional winning strategy. Rather than endorsing a "candidate who blurred party lines, pre-empted the middle of the road, and forced the Democratic aspirant into a posture allegedly left of center," as one leading California electoral observer explained, the GOP offered Californians a "wealthy, arch-conservative, militantly partisan, austere, Protestant Republican." Unable to mend Republican Party fences, Knowland stood even less chance of attracting moderate Democrats, such as those drawn to his party's previous nominees, Knight and Warren. Moreover, by embracing Proposition

18, Knowland inspired organized labor in the state to make "the greatest political effort in its history"—with Brown and his party reaping the benefits.[180]

In July 1957, Brown told a *San Francisco Chronicle* reporter that he was contemplating retirement from politics.[181] Knowland and Proposition 18 put an end to such speculation. As Brown reflected years later, "There was no equivocation. I just made the decision to fight right-to-work." This decision translated to massive support from organized labor. "The money just poured in from the labor leaders. It was like manna from heaven. We didn't have to worry about fundraising drives or anything. They just put it in. . . . In buckets!"[182]

The outpouring of money foreshadowed a resounding victory—both for Brown and his party and against Proposition 18. When the November 4, 1958 ballots were tallied, Brown trounced Knowland by the same decisive, nearly sixty percent, margin that defeated Proposition 18. Moreover, for the first time since 1889, Democrats achieved the "grand slam of state politics." The party took home six out of seven statewide elective offices, assumed control of both the state senate and assembly, and, on the national level, won a majority of the state's congressional delegation and a new United States Senate seat to boot.[183]

When he announced his candidacy for governor, Brown included dispelling discrimination as one of the tasks required to build a "great state."[184] This stood in marked contrast to his predecessor, Knight, who maintained two years before that "strained race relations . . . most certainly [did] not exist" in California.[185] As a result of the 1958 election, then, the prospects for civil rights legislation were brighter than they had ever been. The "laissez-faire" state of "human relations" legislation in California, which the executive director of the CFCU had lamented in 1949, was, nearly a decade later, on the verge of lifting.[186] As Brown and his party prepared to assume power, the question was no longer if or when civil rights legislation would be enacted in California, but what shape that legislation would take? Which of the many "profound problems in the area of human relations," as Brown put it in 1958, which had been reflected in the separate civil rights trajectories in the state since the 1940s, would the new Democratic gubernatorial administration and majority Democratic legislature address, which would they avoid, and with what political consequences? Had the election of 1958 signaled the coalescence of a "natural coalition" of "minority communities" who were "so strongly pro-labor," as the CCFEP's William Becker described the moment years later—the realization of the common ground vision that the CFCU called for in the mid-1940s?[187] Or was that coalition as transitory as the ballot proposition that had done so much to give rise to it—unable to find an issue or set of issues to rally around now that Proposition 18 and the gubernatorial candidate who supported it were no longer there to rally against?

CHAPTER 6

"A COALITION . . .
FOR MANY YEARS"

As the election of 1958 approached, Loren Miller, co-chair of the NAACP-WC's West Coast Regional Legal Redress Committee, groped for a way to praise Democratic gubernatorial candidate Pat Brown. Interviewed for a *New York Times* article, the veteran civil rights lawyer drew a lowest common denominator comparison, crediting Brown for at least distinguishing himself from his Democratic counterparts in the South on civil rights.[1] Miller could have added that Brown had also distinguished himself—at least rhetorically—from California's two previous Republican governors. Unlike Earl Warren and Goodwin Knight, Brown acknowledged "profound problems in the area of human relations" and identified "dispel[ling] discrimination" as one of a handful of tasks necessary for building a "great state." More specifically, his "Statement on Civil Rights" called for the passage of fair employment practices legislation, as well as fair housing legislation for cases in which construction involved government assistance.[2] This delineation of civil rights priorities corresponded with the fair employment practices and fair housing focused agenda that the NAACP-WC had been pursuing since its inception in 1944—a reflection, no doubt, of Miller's influence as an adviser on "the primary issues in the field of minority problems," as Brown's campaign director described Miller's role.[3] Singling out Brown's support for fair employment practices, Miller predicted that the African American vote for Brown would "approach a landslide."[4]

Years later, William Becker, who would serve as the first assistant to the governor for human rights, reflected on Brown's decisive victory. He attributed the outcome to the forging of a "natural coalition" of "minority communities" who were "strongly pro-labor." Becker's claim drew on a long history of work on behalf of some of those communities. Born in Newark, New Jersey, Becker came to California in the late 1940s to organize farm workers, which soon had him working with Ernesto Galarza. Repeatedly foiled in his efforts by the importation of braceros and undocumented Mexican agricultural laborers, Becker abandoned the Central Valley for San Francisco in 1953. There, he took a job with the Jewish Labor Committee, where he sought to "help the labor movement deal with problems and relationships in the area of civil rights." To this end, he became a leading figure in the California Committee for Fair Employment Practices (CCFEP) from its founding in 1953.[5] Closely allied with the NAACP-WC, the CCFEP pressed for fair employment practices legislation. Brown's victory in 1958 boded well for its passage.

It boded less well for the legislative priorities of the Community Service Organization (CSO). As the leading advocacy group for the state's Mexican American population—whose population nearly doubled during the 1950s and was nearly double that of African Americas—the CSO had focused its attention for the five years preceding Brown's election on securing old-age pensions for long-term resident non-citizens.[6] In addition, by the late 1950s, leading CSO member César Chávez identified a range of issues for improving the lives of the state's farm workers whom he deemed "synonymous with the Mexican-American in California."[7] These included stemming the tide of temporary and undocumented farm workers from Mexico, while securing a minimum wage, unemployment insurance, and collective bargaining rights for domestic farm workers. Brown's "Statement on Civil Rights," however, did not mention any of these measures.[8] Nor, for that matter, did the CCFEP reach much beyond fair employment practices. Though it expressed support for old-age pensions for long-term resident noncitizens—just as the CSO supported the NAACP's and CCFEP's push for fair employment practices—the CCFEP, as Becker recollected, considered everything else besides its "very specific goal" of fair employment practices to be "side issues."[9]

The 1958 election brought that goal within reach, elevating civil rights to a place of prominence that it had never before occupied on the state's legislative stage. It also soon elevated Brown's standing in the national Democratic Party. In 1957, the *New York Times* described the second-term state attorney general, and former two-term San Francisco attorney general, as "steady" but not "spectacular;"[10] the *Wall Street Journal* characterized him as "honest, but not extraordinarily smart;"[11] and the *Los Angeles Times* viewed him as "an undistinguished but practical politician."[12] Just two years later, however, the *New York Times* reported that Brown had emerged as a dark horse candidate for the Democratic Party's presidential nomination, adding, "few political prognoses" than those that had attached to Brown "have turned out so wrong."[13] Brown's rising star in the Democratic firmament owed in part to the civil rights record he began to compile. Upon assuming office in 1959, Brown threw his support behind fair employment practices and, four years later, fair housing legislation. He also created a Constitutional Rights Section in the California Office of the Attorney General and placed NAACP-WC regional director Franklin Williams in charge of it. In short, Brown led "racial liberals" in California to "a remarkable string of victories in the late 1950s and early 1960s" and, in the process, became "one of the leading liberal politicians of the 1960s," in the words of two historians.[14]

Yet, the racial liberalism that Brown espoused did not reflect the racial diversity of the state he governed. Instead, Brown's civil rights agenda corresponded with that of the NAACP-WC and CCFEP. As these organizations had done during the 1950s, Brown reasoned by analogy from the plight of African Americans to that of other "minority citizens." He posited a harmony of civil rights interests among them, even as leaders representing organizations from the largest one of those groups, Mexican Americans, pursued a wide range of issues besides fair employment practices and fair housing that Brown and the Democrats did not, with one exception, address with legislation. These divergent civil rights trajectories qualified Brown's 1963 claim about the "tremendous gains for minority citizens" wrought under his watch and help explain why, that same year, Chávez berated the Democrats for failing to deliver "meaningful legislation" for Mexican Americans.[15] These divergent civil rights trajectories also revealed how the "natural [Democratic] coalition" of "minority communities" that Becker described as having come together during the election of 1958, was neither "natural" nor robust.[16] Its emergence owed more to opposition to Proposition 18 and in support for the gubernatorial candidate (Brown) who opposed the "right to work" initiative than in support for a civil rights agenda that bound "minority communities" together. A coalition by default, it would evince strains and fissures from the moment Brown took office and his party assumed control of the California legislature.

At some point during the 1950s—he did not recollect exactly when—Assemblyman Augustus (Gus) Hawkins convened a meeting with California Attorney General Pat Brown. At the time, Brown was California's most prominent Democrat, and Hawkins was California's leading Democratic advocate for a state fair employment practices law, which had been repeatedly rebuffed by the legislature since Hawkins first introduced it in 1943, as well as trounced by the state electorate in 1946. In the face of these recurrent defeats, Hawkins recognized that the only hope for passing fair employment practices would be to elect a governor who would back it. With Brown a likely candidate to be the Democrat's gubernatorial standard-bearer, Hawkins convened a group of people to impress upon Brown their interest in fair employment practices.[17] C.L. Dellums, who was chair of both the CCFEP and NAACP Regional Advisory Committee, led that delegation, which secured Hawkins's objective. "We got him committed," Dellums recollected.[18]

Upon assuming office, Brown quickly began honoring his commitment. His inaugural address, opened by acknowledging both the challenge—in the form of a

$100 million budget deficit—and opportunity—in the form of Democratic control of the governorship and legislature—that his administration faced. He then enumerated a dozen legislative proposals of which a "guarantee of equal job opportunities" was the first. "Discrimination in employment," Brown declared, "is a stain upon the image of California" and legislation to combat it in workplaces and labor unions was "our moral duty."[19] Two days later, Assemblymen Hawkins and William (Byron) Rumford, who joined Hawkins in 1949 as the legislature's only African Americans, introduced their latest fair employment practices bill.[20] Fifty-two other assembly members (out of an eighty member assembly) signed up as co-sponsors.[21] Brown greeted the bill's introduction by noting how "long overdue" it was. California "lagged behind other progressive states" when it came to fair employment practices, and he vowed to do his part to make sure that the bill passed into law.[22]

The CCFEP, which had been coordinating the fair employment practices fight since its inception in 1953, hailed the "fast start" that fair employment practices received when Brown listed it as his first order of legislative business.[23] By throwing his weight behind fair employment practices, Assemblyman Phillip Burton wrote the NAACP-WC's Franklin Williams, Brown not only set himself apart from "his Republican predecessors," but he almost guaranteed the bill's enactment.[24] Assemblyman Edward Gaffney agreed. With the backing of a Democratic majority in the legislature, the "long-delayed triumphant victory for [the] noble cause" that "Byron [Rumford] and Gus [Hawkins]" had been waging for well over a decade was within reach.[25]

Indeed, prospects for passage of fair employment practices shone so bright that Becker urged the CCFEP's leadership to consider revising the organization's name to something "broader . . . than its present emphasis on FEPC." The CCFEP needed to look beyond its single-issue focus in order to continue to "coordinate legislative efforts in the broad civil rights field."[26] Becker also inquired whether the CCFEP should "give support . . . as may be feasible" to other bills pending before the California legislature.[27] These, he subsequently noted, included "a re-introduction of the bill to make it possible for aliens in the United States for twenty-five years or more to receive Old Age Assistance," which was "a major concern of the CSO." However, Becker hastened to add, any additional action the CCFEP took should not detract "from FEPC as our No. 1 priority."[28]

Keeping the focus on fair employment practices, the CCFEP pressed for passage of the Hawkins-Rumford bill as it moved through the legislature. In the process, the financial support the CCFEP received confirmed Dellums's recollection that "labor and NAACP branches supplied over ninety percent of the money."[29] By Becker's accounting, the CCFEP received $2,563 from unspecified "Unions" and $2,017 from the NAACP between November 1958 and May 1959. Contributions from the next largest groups of donors were significantly smaller, with $703 coming from the "Jewish Community," $515 from the California Democratic Committee, and $510 from the JACL. Becker had no line item for contributions, if any, that came from the CSO.[30]

On April 16, 1959, a little over four months after he made it his first legislative priority, Brown signed the California Fair Employment Practice Act. The new law proscribed "discrimination or abridgment on account of race, religious creed, color, national origin, or ancestry" in employment. For enforcement, it established a Fair Employment Practice Commission (FEPC) composed of five gubernatorial appointees, with a staff to investigate employment discrimination cases. If the FEPC then found unlawful discrimination, it could, among other things, order the employer to "take such affirmative action, including (but not limited to) hiring, reinstatement or upgrading of employees, with or without back pay." Refusal to abide by the FEPC's ruling constituted a misdemeanor, punishable by up to six months in jail and a $500 fine.[31] When the FEPC opened in September 1959, Dellums was one of Brown's five appointees, while fellow CCFEP activist Edward Howden was Brown's choice for directing the FEPC's staff.[32]

For Williams, the California Fair Employment Practice Act was "with a few minor provisions . . . everything that we wanted."[33] Brown identified it, along with passage of a bond issue to fund a major water project, as the signal accomplishments of his administration's first legislative session—"a great symbol of human progress."[34] Neither Brown nor Williams, however, noted two critical limitations to the law and the commission it established to enforce it. The law did not cover "agricultural workers residing on the land where they are employed as farm workers," and the initial appointments to the Commission and its staff did not include any Mexican Americans.[35] The first of these limitations reflected a general omission of farm labor-related issues from Brown's civil rights agenda. The second would prompt the CSO, from which César Chávez would soon break to devote himself to the plight of laborers, to demand "expansion of California FEP Commission and Staff in the interest of *all* minorities" as part of the legislative priorities the organization spelled out at its March 1960 annual convention.[36]

The California Fair Employment Practice Act marked the culmination of over fifteen years of plotting and prodding by NAACP-WC leaders. By contrast, the Unruh Civil Rights Act—a second major civil rights law to pass the California legislature and receive Governor Brown's signature in 1959—was the product of civil rights neophytes who faced resistance from veteran civil rights advocates. Yet, despite its unlikely evolution from conception to codification, the Unruh Civil Rights Act proved to be a much bolder and more sweeping law. In particular, it opened the door to a series of successful challenges to discriminatory practices in the housing market. Thus, unlike the California Fair Employment Practice Act, which merely brought the state up to speed with the dozen other states that had similar laws, the Unruh Civil Rights Act placed California at the forefront of the nationwide fight against housing discrimination.

"California's new civil rights tool," as Williams would characterize the Unruh Civil Rights Act, emerged out of the offended conscience of a recent law school graduate.[37] In the fall of 1958, Marvin Holen read a newspaper account of the case of Cynthia Reed. An orphan born and raised in a Burbank foster home, Holen hitchhiked to and from UCLA where he received his bachelor's degree in political science in 1952. He then served in the Marine Corps in the Korean War, returned to UCLA, and earned his law degree. Reed was a five-year-old who had been denied admission to the private Hollywood Professional School because she was African Amercian. Her guardian sued, citing a California law that prohibited discrimination in places of public accommodation.[38] A private school, Reed's advocates argued, fell within the meaning of "all other places of public accommodation" in which the law proscribed discrimination. The school, however, insisted that it was a private institution and thus fell outside the law's purview. Both the trial and appellate courts sided with the Hollywood Professional School.[39]

Reed's case outraged Holen. He conveyed his anger to his friend and boss, Assemblyman Jesse Marvin Unruh, who felt similarly and tasked Holen with drafting a bill to redress Reed's predicament and preclude others like it. Recognizing his and his boss's inexperience with civil rights legislation, Holen sought the counsel of the NAACP-WC's Williams. Williams, Holen understood, "was coming from a movement . . . from long, hard work, from fund-raising efforts, from organizational efforts, from negotiations, from careful calculation of support and opposition." By contrast, Holen continued, "I just wandered in from left field. Jesse Unruh wandered in from left field."[40]

And left field was exactly where NAACP-WC Legal Redress Committee co-chair Nathaniel Colley wished Unruh and Holen would stay. Colley shuddered at the political implications of the sweeping reach of the bill that Holen proposed, covering "all public or private groups, organizations, associations, business establishments, schools, and public facilities." In a memorandum to Williams, Hawkins, Rumford, and Miller, Colley complained, "The limiting clause . . . is almost meaningless." It would allow "a person to legally force his way into a private club, lodge or church, so long as he could show that his exclusion had been based upon race, color, religion, ancestry, or national origin." A Chinese immigrant could not be excluded from the Sons of Italy. An "atheist" could not be denied "full admissions to the privileges of the Catholic Church." The political fallout from attempting to push through such a sweeping bill would ultimately do more harm than good. It would, Colley feared, "simply give our opponents ammunition with which to murder us and drive a wedge between us and many people who are with us 100% on the fundamental issues." Legislators, he believed, who otherwise supported civil rights measures such as fair employment practices might very well recoil at the "prospect of a Negro bringing an action to compel his admission to a Masonic Lodge, rotary club, or even a white citizens council." This, in turn, Colley added, might undermine the prospects for additional civil rights legislation. For this reason, Colley recommended that Unruh "be asked to drop the bill or to amend it to meet the objections raised."[41]

Holen revised it. He re-drew the bill's antidiscrimination boundaries by substituting the phrase "all business establishments of every kind whatsoever" for "all public or private groups, organizations, associations, business establishments, schools, and public facilities." Though less encompassing than its initial iteration, the bill's prohibition against discrimination in "all business establishments of every kind whatsoever" still cut a much wider swath than anything California had ever known. Nevertheless, Holen proceeded without appreciating just how wide. "I didn't know what it meant because I wasn't a lawyer, even though I graduated from law school and all that," he recalled. "No lawyer would write that, no judge would write it, no skilled legislator would draft that. That was just me saying, 'Everybody out there. All you people out there, you are not going to discriminate on irrational grounds.' That was exactly the way Jesse felt about it, and that's where the language came from."[42]

The revised Unruh bill managed to clear the assembly. In the senate, however, it became bottled up in a committee for several months. When it appeared doomed, Unruh wielded his growing political clout to breathe the bill back to life. Though a civil rights novice, Unruh was an expert powerbroker—and as chair of the assembly's Ways and Means Committee beginning in 1959, he had plenty of power. Unruh's committee was the weigh station for any bill with budgetary implications. To prevent his civil rights bill from getting buried in the senate, Unruh ordered all senate bills off his committee's hearing schedule. If Unruh's civil rights bill was going to die in the senate, then all senate bills that needed to go through Unruh's committee would die in the assembly, too.[43]

Left with little choice, the senate committee released Unruh's bill for a vote. This move, however, came on the last night of the legislative session and with the bill in an amended form that bore only partial resemblance to the one that had arrived from the assembly. On first blush, Unruh and Holen felt that the senate amendments had eviscerated their bill, which is what the architects of the amendments intended to do when they stripped it of a list of businesses that would be covered.[44] Upon closer examination, however, Holen realized that the changes inadvertently strengthened the measure. Though the enumeration of specific businesses covered disappeared, the language of "all business establishments of every kind whatsoever" remained. Without that specification, Holen confided to Unruh, "I think they made a mistake . . . I think they broadened it." The more he thought about it, the more he concluded, "I think they've done themselves in."[45]

In its final form, which Governor Brown signed on July 15, 1959, the Unruh Civil Rights Act declared, "All citizens within the jurisdiction of this State are free and equal, and no matter what their race, color, religion, ancestry, or national origin are entitled to the full and equal accommodations, advantages, facilities, privileges, or services in all business establishments of every kind whatsoever."[46] Slated to go into effect two months later, the new civil rights law would soon affirm Holen's intuition about its potential reach, in particular as it applied to the business of housing.

One of the first people to appreciate the potential of the Unruh Civil Rights Act for curbing housing discrimination was Assemblyman Hawkins. Besides the California Fair Employment Practice Act, which Hawkins had been instrumental in securing, the 1959 legislative session also yielded a Hawkins-sponsored fair housing measure, which was limited to "discrimination in publicly assisted housing."[47] Moreover, the law adopted a narrow reading of "publicly assisted," including in its purview tract housing developers who received federal or state backed loans, but excluding individuals who purchased homes in such developments even if they did so with federal or state backed mortgages. This, along with other exclusions written into the Hawkins Act, helped explain why an estimated eighty percent of housing units were beyond law's bounds.[48] Testifying to a United States Commission on Civil Rights hearing in Los Angeles in January 1960, Hawkins attributed the exclusion of "privately owned housing accommodations" to a tactical calculation he and his supporters made. "We were afraid that an act which included private housing would not pass." Consequently, they settled for "half a loaf rather than lose everything." This "deficiency," Hawkins hastened to add, owed to "political expediency," which he hoped to correct with a more inclusive fair housing proposal in a subsequent legislative session. In the meantime, though, Hawkins alluded to the Unruh Civil Rights Act as an example of how the legislature exceeded "our expectations in the enactment of civil rights legislation."[49] With respect to housing, the Unruh Act offered the possibility of reaching beyond the Hawkins Act into the realm of real estate transactions, even if they involved private properties.[50]

As that possibility awaited realization, Brown used the occasion of the United States Commission on Civil Rights hearing in San Francisco in January 1960 to wax proud about his recent accomplishments. "The year 1959 represents a new high water mark in our determined effort to achieve social justice for all our citizens," the governor exclaimed.[51] Brown's director of finance and adviser, Hale Champion, concurred, while placing the 1959 legislative session in historical perspective. "For 14 years," Champion said in 1962, "while other states forged ahead with fair employment and other civil rights legislation . . . California sat unmoved." The election of 1958, however, ushered in a Democratic governor and legislature who brought "the long night of inaction . . . to an end. The lonely years of recurrent defeat through which Gus Hawkins and a few of his colleagues had struggled were finally capped by the decisive action."[52] Champion, like Brown, cited the California Fair Employment Practice Act, Unruh Civil Rights Act, and Hawkins fair housing law as evidence of some of what Brown adviser Richard Kline described as the "enormous changes" wrought during Brown's first year in office, "probably . . . greater . . . than anything since 1911 when Hiram Johnson was governor of the state."[53] In addition, Brown directed the attention of the Commission on Civil Rights to his establishment of a Constitutional Rights Section in the state Office of the Attorney General. Tarea Hall Pittmann, who became acting regional director for the NAACP-WC in September 1959, hailed the new "full civil rights department" as "precedent making."[54] To run it, Brown heeded the advice of newly elected attorney general Stanley Mosk and appointed Pittman's predecessor, Franklin Williams, as assistant attorney general. "I stole Williams from the NAACP," recollected Mosk who had been one of the few California superior court judges in the 1940s to issue a ruling in one of the many racially restrictive housing covenant cases Loren Miller was then litigating.[55] Williams's appointment highlighted the extent to which the Brown administration—along with its legislative allies—understood civil rights in terms synonymous with the NAACP-WC's understanding. "FEPC and Fair Housing," Williams declared in June 1959 had long been "our two priority bills."[56] Having achieved FEPC and a limited fair housing law in 1959, the NAACP and the CCFEP now turned their attention to enacting a more robust fair housing measure.

In May 1960, Fred Dutton offered Governor Brown high praise for what he had accomplished over the course of his first year and a half in office. "You have really made a historical contribution to stabilizing the [Democratic] Party and reducing the internal frictions," Dutton wrote Brown, whose gubernatorial campaign Dutton had directed. Dutton then ventured a bold prediction about the future of the party Brown led in light of his accomplishments. "If the alliance of the Democrats with labor, the minorities, etc., can just be strengthened" beyond the strengthening that had already occurred, Dutton continued, "you will have wrought a completely changed political foundation for the State lasting a decade or two after you leave office. . . . Once a coalition of that nature is put together, its after effects go on for many years."[57]

Dutton's claim about the coalition that Brown had helped forge with "minorities," however, stood in marked contrast to the CSO's assessment of Brown's first year in office. In the summer of 1959, the *CSO Reporter* expressed "bitter . . . disappointment" over the defeat of what it deemed to be "the two most important bills to the Mexican-American community."[58] The first of these was for old-age pensions for long-term resident non-citizens, which the CSO had made its top state legislative priority in the same year (1953) that the CCFEP was formed. In a May 1959 meeting with representatives of the Committee for Extension of Old Age Assistance to Non-Citizens, which included CSO leader Anthony Rios, Brown offered qualified support for the measure, "provided the funds to cover [it] would be made available."[59] Subsequently, when CSO legislative representative Dolores Huerta pressed the issue, a secretary for the governor informed her, "The Governor was not opposed to the measure in principle, [but] it was at the bottom of his priority list, because of the expense involved." When the bill failed, the *CSO Reporter* insisted that the blame for its failure lay "directly with Governor Brown."[60]

A minimum wage for agricultural workers was the second essential bill for Mexican Americans in 1959, according to the *CSO Reporter*. Initially, Brown's support for this measure exceeded his support for old-age pensions for long-term resident non-citizens. Indeed, the sixth point of his twelve-point inaugural address called for the establishment of "$1.25 an hour as the minimum wage for California workers not covered by federal law."[61] A few months later, however, Brown began to backpedal in the face of opposition from agribusiness and its Democratic and Republican allies in the legislature. "I do believe there is danger in California having $1.25 and other states not having a minimum in agriculture," Brown claimed at a news conference in which he announced a cut in his proposal to $1 per hour for farm workers.[62] A subsequent amendment to the minimum wage bill, to which Brown acquiesced, reduced that rate to ninety cents. Despite these concessions, and despite pressure from CSO agricultural workers who were led to Sacramento by César Chávez in April 1959, the minimum wage bill died in the state senate.[63] Its defeat contributed to Brown's realization that the "farm labor lobby" was "one of the toughest" in the state.[64] He would do little to challenge it again in the years ahead.

The defeat of the CSO's two major 1959 legislative priorities was especially "bitter," according to the *CSO Reporter*, given the "hopes and faith" the organization and its constituents vested in Brown. That expectations associated with the "new liberal, enlightened and responsible administration" had been borne out in other legislative areas—including the "historic passage of the . . . FEPC bill," the Unruh Civil Rights Act, and the Hawkins fair housing law—only deepened the disappointment. The *CSO Reporter* praised California's new civil rights laws and credited the NAACP-WC as "the organization responsible" for many of them, along with the CCFEP, which also "played a tremendous role." However, it distinguished these measures from "the needs of the Mexican people," which "were not only ignored, but actually opposed by some key Democrats."[65]

Just as the CSO's disaffection Brown and the Democratic majority legislature in 1959 undermined Dutton's May 1960 assertion of a burgeoning and potentially enduring Brown-led Democratic "coalition" of "labor [and] the minorities, etc.," so, too, did the April 1960 launch of the Mexican-American Political Association (MAPA). Whereas the CSO's disappointment with Brown and the Democrats owed to their failure to enact the legislation the CSO identified as most essential for Mexican Americans, MAPA's grievances focused on political representation and appointments.[66] Although an estimated ninety percent of Mexican Americans supported Brown in his bid for governor in 1958, according to the CSO's Rios, their loyalty, MAPA maintained, was not reciprocated.[67] Thus, MAPA declared independence from both major parties and resolved to serve as an "instrument for the Mexican-American community . . . to place capable and talented Mexican-Americans in elective and appointive offices."[68]

Recognizing the rift within the coalition that Dutton claimed to be coalescing under Brown, Edward Howden, executive director of the newly formed FEPC, wrote Cecile Poole, Brown's legal counsel, in September 1960. "There are," Howden observed, "very serious problems of relations with Spanish-speaking leaders." In response, Howden recommended the appointment of Herman Gallegos to the FEPC staff.[69] Without Gallegos, who had recently assumed the helm of the CSO from Rios, "the Commission would have no Mexican American staffer." This absence threatened to reinforce the Commission's insistence that its "major concern" should be "improvement for employment opportunities for Negroes" since "Negroes file more than 90 percent of the complaints of job discrimination."[70] Gallegos's appointment, Howden suggested, would thus help address the CSO's demand from March 1960 for the "expansion" of the FEPC "in the interest of *all* minorities."[71] Gallegos received the appointment. However, he needed to pressure Brown for the next four years to "finally appoint a Hispanic [FEPC] commissioner." Meanwhile, the operation of the FEPC, according to Gallegos, buttressed the impression that the legislation that created the FEPC "was primarily aimed at blacks."[72]

CSO reservations about the FEPC's composition and operation took a backseat to the other goals the organization spelled out for the 1961 legislative session. At its annual meeting in 1960, the CSO resolved to "go all out" for: "(1) Establishment of a minimum wage of $1.25 and Unemployment Insurance coverage for Farm Workers; (2) Elimination of the Mexican National [i.e., Bracero] Program over a four-year period, by reducing by one-fourth the number of Nationals to be admitted each year; (3) Extension of State Old Age Pensions to non-citizens who entered the country prior to 1932."[73] While the pensions and minimum wage proposals had been identified as top CSO priorities in 1959 (and earlier in the case of pensions), unemployment insurance for agricultural laborers and the phasing out of braceros in 1961 were new proposals. They reflected the influence of César Chávez on shaping the CSO's legislative priorities in the aftermath of his 1958–1959 organizing stint in Oxnard.[74]

Moreover, as in 1959, the CSO's legislative priorities for 1961 cut in a different direction from those of the NAACP-WC and California Committee for Fair Practices (CCFP), which is what the CCFEP morphed into following the enactment of the California Fair Employment Practice Act in 1959. In December 1960, for example, NAACP-WC leader Tarea Hall Pittman identified "hard core resistance to integrated patterns in housing" as "the greatest problem facing Negroes in the West."[75] That same month, the CCFP indicated that it would seek to do for housing what it had done for fair employment practices, namely, spearhead a statewide campaign for fair housing legislation. As with fair employment practices, the CCFP anticipated that its greatest financial support would come from labor and the NAACP.[76]

The CCFP's prioritization of fair housing grew out of meetings it convened in the summer of 1960 in Los Angeles and San Francisco.[77] It was formalized at the end of the year in a CCFP-sponsored "Conference on Civil Rights Legislative Priorities." Following a speech on housing discrimination by NAACP-WC attorney Nat Colley, conference attendees "unanimously agreed that this [i.e., fair housing] would be our No. 1 priority." To be sure, the CCFP also agreed to support a bill for "old age assistance to aliens" that the CSO's Rios discussed. However, the self-proclaimed "Coordinating Committee for Organizations Supporting Civil Rights Legislation" in California also made clear that its "officers were authorized to hold back on items in the program which might impede progress on the No. 1 Objective."[78] One month later, in January 1961, a CCFP letter to "Supporters for Civil Rights Legislation" across the state announced the organization's push for fair housing as "our NUMBER ONE OBJECTIVE." Coming from the organization that an NAACP-WC regional director would later characterize as the "official lobbying arm for the civil rights movement in the State of California," the letter made no mention whatsoever of the "old age assistance to aliens" bill.[79]

That same month, the CSO dispatched Dolores Huerta to Sacramento to serve as its legislative advocate—"the first time in the history of California the Spanish-speaking community had one of their own as a full-time legislative advocate at the State Capitol working towards the solution of their problems."[80] The CSO's long sought pensions bill became Huerta's leading objective for the 1961 legislative session. To this end, Huerta began by approaching Assemblyman Phillip Burton, the "most liberal" member of the California legislature according to a *San Jose Mercury* profile, to whose Committee on Social Welfare Huerta testified on behalf of farm workers in 1959.[81] Burton needed convincing. There was, he told Huerta, little support for such a bill—not the least of which owed to the non-citizen status of its proposed beneficiaries. In addition, he pointed Huerta to the passage of the California Fair Employment Practice Act in 1959 as existing legislation to combat discrimination.[82] This legislation, Huerta no doubt knew, did little for the group that was the target of the CSO's proposed bill. Huerta persisted, and Burton's reservations soon evaporated. In early January 1961, he introduced the measure the CSO sought (AB 5), describing it as "the most important piece of Social Welfare Legislation before us in this Session" and promising to secure passage of "this piece of unfinished business."[83]

Burton's promise quickly foundered on the shoals of the same fiscal constraints claim that Brown made against the bill's 1959 incarnation. "The good Gov. Brown," Huerta wrote, "claims the state budget cannot support the expenditures . . . [and] that the Legislators are not behind it."[84] Refusing to capitulate, Huerta spearheaded letter-writing campaigns and testimony to committee hearings.[85] These efforts helped persuade state officials. On June 23, 1961, J.M. Wedemeyer, head of the California Department of Social Welfare, described the bill as "simple justice" to the non-citizen "long-term residents of this state who have contributed greatly to the progress and development of California during their working lives."[86] Two weeks later, a Brown staffer agreed, calling the measure "an important milestone in the Governor's avowed program for removing from public law the basic elements of discrimination."[87]

Shortly thereafter, on July 18, 1961, Brown signed AB 5 into law. "That was one of the greatest things I ever did," Brown recollected years later. "When I signed that bill, all those old people (who were not only the old Chicanos, but we also had Chinese who have been here a long, long time, and other nationalities), they were all up there . . . and, God, they pretty nearly kissed my feet."[88] Though Brown made no mention of the CSO, the *Los Angeles Times* editors did, viewing the "just and humane bill measure" as the "end of an eight-year fight" waged by the organization.[89] Much more effusive was the CSO member who declared the passage of AB 5 to be "the greatest triumph in the whole history of the CSO."[90]

Obscured in the celebration over the passage of AB 5 was the fate of the other, farm-labor-related bills the CSO also sought in 1961—minimum wage, unemployment insurance, and reduction in the number of braceros imported. Unlike

1959, Brown did not even bother proposing an agricultural minimum wage bill in 1961. "I fought this one out" in the previous legislative session, Brown explained, and "I'm going to leave it to the Legislature, whatever they may come up with."[91] Without Brown "fight[ing] for it," a state senator acknowledged, "there is little likelihood" that the minimum wage bill that was proposed would pass.[92] It did not.

Instead, the senate issued a toothless joint resolution, which reflected Brown's revised view about the federal, rather than state, onus of responsibility for enacting an agricultural minimum wage, lest California find itself "at a tremendous disadvantage in the highly competitive national market for farm products."[93] This resolution—and Brown's support of it—represented a betrayal of the promise that Brown had made in 1959 and reiterated at the signing ceremony for AB 5 in July 1961 to "get a minimum wage for farm workers."[94] As Brown explained his change of heart, "We have on numerous occasions proposed and supported the enactment of a minimum wage law for farm workers. We believe, however, that we should have a federal minimum wage law for farm workers. We recognize that the California farmers must compete with producers of like crops in distant states whose wage rates for farm workers are lower than in California."[95] The farmers Brown invoked could hardly have said it better: let Congress, not California, take up the issue and, in the meantime, stick with the status quo.[96]

Brown proved even less sympathetic to the CSO's demand for phasing out braceros. On the contrary, in May 1960 he called for more of them, vowing, "This administration does not intend to allow crops to rot in the field because of an inadequate labor supply."[97] He reiterated his position in March of 1961, adding, "we . . . are going to need some braceros in the foreseeable future."[98] A few months later, he telegrammed United States Secretary of Labor Arthur Goldberg as well as members of Congress requesting that the "foreseeable future" translate to at least another two-year extension of the Bracero Program.[99] A subsequent appeal from Brown to the Kennedy administration and the California congressional delegation in 1962 to extend the program for two years prompted Chávez to write Huerta, "I'm sick about that Governor of yours." Recognizing that lobbying Brown to oppose the extension of the Bracero Program was a lost cause for the time being, Chávez called for redoubling efforts on behalf of a minimum wage for farm workers by "flood[ing] the Governor['s] office with letters from the workers."[100]

As Brown distanced himself from farm workers, he gravitated toward the victims of housing discrimination. Though his steps in this direction were hesitant during the 1961 legislative session, they accelerated in the 1963 legislative session, following his 1962 re-election over Richard Nixon. As he embraced fair housing as his top civil rights priority by 1963, Brown demonstrated once again how he understood civil rights in terms that were synonymous with the NAACP-WC and CCFP.

Mounting evidence of the depth of housing discrimination in California, especially against African Americans, drove home the need for more fair housing legislation. In December 1959, the Congress of Racial Equality (CORE) published a report of field tests it conducted in Los Angeles. Separate teams of local CORE members—one black, one white—posed as prospective buyers or renters and visited the same apartment complexes, real estate offices, and houses within a few minutes of each other. In almost every instance, the black CORE members found themselves victims of discriminatory treatment not suffered by the white CORE members. One real estate agent informed the black testers that the houses in which they expressed interest required a $300 contract fee, $1250 down payment, and $125 monthly payment. He also claimed that there was neither color choice in houses, nor, for that matter, any houses available. To the white couple that visited the same agent shortly thereafter, the agent mentioned no contract fee, informed them of the array of colors from which to choose, and pointed them to a number of houses currently available. In another test, a real estate agent gave the undercover CORE teams the same information, but assured the white team that the housing development for which he worked "would definitely not sell to Negroes . . . even if [they] had the financial means." Still another agent explained to the white CORE testers that it was easy enough to flout the spirit of the law, while adhering to the letter. "There are always ways to get around," he remarked. "We first ask for their employment verification and consider if their income is substantial enough. We can always tell them 'I don't think you'll qualify.'" Though the agent expressed sympathy for the plight of prospective black buyers, the bottom line, he contended, was that they drove down property values and thus cut housing tract profits. In still another test, one apartment manager informed the white CORE members that, though "we can't . . . advertise restricted or say restricted to anyone . . . we don't and we won't have [Negroes]." Another apartment manager insisted that he engaged in "nothing like [religious discrimination], but of course, no colored."[101]

To this powerful anecdotal evidence, Franklin Williams, added powerful statistical evidence. In an April 1960 magazine article, the former NAACP-WC regional director and current California assistant attorney general in the newly created Constitutional Rights Section of the California Office of the Attorney General, observed, "Fewer than fifty tract houses" of 325,000 new homes built in nine Bay Area counties from 1950 to 1958 "were sold to nonwhite buyers on a first-come first-buy basis." Though Williams referred to "nonwhite buyers," in general, the evidence he cited referred to African

Americans, in particular. Sublegal techniques used to discourage African Americans from buying houses in white neighborhoods included claiming that no listings were available, asking the prospective buyers to come back some other time, referring the prospective buyers to African American areas, overpricing homes and down payments, and insisting that listings were either incorrect or withdrawn.[102] A 1961 report to the United States Commission on Civil Rights from the Commission's California advisory committee expressed the "unanimous view . . . that in California, minority housing is largely a Negro problem." Though other groups were certainly not immune to housing discrimination, the California committee concluded from the testimony given at its hearings, "There is a far greater degree of housing mobility for Orientals and Mexican-Americans in California than exists for Negroes."[103]

In June 1960, the Brown administration sponsored the "First Governor's Conference on Housing." A "Minority Problems in Housing" panel—which included Williams, Miller, Gallegos, and Becker—recommended, among other things, extending the state's limited existing fair housing to "cover all housing and all phases of the housing industry" with an expanded FEPC for enforcement.[104] In January 1961 Assemblyman Hawkins introduced such a measure. Assembly Bill (AB) 801 would place enforcement of housing discrimination within the purview of the FEPC, while extending the state's existing fair housing law "to cover discrimination in the sale, lease, rental or financing of all housing accommodations," with one important caveat, namely, "single unit dwelling[s] occupied in whole or in part by the owner as his residence." To critics who argued that fair housing would send property values plummeting, the CCFP cited studies debunking that myth. To critics who insisted that fair housing laws violated property owners' rights, the CCFP replied, "The property owner retains full authority to set his own standards of financial, personal, cultural and other qualifications. The law merely requires that no one be given separate treatment because of irrelevant standards of race, religion or ancestry."[105]

Despite the CCFP's efforts, Brown and his administration exhibited, at best, lukewarm support for AB 801. On the one hand, Brown issued a call in his 1961 message to the legislature to "extend our laws against discrimination in housing." On the other hand, he buried civil rights near the bottom of his 1961 priorities list, ninth in a ten-point program. Moreover, in terms of specific legislation, Brown made no mention of extending fair housing laws to cover the private housing market.[106] His tepid support also surfaced while addressing the fair housing faithful at an April 1961 CCFP conference on AB 801. Damning the bill with faint praise, Brown offered support in "principle," while conceding that the bill would undergo "revisions" and signaling to the bill's opponents his willingness to "accept reasonable compromises."[107]

Brown's reluctance to throw his weight behind AB 801 reflected advice from his staff. On December 2, 1960, for example, Richard Kline, a veteran political reporter who served as a Brown adviser, deemed it "unsound to initiate any major specific housing legislation at this time." The administration was "simply not prepared" to grapple with "such an explosive subject." Though justice might merit an all-out pursuit of fair housing legislation, politics militated against it. "The question is not what has to be done in this field," Kline maintained, "but what can be done from a politically realistic standpoint."[108]

Absent the full support of California's leading Democrat, AB 801 stood little chance. Though the bill cleared the assembly in May 1961, it died in the senate. In the end, despite numerous studies, hearings, and governor's and CCFP conferences, only a Governor's Advisory Commission on Housing emerged out of the 1961 legislative session.[109] The holes in California's fair housing statutes—the lack of an enforcement agency and the inapplicability to the private housing market—remained. To a letter from a "colored [Air Force] Airman" who kept a "constant watch over our home country" only to "encounter prejudice everywhere" when he tried to rent an apartment, and to the countless other Californians who shared his plight, Brown's office could only offer the stock reply, "At the present time, California laws do not prohibit discrimination in [private] housing based upon race."[110]

While the Brown administration dithered on fair housing, the California Supreme Court took action. In 1962 it handed down two decisions that applied the Unruh Civil Rights Act to the business of housing. Writing in 1960, law professor Harold Horowitz anticipated the broad antidiscriminatory potential inherent in the new Unruh Civil Rights Act, which the California Supreme Court helped realize. Not only did the law preclude racial discrimination in "relationships between private persons in a way which is unique among the states"—that is, without the use of the word *public*, and with the use of the words *business* and *establishments*—but also by leaving the words *business establishments* undefined, it offered judges and lawyers broad interpretive berth. The ambiguity inherent in the Unruh Civil Rights Act provided a powerful lever to pry open the door to California's discriminatory housing market.[111]

Lawyers for the ACLU grasped that lever. On December 31, 1959, Marshall Krause, of the ACLU of Northern California, filed a suit on behalf of Seaborn Burks, Jr. Burks sought to purchase a house in a San Francisco subdivision developed by the Poppy Construction Company. Though Burks was financially qualified, the company refused to sell to him because he was black. This refusal, the suit claimed, violated the Unruh Civil Rights Act, by denying the "plaintiffs the full and equal accommodations, advantages, facilities, privileges and services of their business establishments."[112]

Unlike previous housing discrimination cases (*Shelley, Banks,* and *Ming*), *Burks* did not rely on a Fourteenth Amendment state action claim. Instead, *Burks* leveraged the Unruh Civil Rights Act's prohibition against discrimination in "all business establishments of every kind whatsoever." No philosophical speculation over where state action ended and private action began—the crux of the matter in *Shelley, Banks,* and *Ming*—was necessary to determine the case. Rather, the issue now hinged on whether or not the Poppy Construction Company was a business establishment and thus precluded from discrimination by the Unruh Act.

Though defeated in San Francisco County Superior Court, Krause appealed Burks's case to the California Supreme Court. In a January 1962 brief, he accused the Poppy Construction Company of "attempting to find an exception in the broad language" of the Unruh Act.[113] The company's attorneys agreed, although they insisted that the exception was not theirs but rather the legislature's. In their January 1962 brief, they asserted that "the Unruh Civil Rights Act does not apply to the sale of private housing. . . . The legislature specifically considered, and rejected, the idea of including the purchase and sale of real property within the purview of the act." After all, the same legislature that passed the Unruh Civil Rights Act also passed the Hawkins Fair Housing Act.[114] As the ACLU's Krause paraphrased his opposing counsel's contention, "The Legislature passed the Hawkins Act on discrimination in publicly assisted housing, *ergo* the Unruh Act could not apply to discrimination in housing." He then retorted that one statute covered "racial discrimination in publicly assisted housing," while the other attacked "racial discrimination in business establishments. The Legislature realized that neither Act would do both jobs and enacted both to insure that the field was well covered." What the Poppy Construction Company really sought, Krause maintained, was simply a "constitutional right to discriminate against Negroes."[115]

In March 1962, the California Supreme Court sided with Krause on behalf of his client, Burks. "It is clear that defendants operated 'business establishments' within the meaning of the term as used in the Unruh Act," wrote Chief Justice Phil Gibson. They, therefore, flouted the law by refusing to sell to otherwise qualified African American home buyers. As construed by the California Supreme Court, a law proscribing discrimination in business establishments now began to extend its reach into the business of housing. In so doing, it threatened to disrupt the patterns of residential segregation perpetuated by realtors, developers, and others engaged in sale or rental of housing.[116]

While Marshall Krause of the ACLU of Northern California fought to get the California courts to apply the Unruh Civil Rights Act to housing developers, Al Wirin of the ACLU of Southern California fought to extend the law to cover real estate brokers. In October 1960, Wirin took up the case of Alex Vargas and his wife, a Mexican American couple trying to buy a home in an Orange County development, whose fate demonstrated how housing discrimination was not, of course, an exclusively African American problem. A real estate broker accepted a $100 deposit from the Vargases upon signing a purchase and sales agreement. Four days later, however, the broker reneged and returned the deposit. The Vargases brought suit, citing the broker's actions as violating the Unruh Act.[117]

The Orange County Superior Court, which heard the case in June 1961, acknowledged the applicability of the Unruh Act to real estate agents. As Judge John Shea told Wirin, "You can enjoin [the real estate agent] from discriminating against . . . people of Mexican ancestry." The problem, however, arose over the agent's responsibility and relationship to the seller. The law might indeed bar a real estate agent from discriminating, but what about the private homeowner for whom the agent worked? Wirin sensed that he was pushing the limits of the Unruh Act; indeed, he had already won half the battle—getting the court to view real estate agents within the purview of the Unruh Act's prohibition against discrimination in "all business establishments of every kind whatsoever." Nevertheless, he forged ahead, seeking to persuade the court to hold real estate agents liable for their clients' discrimination. "We think that the Statute imposes liability upon [the agent] if it turns out that the person who has retained him compels him to discriminate," Wirin argued. The law compelled real estate agents to tell homeowners, "I want you to know that under the Unruh Act I must make my services available to all, irrespective of race or ancestry." But what if the agent did that, the increasingly exasperated judge replied, and the seller still chose to discriminate? How, then, could the agents be liable? "That's the one thing that I can't get over," the judge confessed. Though the Vargases did, in fact, experience discrimination, "it [was] not the discrimination of the broker . . . [but rather] the man he represents." The Vargases, the Orange County Superior Court ruled, thus had no claim against the realtor.[118]

In March 1962, the California Supreme Court agreed. Yes, it held, the Unruh Act applied to real estate brokers. This was half of what Wirin sought and which the defendant's lawyers even conceded. As Wirin wrote, "Respondent has eliminated the necessity for us to reply concerning the applicability of the Unruh Civil Rights Act to real estate brokers and salesman." As for the other half, though Wirin argued that real estate agents who did the bidding of homeowners who discriminate are "caught in the cross-fire of [their] own making and should not be permitted to run to [their] principal for cover," the California Supreme Court refused to go that far.[119] In the words of Chief Justice Gibson, "A broker who in good faith does all within his power to serve a member of a racial minority is not liable if the broker's failure to complete the transaction is due solely to the owner's refusal to sell because of the buyer's color." Wirin had to settle for half. Prospective homebuyers had the right to be free from discrimination in obtaining the services of real estate agents, but only up to the point where the real estate brokers' prejudices ended and the homeowners' prejudices began.[120]

With *Vargas* and *Burks*, the California Supreme Court ruled that the Unruh Act's prohibition against discrimination in "all business establishments of every kind whatsoever" applied to both housing tract developers and real estate brokers (up to a point). This represented the "fairly reasonable principle of statutory construction" that Marvin Holen hoped the courts would give to the Unruh Act when he told Jesse Unruh in 1959 that the civil rights act bearing Unruh's name might very well cut a wider antidiscrimination path than its opponents imagined.[121] As Los Angeles County Superior Court Judge Irving Hill rejoiced in a letter to Governor Brown in the wake of *Burks* and *Vargas*, "It now appears that the Unruh and Hawkins Acts are immensely valuable accomplishments which will go a great part of the way in eliminating racial discrimination in the sale and rental of housing. . . . Your administration has made a most valuable contribution to the improvement of our Democracy."[122]

From *Shelley* through *Burks* and *Vargas*, with *Banks, Ming*, and the Unruh Civil Rights and Hawkins Fair Housing Acts in between, California's fair housing advocates had scored a number of critical victories and developed a growing number of legal and legislative tools. Yet, as *Vargas* revealed, they still lacked an essential implement. With *Vargas* the California Supreme Court drew the line against housing discrimination at the door of the private homeowner. Attacking the discrimination practiced by private homeowners—whose sales made up the bulk of California real estate transactions—represented the next fair housing battlefront.

The FEPC's Edward Howden pressed Brown to take up this battle. As significant as the 1959 legislative session had been for the cause of civil rights in California, Howden wrote, the 1961 session proved to be insignificant. A "virtual veil of silence regarding future civil rights program[s]" had descended after 1959. California, he lamented, could make "no honest claim" to being "first in the nation in significant attention to civil rights problems." The time had come for Brown to "give the remaining civil rights challenges," beginning with housing, "the same kind of leadership" in 1963 that he had given to fair employment practices in 1959.[123]

Howden knew just how to prod his boss. Beginning in the middle of 1962, he appealed to Brown's ambition to surpass New York governor Nelson Rockefeller's reputation as the nation's most progressive state chief executive. A recent

San Francisco Chronicle article, Howden wrote Brown, depicted "your civil rights stand . . . [as] 'soft' against Governor Rockefeller's." Inasmuch as a handful of states, including New York, "have added jurisdiction over most private housing, and in some instances over places of public accommodation, to their FEP Commissions," California did in fact lag behind New York. To out-do Rockefeller, Brown thus needed to "forge ahead . . . until all such essential guarantees of equal treatment and opportunity have become law."[124] Howden was not a lone voice in the administration. John Anson Ford, chair of the FEPC, echoed Howden, urging him to mark the upcoming one hundredth anniversary of the Emancipation Proclamation with a civil rights address proposing legislation to attend to the "unfinished business of this nature facing the state." In particular, he focused on California's still unfinished fair housing agenda. "Nine states," he wrote, "have housing antidiscrimination statutes significantly broader in jurisdiction than our Hawkins Housing Act, most with provision for administrative enforcement."[125]

The Governor's Advisory Commission on Housing Problems—the creation of which was the sole piece of fair housing-related legislation to emerge out of the 1961 legislative session—echoed the exhortations of Howden and Ford. Marshall Kaplan, the commission's report coordinator, stressed the need for housing legislation that reached beyond the Hawkins Fair Housing and Unruh Civil Rights acts. He also called for bringing enforcement of fair housing legislation under an administrative umbrella such as the state FEPC. In the absence of an enforcement commission for housing, "It appears that the hardship . . . associated with seeking redress through the judicial process [has] discouraged individuals from enforcing their rights, thus negating the effectiveness of the statutes." As evidence Kaplan noted that, since the establishment of California's FEPC in 1959, over 1,700 employment discrimination complaints had been lodged, whereas fewer than fifty housing discrimination cases had been brought to court.[126]

Other California officials also urged Brown to forge ahead with fair housing. In December 1962, the commissioner of the California Division of Savings and Loan lobbied Brown to harness the "full powers of his office to secure equal housing opportunities." The deputy commissioner concurred, even though he cautioned that doing so threatened to trigger "a period of heightened racial tensions, of bigot-led flareups, of pervading anxiety and uneasiness stemming from ignorance and accentuated by fear."[127]

Brown began to heed these calls. Speaking at an FEPC conference in Los Angeles in September 1962, Brown called for "new legislation against housing discrimination."[128] Though publicly Brown did not yet sketch the contours of the legislation he had in mind, privately he expressed interest "in getting up to date on New York's housing law and experience . . . [and] that, as in 1959, there will be strong legislative program offering [in 1963]." At long last, it seemed to Howden, Brown was preparing to take the battle against housing discrimination to the state legislature, rather than skirt the fight because of "estimates of legislative receptivity" (or lack thereof).[129]

By early 1963, Brown informed Assemblyman Byron Rumford that he intended to "keep abreast of and to eventually surpass the record of accomplishments of other leading states" in terms of fair housing legislation. The governor attributed his gravitation in this direction, in part, to an article by a Catholic priest on housing discrimination that Rumford had forwarded him.[130] One week later, Brown received a memorandum from aide Sherrill Luke with information on fair housing laws in eight states deemed to have more comprehensive statutes than California. "With the exception of Washington," Luke wrote, "the laws of each of these states extend to the most private housing as well as publicly assisted housing, providing for commission enforcement."[131]

Of course, extending the current fair housing legislation to the private market and giving it administrative enforcement teeth was what the CCFP had been calling for since the beginning of 1960. It was also the gist of Assemblyman Hawkins's ill-fated AB 801 in 1961. Not surprisingly, then, the CCFP once again placed fair housing atop its 1963 legislative agenda, declaring "that the top priority civil rights measure in the 1963 session of the state legislature be a comprehensive Fair Housing Act with enforcement powers." As for "all other civil rights bills," the CCFP determined once again that they "should be entirely subordinated to the strategy requirements of passing the Fair Housing Act." Nothing must "endanger the passage of the number one priority, our Fair Housing Bill."[132]

On Valentine's Day, 1963, Brown sent an impassioned "Statement on Human Rights" to the legislature. The time had come to "complete this state's unfinished business in guaranteeing equal rights and opportunity to every California citizen." After sketching some of the "great strides toward our goal of citizenship" taken during his first term—including FEP, the Unruh Civil Rights Act, and the Hawkins Fair Housing Act—Brown exhorted the legislature to go further. "The leading state in the nation"—the union's most populous and "most flourishing economy"—had much work to do for its "minority groups [who] are forced to live in ghettoes." To this end, Brown implored the legislature to "pass legislation to eliminate discrimination in the private housing market in California." Doing so was the key to ameliorating racial tensions and realizing "American principles of equality." Not doing so exacerbated "*de facto* segregation in the schools" and perpetuated ghettoization, which, in turn, bred "poverty, family breakdown, dependency and 'social dynamite.'" More than good public policy, comprehensive fair housing legislation was a moral imperative. "Join me," Brown implored California lawmakers, "in acting now to end the racial nightmare which has so long plagued our nation."[133] Brown's speech drew the praise of California's longtime leading fair housing litigator, Loren Miller, who wrote the governor that he was "particularly impressed by your forthright support for fair housing legislation" and exhorted him to "continue to exert" pressure on the legislature to take action.[134]

Working closely with Brown, Assemblyman Rumford led the fight for fair housing in legislature. Born in the territory of Arizona in 1908, Rumford graduated from a segregated Phoenix high school. He then headed to northern California. Parking cars at night to earn a living, Rumford attended the University of California, Berkeley during the day. He received his pharmacist's degree in 1931, passed the written state exam to earn his license, but failed the oral exam on numerous occasions—a ploy designed to weed out black applicants. After successfully appealing his repeated failures on the oral exam, Rumford landed a job at an Oakland hospital, becoming the first African American employed there. Later, he opened a private practice in Berkeley and became involved in local politics. During World War II, he helped organize the Berkeley Interracial Committee and came to the attention of Governor Earl Warren who appointed Rumford to the Rent Control Board. Shortly after the war, the Appomattox Club—an African American political organization—selected Rumford to make a bid for an assembly seat in the predominantly white Berkeley-Albany district. Rumford won, becoming the first ever African American state assemblyman from northern California. As an assemblyman, Rumford continued his education, earning a bachelor's in political science and master's in public administration from his alma mater. At the same time, his assembly work garnered him a reputation—alongside Los Angeles's Gus Hawkins—as the legislature's civil rights champion. In 1949 he authored a bill that ended segregation of the state's national guard. During the late 1940s and 1950s, he and Hawkins led the battle for fair employment practices. Then, in 1963, after Hawkins retired from twenty-seven years in the assembly to become the first California African American member of Congress, Rumford introduced the fair housing bill—Assembly Bill (AB) 1240—that would become synonymous with his name, as well as the year's most contentious and significant piece of legislation.[135]

The bill's provisions, for the most part, mirrored those of the failed 1961 Hawkins bill (AB 801). As fair housing advocates led by the CCFP and NAACP had been advocating since 1960, AB 1240 sought to prohibit discrimination in the sale or rental of property by owners of any housing accommodation except for "a single unit dwelling occupied in whole or in part by the owner as his residence." It would allow alleged victims of housing discrimination to bring their case before the Fair Practices Commission (the renamed Fair Employment Practices Commission). The commission would, in turn, investigate and resolve the dispute, just as it had been doing since 1959 for employment discrimination cases. For complainants, such administrative enforcement was a less costly and hence less prohibitive option than taking their case to court, which, at the time, was the only recourse available. Though some housing discrimination still fell beyond the antidiscrimination bounds of AB 1240, the bill represented a substantial winnowing away of that which was still permitted.[136]

As 1963 unfolded, Brown's commitment to fair housing deepened. When Berkeley voters defeated a local fair housing ordinance in a hotly contested vote in April—a move which boded ill for the fate of fair housing statewide—the governor urged the fair housing faithful to redouble their efforts. In letters to dismayed constituents who lamented the Berkeley vote, the governor's office responded, "The defeat of the Berkeley ordinance only makes the need for state legislation more urgent. [Governor Brown] accepts it as a greater challenge to press vigorously for a state fair housing law at this session of the Legislature."[137] Indeed, in the aftermath of the failed Berkeley fair housing bid, Brown delivered yet another message to the legislature, this time focusing exclusively on California's pressing housing problems—from construction to discrimination.[138] One month later he appeared at a legislative conference sponsored by the NAACP. Speaking from the capitol steps, Brown lobbied for passage of the AB 1240, which was then stalled in a senate committee. In June 1963, he even reached out to the White House to enlist its support against a recalcitrant state senator in whose committee AB 1240 was stuck.[139] Simply put, Brown poured himself into the fair housing campaign. As he later recalled, "I worked very, very hard for the Rumford bill. . . . I wanted to do the idealistic thing and I felt that the blacks not being able to get houses . . . was an absolute disgrace and I worked like hell. . . . Outside of the water project, I don't think I've lobbied any harder for anything than I did for the Rumford bill. I really put all my gubernatorial pressure on it."[140]

Brown's efforts received a powerful boost from the dramatic events unfolding in 1963. In California, the early part of the year witnessed a wave of protests and pickets against discrimination in businesses and government.[141] Beyond California, civil rights protesters marched in Birmingham, Alabama, where police chief Bull Connor responded to them with baton- and truncheon-wielding police officers, fire hoses, dogs, and the arrest of Martin Luther King, Jr. While in jail, King composed his "Letter from a Birmingham Jail" that stirred the conscience of the nation—and, no doubt, the governor of California. Indeed, in letters to constituents, Brown drew upon the Birmingham analogy. Though quick to acknowledge that California had a better civil rights record than

Alabama, he added, "The injustices, the indignities, and the inequalities which are at the root of what is going on in Birmingham can and do exist here, too."[142]

Meanwhile, California legislators debated and amended AB 1240 and shuttled it from committee to committee and hearing after hearing. On March 27, the bill cleared the critical assembly Committee on Governmental Efficiency. Debate lasted two-and-a-half hours before a standing-room-only audience of nearly four hundred people and featured testimony on the bill's behalf by CCFP, NAACP, AFL-CIO, and Northern California Council of Churches representatives, as well as state Attorney General Stanley Mosk. On the other side of the debate, AB 1240 opponents included, above all, leaders from the California Real Estate Association.[143]

Three weeks later, Rumford announced two significant amendments, both of which reflected lessons learned from the recently defeated Berkeley fair housing proposal. First, he excised a provision similar to one in the Berkeley ordinance that made violation of the fair housing law a misdemeanor, punishable by imprisonment and/or a fine. Second, he reduced the bill's coverage. Whereas the original iteration of AB 1240 exempted only non-publicly-assisted single-unit owner-occupied residences, the amended version exempted non-publicly-assisted dwellings of four units or fewer. According to one estimate, the amended bill covered five percent fewer homes and apartments. With these amendments, AB 1240 passed the assembly by a forty-seven (forty-four Democrats, three Republicans) to twenty-five (all Republicans) vote on April 25, 1963. From there, the bill headed to the senate, where its fate was much less certain.[144]

Rumford's bill quickly became bogged down in the same committee that had buried the Hawkins fair housing bill from 1961 (after which AB 1240 was modeled). Two anti-AB 1240 state senators—Luther Gibson and Hugh Burns—chaired and co-chaired the committee and wielded their procedural prerogatives to ensure that AB 1240 proceeded at a snail's pace.[145] Incensed by the stall tactics, members of the Congress of Racial Equality (CORE) staged a sit-in in the capitol rotunda, a round-the-clock vigil that they hoped would gird the senate into action. Rumford and his allies bemoaned the demonstration. They worried that the protesters—"those wild-and-woolies . . . lying around in the rotunda on their mattresses making threats to stay there till it's passed," as Rumford described them—would antagonize the state senators and that their tactics would in fact backfire.[146] Rumford urged the CORE protesters to "leave, leave. . . . If they were trying to help me, as far as I was concerned, this was a poor way to do it!"[147] Outside the capitol building, the NAACP-WC held a legislative conference and rally. From May 17–19, conference participants attended a luncheon honoring AB 1240's co-sponsors, lobbied legislators, and listened to a speech by Brown.[148]

These efforts, however, appeared to be for naught. On June 14—one week before the legislature's constitutionally mandated final day—the *Sacramento Bee* reported, "Chances for the enactment of a fair housing bill at this session of the legislature today were reduced to practically nil."[149] Failure to broker a compromise between Rumford and Gibson, in whose committee AB 1240 was hanging in the balance, precipitated the *Bee's* dire prediction. Rumford refused to capitulate to Gibson's demand to amend AB 1240 to limit its coverage to publicly assisted housing—an amendment that would have rendered the bill redundant with the existing Hawkins fair housing law from 1959. When Rumford did not yield, Gibson declared negotiations at an impasse.[150] Even threats from Brown— "You're not going to get your legislation through. Forget about it"—failed to prevail upon Gibson and his allies. Nor did strong-arm tactics from the White House's master arm-twister, Vice President Lyndon Johnson, who threatened Gibson, "Senator, that fair housing bill . . . ought to come out. If it doesn't, there won't be any more contracts for the Mare Island Navy Shipyard [in Gibson's district]. There won't be much work over there."[151]

Meanwhile, determined legislators operating outside the public spotlight waged a last-minute campaign to pry the bill loose from committee and move it to the entire senate. Their efforts succeeded, albeit at the price of twenty-three amendments to the bill that further reduced its coverage. On the night of June 21—the final night of the 1963 legislative session—AB 1240 emerged from committee and headed to the senate floor. So, too, however, did hundreds of other bills in the eleventh hour wrangling, and AB 1240 opponents made sure to locate the bill near the bottom of the pile.[152]

In response, AB 1240 proponents flexed their political muscles to force consideration of the fair housing bill. Speaker of the Assembly Jesse Unruh vowed, "There would be no further [Assembly] action on Senate bills until the consideration of Assembly measures [had] been completed [in the Senate]." Specifically, Unruh had AB 1240 in mind. Senator Edward Regan, an AB 1240 supporter, also played political hardball. At eleven P.M., one hour before the curtain descended upon the 1963 legislative session, he motioned to make AB 1240 a special order of business. An outmaneuvered Burns went wild. "You know that we're not supposed to do this!" he exclaimed. "It's a violation of all tradition." Tradition flouted, the senate quickly voted in favor of AB 1240 by a vote of twenty-two (all Democrats) to thirteen (two Democrats, eleven Republicans). The bill headed back to the assembly for a vote in its senate-amended form.[153] Once in the assembly, Unruh requested and received unanimous consent that AB 1240 be taken up, catapulting it past all other bills up for consideration. Shortly thereafter, as the clock ticked toward midnight, the assembly voted for the senate version of the bill by an overwhelming sixty-three (forty-eight Democrats, fifteen Republicans) to nine (nine Republicans) margin.[154]

Eagerly awaiting its passage, Brown signed the bill into law. "It was one of the great victories of my career," he recalled years later.[155] Other AB 1240 supporters spoke in similar glowing tones. Senator Joseph Rattigan located Assemblyman Rumford just after Rumford's bill cleared the senate. In a tearful embrace he confessed to Rumford, "I have just atoned for a Jim Crow boyhood."[156] If Rattigan waxed repentant over his past, John Burby, Brown's press secretary, trained his eyes on the future. Returning home after AB 1240's last-minute victory, Burby gushed to his wife, "Do you realize that our kids may very well grow up in a culture that's really color blind?"[157] Less effusive was the bill's author. For Rumford, the law was not "revolutionary," but rather a logical extension of the antidiscrimination principle embodied in the fair employment practices legislation passed four years earlier.[158] It "simply meant that a person should have the right to select people for the sale, leasing, or rental of their property based on factors other than race, color, or creed."[159] It meant, as well, as Brown's speechwriter later reflected, that "liberalism was . . . rolling, man."[160]

Though Brown, members of his administration and party, and NAACP-WC and CCFP leaders undoubtedly shared the view that "liberalism was . . . rolling" in 1963, César Chávez thought otherwise. Liberalism was certainly not rolling in the direction of the fields and orchards where the state's farm workers, whom Chávez deemed to be synonymous with the state's Mexican Americans, toiled. To improve their plight, Chávez wrote Fred Ross in January 1962 about his "latest dreams" to get the CSO "recognized as THE organization for the farm workers."[161] These dreams had been stoked by the passage of AB 5. After securing the long-sought old-age pensions for long-term resident non-citizens, Assemblyman Burton, according to Chávez, indicated that "the fight for the CSO now is the farm workers."[162] The CSO, however, thought differntly. At the organization's March 1962 convention, according to Dolores Huerta, the majority of delegates insisted that the "CSO was not a labor organization, it was a civic organization." Having realized the potential of a union in Oxnard in the late 1950s, and then having witnessed his efforts there unravel in the absence of one, Chávez knew that the time had now arrived for him to sever ties with the organization to which he had devoted the past decade. As the convention closed, he rose and said, "I have an announcement to make. I resign."[163] Dolores Huerta soon joined him.[164]

A month later, the thirty-five-year-old Chávez and his family moved from Los Angeles to Delano, north of Bakersfield in the San Joaquin Valley. He applied for unemployment, did some part time work in the fields, which made him "feel about 80 years old, like Los Viejitos that come to the CSO for Pensiones," and began organizing farm workers. Over eighty-six days in the summer of 1962, Chávez logged nearly 15,000 miles on his car as he recruited workers, deploying the intensive grassroots organizing techniques that Fred Ross had taught him in the CSO.[165]

Chávez kept Ross apprised of his progress. In May 1962 he said he would only "reconsider" returning to the CSO "when the CSO is willing to fight for field workers." In June he complained that the valley was "teeming" with "Green Card boys" (agricultural workers who commuted from Mexico), though he found it "most encouraging" that many of them were planning to "turn in their cards" and return to Mexico. In July he confessed to having "failed miserably with the Negroes and other groups," though he noted that "there aren't too many of anything else but Chicanos." In July, too, he fretted, "Trying to determine who the farm worker is [is] about as hard as it once was to isolate the atom." In August he resolved this difficulty, identifying "four major groups comprising the farm labor force in California": the "true worker," the "foreign worker," the "industrial worker" who did farm work while receiving unemployment, and the "casual worker," including wives and children of men with "nice" industrial jobs looking for "candy money during the summer" as well as "winos." Only the "true worker" interested Chávez. "All others," he insisted, "are not farm workers."[166]

Chávez's indefatigable efforts in the summer of 1962 culminated on September 30 in an abandoned Fresno theatre. Dolores Huerta led 150 farm workers and their families from fifty-five California communities in the Pledge of Allegiance, thereby opening the convention that launched the Farm Workers Association (which would become the United Farm Workers Organizing Committee in 1966 and the United Farm Workers in 1972). Convention leaders unfurled the organization's symbol: a black eagle in a white circle on a red flag designed by Chávez's brother, Richard. Manuel Chávez, a cousin, explained to the attendees, "The black eagle signified the dark situation in which the worker finds himself, the white circle signifies hope and aspirations, and the red background indicates the toil and sacrifice that the Association and its members will have to contribute in order to gain justice for farm workers."[167]

Under its banner carried by newly elected general director César Chávez, the Farm Workers Association (FWA), according to its constitution, proposed "to unite . . . all workers regardless of race, creed, or nationality, engaged in" farm labor, to secure the "right to engage in collective bargaining" in order to best negotiate hours, wages, working conditions, and labor disputes, and to "guard and further our democratic rights and to become aware of our responsibilities as citizens of the United States of America."[168] The FWA's new constitution reflected the tension over the bonds of ethnicity and the boundaries of citizenship that Chávez's predecessor, Ernesto Galarza, confronted in the 1940s and 1950s during his efforts to organize farm workers. On the one hand, the FWA's founding document spoke of uniting all workers regardless of "nationality" (as well as race and religion). This suggested a broader constituency than Chávez had targeted just a few months earlier when he distinguished between the "true" worker and the "foreign" worker and proposed to focus on the former. On the other hand, the constitution seemed to presume—or at least privilege—citizenship in its members when it spoke of "our responsibilities as citizens." Ultimately, Chávez's union would resolve this tension in a manner similar to Galarza's. It would open its doors to all farm workers, while vigilantly guarding against those, often Mexican nationals, who crossed picket lines. As Chávez chronicler Jacques Levy put it, "All were welcome . . . no questions asked. What the union would not tolerate were strike breakers, and if those were here illegally, [Chávez] felt justified in calling in the INS."[169]

Initially, Chávez sought to steer the fledgling FWA away from strikes. As he explained his recruiting approach to Ross, "I tell them that this is not a union and that we are not involved in strikes," at least not "unless we know we'll win." "A union which tries to organize via the strike route," Chávez believed, "is kidding itself and discouraging workers." For farm workers who wondered what Chávez was then proposing they join, if not a union, Chávez replied, "This is a movement."[170] In this way, Chávez, like Galarza before him, sought to link civil rights and labor rights. He drew parallels between California's "rural Mexican people" and "Mississippi Negroes."[171] More substantively, he called for a "bill of rights for farm workers," which included minimum wage, unemployment insurance, and collective bargaining.[172] The FWA, he announced, had "unanimously voted to establish a minimum wage of $1.50 per hour" as well as "to seek unemployment compensation" for agricultural laborers. These measures became the FWA's top legislative priorities for the 1963 session in California, the same session in which Governor Brown, Assemblyman Rumford, the NAACP-WC, and CCFP, among others, would make fair housing legislation their top civil rights goal. As for collective bargaining, Chávez calculated that it would be best to wait for some other year when the political climate was more conducive and the organization better "set to take advantage of it."[173]

In the meantime, Chávez and Huerta lobbied for the FWA's legislation of choice while recruiting members. To this end, they journeyed to Sacramento where they met with various administrative officials and legislators to press "the great and immediate needs of the Farm Workers and how important it is for them to have the minimum wage and unemployment compensation." They initiated a petition drive hoping to secure "at least 100,000 signatures." They contemplated a letter-writing campaign to "raise cain." Beyond the drive for minimum wage and unemployment insurance, the FWA sent a group of sixty members to Sacramento to fight against the importation of workers from Mexico and urged California's congressional delegation to vote against extending PL 78, the Bracero Program.[174]

Their efforts, however, came to naught. Shortly after the 1963 legislative session began, the executive vice president of the Council of California Growers informed his organization's members and allies, "Governor Brown has assured us he is not in favor of a minimum wage for farm workers." Moreover, "The governor also says . . . he favors a two year extension of Public Law 78, the bracero program."[175] Brown's opposition to a minimum wage for farm workers represented a continued abdication of a 1959 inaugural address promise, while his support for extending the Bracero Program represented an affirmation of a 1962 campaign promise. On the latter, Brown not only issued an April 1963 call to Washington, D.C. to add two more years to the life of the two decade old Bracero Program, but he also dispatched his director of employment to Congress, where he testified that California would "face rather serious labor shortages in many crop activities if Congress fails to extend the (bracero) law."[176] Brown's efforts, he asserted in a speech to the Agricultural Council of California in May 1963, demonstrated how his campaign "pledge is being kept. I have informed Congress and President Kennedy's administration that California needs a two-year extension of the law."[177] They also provided comfort to growers who anticipated "measures that will make your hair stand on end" in the 1963 legislative session given changes in the composition of the state senate labor committee.[178] As for unemployment insurance for farm workers, Brown never had to take a stand. Though a bill introduced by Burton in 1963 passed the assembly—"the first piece of legislature [sic] extending these benefits to farm workers" ever to make it this far, according to Burton—it died in the senate.[179]

As the 1963 legislative session unfolded, Speaker of the Assembly Unruh told Chávez to prepare for disappointment on the farm labor-related bills that Chávez and his fledgling FWA wanted. As Chávez wrote Huerta about a "bull session" he had with "Big Daddy" (a nickname for Unruh) in April 1963, "He is certain that nothing can be done [legislatively for farm workers] until senate make up is materially improved. . . . Says he will work for both Unemployment and Minimum wage but senate will not pass it." However, Chávez hastened to add, "I don't think he is hot on this." Chávez then sought to reassure Huerta and encourage her to redouble her organizing efforts, "Don't worry your head on account of the Farm labor legislation. We won't get anything anyway and even if we did, it wouldn't be fair because the people haven't worked for it" like they had worked for "pensions." The task at hand, then, was to build membership. "Without that," he asserted, "we haven't got anything and we are nothing."[180]

While Chávez exhorted Huerta to organize, he implored Brown and his fellow Democrats to act on behalf of farm workers. Just one month after Brown delivered his February 1963 "Statement on Human Rights" in which he called for passage of what would eventually become the Rumford Fair Housing Act, Chávez wrote Brown, "Recognizing that the farm worker has neither the power nor wealth with which to make its demands heard, we appeal to you, praying that at great personal sacrifice you will make a decision to carry the legislative banner on behalf of these workers and families."[181] At the same time, Chávez lobbied other Democratic state legislators. "The farm worker," he declared, "is synonymous with the Mexican-American in California, and the Mexican-American voter is synonymous with the Democratic party in California." Though the Democrats led by Brown and backed by the NAACP and CCFEP/CCFP had passed civil rights laws between 1959 and 1963, which Brown detailed in his "Statement on Human Rights," only one of these—old-age pensions for long-term resident non-citizens—corresponded to the leading legislative priorities laid out by Chávez, the FWA, and the CSO in 1950s and early 1960s. Their other legislative goals—minimum wage, unemployment insurance, and collective bargaining for farm workers, as well as an end to bracero importation—still remained unfulfilled. Not surprisingly, then, Chávez wondered, "When will the Mexican-American and other farm workers receive some meaningful legislation from those Democrats whom they so loyally support year in and year out?"[182]

Chávez's disaffection with Brown and the Democrats resonated with other Mexican American leaders and organizations. In February 1963, for example, just one day before Brown issued his "Statement on Human Rights," *Los Angeles Times* correspondent Ruben Salazar reported that the organization that "spearheaded the governor's campaign among Spanish-speaking groups" in 1962—the Mexican-American Committee to Re-elect Gov. Brown—had reconstituted itself as the Mexican-American Citizens Committee of California and charged Brown with not appointing enough Mexican Americans to key positions. In response, the new committee threatened to launch a campaign, this time to "change the registration of Mexican-Americans from Democrats to Republicans . . . 'unless the governor keeps his promises.'"[183] Julius Castelan, president of MAPA, levied the same charge and, implicitly, threat. "Our percentage of voters in the state," he said in reference to Mexican Americans, "is higher than any other minority group," yet Brown "has not appointed anywhere near the percentage."[184]

Brown's Mexican American executive secretary, Arthur Alarcon, issued a press release, insisting that Brown "has more than kept his promises to the minorities in California." As evidence, Alarcon pointed to "the governor's record on human rights legislation [which] speaks for itself." In particular, Alarcon noted Brown's support for "this state's first Fair Employment Practices Commission," as well as his support for "a broad new program for human rights to eliminate discrimination in housing and other areas," which Brown intended to propose to the legislature the following day. As for appointments of Mexican Americans, Alarcon maintained that Brown doled these out "on the basis of the individual's qualifications and the position's requirement." Anything else would amount to "a 'quota' system," which "would lead to the very worst kind of patronage and spoils."[185]

Not surprisingly, Alarcon's press release made no mention of the absence of a Mexican American commissioner on the state FEPC. Nor, for that matter, did it make mention—for none could be made—of Brown's record on farm-labor-related legislation, focusing instead on what he had done for fair employment practices and what he intended to do on fair housing as the core of Brown's "human rights" record. By 1963, this particular understanding of civil rights joined the issue of appointments (or lack of them) as a source of friction between Brown, his administration, and their Democratic supporters, on the one hand, and Mexican American leaders, on the other hand. As the *Los Angeles Times*'s Salazar reported in October 1963, "Mexican-American leaders—a highly individualistic and faction-ridden breed"—had achieved a "new" degree of unanimity in their opposition to the Bracero Program, in particular, and "support for domestic agricultural workers," in general. As evidence, Salazar pointed to an August 1963 meeting in Los Angeles between a group of "50 Mexican-American leaders" and Vice President Johnson, Governor Brown, Senator Clair Engle, and a handful of California members of Congress. There, all but one of the Mexican American leaders endorsed the anti-bracero, pro-domestic agricultural worker message: "the bracero program must end because it's taking jobs away from our people." This message and the novel near consensus with which it was delivered, Salazar maintained, reflected how the plight of "domestic agricultural workers" provided "the one common issue throughout the Southwest" for Mexican American leaders to unite around. For "like the Negroes in the South, the Mexican-Americans in the Southwest (especially California and Texas) comprise most of the domestic agricultural workers."[186]

If Chávez—and other Mexican American leaders—expressed doubts about the California Democratic Party's legislative plans for farm workers, Unruh confirmed them. The Speaker of the Assembly advised Chávez to persuade farm workers to register to vote as Republicans in order to pressure the Democrats. "It is only by punishing your friends," Unruh told Chávez, "that you get something from them."[187] Unruh's advice echoed the course of action that

MAPA president Castelan, as well as the Mexican-American Citizens Committee of California, urged Mexican Americans to take in February 1963, albeit in response to the Democrat's inaction on appointments, rather than on farm labor.

While Unruh suggested that one solidly Democratic constituency break ranks in order to exert pressure on the party to pass farm labor related legislation, he worried that another solidly Democratic constituency might do precisely that if the party's fair housing legislation passed. As veteran California political reporter—and Unruh biographer—Bill Boyarsky described Unruh's concerns about the Rumford fair housing bill in the spring of 1963, "He knew that the white union members, an essential component of the [New Deal] coalition . . ., would tolerate no state interference in what they considered their right to keep their neighborhoods white." The failure of the Berkeley fair housing ordinance in April 1963—in which over ninety percent of the city's black residents voted in favor, while sixty-three percent of white residents voted in opposition—only reinforced Unruh's worries. As the Berkeley vote approached, Unruh urged his fellow Democrats, "If Berkeley residents repealed that city's fair housing ordinance in a referendum on April 2 the 'legislature should take a long look at the state level. If it is defeated badly it may well be a warning sign.'"[188]

In the end, Unruh supported the Rumford bill. When it passed, however, his reservations remained. As Brown adviser Richard Kline recalled, "Jesse cautioned that this thing might reverberate against us, people weren't ready for this."[189] Unruh's concerns stood in marked contrast to the euphoria that characterized so many of his fellow Democrats. Taken together, Unruh's advice to Chávez and his apprehensions about the Rumford Fair Housing Act underscored the fragility of the "coalition" of "labor" and "minorities" that Fred Dutton forecasted in 1960 to last for "many years."[190] Put another way, if liberalism was rolling in one direction in California during the years 1959 to 1963, it was not rolling in the direction that Chávez and an increasing number of Mexican American leaders wanted to see it rolling. Moreover, with the passage of the Rumford Fair Housing Act, it would soon be rolling off a cliff.

CHAPTER 7

"THE DEMOCRATIC . . . SPLINTERING"

As 1963 drew to a close, Governor Brown wrote his Alabama counterpart, George Wallace. Still riding high from the passage of the Rumford Fair Housing Act, Brown contrasted California's race relations with Alabama's and extended an invitation to the Alabama governor. "One of these days, come out to California," Brown urged Wallace, "where we have a very substantial minority population consisting of Negroes, Mexican-Americans, Japanese and Chinese and we work side by side, go to school side by side, and nobody thinks a single, solitary thing about it."[1] Curiously, given California's recently passed fair housing legislation, Brown omitted "live side by side" from this list. Perhaps the oversight was unwitting. Or perhaps it was intentional, for at the very moment when Brown was beckoning Wallace to California to marvel at the state's racial harmony, a grassroots movement to nullify the recently passed fair housing law and amend the state constitution to forbid the passage of similar measures was spreading like a Santa Ana wind-stoked wildfire.

The California Real Estate Association (CREA) spearheaded this drive. They blanketed the state with petitions and within three months secured some 767,000 signatures in support of submitting what would become known as Proposition 14 (or, Prop 14) to a November 1964 vote. For Brown, Prop 14 was "one of the most dangerous and inflammatory initiatives I have ever seen."[2] Martin Luther King, Jr. insisted that passage of Prop 14 would mark "one of the great tragedies of the 20th century."[3] *Time* magazine described Prop 14 as a "bitterly fought issue," and added that the 1964 presidential race between Lyndon Johnson and Barry Goldwater was, by comparison, a "relatively piddling contest."[4] Prop 14 and Goldwater, opponents of both believed, were cut from the same repugnant cloth. Defeat of one, therefore, did not make sense without defeat of the other. Linking the two at the Democratic National Convention in Atlantic City in August 1964, Brown vowed, "We will defeat Proposition 14 and we will elect Lyndon Johnson. But we will do so only if we remember that these two goals are inseparable, and remain aware that bigotry, racism, and Goldwaterism feed on one another, and lead to the destruction of Democratic politics."[5]

Brown was only half right. On November 3, 1964, in what struck the California governor and numerous other Prop 14 opponents as a case of ideological schizophrenia, Californians cast ballots in the same overwhelming numbers *against* Goldwater as they did *for* Prop 14. The crushing defeat of fair housing befuddled and dismayed the Rumford Fair Housing Act's supporters led by Brown, the NAACP-WC, and CCFP. In their estimation, passage of Prop 14 not only bucked historical trends and defied political odds, but also flouted logic and moral decency. Many of the same Californians who had earlier embraced antidiscrimination legislation in employment and businesses recoiled at the prospect of extending antidiscrimination legislation into segments of the private housing market. What fair housing proponents touted as the next logical step down the civil rights road that the state had been traveling since litigating away legalized segregation in the late 1940s, a sizeable majority of the state's voters viewed as a step too far. With Prop 14, they served notice about just how much civil rights they would tolerate.

Two years later, Californians catapulted Ronald Reagan into the governor's office. Reagan's trouncing of Brown owed in good measure to Reagan's support of Prop 14, which the California Supreme Court overturned in May 1966, to the outrage of millions of voters. While Reagan campaigned against fair housing, and for the disgruntled white voters—especially white working class voters—who supported Prop 14, he also campaigned for a growing number of Mexican American voters for whom the Brown administration had proven to be a disappointment on a host of other issues unrelated to fair housing. In his pursuit of these two disproportionately Democratic constituencies, Reagan targeted two of the four groups that Brown's human rights adviser, William Becker, identified in 1965 as "the base of any Democratic vote and the possibilities of any Democratic victory" (the other two being African Americans and Jews).[6] In the process, Reagan exploited fissures in the Democratic base that were evident from the beginning of Brown's administration with Mexican Americans and exploded to the fore in the aftermath of the Rumford Fair Housing Act with white laborers.

Members of the California Real Estate Association (CREA) did not just sell houses. They promoted "American ideals and free institutions," as their leaders put it. With over 40,000 members drawn from 171 local real estate boards, CREA claimed to be the state's guardian of the "basic human right of private ownership of property." No right, the association believed, did more to promote America's "great social progress." No right was more sacred, and, by the fall of 1963, no right was more imperiled.[7] CREA president L.H. "Spike" Wilson invoked Lincoln at Gettysburg to emphasize the gravity of the "great battle for liberty and freedom" in which his organization was involved. "We are engaged in a great war over civil rights," he declared. Wilson did not have Bull Connor and Birmingham in mind, but rather Governor Brown, Assemblyman Rumford, and the Rumford Fair Housing Act. Could "equal rights for all . . . be achieved without losing freedom of choice, freedom of association and the sacrifice of private property rights," Wilson asked rhetorically.[8] His question revealed the tension between the quest for antidiscrimination, on the one hand, and the protection of private property, on the other hand, that figured prominently in California's heated political and legal battles over fair housing in the 1960s.

The Rumford Act, which went into effect on September 20, 1963, covered two new segments of the California housing market: owner-occupied, single-family homes that were "financed in whole or in part by a loan . . . which is guaranteed or insured" by federal or state government, and apartments in buildings containing five or more units, regardless of how they were financed.[9] The law charged the state FEPC with the responsibility "to receive, investigate and pass upon verified complaints alleging discrimination in housing accommodations . . . because of race, religious creed, color, national origin or ancestry." Where probable cause for unlawful practices was found, the FEPC sought to resolve complaints through "conference, conciliation, and persuasion." If this failed, a public hearing was to be conducted before a panel of FEPC commissioners, where a handful of potential remedies existed.[10] In this way, the Rumford Act offered victims of housing discrimination a cheaper, faster, and more accessible alternative to litigation.

Before the Rumford Act, owners of single-family homes—including those receiving government backed mortgages—were free to dispose of their property as they saw fit. After its passage, some of that freedom was restricted. According to one study, the Rumford Act brought approximately 950,000 (or, roughly twenty-five percent) of the 3,779,000 single-family homes in the state within its purview. All told, the Rumford Act covered about one-third of the state's housing, leaving the other two-thirds uncovered. The uncovered swaths included, most significantly, owner-occupied single-family homes that were not "financed in whole or in part by a loan . . . which is guaranteed or insured" by federal or state government (approximately seventy-five percent of the single-family homes), as well as apartments in duplexes, triplexes, and fourplexes (approximately fifty percent, or 800,000, of the non-single-family residences). Even with the Rumford Act, then, the bulk of California home and apartment owners remained free to discriminate on the basis of race when selling or leasing.[11]

Though Rumford Act supporters viewed the legislation as a modest extension of the antidiscrimination principle embodied in the existing fair employment practices and fair housing legislation, the law's opponents found nothing modest about it. Indeed, a little over a month after the law went into effect in

November 1963, CREA announced the creation of Americans to Outlaw Forced Housing an umbrella organization led by CREA, which also included the California Apartment Home Owners Association and the California Home Builders. Two days later, the new organization received permission from the California Office of the Attorney General to begin gathering the requisite signatures to place what would eventually become Prop 14 on the November 1964 ballot.[12]

The proposed initiative sought to modify the state constitution. It would add a provision stipulating, "Neither the State nor any subdivision or agency thereof shall deny, limit or abridge, directly or indirectly, the right of any person, who is willing or desires to sell, lease or rent any part or all of his real property, to decline to sell, lease or rent such property to such person or persons as he, in his absolute discretion, chooses." In other words, neither the state nor its local subsidiaries, could infringe upon the right of private property owners to dispose of their property as they saw fit. As the California Office of Legislative Counsel explained in February 1964, "What the measure does is to prohibit the State (including the legislative, executive, and judicial branches thereof)" from "denying, limiting, or abridging the right of a *private individual or entity to decline to sell, lease, or rent his residential real property* to such person or persons as he chooses."[13] The key word here was "private." Prop 14 did not threaten to undo civil rights legislation that California courts had interpreted as forbidding discrimination practiced by real estate brokers and housing tract developers; these, the California Supreme Court had recently ruled, were "businesses" open to the public and, therefore, encompassed by the 1959 Unruh Civil Rights Act. Prop 14, however, did propose to nullify provisions of the Rumford Fair Housing Act that outlawed discrimination practiced by owners of owner-occupied, single-family homes with government-backed mortgages.

As an amendment initiative, rather than a referendum, Prop 14 would not formerly repeal the Rumford Act. It would, however, nullify the Rumford Act and amend the state constitution to preclude the passage or enforcement of any state or local ordinances similar to the Rumford Act, unless the amendment was first repealed through another amendment. With Prop 14, according to its supporters, Californians would reclaim what the legislators had taken. As CREA's president put it, "A mandate from the voters of California will provide a permanent settlement for the forced housing law . . . [and] return control of private property once again to the individual home owners of California."[14]

Having received the go-ahead from the attorney general in November 1963, Americans to Outlaw Forced Housing began gathering the requisite signatures to qualify the proposed initiative for the November 1964 ballot.[15] During the signature-gathering drive, Prop 14 leaders established the themes that suffused their campaign over the course of the next year. Above all else, they claimed to be fighting to protect Californians from the evils of "forced housing." Private property owners, they insisted, had an unfettered right to choose to whom to sell, rent, or lease their property. As a *California Real Estate Magazine* (of CREA) editorial entitled "The Forced Housing Issue" attempted to frame the issue, "What possible authority could anyone have to knock on a property owner's door and demand that he be selected as the one with whom to deal, simply because he desires that particular property?" The Rumford Act violated "the most fundamental right Americans enjoy—the right to own property, to use it as they see fit, and to dispose of it without governmental interference." A vote for Prop 14 was a vote to "restore the right of choice to the property owner in this state."[16]

Prop 14 supporters also invoked the Fourteenth Amendment's equal protection clause and, more generally, appropriated civil rights rhetoric. The Rumford Act did "not treat all of our citizens equally," the *California Real Estate Magazine* proclaimed. Rather, "It grant[ed] special privilege to those who want to buy, rent, or lease."[17] Thus, the fair housing law overstepped the bounds of anti-discrimination, becoming a form of discrimination itself. "It is a dangerous precedent when one group is conceded rights over others because of an accident of birth or belief," declared a CREA editorial.[18] When Congress of Racial Equality (CORE) activists picketed CREA offices in Los Angeles to protest the realtors' amendment initiative, CREA president Wilson accused them of hypocrisy. How "ironic," he seethed, "that an organization that uses the word 'equality' in its name should be picketing us." Whereas CREA endeavored to "restore equality for all citizens of California in the sales and rentals of residential property," Wilson continued, fair housing supporters, like CORE, sought to "perpetuate racial discrimination in favor of so-called minority races and against other Americans."[19]

Touting these themes, local real estate boards from across the state quickly drummed up the necessary signatures to qualify their amendment initiative for the California ballot. In January 1964, the *California Real Estate Magazine* reported, "95% of the people approached are willing and eager to sign the petitions."[20] By February, an armored vehicle deposited the petitions bearing signatures of the necessary half million voters—plus another quarter million for good measure—at the California Secretary of State's office in Sacramento. The *California Real Estate Magazine* declared this "the largest number of signatures on petitions ever submitted on a first filing."[21]

Despite its supporters' convictions, a Las Vegas handicapper would have been hard-pressed to give anything but extremely long odds for the passage of Prop 14. A glance at the raw number of prominent individuals and organizations arrayed on either side of the Prop 14 battle line suggested a mismatch of

David-and-Goliath proportions. On paper at least, the Prop 14 forces appeared hopelessly outgunned. They were initially little more than a smattering of angry and anxious realtors, apartment owners, and tract developers. Later, the 6,000-member United Republicans of California announced its support for the initiative. So, too, did the American Council of Christian Churches of California, an organization embracing fifteen Protestant fundamentalist denominations. Whereas the Republican group invoked libertarian ideals in defense of its opposition to fair housing legislation, the American Council of Christian Churches invoked the Old Testament. The Rumford Act did not simply raise the specter of a police state wielding a legislative baton to beat back the rights of property owners and, in the process, pummel the Constitution, but it also violated one of the Ten Commandments: "The right of private property is a human right required by the commandment, 'Thou shall not steal,' and is absolutely fundamental to all other rights guaranteed in the Bill of Rights."[22]

Shortly after CREA launched its attack on the Rumford Act, Speaker of the Assembly Jesse Unruh warned that the Prop 14 campaign would "sow the dragon's teeth of hate and suspicion."[23] As the campaign gathered momentum, Unruh's dire prognostication seemed to be coming to fruition. In January 1964, the National States' Rights Party of California threw its support behind the effort to undo fair housing legislation—a position that stood alongside the party's endorsement of "complete separation of all non-Whites and dissatisfied racial minorities from our White Folk Community," deporting African Americans to Africa, and restricting immigration to whites only.[24] In February 1964, William Shearer, a leading figure in the initiative movement, endorsed the "right to discriminate . . . We may question [the] wisdom to do so, but not [the] right."[25] Three months later, the *New York Times* reported that "extreme right-wing organizations have attached themselves" to the pro-Prop 14 forces. For example, Shearer, the *Times* revealed, had also written numerous anti-civil rights tracts in *The Citizen*, voice of the Mississippi White Citizens Councils.[26]

In response, opponents of Prop 14 mocked the initiative's supporters and derided their motives. They ridiculed them as "crackpots for housing," victimized by a "conspiracy of ignorance," and peddling a "hate" / "segregation" amendment that would place California in the company of Mississippi.[27] Cooler heads and kinder hearts, fair housing advocates predicted in late 1963 and early 1964, would undoubtedly prevail. The *San Francisco Chronicle*, for example, declared, "We have never believed California voters would approve the repeal of the Rumford law if it were put to them by an initiative on the ballot."[28] Assemblyman Rumford concurred. "When people understand the law," he believed, "they will reject the petition presented by the CREA."[29] California Attorney General Stanley Mosk voiced an equally hopeful sentiment. California voters, he was convinced, would spurn the initiative and "stay in the 20th Century."[30] More than hopeful, Brown speechwriter Lu Haas recalled being downright dismissive. "I was unaware that the Rumford Fair Housing [Act] was controversial in the beginning" except among the realtors, Haas explained. "But then, that was only the real estate lobby . . . . Nobody had any respect for those assholes."[31]

Though confident that Prop 14 would suffer defeat, Prop 14 opponents did not take that outcome for granted. On the contrary, from the moment CREA launched its crusade against "forced housing," their opponents vowed to "do everything that can be done on all fronts to fight the initiative to the death!"[32] To this end, they assembled a political strategist's dream team coalition. Leaders of Californians Against Proposition 14 hailed from almost every liberal, labor, civil rights, and religious organization in the state. "I am most encouraged by the broad support we are attracting," reported one anti-Prop 14 activist to Governor Brown. "We will, I am convinced, receive endorsements from 90 percent of California's leaders—political, social, intellectual, business, church, labor, professional."[33]

This ostensibly formidable coalition even included moderate Republicans, like Caspar Weinberger, chair of the Republican State Central Committee. Weinberger urged his fellow GOP-mates to steer clear from endorsing Prop 14, which threatened to trigger a political backlash as happened in 1958 when the "right-to-work initiative [Proposition 18] brought out an unusually large . . . anti-Republican vote."[34] In October 1964, Weinberger joined two hundred other Republican leaders in forming Republicans in Opposition to Proposition 14. Rather than remaining on the fringe of the struggle, registering at best silent disapproval, Weinberger and Republicans in Opposition to Proposition 14 allied with many of their erstwhile rivals in pressing for the initiative's defeat. The party of Lincoln, they maintained, must combat the scourge of racial segregation that passage of Prop 14 portended. Moreover, they must defend basic Republican principles of governance, including the right and duty of elected representatives—and not a plebiscite of the people—to enact legislation such as the Rumford Fair Housing Act. "The passage of this Initiative," the Republican anti-Prop 14 organization declared, "would be a severe blow to the efforts of responsible leaders who are attempting to solve our racial problems through voluntary action or in our legislative halls and our courts."[35] California Republican United States Senator Thomas Kuchel minced fewer words. Passage of Prop 14, he pronounced, would "mock the American Constitution and American conscience."[36] Even some GOP leaders who had voted against the Rumford Act refused to endorse Prop 14. State Senator Hugh Burns, for example, implored voters to give the new law a trial period, to "determine once and for all whether it creates any unreasonable hardships as well as whether it does aid minority groups in finding decent housing."[37]

The fault line that Prop 14 cut through the California GOP even ran through the ranks of California's realtors, Prop 14's most likely supporters. Leading Brown administration officials detected such rumblings almost from the moment that CREA launched its initiative. In October 1963, William Becker observed "considerable confusion" among realtors about the direction their organization was headed. This confusion, Becker believed, presented a good opportunity to persuade rank-and-file realtors to "back away from their leaderships' position to a more rational one."[38] One month later Edward Howden, chief of the California Division of Fair Employment Practices, offered a similar assessment: "There seems to be, among some homebuilders, less than full enthusiasm for the costly ballot initiative to which their state organizations appear to be committed."[39] The San Francisco Realtors for No on 14 confirmed the impressions of Becker and Howden, blasting CREA for "discredit[ing] . . . the entire industry."[40]

Some apartment owners and builders also opposed Prop 14. A Los Angeles apartment owner cajoled his peers to give the Rumford Fair Housing Act a chance before attacking it.[41] A Sacramento developer admonished Prop 14 proponents for launching California down a path of "racial and religious warfare."[42] A Palo Alto homebuilder encouraged Brown to "brandish the supporters of the initiative as extremists or irresponsible real estate brokers."[43]

Other anti-Prop 14 coalition members included prominent labor leaders and organizations. The California AFL-CIO viewed Prop 14 as the "most important single issue" in California politics in 1964. The president of the California Building and Construction Trades Council fretted that Prop 14 would result in the withdrawal of federal housing funds, which would, in turn, cost his union jobs. He pledged to lead "an all-out fight to defeat this scheme to ban fair housing for all."[44] A leader of the California Labor Federation warned that passage of Prop 14 loomed as the "greatest set-back [to California labor] since [the 1947] Taft-Hartley [Act]."[45] California Teamsters Union officials also urged their members to reject Prop 14.[46]

So, too, did California religious leaders. "By signing such a petition," the *Catholic Voice* of the Oakland Diocese instructed parishioners, "you will be taking a giant step backwards from the road to community peace and understanding."[47] The Western Association of Reform Rabbis denounced the initiative as "contrary to the religious ideals of brotherhood, justice and equality."[48] Over one thousand southern California Protestant clergy members formed Protestant Clergy Against Proposition 14, which declared, "Not even Mississippi or Alabama have such a Constitutional provision," and noted the unprecedented "unanimity [against Prop 14] among religious organizations (Catholic, Protestant, Jewish and others)."[49]

In a memo to Brown, Haas marveled at the "diversity of individuals and organizations in opposition to [Prop] 14."[50] Richard Kline, a Brown adviser and director of Californians Against Prop 14, described the coalition as "probably the greatest organization put together for a California political campaign."[51] Similarly, Becker recalled, "There were more people involved in the [anti-Prop 14 campaign] than almost any other issue that I have watched."[52] The Prop 14 foes had indeed assembled a seemingly unbeatable coalition.

The diversity of Prop 14 opponents was matched by the plethora of arguments they deployed. A July 1964 Californians Against Proposition 14 progress report delineated at least eleven arguments, insisting that they "all . . . must be used for all groups."[53] As early as October 1963, Howden sketched many of these arguments in an impassioned speech delivered to the California Apartment Owners' Association's convention in San Diego. Howden's address came on the heels of CREA's pledge to launch its amendment initiative. He hoped to dissuade the Apartment Owners' Association from allying with CREA. To this end, he began by stressing the moderate, middle-class nature of the Rumford Act. Since World War II, California had experienced unprecedented economic and population growth. As a consequence, a new middle-class was emerging with two distinctive characteristics. First, its members were increasingly white-collar and, second, they were increasingly non-white. Though distinguished by color, creed, and/or culture, class bound these new non-white, white-collar Californians with their white, white-collar counterparts. As middle-class mates, it was only fitting to grant them equal treatment in the sale or rental of property. "You many not have met them before," Howden remarked, "because Californians who are Negro, or Mexican-American, or of Japanese or Chinese or Filipino or Indian descent, have generally been excluded from the social and economic life. . . . Now, however, they are entering the better careers, and the time has come for them to have access to the good homes." To the extent that Apartment Owners' Association members equated non-white with poor, Howden's first line of defense for Rumford Act was to drive a wedge into that thinking—to soothe their class anxieties. They must only "open the doors" of their apartments to "qualified minority families" in order to comply with the law. Howden referred the apartment owners to an FEPC publication entitled "Success Story." "My purpose in giving you this pamphlet," he explained, "is simply to introduce to you, by way of pictures, a cross-section of minority individuals who are employed in good positions today in California." He urged his audience to "look at their faces, check their jobs and their demeanor." It was these upwardly mobile "minority individuals" who had the means to rent apartments and buy houses in places where the "doors have usually been closed to them." Surely, the apartment owners had nothing to fear from them.

Howden next sought to reframe CREA's approach to the question of just whose property rights were being gored by the new fair housing legislation. Fair housing opponents tended to reduce property rights to the right to *dispose* of one's property as one saw fit. Howden agreed, but added that the right to property also included the right to *acquire* property, and that the right to acquire property free from discrimination superseded the right to dispose of property. He explained, "The right to secure [that is, to acquire] . . . property is a vital human right . . . [that] cannot be a right for white folks only—unless we wish to be classed as liars and hypocrites who pay no more than lip service to the principles of free enterprise and equality of opportunity for all."

Howden then directed his audience's attention to California's experience with fair employment practices legislation. Opponents of fair employment practices legislation had once trotted out arguments similar to those being bandied about by fair housing opponents. Their fears, however, proved unfounded. "Business activity has soared. New industry continues to come into the State, and existing industry has expanded. . . . Customers quietly accept good service from Negro, Oriental, and Mexican American sales personnel." No evidence existed of "forced hiring" or FEPC "harassment of business." Fair housing opponents should heed these lessons.

As his address built toward its conclusion, Howden revealed the anger that roiled up inside him as he contemplated what he took to be the real motives driving the amendment initiative. CREA's purported defense of white picket fences was in fact a defense of lily-white neighborhoods. "When you read and re-read the CREA statement of last week," Howden inveighed, "it becomes unmistakably clear that when the gentlemen speak of the property rights 'of every person' they mean every *white* person, no more and no less. For they know full well that nonwhite Americans in our State are generally unable to acquire or occupy housing as are other citizens." As such, the campaign against the recently enacted fair housing legislation threatened to roll back the significant strides that had been taken since World War II to give, "the Negro his long-overdue full citizenship!" He then concluded with the warning, "The turmoil in community and race relations which would boil to a fever pitch during the mass campaign . . . would leave scars for years to come."[54]

Besides articulating many of the basic arguments advanced by Prop 14 foes, Howden's speech also reflected a tension that cut through the entire anti-14 campaign: how to balance between "arguments appeal[ing] to the intellect, to the heart, and the viscera . . . i.e., from head to gut."[55] To be sure, opponents of Prop 14 utilized numerous arguments from the "head." Above all, they stressed that the Rumford Act was, at most, a "moderate, fair, and workable" extension of existing laws, as Unruh characterized it.[56] As evidence, FEPC commissioner Carmen Warschaw observed that only 159 complaints about the Rumford Act had been filed during the law's first ten months on the books, the vast majority of which involved segments of the housing market in which pre-Rumford Act legislation proscribed discrimination. From this she concluded, "To say that the fair housing law 'invades the rights' of individual home owners [as did Prop 14 proponents] is nonsense."[57] The facts belied such inflammatory rhetoric. The second main argument from the "head" revolved around recasting the property rights argument advanced by Prop 14 proponents. Echoing Howden from the year before on this point, the state real estate commissioner expressed this alternative, more robust reading of property rights when he insisted, "One cannot dispose of property unless one has property."[58] For this reason, the right to acquire property free from racial, religious, or national origin-based discrimination was, according to California's attorney general, "the most basic of all property rights."[59] A third argument from the "head" stressed the threat to representative government posed by Prop 14. It would "void in one fell swoop laws arrived at through representative governmental processes." Moreover, it would amend the California Constitution to prevent state and local government from taking similar steps to combat housing discrimination. As a result of Prop 14, "All levels of government . . . would be unable to take affirmative action against discrimination in the rental or sale of housing." Consequently, "This is not just a fight of civil rights," declared the CCFP, but rather one over the viability of representative democracy itself.[60]

As the campaign unfolded, however, arguments from the "head" were dwarfed by those from the "gut," becoming more like the occasional rattle of small munitions fire punctuating the din of heavy artillery bombardment. Prop 14 foes cast their effort as a morality play, pitting the forces of "right and tolerance," in the words of one gubernatorial aide, against those of "hate and bigotry."[61] What began as an attack on recently enacted fair housing legislation by what appeared to be a hopelessly outgunned cabal of real estate agents quickly evolved into a crusade.

Anti-Prop 14 campaign materials reflected this moralistic tone. Pamphlets with images of Abraham Lincoln and John F. Kennedy adorning their covers urged voters, "Don't Legalize Hate: No on 14."[62] Fliers drew attention to the "bigots," "racists," "extremists," and other "opponents of democracy" who supported Prop 14, including the White Citizens Council, American Nazi Party, National State's Right Party, "anti-Catholic" American Council of Christian Churches, "ultra-right wing" United Republicans of California, and John Birch Society.[63] They attacked the "Jim Crow Wall" that Prop 14 "segregationists" sought to erect with their "segregation Amendment" that would "legalize racism" and render California worse than Mississippi, which lacked such a restriction. A Jewish Federation Council of Greater Los Angeles pamphlet recalled "when 'restricted' meant: For Rent—No Jews or Dogs Allowed."[64] A Japanese American Citizens League advertisement bearing the picture of a Japanese American girl clutching a doll invoked World War II internment: "She can't remember 1942. But you can. . . . Remember how it felt to be unfairly and illegally segregated. . . . For ourselves and for our children, prevent legalized racism in housing. Fight now against Proposition 14."[65] A Mexican American Political Association publication insisted, "Discrimination and Segregation is Aimed at Us!! Vote No on 14."[66] "Catholics Against Proposition 14" cited Pope John XXIII, the prophet Isaiah, and Saints Paul, John, and Matthew in a pamphlet excoriating Prop 14 as, among other things, "immoral," "un-Christian," and "un-American." Catholics had a "moral obligation" to not commit the "ERROR OF CONSCIENCE" that a vote for Prop 14 would represent.[67]

Anti-Prop 14 leaders who canvassed the state were equally outraged. Howden described the measure as an "open declaration of war upon the legitimate housing aspirations of at least three million Californians who are of nonwhite or Mexican American identity."[68] FEPC commissioner John Anson Ford urged Becker to press "the moral issue presented by racial discrimination" in order to coax "the majority of Protestants to our side," including the conservative Republicans among them.[69] Becker exhorted Brown to accentuate "THE MORAL ISSUE AT STAKE" for the same reason as Ford.[70] He later denounced Prop 14 as an "irresponsible" and "radical amendment . . . worthy of the extremists who support it."[71]

The most vocal and prominent Prop 14 opponent was also the most conflicted about how best to rally voters to his side. On the one hand, Brown's political instincts counseled a course of moderation. As early as November 1963, he wrote of how "tragic" it would be to adopt the "inflammatory terms" being bandied about by fair housing opponents.[72] He reiterated this advice in February 1964 in an address to the California Democratic Council convention in Long Beach: "It will be hard for us not to respond in kind to the ranting of the racists who even now are infiltrating the ranks of our opposition. But we must resist that temptation. We must hold the argument to . . . a conflict of principle, not of emotion."[73] On the other hand, Brown proved almost constitutionally incapable of heeding his own advice. He described support for fair housing as "the idealistic thing," and opposition "an absolute disgrace" that would "cause blood to run in the streets." He was quick to lump together Prop 14 supporters as "bigots," and loath to consider the possibility that something other than bigotry might have animated them.[74] "The real purpose [of Prop 14]," he fumed, "is clearly legalized discrimination against our minority citizens."[75]

Brown often evinced the conflict between his political instincts and his moral outrage in a single speech. In a February 1964 address, he exhorted Prop 14 foes to stick to "principle" and eschew "emotion," but subsequently fulminated over the "ranting of racists infiltrating the ranks of our opposition" and how "nowhere—nowhere—do we face [a] greater threat to California's liberal tradition than in the current initiative to repeal the Rumford Fair Housing Act."[76] As the Prop 14 vote drew near and the battle intensified, so, too, did Brown's assessment of the historical stakes, as well as his rhetoric. In letters and speeches during July and August 1964, the governor called leading Prop 14 proponents the "shock troops of bigotry." Their efforts had "echoes . . . of another hate binge which began more than 30 years ago in a Munich beer hall," Brown charged, linking Prop 14 with Nazism. "The future of American Democracy," he declared forebodingly, hinged on defeating Prop 14, "the most basic moral challenge in our nation's history."[77]

The *Los Angeles Times*, which endorsed Prop 14, admonished the governor for his "inflammatory talk." Brown demeaned his office through "villification-by-association" attacks on Prop 14 supporters and a sanctimonious refusal to grant "good faith to those who don't share his opposition."[78] Brown retorted indignantly, "It is not the governor who is inflammatory" but the "racists and bigots" who support Prop 14.[79] Brown's speechwriter Haas also took umbrage with the *Times*'s indictment of his boss. He pointed to "the massive problems of ghettos that are growing like black cancers in the hearts of our cities" and insisted that it is, therefore, "not intemperate to shout 'fire' when the blaze is already licking at our feet. It's folly not to shout."[80]

Only when admonishments came from ordinary, but sympathetic, voters did Brown heed his political intuitions to tone it down, but never for long. A woman active in a local anti-Prop 14 group expressed concern that the governor's intemperance did more to stymie than spur the campaign. The "fearful" far outnumbered the "bigots," she insisted and then advised, "Rather than hurling epithets at the opposition, we shall gain more allies by interpreting the changes that are happening in race relations." The governor must devote himself to dispelling the "false fears . . . that worry John Q. Citizen." To this end, "reasoned and logical arguments" are the best approach. "I just wish you'd temper your remarks a bit."[81] Jack Burby, a Brown adviser, brought the letter to the governor's attention. Upon it the governor scribbled, "Jack, I want to become more temperate."[82]

Temperance, however, eluded him. Less than a month after expressing his desire to tone down, and less than a month before the November election, Brown appeared before the "California Democratic Women's Forum" and blasted the pro-Prop 14 "campaign of deception and deceit." He railed against the "false shibboleth" of "freedom to sell or rent to whom you choose" being dangled like poisoned fruit before unwitting Californians. "Freedom to discriminate. Freedom to segregate"—these were "imaginary freedoms" that masked "the age-old cudgel of bigotry" with which the money-grubbing, racist realtors sought "once again" to bludgeon "Negroes, Mexican-Americans and other minority groups in this state."[83]

In the end, all the arguments deployed against Prop 14 had as much impact as rocks hurled by hand at an oncoming tank. When November 3, 1964 arrived, California voters confronted a choice on Prop 14 as stark as the one between Lyndon Johnson and Barry Goldwater. Though Brown and other anti-Prop 14 leaders insisted that defeating Goldwater did not make sense without defeating Prop 14, the electorate thought otherwise and delivered overwhelming victories to both Lyndon Johnson (4,171,877 to 2,879,108) and Prop 14 (4,526,460 to 2,395,747). Of California's fifty-eight counties, only sparsely populated Modoc county rejected the measure (and there only barely so—1,536 yes to 1,555 no).[84] In the "confrontation of a choice between good and evil" that Prop 14 represented to Brown the forces of evil had won in a rout.[85]

The lopsided vote stunned many of Prop 14's opponents. In July 1964, Lu Haas, Brown's speechwriter, boasted about the breadth of the anti-Prop 14 coalition. "Nearly all churches and unions oppose [Prop 14]," he wrote Brown, "as do many civic organizations and hundreds of prominent business, civic and political leaders in both parties."[86] This breadth of leadership, however, was not matched by depth of rank-and-file support. Anti-Prop 14 leaders, according to Becker, "weren't able to influence (very strongly, at any rate) the membership" of their various constituencies.[87]

This disconnect appeared even among some of the non-African American groups that opponents of Prop 14 sometimes portrayed as potential victims of its passage. For example, in July 1964, leaders of the JACL and formed a California State Committee Against Prop 14. From the outset, though, the JACL committee conceded that it faced an uphill battle with Japanese Americans who "may resent our campaigning for something which they claim does not involve them."[88] Similarly, following a July 1964 meeting in Los Angeles with some "40 Mexican-American leadership people" representing "all the organizations," Becker wrote Brown, "There was more real concern [about Prop 14] than I had been led to expect, but also some doubt that the rank and file really saw this as *their* issue."[89] The gap between leaders and rank-and-file was perhaps greatest within unions. Nearly seventy percent of white union members supported Prop 14, which was substantially greater than the fifty-six percent of support given for the measure by those without union affiliation.[90] In short, ordinary California voters delivered a powerful rebuke to the people who ostensibly spoke on their behalf. As Haas quipped, "We had everybody on our side. Everybody but the voters."[91]

In the postmortem that followed, Prop 14 opponents chalked up the vote to anti-black racism. At a press conference one week after the election, a crestfallen Brown described the outcome as evidence that "a majority of whites in the state don't want Negroes living in the same neighborhood with them."[92] Likewise, for Becker a vote for Prop 14 was a vote "against the possibility that a Negro might move in next door."[93] Years later, however, both Becker and Brown revised their original explanations. Of course, there was "prejudice" and economic self-interest involved, Brown maintained. But he added, "I don't think that Proposition 14 was essentially an anti-black vote." Rather, "I think it was the freedom to use your own property. . . . You own your own property, you work for it, you fight for it and, by golly, you can rent or lease it to anybody you want."[94] Similarly, Becker recalled how the Prop 14 supporters "formulat[ed] the issue in terms of 'Every man's home is his castle' and 'What the hell is government doing in telling me I can't sell my home to whomever I want, I can't rent my apartments to whomever I want?'" When framed in this way during debates, Becker recollected, "you could just see the faces [in the audience] take on a different look." Consequently, while he did not repudiate his original explanation about the "heavy element of bigotry" involved in Prop 14's passage, Becker supplemented it with an account that factored in the value placed on "ownership of a piece of land, a piece of property . . . with being a free yeoman in the Jeffersonian sense."[95]

The revised explanations of Brown and Becker perhaps best capture the motives of those Californians who voted for Prop 14 but against Goldwater. Members of this slice of the California electorate were often as adamant in their opposition to the Rumford Fair Housing Act as they were in their support for many other forms of antidiscrimination legislation such as the 1964 Civil Rights Act and its California precursors, the Unruh Civil Rights Act and the California Fair Employment Practices Act. For all the letters that poured into the governor's office during the Prop 14 battle denouncing the "Rumford Mongrelization Act" and declaring "Can't you get it through your thick head that the majority of Christian White people don't want to live with niggers," there were others insisting, "I would have protested just as vehemently had they said I could not sell to a Negro." Similarly, "Twenty-one years ago, long before support for civil rights became 'fashionable,' I joined the NAACP. . . . I firmly believe that minority groups . . . are entitled to every right of every other citizen in the United States. . . . With the laws which require a business, open to the public, to admit all of the public, I am in complete accord. This also applies to any public facility. However, with regards to any law which denies a person the right to personally dispose, or make available, his personal property as he sees fit, I am unalterably opposed. It is my belief that a free people cannot be denied a free choice in such a personal area, and yet be deserving of all that is contained in the word 'free.' "[96]

In the heat of the battle, anti-Prop 14 leaders failed to detect a distinction between these two types of Prop 14 supporters—the one unabashedly racist, the other doggedly principled. This tone deafness exacted a political price. Though Brown had urged Prop 14 opponents to "hold the argument . . . to a conflict of principle, not emotion," his own failure to do so sent letters streaming into his office that accused him of "foaming at the mouth," being a "breeder of hate," and following in the "footsteps of McCarthy and the John Birch Society." Other constituent letters implored the governor to "stop hurling epithets" and "impugning the motives of the [pro-14-ers] in a most inflammatory manner." Such "tactics," one self-proclaimed "strong opponent of Proposition 14" warned, "are not only unfair . . . [but] will seriously backfire." Righteousness, letters like these implied, would only beget righteous indignation—a warning borne out by at least one man who wrote, "Governor Brown, I was not for the Initiative to nullify the Rumford bill. However, with your attitude you caused many of our friends as well as myself and family to vote for it."[97]

It is, of course, impossible to know if a change in tone would have swung many votes in the opposite direction. Surely, the "bigots" among Prop 14 sympathizers were beyond the pale of persuasion. But what about the "fearful," who, according to one Californian active in the anti-Prop 14 effort, far outnumbered the "bigots"?[98] And what about those who claimed to support Lyndon Johnson and all other antidiscrimination legislation with the exception of that targeting private homes and apartments?[99] Could enough of them have been persuaded if the anti-Prop 14 forces had plotted a course that was less tilted toward "right and tolerance versus hate and bigotry" and more toward competing property rights claims, as one Brown administration official recommended in July 1964?[100] Probably not. After all, Prop 14 was 1.1 million votes short of being defeated.

Less doubtful, though, is how greater attentiveness to the more principled supporters for Prop 14 would have helped the measure's opponents anticipate and understand the drubbing they took at the polls, as well as how to reconcile it with the equally overwhelming drubbing that Barry Goldwater took. Had Prop 14 foes listened more carefully to the principled arguments advanced on behalf of the measure, they would have heard what one noted legal scholar describes as a conflict between "the nondiscrimination principle . . . [and] private property rights."[101] Where private property rights clashed with the antidiscrimination principle in workplaces or businesses serving the public, the majority of Californians weighed the competing rights claim scale in favor of antidiscrimination. This stood in contrast to Goldwater who opposed the 1964

Civil Rights Act precisely because he viewed its public accommodations provisions to be an attack on private property.[102] Where private property rights clashed with the antidiscrimination principle in private homes and apartments, however, the majority of Californians tilted the scale toward the private property rights claim. As Cecil Poole, Brown's African American legal affairs secretary from 1959 to 1961, later put it, "A lot of people who could accept the philosophy of equality in employment couldn't see the guy with that new job living next door to them."[103]

Viewing the 1964 election in California from this vantage point helps clarify some of the confusion expressed in Brown's post-election observation: Californians "wanted Proposition 14, but they also wanted President Johnson, despite the president's stand on civil rights."[104] Californians who voted *for* Prop 14 but *against* Goldwater were not so much signaling a wholesale rejection of civil rights—as Brown seemed to suggest. They were, however, hoisting a "no trespassing" sign. They drew a line that cordoned off a more public sphere where the state could and should protect against discrimination from a more private sphere where no such state laws could tread. This line separated Brown (and the Rumford Act) from Lyndon Johnson (and the 1964 Civil Rights Act) as much as it did Johnson from Goldwater.

Of course, the anti-Prop 14 side had a property rights argument of its own: the primacy of the right to acquire property over the right to dispose of property. This argument, however, failed to reach voters. "We have missed something," wrote one politically perceptive Californian to the governor in September 1964. "We have allowed the opposition to gain the propaganda advantage by their claim to 'restore property rights.' . . . The only way that their argument can be met head on is to promise 'property rights' in greater proportion. . . . Property owners have more 'rights' to lose with 14 than they have to gain, and this must be emphasized."[105] Speaking about the Prop 14 outcome in 1965, Howden criticized "our realtor-philosopher friends" for failing to "address themselves in a serious, sustained way to the elementary, prior problem of *acquiring* that property in the first place."[106] This criticism, however, could have been just as easily self-directed. Instead of meeting Prop 14 proponents with their own arguments about property rights, Prop 14 opponents mostly vilified the "segregation amendment" and, by extension, impugned as racist those who supported it. In this way, according to Speaker of the Assembly Unruh, leaders in the campaign against Prop 14 "did little more than echo back the charges of the sponsors [of the measure]." They then listened as their voices got drowned out in the echo chamber.[107]

Whatever the causes of Prop 14's passage, the consequences could hardly be graver, in the view of some leading Prop 14 opponents. On August 11, 1965, a white highway patrol officer arrested a black motorist for allegedly driving under the influence of alcohol in the Watts section of Los Angeles. Word soon reached the driver's mother, who arrived on the scene and berated her son for drinking. The son waded into the crowd that was beginning to mill around him. As the circle of spectators grew, so, too, did the police presence, which only inflamed the crowd in a neighborhood where the police had long been associated with harassment and brutality. An officer accused a woman of spitting on her, plucked her from the crowd, and placed her under arrest. Rumors and then rocks flew, the police fled, and some of the crowd began venting their anger elsewhere. Watts exploded, ultimately engulfing its central business district in flames, claiming thirty-four lives, and injuring over one thousand others.[108]

A little over a year before the conflagration, Loren Miller warned Howard Jewel, an assistant attorney general, "violence in Los Angeles is inevitable" owing to the miserable relations between the police and the African American community.[109] When Miller's prediction came to fruition, he offered a second explanation, racially restrictive housing covenants—which had served to segregate Watts decades earlier—for Watts's "fire this time," as he described it.[110] Though Miller did not mention Prop 14, Edward Howden did. "The two-to-one victory of the amendment struck minority group Californians like a smashing blow to the teeth," Howden told the Governor's Commission on the Los Angeles Riots in November 1965. "Negro and other nonwhite residents felt this as a stinging and deeply damaging expression of persistent and implacable racism. No other interpretation of the vote was felt to have any value. Once again, in a vital test, the white man had resoundingly and cruelly rejected the legitimate needs and aspirations of nonwhite fellow citizens for reasonable housing opportunity."[111] Years later, Richard Kline, another Brown administration official and leader in the anti-Prop 14 campaign, drew the same connection. "My view," he maintained, "is that the Watts riot was a direct result of Proposition 14."[112]

Howden's linkage of Prop 14 to all nonwhite Californians reflected a pre-Prop 14 vote effort by the measure's opponents to reach out to Mexican Americans. In late September 1964, Brown delivered a speech to a dinner of the Council of Mexican-American Affairs. He used the platform to rally support for the campaign against Prop 14, the vote for which was a little more than a month away. Prop 14, he told the audience gathered to honor Mexican-American judges, "is aimed squarely at the Mexican-American community of this state. Just as squarely as it is aimed at Negro Californians."[113] Brown's effort to link Prop 14 to Mexican Americans reflected a concern expressed by anti-Prop 14 leaders about the depth of Mexican American opposition to the measure. As early as March 1964, for example, Becker wrote CSO founder Fred Ross an urgent letter, asking him to respond "as soon as possible" to a series of queries. "Has much interest been developed in the Mexican-American communities" for what Becker referred to as "the segregation initiative"? "Has CSO done anything on this as yet? Can CSO mount a campaign on this?"[114] The following month, Becker reiterated his reservations. In a letter to CSO leader Anthony Rios, Becker complained about the "absence of Mexican-American activity on the initiative question." He could point to "few actions in support of us" and found no evidence of "Mexican-American activity" on the matter as communicated through the CCFP.[115]

By contrast, the NAACP-WC never gave Becker similar cause for concern. The organization's regional director Tarea Hall Pittman described Prop 14 as the "biggest political challenge" of 1964, and its leading lawyers—Loren Miller and Nathaniel Colley—sought to meet that challenge beginning with a December 1963 suit to "stop the initiative cold."[116] In a letter to long-time NAACP-WC leading figure C.L. Dellums, Colley explained, "It is our decision to make it an NAACP suit. . . . We cannot share this with anyone. This is not selfishness but rather self-preservation."[117] Though Brown would later try to portray Prop 14 as "aimed squarely" at both Mexican Americans and African Americans, at least when speaking to a Mexican American audience, the NAACP-WC understood Prop 14 as "aimed squarely" at African Americans.

While the NAACP-WC—along with the Brown administration and CCFP—threw itself into the campaign against Prop 14, Becker continued to find little comparable energy emanating from Mexican American advocacy groups. "Opposition to the initiative is forming," he wrote Louis Garcia, the FEPC's lone Mexican American commissioner, in May 1964, "but slowly, among the Mexican American organizations."[118] That momentum, however, never gathered much steam. Though MAPA adopted an anti-Prop 14 resolution, it did so, according to Ruben Salazar of the *Los Angeles Times*, in order to consummate a "shaky trial marriage" on behalf of "Latin-Negro Unity." That union, according to Salazar, was based on a prenuptial: " 'You help us defeat the initiative to repeal the Rumford Housing Act,' the Negroes ask of the Mexican-Americans. 'Yes,' they answer, 'if you help us elect a Mexican-American to the State Assembly.' "[119] Whether MAPA could hold up its end of the agreement struck Becker as doubtful in July 1964. Following a meeting in Los Angeles with some "40 Mexican-American leadership people" representing "all the organizations," Becker wrote Brown, "There was more real concern [about Prop 14] than I had been led to expect, but also some doubt that the rank and file really saw this as *their* issue."[120] An August 1964 study of Mexican American voters in East Los Angeles conducted by two UCLA researchers confirmed these doubts. "Fair housing is not a 'gut' issue of itself for the community," the report concluded, noting that some seventy-five percent of those surveyed had "no knowledge of Proposition 14."[121]

To build support against Prop 14 among Mexican Americans, the FEPC, whose task it was to handle complaints brought under the state's fair employment and fair housing laws, dispatched commissioner C.L. Dellums to a "Mexican-American Luncheon Forum" in late July 1964. Dellums noted how few of the employment and housing cases received by the FEPC came from Mexican Americans as compared to those from African Americans. By the FEPC's own count, during the Rumford Act's first year on the books, African Americans brought 125 housing discrimination cases, while Mexican Americans brought three (as did Asian Americans).[122] Four years earlier, a similar disparity in employment discrimination complaints led the FEPC to conclude that its "major concern" should be "improvement for employment opportunities for Negroes" since "Negroes file more than 90 percent of the complaints of job discrimination received by the Commission."[123] In 1964, however, the FEPC's Dellums struck a different chord. The data, he insisted, did not make sense. "I just can't believe we are that free of discrimination," Dellums explained in reference to the paucity of Mexican American complaints. He then exhorted his audience's members and the people they represented to avail themselves of the FEPC's services.[124]

To underscore its commitment to Mexican Americans, the FEPC also released two reports. The first—"Californians of Spanish Surname"—came out in May 1964 and represented a counterpart to the FEPC's previously published "Negro Californians."[125] The publication of "Negro Californians" had prompted Carlos Borja, Jr., president of the Council of Mexican-American Affairs and leader in MAPA, to urge FEPC chair John Anson Ford to push for a similar publication for the "Spanish surname population . . . in order that we might be able to ascertain statistically what the problems of the Spanish surname population are in the State of California." Borja then added, "I know that I do not need to point out to you that the Spanish surname population has greater numbers in the State of California, and in some cases greater problems than any other minority group."[126] The second FEPC report—"Si Se Puede! It Can Be Done!"—came out in August 1964 and focused on the FEPC's role in combating discrimination against Mexican Americans. In doing so, it sought to demonstrate, according to a *San Jose Mercury News* report, how the Brown administration "isn't forgetting . . . Mexican-Americans" even amidst "all the hubbub over rights and responsibilities of Negroes in California." The article also linked the FEPC's overtures to Mexican Americans to Prop 14. "Most Democratic sources," it reported, "will frankly admit that it's an uphill battle to defeat the initiative." To this end, a "Mexican-American vote solidly against the proposition" was essential. By publishing "Si Se Puede! It Can Be Done!" and "Californians of Spanish Surname" and appointing Louis Garcia, a San Francisco attorney and MAPA leader, as the

FEPC's first Mexican American commissioner, the Brown administration hoped to attract Mexican American voters.[127]

Despite these overtures, a leader in the campaign against Prop 14 fretted in October 1964, "We have not yet reached the Latin community by traditional means."[128] MAPA president Eduardo Quevedo voiced a similar concern two weeks prior to the election. "No one," he said, "is helping us on Proposition 14."[129] Quevedo's observation foreshadowed Brown's rueful recollection years later. "They [i.e., Mexican Americans] didn't help very much [on Prop 14]," he maintained in a tone that was as matter of fact as it was miffed.[130] It also helped explain Dellums's understanding of the Prop 14 vote as a hateful message delivered to African Americans, in particular, rather than "nonwhite citizens," in general, as Howden interpreted it, and Dellums had tried to help Mexican Americans see in the months before November 1964. The Rumford Act, Dellums explained, had been a "symbol of hope" for "Negro citizens," which Prop 14 dashed. This "stunned loss of hope [was] discernible in the faces and actions of Negro Californians" in Watts the following year.[131] It was also discernible in the widely divergent poll responses to Watts by Mexican Americans and whites, on the hand, and African Americans, on the other hand. For example, sixty-eight percent of Mexican Americans and sixty-six percent of whites said that authorities responded "well" to the violence versus only twenty-eight percent of African Americans.[132]

What Brown took to be befuddling indifference by Mexican Americans to Prop 14, Mexican American leaders understood as a reflection of different civil rights priorities. "We are sympathetic to the problems of the Negroes and we should help them fight for their rights," declared Borja at the June 1964 MAPA convention, which passed a resolution against Prop 14. "But," he added, "Mexican Americans have unique problems."[133] MAPA vice president Bert Corona offered a similar assessment. "You have to take a special approach to solve a special problem," Corona told the FEPC in a meeting with Mexican American leaders in Los Angeles on November 10, 1964. "The Commission," Corona continued, "must reorient itself. It cannot deal with Mexican-Americans as it deals with the Negro community. And if this is the way you have been viewing it, no wonder you have done very little." Manuel Ruiz, Jr., a consulting attorney for MAPA whose advocacy on behalf of Mexican Americans ran back to the 1940s, echoed Corona. "Our particular problems," Ruiz asserted, "have not been considered up to now." To remedy this, Ruiz called for the FEPC to be "alerted to our grievances."[134]

These concerns did not include Prop 14, which helps explain a 1965 poll of Mexican Americans in East Los Angeles that unearthed only sixteen percent support for "political efforts in conjunction with Black Americans."[135] As Becker discovered the previous summer during a meeting with a group of Mexican American leaders he convened to drum up opposition to Prop 14, "The meeting, as expected, provided an opportunity for some of them to express their grievances" and for "most of the complainers" the problem was not Prop 14 but rather "'not enough appointments.'"[136] Four months later, the meeting between the FEPC and Mexican American leaders revealed a similar frustration. Though convened one week after the Prop 14 vote, Prop 14 received mention only in passing. Corona touched upon the "defeat that we have suffered" as a result of Prop 14, which Ruiz cast as an opportunity for Mexican Americans. "All of the [FEPC's] energies that were to be directed into the Rumford Act," Ruiz said, could, instead, be channeled into tackling the "pressing need" for "recruitment, hiring and upgrading of Mexican Americans" through the California Department of Employment. Corona also emphasized public employment, noting that "less than two per cent" of state government employees were Mexican American even though "we represent 10 to 12 percent of the population." Among the Mexican American state employees he hoped to be hired, Corona called for a second Mexican American commissioner on the FEPC. Quevedo added that the FEPC needed to employ more "staff to speak Spanish," lest it continue to do a "fine job for our brothers in the Negro community" while "missing the boat" with Mexican Americans.[137] One month later, in a follow-up meeting with FEPC representatives, Mexican American leaders, including Quevedo, Corona, and Gallegos, insisted "Mexican Americans need the kind of attention" from the state Department of Employment "that the Negro community has been getting."[138]

That same day, those same Mexican American leaders appeared before a San Francisco hearing of the United States Department of Labor to address their other major civil rights concern, besides underrepresentation in political appointments and state employment, namely, the plight of domestic farm workers. In anticipation of their appearance, the organizations they represented—including MAPA and the CSO—issued a press release, denouncing "the importation of braceros because it lowers wages and eliminates the decency of farm work" and demanding that their "importation be cut off entirely" rather than through "a gradual phase out." Though the press release sympathized with "the poor Mexicans in Mexico who are desperate to indenture themselves as braceros," it insisted, "we should not steal jobs from our own people to give jobs to them." After all, there were, MAPA leader Quevedo maintained in his testimony, "sufficient workers in the United States who are able, willing, qualified, and available."[139]

Brown took a different view—and crossed an anti-bracero picket line to convey it to the Department of Labor hearing. Though he lamented the "miserable and degrading poverty" in which many farm workers and their families were forced to live, he placed the burden for remedying it on the federal government. Since "agriculture truly is a national industry," Brown contended, "it is primarily a federal responsibility to take the first steps toward correcting the long-standing injustices against our farm workers." Until then, he did not believe that growers could attract workers from among "the 355,000 currently unemployed Californians" and must, therefore, be allowed to continue to import braceros according to a four-year phase-out plan he announced the previous month.[140]

Brown's proposal betrayed a promise he had made to MAPA. Having "reluctantly supported" a one-year extension of the Bracero Program through 1963, Brown vowed, "It was the last time it will receive my support." Growers would have to "buckle down to the job of finding and developing domestic workers."[141] In 1964, however, rather than growers buckling down, Brown buckled under. As Albert Tieburg, director of the Department of Employment, explained, "The Governor had a lot of good friends and supporters who were big farmers who used foreign workers. And, boy, he was getting heat from them."[142] In response, Brown invoked Public Law (PL) 414, as a means for providing for the additional importation of foreign agricultural workers after PL 78 ended.[143] That "the governor did not keep his word when he promised this would be the last year for the bracero program," FEPC commissioner Garcia charged, was a source of profound "disappoint[ment]" for the Mexican Americans.[144] It was also, Ernesto Galarza wrote, the latest chapter in the "pitiful story" of farm workers and "politicians in California."[145] Though neither Garcia nor Galarza mentioned it, they could have added that Brown's "vacillation and eventual abandonment of the farm worker's cause," as one journalist put it in 1965, stood in marked contrast to his staunch support for fair employment and fair housing and equally staunch opposition to Prop 14 for which the NAACP-WC credited him for "campaign[ing] vigorously."[146] "Politics," one farm worker advocate commented on this ostensibly ironic limit to Brown's civil rights reach, made "strange bedfellows."[147]

On the same day that the Department of Labor heard testimony from Mexican American leaders against extending the Bracero Program and from Brown in favor of doing so, the NAACP-WC met to plan its legal campaign against Prop 14. National NAACP general counsel Robert L. Carter flew from New York to attend. Not since the housing covenant cases in the 1940s, in Carter's view, did his organization confront a housing discrimination case of such magnitude. "California is the first state, North or South, to enact a law, that, in purpose and effect, accomplishes a restriction based upon race, believed to have been outlawed by the United States Supreme Court a decade ago," Carter insisted. "A case testing the law's constitutionality, therefore, is made mandatory, and its outcome will have considerable bearing on the course this country will take in the years ahead in dealing with the unresolved issue of the place of the Negro in this society."[148] Carter's comment underscored just how much NAACP leaders understood Prop 14—and the case the NAACP called for to overturn it—as an African American issue.

As NAACP-WC lawyers launched a three-year legal campaign against Prop 14 in order to help resolve "the place of the Negro in this society," Mexican American organizations continued to focus their attention on the plight of domestic farm workers and underrepresentation in political appointments and state employment. In January 1965, a group designating itself the Mexican-American Unity Council Task Force, whose members included Corona, Galarza, Quevedo, and Ruiz, met with Brown. First among the "gripes" they voiced was the stance that Brown had taken on the "importation of foreign labor." Next was the absence of a Mexican American on the California Agricultural Board and, more generally, the way in which Mexican American state employment was "out of balance" in comparison to the "higher percentage of Negro employees." This imbalance underscored how, in Corona's words, "many of us Mexican Americans feel that we have been left out." He recommended expanding the FEPC budget to ensure that Mexican Americans "receive the same recognition as other minority groups."[149]

Four months later, little had changed. A meeting of the MAPA executive board prompted angry resolutions aimed at Brown's failure to resolve "the most pressing problems facing our people." Among these, one insisted that the "first order of business of [Brown's] administration" needed to be the appointment of Mexican Americans to "at least 10% proportions to the powerful and policy-making positions" in the state such as the Board of Education and Regents of the University of California. More generally, the minutes recorded Corona's discussion of a meeting he had with Brown and Tieburg on state employment of Mexican Americans. In that meeting, Corona pointed out how the "proportion of Negroes holding state jobs is 8% to 5% population, whereas Mexican-American population is 10.9% and only 2% holding state jobs." In addition, the MAPA executive board issued a "Resolution on Farm Labor," which blasted Brown for his "utter disregard for the welfare of domestic farm workers" by repeatedly caving into growers' demands for non-domestic employees. Still another resolution reiterated a longstanding indictment of the FEPC, claiming the agency had done "very little or nothing . . . to serve the pressing needs of the 2,000,000 Mexican-Americans" in the state.[150]

The Brown administration attempted to rebut the charges. In May 1965, for example, Howden reminded Corona how the FEPC had met several times to "listen further to the needs and concerns of the Mexican American community."

More substantively, he singled out the appointment of two consultants—one in the FEPC's Los Angeles office and the other in the FEPC's San Francisco office—to "work on matters of special concern to Californians of Spanish surname, principally those of Mexican ancestry."[151] These efforts, however, did little to address the underrepresentation of Mexican Americans in state employment. As a July 1965 "Second Ethnic Survey of Employment and Promotion in State Government" revealed, "As in 1963 [when the first such survey was conducted] we find an under-representation of Mexican-Americans who are over 10% of our population." Though the number of Mexican American state employees had increased from 2,382 to 2,645, the proportion remained static at roughly 2.5 percent. By contrast, African American state employment increased from 5,390 to 6,001, which was "about their proportion of the population (6%)." This discrepancy between Mexican Americans and African Americans, the survey's authors contended, was due to the "high rate of participation in civil service competition" on the part of African Americans. In other words, unlike African Americans, Mexican Americans were not applying.[152]

Meanwhile, Brown responded to the "Resolution on Farm Labor," which Quevedo conveyed to him in May 1965. "Your letter," the governor replied, "puzzled me." The "problems . . . outlined in the resolution," Brown insisted, would receive a sympathetic hearing from Tieburg—"an understanding and cooperative state official." Besides Tieburg, Brown wrote, "I can soundly advise you" to speak with Becker. Brown did not address the resolution's substance. Instead, he concluded, "I am certain that we will have minor disagreements, but certainly in the long run you and MAPA and the people for whom you speak are together with me on the same side."[153] Brown's assurance must have rung hollow to Quevedo, given that MAPA's "Resolution on Farm Labor" criticized Tieburg for his "avid encouragement" of continuing to import farm workers from abroad while "'holding hands' with the growers."[154] It must have rung even more hollow when Brown reiterated his call for a protracted phase out of the Bracero Program to the House Committee on Education and Labor in July 1965.[155] Brown's testimony lent further credence to César Chávez's claim that the governor "never did anything on the braceros" because of the "tremendous political pressure" he was under.[156]

Brown's inaction, however, did not preclude Congress's 1963 decision to draw the Bracero Program to a close at the end of 1964, after the importation of more than four million braceros over more than two decades. In late March 1965, United States Secretary of Labor Willard Wirtz—whose efforts the Mexican-American Unity Council Task Force praised in its "Resolution on Farm Labor"—came to California to evaluate the fate of agribusiness in the aftermath of the Bracero Program. Prior to his trip, Wirtz wrote Brown that talk about "our own people 'not wanting to do stoop labor' gets pretty thin when we know that the real point is that they are being expected to do it at a wage which averages less than half of what they are for other work that is generally easier." Even in the face of such wage disparities, Wirtz insisted that there had been "no significant losses resulting from labor shortages," despite the "good deal of talk" to the contrary.[157] His visit confirmed what he had written Brown. After four sixteen-hour days trudging through fields and orchards and talking with hundreds of workers, employers, and officials, Wirtz told reporters that he did not believe that California farm workers had a "fair and equitable part in society," and that terminating the Bracero Program would help correct that. "From here on there will be a competitive factor in the labor situation which there had not been before," Wirtz explained. "Unionism," he predicted, would soon grow in the fields.[158]

Six months later farm workers in California began proving Wirtz right. On September 8, 1965, a group of Filipino grape workers walked off their jobs at Delano's Schenley Corporation, the region's second largest grape grower. They sought a pay increase from $1.20 per hour to $1.40 per hour and recognition of their union, the Agricultural Workers Organizing Committee (AWOC).[159] Some 1,100 workers from Chávez's National Farm Workers Association soon joined their AWOC counterparts. The grape strike had begun—an "historic movement of Mexican-Americans," as Chávez described it.[160]

As the strike unfolded, MAPA expressed solidarity with the strikers. Echoing Chávez's earlier assertion about the farm workers' inextricable relationship to Mexican Americans, a November 1965 MAPA statement inquired, "Have not the bulk of the Spanish-speaking people of our country been farm workers at one time or another?" Being "true to the needs of the Mexican-Americans meant taking a "firm and clear stand against the naked exploitation of farm workers."[161]

Assemblyman Phillip Soto also called attention to the solidarity between Mexican Americans as a whole and the striking farm workers. In a letter to Brown, he pointed out that he was the "only elected State Representative with a Spanish Surname." He then informed the governor of the "heavy sentiment and concern" for the strikers among the "the Spanish-speaking community in Los Angeles" and elsewhere, which "should not be passed off too lightly." The "Delano situation," he believed, reverberated far beyond Delano and farm labor. It joined the "same old criticism" of the Brown administration for failing to help increase the numbers of Mexican American elected officials as well as appointees. If Brown did not help resolve the strike in a way that redounded in the strikers' favor, Soto warned, he would "wind up with a large black eye from the Spanish-speaking community."[162]

In fact, the black eye that Brown already had was self-inflicted and would only swell. "Your letter to the Governor back in November," Becker wrote Soto at the end of January 1966, "was copied and sent to a large number of people." Beyond disseminating the letter, Becker urged Soto to understand, there was little Brown could do. The responsibility resided with Soto's colleagues in the legislature to enact "legislation to deal with problems in the area of farm labor." As for Mexican American appointments and resolving the strike, Becker insisted that they were doing as much as they could, which was not much when it came to the strike.[163] In February 1966—as the strike dragged into its sixth month—a group of some thirty strikers, including Dolores Huerta, confronted Brown as he was entering the California Democratic Council convention in Bakersfield. They carried signs requesting his intervention to help settle the strike. In response, Brown told reporters, "I can't go to Delano this trip. I'll be down there one of these days." He then added, "The governor can't get into every strike in the state. . . . This is a pure, out-and-out disagreement on unionization. All I could do is take one side or the other." He did not want to take sides—a reluctance which stood in marked contrast to the unequivocal and vocal stance he had taken on the civil rights priorities articulated by the NAACP-WC and CCFP since he had assumed office.[164]

If Brown would not go to the strikers, they would go to him. On March 17, 1966, they began a Chávez-led march from Delano to Sacramento. This 300-mile "pilgrimage," as Chávez and the marchers often referred to it, came on the heels of a U.S. Senate Subcommittee on Migratory Labor hearing, which was held in Delano and included Senator Robert Kennedy.[165] Brown, however, did not attend the hearing. Instead, a spokesperson delivered a statement on the governor's behalf. It claimed that California was a "leading state in the protection of farm workers by law" and urged the federal government to legislate in the areas where California had not when it came to agricultural labor, including minimum wage, unemployment coverage, and expansion of the National Labor Relations Act.[166]

The marchers, however, did not intend to let California slough off these legislative responsibilities onto the federal government without a fight. They arrived in Sacramento on Easter Sunday—by then 8,000 strong, up from 150 at the outset—and called upon Brown to convene a special legislative session to enact a collective bargaining law. Brown, who was in Palm Springs with his family and Frank Sinatra for the holiday, refused to heed the farm workers' request. "There is no possibility for enactment of such legislation at this time," Brown wrote Chávez a few days later. Still, the governor expressed his support for the farm workers' "struggle for justice," defended his farm labor record, reminded Chávez that "there is no state collective bargaining act for any workers," but vowed nonetheless to "see that this matter is presented at the next General Session of the Legislature in 1967."[167] Brown's promise, of course, presumed his gubernatorial presence in Sacramento when the next legislative session convened. That, however, would require his re-election.

With the election of 1966 over a year away, Becker sent Brown a memorandum on July 30, 1965 entitled "Minorities in the 1966 Election." "We must recognize," Becker wrote, "these four groups as the base of any Democratic vote and the possibilities of any Democratic victory," namely, African Americans, Jews, Mexican Americans, and white labor.[168] Becker's delineation of the groups comprising the Democratic Party's base echoed Dutton's claim from 1960 about the "alliance" Brown was forging "with labor, the minorities, etc." and its long-term prospects.[169] Becker, however, did not simply echo Dutton. Rather, he implied that Dutton had overestimated the coherence and endurance of the Democratic coalition. Implicit in Becker's concern was a development that Dutton himself would concede many years later: the election of 1966, in which Dutton directed Brown's campaign as he had in 1958, revealed that "the Democratic base was splintering its power."[170] Becker sensed that splintering in 1965. So, too, did Brown's opponent, Ronald Reagan, who would seek to exploit it to his political advantage.

Among Mexican Americans, the grievances that organizations, like the CSO and MAPA, and individuals, such as Chávez, Corona, and Quevedo, had voiced to Brown over the years came to a head with his handling of the grape strike. Indeed, at least some of Brown's advisers had Mexican American voters in mind when, according to a *New York Times* account, they "urged him to greet the marchers" in Sacramento, even if it meant cutting short his Easter holiday. That Brown had informed Chávez and Huerta in early April that he had previously "committed [himself] to spend Easter Sunday with [his] family" and offered to meet on the following Monday instead, these Brown advisers contended, would not suffice to quell the warnings he received "that two million Mexican-Americans . . . who had supported him in the past would weigh his action carefully at the polls."[171] William Bennett, a state Public Utilities Commission member who was seeking the Democratic nomination for state attorney general, also spelled out the political pitfalls of the governor's refusal to act more forthrightly. "The Delano situation," he wrote Brown in early April, afforded the "opportunity for [California to become] the first State in the Nation to pass a mandatory collective bargaining statute for agricultural workers." If Brown squandered that opportunity, if his administration failed to give "more than lip service to ideals, then we come down to the very uncomfortable fact that in terms of seeking to help the people in Delano there is no difference between that which Mr. Reagan is not doing and that which we as Democrats are not doing."[172] A chant by some of the marchers who arrived in Sacramento on the Easter Sunday when Brown was in Palm Springs put the matter simply, "No Brown, No Vote!"[173]

A month later, Becker sent Brown a memorandum on "The Mexican-American Front." He reiterated Assemblyman Soto's point from the previous November about the "heavy sentiment and concern" for the grape strikers, in particular, among the "the Spanish-speaking community." As Becker explained, he was "impressed" in meetings he had held "by the degree to which the local Mexican-American communities identified with the Easter Sunday March." Though Brown's handling of the grape strike had cost him support among Mexican Americans, Becker discerned "a considerable shift to a more positive" view of the governor because of "strong speeches and commitments on the farm labor issue" since the grape strike marchers descended on Sacramento. Becker thus expected Brown to receive "good support from the Mexican-Americans" going forward provided he "follow[ed] through on [his] program and appointment commitments to them." At the same time, Becker hastened to add, Brown needed to avoid "get[ting] close to the Chavez-Huerta movement."[174]

The June 1966 Democratic primary suggested that Becker had overestimated Brown's Mexican American support. Overall, Brown received a narrow majority of fifty-one percent, while his main rival, Samuel Yorty, the mayor of Los Angeles, garnered thirty-nine percent. Physician and Pan American Bank founder Francisco Bravo spearheaded Yorty's campaign for Mexican American voters. His efforts, according to a MAPA spokesperson paraphrased in the *Los Angeles Times*, helped Yorty run "well in predominantly Mexican-American areas."[175]

Brown's campaign strategists recognized the erosion of Mexican American support that the Yorty vote reflected. As they grasped for explanations, one observed, "Mexicans shared in the anti-Negro sentiment at large and focused that feeling on the Governor as did many of their fellow Caucasians. Indeed, that sentiment may have been sharpened by the quiet but real resentment over the Negroes' seeming monopoly of the anti-poverty programs."[176] Another understood the Mexican American vote for Yorty as a "protest to the Governor's actions with reference to Delano and with reference to a general discontentment [against Brown] in the Mexican American community."[177]

Consequently, as Brown prepared to speak to the "MAPA Statewide Endorsing Convention" in Fresno on June 25, 1966, on the heels of the Democratic primary vote, a *Los Angeles Times* reporter predicted a "dogfight" between Brown and Reagan for MAPA's endorsement. MAPA members had grown disillusioned with Democrats, in general, and Brown, in particular, for not devoting "enough of the administration's attention . . . to the Mexican-American." Though the reporter attributed this disaffection to charges levied by MAPA leaders "since the Watts riots last year [that] the Negro has been given preference over the Mexican-American in a number of political and governmental arenas," its roots, in fact, preceded Watts, running back to the beginning of Brown's tenure.[178] The *Eastside Journal* of heavily Mexican American East Los Angeles echoed the *Times*. It reported rumors circulating at the MAPA convention that "the Governor was losing his power among Mexican-Americans" because "he was paying too much attention to the Negro and not enough the Mexican-American," especially when it came to his lack of support for the grape strikers and opposition to imposing a ban on the importation of farm workers from Mexico.[179]

In his speech to the MAPA convention, Brown maintained "we have done more for the farm laborer in California than any other state," despite the unfulfilled demands of farm labor advocates since he assumed office. Brown also touted his appointments of "Mexican-American citizens [to] ever more important leadership [positions] in government on every major front"—a claim that belied MAPA's recent charges against him. More persuasively, however, Brown skewered Reagan and his supporters as "bitter" opponents of "everything you have ever stood for—whether it concerned economic opportunity, education or civil rights." On the "key issue" of "farm labor," for example, Brown contrasted his record—meager as it was—with the "hard-shell conservatism" of his opponent who "called the Delano farm strikers 'bleeding hearts.' "[180]

In response, Reagan spoke by phone, rather than in person. His performance flopped. Quevedo, who presided at the convention as MAPA's state chair, blasted "the Hollywood actor [for being] guilty of the worst sort of hypocrisy in soliciting our endorsement with a speech filled with platitudes and then refusing to answer our questions." Not surprisingly, Reagan failed to come anywhere near receiving the MAPA endorsement, which went to Brown by a vote of 147 to 19.[181]

Despite this drubbing, Reagan did not concede Mexican American votes. His appearance, albeit by phone, at the MAPA convention was unprecedented for a Republican gubernatorial candidate.[182] He also redoubled his efforts to capitalize upon at least some of the well-documented Mexican American discontent with Brown. As William Roberts, who helped manage Reagan's campaign, explained years later, "We did a lot of work in the Mexican-American community. Almost none in the black. There were no votes there to speak of."[183] In this effort, Reagan enlisted Bravo, on Yorty's recommendation, to lead his appeal to Mexican American voters, just as Bravo had done for Yorty during the Democratic primary.[184] Bravo, in turn, introduced Reagan to the Spanish slogan "Ya Basta" (we've had enough), which Reagan repeatedly invoked in stump speeches in the campaign's waning months.[185] "Ya Basta" also became the expression associated with the "Mexican-American Democrats for Reagan," which Bravo chaired.[186] They carried placards at Reagan rallies emblazoned with the words "Ya Basta! Vote for Ronald Reagan" and were accompanied by mariachi bands. A *Los Angeles Times* reporter who covered a Reagan rally in East Los Angeles commented, "Reagan made it plain he was gunning for those Democratic voters who deserted Brown in the primary to vote for Mayor Samuel W. Yorty."[187]

Although some of these disaffected Democrats were Mexican Americans, many more were what Becker referred to as "labor," and the columnists Rowland Evans and Robert Novak described as "lower income and lower middle income white" voters who had joined "Mexican Democrats in the Los Angeles area [to give] May Sam Yorty his anti-Negro backlash vote against Brown in last June's primary." Evans and Novak added, "Spencer-Roberts and Associates, the political management firm running the Reagan campaign, has been scouring these precincts in search of Reagan supporters."[188] For many of these voters, the California Supreme Court reignited the smoldering issue of fair housing in May 1966 when it overturned Prop 14 and thereby reinstated the Rumford Fair Housing Act.

Handled by Al Wirin, the veteran ACLU of Southern California attorney, the Prop 14 case involved Lincoln Mulkey and his wife who sought to rent a vacant apartment in May 1963 in an Orange County apartment building owned by Neil Reitman. Though the Mulkey's were financially qualified, Reitman refused to rent to the couple for the sole reason that they were black. In the aftermath of Prop 14, the Orange County Superior Court ruled in favor of Reitman, declaring that the measure voided fair housing statutes on the books. On May 10, 1966, however, the California Supreme Court reversed the lower court ruling and declared Prop 14 unconstitutional. What 4.5 million California voters cast their ballots for, five California Supreme Court judges (versus two dissenters) overturned.

With their Prop 14 vote, the majority opinion explained, California voters had amended the state constitution to grant private citizens the right to discriminate in the sale or rental of their private property. In denying the Mulkeys an apartment because they were black, Reitman sought to exercise this right. The court majority did not dispute the right of private citizens to discriminate. It did, however, contend that Reitman's discrimination against Mulkey—given sanction by Prop 14—was not simply a private action, but rather one that "results at least in part from state action which is sufficiently involved to bring the matter within the proscription of the Fourteenth Amendment." Laws approved by popular vote, no less than laws approved by elected representatives, constituted "state action." "When the electorate assumes to exercise the law-making function," the California Supreme Court ruled, "then the electorate is as much a state agency as any of its elected officials." Since a plebiscite such as Prop 14 counted as state action, and since Prop 14 wrote into the state constitution a right to discriminate, Prop 14 amounted to state complicity in discrimination. That "the final act of discrimination is undertaken by a private party" did not deny the fact that "the state has acted affirmatively to change its existing laws from a situation wherein the discrimination practiced was legally restricted to one wherein it is encouraged within the meaning of the cited decisions."[189] Such state action in the service of racial discrimination rendered Prop 14 unconstitutional.

The California Supreme Court's *Mulkey* ruling incensed many of the millions of Californians who had voted for Prop 14. Letters sent to Brown in the wake of the decision captured some of the fury that the case unleashed. Besides the expected antipathy of right-wing Californians, there was the less expected groundswell of discontent from traditional Democrats, the once core elements of Brown's constituency. "How can a landslide be canceled by the State Supreme Court? Is this democracy? After 52 years as a Democrat I'll vote Republican this year," announced an Oakland man.[190] A lifelong Burbank Democrat also tendered his party resignation: "You have done more than any man in the history of the democratic party to drive me over to the G.O.P."[191] Another apostate explained, "I have voted for every Democratic President since 1928 . . . but the plan of forced housing is not Democracy. . . . I know of several thousand that are registered Democrats that feel the same way."[192] Still another disaffected Democrat wrote, "I have been a model Democrat for over 50 of my years . . . [but] your stand on forcing integration has affected me so deeply that I have recently changed my political ties. . . . Each and every race are certainly entitled to everything that the Constitution provides but nothing justifies taking rights away from a majority race in order to satisfy the whims of a minority."[193]

Although not renouncing her party membership, a Democratic voter registrar conveyed the wholesale defection of party members she was witnessing in the wake of the California Supreme Court's rejection of Prop 14. "I am very depressed lately," she complained. "I am astounded at the number of applicants changing their party to Republican. At the time of registering I cannot say anything, but when they are through I ask why? All their answers are the very same—all concerning proposition 14." Reflecting some of the smoldering class resentments that California's fair housing struggles ignited, the letter continued, "The property owners, mostly poor, are retired people around in my neighborhood. They are afraid they will have to rent or sell to the first persons that come along."[194] Similarly, a Salinas woman lashed out at the hypocrisy she believed characterized fair housing proponents. "I have been a Democrat for 59 years until the last year I registered as a Republican, and I know a lot of people who did the same thing. . . . You are just like L.B.J. Both of you are wealthy men and you can live in such high priced homes that none but others like you can move in next door to you. Prop 14 is the only thing we the middle class people have to keep our neighborhood a decent place to live."[195] Defense of property rights, disgust with a political process that allowed the will of some 4.5 million Californians to be trumped by five California Supreme Court judges, resentment at the class privilege of those Prop 14 foes who did not have to bear the burdens they seemed willing to foist upon others, rejection of the Democratic Party to which many of them had been lifelong members, racist fears of being overrun by African Americans (especially) who would drive down property values— these were the sentiments that coursed through the angry letters that poured into Brown's office in the wake of the California Supreme Court's *Mulkey* decision.

In his 1966 bid for governor, Reagan capitalized on Prop 14 and its aftermath. His winning strategy owed in part to his opposition to the Rumford Fair Housing Act. Whereas Brown often equated opposition to Rumford (and support for Prop 14) with racism, Reagan framed anti-Rumford sentiment in terms of support for property rights. He frequently voiced the antidiscrimination ends envisioned by Rumford Act supporters. "I worked for equality of opportunity before it ever became the popular issue that it is today," he asserted in a March 1966 speech, "and I could not consciously use prejudice. I would not consciously patronize any business that discriminated against any human being on the basis of prejudice."[196] That said, Reagan insisted that he rejected the Rumford Act for the same reasons he had once condemned racially restrictive housing covenants. Both were examples of unacceptable infringements upon private property rights. As Reagan explained in a letter to a Los Angeles clergyman, "I oppose restrictive covenants, not only from the moral stand against discrimination, but because I do not believe the majority has a right to impose a restriction on the individual in their midst who chooses to dispose of his property contrary to the will of the majority. It is just as wrong to do the same thing by legislation as in the Rumford Act."[197]

In framing opposition to fair housing in this way, Reagan appealed to Californians who opposed all civil rights legislation, but also to those crucial swing voters who opposed only the Rumford Act and resented the charges of racism that Brown and his allies often hurled in their direction during the Prop 14 battle. Rather than a clash between the forces of good and evil—as Brown often framed the issue—Reagan offered a vision of what California pollster Mervin Field described as "the collision of two opposing philosophies." On the one hand, there were "the rights of private citizens to dispose of their property as they see fit." On the other hand, there were the "rights of minority groups . . . to a fair chance to obtain housing of their choice." Reagan thus appealed to the majority of Californians who sought to protect their property rights from the perceived encroachment of the Rumford Act, "even though many of them may also deplore discrimination."[198]

A similar conflict of constitutional rights gripped the American South and captured national attention during the South's sit-in beginning in 1960. Sit-ins, according to one leading legal scholar, involved a clash between "the nondiscrimination principle as well as private property rights." Sit-in participants sought to extend the "fundamental constitutional principle of nondiscrimination" established by *Brown* into the realm of private businesses that served the public. In doing so, they challenged the more established fundamental constitutional principle of private property. In addition, they pushed against the outer limits of tolerance that many Americans possessed for civil rights goals and tactics. "The infringement on private property rights entailed by sit-ins" even troubled "some 'well-meaning' northern liberals, not to mention centrists."[199]

The uneasiness about how far to extend the antidiscrimination principle wracked the United States Supreme Court during deliberations over the sit-in case, *Bell v. Maryland*. In the same year (1964) that Justice Hugo Black declared that the "time for 'deliberate speed' has run out" in regard to the South's foot-dragging on school desegregation, Black and five other justices expressed deep reservations about the Fourteenth Amendment's applicability to private businesses—a position that foreshadowed the one Black would take in dissent in 1967 in the Prop 14 case over extending the antidiscrimination principle into the realm of private housing. Segregated public schools were one thing; segregated lunch counters in private businesses were quite another. According to a Black biographer, "Since the 1940s the Court had consistently applied the Fourteenth Amendment to overturn racial segregation imposed by the state, but it never questioned that private individuals could refuse to associate with those of another race." Black's support of judicial support for antidiscrimination ended where private property began. "Recalling his 'Pappy's' store, Black declared . . . 'I don't think the Constitution forbids the owner of a store to keep people out,' so long as the business was 'really wholly your own and neither in its origin nor in its maintenance' was involved 'directly or indirectly' in issues of state or federal authority."[200]

Though the 1964 Civil Rights Act helped resolve the tension between antidiscrimination and private property as applied to public accommodations, Prop 14 reignited it with respect to housing. Unlike Justice Black, most Californians did not balk at the notion of extending the antidiscrimination principle into some private spheres, as evidenced by the passage of the state's fair employment practices and Unruh Civil Rights acts in 1959. In neither case did the state's voters seek to undo these laws via the referendum or initiative process. However, when the Rumford Fair Housing Act extended the antidiscrimination principle into the realm of some private homes and apartments, a majority of voters recoiled and passed Prop 14. The quest for antidiscrimination legislation in California ended where private housing began. As one California woman put it, "As a free person I should be able to, and will sell to whoever I please. That's MY RIGHT under the CONSTITUTION and YOUR RIGHTS END WHERE MY PROPERTY BEGINS. I don't care if you are white, black, blue or green."[201]

During the 1966 California gubernatorial race, Democrats, like Unruh, commented that Reagan was "running against fair housing."[202] Reagan's strategy, they believed, was drawn from Machiavelli rather than Locke. His defense of property rights struck them as disingenuous, a thinly veiled ruse that masked a more sinister race-based divide-and-conquer campaign. Becker, for example, spoke of the "conspiracy to divide labor, by using the race issue." The former union organizer recalled the days "when employers broke strikes by hiring Negroes from the South to work behind picket lines." Just as working people then eventually wised up to the employer's divide-and-conquer tactics, so, too, should working people of California recognize and respond to the seeds of dissension being sown by Reagan's run to unseat Brown. The "reactionaries" led by Reagan "can only win . . . if [they] can divide the working people," which is precisely what Becker accused them of "trying to do on the issue of race, especially in the field of housing."[203]

Whether Becker was right about Reagan's motive, he was certainly right about Reagan's effect. As the 1966 election made clear, Brown and the Democrats paid a heavy price for their fair housing stance. On November 8, 1966, Reagan trounced Brown garnering fifty-eight percent of the popular vote. Reagan also led the Republican ticket to triumphs approaching the Democrat's 1958 landslide. The GOP took home five of six statewide offices, five new state senate seats, and seven new assembly seats, winnowing Democratic control of the state legislature to twenty-one to nineteen in the senate and twenty to eighteen in the assembly.[204] Since 1963, California had been, according to Howden, "the nation's number one battleground over fair housing."[205] In 1966, in the wake of Prop 14 and the California Supreme Court case that overturned it, Californians struck a lethal blow to the leader and political party they associated with promoting fair housing. Rumblings of discontent that had been registering on civil rights seismographs since passage of the Rumford Fair Housing Act had coalesced into an electoral earthquake.

Prop 14 marked a pivotal moment in California politics and foreshadowed a similar one for the nation as a whole. Though Barry Goldwater took a beating at the hands of California voters in November 1964, the equally decisive vote for Prop 14 nevertheless represented a vindication of essential ideas that Goldwater espoused. With Prop 14, a majority of Californians served notice about just how much racial liberalism they would tolerate. Many did so while remaining tethered, albeit tenuously, to the Democratic Party. They cast ballots for both Lyndon Johnson and Prop 14. Although such voting behavior struck Brown and his allies as a form of ideological schizophrenia, those "schizophrenic" voters considered their behavior perfectly consistent. As good Democrats they claimed to abhor discrimination in public accommodations, champion equal rights, but oppose perceived encroachments upon property rights. Other voters, however, renounced their party affiliation altogether. Over and over, their resignation letters blamed the Rumford Act and Brown's strident opposition to Prop 14.

Such letters signaled the beginnings of a tectonic shift in California (and American) politics.[206] In 1958, Brown's opposition to Proposition 18—the controversial right-to-work initiative—earned him the allegiance of blue-collar Californians and catapulted him into office. In 1964, as a result of his opposition to Prop 14, Brown declared, "I lost support of the unions." Prop 14, Brown believed, "was a big contributing force in my defeat [by] Reagan."[207] Brown aides offered similar assessments. Brown's press secretary placed the governor's stance on fair housing "no more than one percentage point below" his handling of the contemporaneous University of California, Berkeley free speech protests on a list of factors contributing to Brown's loss.[208] Becker also attributed "some of the opposition that developed to [Brown] in the white community" to the governor's support of fair housing.[209] For Brown's speechwriter, Haas, the day that Prop 14 passed marked the day that "liberalism died."[210]

Though the "Ya Basta" issued by supporters of Prop 14 proved to be a far greater "contributing force," as Brown put it, to his loss to Reagan, the "Ya Basta" issued by "Mexican-American Democrats for Reagan" also contributed to Brown's defeat. Their "Viva Reagan" clubs, according to two scholars, "played an instrumental role in Reagan's victory," garnering him "nearly 30 percent of the Mexican-American vote in California."[211] William Roberts's estimate was slightly lower. "We managed to get almost 25 percent of the Mexcian-American vote who were unhappy with Brown over a lot of things, appointments and so forth, and so we took advantage of that unrest," Roberts recollected. "Ya Basta," Roberts added, "served as a pretty good battle cry for our campaign in the Mexican-American community and it worked"—perhaps more so than Roberts realized.[212] According to Reagan's leading biographer, "Despite Brown's jibe that Reagan was an enemy of Mexican Americans, he ran more strongly in this community (the estimates range from 38 to 40 percent) than any Republican had ever done."[213]

If the exact numbers of white working-class and Mexican American voters are hard to pin down, the final, decisive vote for Reagan over Brown in 1966 is indisputable. The "coalition . . . for many years" that Brown's 1958 and 1966 campaign manager, Fred Dutton, credited the governor with forging during his first term had unraveled. "The Democratic base," Dutton would acknowledge years later as he reflected on Brown's 1966 gubernatorial bid, "was splintering its power."[214] As governor, Reagan would continue to exploit that splintering to his political advantage.

Virna Canson feared the implications of the election of 1966. Ronald Reagan's trouncing of Pat Brown, she wrote, meant that "many of our gains [were] in jeopardy." To meet "their greatest . . . challenge in many years," the NAACP-WC opened a Sacramento legislative office with Canson in charge. Canson's first newsletter from her new position, issued in March 1967, was unequivocal about what needed to be done. Above all, she proclaimed, "We must fight to the last ditch" to "defend the Rumford [Fair Housing] Act."[1]

The NAACP-WC's top civil rights priority corresponded with that of the California Committee for Fair Practices (CCFP), as had been the case since the 1953 formation of the CCFP's predecessor, the California Committee for Fair Employment Practices. In late December 1966, a CCFP newsletter warned against the impending "powerful attack against all the gains made in the past." Among these attacks, emphasis needed to be placed on preventing the Rumford Act from being gutted or repealed.[2] To direct this effort, Nathaniel Colley succeeded C.L. Dellums as the CCFP's chair in January 1967, replacing one longtime NAACP-WC leader with another. A few months later, a CCFP newsletter pronounced preservation of the Rumford Act to be "STILL TOP PRIORITY."[3]

While the NAACP-WC dispatched Canson to Sacramento, MAPA appointed Jack Ortega to an equivalent post. From it, Ortega wrote in 1967, "There are problems that are peculiar to the Mexican-Americans." They "must be pointed out" to California lawmakers, he continued, who "have forgotten . . . that Mexican-Americans . . . deserve consideration and respect despite the cultural and language differences." In contrast to his NAACP and CCFP counterparts, Ortega made no mention of the Rumford Act. Instead, he singled out the paucity of Mexican Americans in the California legislature. In addition, Ortega's reference to "cultural and language differences" alluded to the issue of bilingual education, which would become a top legislative priority for MAPA, and other Mexican American organizations, beginning in 1967.[4] These included the Mexican American Legal Defense and Educational Fund (MALDEF), launched in 1967 as a Mexican American equivalent of the NAACP's Legal Defense and Educational Fund and initially headquartered in San Francisco. Speaking about a bilingual education case MALDEF brought in New Mexico in the early 1970s, Vilma Martinez, the organization's president and general counsel, described bilingual education as to "Chicanos what *Brown [v. Board of Education]* is for Blacks."[5]

Having campaigned against the Rumford Act, Reagan unsurprisingly supported efforts launched in 1967 to either revise or repeal the law. "If revision could solve the problems that caused the passage of [Proposition] fourteen," Reagan said at an April 1967 press conference, "I could go for revision." If, however, the legislature passed a bill to repeal the Rumford Act, Reagan added, "I'll sign it."[6] In fact, neither option presented itself. The United States Supreme Court upheld the California Supreme Court's overturning of Prop 14 in 1967, and Congress then passed the Fair Housing Act in 1968.[7]

With the Rumford Act secure, the NAACP-WC announced its intention in 1969 to switch its "major emphasis" to other areas it had hoped to devote attention, including, above all, school desegregation.[8] When school desegregation litigation yielded victories for its proponents in Los Angeles in 1970 and San Francisco in 1971, "forced busing" became to its opponents, like Reagan, the lightning rod that "forced housing" had been in the 1960s. The NAACP-WC, it turned out, got what it had wished for and more, prompting its regional director Leonard Carter to quip in June 1971, "It seems like all hell is breaking loose in the educational arena."[9]

If busing to promote desegregation was not combustible enough in California, as it was across the country, it was complicated in California by bilingual education. The latter stood at least in tension, if not at loggerheads, with the former. As one MALDEF lawyer explained in 1971, "The danger" in multiracial school systems undergoing court-ordered desegregation "is that the Chicano and Chinese minorities will be so dispersed [to achieve desegregation] that they will lose or fail to receive needed educational programs," most notably "bilingual education."[10]

Reagan quickly apprehended and exploited this tension. Campaigning for re-election in 1970, he insisted that busing would undermine fledgling bilingual education initiatives, which he supported. If Reagan's opposition to busing in the 1970 campaign was an extension of his opposition to fair housing in the 1966 campaign, so, too, was his support for bilingual education an extension of his efforts in both 1966 and 1970 to win Latino voters. Unlike Brown, the NAACP-WC, and the CCFP—who reflected the historical tendency in California for black and white racial liberals, in particular, to reason by analogy and posit a harmony of civil rights interests among Californians of color—Reagan drew a sharp distinction between desegregation through busing, which the NAACP-WC prioritized, and bilingual education, which MALDEF, MAPA, and other Mexican American organizations prioritized.

The tension between desegregation and bilingual education revealed itself dramatically in San Francisco during the early 1970s. There, a desegregation suit brought in federal court by the local NAACP encountered stiff resistance from members of the city's Mexican descent and, especially, Chinese descent communities. Concurrently, a bilingual education suit brought by attorneys acting on behalf of non-English-speaking Chinese descent students, with input from attorneys representing non-English-speaking Mexican descent students, would culminate in the United States Supreme Court in 1974. Though these cases unfolded on separate tracks, they had profound implications for one another. The thrust of desegregation was centrifugal—requiring the dispersal of racial concentrations of students—while the thrust of bilingual education was centripetal—requiring the concentration of students along racial/linguistic lines. For this reason, desegregation activist and Harvard professor Gary Orfield fretted in 1977, "I think that one of the reasons I have become interested in the bilingualism movement and the way it crosses the desegregation issue is that it seems to break up coalitions of minority people in city after city."[11] In California, in general, and San Francisco, in particular, in the 1970s the intersection of desegregation and bilingual education as approaches to promoting equality of educational opportunity did not so much break up the coalitions of which Orfield spoke, which were never that substantial to begin with, but rather impeded their formation. Prior to this time, California's different axes of discrimination had translated into merely *different* avenues of redress. Now, however, the educational civil rights goals pursued through litigation for race-based discrimination, on the one hand, and language-based discrimination, on the other hand, translated into *conflicting* avenues of redress.

When Ronald Reagan assumed the governorship in January 1967, California was approaching the hundredth anniversary of a law enacted in 1872 that stipulated, "All schools shall be taught in the English language."[12] Recently re-elected state Superintendent of Public Instruction Dr. Max Rafferty, whom the *New York Times* described as a "national symbol of the ultraconservative approach to education," drew the newly elected governor's attention to California's English-only instruction law in a November 30, 1966 memorandum—to bury it, however, not to praise it. Among the educational legislation he recommended, Rafferty included a call to "permit initial instruction in native tongue—a bilingual approach. Not require all instruction to be in English." Next to this, Reagan's communications director scribbled, "with limits."[13]

Rafferty's recommendation would have heartened Mexican American advocacy groups and educators, who had been clamoring for something like it for several years. At an August 1963 "Mexican-American Education Conference" in

Los Angeles, for example "Mexican-American community leaders," according to a *New York Times* report, identified language as the "major barrier" to be tackled in schools. In so doing, they joined a growing "wave of Mexican-American concern that the . . . national drive for Negro rights was eclipsing urgent needs of a minority group that, regionally, is quite numerous."[14]

One month later, the Mexican American Ad Hoc Committee on Education admonished the Los Angeles Board of Education's Ad Hoc Committee on Equal Educational Opportunity for not fielding any Mexican American testimony during its year-long public hearings. According to *Los Angeles Times* reporter Ruben Salazar, the Mexican American Ad Hoc Committee on Education "urged the Board of Education to consider Mexican-American problems apart from those of Negroes." In particular, they stressed, "the problems of Mexican-American students do not necessarily stem from de facto segregation or inadequate school boundaries but from curriculum." Rather than desegregation, then, they delineated a handful of proposals, including the teaching of Spanish language and Mexican, Spanish, and Latin American literature, and the hiring of "bilingual teachers, counselors, and administrators who have an understanding of the Mexican-American child and his community."[15]

In May 1964, Carlos Borja, Jr., president of the Council of Mexican-American Affairs and also MAPA leader, delivered a speech to the League of United Latin American Citizens (LULAC) state convention in Long Beach. Borja placed "education" at the top of his list of "state level problems" faced by Mexican Americans (followed by farm labor, English literacy tests as a bar to voting, and under-representation of Mexican Americans in War on Poverty programs). He called for schools to devote more time to letting "the [Mexican American] child develop a pride in his culture, heritage and language."[16]

On the heels of the passage of Prop 14 in November 1964, Dr. Manuel Guerra, MAPA's Education Council chair, echoed and amplified Borja. In testimony to the California FEPC, Guerra maintained that the "educational problems" of Mexican American students "cannot be identified with the problems of Anglo-American children nor those of other minorities." Of particular concern to Guerra was, he charged, the Brown administration's decision to "maintain its original opposition to Spanish instruction in the elementary school program." Following Guerra, Manuel Ruiz, Jr., who had fought for school desegregation of Mexican Americans during the 1940s, urged California legislators to distinguish between the "totally different problem[s]" of "race and color," such as desegregation, and those of "national origin and ancestry," such as bilingual education. What might be the proper response to the "question of segregation and discrimination on account of race and color may be a highly improper approach on the question of discrimination because of national origin and ancestry. Color and race may have no relation to language barriers, lack of communication or bilingual culture."[17]

In May 1966, Assemblyman Philip Soto made a similar point in a letter to the federal Equal Employment Opportunity Commission (EEOC). Mexican Americans, Soto asserted, had "problems that are different and unique to this group alone." First among these, Soto singled out "cultural and language difference," with which, he maintained, "no other large ethnic group is handicapped."[18] George Sánchez, who like Ruiz had fought for school desegregation of Mexican Americans students during the 1940s, echoed Soto. In a 1967 letter to MALDEF founder, Pete Tijerina, Sánchez wrote, "Though we should make common cause with the Negroes from time to time, we should not blend their issues with ours. . . . [W]hile the effects of discrimination against Negro and 'Mexican' are essentially the same, the causes, the history, and the remedies differ broadly. . . . The bases for mistreatment of the *Mexicano* are much more varied and very different."[19] In their reflections on desegregation and bilingual education, Ruiz, Soto, and Sánchez were, in effect, pointing to a pattern that California's multiracial civil rights struggles had long revealed: different axes of discrimination—in this case, race/color versus national origin/ancestry, as Ruiz distinguished— necessitated different avenues of redress—in this case, desegregation versus bilingual education.

Soto's letter to the EEOC came amidst California's gubernatorial race, during which Reagan campaigned hard for Mexican American voters, while making no comparable effort among African Americans.[20] Following Reagan's election, Rafferty's recommendation to support a bill abolishing California's ninety-five-year-old English-only instruction law afforded Reagan the chance to burnish his appeal to Mexican American voters. Shortly after assuming office, that opportunity presented itself. On January 12, 1967, Senator Alan Short, a Democrat representing Sacramento and San Joaquin Counties, introduced Senate Bill (SB) 53. In a letter to Reagan, Short explained that "the essence of the bill" was "to insure the mastery of English by all pupils, but to permit bilingual instruction to the extent it does not interfere with systematic, sequential, and regular instruction in English." This, Short explained, would help reduce the "extremely high" rate of school attrition "among children with a language handicap." Such students were at a "severe disadvantage" in classrooms where they could not "comprehend instruction." Moreover, when they finally acquired English proficiency, they lagged "far behind" their English-speaking classmates and were, therefore far more likely to become "school failure[s] and . . . dropout[s]." As evidence, Short singled out "Spanish surname[d]" Californians, half of whom had "not gone beyond the 8th grade."[21]

Shortly after Short's bill cleared the senate by a unanimous vote in March 1967, representatives from the state's leading Mexican American advocacy organizations, including MAPA and CSO, convened a "Mexican American Legislative Conference." "A new administration in Sacramento," the conference announcement declared, provided the occasion to "unite and plan a course of action for the next four to eight years." For "too long the Mexican-American viewpoint has been missing from the legislation of this State." To correct this in realm of education, conference participants endorsed SB 53 as their top educational priority.[22]

One month after the Mexican American Legislative Conference, the California State Department of Education, at Superintendent of Public Instruction Rafferty's behest, sponsored the "First Annual Nuevas Vistas Conference." Associate Superintendent of Public Instruction, Euguene Gonzales, whom the *Fresno Bee* described as the "first administrator of Mexican descent to hold a high post in the department," chaired the conference planning committee. Some five hundred educators came to the conference, which, according to Rafferty, focused on "the problems that face us in meeting the needs of the Mexican-American" student. Attendees embraced what Horatio Ulibarri, a University of New Mexico professor, described as the "need to revise our curriculum to give the child an opportunity to grow into bilingualism." Rafferty concurred. He spoke of the need for "bilingual teachers who know the language and the culture of the Spanish-speaking child and who can become the bridge for them into a bicultural world." He also spoke about the inappropriateness of conflating Mexican American and African American educational interests. "The needs of the children of Mexican descent are different from those of the Negro minority," he insisted, "and the same techniques or the same materials applied in the one case are not necessarily applicable to the other."[23] Few examples illustrated Rafferty's point better than bilingual education.

On the heels of the first "Nuevas Vistas Conference," the assembly followed the senate's lead and passed SB 53 by an overwhelming margin. Shortly thereafter, on May 24, 1967, Reagan signed the bill into law. "This measure will be of tremendous benefit to many Californians," the governor announced in a press release that accompanied his signing. "It will be particularly valuable," he added, "in giving Spanish-speaking California children more and better opportunities for quality education." They would now have the opportunity to learn subjects in Spanish until they acquired proficiency in English. This, Regan continued, would reduce the "high drop-out rate among Spanish-speaking children," which was due, in part, to "their difficulty in understanding basic subjects which are only taught in English."[24]

The editors of the *Los Angeles Times* hailed the new law a "major breakthrough" for overcoming "the language barrier that has denied a full education to tens of thousands of Spanish-speaking students in Los Angeles schools."[25] Their counterparts at the *Independent Press-Telegram* in nearby Long Beach also praised the law's impact on "Spanish-speaking youngsters, many thousands of whom have been deprived of a fair chance in monolingual classes." That the measure passed "with hardly a whisper of opposition," the editors of the *Independent Press-Telegram* added, owed to the "rising aggressiveness and voting power of the Mexican-American community."[26] As a testament to the growing political power of Mexican Americans, whose votes Reagan had actively pursued in 1966, Reagan himself spoke to the "Third Annual Nuevas Vistas Conference." Waxing proto-multicultural, Reagan declared, "We must find ways to preserve among those of Spanish heritage a proud sense of cultural identity, yet at the same time equip the youngster from a bilingual home to compete and to succeed in the pluralistic melting pot society that we call America."[27]

Reagan's overtures to Mexican Americans through bilingual education anticipated those of fellow California Republican Richard Nixon as president.[28] They were also part of what some Latino political analysts referred to as a "Southwest strategy," which Reagan began employing during his gubernatorial campaign in 1966 in his effort to court Latino voters.[29] This strategy foreshadowed and served as a complement to the GOP's much better-known and infamous "Southern strategy." The brainchild of Republican strategist and Nixon adviser Kevin Phillips, the Southern strategy involved using wedge issues—like school busing for desegregation—to win support from working class white voters (in the South and elsewhere, too) who had historically voted Democratic.[30] The Southwest strategy was a variation on the Southern strategy, but with a Latino twist. The Republicans, led by Reagan in 1966 and Nixon in 1968, also tried to court a traditionally Democratic constituency, Latinos, by supporting bilingual education, which they subsequently pitted against desegregation.[31]

If the significance of the 1967 legislative session to Mexican American advocacy organizations was due, in part, to legislation that passed—SB 53—its significance to the NAACP-WC was due to legislation that did not pass. "As you will recall," wrote Virna Canson in 1969, "many candidates [led by Reagan] who came into office in the Fall of 1966 came in with the promise to repeal the Fair Housing Act." In the face of this threat, the NAACP-WC's "principal achievement in 1967" was the "preservation of the Rumford Fair Housing Act. Through our efforts we were able to weather a storm."[32] A similar storm threatened in 1968. As Canson reported, "Again in 1968, preservation of the fair housing law was the immediate goal," which again her organization achieved. Thwarted for two years running, Canson observed, "even the most rabid anti-fair housing legislators remained silent" in 1969. This silence allowed the NAACP-WC's "major emphasis [to] shift from preservation of fair housing" to other priorities it had previously identified, including, most notably, school desegregation.[33]

Though the California legislature had struck down the state's school segregation statute in 1947 in the immediate aftermath of *Mendez v. Westminster*, de facto school segregation persisted and was a major NAACP-WC concern throughout the postwar period. As early as 1952, for example, Franklin Williams, NAACP-WC regional director, observed, "The large influx of Negroes into . . . cities and the growing pattern of residential segregation is beginning to create substantially segregated schools." School officials, Williams added, "gerrymandered" district lines, which served to "extend the pattern of segregation."[34] Two years later Williams's organization published a pamphlet entitled "Freedom's Frontier," as part of the national NAACP's "Fight for Freedom" campaign to culminate in 1963, the one-hundredth anniversary of the Emancipation Proclamation. At the time, only one state, Arizona, within the NAACP-WC's purview had a school segregation statute. The rest, however, had patterns of "residential segregation" as well as "carefully drawn district boundary lines to enclose areas of Negro occupancy." This gerrymandering contributed to a "species of school segregation."[35] By fighting housing segregation—as it did in the 1950s and 1960s—the NAACP-WC was also, indirectly, fighting school segregation. When the fair housing battles abated in the late 1960s, the NAACP-WC turned its attention more squarely to school segregation.

In the fall of 1966, California published its first annual "Racial and Ethnic Survey of California Public Schools." It revealed that 75.7 percent (3,200,496) of all public school students were white, 13.3 (562,943) percent were Spanish surnamed, 8.05 percent (340,833) were black, 2.1 percent (89,474) were Chinese, Japanese, or Korean, 0.3 percent (11,060) were American Indian, and 0.6 percent (25,819) were other nonwhite. The survey defined a racially "imbalance[d]" school as one in which "the enrollment of pupils of any racial or ethnic group differs by more than 15 percentage points from that for all the schools of the district." By this definition, it found that eighty-five percent of black students and fifty-seven percent of Spanish-surnamed students attended racially imbalanced schools in California's eight largest school districts.[36] Two years later, those percentages, more or less, persisted. A 1969 report prepared by Wilson Riles, the state's deputy superintendent of public instruction reported, "In 1968 three-quarters of all Negro pupils in California attended imbalanced schools, as did more than half of all Oriental pupils and nearly half of all Spanish-surname pupils."[37]

In response, the state Board of Education incorporated the "15 percentage point formula" into its existing integration guidelines in February 1969. Just what actual impact the board's action would have, however, was a matter of dispute. State Superintendent of Public Instruction Rafferty insisted that it would have none whatsoever. "The Board," he exclaimed, "has no legal power to tell the local districts to do anything. It can tell them, but the (local) board can tell them to 'Go jump in a lake.' " At best, the board's decision could have a "moral effect." It lacked, however, the force of a "legal mandate."[38] By contrast, the *Los Angeles Times* reported that the board's newly adopted integration guidelines—"the first such decision anywhere in the nation"—provided the state "with a firm basis for taking school districts to court and cutting off funds if they fail to comply with the new provisions."[39] A few days later, the *Times* reiterated this position, and sketched the implications for the city's nearly one million students. "A strict interpretation of the Board rule," the paper announced, "might lead to extensive dislocation of present student bodies," nearly half of whom were "members of a minority." Hoping to avert such dislocation, the *Times* recommended alternatives short of busing to "meet the problem of de facto segregation" about which "precious little has been done."[40] This inaction, however, was about to change.

The United States Supreme Court paved the way. Though various lower courts wrestled with the exact meaning of *Brown*, by 1968 no legal consensus had emerged. Instead, the debate divided into two camps: those who insisted that *Brown* called only for an end to legalized segregation (via striking segregation statutes from the books) and those who insisted that *Brown* required an affirmative duty to integrate.[41] In *Green v. County School Board*, the Supreme Court entered the debate. The case involved the two New Kent County, Virginia schools, both of which remained as segregated in 1968 as they were before *Brown* in 1954. Speaking on behalf of a unanimous Court, Justice William Brennan did not mince words. *Brown*, he held, left no room for debate. School boards such as New Kent County's were "clearly charged with the affirmative duty to take whatever steps might be necessary to convert to a unitary system in which racial discrimination would be eliminated root and branch." It was not enough that the county offered students the freedom to choose which school they would attend if such "freedom of choice" did not result in integration. Instead, Brennan wrote, "The burden on a school board today is to come forward with a plan that promises realistically to work now."[42]

Like *Brown*, *Green* was a watershed in the nation's long history of school desegregation litigation. But like *Brown*, *Green* raised as many questions as it resolved. Foremost among them, according to legal scholar Alexander Bickel, who clerked for Justice Felix Frankfurter during the *Brown* deliberations, was "whether racial balance must be achieved in each school, or whether zoning which causes residential patterns to be reflected in the schools is unconstitutional as such"? As Bickel saw it, desegregation jurisprudence was at a crossroads. "It is," he wrote in August 1970, "poised to make—or not make—a transition from the disestablishment of segregation to the imposition, in the South initially and then perhaps elsewhere, of a requirement of racial balance in the schools."[43]

In fact, the transition to which Bickel referred was already under way in southern California in the case of *Crawford v. Board of Education of the City of Los Angeles*. "Negro and Mexican children suffer serious harm when their education takes place in public schools which are racially segregated, whatever the source of such segregation may be," announced Judge Alfred Gitelson of the Los Angeles County Superior Court in a February 11, 1970 decision that sent shock waves across California and the country. "It applies equally to segregation not compelled by law (allegedly *de facto*) as when compelled by law (allegedly *de jure*)."[44] With this ruling, Gitelson launched California down a desegregation path that was as precedent setting as it was contentious. Not only did Gitelson read *Brown* and its progeny as applying beyond the South and requiring Los Angeles to take affirmative, corrective steps to redress the racial imbalances in its public schools, but he also applied *Brown* beyond the black and white racial categories in which it had originally been cast and beyond distinctions of whether the source of school segregation was de jure or de facto. Little wonder, then, that the *Los Angeles Times* described *Crawford* as "the most significant court decision on racial segregation outside the South."[45] Implementing it, however, would require busing, which a *Sacramento Bee* columnist predicted "could become the biggest racial backlash issue in California politics since the mid-1960s furor over the Rumford Act."[46]

Running for re-election in 1970, Reagan seized the political opportunity *Crawford* presented. Shortly after Gitelson handed down his decision, Reagan denounced it as "utterly ridiculous . . . shatter[ing] the concept of the neighborhood school as the cornerstone of our educational system."[47] Seven months later, as the election approached, Reagan insisted, "No single issue has produced a greater overall expression of concern—from every ethnic segment of our citizenry—than that of forced busing of school children." Though "the vast majority" of Californians "strongly oppose racial discrimination," Reagan contended, they "understandably view mandatory busing as a ridiculous waste of time and public money which could seriously undermine all efforts to improve the quality of our schools."[48] Reagan's strident opposition to school desegregation via busing in 1970 echoed his strident opposition to fair housing in 1966. As NAACP-WC regional director Leonard Carter remarked in a press release, "The Reagan Southern strategy is no secret. In 1966 his campaign issue was 'forced housing.' Today, his campaign issue is 'forced busing.'"[49] Carter echoed fellow NAACP-WC leader, attorney Nathaniel Colley. Four years earlier, Colley noted the Catch-22 in which proponents of both fair housing and school desegregation found themselves ensnared. "Proposition 14 is tied in with inferior schools," Colley, who was then a member of the California State Board of Education, explained. "The same people who say to us when we try to fight school segregation, 'this is a housing problem,' you'll find them to be the same ones who voted in Proposition 14. Now this is certainly a good double play."[50]

Executing the second half of this double-play, Reagan vowed to "take all legal steps possible to oppose mandatory student busing."[51] His efforts, according to the NAACP-WC's Canson, included prevailing upon the California Board of Education to rescind its 1969 "15 percentage point formula" as a guideline for determining racial imbalance. "The Board's hasty actions," wrote Canson, had been "triggered" by the *Crawford* decision with "pressure exerted through the Governor's office . . . as an 'assist' to the Los Angeles School District in their fight AGAINST complying with the Judge's decision."[52] In addition, Reagan endorsed Assemblyman Floyd Wakefield's Assembly Bill (AB) 551, which proposed to prohibit school districts from transporting students by bus to promote integration without parental permission. His endorsement came despite a warning from the state attorney general's office that AB 551 "could well be held to be unconstitutional."[53] Finally, Reagan linked what Carter referred to as his "Southern strategy" with the Southwestern strategy Reagan employed in his 1966 campaign for Mexican American voters and his 1967 support for abolishing California's English-only law. In a press conference following the *Crawford* decision, he insisted that busing for desegregation would undermine bilingual education. "We have in Los Angeles the community of Americans of Mexican Descent . . . [and] our problem there in the schools of trying to bring about this understanding of the bi-lingual situation to meet the language problem in those schools. I don't know how we'd meet it if you disperse those students out of that neighborhood and scatter them all over the Los Angeles School District."[54] A little over half a year later, in a press release that accompanied his signing of AB 551 into law, Reagan reiterated his contention that busing jeopardized bilingual programming. "Mandatory busing," he asserted, "could imperil some of the most innovative and worthwhile projects for minority children ever instituted in our public schools—vital bilingual teaching programs in neighborhood schools located in Spanish-speaking areas."[55]

Though Carter viewed Reagan's opposition to busing through the prism of the Southern strategy, Reagan's exploitation of the tension between desegregation and bilingual education—pitting them against one another as a zero sum choice between educational civil rights policies—was better viewed as an extension of the Southwest strategy he adopted during his run for governor in 1966.[56] Reagan's efforts were mirrored on a national stage, as President Nixon also demonstrated support for bilingual education while opposing school desegregation through busing.[57]

To avert the damage that "political exploitation of the controversial busing issue" threatened, as Canson put it, the NAACP-WC sought to "take leadership in this fight to get California back on the track in the school situation."[58] In May 1970, the organization sponsored a "Call to Conscience Caucus" in Sacramento to mark the sixteenth anniversary of *Brown* and "reaffirm our commitment to integrated, quality education." NAACP-WC attorney Colley blasted the "right wing bigots" on the California State Board of Education, on which he had recently served, for rescinding the desegregation guidelines that he had helped formulate. "Hell, I wrote those regulations," Colley exclaimed. "They sprang from my heart because I had walked to school in Snowhill, Alabama. The buses passed me loaded with white kids . . . yell[ing], 'Nigger, Nigger!' "[59] Other speakers included state Senator Mervyn Dymally, the only African American member of the senate, who had previously praised *Crawford* as good for "all minorities, not only Blacks."[60] A similar sentiment had prompted Canson's decision for the "Call to Conscience Caucus." As she explained in a letter to national NAACP leader Roy Wilkins in September 1970, after a meeting with a "Chinese-lady Assemblyman from Oakland" who was "really having second thoughts about integration. . . . It hit me hard; I concluded this was rock bottom—a Chinese person deliberating that kind of concept."[61] Despite her and Dymally's conviction about the benefits of desegregation for all minority students, the "Call to Conscience Caucus" acknowledged that future caucuses needed to be more inclusive than it had been, adopting a resolution to "involve leaders from the Mexican-American community."[62]

A little over a month later, the NAACP's San Francisco branch filed a lawsuit in the United States District Court against the city's segregated public elementary schools. Since 1963 the San Francisco Board of Education had issued numerous reports on how to improve racial balance. Not until May 1970, however, did the board approve the implementation of two racially balanced schools slated to open in the upcoming school year. The board's approval of the Richmond and Park South schools came in the face of Mayor Joseph Alioto's staunch opposition. Taking his case to the people, Alioto, who would join the MALDEF Board of Directors in March 1971 and later be hailed by the organization as someone who "tirelessly fought for programs that help the poor, urban Chicanos," urged parents to sue the school district to prevent it from proceeding with its "forced busing" plan.[63]

Frustrated by Alioto's actions, twenty-nine-year-old Charles Belle, NAACP San Francisco chapter president, said he was "tired and ashamed of the segregated schools in the city," which he considered "behind . . . Mississippi and Texas in offering equal educational opportunities to black students."[64] He vowed to sue the school district if it failed to proceed, not just with its plans to open the two new integrated schools, but also with district-wide integration. In June 1970, after the district announced that it only had enough funds to open one of the schools in September, Belle followed through on his promise. A memorandum from Belle's NAACP chapter sought to answer the question it posed, "Why This Lawsuit?" It read, "On June 24, 1970, the case of David Johnson v. San Francisco Unified School District was filed in the Federal District Court in San Francisco. After more than 15 years of unproductive protest to the San Francisco Board of Education, the San Francisco N.A.A.C.P. was finally taking firm steps to end racial discrimination in public education."[65] The legal battle had been joined.

The San Francisco NAACP's suit focused on elementary schools, which housed the school district's most pronounced racial imbalances. Though twenty-nine percent of San Francisco's student population was black in 1969–1970, twenty-seven of the city's ninety-six elementary schools contained black student populations ranging from forty-seven to ninety-seven percent. These percentages, however, only conveyed part of the story. More than the de facto result of "freedom of choice" in neighborhood selection, the NAACP claimed that the segregation in San Francisco Unified School District's (SFUSD) elementary schools had a more insidious basis, including the school district's unequal allocation of resources between schools, its invidious consideration of race in the assignment of school personnel, its racial gerrymandering of school attendance zone lines, and its school site construction which exacerbated segregation. Collectively, according to the NAACP, these acts and omissions denied black elementary school students the "right to be educated under the same and equal terms as white minor residents."[66]

By September 1970, the judge in *Johnson*, Stanley Weigel, announced his intention to issue his decision at some point during the school year. At the same time, he tipped his hand by suggesting that the school district begin preparing for elementary school desegregation. Six months later, the Citizens Advisory Committee on Desegregation and Integration, formed in response to Judge Weigel's suggestion, had barely set about its task when, on April 21, 1971, Weigel announced his impending desegregation order and called for both sides to submit desegregation plans by June 10, 1971.[67]

As the June deadline approached, NAACP-WC regional director Carter touted the virtue of his organization's desegregation litigation for all students. Echoing state Senator Dymally from the year before in reference to *Crawford*, Carter maintained, "Black, brown, yellow and white kids are all being cheated out of a meaningful education opportunity by segregation."[68] The desegregation of San Francisco's elementary schools that the NAACP sued for on behalf of black students was, according to Carter's reasoning by analogy, a means to equality of educational opportunity for all students.

Representatives of San Francisco's Mexican American and Chinese American communities took a different view. In late June 1971, for example, Robert Gonzales, a member of the San Francisco Board of Supervisors and board of director member of MALDEF, echoed Reagan from the year before when he insisted, "The children of the Latino and Chinese communities must not be deprived of the few, hard-won, bilingual/bicultural programs which now exist in San Francisco." These, he feared, would be rendered "economically infeasible" by "too great a dispersal of these communities throughout the City" as a result of *Johnson*. For this reason, though Gonzales claimed to be a strong supporter of integration, he did not think that the plans considered during the *Johnson* litigation addressed "the crucial need for preserving," much less increasing, the district's bilingual/bicultural offerings.[69] The court in *Johnson*, Gonzales charged one month later, "did not exhibit any sensitivity" to the "need" for "bilingual and bicultural programs for children from non-English-speaking home."[70] A local community organization—La Raza Caucus—agreed. Any "integration" plan that emerged from *Johnson*, it insisted, must accommodate "the particular educational needs of the Latino community" for whom "equality of educational opportunity means bilingualism and biculturalism." Like Gonzales, La Raza Caucus worried, "If the Latino community is so dispersed throughout the San Francisco schools that bilingualism is not economically feasible then integration will not be acceptable."[71]

Similar reservations emanated from segments of the city's Chinese descent community. On May 30, 1971, for example, a *San Francisco Examiner and Chronicle* reporter wrote, "Chinese parents argue that if their children are bused far from Chinatown, the children will miss the special Chinese language and cultural schools and lose the special bilingual training in English and Chinese that will enable them to more quickly make their way in Western society."[72] Less than two weeks later, *East/West: The Chinese-American Journal* reported that a record turnout of more than six hundred Chinese descent San Franciscans voiced their opposition to desegregation at the school board's bimonthly public meeting.[73] Similar protests took place throughout the summer. Together, they prompted MALDEF's general counsel Mario Obledo to comment in September 1971, "The Chinese community opposed the busing aspect of the integration order" that Judge Weigel would eventually deliver.[74]

A handful of Chinese community members took their opposition to court. Represented by attorneys Quentin Kopp and William Jack Chow, they sought to intervene in the *Johnson* proceedings in order to win exemption from any desegregation through busing plan that might and eventually did emerge from the NAACP's suit. In making their case, Kopp and Chow lumped together the opposing sides of the *Johnson* litigation. They charged both the school district and the NAACP with ignoring "the wishes and needs of pupils of Chinese extraction." Those needs included after-school "Chinese cultural education" and in-school "access to bi-lingual teachers and administrators," both of which, they argued, would be jeopardized by desegregation through busing. This, in turn, would cause "irreparable harm." In the process, Kopp and Chow offered a reading of what equal protection of the laws entailed for equal educational opportunity that differed from the NAACP's. Desegregation and equal educational opportunity were not inextricably bound, as the NAACP lawyers argued in *Johnson*. Instead, when it came to Chinese American students, desegregation had the effect of "denying [them] an equal educational opportunity."[75] Put another way, what was good for one group was not necessarily good or legal for another. "Pupils classified racially otherwise than as negroes are entitled to that educational opportunity which constitutes an equal educational opportunity for their racial classification," Kopp and Chow contended. "What is good for one racial classification," they insisted, "is not necessarily good for another, and to achieve equality one must take into account the special problems of particular racial groups."[76] This argument bore a striking resemblance to one advanced by MALDEF staff attorney Alan Exelrod that same year. After ruminating over the difficulty of reconciling desegregation with bilingual education, Exelrod suggested, "The solution is to view identifiable minority groups—black, brown, yellow, and red—as separate and distinct classes for purposes of equal protection analysis and equitable relief."[77]

The resistance to desegregation on the part of some Chinese San Franciscans garnered national attention. One *Wall Street Journal* reporter, for example, noted the novelty and, in his view, irony of it all. "In few cities have minority groups with a legacy of deep discrimination against them . . . so loudly protested a desegregation move designed primarily to aid minorities." This observation betrayed the very tendency that the Chinese San Franciscans seeking exemption from desegregation challenged. From their vantage point, there was nothing at all ironic about their resistance, unless one conflated—as did the *Wall Street Journal Reporter* and NAACP—the educational civil rights interests of African Americans with Chinese Americans.[78]

There was, however, something morally and legally compelling about the Chinese American opposition to desegregation—or so their lawyers claimed and the *Wall Street Journal* reporter acknowledged. Unlike white resistance in other parts of the country, the Chinese American appeal merited and indeed legally mandated a special hearing. For like the African American plaintiffs that the NAACP represented in *Johnson*, Chinese Americans, in their attorneys' words, "have been and continue to be every bit as subject to the residual and continuing effects of racial classification by law and racial discrimination." They were, by the Supreme Court's definition, a "discrete and insular" minority. And, as such, any government actions that implicated them—such as Judge Weigel's impending desegregation ruling—must receive "more exacting" (or, strict) judicial scrutiny before being applied to them. As Kopp and Chow asserted on behalf of their Chinese American litigants, "The victims of such denial of equal protection of the law should not without hearing be subjected to a 'cure' they neither need nor want, for to do so merely perpetuates the invidious racial discrimination."[79]

Judge Weigel disagreed. In his July 9, 1971 decision in *Johnson*, he rejected the claim for Chinese American exemption. In addition, like Judge Gitelson in Los Angeles the year before in *Crawford*, Weigel adopted a definition of desegregation that reached beyond the black and white categories in which it had typically been cast. He explained, "It has been repeatedly urged upon the Court that, since the racial population of San Francisco (and its elementary school children) is more diverse than in other communities, racial segregation in the elementary schools ought to be permitted. The law allows no such latitude."[80]

Not to be denied, lawyers for the Chinese Americans seeking exemption from desegregation made one last ditch effort before the 1971 school year began. Their eleventh-hour appeal went to Supreme Court Justice William O. Douglas who agreed that what was good for one group was in fact good for another. In Douglas's opinion, "*Brown v. Board of Education* was not written for blacks alone. . . . The theme of our desegregation cases extends to all racial minorities treated invidiously by a State or any of its agencies."[81] Douglas's reasoning must have struck the Chinese American petitioners as maddeningly ironic. For they were indeed saying that the state was treating them invidiously, but *because* of desegregation, not *despite* it. Ironies aside, the outcome remained: elementary pupils of Chinese descent were to be included in San Francisco's new desegregation-via-busing plan.

On Monday, September 13, 1971 a fleet of 130 school buses took to the hilly San Francisco streets on the first day of the school year. Thousands of elementary school children flocked to street corners and awaited those buses as they anticipated the new school year. "For the first time in San Francisco's long history of good race relations," wrote a *San Francisco Chronicle* reporter, "the city's 97 elementary schools will be totally integrated."[82] Or would they?

Judge Weigel hoped that "the school children of San Francisco can be counted upon to lead the way to unity."[83] For many of the 25,000 elementary schoolers slated to board buses on the first day of the 1971 school year, however, the question of the day was whether they would do so.[84] While Mayor Alioto sought to allay fears about safety and warned against violent protest, representatives from

WALK, a coalition of anti-busing groups, predicted that all 25,000 children would remain at home on the first day.[85] Thereafter, according to WALK's co-chair, another half would be kept out of school until the court reversed course.[86]

This prediction would prove exaggerated. Still, many seats were empty on the buses that opening day, as were many desks at the schools to which they were bound. Overall, an estimated forty-four percent of the city's elementary school students did not report to class, with absentee rates peaking in Chinatown. There a mere forty pupils—fewer than half of them Chinese—boarded their designated buses, a far cry from the 750 that the city assigned.[87] By October 1971, the number of boycotters had dropped precipitously. Citywide, school bus ridership rose to seventy-one percent, while the percentage of elementary school students still boycotting classes hovered around fifteen percent (eighty percent of whom were assigned to be bused).[88]

Chinatown, however, was the exception to this trend. There, the resistance, which had been stiff since before the desegregation order, not only persisted but evolved into an alternative to busing. During the first week of the school year, four Chinese Community Schools opened their doors to some 1,000 of Chinatown's 5,500 elementary school children, with another 1,000 on a waiting list.[89] In an ironic twist, these "freedom schools," as they soon came to be known, borrowed their name from schools established by civil rights activists in the South in response to the region's massive resistance to desegregation. Less ironic was the "freedom-of-choice" argument against busing that was expressed by various leaders in the Chinatown community, including James Wong of Chinese Parents for Quality Education. He explained, "We were forced to set up these schools because of the strong desire of parents to have a free choice of where to send their children."[90] Such freedom-of-choice plans had been the remedy of choice for many school districts in the South following *Brown* and had done little more than replicate the segregated systems of schooling, albeit without an explicit statutory sanction. Leaders of the San Francisco "freedom schools," however, insisted that they were not opposed to integration, per se, but rather to busing. Busing, they feared, would have numerous adverse consequences, including pulling Chinatown students away from the benefits of special English language programs established in local schools, limiting student access to private Chinese language and cultural after-school programs because of the time required to transport students, driving a wedge between Chinese-speaking parents and the new schools because of language barriers and distance, and fomenting tensions between Chinese and non-Chinese children at the new schools.[91]

Nathan Glazer, a Harvard sociologist on sabbatical at Stanford, followed the drama unfolding to his north as the San Francisco Unified School District began its first year under court-ordered desegregation. Something, he thought, was terribly as what had once been a "Southern issue [now] became a national issue." "How," he asked, "have we come from a great national effort to repair a monstrous wrong to a situation in which the sense of right of great majorities is offended by policies which seem continuous with that once noble effort?" Unlike *Brown*, to whose lineage *Johnson* laid claim, the thrust of the *Johnson* decision, in Glazer's view, "turned from one in which the main note is the expansion of freedom into one in which the main note is the imposition of restrictions." This might have made legal and ethical sense in the South where history was cast in black and white and the "whites in question were the children or grandchildren of those who had deprived black children of their freedom in the past." Beyond the South, however, beyond black and white, what did equal protection entail? "Is it 'equal protection of the laws,'" Glazer asked, "to prevent Chinese-American children from attending nearby schools in their own community, conveniently adjacent to the afternoon schools they also attend? Is it 'equal protection of the laws' to keep Spanish-speaking children from attending school in which their numerical dominance has led to bilingual classes and specially trained teachers? Can the Constitution possibly mean that?" In the name of promoting equal protection for one group of students— for black students via desegregation—was the court now riding roughshod over the equal protection of another?[92]

Glazer's query echoed that of Manuel Ruiz, Jr. of the United States Civil Rights Commission from 1970 and anticipated that of San Francisco Board of Education member David Sanchez in 1972. "Assuming desegregation resulted in perfect racial balance between black and white," Ruiz observed, "the problem of the Mexican American would not be solved." School curricula remained "oriented for persons whose first language, whether black or white, is English— persons not beset by bi-lingual problems."[93] Two years later, as the *Johnson* decision was being implemented in San Francisco, Sanchez contended that he "saw no way a busing plan would help the Spanish-speaking people, who need more bilingual programs rather than integration."[94]

While SFUSD proceeded with the desegregation ordered by Judge Weigel, city attorneys appealed to have the verdict overturned. The case dragged on for several years before the Ninth Circuit Court of Appeals rendered its verdict on June 21, 1974. Waiting for a cue from the Supreme Court in *Keyes v. School District No.1*, a Denver-based desegregation case, the court of appeals held that the trial court in *Johnson* "applied an erroneous legal standard in determining that a constitutional violation had occurred." As *Keyes* had stipulated, determining whether school districts *intended* to segregate was critical to differentiating between de jure and de facto segregation.[95] Though it was "quite understandable" that the trial court "made no finding as to whether the School Board possessed the requisite segregatory intent," in *Johnson* since *Johnson* had, after all, preceded *Keyes*, it was now neither sufficient nor legal. "Because the litigants, like the district court, did not focus on the issue of intent," the court of appeals held, "we cannot be confident that all of the relevant and reasonably available evidence is now before us." *Johnson* was to be "vacated and remanded for further consideration."[96] Though legally the Ninth Circuit ruled that the *Johnson* desegregation order would remain in effect until the litigation reached a final resolution, practically speaking that order seemed to have had little effect on reducing SFUSD's racial imbalance. In 1971 thirty-eight percent of the city's elementary school students attended racially imbalanced schools. In 1974, forty-three percent did.[97] In 1971, court-ordered integration in San Francisco inflamed passions and attracted national attention. By 1974, it seemed to have left little imprint on the city's schools and fizzled to a temporary close.[98]

Although some Chinese Americans in San Francisco fought *against* the NAACP's chosen path to equal educational opportunity (i.e., desegregation), others fought *for* an alternative path along an altogether separate track. For them, language—or, more specifically, English-only instruction—was the root cause of the educational discrimination they faced. As community organizer Ling-chi Wang explained at a March 1969 Chinatown meeting between parents and SFUSD's superintendent, "Language handicaps are depriving many Spanish- and Chinese-speaking children from getting an education. . . . Classes are irrelevant and create more anger and frustrations."[99] The following school year, *East/West* reported, Chinese-speaking students "languish in classes for which they are not linguistically equipped, marking time, bored, frustrated, building a tension to a near-breaking point."[100]

In response, lawyers acting on behalf of non-English-speaking Chinese students in SFUSD filed suit in the United States District Court in San Francisco on March 23, 1970. Ed Steinman, a twenty-five-year-old Stanford Law School graduate and Freedom Summer participant with one year of federal clerkship experience and a few months as a public interest attorney in Chinatown, served as lead counsel. Reflecting on how often he needed a translator to conduct his legal work—which typically involved representing Chinese immigrant tenants and employees against their landlords and employers—Steinman began wondering about the educational plights of his clients' children. He started attending community and school board meetings, where he soon discovered an enormous unmet educational need: "thousands of kids who were getting nothing" in the classroom as a result of their inability to comprehend English. Having represented the mother of six-year-old Kinmon ("Kinney") Lau, a recent Chinese immigrant, in a wage garnishment dispute with her employer, Steinman found his way to his lead plaintiff in *Lau v. Nichols*.[101]

Unlike the contemporaneous *Johnson* case, *Lau* did not challenge segregation. Quite the opposite. For the non-English-speaking students represented in *Lau*, integration was the problem —integration, that is, into classes where English was the sole language of instruction. Thus, while Johnson's lawyers called for "complete desegregation of the student bodies, faculties, and administrative personnel," Lau's lawyers sought "special instruction in English, taught by bilingual teachers."[102] Absent that instruction, they argued, SFUSD denied "the right to an education" to some 1,800 non-English-speaking Chinese students— a number that was growing rapidly in the wake of the demographic changes ushered in by the 1965 Immigration Act.[103]

Whatever his case's merits, Steinman believed that he stood no chance when he drew Lloyd Burke as the trial court judge in his case. From his previous year as a clerk in the Ninth Circuit, Steinman knew Judge Burke. "Once I get Burke I know that's it," Steinman later recollected. "Lloyd Burke would come in at 11 o'clock and leave at 2 o'clock every day. . . . Very much a right winger. . . . I knew his politics. I knew his style. I knew I had no chance to win." He was right. Judge Burke needed only two-and-a-half hours to hear the case and two weeks to cobble together a written opinion. On May 26, 1970, he concluded that to grant the Chinese-speaking students the relief they sought would be to confer upon them rights denied to other students. "Plaintiffs have no right to a bilingual education," Burke's opinion read, however "desirable and effective" such education might be. "Their special needs, however acute, do not accord them special rights above those granted other students."[104]

Curiously, though Burke signed the opinion, the words were all Steinman's. "I wrote the order against me which he signed," Steinman explained years later. At the time, according to Steinman, overworked and understaffed state court judges often had the winning attorneys write the opinions that the judges would then read, edit, and sign. Though Burke was a federal judge, he did not have a clerk. Moreover, Steinman's opposing counsel was a city attorney with a heavy caseload. With his eye on winning on appeal, Steinman approached Burke and "did something which was chutzpah. . . . I say, 'You know what Judge Burke . . . I know you don't like this case and lookit I'm a young attorney; I've got nothing to do. . . . Tell you what, I will take a stab at writing the order that you're going to issue against me.'" Burke agreed, and Steinman wrote a short opinion in a way that he knew the judge would approve but hoped that the Ninth Circuit Court of Appeals or United States Supreme Court would not. "I didn't go crazy, I didn't write it long, and I didn't do anything at all that was dangerous," Steinman remembered. "But I wrote in the way . . . [that] captured what he felt: you don't second guess schools, that's not what courts do, and if every kid's getting the same thing that's equality."[105] Of course, Steinman did not subscribe to such a rigid view of equality and he hoped that the Ninth Circuit would not either.

While Steinman appealed *Lau*, California legislators wrangled over appropriating funds for bilingual education. Assemblyman Peter Chacon led the effort. "The California Legislature has not provided monies for bilingual-bicultural education," Chacon wrote, "even though we have a law," signed by Reagan in 1967, "that permits a language other than English to be used as a medium of instruction."[106] In 1971, a state Bilingual-Bicultural Task Force counted nearly 200,000 students in the state "whose primary language is other than language"—160,000 of them being Spanish speakers—and who were "not being educated in their mother tongue."[107] Though no law precluded such instruction, no state funds—and minimal federal funds —existed to provide it. By Chacon's estimate, "If we were to service the 200,000 plus youngsters in our schools in California who have a language other than English, we would need 20–30 million more dollars." An effort to procure $3 million worth of that funding passed the state legislature in 1971, only to be vetoed by Reagan.[108]

Undeterred, Chacon introduced the Bilingual Education Act of 1972 (AB 2284). Like its forerunner from the year before, AB 2284 passed both houses of the California legislature by overwhelming majorities. Unlike its predecessor, however, the Bilingual Education Act of 1972 received support from Reagan. A December 22, 1972 press release accompanying his signature hailed the law's $5 million appropriation for "more effective bilingual education programs in California" as a "key element of [the governor's] 1972 legislative program." It would target "youngsters in the earliest elementary grades, particularly children of Mexican descent who have learned little or no English before enrolling in school." This, in turn, Reagan believed, would help steer these students "into the mainstream of our educational system and ultimately into the mainstream of our economic system."[109] Though the funds fell far short of what Chacon deemed necessary, they nevertheless marked "the first time the State of California has made a genuine commitment to our non-English-speaking and limited-English-speaking school children." Noting Reagan's support for establishing a "comprehensive bilingual program," Chacon remarked, "This is a major gain."[110] What Chacon probably did not know was that it was a gain that came against the advice of Reagan's own Department of Finance, which recommended that he "sign but delete the appropriation."[111]

Unmentioned by Reagan and Chacon was any connection between Reagan's support for bilingual education and opposition to desegregation, which Reagan had juxtaposed in 1970 in the wake of the *Crawford* decision. This connection, however, would not have been far from Reagan's mind in 1972. That year Reagan reinforced his commitment to bilingual education, while he also reiterated his opposition to desegregation through school busing. In September 1972, he threw his support behind Proposition 21. Spearheaded by Assemblyman Floyd Wakefield, Proposition 21 proposed to add a section to the California Education Code stipulating, "No public school student shall, because of his race, creed, or color be assigned to or be required to attend a particular school." Proponents of the measure referred to it as "The Neighborhood School Initiative." It aimed to "preserve" the "right" of parents to have their children "attend schools in the neighborhood where [they] choose to live." Opponents of the measure, such as Senator Dymally, cast it as an attempt to "outlaw integrated schools in California," and, more generally, "the most vicious, racist proposal to be offered to the public" since Prop 14. As with Prop 14, the proponents won in a rout—4.96 million (63.1%) to 2.91 million (36.9%).[112] However, as with Prop 14, Proposition 21 would eventually be declared unconstitutional by the California Supreme Court in 1975.[113]

In the meantime, the Ninth Circuit issued its *Lau* decision in January 1973, upholding the trial court's ruling, but with one ultimately lethal addition. Unlike the African American plaintiffs in *Johnson*, the Ninth Circuit ruled, the Chinese American plaintiffs in *Lau* made "no showing that [their] lingual deficiencies are at all related to any such past [state-based] discrimination. . . . The classification claimed invidious is not the result of laws enacted by the State presently or historically, but the result of deficiencies created by appellants themselves in failing to learn the English language." In other words, it was the immigrant kids' fault that they did not speak English. The San Francisco schools met the Fourteenth Amendment's equal protection mandate by treating English-speaking and non-English-speaking students the same. Absent a finding of intentional discrimination by the state, the *Lau* plaintiffs were not legally entitled to anything more than "the same facilities, textbooks and curriculum." An educational "need"—in this case, supplemental English-language instruction—did not rise to the level of an educational "right."[114]

When Steinman read the Ninth Circuit's opinion, he rejoiced. True, the court had rebuffed his appeal, but it did so in part by attributing the so-called "lingual deficiencies" to the Chinese-speaking students themselves. Steinman recalled thinking, "My God how could you not be happier?! You schmucks! You idiots! Blame the kids?!"[115] In so doing, the Ninth Circuit paved *Lau*'s way to the Supreme Court.

Steinman's briefs presented two basic arguments. First, the Chinese-speaking students were a "discrete and insular" minority who were entitled to the same level of judicial protection as African Americans, and, second, that equal treatment sometimes entailed different treatment. Thus, whereas the NAACP lawyers in *Johnson* fought for the right of black children to be "educated under the same and equal terms" as white students, Steinman argued that the "same and equal" treatment between English-speaking and non-English-speaking students constituted a denial of equal educational opportunity. "The Equal Protection Clause forbids not only different treatment of similarly situated persons, but also identical treatment of persons who are not similarly situated." Indeed, if anything the *Lau* plaintiffs had a more compelling equal protection claim than did the *Johnson* plaintiffs. After all, Steinman reasoned, black students in segregated schools could at least "understand their teachers, fellow students, and the materials of instruction." By contrast, non-English-speaking students were completely cut off from equal educational opportunity. In terms of promoting such opportunity, then, language was as least as salient a prism through which to view diversity and discrimination as race.[116]

A number of amici curiae briefs accompanied Steinman's case to the Supreme Court. A group of Chinese organizations, including the Chinese Consolidated Benevolent Association, the Chinese Chamber of Commerce, and the Chinese for Affirmative Action, maintained that equal treatment for students unequally situated did not amount to equal educational opportunity.[117] In addition, a group of Mexican American organizations, including MALDEF, sought to link the plight of the *Lau* students to that of Spanish-speaking students. This decision, at least on MALDEF's part, involved overcoming an initial reluctance to even participate in the *Lau* litigation. In an April 1973 letter sent from MALDEF legal director Sanford Jay Rosen to MALDEF staff attorney Alan Exelrod, Rosen fretted, "This is the wrong case to go to the Supreme Court first." Instead, Rosen preferred a case in which "the vast majority of the 5,000,000 . . . Spanish-speaking children" were the lead plaintiffs. Only in such a case was "the potentiality of success . . . greatest, and the risks smallest."[118]

Rosen even went so far as to phone Steinman, exhorting him not to press the case to the Supreme Court. "They [Rosen and MALDEF] were scared shitless that we're going to lose this case," remembered Steinman, "that I would just destroy it."[119] Steinman, not surprisingly, took a different view. Given the "model minority" stereotype, Steinman thought "the courts might have an easier time dealing with children from [Chinese] backgrounds than with children from Spanish-speaking backgrounds." A legal victory for Steinman's Chinese immigrant students would, Steinman believed, pave the way for other non-English-speaking students.[120] Moreover, even if he lost—as had happened in the trial and appellate courts—Steinman felt that MALDEF could just distinguish *Lau* as an exceptional case, not applicable to Spanish-speaking students. Unable to dissuade Steinman from forging ahead, MALDEF participated in an amicus brief, noting, "This denial of an equal educational opportunity presently taking place in the Chinese community in San Francisco is but a microcosm of the situation facing Spanish-speaking communities in the United States today." It also suggested that compensatory language instruction was necessary to "remedy a past history of segregation" for students of Chinese and Mexican descent, although it did not address the issue of how such instruction might foster another kind of segregation.[121]

A few years before MALDEF filed its *Lau* amicus brief, a newsletter published by the organization observed how Nixon, like Reagan in 1970, had staked out positions against desegregation through busing but for bilingual education. "It was clear to MALDEF attorneys," the newsletter reported, "that no more action to eliminate segregation can be expected from HEW than from the Justice Department. (This impression has since been reaffirmed by the Administration's public statements). In other educational areas, however"—including bilingual education—"we are much more hopeful."[122] This hope was borne out, in part, by the filing of an amicus brief on the side of the *Lau* petitioners by Nixon's Department of Justice, led by Solicitor General Robert Bork and joined by Assistant Attorney General Stanley Pottinger, among others. In their brief, Bork and Pottinger maintained that failure to "provide some special instruction to national origin-minority group students . . . who do not have proficiency in the English language sufficient to allow them meaningfully to participate in the educational program which is readily accessible to their English-speaking classmates" constituted a violation of both the equal protection clause of the Fourteenth Amendment and Title VI of the Civil Rights Act of 1964.[123]

Arrayed against such formidable opponents, attorneys for the city of San Francisco reiterated their winning lower court formula; namely, that equal treatment did in fact amount to equal educational opportunity, and that where there was no intentional discrimination, there need not be any more corrective action taken by the school district than the programs already in place. Yes, there might be a "need" on the part of Chinese-speaking students for special English-language instruction, but a "need" did not constitute a "right." "Something more than 'racial imbalance' or hardship on an 'insular minority' is needed to justify judicial intervention with a state's social policies and educational programs." Under such circumstances, legislation, not litigation, was the proper course of action. In addition, the city attorneys touched upon the legal incompatibility (in their view) between desegregation and bilingual education. How could the plaintiffs accuse the school district of discriminating against non-English-speaking students when in fact the district had not attempted "to set them apart and accord to them special treatment on the basis of their language difficulties?" How could the *Lau* plaintiffs reconcile their remedy of choice (i.e., bilingual education) with legal precedents prohibiting state-sanctioned segregation? As the city attorneys stated, "The petitioners are complaining because there has been no segregation and, in fact, that is just what they seek."[124]

The Supreme Court avoided addressing the tension between desegregation and bilingual education. Instead, on January 21, 1974—a little more than a month after twenty-nine-year-old Ed Steinman, who was then a Santa Clara University law professor, appeared for oral argument before the Supreme Court—Justice Douglas delivered a short, unanimous, and ringing vindication of the *Lau* plaintiffs, best described as the *Brown v. Board of Education* for language minority students.[125] Equality of educational opportunity meant more than mere similar treatment of dissimilarly situated students. Implicitly referencing and renouncing the Ninth Circuit's attribution of "lingual deficiencies" to the *Lau* students themselves, the Supreme Court pronounced, "There is no equality of treatment merely by providing students with the same facilities, textbooks, teachers, and curriculum; for students who do not understand English are effectively foreclosed from any meaningful education." To make the "very core" of what public schools teach a prerequisite to "effectively participate" in public schools is to "make a mockery of public education." The Supreme Court based its decision not on the equal protection clause but rather on Title VI of the 1964 Civil Rights Act, which banned discrimination "on the ground of race, color, or national origin" in "any program or activity receiving Federal financial assistance." By this statutory standard, effects, not intentions, were what mattered in determining discrimination. "Discrimination is barred which has that *effect* even though no purposeful design is present." Inaction on the part of the school district to meet the linguistic needs of its non-English-speaking Chinese students thus amounted to discrimination. The Court did not indicate a specific program to redress that discrimination. Instead, it "remand[ed] the case for the fashioning of appropriate relief."[126]

Just what form that "appropriate relief" should take would be a question that educators and policy makers would begin to wrestle with following *Lau*. As complicated and fraught as it would be to arrive at an answer, it would prove even more complicated and fraught in school districts, like San Francisco's, operating under desegregation orders. As a MALDEF Education Task Force convened in the aftermath of *Lau* asked about one of the "many questioned unanswered" in the decision, "Is segregation the only feasible manner to achieve bilingual education?"[127] This question captured the tension between desegregation and bilingual education. More broadly, it dramatized how California's largely separate struggles for civil rights since the 1940s had come into collision, at least where desegregation and bilingual education were concerned as paths to equality of educational opportunity.

At a heated San Francisco school board meeting held in the immediate wake of the *Johnson* decision in July 1971, a Chinese Chamber of Commerce member vowed, "The sleeping giant of San Francisco is waking up. We will fight all the way to the Supreme Court." Three months later, the writer Tom Wolfe reported on the contentious opening of the 1971 school year in San Francisco. "School integration," Wolfe wrote in *New York* magazine, "has set off the first militant movement ever to sweep Chinatown." Yet this was a curious militant movement in Wolfe's eyes, for its participants "were not demonstrating for civil rights, a bigger slice of the pie, the release of political prisoners, the uplift of the people, or for even a slightly new deal." On the contrary, "All they were saying was: no favors, thank you, you lunatics. Include us out of your politics and your orgies of guilt." Thus, the stirring of San Francisco's "sleeping giant" was, in Wolfe's estimation, "a mighty blow for the status quo."[128] Wolfe, however, was only half right. Members of San Francisco's Chinese descent community had not eschewed the quest for civil rights, nor was their struggle merely a reactionary reflex to desegregation. Far from it. Although some of them were, indeed, fighting *against* one form of educational civil rights (desegregation) in the courtrooms, streets, and "freedom schools" of San Francisco, others were, in fact, fighting *for* another form of educational civil rights (bilingual education).

Like most cities across the country, San Francisco grappled with issues of educational discrimination during the 1960s along a black/white axis: racial segregation being seen as the equal protection violation, racial desegregation was the chosen remedy. As one Chinese American community leader explained, the San Francisco school board "was so divided and preoccupied with the whole integration and busing program that they couldn't care less about [bilingual education]."[129] Unlike most cities across the country, however, the growing and increasingly vocal Chinese descent population challenged what historian Matthew Jacobson has described as a "civil rights politics . . . [that] pressed an agenda of racial justice defined by the binary logic of the Jim Crow South."[130] They bucked this "binary logic" when they insisted that what was good for African American students was not necessarily good or even legal for students of Chinese descent.[131]

The Chinese American campaign against desegregation was a negative challenge to the reigning remedy to educational discrimination—"negative" in the sense that it did not advance an alternative remedy, but rather only sought exemption from the NAACP's remedy. By contrast, the separate but concurrent Chinese American campaign for bilingual education was a positive one. Bilingual education proponents did not oppose desegregation, per se. Rather, they supported bilingual education and, in the process, presented what attorney Ed Steinman described as a "different notion of equality" than the one undergirding the NAACP's defense of desegregation. He explained, "At that time, the country was focused on problems of racial segregation. A focus on segregation and the treatment of blacks, in essence, provides one notion of inequality: taking people who are the same and treating them differently. That is only half the coin. The other side of inequality is more subtle, less visible, and equally invidious. It is taking kids who are different and treating them the same."[132]

Philosophically speaking—to the extent that they reflected upon it—bilingual education advocates like Steinman did not detect any fundamental contradiction between the "old" and "new" notions of what equal protection of the laws entailed for equal educational opportunity. The two remedies to educational discrimination were, as Steinman put it, flip sides of the same equal protection coin. In some cases equal protection meant same and equal treatment; in other cases it meant different treatment. Supreme Court Justice Douglas, in fact, conveyed as much with opinions that first rejected the Chinese American request for exemption from desegregation in *Johnson* and later supported the Chinese American call for bilingual education in *Lau*.

Practically speaking, however—as a matter of educational policy to be implemented—bilingual education and desegregation proved much harder to reconcile. Though Steinman would eventually recognize the "agonizing tension" between desegregation and bilingual education, in the early 1970s he did not detect any such tension. Instead, he hoped for a fusion of both.[133] Like Steinman, MALDEF also hoped to secure both desegregation and bilingual education. "In adopting the appropriate desegregation plan," the organization wrote in its *Johnson* amicus brief, "this Court should not only safeguard the existing, although limited Spanish-English bilingual-bicultural program, but should also reflect in such a plan the right of all Spanish-speaking children to bilingual-bicultural instruction." Though school desegregation and bilingual education were not antithetical in MALDEF's view, MALDEF warned against privileging the former over the latter. "Whenever a state undertakes to provide educational opportunities, it must do so in a manner that meets the educational needs of all classes of children equally and not just those of a particular racial or linguistic group."[134] Unlike Steinman, however, MALDEF recognized from the outset the practical challenge of reconciling desegregation and bilingual education. A September 1971 report commissioned by MALDEF, for example, cautioned, "It should be noted that the goal of school integration possibly conflicts with another goal sought to be effected by MALDEF, that of bilingual education for Chicano students. As the goal of a unitary [integrated] system is approached, the difficulties for providing a bilingual education are compounded and perhaps impossible to overcome. It would seem, then, that only one of these goals can be vigorously pursued and that whichever goal is selected should be that one which in the long run would provide the greatest opportunity for Chicano students to truly improve their position vis-à-vis Anglo society."[135] Several years later, MALDEF's Vilma Martinez questioned "whether rules which are formulated to protect Southern Blacks are applicable by extension to Chicanos." In particular, Martinez noted how "bilingual-bicultural education may itself be at odds with *Brown* and its progeny" since "true bilingual-bicultural education classes may at times call for separate classes in substantive subjects."[136] As Martinez saw it, "bilingual education" was to "Chicanos what *Brown* is for Blacks." Because language "define[d] the Chicano and his culture," bilingual education cut to the core of the "problems the Chicanos face" and could, therefore, serve as the "star on which to hitch MALDEF's wagon."[137]

Martinez's suggestion that MALDEF privilege bilingual education over desegregation reflected an ironic trajectory that MALDEF attorney Carlos Alcala attributed to Mexican American history more broadly. Writing in 1974 and alluding to the 1947 *Mendez* desegregation case, Alcala observed, "Where Chicanos formerly argued for an eradication of segregation resulting from educators allegedly benign pedagogical motives"—the "language handicaps" that school officials in southern California in the 1940s trotted out to defend their segregation policies—"Chicanos are now arguing for bilingual-bicultural classrooms that may well remain segregated." What was once an "an excuse for segregation" and was vehemently opposed by the likes of George I. Sánchez in Texas and Manuel Ruiz in Los Angeles had, by 1974, "reached popular acceptance in an equal educational opportunity milieu and is being advanced in a series of suits across the nation." Simply put, according to Alcala, "The current legal status of bilingual education is full circle from its original position—an irony of history."[138]

Rather than choose between the two, MALDEF continued to search for ways to reconcile them. In July 1976, MALDEF's director of education litigation Peter Roos proposed a project whose "basic thrust . . . should be toward a reconciliation of the needs of a bilingual program and the legal requirements against segregation. The issue has most frequently come up in the context of an order to desegregate." As Roos explained the following year at a conference on "Desegregation and the Education Concerns of the Hispanic Community," "Simply stated, the threat to bilingual programming derives from the dispersal aspects of a desegregation decree. Students are dispersed to various schools in order to break down ethnic or racial concentration. It is just such concentration that many feel to be a predicate for effective bilingual programming. Can these apparently contradictory goals be reconciled?"[139]

Speaking at the same conference, Gary Orfield, a leading desegregation advocate and scholar, lamented the political consequences of the tension that MALDEF sought to resolve. He explained, "I think that one of the reasons I have become interested in the bilingualism movement and the way it crosses the desegregation issue is that it seems to break up coalitions of minority people in city after city."[140] Orfield could very well have had Ronald Reagan and Richard Nixon in mind, both of whom sensed the political payola to be gleaned from pitting bilingual education against desegregation. Alternatively, and coming from the opposite end of the ideological spectrum, Orfield could have had the NAACP-WC in mind. Leading members of that organization also presented a zero-sum assessment, like Reagan and Nixon, only in their view bilingual education imperiled desegregation, rather than vice versa. During the heat of the *Johnson* litigation, for example, San Francisco NAACP president Charles Belle put the matter bluntly, "If they want to be Chinese, then they should go back to China. If they want to be Chinese-Americans, then they have to participate" in the NAACP-driven desegregation plan.[141] Even more tellingly, in a 1976 letter, NAACP-WC regional director Virna Canson linked what she called "the Chinese community . . . offensive against . . . integration" led by Quentin Kopp with "the concept of bi-lingualism which has culminated in the *Lau* decision." That Canson falsely credited Kopp ("a stone racist") with having "fathered the concept of bi-lingualism"—and thereby conflated opposition to desegregation with support for bilingual education—attests to just how incompatible she viewed the two.[142] For California NAACP leaders, like Reagan, bilingual education, it seemed, could not coexist with desegregation.

Whether desegregation and bilingual education were, as a practical policy matter, really at loggerheads would be a question for educational policymakers to tackle in subsequent years. Certainly, less partisan observers of the day than Reagan and the NAACP recognized at least a tension between desegregation and bilingual education, while the more hopeful among them, like Roos and Orfield, believed that that tension could be reconciled. As of the late 1970s, however, according to Orfield, little by way of the creative policy thinking necessary to effect this reconciliation had been done. The tension remained.[143]

Writing about the desegregation side of San Francisco's struggles over desegregation, bilingual education, and the tension between them, Harvard sociologist Nathan Glazer described the city as in the throes of a "great enterprise to determine what the 'equal protection of the laws' should concretely mean in a multi-racial and multi-ethnic society."[144] Had Glazer also reflected on the concurrent litigation over bilingual education and the tension between desegregation and bilingual education, his observation would have applied with even greater force. Taken together, they made San Francisco the epicenter of a civil rights earthquake. They also provided yet another example of America's racial frontier as America's civil rights vanguard.

CONCLUSION:
"DILEMMAS OF RACE
AND ETHNICITY"

Thirty-five years after Carey McWilliams declared that the "color of America has changed," the United States Supreme Court confronted the implications of that change.[1] On June 28, 1978, in the landmark case of *University of California Regents v. Bakke*, four justices joined parts of Justice Lewis F. Powell, Jr.'s opinion to cobble together a one-vote majority on behalf of a limited defense of affirmative action in university admissions.[2]

Though Thurgood Marshall was one of those four justices, he also filed a separate opinion. In it he blasted the limited reach of the majority decision. Focusing exclusively on African Americans, and echoing Gunnar Myrdal from over three decades earlier, Marshall described their history as "different in kind, not just degree, from that of other ethnic groups." For this reason, Marshall found it "difficult . . . to accept that Negroes cannot be afforded greater protection under the Fourteenth Amendment where it is necessary to remedy the effects of past discrimination." The exceptionally invidious history of antiblack racism in the United States merited at least that much jurisprudential consideration.[3]

At issue in *Bakke*, however, was a University of California, Davis medical school admission's program that reserved sixteen (out of one hundred) slots for not only "Blacks," but also "Chicanos," "Asians," and "American Indians."[4] Whether these other groups should be included alongside African Americans for affirmative action as a partial remedy for their past discrimination, Marshall did not say. By remaining silent on this issue, he failed to confront the full complexity—both demographic and, by extension, legal—of the case at hand.

"What should be the policy of a federal government toward racial minorities in a multi-racial, multi-ethnic republic?"[5] This question, which Carey McWilliams posed in 1947, cut to the core of *Bakke* and the complex civil rights politics and law that the case signaled for a country that increasingly resembled multiracial and multiethnic California. Marshall's opinion avoided addressing it. Powell's, however, did not. Playing a version of McWilliams to Marshall's Myrdal, Powell spoke to what McWilliams had described in 1943 as a plurality of "race problems" that included but were not limited to the "Negro problem."[6]

In particular, Powell noted that adjudicating affirmative action programs premised on providing redress for past discrimination would require judges to weigh "the extent of the prejudice and consequent harm suffered by various minority groups." This kind of evaluation was one thing where there were two groups involved, namely, whites and blacks; it was quite another matter where the "'two-class theory' of the Fourteenth Amendment is put aside," as in the affirmative action program at issue in *Bakke*. UC Davis, in Powell's view, failed "to explain its selection of only the four favored groups—Negroes, Mexican Americans, American Indians, and Asians—for preferential treatment." Nor could it have offered a legally satisfactory answer even if it tried, for, in Powell's estimation, "the concepts of 'majority' and 'minority' necessarily reflect temporary arrangements and political judgments." Even the "white 'majority' itself," Powell reasoned, consisted of groups who could "lay claim to a history of prior discrimination at the hands of the State and private individuals." For these reasons, Powell could find "no principled basis for deciding which groups would merit 'heightened judicial solicitude' and which would not." Courts simply lacked the "competence" required to engage in the "kind of variable sociological and political analysis" to make these sorts of determinations. However, Powell added, building "a diverse student body . . . is clearly a constitutionally permissible goal for an institution of higher education." Such "ethnic diversity" helped "contribute . . . to the 'robust exchange of ideas.'" Although explicit reservations of racial slots could not be employed, race could be considered as one criteria among many for achieving a diverse student body.[7]

Bakke thus marked a crucial step beyond the black/white, "'two-class theory' theory of the Fourteenth Amendment" in United States history. It also gave the Supreme Court's imprimatur to the categories of "official minorityhood," as historical sociologist John David Skrentny has described them.[8] The groups UC Davis singled out for affirmative action corresponded with those identified by federal officials, beginning with the Equal Employment Opportunity Commission (EEOC) in the mid-1960s. These "official minorities" included African Americans and those groups EEOC bureaucrats reasoned by analogy to be *like* African Americans, namely, Latinos, Native Americans, and Asian Americans.[9] Advocates of ethnic studies followed the EEOC's lead in the late 1960s when it came to the groups they targeted for analysis. For example, one of the very first ethnic studies departments in the United States, established at the University of California, Berkeley in 1969, encompassed programs in Black, Asian American, Chicano, and Native American studies.[10]

What *Bakke* solidified in the 1970s, leading race theorists and multicultural historians reinforced during the 1980s and 1990s. The former, led by Michael Omi and Howard Winant, argued for the "qualitative differences between white and non-white groups' encounters with U.S. society," while the latter, led by Ronald Takaki, sought to promote ethnic studies teaching beyond ethnic studies departments in an effort to expose more students to the "viewpoints" of "racial minorities" who were "historically set apart" from "European immigrant groups" and relegated to the margins of "a history that has viewed America as European in ancestry."[11]

These critical steps toward diversifying dominant notions about the history and theory of race and racism in the United States echoed McWilliams's exhortation from 1943 to reach beyond a binary, black/white understanding of the "race problem." At the same time, they also followed in McWilliams's footsteps by supplementing the longstanding black/white dichotomy, without supplanting or subverting it. Despite his insistence that the "color of America has changed" and his call to pluralize the "race problem," McWilliams still drew a singular color line between "colored minority groups," on the one hand, and "foreign-born 'white' immigrants" and their descendants, on the other hand.[12] Similarly, race theorists and multicultural historians of the 1980s and 1990s, like Omi and Winant and Takaki, posited a dichotomous white/non-white framework, with the experiences *between* the halves different enough, and the experiences *within* the halves similar enough, to warrant the continued division down the middle.[13] In this way, "intellectual affirmative action," as some proponents of multiculturalism described the curricular changes they advocated, adopted the same categories and binary logic of affirmative action in higher education admissions.[14]

The effort to reach beyond black and white without reaching beyond binaries culminated on June 13, 1997 with President Bill Clinton's Executive Order 13050, establishing a President's Advisory Board on Race. Chaired by the eminent historian John Hope Franklin, the "President's Initiative on Race" marked the first major executive undertaking on "race and racial reconciliation" since President Johnson convened the National Advisory Commission on Civil Disorder (the Kerner Commission) in 1967.[15] A day after he signed Executive Order 13050 on June 13, 1997, Clinton delivered a commencement address at the University of California, San Diego. In his speech, he announced his race initiative, as well as the dawn of a new day in American race relations. Acknowledging the "old, unfinished business between black and white Americans," the president added, "the classic American dilemma has now become many dilemmas of race and ethnicity." In choosing the word "dilemmas," Clinton implicitly invoked and revised Myrdal's *An American Dilemma*, which equated America's "dilemma" with "the Negro problem." To underscore the implications of America's "dilemmas," Clinton explicitly invoked and revised the Kerner Commission's report, which concluded, in

Clinton's paraphrasing, "We were becoming two Americas, one white, one black, separate and unequal." Nearly three decades later, Clinton continued, "We face a different choice: will we become not two, but many Americas, separate, unequal and isolated?"[16]

Though he did not mention McWilliams, Clinton's pluralization of Myrdal's "dilemma" echoed McWilliams's pluralization of the "race problem" in *Brothers Under the Skin*. So, too, did the views of advisory board member Angela Oh. During the board's first meeting, Oh urged her colleagues to "go beyond the black-white paradigm." Oh's exhortation prompted one observer to comment, "She has single-handedly introduced many Americans, experts among them, to the notion that race relations are more than literally black and white." Oh's efforts also prompted Franklin to retort, "This country cut its eyeteeth on racism in the black-white sphere. . . . It's not to neglect [others] . . . but it's to try to understand how it all started."[17]

Press accounts portrayed the exchange between Oh and Franklin as evidence of a fundamental rift on the advisory board. It was not. As Oh explained, "I voiced an opinion that any relevant framework around race relations in this country would have to include the experiences of people who are neither black or white. . . . I did not try to diminish the chasm between blacks and whites. . . . John Hope did not disagree with me at all. . . . He simply asserted . . . that we should not forget the unique history of white/black relationships. . . . The media blew this thing up."[18]

Oh's recollection of the basic agreement between her and Franklin was corroborated by the race initiative's two major reports published in 1998, *One America in the 21st Century: Forging a New Future* and *Changing America: Indicators of Social and Economic Well-Being by Race and Hispanic Origins*. These reports neither "ignore[ed] the growing racial diversity of the American people," nor ventured much beyond the binary "black-white paradigm," except to replace it with an equally binary, non-white/white paradigm. What the initiative hailed as a paradigm shift—"the discussion of race in this country is no longer between and about blacks and whites"—was in fact little more than a demographic tweak. Rather than limiting its focus to blacks and whites, the initiative distinguished between "minorities and people of color," on the one hand (which it defined as "the collective group of principal American minorities"—"Hispanic, may be of any race," "Black, not of Hispanic origins," "Asian, including Pacific Islander," "American Indian, including Alaska Native")—and "white Americans," on the other hand. This revised configuration remained binary, just not black and white. What bound "minorities and people of color" together was "a common history of legally mandated and socially and economically imposed subordination to white European-Americans and their descendants," the consequences of which, according to the initiative, were reflected in "troubling disparities between people of color and other Americans."[19]

Though the initiative's aspiration for "resolving the 'problems of the color-line'" included a recognition of multiple problems reflective of each "minority group['s] . . . distinct and unique historical experience with racism and oppression," that multiplicity did little to disrupt the notion of a singular "color-line." The initiative's findings, however, did. The racial disparities delineated in the report frequently belied the initiative's basic binary ("minorities and people of color"/"white Americans") premise. For example, Asian Americans in the late 1990s had higher median family incomes, higher levels of educational attainment, greater representation in the white collar ranks, and lower homicide and HIV infection rates than any other group, including whites. On these scores, at least, the proximity of whites to Asian Americans and distance of Asian Americans and whites from the rest pointed to an Asian American/white vs. black/Hispanic/Native American division. This configuration also characterized the data for poverty rates for individuals and children, though on these scores whites fared slightly better than Asian Americans. Still, whites and Asian Americans were much closer to one another than they were to Hispanics and blacks.[20]

Other data revealed racial disparities better characterized as black versus everyone else, rather than the report's "minorities and people of color" vs. "white Americans." For example, the rates of intermarriage for Asian American/white, Hispanic/white, and Native American/white couples between the ages of 25–34 in 1990 were four to seven times greater than black male/white female marriage rates, and eight to thirteen times greater for black female/white male marriage rates.[21] Similarly, African Americans stood significantly apart from all other groups when it came to rates of infant mortality, homicide, HIV infection, heart disease, cancer, and incarceration.[22] On incarceration, the initiative was so committed to its "minorities and people of color"/"white Americans" binary that the "approximately 50 percent" of state and federal prison inmates who were African American and the "approximately 15 percent" who were Hispanic served as evidence of "policies and practices that have an unjustified disparate impact on minorities and people of color." To be sure, the incarceration rate for Hispanics was slightly higher than the overall percentage of the Hispanic population in the late 1990s, but it paled in comparison to the four-fold over-representation of African American state and federal inmates relative to the overall percentage of the African American population.[23]

In other instances, the data fell along a kind of hierarchical tier. Unemployment rates for persons sixteen and older, for example, had whites at the lowest percentage, followed by Hispanics and then blacks.[24] Similarly, median weekly earnings for male and female full-time workers had whites at the top, followed by blacks and Hispanics.[25]

In the face of this kind of binary bucking evidence, the initiative could have made the case for a genuine paradigm shift. It did not. However, a growing chorus of scholarly publications in the late 1990s and early 2000s did. In 1999, for example, Asian American studies scholars Edward S.W. Park and John S.W. Park decried approaches to "race theorizing" that lumped together Asian Americans and Latinos with African Americans. "To redefine Blackness to be more inclusive [of Asian Americans and Latinos] might make for desirable political strategy," they wrote, "but it still ignores the substantial differences *between* Asian Americans, Latinos, and African Americans" (to say nothing of the cleavages *within* any one of the groups that are subsumed by the categories themselves).[26]

One year later, historian Manning Marable described the "cultural amalgamation" embodied in the "concept 'people of color,'" as one of the "problematics of ethnic studies." While the "concept 'people of color'" has served to highlight commonalities among "racialized ethnic groups"—"Asian Americans, American Indians, Latinos, and black Americans"—it has also buttressed the notion that "all people of color are . . . equally oppressed and share the objective basis for common politics." That idea, Marable said, was "dubious at best."[27]

Other scholars also mounted challenges to the white/non-white framework in the new millennium. Political scientist Claire Jean Kim, for example, posited a kind of racial hierarchy model—"a racial order . . . in which each group occupie[s] a distinct status and possesse[s] a distinct set of burdens and privileges" with whites on top, blacks on bottom, and the rest in between.[28] Sociologists Jennifer Lee and Frank D. Bean advanced an altogether different dichotomy, a "black/nonblack divide" in which "Latinos and Asians [increasingly] fall into the nonblack category."[29]

In explicitly arguing for the revision of the familiar black/white or non-white/white binary approaches to race theorizing, these various academic works implicitly argued for what legal scholar Kevin R. Johnson described in 2002 as the "end of 'civil rights' as we know it." As a result of changes wrought by the post-1965 spike in immigrants from Asia and Latin America, "civil rights issues," according to Johnson, had become more "complex and perplexing" than ever.[30]

Late twentieth and early twenty-first century events and developments that captured this complexity included resistance to affirmative action on the part of some Asian Americans;[31] deep reservations about immigrants voiced by a majority of African Americans and whites (though not Hispanics) polled;[32] and, most dramatically, the dynamics of the "nation's first multiracial riot"—as cultural critic Mike Davis described the explosion unleashed by the 1992 acquittal of four police officers who had been videotaped beating African American motorist Rodney King—in which Korean American businesses were targeted for half of the property damage sustained and Latinos were the majority of those arrested.[33] Surveying the devastation—52 dead, 2,499 injured, 6,559 arrested, 3,000 businesses damaged or destroyed, $800 million in property lost—*Newsweek* also commented on the "multicultural" nature and meaning of the conflagration. The "old [black/white] vocabulary of race relations in America" no longer sufficed to "depict the American social reality." Instead, "The nation is rapidly moving toward a multiethnic future in which Asians, Hispanics, Caribbean islanders, and many other immigrant groups compose a diverse and changing social mosaic."[34] Performer Anna Deveare Smith sought to capture "this new racial frontier" in her one-woman show, *Twilight: Los Angeles, 1992*. "It isn't about black and white," Smith told the *New York Times*, "and that's thrilling to me because I'm a product of the civil rights movement. This story is about multiple conflicts. Latinos, Blacks, Asians, Police."[35]

A decade later, in 2003, the editors of the *New York Times* echoed Smith, albeit in response to another watershed moment in United States history. They viewed a United States Census Bureau announcement that "Hispanics" surpassed African Americans as "the nation's largest minority" as "part of a larger trend that makes old views of race, in terms of black and white, incomplete and in need of rethinking."[36] Shortly thereafter, the Harvard Civil Rights Project convened a Conference to foster precisely that kind of "rethinking." The "Color Lines Conference," according to Christopher Edley, Jr., one of the Harvard Civil Rights Project's co-founders, hoped to encourage a "new generation" of scholarship to analyze the country's "complex multiracial dynamics that are both underexposed and misunderstood."[37] It sought "new paradigms" for understanding the nation's "confusing array of new color lines and color blends," in the words of Gary Orfield, the Harvard Civil Rights Project's other co-founder.[38]

Both Edley and Orfield, like so many other professors, pundits, and policymakers who reflected on race and racism in the late twentieth and early twenty-first centuries, viewed the recent past—from roughly the 1980s to the present—as having "no precedent in American history," as Orfield put it. What was once a "color line" with "obvious meanings" and "clear . . . targets for legal reform" in the mid-twentieth century possessed "none of these things" by the turn of the century.[39]

The history recounted in this book belies such claims. The country's increasingly complex, nonbinary, multiracial civil rights law, policy, and politics have long been California's. If the ultimate goal of the "Color Lines Conference" was to lay the intellectual foundation for a "second civil rights movement . . . with a decidedly multiracial focus," then the events narrated in these pages provide a usable past for that momentous task.[40] They demonstrate the difference (political and legal) that difference (demographic) made—the challenge of civil rights making in multiracial settings. To rise to this challenge, California civil rights advocates from Carey McWilliams and the CFCU in the 1940s forward often reasoned by analogy from the plight of African Americans to that of other non-white Californians and assumed a harmony of civil rights interests among them. As well-intentioned and politically sensible as this was, it also proved ill-equipped for building the multiracial civil rights movement its proponents sought. Time and again, the different axes of discrimination confronted by the state's different racial groups translated into different avenues of legal and legislative redress. For this reason, though much precedent-setting action (and reaction) occurred during California's civil rights era, most of it took place in the large space between the poles of civil rights making that was either coalition-based or conflict-ridden. Through this wide terrain flowed the separate streams of California's civil rights history that never came together for long enough to form a river.

Put another way, from the moment that the attack on the "problem of the color line" (as W.E.B. DuBois famously characterized the problem of the twentieth century) began to gather momentum nationally during World War II, California demonstrated that the problem was one of color lines. No single "color line" with "obvious meanings" existed then, as revealed by the (mostly) parallel legal campaigns mounted in the 1940s against California's multiracial manifestations of state-sanctioned segregation by lawyers representing groups of Japanese Americans, Mexican Americans, and African Americans. Nor did the "targets for legal reform" become any clearer thereafter, as Orfield himself discovered in the mid-1970s when he lamented the coalition-disrupting implications of bilingual education for desegregation. In short, California's multiracial struggles for civil rights demonstrated how the state's—and, by extension, the country's—civil rights past must not only be understood as "long," as recent civil rights historians have argued, but "wide"—wide regionally, wide racially, and, above all, wide substantively with respect to the axes of discrimination that civil rights reformers tackled and the avenues of redress they pursued. Understanding this history not only helps nationalize America's civil rights past, but also offers a glimpse into its civil rights present and future.

Abbreviations of Archival Collections Cited

ACLU   ACLU Records, Seeley G. Mudd Manuscript Library, Princeton University, Princeton, New Jersey.

ACLU-MF   The American Civil Liberties Union Archives: The Roger Baldwin Years, 1917-1950, Microfilm Edition.

AD   Anne Draper Papers, Department of Special Collections, Stanford University, Stanford, California.

BvP   Burks v. Poppy Construction Company, S.F. 20809, Supreme and Appellate Court Cases Collection, California State Archives, Sacramento, California.

BBTF   Bilingual-Bicultural Task Force, California State Archives, Sacramento, California.

BR   William Byron Rumford Papers, Bancroft Library, University of California, Berkeley.

CA-AG   California Attorney General Records, California State Archives, Sacramento, California.

CIC-LA   Catholic Interracial Council of Los Angeles Papers, Center for the Study of Los Angeles Collection, Loyola Marymount University, Los Angeles, California.

CFCU   California Federation for Civic Unity Records, Bancroft Library, University of California, Berkeley.

CM-B   Carey McWilliams Papers, Bancroft Library, University of California, Berkeley.

CM-Y   Carey McWilliams Papers, Department of Special Collections, Charles E. Young Research Library, University of California, Los Angeles.

DC   Frank B. and Josephine Whitney Duveneck Collection, Hoover Institution Archives, Stanford, California.

EG   Ernesto Galarza Papers, Department of Special Collections, Stanford University Libraries, Stanford, California.

EQ   Eduardo Quevedo Papers, Department of Special Collections, Stanford University Libraries, Stanford, California.

EW   Earl Warren Papers, California State Archives, Sacramento, California.

FC   Frank F. Chuman Papers, Department of Special Collections, University Research Library, University of California, Los Angeles.

FR   Fred Ross Papers, Department of Special Collections, Stanford University Libraries, Stanford, California.

GCBF   Governor's Chaptered Bill Files, California State Archives, Sacramento, California.

GK-CA   Goodwin J. Knight Papers, California State Archives, Sacramento, California.

GK-S   Goodwin J. Knight Papers, Department of Special Collections, Stanford University Libraries, Stanford, California.

GS   George I. Sánchez Papers, Benson Latin American Collection, General Libraries, The University of Texas at Austin.

HC   Hale Champion Papers, Bancroft Library, University of California, Berkeley.

JACL   Japanese American Citizens League History Collection, Japanese American National Library, San Francisco, California.

JL   Jacques E. Levy Research Collection on César Chávez, Yale Collection of Western Americana, Beinecke Rare Book and Manuscript Library, Yale University, New Haven, Connecticut.

JU   Jesse Unruh Papers, California State Archives, Sacramento, California.

LM   Loren Miller Papers, Huntington Library, San Marino, California.

MALDEF   Mexican American Legal Defense and Educational Fund Records, 1967-1984, Department of Special Collections, Stanford University Libraries, Stanford, California.

MM   Mike M. Masaoka Papers, J. Willard Marriott Library, University of Utah, Salt Lake City, Utah.

MR   Manuel Ruiz Papers, Department of Special Collections, Stanford University Libraries, Stanford, California.

MvW-DC   Mendez v. Westminster, No. 4292-M-Civil, Records of the District Courts of the United States (RG 21), Records of the United States Southern District Court of California, Central Division (Los Angeles), National Archives and Records Administration, Pacific Region, Perris, California.

NAACP-MF   National Association for the Advancement of Colored People Records, Microfilm Edition.

NAACP-WC   National Association for the Advancement of Colored People, West Coast Regional Office, Region I, Records, Bancroft Library, University of California, Berkeley.

NAACP-WC (previous)   National Association for the Advancement of Colored People (NAACP), West Coast Regional Office, Region I, Records, Bancroft Library, University of California, Berkeley.*

NLG   National Lawyer's Guild Records, 1936-1999, Bancroft Library, University of California, Berkeley.

Oyama-CA   People v. Oyama, L.A. 19533, Supreme and Appellate Court Cases Collection, California State Archives, Sacramento, California.

* *Endnotes with this abbreviation refer to items in the NAACP-WC collection prior to being re-catalogued.*

Oyama-USSC	Oyama v. California, 332 U.S. 633 (1948), U.S. Supreme Court Records and Briefs, 1832-1978, Gale, Cengage Learning.
PB	Edmund G. (Pat) Brown Papers, Bancroft Library, University of California, Berkeley.
PBu	Phillip Burton Papers, Bancroft Library, University of California, Berkeley.
PC	Peter Chacon Papers, California State Archives, Sacramento, California.
Perez	Perez v. Sharp, L.A. 20305, Supreme and Appellate Court Cases Collection, California State Archives, Sacramento, California.
RFHAF	Rumford Fair Housing Act Files, California State Archives, Sacramento, California.
RK	Ruth Kingman Papers, Department of Special Collections, Charles E. Young Research Library, University of California, Los Angeles.
RR	Ronald Reagan Governor's Papers, Ronald Reagan Library, Simi Valley, California.
RR-H	Ronald Reagan Governor's Papers, Hoover Institution Archives, Stanford, California.*
RWK	Robert Walker Kenny Papers, Bancroft Library, University of California, Berkeley.
SACCC	Supreme and Appellate Court Cases Collection, California State Archives, Sacramento, California.
SRRC	State Reconstruction and Reemployment Commission, California State Archives, Sacramento, California.
STFU	Southern Tenant Farmers Union Papers, Microfilm Edition.
Takahashi-CA	Takahashi v. Fish and Game, L.A. 19835, Supreme and Appellate Court Cases Collection, California State Archives, Sacramento, California.
Takahashi-USSC	Takahashi v. Fish and Game Commission, 334 U.S. 410 (1948), U.S. Supreme Court Records and Briefs, 1832-1978, Gale, Cengage Learning.
THP	Tarea Hall Pittman Papers, Bancroft Library, University of California, Berkeley.
VvH	Vargas v. Hampson, L.A. 26594, Supreme and Appellate Court Cases Collection, California State Archives, Sacramento, California.
WB	William Bagley Papers, Bancroft Library, University of California, Berkeley.
WvM-9C	Westminster v. Mendez, No. 11310, Records of the United States Circuit Court of Appeals for the Ninth Circuit, National Archives and Records Administration, Pacific Region, San Bruno, California.

Endnotes with this abbreviation refer to items in the Ronald Reagan Governor's Papers at the Hoover Institution prior to being moved to the Ronald Reagan Library and re-catalogued.

Notes

Introduction

1. Carey McWilliams, *Brothers Under the Skin* (Boston: Little, Brown, 1943), 49.

2. For example, the cover of *Time* on April 9, 1990 read, "America's Changing Colors." A decade later, the cover of *Newsweek* on September 18, 2000 read, "Redefining Race in America," while an article in that issue devoted to "The New Face of Race," noted in its subtitle, "Every day, in every corner of America, we are redrawing the color lines and redefining what race really means. It's not just a matter of black and white anymore." Thereafter, the article proclaimed, "We are now in an Age of Color in which the nuances of brown and yellow and red are as important, if not more so, than the ancient divisions of black and white." That same year, the *New York Times* launched its Pulitzer-prize winning series, "How Race Is Lived in America," with an article on "Race in America" on June 4, 2000 that observed, "America is now an inescapably multiracial society from which there is no turning back for whites and blacks." For more, see Conclusion.

3. Betsy Hutchinson, "Our 'Forgotten Men,'" review of *Brothers Under the Skin*, by Carey McWilliams, *Nation*, September 4, 1943: 271. Four years later, McWilliams offered the same observation. "Race problem," McWilliams noted in 1947, "in our loose and general speech, usually means Negro" (Carey McWilliams, "Equality - a Political Problem," *Survey Graphic* [December 1947]: 690). On this point, Matthew Frye Jacobson writes that McWilliams refused "to make 'race' identical with 'the Negro' in American political life" at a time when "'the Negro' represented the single racial problem to be solved" (Matthew Frye Jacobson, *Whiteness of a Different Color: European Immigrants and the Alchemy of Race* [Cambridge: Harvard University Press, 1998], 258, 265).

4. Gunnar Myrdal, with the assistance of Richard Sterner and Arnold Rose, *An American Dilemma: The Negro Problem and Modern Democracy*, with a new introduction by Sissela Bok (New Brunswick: Transaction Publishers, 1996), lix. Harper & Brothers originally published *An American Dilemma* in 1944.

5. According to a biographer, Myrdal believed "that the problems of blacks differed significantly from those of other minorities" (David W. Southern, *Gunnar Myrdal and Black-White Relations: The Use and Abuse of* An American Dilemma, *1944–1969* [Baton Rouge: Louisiana State University Press, 1987], 59).

6. Myrdal, lxxxix. On this point, see also, Jacobson, 258: "Myrdal . . . would effectively expel from consideration those pegged neither as 'white' nor as 'black.'"

7. Myrdal, 28–29, 1020.

8. McWilliams, *Brothers Under the Skin*, 48–49; Carey McWilliams, "Minorities in California," speech, October 20, 1944, Carton 4, Folder 43, CM-B. McWilliams borrowed the phrase "racial frontier" from sociologist Robert E. Park, "Our Racial Frontier on the Pacific," *Survey Graphic* 56 (May 1926): 192–196. In 1945 sociologist L.D. Reddick also used the phrase "racial frontier" in reference to the Pacific Coast. He wrote, "Definitely, the race-relations frontier has shifted to the West, particularly the

West Coast" (L.D. Reddick, "The New Race-Relations Frontier," *Journal of Educational Sociology* 19, no. 3 [1945]: 137).

9. By "colored minorities," McWilliams meant those whose "degree of color visibility or physical differentiation [were] sufficient to constitute a recognizable difference" from "foreign-born 'white' immigrants" (McWilliams, *Brothers Under the Skin*, 10; Carey McWilliams to Angus Cameron, November 19, 1942, Box 31, Folder 7, CM-Y).

10. McWilliams, *Brothers Under the Skin*, 49.

11. McWilliams, *Brothers Under the Skin*, 42; Carey McWilliams, "Racial Relationships in California: Changes Brought About by the War," circa 1943, Carton 3, Folder 79, CM-B. The population percentages and numbers in this paragraph come from *Californians of Japanese, Chinese, and Filipino Ancestry* (San Francisco: Department of Industrial Relations, Division of Fair Employment Practices, 1965), 17. The figures for "Persons of Spanish Surname" in 1940 are "not available," according to this particular report.

12. These cases are the subjects of Chapters 2, 3, and 4.

13. Robert O. Self, *American Babylon: Race and the Struggle for Postwar Oakland* (Princeton: Princeton University Press, 2003), 178.

14. These cases are discussed in Chapter 5.

15. See Chapter 6 and 7.

16. See Chapter 8 and Conclusion.

17. See Chapters 7 and 8.

18. Franklin Roosevelt quoted in David M. Kennedy, *Freedom From Fear: The American People in Depression and War* (New York: Oxford University Press, 1999), 247.

19. Philip Gleason, "Minorities (Almost) All: The Minority Concept in American Social Thought," *American Quarterly* 43, no. 3 (1991): 392–424. On the New Deal's privileging of white Americans, see, for example, Ira Katznelson, *When Affirmative Action Was White: An Untold Story of Racial Inequality in Twentieth-Century America* (New York: Norton, 2005), chapters 2 and 3. On the New Deal's privileging of "statist quests for economic stability" over "concern with race and ethnic relations," see Mae Ngai, *Impossible Subjects: Illegal Aliens and the Making of Modern America* (Princeton: Princeton University Press, 2004), 232.

20. McWilliams, *Brothers Under the Skin*, 301.

21. Carey McWilliams, "How We Felt About Minorities," circa 1945, Carton 3, Folder 44, CM-B.

22. Historian David M. Kennedy distills the overarching aim of New Deal liberalism into a single word: security. "Security," Kennedy asserts, "was the touchstone, the single word that summed up more of what Roosevelt aimed at than any other" (Kennedy, 245).

23. What legal historian Mark Tushnet has written about "advocates of African American interests" and their pursuit of different forms of fair employment practices (initially nondiscrimination and subsequently proportional-based) applies to California racial liberals more generally. They were, as Tushnet writes, "continually making and adjusting strategic judgments about what would succeed in the existing political climate. Operating in a political world dominated by white interests, they initially

believed that the most they could achieve was a law requiring nondiscrimination. They did not regard getting such a law as a trivial accomplishment. But, as soon as they saw the possibility for getting a more far-reaching policy that would, in their view, better advance the interests of the African American community, they sought proportionality" (Mark Tushnet, review of *From Direct Action to Affirmative Action: Fair Employment Law and Policy in America, 1933–1972*, by Paul D. Moreno, *American Journal of Legal History* 42 [July 1998]: 338).

24. See, for example, Lani Guinier, who juxtaposes racial liberalism with racial literacy, thereby suggesting that racial liberals were racial illiterates. In this sharply drawn dichotomy, racial liberals naively espoused a tepid and fixed ideology that sought to "redefine equality, not as a fair and just distribution of resources, but as the absence of formal, legal barriers that separated the races" (Lani Guinier, "From Racial Liberalism to Racial Literacy: *Brown v. Board of Education* and the Interest-Divergence Dilemma," *Journal of American History*, 91, no. 1 [2004]: 93). Guinier's take on racial liberalism echoes that of Peter Kellogg on "civil rights consciousness in the 1940s" from twenty-five years earlier. "The Second World War," Kellogg argues, "had made white racism a national shame and had provided a powerful, though not overwhelming, motive for at least limited reform to end overt forms of racial discrimination. Unfortunately, the issue of race, by the nature of white America's confrontation with its own conscience, had been removed from the realm of social, political, and economic restructuring and had called forth a movement for legal equality only. Social and economic justice were not seen as elements of the new crusade and were not to be a central concern of the new civil rights consciousness" (Peter J. Kellogg, "Civil Rights Consciousness in the 1940s," *Historian* 42, no. 1 [1979]: 40–41). For a more nuanced view of racial liberalism, more consistent with the one presented in this book, see, for example, Tushnet, review of *From Direct Action to Affirmative Action*. See, too, Gary Gerstle, "The Crucial Decade: The 1940s and Beyond," *Journal of American History* 92, no. 4 (2006): 1292–1299. Gerstle observes how the passage of a fair employment practices law in New York in 1945—the first of many such laws passed in states outside the South in the years before the 1964 Civil Rights Act—"points to the power of the emerging liberal consensus on racial equality, not its fragility or weakness. It does more to rehabilitate the older historiographical view of the 1940s as a decade of liberal possibility and achievement than to reinforce the more recent view of the period as one of lost or compromised opportunity." Similarly, David Roediger disputes the claim that the civil rights movement focused on race to the exclusion of class. He writes, "The former movement, we learn, emphasized a 'liberal, rights-centered political agenda [that] undermined the development of a coherent working class movement in the United States.'" This, Roedgier argues, is simply wrong. On the one hand it "lets white supremacist trade unionism off the hook." On the other hand, it "leads to the missing of the centrality of jobs, union organizing, welfare rights, poor people's campaigns, and point-of-production organizing—of class— to the civil rights and Black Power movements" (David Roediger, "The Retreat from Race and Class," *Monthly Review* 58, no. 3 [2006]). If the push for fair employment practices is one example of how civil rights and economic rights were intertwined for racial liberals, so, too, was the pursuit of a host of agricultural labor oriented issues, including

the right to organize and bargain collectively, advocated by Mexican American civil rights leaders in California from Ernesto Galarza, beginning in the 1940s, to César Chávez afterwards, as discussed in subsequent chapters. For more on the connection between labor rights and civil rights in Mexican American history, see Zaragosa Vargas, *Labor Rights Are Civil Rights: Mexican American Workers in Twentieth-Century America* (Princeton: Princeton University Press, 2005). In short, racial liberalism was not a panacea, but it was more robust and less ideologically fixed on the attainment of mere formal equality than its critics allow.

25. Nancy MacLean, *Freedom Is Not Enough: The Opening of the American Workplace* (Cambridge: Harvard University Press, 2006), 30.

26. Jacquelyn Dowd Hall, "The Long Civil Rights Movement and the Political Uses of the Past," *Journal of American History* 91, no. 4 (2005): 1250.

27. Robert Rodgers Korstad, *Civil Rights Unionism: Tobacco Workers and the Struggle for Democracy in the Mid-Twentieth Century South* (Chapel Hill: University of North Carolina Press, 2003), 417.

28. Robert Korstad and Nelson Lichtenstein, "Opportunities Found and Lost: Labor, Radicals, and the Early Civil Rights Movement," *Journal of American History* 75, no. 3 (1988): 786–811. See also William H. Chafe, "Race in America: The Ultimate Test of Liberalism," in *The Achievement of American Liberalism: The New Deal and Its Legacies*, ed. William H. Chafe (New York: Columbia University Press, 2002), 166: "The focus on economic and systemic change as a solution to racial inequality faded into oblivion [as a result of the Cold War], and more and more of the energies of civil rights groups went into legal challenges, within the constitutional structure, to patterns of segregation."

29. For similar renderings of this declensionist civil rights narrative and challenges to it more consistent with the one advanced in these pages, see Shana Beth Bernstein, *Bridges of Reform: Interracial Civil Rights Activism in 20th Century Los Angeles* (New York: Oxford University Press, forthcoming); Eric Arnesen, "Reconsidering the 'Long Civil Rights Movement,'" *Historically Speaking* (April 2009): 31–34; Gerstle, "The Crucial Decade"; Jess M. Rigelhaupt, "'Education for Action': The California Labor School, Radical Unionism, Civil Rights, and Progressive Coalition Building in the San Francisco Bay Area, 1934–1970" (PhD diss., University of Michigan, 2005), 16.

30. Sundiata Keita Cha-Jua and Clarence Lang apply this distinction to the North versus the South. They write, "One may also consider the enactment of local fair employment practice laws in the 1940s and 1950s. Although they were limited and easily subverted, they nonetheless represented reforms achieved largely in the North" (Sundiata Keita Cha-Jua and Clarence Lang, "The 'Long Movement' as Vampire: Temporal and Spatial Fallacies in Recent Black Freedom Studies," *Journal of African American History* 92, no. 2 [2007]: 283).

31. "Brief of the Japanese American Citizens League—Amicus Curiae," 2, December 1, 1947, *Hurd v. Hodge* 334 U.S. 24 (1948), *U.S. Supreme Court Records and Briefs, 1832–1978*, Gale, Cengage Learning.

32. "Brief of the Japanese American Citizens League—Amicus Curiae," 2.

33. Carey McWilliams, "Spectrum of Segregation," *Survey Graphic* 36, no. 1 (1947): 22.

34. For example, Laura Pulido notes how the "racialization of many Latinas/os in the Western United States" is linked to "the intimate relationship between Mexicans and farm work" (Laura Pulido, *Black, Brown, Yellow, and Left: Radical Activism in Los Angeles* [Berkeley: University of California Press, 2006]), 27. For Asian immigrants until the mid-twentieth century, to cite another example, citizenship status, or, more specifically, racial ineligibility to naturalized citizenship was one manifestation of what Neil Gotanda refers to as "Asiatic racialization" (Neil T. Gotanda, "Citizenship Nullification: The Impossibility of Asian American Politics," in *Asian Americans and Politics: Perspectives, Experiences, Prospects*, ed. Gordon H. Chang [Stanford: Stanford University Press, 2001], 80). Relatedly, citizens and noncitizens of both Asian and Latino descent confronted what Mae Ngai characterizes as "alien citizens[hip]," by which she means the "racialization of these ethnic groups' national origin . . . as permanently foreign and unassimilable to the nation" (Ngai, 7–8). Language, or, more specifically, being a non-native English speaker, served as the basis for still another axis of racialized discrimination, which the United States Supreme Court confronted in 1973 as it struggled to reconcile what Tom Romero describes as "the unique needs and concerns of Mexican Americans students" for bilingual education in Denver's public schools, on the one hand, with the NAACP's demand for desegregation, on the other hand (Tom I. Romero, II, "Our Selma is Here: The Political and Legal Struggle for Educational Equality in Denver, Colorado and Multiracial Conundrums in American Jurisprudence," *Seattle Journal of Social Justice* 3 [Fall/Winter 2004]: 73–123).

35. For similar formulations in different California contexts, see Tomás Almaguer on the "varieties of racialized experiences" in the origins of white supremacy in nineteenth and early twentieth century California and Laura Pulido on "differential racialization" reflective of "distinct experiences of racism" confronted by "various racial/ethnic groups" in the "Third World Left" in 1970s Los Angeles (Tomás Almaguer, *Racial Fault Lines: The Historical Origins of White Supremacy in California* [Berkeley: University of California Press, 1994], 4; Pulido, 4).

36. Joseph James to Thurgood Marshall, May 6, 1944, Part 13C, Reel 1, Frame 152, NAACP-MF.

37. Carey McWilliams, "Minority Rights on the West Coast," speech, July 1949, Part 1, Reel 12, Frames 717–727, NAACP-MF.

38. Lucien C. Haas, Oral History Interview, Conducted 1989 by Carlos Vasquez, UCLA Oral History Program, for the California State Archives State Governmental Oral History Program, 76.

39. Peter Richardson, *American Prophet: The Life and Work of Carey McWilliams* (Ann Arbor: University of Michigan Press, 2005).

40. Michael Denning, *The Cultural Front: The Laboring of American Culture in the Twentieth Century* (London: Verso, 1997), 450.

41. McWilliams, *Brothers Under the Skin*, 309.

42. After all, as Eric Arnesen writes, the "movement [in the South] *was* distinctive. It was significantly larger than its predecessors; it was visible nationally and consistently in a way unmatched by earlier organizations; it attained a genuinely mass character; it provoked a violent backlash of unprecedented proportions; and it ultimately succeeded

in toppling legalized segregation and enfranchising black Southerners" (Arnesen, 34). Similarly, on "Dixie's distinctiveness," see Cha-Jua and Lang, 282–283.

43. For an overview of the "long civil rights movement" historiography and the challenge that the works comprising it pose for the "dominant narrative of the civil rights movement," see Hall, as well as Jeanne Theoharis, "Black Freedom Studies: Re-imagining and Redefining the Fundamentals," *History Compass* 4, no. 2 (2006): 348–367. According to the "dominant narrative of the civil rights movement," which proponents of the "long civil rights movement" challenge, like a stone dropped in a pond, the civil rights movement begins in the mid-1950s with the Supreme Court's ruling in *Brown v. Board of Education* followed the next year by the Montgomery Bus Boycott led by a young Martin Luther King, Jr. It ripples to the nation's capital in the mid-1960s, with the March on Washington in 1963 in which King tells America about his "dream," which is then written into law, in part, in 1964 with the Civil Rights Act and 1965 with the Voting Rights Act. Then, and only then, does the civil rights movement wash upon shores beyond the South and groups other than the South's African Americans, only to founder over developments such as the conflagrations in urban ghettoes such as Watts in 1965 (just days after President Johnson signed the Voting Rights Act), the angry "white backlash" that King, for example, confronted when he moved to Chicago in 1966 to campaign for neighborhood integration (among other things), the Black Power separatism (as opposed to the civil rights integrationism) associated with groups such as the Black Panther Party (founded in Oakland in 1966), and the assassination of King in 1968 and the election of Richard Nixon later that same year. For similar renderings of the "dominant narrative of the civil rights movement," see Thomas J. Sugrue, *Sweet Land of Liberty: The Forgotten Struggle for Civil Rights in the North* (New York: Random House, 2008), xiii–xiv; Jeanne Theoharis, "From the Stone the Builders Rejected: Towards a New Civil Rights Historiography," *Left History* 12, no. 1 (2007): 103; Hall, 1234; Nikhil Pal Singh, *Black is a Country: Race and the Unfinished Struggle for Democracy* (Cambridge: Harvard University Press, 2004), 5; Self, 178. For critiques of the "long civil rights movement" interpretation, see Arnesen, 31–34 and Sundiata Keita Cha-Jua and Clarence Lang, 265–288.

44. Sugrue, xiii, xxvii. Sugrue "focuses on the states with the largest black populations outside the South," led by New York, but also including "occasionally" California and Washington. Similarly, Jeanne Theoharis defines the North as "everywhere not in the South (i.e., not the Confederacy) despite the regional variations that existed between the Northeast, Midwest, and West" (Theoharis, "Black Freedom Studies: Re-imagining and Redefining the Fundamentals," footnote 24, 362). Both Sugrue and Theoharis acknowledge the influence of Latinos and Asian Americans in shaping the West's civil rights history. Sugrue, for example, cites "recent scholarship on Texas and California" that "considers the intersections and tensions among black, Asian, and Latino civil rights struggles" (551, footnote xv), while Theoharis references "new scholarship [that] has shown the interconnections between the black struggle and international movements and between Latino and Asian American organizing and African American organizing in the United States" (361, footnote 8). Nevertheless, their focus on "whites and African Americans," as Sugrue puts it, and "the black freedom struggle,"

as Theoharis puts it, provides little insight into how those groups fit into the history of the civil rights era. For a similar acknowledgment and omission, see Hall: "The meaning of race and racism in America has always been inflected by ethnic exclusions and identities, and it has been complicated by the demographic changes in the late twentieth century. In this essay, however, I limit my focus to the black-white divide" (1235, footnote 5). By doing so, Hall, like Sugrue and Theoharis, does not account for how nonblack civil rights struggles figure into the "long civil rights movement."

45. Sugrue, xv.

46. Richard White, "Race Relations in the American West," *American Quarterly* 38, no. 3 (1986): 397; Elliott West, "Expanding the Racial Frontier," *The Historian*, 66, no. 3 (2004): 556.

47. John Mack Faragher, "The Social Fabric of the American West," *The Historian*, 66, no. 3 (2004): 448; Patricia Nelson Limerick, "The American West: From Exceptionalism to Internationalism," in *The State of U.S. History*, ed. Melvyn Stokes (Oxford: Berg, 2002), 291; West, 556.

48. There have been numerous other calls for scholars to reach beyond the black/white binary, though they have offered limited clues about what analytic insights the more demographic inclusiveness promises to yield. See, for example, Jacqueline Jones, "Race and Gender in Modern America," *Reviews in American History* 26, no. 1 (1998): 222; George J. Sánchez, "Reading Reginald Denny: The Politics of Whiteness in the Late Twentieth Century," *American Quarterly* 47, no. 3 (1995): 393; Gary Y. Okihiro, *Margins and Mainstreams: Asians in American History and Culture* (Seattle: University of Washington Press, 1994), 62. Similarly, among nonhistorians, especially legal scholars, see Richard Delgado, "Derrick Bell's Toolkit—Fit to Dismantle that Famous House," *New York University Law Review* 75, no. 2 (2000): 290; Juan F. Perea, "The Black/White Binary Paradigm of Race: The 'Normal Science of American Racial Thought," *La Raza Law Journal* 10 (Spring 1998), 135; Angelo N. Ancheta, *Race Rights, and the Asian American Experience* (New Brunswick: Rutgers University Press, 1998), 12; Kevin R. Johnson, "Racial Hierarchy, Asian Americans and Latinos as 'Foreigner,' and Social Change: Is the Law the Way to Go?" *Oregon Law Review* 76 (Summer 1997): 350; Adrienne D. Davis, "Identity Notes Part One: Playing in the Light," *American University Law Review* 45 (February 1996): 696; William Tomayo, "When the 'Coloreds' Are Neither Black Nor Citizens: The United States Civil Rights Movement and Global Migration," *Asian Law Journal* 2 (May 1995): 24–25.

49. On Los Angeles, see, for example, Bernstein; Scott Kurashige, *The Shifting Grounds of Race: Black and Japanese Americans in the Making of Multiethnic Los Angeles* (Princeton: Princeton University Press, 2008); Kevin Allen Leonard, *The Battle for Los Angeles: Racial Ideology and World War II* (Albuquerque: University of New Mexico Press, 2006); Pulido; George J. Sánchez, "What's Good for Boyle Heights Is Good for the Jews: Creating Multiracialism on the Eastside During the 1950s," *American Quarterly* 56, no. 3 (2004): 633–661; Daniel Widener, "'Perhaps the Japanese Are to Be Thanked?' Asia, Asian Americans, and the Construction of Black California," *Positions* 11, no. 1 (2003): 135–181. On San Francisco and the Bay Area, see, for example, Scott H. Tang, "Becoming New Objects of Racial Scorn: Racial Politics and Racial Hierarchy in

Postwar San Francisco, 1945–1960" in *The Political Culture of the New West*, ed. Jeff Roche (Lawrence: University Press of Kansas, 2008), 219–245; Rigelhaupt; Jason Michael Ferreira, "All Power to the People: A Comparative History of Third World Radicalism in San Francisco, 1968–1974" (PhD diss., University of California, Berkeley, 2003). On California more generally, see, for example, Charlotte Brooks, *Alien Neighbors, Foreign Friends: Asian Americans, Housing, and the Transformation of Urban California* (Chicago: University of Chicago Press, 2009); Allison Varzally, *Making a Non-White America: Californians Coloring Outside Ethnic Lines, 1925–1955* (Berkeley: University of California Press, 2008); Albert M. Camarillo, "Cities of Color: The New Racial Frontier in California's Minority-Majority Cities," *Pacific Historical Review*, 76, no. 1 (2007): 1–28; Daneil Wei HoSang, "Racial Proposition: 'Genteel Apartheid' in Postwar California" (PhD diss., University of Southern California, 2007); Lauren Araiza, "'For Freedom of Other Men': Civil Rights, Black Power and the United Farm Workers, 1965–1973" (PhD diss., University of California Berkeley, 2006); Almaguer. Beyond California, see for example, Neil Foley, *Quest for Equality: The Failed Promise of Black-Brown Solidarity* (Cambridge: Harvard University Press, 2010); Carlos K. Blanton, "George I. Sánchez, Ideology, and Whiteness in the Making of the Mexican American Civil Rights Movement, 1930–1960," *Journal of Southern History* 72, no. 3 (2006): 569–604; Thomas A. Guglielmo, "Fighting for Caucasian Rights: Mexicans, Mexican Americans, and the Transnational Struggle for Civil Rights in World War II Texas," *Journal of American History* 92, no. 4 (2006): 1212–1237; Ngai; Tom I. Romero, II, "The 'Tri-Ethnic' Dilemma: Race, Equality, and the Fourteenth Amendment in the American West," *Temple Political and Civil Rights Law Review* 13 (2004): 817–855; Romero, "Our Selma is Here"; Hugh Davis Graham, *Collision Course: The Strange Convergence of Affirmative Action and Immigration Policy in America* (New York: Oxford University Press, 2002); John David Skrentny, *Minority Rights Revolution* (Cambridge: Harvard University Press, 2002); Neil Foley, *The White Scourge: Mexicans, Blacks, and Poor Whites in Texas Cotton Culture* (Berkeley: University of California Press, 1997); Quintard Taylor, "The Civil Rights Movement in the Urban West: Black Protest in Seattle, 1960–1970," *Journal of Negro History* 80, no. 1 (1995): 1–14.

50. See, for example, Kurashige. Among the major themes in Kruashige's book about "multiracial relations" are "the omnipotence of white racism, the specter of interethnic conflict, and the promise of interethnic coalitions" (2, 285). Other works that focus on cooperation and/or conflict in "multiracial relations" include: Bernstein, who examines "an interracial version of persistent civil rights"; Varzally, who traces the "hidden history of mingling and mixing among minorities" and how that laid the "foundation for multiethnic civil rights activism" (2); Camarillo, who discusses "conflict and adversarial inter-group relations" as well as the "other story" of "cooperation, collaboration, and the possibilities of coalition building" (24); Rigelhaupt, who argues for the "enduring Popular Front orientation and the coalescence of progressive social movement activism in unions and civil rights" (3); and Sánchez, who concentrates on "ethnic cooperation" between Jewish Americans and Mexican Americans (657).

51. This book's approach to understanding civil rights making in multiracial contexts, might also very well apply to the civil rights era history in non-Western U.S.

places with multiracial populations, such as Boston, Chicago, Houston, Miami, and New York. After all, California and the West have never had a monopoly on racial diversity. As such, one wonders what Sugrue's "forgotten struggle for civil rights in the North" would look like if it reached beyond its parameters of "whites and African Americans" and included, for example, Mexican Americans in Chicago or Denver (551, footnote, xv). Denver, for example, was the site of what Sugrue describes as the "first major [Supreme Court] decision with the potential to clarify the meaning of *Brown* in the North" (480). Yet, the role of Mexican Americans in that case—*Keyes v. Denver School District #1*—introduced an element of western, multiracial complexity that is lost if one focuses on blacks and whites only. On this point, see Romero, "Our Selma is Here." Similarly, one wonders what shape Martha Biondi's "struggle for civil rights in postwar New York City" would take if it looked past "Black New York" to include, for example, Puerto Ricans (Martha Biondi, *To Stand and Fight: The Struggle for Civil Rights in Postwar New York City* [Cambridge: Harvard University Press, 2003]). Most generally, one wonders how Jacquelyn Dowd Hall's synthetic description of the "long civil rights movement" would change if it did not confine itself to the "black-white divide" (1235, footnote 5).

52. Patricia Nelson Limerick, "The Case of the Premature Departure: The Trans-Mississippi West and American History Textbooks," *Journal of American History* 78, no. 4 (1992): 1390–1391. Limerick writes of the "truly national view of the movement against racial discrimination," which has been obscured by "the usual eastward tilt of historical significance." This, in turn, has obscured a history of "activism on the part of western American minorities" and perpetuates the belief that Mexican Americans and Asian Americans "remained passive and quiet until eastern African Americans gave them a better idea." On this point, see also Quintard Taylor, *In Search of the Racial Frontier: African Americans in the American West, 1528–1990* (New York: Norton, 1998), 278: "The civil rights movement was national in scope, its western version integral to the effort to achieve a full, final democratization of the United States."

Chapter 1

1. "Frisco Boilermakers' Leader Was a Local WPA singer," *Los Angeles Tribune*, January 15, 1945, in Reel 232, Frame 2693, ACLU-MF; "Collective Bargaining—California Style," *The Crisis*, February 1945: 43–44; Charles Wollenberg, "*James v. Marinship:* Trouble on the New Black Frontier," *California History* 60, no. 3 (1981): 269.

2. Wollenberg, 267–268; *James v. Marinship*, 25 Cal. 2d 721, 725–726 (1944).

3. Joseph James quoted in Albert S. Broussard, *Black San Francisco: The Struggle for Racial Equality in the West, 1900–1954* (Lawrence: University of Kansas Press, 1993), 160; Joseph James, "Statement by the San Francisco Committee Against Discrimination and Segregation," news release, March 4, 1944, Part 13C, Reel 1, Frame 102, NAACP-MF; Wollenberg, 269–270.

4. "NAACP Aids Coast Shipyard Workers," news release, December 3, 1943, Part 13C, Reel 1, Frame 42, NAACP-MF; Joseph James to Thurgood Marshall, May 6, 1944, Part 13C, Reel 1, Frame 152, NAACP-MF; Wollenberg, 271.

5. "Articles of Incorporation," Carton 3, Folder Bd. of Directors Meetings—Minutes & Reports, CFCU; *A Monthly Summary of Events and Trends in Race Relations* 1, no. 3 (1943): 3.

6. Marshall Field, speech, July 16, 1944, Part I, Reel 11, NAACP-MF.

7. A.A. Liveright, "The Community and Race Relations," *The Annals of the American Academy of Political and Social Science* 244 (1946): 106. For a directory of many of these "Race Relations Action Committees," see "Programs of Action on the Democratic Front," *A Monthly Summary of Events and Trends in Race Relations* 2, no. 1–2 (1944): 23–32.

8. Joseph James, speech, June 1946, Part I, Reel 11, NAACP-MF.

9. Carey McWilliams, "Minorities in California," speech, October 1944, Carton 4, Folder 42, CM-B.

10. John Gunther, *Inside U.S.A.* (New York: Harper and Brothers, 1947), 1.

11. California Council for Civic Unity, minutes, February 19, 1946, Carton 3, Folder Minutes 46–47, CFCU; California Council for Civic Unity, advisory council membership list, April 27, 1946, Carton 3, Folder Minutes 46–47, CFCU.

12. "First State-Wide Council Organized," *American Council on Race Relations Report*, April 1946: 2.

13. Dorothy Handy to Laurence Hewes and Ruth Kingman, September 1946, Box 5, Folder Correspondence Re: Separation, CFCU.

14. "What Is the CCCU?" circa 1947, Carton 2, Folder McCarran-Walter Act, CFCU.

15. Laurence I. Hewes, Jr., "Race Relations on the West Coast," *The Nation*, September 21, 1946: 25. Hewes was the regional director of the American Council on Race Relations, which helped launch the CFCU. He also served on the CFCU's first board of directors.

16. Hewes, 25.

17. *James v. Marinship*, 25 Cal. 2d 721, 745 (1944).

18. Press release [?], circa January 1945, Part 13C, Reel 1, Frame 306, NAACP-MF;

19. Herbert Resner to Thurgood Marshall, April 4, 1945, Part 13C, Reel 1, Frame 234, NAACP-MF.

20. Joseph James, "Profiles: San Francisco," *Journal of Educational Sociology* 19, no. 3 (November 1945): 171.

21. California State Reconstruction and Reemployment Commission, *Report and Recommendations* (Sacramento: California State Printing Office, 1945), 11, 13.

22. C.H. Purcell, "Introductory Remarks," in "Transcript of Addresses," March 22, 1944, File 775 (Meetings 1944), SRRC.

23. Earl Warren, "California After the War," in "Transcript of Addresses," March 22, 1944, File 775 (Meetings 1944), SRRC.

24. California State Reconstruction and Reemployment Commission, *Objectives, Organization, Program* (Sacramento: California State Printing Office, March 1944), File 396, SRRC.

25. *Report and Recommendations* (1945), 21.

26. "Predated Disaster—Unless!" *Fortune*, February 1945, quoted in Samuel C. May, "Prospects for Postwar Employment in California," *Postwar California*, 2, no. 2 (1945): 1–2.

27. California State Reconstruction and Reemployment Commission, *Report and Recommendations* (Sacramento: California State Printing Office, 1946), 4.

28. "Warren to Hand Housing Program to Legislature," *Los Angeles Times*, December 13, 1945: 1.

29. *Report and Recommendations* (1946), 69–72.

30. "Governor Urges Equality Commission," *Los Angeles Sentinel*, January 11, 1945: 1.

31. *Report and Recommendations* (1945), 22.

32. Alexander Heron to Elam Anderson, April 14, 1944, File 664, SRRC.

33. Alexander Heron to Edgar Johnson, December 5, 1944, File 664, SRRC.

34. "Recommendation on Fair Employment Practices," October 16, 1945, File 802, SRRC.

35. Paul Scharrenberg, "Digest of Presentation," October 16, 1945, File 805, SRRC.

36. "The Work of Race Relations Action Committees, 1943–1945: An Overview," *A Monthly Summary of Events and Trends in Race Relations* 3, no. 3 (1945): 116.

37. John H. Burma, "Race Relations and Antidiscriminatory Legislation," *American Journal of Sociology* 56, no. 5 (1951): 416–418. For more on the distinction between prejudice and discrimination and the need to target the latter with legislation and litigation versus the former with education, see Carey McWilliams, "Race Discrimination and the Law," *Science and Society* 9, no. 1 (1945): 1–22 and Will Maslow, "The Law and Social Relations," *The Annals of the American Academy of Political and Social Science* 244 (March 1946): 75–81.

38. "Reporter's Transcript of Commission Meeting," November 5, 1945, File 425, SRRC.

39. *Report and Recommendations* (1946), 100–136.

40. Miriam Roher, "Trouble Coming in California," *New Republic*, January 21, 1946: 84–85.

41. California State Reconstruction and Reemployment Commission, *Report and Recommendations* (Sacramento: California State Printing Office, 1947), 17, 34; *Report and Recommendations* (1946), 119.

42. "Governor Urges Equality Commission," 1.

43. Beach Vasey to Earl Warren, March 13, 1945, Folder 8038, EW. For more on the fight for fair employment practices in California, see Chapters 4 and 5.

44. Carey McWilliams, "Earl Warren—A Likely Dark Horse," November 29, 1947, Box 80, Folder 3, CM-Y.

45. Ed Cray, *Chief Justice: A Biography of Earl Warren* (New York: Simon and Schuster, 1997), 166–167.

46. Beach Vasey to Jim Welsh, March 21, 1945, Folder 6100, EW.

47. Jim Welsh to Beach Vasey, March 23, 1945, Folder 6100, EW.

48. Pauli Murray, ed., *States' Laws on Race and Color* (Cincinnati: Women's Division of Christian Service, Board of Missions and Church Extension, Methodist Church, 1950), 51–58.

49. Carey McWilliams, *Brothers Under the Skin* (Boston: Little, Brown and Company, 1943), 301.

50. California Poll Release 8, February 22, 1947; California Poll Release 85, August 14, 1948.

51. Ruth Kingman to Josephine Duveneck, September 2, 1974, Box 1, Folder 6, DC.

52. Handy to Hewes and Kingman.

53. "What Is the CCCU?" Ruth Kingman, "A Brief Historical Report of the Pacific Coast Committee on American Principles and Fair Play," circa 1946, Box 154, Folder 9, RK.

54. "Application for Financial Grant," December 4, 1947, Box 1, Folder Outgoing Correspondence 1948, CFCU.

55. "What Is the CCCU?"

56. Kingman to Duveneck.

57. "What Is the CCCU?"; Kingman, "A Brief Historical Report of the Pacific Coast Committee on American Principles and Fair Play."

58. Josephine Whitney Duveneck, *Life on Two Levels: An Autobiography* (Los Altos, CA: William Kaufman, Inc., 1978), 248. On this point, see also Ruth Kingman to Laurence Hewes, September 16, 1946, Box 5, Folder Correspondence Re: Separation, CFCU: "The evacuation of persons of Japanese ancestry from the Pacific Coast had created problems which were becoming increasingly complex. The influx of Negro and white war workers from the South provided an additional challenge. . . . During the closing months of the war, it became evident that much of the wartime population would become permanent. Officers and members of many of California's organizations working in the general field of race relations came to feel that some over-all organization would strengthen and supplement the work that each was undertaking more or less alone. This feeling led to the formation of the CCCU in February of 1946."

59. "Application for Financial Grant."

60. Joseph James, speech.

61. "First State-Wide Council Organized," *American Council on Race Relations Report* 1, no. 1 (1946): 2.

62. Charles S. Johnson, "National Organizations in the Field of Race Relations," *The Annals of the American Academy of Political and Social Science*, 224 (March 1946): 126.

63. Liveright, 106.

64. Hewes, 25.

65. Josephine Duveneck and Ruth Kingman, "Brief Statement Covering Problems Facing California Federation for Civic Unity," February 26, 1948, Carton 3, Folder Board of Directors Meetings, CFCU.

66. Board of Directors meeting, minutes, June 19, 1948, Carton 3, Folder Minutes—Board of Directors, CFCU; "The Civic Unity Movement: What? Why? How?" *Blueprint for Action*, June 7, 1949, in Carton 4, Folder Race Relations on the West Coast, CM-B.

67. Duveneck, *Life on Two Levels*, 248.

68. "Report on Conference of California's Councils of Civic Unity and Similar Organizations," July 6, 1945, Box 1, Folder 11, CFCU.

69. "Report on Conference of California's Councils of Civic Unity and Similar Organizations."

70. Preoccupied with the "betterment of their own group's condition," as historian Cheryl Greenberg has written, the NAACP "remained silent on internment"

(Cheryl Greenberg, "Black and Jewish Responses to Japanese Internment," *Journal of American Ethnic History* 14, no. 2 [1995]: 5). On this silence, see also Scott Kurashige, *The Shifting Grounds of Race: Blacks and Japanese in the Making of Multiethnic Los Angeles* (Princeton: Princeton University Press, 2008), 177; Roger Daniels, "The Japanese American Cases, 1942–2004: A Social History," *Law and Contemporary Problems* 68 (Spring 2005): 162. Years after the war, the African American writer Maya Angelou suggested another explanation for the NAACP's inaction on internment. In her childhood memory of the "visible revolution" that transformed San Francisco's Japantown into "San Francisco's Harlem" in a few short months in 1942, Angelou recalled the "indifference" of the "Black newcomer" to the "Japanese removal," adding, "The Japanese were not whitefolks" and as such "since they didn't have to be feared, neither did they have to be considered" (Maya Angelou, *I Know Why the Caged Bird Sings* [New York: Random House, 1969], 178–179).

71. Kurashige, 166.

72. "Report on Conference of California's Councils of Civic Unity and Similar Organizations."

73. "Report on Conference of California's Councils of Civic Unity and Similar Organizations."

74. "The Civic Unity Movement: What? Why? How?"

75. "Brief Statement Covering Problems Facing California Federation for Civic Unity."

76. Richard Dettering, "The Job the Federation Can Do," May 12, 1950, Carton 3, Folder Bd. of Directors Meetings – Minutes & Reports, CFCU; Richard Dettering, report, December 3, 1949, Carton 3, Folder Board of Directors Material, CFCU.

77. Carey McWilliams, *Prejudice—Japanese-Americans: Symbol of Racial Intolerance* (Boston: Little, Brown, 1944), 82.

78. "The Job the Federation Can Do"; Conference on Fair Employment Practices Legislation, minutes, August 13, 1949, Carton 3, Folder Bd. of Directors Meetings—Minutes & Reports, CFCU; "The Civic Unity Movement: What? Why? How?" Writing about Los Angeles in the immediate postwar years, historians have corroborated Dettering's observation. See, for example, Douglas Flamming, *Bound for Freedom: Black Los Angeles in Jim Crow America* (Berkeley: University of California Press, 2005), 360–361 and Kurashige, 173–185.

79. James, "Profiles: San Francisco," 171; Wollenberg, 277.

80. Duveneck, *Life on Two Levels*, 256.

81. Carey McWilliams, "Spectrum of Segregation," *Survey Graphic* 36, no. 1 (1947): 22. On this point, McWilliams wrote elsewhere, "The dominant characteristic of our prewar policy toward racial minorities was the practice of segregation. While this practice varied regionally, it prevailed throughout the nation. It was imposed furthermore, not merely against Negroes but, with variations, against Mexicans in the Southwest, Indians throughout the West, and Orientals on the west coast" (Carey McWilliams, "How We Felt About Racial Minorities," circa 1945, Carton 3, Folder 44, CM-B).

Chapter 2

1. Larry Tajiri, "Farewell to Little Tokyo," *Common Ground* 4, no. 2 (1944): 94.

2. Bill Hosokawa, *JACL in Quest of Justice* (New York: William Morrow and Company, 1982), 156; David Yoo, "Tajiri, Larry (1914–1961)," in *Japanese American History: An A-to-Z Reference from 1868 to the Present*, ed. Brian Niiya (New York: Facts on File, Inc.), 322.

3. Of the 126,947 Nikkei in the United States in 1940, 79,642 (or nearly 63 percent) were Nisei (first generation immigrants) and 47,305 were Issei (second generation, United States born children of Issei) (Jere Takahashi, *Nisei/Sansei: Shifting Japanese American Identities and Politics* [Philadelphia: Temple University Press], 35). The vast majority of Nikkei—93,717—resided in California. They represented 1.4 percent of the total state population (*Californians of Japanese, Chinese, and Filipino Ancestry* [San Francisco: Department of Industrial Relations, Division of Fair Employment Practices, 1965], 17).

4. Roger Daniels, "Incarceration of the Japanese Americans: A Sixty Year Perspective," *History Teacher* 35, no. 2 (2002): 301; Hosokowa, 178.

5. Tajiri, 93.

6. Carey McWilliams, *Brothers Under the Skin* (Boston: Little, Brown, 1943), 309.

7. Tajiri, 94–95.

8. "Report on Conference of California's Councils of Civic Unity and Similar Organizations," July 6, 1945, Box 1, Folder 11, CFCU.

9. Joseph James to Thurgood Marshall, May 6, 1944, Part 13C, Reel 1, Frame 152, NAACP-MF.

10. Joseph James, "Profiles: San Francisco," *Journal of Educational Sociology* 19, no. 3 (1945): 175.

11. "Report on Conference of California's Councils of Civic Unity and Similar Organizations."

12. *Plessy v. Ferguson*, 163 U.S. 537, 560–561 (1896).

13. For more on the limits of Harlan's "color blind" jurisprudence, see Gabriel J. Chin, "The Plessy Myth: Justice Harlan and the Chinese Cases," *Iowa Law Review* 82 (October 1996): 151–182. On the expansion of Asian immigration exclusion beyond the Chinese, see Mae M. Ngai, *Impossible Subjects: Illegal Aliens and the Making of Modern America* (Princeton: Princeton University Press, 2004), 21–50.

14. These eleven states were California (1913), Arizona (1917), Louisiana (1921), New Mexico (1922), Idaho (1923), Montana (1923), Oregon (1923), Kansas (1925), Florida (1926), Utah (1943), Wyoming (1943), and Arkansas (1943) (Dudley O. McGovney, "The Anti-Japanese Land Laws of California and Ten Other States," *California Law Review* 35 (1947): 7–11). Based on 1940 Census figures, McGovney counted 48,158 "aliens racially ineligible to citizenship under present [1947] law" (McGovney, 11). The vast majority of these—47,305—were Japanese, along with 749 Korean, 9 Polynesian, and 95 Other Asian. Prior to 1947, Alien Land Laws in other states applied to Chinese and Filipinos, but Congress extended naturalization rights to Chinese in 1943 and Filipinos in 1946. Including the states where the Alien Land Law provisions targeted Chinese and/or Filipinos, even though they were no longer ineligible for naturalized citizenship

after 1943 and 1946, respectively, perhaps explains why the *Pacific Citizen* counted eighteen states with Alien Land Laws in November 1946 ("Oyama Test Case to Taken to U.S. Court," *Pacific Citizen*, November 2, 1946: 1).

15. "Escheat Cases," *Pacific Citizen*, November 22, 1947: 4; "California's Supreme Court Says 39-Year-Old Measure Violates U.S. Constitution," *Pacific Citizen*, April 19, 1952: 1; "California's Alien Land Law is Buried," *Open Forum*, May 10, 1952: 1–2.

16. Saburo Kido, "Nisei Problems Go to Court," *Pacific Citizen*, December 28, 1946: 2. For a powerful argument about how these cases—and their World War II predecessors—laid the "foundation for the doctrine of strict scrutiny on which *Brown*" would draw, see Greg Robinson and Toni Robinson, "*Korematsu* and Beyond: Japanese Americans and the Origins of Strict Scrutiny," *Law and Contemporary Problems* 68, no. 2 (2005): 29–55.

17. "Statement of Policy," January 16, 1947, Box 16, Folder ADC-Statements, 1944–53, JACL.

18. Fred Okrand, "Forty Years Defending the Constitution," oral history conducted by Michael Balter, Oral History Program, University of California, Los Angeles (1984), 219–220.

19. Larry Tajiri, "Farewell to the Land Law," *Pacific Citizen*, April 19, 1952: 4.

20. "The Story of the *Oyama* Case," *JACL Reporter* 4, no. 2 (February 1948): 1.

21. "Angelenos Polled on Postwar Views," *Los Angeles Times*, January 16, 1944: A1.

22. Abraham Lincoln Wirin, partially completed oral history conducted by Joel Gardner in 1974, Record Series 501, Box 21, University Archives, University of California, Los Angeles; "Interview of Al Wirin" by Frank Chuman, December 17, 1971, Los Angeles, Box 534, Folder Misc. Notes, A.L. Wirin Interview, FC; Donald E. Collins, "Wirin, Abraham Lincoln (1901–1978)," in *Japanese American History*, ed. Brian Niiya (New York: Facts on File, 1993), 350–351. For more on Wirin's role in the Japanese American incarceration cases, see Peter Irons, *Justice at War: The Story of the Japanese American Internment Cases* (New York: Oxford University Press, 1983).

23. Wirin, partially completed oral history; Alice Sumida, "Civil Rights Defender: A.L. Wirin Jeopardized Career in Backing Japanese Americans," *Pacific Citizen*, January 24, 1948: 2; Collins, 350–351; Irons, 192, 222–226.

24. Irons says the JACL's participation in *Hirabayashi* "signaled a turnabout of the JACL's policy of withholding support from the Japanese Americans who challenged DeWitt's orders" (Irons, 192). This "turnabout" continued after the war, when, according to Jere Takashi, "the JACL became the major community organization to deal with the racial discrimination and differential treatment [Nikkei] confronted" (Takahashi, 125). See also Toni Robinson and Greg Robinson, "The Limits of Interracial Coalitions: Méndez v. Westminster Reexamined," in *Racial Transformations: Latinos and Asians Remaking the United States*, ed. Nicholas DeGenova (Durham: Duke University Press, 2006), 98; Roger Daniels, *Asian America: Chinese and Japanese in the United States Since 1850* (Seattle: University of Washington Press, 1988), 295.

25. Kajiro Oyama, interview by Don Estes, 1975, on file at the Japanese American Historical Society of San Diego; Fred Oyama and Alice (Oyama) Yano, interview by Robin Li and Mark Brilliant, June 23–24, 2009.

26. Kajiro Oyama, interview; Fred Oyama and Alice (Oyama) Yano, interview. Following Glower's death, Oyama made a point of honoring him each year by bringing flowers to his grave.

27. Fred Oyama and Alice (Oyama) Yano, interview; Petition to Declare an Escheat to the State of California, August 28, 1944, Clerk's Transcript, Oyama-CA.

28. Fred Oyama, letter to author, May 25, 2009; Kajiro Oyama, interview; Fred Oyama and Alice (Oyama) Yano, interview.

29. "Petition to Declare an Escheat to the State of California," August 28, 1944, in "Clerk's Transcript," Oyama-CA.

30. Fred Oyama, letter to author; Fred Oyama and Alice (Oyama) Yano, interview.

31. Kajiro Oyama, interview.

32. Alien Land Law, Statutes of California, 1913, Chapter 113, 206–208.

33. Ian F. Haney López, *White By Law: The Legal Construction of Race* (New York: New York University Press, 1996).

34. Edwin E. Ferguson, "The California Alien Land Law and the Fourteenth Amendment," *California Law Review* 35 (1947): 62; Ronald T. Takaki, *Strangers from a Different Shore* (Boston: Little, Brown, 1998), 203–204; Frank F. Chuman, *The Bamboo People: The Law and Japanese-Americans* (Chicago: Japanese American Research Project, 1981), 50.

35. *Californians of Japanese, Chinese, and Filipino Ancestry*, 17; Carey McWilliams, *Factories in the Field: The Story of Migratory Farm Labor in California* (Boston: Little, Brown and Company, 1939), 66–71; Masao Suzuki, "Important or Impotent? Taking Another Look at the 1920 California Alien Land Law," *Journal of Economic History*, 64, no. 1 (2004): 128; Yuji Ichioka, "Japanese Immigrant Response to the 1920 California Alien Land Law," *Agricultural History*, 58, no. 2 (1984): 158.

36. U.S. Webb quoted in *Oyama v. State of California* 332 U.S. 633, 657 (1948).

37. As legal scholar Milton Konvitz wrote in 1947, California "could not pass an exclusion act, but it did pass an act which, it was hoped, would tend to keep the Japanese from California" (Milton R. Konvitz, "Alien Land Laws Before the Supreme Court," *Common Ground*, 7 no. 4 [1947]: 92).

38. *Californians of Japanese, Chinese, and Filipino Ancestry*, 17; Suzuki, 128.

39. Ichioka, 158, 162.

40. Carey McWilliams, *Prejudice—Japanese-Americans: Symbol of Racial Intolerance* (Boston: Little, Brown, 1944), 65; "Treasure Hunt," *Business Week*, August 4, 1945: 52; Park, 112.

41. Suzuki, 132.

42. Ferguson, 69–70; Chuman, 78–80.

43. *Ozawa v. U.S.*, 260 U.S. 189 (1922).

44. *Porterfield v. Webb* 263, U.S. 225 (1923), *Webb v. O'Brien*, 263 U.S. 313 (1923), *Frick v. Webb*, 263 U.S. 326 (1923). For a summary of these cases, see Chuman, 83–87.

45. *Cockrill v. California*, 268 U.S. 258 (1925), *Morrison v. People of the State of California*, 291 U.S. 82 (1934). For a summary of these cases, see Chuman, 83–87

46. On the 1923 amendments to the Alien Land Law, see Chuman, 87–88.

47. Johnson-Reed Immigration Act of 1924, quoted in *Asian Americans and the Supreme Court: A Documentary History*, ed. Hyung-Chan Kim (New York: Greenwood Press, 1992), 44.

48. Lucy Salyer, *Laws Harsh as Tigers: Chinese Immigrants and the Shaping of Modern Immigration Law* (Chapel Hill: University of North Carolina Press, 1995), 135; Ngai, 21–50.

49. *Californians of Japanese, Chinese, and Filipino Ancestry*, 17.

50. Suzuki, 128; Ichioka, 170; Robert Higgs, "Landless by Law: Japanese Immigrants in California Agriculture to 1941," *Journal of Economic History* 38, no. 1 (1978): 222,

51. Ferguson, 72.

52. Article from Selma, California *Enterprise*, January 24, 1946, in "Escheat Proceedings," *A Monthly Summary of Events and Trends in Race Relations* 3, no. 7 (1946): 183, 217.

53. "Treasure Hunt," 52.

54. Warren to various California county district attorneys, January 26, 1942, Box 1, Folder Meeting re Alien Land Owners, CA-AG; "Ouster of Foe on Coast Sought," *Los Angeles Times*, February 3, 1942: 6.

55. "Memorandum on Alien Land Law," circa 1942, Box 19/3a, Folder Alien Land Law, CA-AG.

56. "Warns Saboteurs Wait for Deadline," *New York Times*, February 22, 1942: 22.

57. "Alien Land Hearing Set," *Los Angeles Times*, March 11, 1942: 24.

58. Irons, 180–181.

59. Robert Kenny, press release, August 17, 1943, Box 12, Folder 1943 Press Releases, RWK; Robert Kenny, press release, May 29, 1944, Box 12, Folder 1944 Press Releases, RWK. Though the press release is dated May 29, 1944, it refers to Kenny's request to California District Attorneys to investigate Alien Land Law violations as having been issued the year before.

60. Robert Kenny, speech, June 7, 1944, Box 12, Folder Speeches January 1944–June 1944, RWK; Kenny, press release, May 29, 1944.

61. Native Sons of the Golden West, Santa Cruz Parlor No. 90 to Robert Kenny, April 25, 1944, Box 30, Folder Native Sons of the Golden West, RWK.

62. Suzuki, 132.

63. Suzuki, 132; *Californians of Japanese, Chinese, and Filipino*, 17; McWilliams, *Prejudice*, 87. For another accounting, see Victor Boesen, "The Nisei Come Home, *New Republic*, April 26, 1948: 16–17: "On 3.9 percent of the state's farms which the Japanese operated before the war, they produced 35 percent of the state's total truck crop annually. In Los Angeles County, they accounted for 64 percent of all truck crops for processing and 87 percent of the supply of fresh vegetables."

64. McWilliams, *Prejudice*, 87.

65. Larry Tajiri, "Rich California Grabs Land from Weakest Citizens," *Open Forum*, March 2, 1946: 1. For similar characterizations, see Bradford Smith, "The Great American Swindle," *Common Ground* 7, no. 2 (1947): 34; "Treasure Hunt," 50.

66. "Appendix B: Civil Escheat Proceedings Instituted by the California Attorney General's Office Under the Alien Land Law" in "Brief for Petitioners," September 30,

1947, Oyama-USSC. On the "first of a series of suits" during World War II brought by the Los Angeles County District Attorney's office, headed by future California Attorney General Fred Howser, see "Suit Filed on Jap Land," *Los Angeles Times*, April 13, 1944: A1. On the "first action against Japs alleged to own lands in Orange County in violation of the alien land law," see "Orange County Attacks Title of Jap-Held Lands," *Los Angeles Times*, September 3, 1944: A8.

67. "Hearing on Anti-Jap Feeling Opens at Fresno," *Los Angeles Times*, 27 August 1943: A2.

68. "Race Issues to Feature Election," *Open Forum*, September 21, 1946: 2. Of these cases, the first one was decided in favor of the state in October 1944, after which "the district attorney declared that the case was a test and that many other suits like it would be filed" ("First Case on Anti-Alien Law Won by California," *Open Forum*, October 21, 1944: 2).

69. Grace Cable Keroher, "California's Proposition 15," *Common Ground* 7, no. 2 (1947): 30; Eiji Tanabe, "JACL and the Oyama Case," *Pacific Citizen*, January 24, 1948: 5.

70. Kenny, press release, May 29, 1944.

71. "Petition to Declare an Escheat to the State of California."

72. McGovney, 16.

73. On paying fees to avoid prosecution, the *New York Times* reported a $100,000 "out-of-court settlement" in November 1946 ("California Alien-Land Curbs Upheld Again as Court Rules Against Nisei Over Property," *New York Times*, November 1: 1946). More generally, Larry Tajiri wrote in 1952, "A number of escheat cases were compromised with the State through the payment of money to quiet title to the property. Nearly $500,00 was paid by Japanese Americans to settle escheat cases" (Tajiri, "Farewell to the Land Law," 4). According to Masaoka, "The state was practicing a form of blackmail by paying a reward for information about alleged violations of the land law and offering to 'sell' the escheated farms back to the owners after charges were filed" (Mike Masaoka with Bill Hosokawa, *They Call Me Moses Masaoka* [New York: William Morrow, 1987], 83).

74. "The Story of the *Oyama* Case," 4.

75. "Rich California Grabs Land from Weakest Citizens," *Open Forum*, March 2, 1946: 4.

76. Galen M. Fisher, "The Nisei Return," *Common Sense*, November 1945: 7.

77. Robert Kenny, speech, March 16, 1945, Folder 2579, EW.

78. "Anti-Lynching Law," *Pacific Citizen*, February 7, 1948: 4. Kenny himself pointed to "more than eighty reports of arson and other destructive acts or threats made to authorities" in an address to the "Conference of California's Councils of Civic Unity and Similar Community Organizations" ("Report on Conference of California's Councils of Civic Unity and Similar Organizations").

79. Earl Warren to Eleanor Roosevelt, January 8, 1946, Folder 2583, EW.

80. Earl Warren to Loren Grey, July 7, 1945, Folder 3675, EW.

81. "Why, Mr. Kenny?" *Open Forum*, March 2, 1946: 3.

82. Chas Johnson to Earl Warren, July 9, 1945, Box 2, File Chapter 1129, E5927, EW.

83. Letter to Earl Warren, July 5, 1945, Box 2, File Chapter 1129, E5927, EW.

84. Beach Vasey to Earl Warren, July 2, 1945, Box 2, Folder Chapter 1129, E5927, EW.

85. Fred Oyama, letter to author.

86. *People v. Fred Y. Oyama*, September 17, 1945, in "Clerk's Transcript," Oyama-CA.

87. "The Story of the *Oyama* Case," 4.

88. "Memorandum of Japanese American Citizens League in Support of the Appellants' Request that the Supreme Court Retain Jurisdiction," November 5, 1945, Oyama-CA.

89. "Application for Leave to File Memorandum in Support of Appellants' Request for Supreme Court to Retain Jurisdiction of Appeal and Said Memorandum," November 6, 1945, Oyama-CA; Morris E. Cohn to Phil S. Gibson, Chief Justice of the California Supreme Court, November 9, 1945, Oyama-CA.

90. Al Wirin to Loren Miller, October 30, 1945, Box 5, Folder 2, LM.

91. "Escheat Cases Set for Hearing," *Open Forum*, February 23, 1946: 1.

92. For more on Miller and his racially restrictive housing covenant litigation, see Chapter 4.

93. Minutes of meeting, December 6, 1945, Box 16, Folder Civil Rights Defense Union, JACL.

94. "A Program of Action for the J.A.C.L., For All Isseis and For All Lovers of Freedom," circa 1946, Box 38, Folder Escheat Cases, JACL Program of Action, 1944–1945, JACL.

95. "Japanese Americans," *A Monthly Summary of Events and Trends in Race Relations*, 3, no. 6 (January 1946): 183.

96. "An Historic Day," *Open Forum*, June 1, 1946: 2.

97. *People v. Fred Y. Oyama* 29 Cal. 2d 164, 178 (1946).

98. *People v. Fred Y. Oyama* 29 Cal. 2d 164, 181 (1946). Two other justices—Chief Justice Phil S. Gibson and Justice Jesse W. Carter—neither concurred with Justice Edmonds's opinion, which was "fully concurred" by three other justices, nor dissented from it ("Supreme Court OK's Alien Land Law," *Open Forum*, November 17, 1946: 1).

99. "Decision Delivered by Four of Seven Justices is Based on Earlier U.S. Court Verdict," *Pacific Citizen*, November 2, 1946: 1.

100. "Reporter's Transcript," August, 21, 1945, Oyama-CA.

101. "Oyama Test Cast to be Taken to U.S. Court," *Pacific Citizen*, November 2, 1946: 1.

102. "Proposition 15: Validation of Legislative Amendments to the Alien Land Law," 1946. Available online through: http://library.uchastings.edu/library/california-research/ca-ballot-measures.html#ballotprops.

103. Larry Tajiri, "Fighting the Alien Land Law," *Pacific Citizen*, November 2, 1946: 4.

104. *Report of the Joint Fact-Finding Committee on Un-American Activities in California* (Sacramento: Senate of the State of California, 1945), 65.

105. Daniel Marshall quoted in "Propositions 11 and 15 Civil Liberties Issues," *Open Forum*, October 19, 1946: 1.

106. Chuman, 205, 220; Keroher, 31.

107. "Argument Against Senate Constitutional Amendment No. 17, Proposition 15: Validation of Legislative Amendments to the Alien Land Law," 1946. Available online through: http://library.uchastings.edu/library/california-research/ca-ballot-measures. html#ballotprops.

108. Joseph Stillwell quoted in Ruth W. Kingman and Joe Grant Masaoka, "A Measure of Things to Come," *World Call*, July-August 1946," in Box 1, Folder Race Relations, CFCU.

109. "Vote 'No' On 15," 1946, Box 154, Folder 10, FC; "Ex-Sgt. Akira Iwamura Is Puzzled," *Los Angeles Times*, October 14, 1946: A4.

110. Sophia Booth to Earl Warren, October 14, 1946, Folder 3675, EW,

111. Beach Vasey to Sophia Booth, October 21, 1946, Folder 3675, EW.

112. "Oyama Test Cast to be Taken to U.S. Court," *Pacific Citizen*, November 2, 1946: 1.

113. "Some 100 proceedings charging Alien Land Act violations were initiated in 1946 and 1947." (Tajiri, "Farewell to the Land Law," 4). According to Wirin, approximately seventy-five Alien Land Law cases were pending (Boesen, 19).

114. "Proposition 15," *Pacific Citizen*, November 9, 1946: 4.

115. Saburo Kido, "Defeat of Proposition 15 Shows Opposition of Voters to Race-Baiting Legislation," *Pacific Citizen*, November 9, 1946: 3.

116. "People's Mandate Has Upset 50 Years of Anti-Orientalism in California, Says Masaoka," *Pacific Citizen*, November 9, 1946: 1. On this point, see also Larry Tajiri, "Fighting the Alien Land Law," *Pacific Citizen*, November 2, 1946: 4: "For the first time in CA political history, an imposing number of individuals, organizations, and newspapers have stood up to be counted on an issue involving discriminatory legislation against persons of Japanese ancestry."

117. "Supreme Court OK's Alien Land Law," *Open Forum*, November 17, 1946: 1.

118. "Petition for Rehearing Filed in the Oyama Land Law Case," *Pacific Citizen*, November 16, 1946: 1.

119. "Petition for A Writ of Certiorari," February 25, 1947, Oyama-USSC.

120. Al Wirin to Thurgood Marshall, December 3, 1946, Box 558, Folder 19, ACLU.

121. "California Supreme Court Rejects Oyama Petition," *Pacific Citizen*, 30 November 1946: 2.

122. "Why an Additional Appropriation for the Alien Land Law is Ill-Advised," May 8, 1947, Box 19, Folder Alien Land Law—Masaoka, 1947–1950, 1952, JACL.

123. Memorandum from Northern California JACL-ADC to National Headquarters, Box 17, Folder ADC Calif. Legislative, 1947, JACL; "Order Allowing Certiorari," April 7, 1947, in "Transcript of Record," Oyama-USSC.

124. At this point, Wirin's "associates" were Saburo Kido and Fred Okrand. They were "supported" by James Purcell, William Ferriter, and Guy C. Calden of San Francisco; and Charles A. Horsky and Ernest W. Jennes, of Washington, D.C. ("U.S. Supreme Court to Hear Oyama Case," *Open Forum*, April 19, 1947: 1). The "Petition for a Writ of Certiorari" and "Brief for Petitioners" list Horsky and Jennes as "Counsel for Petitioners" and Purcell, Ferriter, Calden, Kido, and Okrand as "Of Counsel." Purcell,

Ferriter, and Caldren were affiliated with the Civil Rights Defense Union, while Kido, the former JACL president, and Okrand were in practice with Wirin (Oyama-USSC).

125. "Defendants' Supplemental Memorandum on Demurrer," March 2, 1945, in "Transcript of Record," Oyama-USSC.

126. "Petition for a Writ of Certiorari," February 25, 1947, Oyama-USSC.

127. "The Story of the *Oyama* Case," 4.

128. Masaoka, 213.

129. David Mao, Covington and Burling Librarian, e-mail message to author, May 2003. Mao said that the firm undertook the case on behalf of the ACLU, but, unfortunately, destroyed the case records in 1996; Dean Acheson, *Present at the Creation: My Years at the State Department* (New York: Norton, 1969), 239; "Horsky to Aid Preparation of Oyama Appeal," *Pacific Citizen*, December 7, 1946: 1. Horsky had ACLU connections and had been responsible for the organization's amicus brief in *Korematsu* (Robinson and Robinson, "*Korematsu* and Beyond," 36).

130. Al Wirin to Roger Baldwin, April 9, 1947, Box 558, Folder 19, ACLU.

131. Masaoka, 213. In Masaoka's recollection, Acheson agreed to join on the spot. In Wirin's recollection, he did not receive word that Acheson would join until the day before oral arguments were slated to begin (Wirin, partially completed oral history).

132. "Wirin, Acheson Hold Anti-Alien Land Law Restricts Citizen Rights of Japanese Americans," *Pacific Citizen*, October 25, 1947: 5.

133. John Kitasako, "Supreme Court Justices Fire Sharp Queries on Land Law," *Pacific Citizen*, November 1, 1947: 5.

134. Kitasako, 5.

135. General Report, October 26, 1947, Box 5, Folder 8, MM.

136. *Oyama v. State of California*, 332 U.S. 633, 641–647 (1948).

137. *Oyama v. State of California*, 332 U.S. 633, 647–650 (1948).

138. *Oyama v. State of California*, 332 U.S. 633, 650, 673 (1948).

139. Al Wirin to Roger Baldwin, January 24, 1948, Reel 256, Volume 96, ACLU-MF. Half a century later, Harvard Law School professor Randall Kennedy was even more effusive. He described Justice Murphy's concurrence as "my favorite judicial opinion," one of the few "Supreme Court opinions in the area of race relations law that I wholeheartedly admire" (Randall Kennedy, "Justice Murphy's Concurrence in Oyama v. California," *Texas Law Review* 74 [1996]: 1245).

140. "California Alien Land Law Dead!" *Open Forum*, February 7, 1948: 1–2. By contrast, Justice Felix Frankfurter wrote in his diary that Justice Murphy's concurrence was a "long-winded, soap-boxy attack against racism" (Felix Frankfurter quoted in "Nationality and Aliens, *Oyama v. California*," *The Supreme Court in Conference (1940–1985),* ed. Del Dickson [New York: Oxford University Press, 2001], 756).

141. *Oyama v. State of California*, 332 U.S. 633, 684, 688 (1948). During deliberations, Jackson observed, "the only plausible way" to reverse the California Supreme Court's ruling "would be on Dean Acheson's ground." He indicated that he "could go that way," but, in the end, did not (*The Supreme Court in Conference (1940–1985),* 755).

142. "Oyama Case Decision Upholds Nisei Rights," *Pacific Citizen*, January 24, 1948: 1.

143. "The Story of the Oyama Case," 4.

144. Editorials quoted in "Editorial Comment," *Pacific Citizen*, January 31, 1948: 4.

145. Tanabe, 5.

146. Fred Howser quoted in "California Alien Land Law Dead!"

147. Al Wirin to Mike Masaoka, January 30, 1948, Box 6, Folder A.L. Wirin, 1947–1948, JACL.

148. Al Wirin to Clifford Forster, January 28, 1948, Reel 256, Volume 96, ACLU-MF.

149. Fred Howser quoted in Kevin Allen Leonard, *The Battle for Los Angeles: Racial Ideology and World War II* (Albuquerque: University of New Mexico Press, 2006), 244.

150. "New California Budget Contains No Provision for Funds to Enforce State's Alien Land Law," *Pacific Citizen*, March 20, 1948: 3.

151. Boesen, 19; "California Alien Land Law Dead," 1.

152. Robert M. Cullum, "Japanese American Audit—1948," *Common Ground* 9, no. 2 (1949): 90.

153. "Petition for Writ of Mandamus," May 6, 1946, in "Transcript of Record," Takahashi-USSC; Chuman, 229.

154. Chuman, 228.

155. Donnelly Committee on Japanese Resettlement quoted in "Memorandum of Opinion," June 13, 1946, in "Transcript of Record," Takahashi-USSC.

156. "Supreme Court Voids California Fishing Ban," *Open Forum*, June 26, 1948:1.

157. Ralph Scott to Earl Warren, April 26, 1945, Chapter 181, MF3:1 (35), GCBF.

158. "Petition for Writ of Mandamus," May 6, 1946, in "Transcript of Record," Takahashi-USSC; "Jap Fisherman Asks Court Relief," *Los Angeles Times*, May 7, 1946: A2.

159. "Memorandum of Opinion," June 13, 1946; "Notice of Appeal," August 26, 1946, in "Transcript of Record," Takahashi-USSC.

160. "Memorandum of Opinion," June 13, 1946.

161. *Torao Takahashi v. Fish and Game Commission*, 30 Ca1.2d 719, 731, 737, 745 (1947).

162. Al Wirin to the Justices of the California Supreme Court, November 13, 1946, Takahashi-CA; "Memorandum of Opinion," June 13, 1946.

163. *Torao Takahashi v. Fish and Game Commission*, 30 Ca1.2d 719, 741, 745 (1947).

164. "Let Aliens Die Supreme Court Holds," *Open Forum*, November 1, 1947: 1.

165. Samuel Ishikawa to Roger Baldwin, January 21, 1948, Reel 256, Volume 96, ACLU-MF.

166. Samuel Ishikawa to Marian Wynn Perry, January 21, 1948, Part 15 A, Reel 8, Frame 194, NAACP-MF; Mike Masaoka, "General Report," October 26, 1947, Box 5, Folder 8, MM.

167. "Petition for a Writ of Certiorari," January 16, 1948, Takahashi-USSC.

168. Risa L. Goluboff, *The Lost Promise of Civil Rights* (Cambridge: Harvard University Press, 2007), 43–44.

169. "Order Allowing Certiorari," March 15, 1948, in "Transcript of Record," Takahashi-USSC.

170. "U.S. Attorney General Enters Fishing Case," *Open Forum*, February 21, 1948: 1.

171. *Torao Takahashi v. Fish and Game Commission*, 334 U.S. 410, 418–420 (1948).

172. *Torao Takahashi v. Fish and Game Commission*, 334 U.S. 410, 428 (1948).

173. Masaoka, 214.

174. "Reporters Transcript," *Sei Fujii v. State*, L.A. 21149, SACCC.

175. *Sei Fujii v. State* 38 Ca1.2d 718 (1952); *Haruye Masaoka v. People* 39 Cal. 2d 882 (1952); Chuman, 218–221.

176. Pat Brown quoted in "California Will Not Appeal Alien Land Law to U.S. Supreme Court," in *Los Angeles Daily Journal*, May 12, 1952, Box 584, Folder 8, ACLU. See also, "Will Not Appeal Alien Land Law Decision," *Open Forum*, June 7, 1952: 2; "California Drops Fight to Curb Aliens," *Washington Post*, May 13, 1952: 5.

177. "Escheat Cases," *Pacific Citizen*, November 22, 1947, 4; "California's Supreme Court Says 39-Year Old Measure Violates U.S. Constitution," *Pacific Citizen*, April 19, 1952: 1; "California's Alien Land Law is Buried," *Open Forum*, May 10, 1952: 1–2.

178. Saburo Kido, "Epilogue for the Alien Land Law," *Pacific Citizen*, April 19, 1952: 4.

179. Fred Oyama, letter to author; Fred Oyama and Alice (Oyama) Yano, interview.

180. Al Wirin quoted in Hosokawa, 266.

181. Tajiri, "Farewell to Little Tokyo," 90–94.

182. Wirin, partially completed oral history, 77, 115–117.

183. Samuel Ishikawa to Roger Baldwin, January 21, 1948, Reel 256, Volume 96, ACLU-MF.

184. "JACL Establishes Defense Fund for Civil Rights Cases," *Pacific Citizen*, December 7, 1946: 1.

185. Mike Masaoka, statement, May 1, 1947, Box 27, Folder Civil Rights, JACL.

186. "JACL National Planning Committee Report," 1948, Reel 256, Volume 94, ACLU-MF. See also, "In the field of state and municipal legislation, this Committee recommends that the National Organization concern itself with discriminatory or prejudicial legislation that affects the welfare of persons of Japanese ancestry, as well as other American[s], whenever and wherever it is appropriate and proper" ("Report of JACL National Committee on Legislative Matters," September 5, 1948, Box 16, Folder Committee on Legislative Matters, 1948–1951, JACL).

187. "Statement of Policy," January 16, 1947, Box 16, Folder ADC-Statements, 1944–1953, JACL. For a similar statement from a year or two before, see "Program of Action for the J.A.C.L." which called for assisting "other minority groups" with issues particular to them. "The time has come . . . when we can demonstrate the sincerity of our appreciation to the many groups whose members are not of Japanese descent, who have helped us, by our aiding other minority groups when their rights are denied." Doing so would "afford us an opportunity to prove our claims . . . that a race-baiting attack upon any minority racial groups is a danger equally to every minority groups in the United States" ("A Program of Action for the J.A.C.L., For All Isseis and For All Lovers of Freedom," circa 1946, Box 38, Folder Escheat Cases, JACL Program of Action, 1944–1945, JACL).

188. These cases, including the JACL's contribution to them, will be discussed in Chapters 3 and 4, respectively.

189. Joe Grant Masaoka, "Unfinished Business on Erasing Discrimination Toward Japanese Americans," November 29, 1948, Carton 1, Folder Race Relations, CFCU.

190. Al Wirin to James Purcell, April 25, 1949, Box 38, Folder Attorneys 1948–1950, JACL.

191. Organizational Meeting for JACL-ADC, minutes, September 13, 1951, Box 42, Folder JACL-ADC Calif. Legislative Committee, JACL. For a different interpretation of the JACL and interracial coalition-building in the second half of the 1940s, see Robinson and Robinson, "The Limits of Interracial Coalitions: Méndez v. Westminster Reexamined," who argue that "the JACL became heavily invested in intergroup alliances" (100).

192. "Report of JACL National Committee on Legislative Matters," September 5, 1948, Box 16, Folder Committee on Legislative Matters, 1948–1951, JACL.

193. "JACL National Legislative Program—1949," Part 18B, Reel 23, Frames 480–485, NAAC-MF.

194. "Oyama Test Case to Be Taken to U.S. Court," *Pacific Citizen*, November 2, 1946: 1; Tosuke Yamaski, "Prominent Americans Join Effort to Erase Bias From Natrualization Law," *Pacific Citizen*, December 27, 1947: 1.

195. Cullum, 87–88.

196. Tajiri, "Farewell to the Land Law," 4.

197. "Unfinished Business on Erasing Discrimination Toward Japanese Americans."

198. "Nisei USA: Racists Repudiated," *Pacific Citizen*, April 24, 1948: 4.

199. For more on the Immigration and Naturalization Act of 1952, see Ngai, 196–197, who describes the new law as part of "a general rehabilitation of Japanese Americans' citizenship."

200. Fred Oyama and Alice (Oyama) Yano, interview.

Chapter 3

1. Fred Ross, "Workbook of a Wayfaring Organizer," no date, Box 20, Folder 1, FR.

2. Carey McWilliams, *North from Mexico: The Spanish-Speaking People of the United States* (1949; New York: Greenwood Press, 1968), 280, 283.

3. For more on Ross's Unity Leagues organizing, see "Community Organizing in Mexican American Colonies," 1947, Box 20, Folder 19, FR; McWilliams, *North from Mexico*, 280; Matt Garcia, *A World of Its Own: Race, Labor, and Citrus in the Making of Greater Los Angeles, 1900–1970* (Chapel Hill: University of North Carolina Press, 2001), 234–236.

4. Fred Ross to Laurence Hewes, February 2, 1947, Box 5, Folder Incoming Correspondence: R: Ross, Fred, CFCU.

5. McWilliams, *North from Mexico*, 283.

6. "Petition," March 2, 1945, MvW-DC. Throughout this chapter (and book), I refer to the case and case filings as *Mendez* (without an accent) in keeping with how it was referenced in the legal documents. In all other instances, I use the accent (Méndez).

7. Philippa Strum, *Mendez v. Westminster: School Desegregation and Mexican-American Rights* (Lawrence: University of Kansas Press, 2010), 41.

8. David Marcus quoted in Fred Ross, "Bell Town Unity League," no date, Box 20, Folder 4, FR.

9. Carey McWilliams, "Spectrum of Segregation," *Survey Graphic* 36, no. 1 (1947): 22.

10. Robert Carter to Leon Silverman, March 24, 1947, Papers of the NAACP, Part 3B, reel Reel 1, frame Frame 296, NAACP-MF.

11. Ronald Takaki, *Double Victory: A Multicultural History of America in World War II* (Boston: Little, Brown, and Company), 223; Richard B. Valencia, "The Mexican American Struggle for Equal Educational Opportunity in *Mendez v. Westminster*: Helping Pave the Way for *Brown v. Board of Education*," *Teachers College Record* 107, no. 3 (2005): 389–423. See also Jennifer McCormick and César J. Ayala, "Felícita 'La Prieta' Méndez (1916–1998) and the End of Latino School Segregation in California," *CENTRO Journal* 19, no. 2 (2007): 28; Frederick P. Aguirre, "*Mendez v. Westminster School District*: How it Affected *Brown v. Board of Education*," *Journal of Hispanic Higher Education* 4, no. 4 (2005): 321–332; Bob Egelko and Vanessa Hua, "California Latinos' Suit in '47 Set Stage for *Brown* Decision," *San Francisco Chronicle*, May 16, 2004; Vicki L. Ruiz, "Tapestries of Resistance: Episodes of School Segregation and Desegregation in the Western United States," in *From the Grassroots to the Supreme Court: Brown v. Board of Education and American Democracy*, ed. Peter F. Lau (Durham: Duke University Press, 2004), 62; Christopher Arriola, "Knocking on the Schoolhouse Door: *Mendez v. Westminster*—Equal Protection, Public Education and Mexican Americans in the 1940's," *La Raza Law Journal* 8 (1995): 207; Mario T. García, *Mexican Americans: Leadership, Ideology, and Identity* (New Haven: Yale University Press, 1989), 57.

12. "Petitioners' Opening Brief," 15–16, September 29, 1945, MvW-DC.

13. "Plaintiffs Reply Brief," 11, November 1, 1945, MvW-DC.

14. *Brown v. Board of Education*, 347 U.S. 483, 493, 495 (1954).

15. *Mendez v. Westminster*, 64 F. Supp. 544 (1946); *Westminster v. Mendez*, 161 F.2d 774 (1947).

16. "Reporter's Transcript of Proceedings," 84, June 26,1945, MvW-DC.

17. For more on this point, see Chapter 8.

18. Roger Baldwin to Thurgood Marshall, June 3, 1955, Box 2, Folder 20, GS.

19. "Proceedings of Third Annual Convention for Civic Unity," December 1948, Carton 4, Folder Race Relations on the West Coast, CM-B.

20. The details from this paragraph come from a variety of sources, all of which draw on interviews with various Méndez and Munemitsu family members: *Mendez vs. Westminster: For All the Children*, prod. and dir. Sandra Robbie, 27 min., KOCE-TV Foundation, 2002, DVD; David Montgomery, "A First-Class Civil Rights Lesson," *Washington Post*, October 9, 2007: C1; Gilbert G. Gonzalez, *Chicano Education in the Era of Segregation* (Philadelphia: Balch Institute Press, 1990), 149–150; McCormick and Ayala, 12–35.

21. "Reporter's Transcript of Proceedings," 462–463, July 10, 1945, MvW-DC.

22. "Reporter's Transcript of Proceedings," 461, July 10, 1945, MvW-DC.

23. "Reporter's Transcript of Proceedings," 445, July 9, 1945, MvW-DC.

24. Toni Robinson and Greg Robinson, "The Limits of Interracial Coalitions: Méndez v. Westminster Reexamined," in *Racial Transformations: Latinos and Asians Remaking the United States*, ed. Nicholas DeGenova (Durham: Duke University Press, 2006), 96; Fred Oyama, letter to author, May 25, 2009.

25. "Reporter's Transcript of Proceedings," 462, July 10, 1945, MvW-DC.

26. Felícitas Méndez quoted in McCormick and Ayala, 24.

27. Strum, 1; Gonzalez, 150; Maria Fleming, "A Tale of Two Schools," in *A Place at the Table: Struggles for Equality in America*, ed. Maria Fleming (New York: Oxford University Press, 2001), 92.

28. "Reporter's Transcript of Proceedings," 445–446, July 9, 1945, MvW-DC.

29. "Reporter's Transcript of Proceedings," 446, 450, 455, July 9, 1945, MvW-DC.

30. "Reporter's Transcript of Proceedings," 435–439, July 9, 1945, MvW-DC.

31. "Reporter's Transcript of Proceedings," 456, July 9, 1945, MvW-DC.

32. Curiously, Marcus is sometimes referred to as an "African American civil rights lawyer." See, for example, Jeanne M. Powers and Lirio Patton, "Between *Mendez* and *Brown*: *Gonzalez v. Sheely* (1951) and the Legal Campaign Against Segregation," *Law and Social Inquiry* 33 (Winter 2008): 138; Valencia, 401; Arriola, 193.

33. Gigi Marcus Lane (daughter of David C. Marcus and Yrma Maria Davila, Marcus's second wife), phone interview with author, May 21, 2009; Melissa Marcus (granddaughter of David C. Marcus and his first wife), phone interview with author, June 21, 2003.

34. Strum, 40.

35. *Lopez v. Seccombe*, 71 F. Supp. 769 (1944); Strum, 38–39; Mario T. García, 86–88; Matt Garcia, 228–242.

36. Strum, 41, 53; *Mendez vs. Westminster: For All the Children*; Gonzalez, 150.

37. "Petition," March 2, 1945, MvW-DC. Elsewhere in the court records, El Modena is spelled El Modeno and El Modino. The other named petitioners in the case were William Guzmán, Frank Palomino, Thomas Estrada, and Lorenzo Ramirez, and their respective children. For more on the other named plaintiffs, see Strum, 43–46.

38. These states also included those in the South and states bordering the South such as Kansas, Texas, and Delaware, plus Arizona and Wyoming in the West. Pauli Murray, ed., *States' Laws on Race and Color* (Cincinnati: Women's Division of Christian Service, Board of Missions and Church Extension, Methodist Church, 1950), 14.

39. Charles Wollenberg, *All Deliberate Speed: Segregation and Exclusion in California Schools, 1855–1955* (Berkeley: University of California Press, 1976), 13–14. This chapter focuses on the segregation of school children of Mexican descent. With respect to African American, Chinese- and Japanese-descent students, here is a capsule history, drawn from Wollenberg: In 1854, the San Francisco Board of Education opened California's first "colored school." Less than a decade later, the state legislature forbade "Negroes, Mongolians and Indians" admittance into public schools attended by white children. In 1874, the California Supreme Court ruled on the matter of de jure school segregation. In a test case brought by an African American woman who tried but failed to register her daughter in a white San Francisco public school, the California Supreme Court in *Ward v. Flood* promulgated a "separate but equal" opinion, some twenty-two years before the U.S. Supreme Court did the same in *Plessy v. Ferguson*. After 1880, due to African American lobbying efforts, African Americans successfully removed themselves from the state's school segregation law and were never again inserted. Unlike their African American counterparts, Chinese Californians prior to 1947 never managed

to prevail upon the state legislature to strike "Mongolian" or "Chinese" from the educational code. In theory, this meant that local school boards had the option to establish separate schools for children of "Chinese" or "Mongolian parentage." In practice, however, according to Wollenberg, "the rigid policy of segregation [of Chinese] broke down" over the course of the twentieth century. Beginning in1905, parents of Chinese-descent school children in San Francisco did much to force this change. That year they threatened to boycott the Chinese elementary school unless the San Francisco Board of Education admitted their children into regular city high schools. Fearing the loss of state educational funds, the San Francisco Board of Education capitulated. By 1947, no de jure Chinese school existed in San Francisco, although a de facto one operated in Chinatown due to patterns of residential segregation. In 1921, the state legislature inserted "Japanese" into the school segregation law. However, only four Sacramento County school districts—where Japanese American students composed a majority of the school population—availed themselves of the segregation option the law afforded them. By decade's end, 575 Japanese American students attended Sacramento County's segregated schools, while 30,000 attended integrated schools in the rest of the state. When World War II began, according to the *Pacific Citizen*, the official publication of the Japanese American Citizens League, "the only [remaining] segregated school in California for children of Japanese ancestry" was in Sacramento County.

40. "Segregated Schools," *Pacific Citizen*, February 23, 1946: 4. See also McWilliams, *North from Mexico*, 281: "The School Code . . . says nothing about Mexicans or Negroes."

41. *Mendez v. Westminster*, 64 F. Supp. 544, 548, footnote 5 (1946).

42. Grace Stanley, "Special School for Mexicans," *The Survey*, September 15, 1920: 714.

43. Mae M. Ngai, *Impossible Subjects: Illegal Aliens and the Making of Modern America* (Princeton: Princeton University Press, 2004), 50.

44. *Mexicans in California: Report of Governor C.C. Young's Mexican Fact-Finding Committee* (San Francisco: State Building, 1930), 44.

45. Wollenberg, 109.

46. Ruiz, 57.

47. Strum, 27; Arriola, 171.

48. Wollenberg, 112.

49. Mary Peters, "The Segregation of Mexican American Children in the Elementary Schools of California: Its Legal and Administrative Aspects" (M.A. Thesis, University of California, Los Angeles, 1948), 35, in Wollenberg, 112.

50. Simon Ludwig Treff, "The Education of Mexican Children in Orange County," (M.A. Thesis, University of Southern California, 1934), 22–24, in Wollenberg, 116; Strum, 19–20.

51. "Reporter's Transcript of Proceedings," 73, June 26, 1945, MvW-DC.

52. McWilliams, "Spectrum of Segregation," 24.

53. McWilliams, "Spectrum of Segregation," 24.

54. "Segregated Schools," *Pacific Citizen*, February 23, 1946: 4; *Mendez v. Westminster*, 64 F. Supp. 544, 548, footnote 5 (1946); Wollenberg, 26, 118; Gonzalez, 24.

55. Francisco E. Balderrama, *In Defense of La Raza: The Los Angeles Mexican Consulate and the Mexican Community, 1929–1936* (Tucson: University of Arizona Press, 1982), 63–67.

56. U.S. Webb quoted in "Montoya Takes New Step," *Los Angeles Times*, April 13, 1931: 8; Balderrama, 62–63.

57. Manuel Ruiz, Jr. to Herbert Slater, May 14, 1945, 16, Folder 3, MR. On the bill's defeat, see Strum, 14; Balderrama, 65–67.

58. Section 8004, California Education Code, 1946, in *Mendez v. Westminster*, 64 F. Supp. 544, 548, footnote 5 (1946).

59. W. Henry Cooke, "The Segregation of Mexican-American School Children in Southern California," *School and Society* 67 (1948): 417.

60. *Mendez v. Westminster*, 64 F. Supp. 544, 550 (1946).

61. "Answer of El Modeno School District," May 5, 1945, MvW-DC.

62. "Reporter's Transcript of Proceedings," July 5, 1945, 27–29, MvW-DC.

63. "Answer of Santa Ana City Schools," May 5, 1945, MvW-DC.

64. "Reporter's Transcript of Proceedings," 228, 580, 591, MvW-DC.

65. "Brief for the National Association for the Advancement of Colored People as *Amicus Curiae*," 12, October 2, 1946, MvW-DC.

66. Fred Ross, report, October 13, 1946, Box 5, Folder Incoming Correspondence: R: Ross, Fred, CFCU; Manuscript about LULAC, circa 1946, Box 22, Folder 2, FR.

67. Cooke, 417; Wollenberg, 116–117; Arriola, 176–177.

68. "Reporter's Transcript of Proceedings," July 5, 1945, 17, 28–29, MvW-DC.

69. For example, leaving aside those who never even matriculated, Christopher Arriola notes that of the fifty-seven students of Mexican descent who entered high school in El Modena in 1940, only eight made it to their senior year (Arriola, 179; Strum, 20).

70. Strum, 18–19; Arriola, 172–176.

71. "Reporter's Transcript of Proceedings," 12, 27, 58, 65, July 5, 1945, MvW-DC.

72. "Reporter's Transcript of Proceedings," 229, 230, 240, 249, July 6, 1945, MvW-DC.

73. "Reporter's Transcript of Proceedings," 442, July 9, 1945, MvW-DC.

74. "Reporter's Transcript of Proceedings," 3, 43, 84, June 26, 1945, MvW-DC.

75. McWilliams, *North from Mexico*, 298; Strum, 52.

76. Roger Baldwin to Thurgood Marshall, June 3, 1955, Box 2, Folder 20, GS.

77. Ricardo Romo, "George I. Sánchez and the Civil Rights Movement: 1940–1960," *La Raza Law Journal* 1 (1986): 343–346.

78. George Sánchez to Roger Baldwin, September 15, 1942, Box 2, Folder 17, GS.

79. George Sánchez to Roger Baldwin, January 4, 1942, Box 2, Folder 17, GS.

80. George Sánchez to Roger Baldwin, September 21, 1942, Box 2, Folder 17, GS.

81. George Sánchez to Roger Baldwin, September 15, 1942, Box 2, Folder 17, GS.

82. George Sánchez to Roger Baldwin, September 21, 1942, Box 2, Folder 17, GS; George Sánchez to Roger Baldwin, January 25, 1945, Reel 232, Volume 2686, ACLU-MF; George Sánchez to Roger Baldwin, March 8, 1945, Box 2, Folder 17, GS. See also George Sánchez to Roger Baldwin, March 21, 1945, Box 2, Folder 17, GS: "No one has

saught [sic] to . . . dispute the pedagogical reasons under which school boards find it possible to maintain segregated schools."

83. George Sánchez to Roger Baldwin, March 8, 1945, Box 2, Folder 17, GS.

84. George Sánchez to Roger Baldwin, May 2, 1945, Box 2, Folder 17, GS.

85. George Sánchez to Roger Baldwin, March 8, 1945, Box 2, Folder 17, GS.

86. George Sánchez to Roger Baldwin, March 21, 1945, Box 2, Folder 17, GS.

87. George Sánchez to Roger Baldwin, March 8, 1945, Box 2, Folder 17, GS; George Sánchez to Roger Baldwin, May 2, 1945, Box 2, Folder 17, GS; George Sánchez to Al Wirin, October 3, 1947, Box 62, Folder 15, GS.

88. "Petition," March 2, 1945, MvW-DC. Marcus's use of "American Mexican" is in his "Petitoners' Opening Brief," September 29, 1945, MvW-DC.

89. "Answer of Westminster School District," May 5, 1945, MvW-DC.

90. "Answer of El Modeno School District," May 5, 1945, MvW-DC; "Answer of Garden Grove School District," May 5, 1945, MvW-DC; "Answer of Santa Ana School City Schools," May 5, 1945, MvW-DC.

91. George Sánchez to Roger Baldwin, March 8, 1945, Box 2, Folder 17, GS.

92. "Reporter's Transcript of Proceedings," 43, 67, 77, 79, 104, June 26, 1945, MvW-DC. On this last point, see also "Reporter's Transcript of Proceedings," 33, July 5, 1945, MvW-DC.

93. "Reporter's Transcript of Proceedings," 60, 67, 68, 70, 75, 76, June 26, 1945, MvW-DC.

94. "Reporter's Transcript of Proceedings," 5, 24, 33, 34, 75, 103, June 26, 1945, MvW-DC.

95. "Reporter's Transcript of Proceedings," 83, July 5, 1945, MvW-DC.

96. "Reporter's Transcript of Proceedings," 404, July 9, 1945, MvW-DC.

97. "Reporter's Transcript of Proceedings," 255, 301–304, July 6, 1945, MvW-DC; see also "Reporter's Transcript of Proceedings," 618, 619, July 11, 1945, MvW-DC.

98. "Reporter's Transcript of Proceedings," 48, 36, 69, 444, MvW-DC.

99. "Reporter's Transcript of Proceedings," 9, 14, 41, 45, 48, 61, 168, 260, MvW-DC.

100. "Reporter's Transcript of Proceedings," 258–268, 306, July 6, 1945, MvW-DC.

101. "Petitioners' Opening Brief," 9, 11, September 29, 1945, MvW-DC.

102. "Reply Brief of National Lawyers Guild, and the American Civil Liberties Union, Amici Curiae," 8, October 25, 1945, MvW-DC.

103. "Answer of Garden Grove School District," May 5, 1945, MvW-DC.

104. "Reporter's Transcript of Proceedings," 85, 86, 88, 116, 120, 124, 138, 139, July 5, 1945, MvW-DC.

105. "Reporter's Transcript of Proceedings," 520–522, July 10, 1945, MvW-DC.

106. "Petitioners' Opening Brief," 15, 16, September 29, 1945, MvW-DC.

107. "Reporter's Transcript of Proceedings," 309, 326, 335, July 6, 1945, MvW-DC.

108. "Reporter's Transcript of Proceedings," 381, 402, 419, July 9, 1945, MvW-DC.

109. "Reporter's Transcript of Proceedings," 668, 669, 675, 676, July 11, 1945, MvW-DC.

110. Carey McWilliams, "Is Your Name Gonzales?" *Nation*, March 15, 1947: 302.

111. "Petitioners' Opening Brief," 33, September 29, 1945, MvW-DC. On this point, see also "Brief of National Lawyers Guild, and American Civil Liberties Union, Amici

Curiae," October 1, 1945, MvW-DC: "The evidence is without contradiction that children of Mexican descent have been segregated in separate school houses. Such segregation was demonstrated to be based upon the ancestry of the pupils, that of being descendants of Mexicans. The defense contention that the segregation was based upon other reasons [presumably language-based pedagogical reasons] was not supported at the trial."

112. "Petitioners' Opening Brief," 7, September 29, 1945, MvW-DC; "Plaintiffs Reply Brief," 4, November 1, 1945, MvW-DC.

113. "Plaintiffs Reply Brief," 12, November 1, 1945, MvW-DC.

114. Strum, 64.

115. "Reporter's Transcript of Proceedings," 108, 44, June 26, 1945, MvW-DC.

116. "Petitioners' Opening Brief," 11, 13, 15, September 29, 1945, MvW-DC.

117. "Brief of National Lawyers Guild, and American Civil Liberties Union, Amici Curiae," 17, October 1, 1945, MvW-DC.

118. "Plaintiffs Reply Brief," 12, November 1, 1945, MvW-DC.

119. Robinson and Robinson, 100–101. Robinson and Robinson view Marcus's decision as less tactical than ideological. "Marcus and his clients," they argue, "were clearly aware of the 'social value of whiteness' and the potential detriment to Mexican Americans of being classed as a nonwhite race" (104).

120. "Brief of National Lawyers Guild, and American Civil Liberties Union, Amici Curiae," 17, October 1, 1945, MvW-DC

121. "Reporter's Transcript of Proceedings," June 26, 1945, 108, MvW-DC.

122. "Petitioners' Opening Brief," 7, September 29, 1945, MvW-DC.

123. *Mendez v. Westminster School District of Orange County*, 64 F. Supp. 544, 546–551 (1946).

124. *Mendez v. Westminster School District of Orange County*, 64 F. Supp. 544, 549 (1946).

125. *Mendez v. Westminster School District of Orange County*, 64 F. Supp. 544, 548–549 (1946). On the "revolutionary" nature of McCormick's decision and how it "anticipated the Supreme Court by almost a decade," see Strum, 125–127. For a more tempered reading of McCormick's ruling, like the one advanced here, see Powers and Patton, 137–148.

126. "Judgment and Injunction," March 21, 1946, MvW-DC. With respect to the first blush reading of McCormick's decision presented in this paragraph, see also the NAACP-LDF's Constance Baker Motley: "The district court's unequivocally strong language was radically new at the time the decision was issued." It buoyed the hope that "integrated education was an idea whose time had truly come" (Constance Baker Motley, "Standing on His Shoulders: Thurgood Marshall's Early Career," *Howard Law Journal* 23 (1991): 26, footnote 10).

127. "Opinion No. V-128, Re: Legality of Separate School Buildings for Instruction of Latin-American Students," April 8, 1947, Box 32, Folder 15, GS.

128. Fred Ross, report, October 13, 1946, Box 5, Folder Incoming Correspondence: R: Ross, Fred, CFCU.

129. Fred Ross, "Bell Town Unity League," circa 1946, Box 20, Folder 4, FR.

130. *La Opinión* and David Marcus quoted in Wollenberg, 128.

131. Strum, 128.

132. Lawrence E. Davies, "Segregation of Mexicans Stirs School-Court Fight," *New York Times*, December 22, 1946: 80; McWilliams, *North from Mexico*, 283.

133. Fred Ross to Laurence Hewes, October 13, 1946, Box 5, Folder Incoming Correspondence: R: Ross, Fred, CFCU; "Riverside Schools Become American," *Open Forum*, November 30, 1946: 2.

134. McWilliams, "Is Your Name Gonzales?" 302.

135. "Answer of Westminster School District of Orange County, et al.," May 5, 1945, MvW-DC.

136. *Mendez v. Westminster School District of Orange County*, 64 F. Supp. 544, 546 (1946).

137. "Apellants' Reply Brief," 1, 3, October 17, 1946, WvM-9C.

138. "Appellees' Reply Brief," 8–10, October 11, 1946, WvM-9C; "Apellants' Reply Brief to the American Civil Liberties Union, National Lawyers Guild, Los Angeles Chapter, and the Attorney General of the State of California, as Amici Curiae," 10, October 17, 1946, WvM-9C.

139. "National JACL Enters Case Challenging Segregation of Mexican American Children," *Pacific Citizen*, November 23, 1946: 1; Mike Masaoka quoted in "JACL Establishes Defense Fund for Civil Rights Cases," *Pacific Citizen*, December 7, 1946: 1.

140. "Brief for the American Civil Liberties Union, and the National Lawyers Guild, Los Angeles Chapter, as Amici Curiae," 9, 13, 19, November 12, 1946, WvM-9C.

141. "Motion and Brief of the Attorney General of the State of California as Amicus Curiae," 7, 11, November 12, 1946, WvM-9C.

142. William Hastie to Thurgood Marshall, September 13, 1946, 3B, Reel 1, Frame 261, NAACP-MF.

143. The NAACP files on *Mendez v. Westminster* begin with a letter from Thurgood Marshall to Loren Miller on April 16, 1946, 3B, Reel 1, Frame 224, NAACP-MF.

144. Robert Carter to Leon Silverman, March 24, 1947, Part 3B, Reel 1, Frame 296, NAACP-MF.

145. On this point, see also Strum, 136: "The NAACP was therefore somewhat curious in context, because its argument had everything to do with race and focused primarily on African-Americans, with Mexican-Americans a seeming afterthought." For example, the NAACP brief's statistical information focused exclusively on African Americans in the South.

146. "Brief for the National Association for the Advancement of Colored People," 31, October 2, 1946, WvM-9C.

147. Robert L. Carter, review of *The NAACP's Legal Strategy Against Segregated Education, 1925–1950*, by Mark Tushnet, *University of Michigan Law Review* 86 (May 1988): 1087, footnote 16, 1084, footnote 5.

148. Powers and Patton, 148, footnote 17.

149. "Brief for the American Jewish Congress," October 1946, 34, October 17, 1946, WvM-9C.

150. Noah Griffin to Thurgood Marshall, Part 3B, Reel 1, Frame 286, NAACP-MF; "School Segregation Case Is Before U.S. Court Here," *San Francisco Chronicle*, December 10, 1946, in Part 3B, Reel 1, Frame 287, NAACP-MF.

151. *Westminster School District of Orange County v. Mendez*, 161 F.2d 774, 780 (1947).

152. *Westminster School District of Orange County v. Mendez*, 161 F.2d 774, 780 (1947).

153. On "the Ninth Circuit's support for language-based segregation in *Mendez*, see also Steven H. Wilson, "Brown over 'Other White': Mexican Americans' Legal Arguments and Litigation Strategy in School Desegregation Lawsuits," *Law and History Review* 21 (Spring 2003): 158.

154. "Federal Court Bans Segregation," *Open Forum*, May 3, 1947: 1.

155. Robert Carter to NAACP Public Relations Department, April 24, 1947, Part 3B, Reel 1, Frame 298, NAACP-MF.

156. George Sánchez to Ernesto Galarza, April 14, 1947, Box 16, Folder 13, GS.

157. Manuel Ruiz to Herbert Slater, May 15, 1945, Box 16, Folder 3, MR.

158. News release, April 30, 1945, Box 16, Folder 3, MR.

159. The biographical details about Ruiz in this paragraph come from the introduction to the finding aid to his papers, MR.

160. William Rosenthal to Manuel Ruiz, January 17, 1945, Box 16, Folder 3, MR.

161. Manuel Ruiz to William Rosenthal, January 20, 1945, Box 16, Folder 3, MR.

162. Manuel Ruiz to Herbert Slater, May 15, 1945, Box 16, Folder 3, MR.

163. Manuel Ruiz to California Legislature Assembly Education Committee, April 13, 1945, Box 16, Folder 3, MR.

164. News release, June 20, 1945, Box 16, Folder 3, MR.

165. Manuel Ruiz to Earl Warren, October 1, 1945, Box 16, Folder 3, MR.

166. Beach Vasey to Manuel Ruiz, October 3, 1945, Box 16, Folder 3, MR.

167. Manuel Ruiz to Beach Vasey, October 8, 1945, Box 16, Folder 3, MR.

168. Manuel Ruiz to Earl Warren, October 31, 1945,Box 16, Folder 3, MR.

169. Earl Warren to Herbert Slater, April 18, 1947, File Legislative Correspondence, 1947, AB 1375—AB 1458, EW.

170. William Denman to Warren, April 16, 1947, File Legislative Correspondence, AB 1375—AB 1458, 1947, EW; Earl Warren to Herbert Slater, April 18, 1947, File Legislative Correspondence, 1947, AB 1375—AB 1458, EW.

171. AB 1375, Chapter 737, MF3:1, 43, GCBF.

172. Strum, 159.

173. Thurgood Marshall to Carl Murphy, December 20, 1946, Part 3B, Reel 1 , NAACP-MF.

174. Abraham Lincoln Wirin, partially completed oral history conducted by Joel Gardner in 1974, Record Series 501, Box 21, University Archives, University of California, Los Angeles, 117.

175. *Delgado v. Bastrop Independent School District*, Civ. No. 388 (W.D. Tex. June 15, 1948). In 1951 a federal district court in Arizona invoked "the principle established" in *Mendez* when it denounced "omnibus segregation of children of Mexican ancestry," but upheld "separate treatment in separate classrooms" for students with "foreign

language handicaps" provided that school authorities administered "credible examination[s]" (*Gonzales v. Sheely*, 96 F. Supp. 1004 [1951]).

176. Thurgood Marshall to George Sánchez, July 1, 1948, Box 24, Folder 8, GS; George Sánchez to Thurgood Marshall, July 6, 1948, Box 24, Folder 8, GS.

177. George Sánchez to Al Wirin, October 14, 1953, Box 62, Folder 18, GS.

178. Al Wirin to Roger Baldwin, October 9, 1953, Box 62, Folder 18, GS.

179. Executive committee meeting, minutes, April 21, 1947, Box 456, Folder 5, ACLU.

180. Al Wirin to James Marshall, September 30, 1953, Box 62, Folder 18, GS.

181. See Earl Warren Papers, Box 570, Folder October Term, 1952, Segregation Cases; Box 571, Folders Segregation Cases (including State Cases); and Box 574, Folders Segregation Cases, Library of Congress, Washington, D.C. Thanks to Rachel Bernard, University of California, Berkeley history PhD student, for investigating these files for me in May 2009.

182. "Proceedings of Third Annual Convention for Civic Unity," December 1948, Carton 4, Folder—Race Relations on the West Coast, CM-B.

183. "The First House Meeting," no date, Box 21, Folder 10, FR. On this point, see also George Sánchez to Roger Baldwin, June 29, 1948, Box 2, Folder 18, GS.

184. Ernesto Galarza, "The Mexican American: A National Concern—Program for Action," *Common Ground*, 9, no. 4 (1949): 37.

185. Galarza, "The Mexican American," 37.

186. Second Quarterly Board of Directors Meeting, minutes, March 1952, Box 10, Folder 8, FR.

187. Galarza, "The Mexican American," 37.

188. Second Quarterly Board of Directors Meeting, minutes, March 1952, Box 10, Folder 8, FR.

189. "Program of the Industrial Areas Foundation—LACSO," 1949, Box 5, Folder 11, FR; Galarza, "The Mexican American," 34; "Community Organizing in Mexican American Colonies: A Progress Report Undertaken in Several Mexican American Communities in Southern California, 1946–1947," Box 20, Folder 19, FR.

190. McWilliams, "Is Your Name Gonzales?" 304.

191. This is the subject of Chapter 8.

Chapter 4

1. Curiously, the various autobiographical writings contained in Miller's personal papers do not discuss his parents' anomalous interracial marriage, though they do contain the marriage certificate, which Miller held onto for his entire life. According to the marriage certificate, a justice of the peace in Council Bluffs, Iowa, married Miller's father, John B. Miller, and mother, Nora Harbaugh, both of whom were then living in Ravenna, Nebraska. The year of the marriage is obscured in the certificate (Box 58, Folder 5, LM).

2. "Biographical Data: Loren Miller," Box 21, Folder 1, LM; Carton 2, Folder Miller, NAACP-WC; Paul Weeks, "New Judge Reluctant Member of Profession," *Los Angeles Times*, May 17, 1964: F4; Josh Sides, *L.A. City Limits: African American Los Angeles from*

the Great Depression to the Present (Berkeley and Los Angeles: University of California Press, 2003), 30–31; Douglas Flamming, *Bound for Freedom: Black Los Angeles in Jim Crow America* (Berkeley: University of California Press, 2005), 302–303.

3. Carey McWilliams, "The House on 92d Street," *Nation*, June 8, 1946: 690–691.

4. "Appellants' Opening Brief," 59, February 8, 1946, *Cumings v. Hokr*, L.A. Nos. 19588–19594, SACCC.

5. Loren Miller to Clore Warne, November 2, 1947, Box 7, Folder 11, LM.

6. "Biographical Data: Loren Miller," Box 21, Folder 1, LM.

7. Prentice Thomas to Thomas Griffith, January 11, 1943, Part 5, Reel 20, Frame 247, NAACP-MF.

8. Loren Miller to Selma Mikels Bachelis, July 26, 1946, Box 6, Folder 2, LM.

9. Report to the Board of Directors, April 20–May 20, 1945, Carton 1, Folder 46, NAACP-WC.

10. Noah Griffin to Walter White, et al., September 8, 1944, Part 17, Reel 15, Frame 491, NAACP-MF.

11. "Jim Crow Is Dying," *Los Angeles Sentinel*, October 7, 1948: 25.

12. Loren Miller, "The Coast Housing Problem and Its Solutions," speech to NAACP West Coast Regional Conference, March 1947, Carton 1, Folder 41, NAACP-WC.

13. *Californians of Japanese, Chinese, and Filipino Ancestry* (San Francisco: Department of Industrial Relations, Division of Fair Employment Practices, 1965), 17.

14. "Monthly Report," July 1945, Carton 1, Folder 46, NAACP-WC.

15. "Appellants' Opening Brief," February 8, 1946, *Cumings v. Hokr*, L.A. Nos. 19588–19594, SACCC.

16. Loren Miller, "Covenants in the Bear Flag State," *The Crisis*, May 1946: 140.

17. Loren Miller, "A Right Secured," *Nation*, May 29, 1948: 600.

18. Carey McWilliams, "Los Angeles: An Emerging Pattern," *Common Ground*, Spring 1949: 5.

19. Loren Miller, "Restrictive Covenants Versus Democracy," in *Racial Restrictive Covenants* (Chicago: Chicago Council Against Racial and Religious Discrimination, 1946), 5, in Reel 239, Volume 16, ACLU-MF.

20. Sara Lamport, "A New Dred Scott Case," *Nation*, January 31, 1948: 124.

21. Miller, "Covenants in the Bear Flag State," 139.

22. Larry Tajiri, "Ghettos in Our Cities," *Pacific Citizen*, May 18, 1946.

23. National JACL Staff Meeting, minutes, August 13, 1947, Box 16, Folder ADC 1947, JACL.

24. "Negro Wins Right to Live in New Home," *Los Angeles Times*, January 18, 1946: A3.

25. "Appellants' Opening Brief," February 8, 1946, *Cumings v. Hokr*, L.A. Nos. 19588–19594, SACCC.

26. Loren Miller, "Test for Covenants," *The Crisis*, November 1947: 329.

27. Al Wirin to Roger Baldwin, October 5, 1945, Reel 232, Volume 2686, ACLU-MF.

28. Loren Miller, "The Power of Restrictive Covenants," *Survey Graphic*, 36, no. 1 (January 1947): 46. On this point, see also Toni Robinson and Greg Robinson, "The

Limits of Interracial Coalitions: Méndez v. Westminster Reexamined," in *Racial Transformations: Latinos and Asians Remaking the United States*, ed. Nicholas DeGenova (Durham: Duke University Press, 2006), 100–101. Robinson and Robinson refer to the case of *A. T. Collison and R.L. Wood v. Nellie Garcia et al.* (Superior Court of the Country of Los Angeles, Civil Case ser. I, no. 498206, February 9, 1945) in which Judge Alred E. Panoessa dismissed an attempt to enforce a racially restrictive housing covenant against a Mexican American woman on the grounds that there was no such thing as a "Mexican race."

29. Loren Miller to Vianna Evans, January 26, 1945, Box 5, Folder 3, LM.

30. "Reporter's Transcript," 74–75, *McCormick vs. Howard*, L.A. 19592–19593, SAC-CC.

31. "Reporter's Transcript on Appeal," 288–293, *Merriweather v. Fleming*, L.A. 19916, L.A. 19916, October 2, 1946, SACCC.

32. Miller, "Covenants in the Bear Flag State," 139.

33. Loren Miller to Clore Warne, November 2, 1947, Box 7, Folder 11, LM; Loren Miller to Selma Mikels Bachelis, July 26, 1946, Box 6, Folder 2, LM.

34. Miller, "Covenants in the Bear Flag State," 140.

35. *Corrigan v. Buckley*, 271 U.S. 323 (1926).

36. Miller, "Covenants in the Bear Flag State," 140.

37. Loren Miller, "The Coast Housing Problem and Its Solutions," speech, March 1947, Carton 1, Folder 41, NAACP-WC.

38. "Supreme Court," *The Crisis*, June 1948: 179.

39. "Appellants' Opening Brief," 79, 86, 89, February 8, 1946, *Cumings v. Hokr*, L.A. Nos. 19588–19594, SACCC; Dudley O. McGovney, "Racial Residential Segregation by State Court Enforcement of Restrictive Agreements, Covenants or Conditions in Deeds Is Unconstitutional," *California Law Review* 33, no. 1 (March 1945): 5–39.

40. "Celebrities in Spotlight as 'Sugar Hill' Trial Begins," *California Eagle*, December 6, 1945: 4.

41. Loren Miller to Thurgood Marshall, December 6, 1945, Part 5, Reel 20, Frame 302, NAACP-MF; Willis O. Tyler, "Defense Attorney Analyzes Historic 'Sugar Hill' Decision," *California Eagle*, December 13, 1945: 24.

42. Loren Miller to Thurgood Marshall, December 12, 1945, Part 5, Reel 20, Frame 306, NAACP-MF; Justice Thurman [Sic] Clark's [sic] Decision in the Restrictive Covenant Case in Los Angeles," December 19, 1945, Part 5, Reel 20, Frame 314, NAACP-MF.

43. Walter White to Loren Miller, December 19, 1945, Part 5, Reel 20, Frame 310, NAACP-MF.

44. Marian Wynn Perry to Arthur McNulty, March 26, 1947, Part 5, Reel 20, NAACP-MF.

45. Loren Miller to Lester Granger, December 18, 1945, Box 3, Folder 1, LM.

46. "Answer," February 27, 1945, *Merriweather v. Fleming*, L.A. 19916, SACCC.

47. "Respondents' Reply Brief," *Sandel v. Saunders*, L.A. No. 19783, SACCC.

48. "Appellants' Opening Brief," February 8, 1946, *Cumings v. Hokr*, L.A. Nos. 19588–19594, SACCC.

49. "Appellants' Opening Brief," 65–68, February 8, 1946, *Cumings v. Hokr*, L.A. Nos. 19588–19594, SACCC.

50. "Appellants' Opening Brief," January 26, 1946, *Thompson v. Clarke*, L.A. No. 19578, SACCC.

51. Loren Miller to Thurgood Marshall, October 24, 1947, Part 5, Reel 20, Frame 412, NAACP-MF; "Judge Stanley Mosk Rules Race Covenants Illegal, 'Un-American,'" *Los Angeles Sentinel*, October 30, 1947: 1.

52. "Reporter's Transcript," 71–72, December 20, 1945, *Hester v. Barbe*, L.A. No. 19588, SACCC.

53. "Reporter's Transcript on Appeal," 69–70, October 2, 1946, *Merriweather v. Fleming*, L.A. No. 19916, SACCC.

54. "Reporter's Transcript," 15–30, *Bushelman v. Cooper*, December 20, 1945, L.A. No. 19593, SACCC.

55. "Complaint to Enforce Restrictions of Real Property and for Injunctive Relief, November 16, 1944," in "Clerk's Transcript," April 2, 1946, *Davis v. Carter*, L.A. No. 19696, SACCC.

56. "Reporter's Transcript on Appeal," 199, 392, *Davis v. Carter*, April 2, 1946, L.A. No. 19696, SACCC.

57. Flaming, 50, 198.

58. "Answer of Defendant Benny Carter," January 18, 1945, in "Clerk's Transcript," April 2, 1946, *Davis v. Carter*, L.A. No. 19696, SACCC.

59. "Answer," October 1944, in "Clerk's Transcript," *Cumings v. Hokr*, L.A. Nos. 19588–19594, SACCC; "Answer," October 1944, in "Clerk's Transcript," *Hester v. Barbe*, L.A. Nos. 19588, SACCC.

60. "Reporter's Transcript on Appeal," 2, 3, 52, April 2, 1946, *Davis v. Carter*, L.A. No. 19696, SACCC.

61. "Reporter's Transcript on Appeal," 311–325, 600, 458, April 2, 1946, *Davis v. Carter*, L.A. No. 19696, SACCC.

62. "Reporter's Transcript on Appeal," 58, 519, April 2, 1946, *Davis v. Carter*, L.A. No. 19696, SACCC.

63. "Reporter's Transcript on Appeal," 152, 575, 598, 607, April 2, 1946, *Davis v. Carter*, L.A. No. 19696, SACCC.

64. "Reporter's Transcript on Appeal," 461, 464, 465, 468, April 2, 1946, *Davis v. Carter*, L.A. No. 19696, SACCC.

65. "Reporter's Transcript on Appeal," 574, April 2, 1946, *Davis v. Carter*, L.A. No. 19696, SACCC.

66. "Reporter's Transcript on Appeal," 608, April 2, 1946, *Davis v. Carter*, L.A. No. 19696, SACCC.

67. Clement E. Vose, *Caucasians Only: The Supreme Court, the NAACP, and the Restrictive Covenant Cases* (Berkeley: University of California Press, 1959), 157; "2 Judges Own Covenanted Property," *Los Angeles Sentinel*, January 22, 1948: 1.

68. Vose, 158, 159, 163, 168–170; Stephen Grant Meyer, *As Long as They Don't Move Next Door: Segregation and Racial Conflict in American Neighborhoods* (Lanham: Rowman & Littlefield, 2000), 93.

69. Eiji Tanabe to Loren Miller, May 14, 1947, Box 7, Folder 3, LM.

70. Fred Fertig to Loren Miller, October 23, 1947, Box 7, Folder 1, LM. The absence of JACL/NAACP collaboration up to this point, would appear to undermine the claim of Robinson and Robinson that the "JACL became heavily invested in intergroup alliances," as evidenced by how they, led by Wirin, "collaborated with NAACP attorney Loren Miller in a series of legal cases challenging restrictive covenants against nonwhites in housing" (98–100). The point here is not that there was no collaboration—there clearly was some, as discussed in the paragraphs following this one—but rather how "heavily invested" in it the JACL (or, the NAACP for that matter) was.

71. Mike Masaoka, "General Report," October 26, 1947, Box 5, Folder 8, MM.

72. "Brief of the Japanese American Citizens League—Amicus Curiae," December 1, 1947, *Hurd v. Hodge* 334 U.S. 24 (1948), *U.S. Supreme Court Records and Briefs, 1832–1978*, Gale, Cengage Learning. *Hurd v. Hodge* was one of the companion cases in *Shelley v. Kraemer* 334 U.S. 1 (1948).

73. Larry Tajiri, "Ghettos in Our Cities," *Pacific Citizen*, May 18, 1946.

74. "Brief of California Amici Curiae," December 1, 1947, *McGhee v. Sipes* 334 U.S. 1 (1948), *U.S. Supreme Court Records and Briefs, 1832–1978*. Gale, Cengage Learning.

75. "Add New 'Color' to Supreme Court Cases," *Open Forum*, October 18, 1947: 1; Consolidated Petitions for Writs of Certiorari to the Supreme Court of the State of California, November 6, 1947, *Amer v. Superior Court*, 334 U.S. 813 (1948), *Kim v. Superior Court*, 334 U.S. 813 (1948), *U.S. Supreme Court Records and Briefs, 1832–1978*. Gale, Cengage Learning.

76. "California Native Sons Fight for Homes," *Open Forum*, August 23, 1947: 1; *Amer v. Superior Court*, 334 U.S. 813 (1948); *Kim v. Superior Court*, 334 U.S. 813 (1948).

77. National JACL Staff Meeting, minutes, August 13, 1947, Box 16, Folder ADC 1947, JACL.

78. "Brief of Japanese American Citizens League, Amicus Curiae, on Petitions for Writs of Certiorari to the Supreme Court of the State of California," December 26, 1947, *Amer v. Superior Court*, 334 U.S. 813 (1948), *Kim v. Superior Court*, 334 U.S. 813 (1948), *U.S. Supreme Court Records and Briefs, 1832–1978*. Gale, Cengage Learning.

79. Al Wirin to Thurgood Marshall, December 16, 1947, Part 5, Reel 20, Frame 422, NAACP-MF.

80. Al Wirin to Loren Miller, December 16, 1947, Box 7, Folder 1, LM.

81. Thurgood Marshall to Roger Baldwin, December 30, 1947, Box 564, Folder 24, ACLU.

82. Clifford Forster to Thurgood Marshall, December 31, 1947, Part 5, Reel 20, Frame 426, NAACP-MF.

83. Miller, "A Right Secured," 599.

84. *Shelley v. Kraemer*, 334 U.S. 1, 20 (1948).

85. Stanley Mosk to Loren Miller, May 10, 1948, Box 8, Folder 3, LM.

86. Noah Griffin to Thurgood Marshall, May 3, 1948, Part 5, Reel 20, Frame 455, NAACP-MF.

87. Letter to Noah Griffin, May 6, 1948, Part 5, Reel 20, frame 456, NAACP-MF.

88. *Cumings v. Hokr*, 31 Cal.2d 844 (1948).

89. See, for example, *Davis v. Carter*, 31 Ca1.2d 870 (1948), which was a consolidation of eleven cases; *In re Henry Laws*, 31 Ca1.2d 846 (1948); *Cassell v. Hickerson* and *Fairchild v. Raines* 31 Ca1.2d 869 (1948); *Lippold v. Johnson*, 32 Ca1.2d 894 (1948), which was a consolidation of eight cases; *Morin v. Crane* 32 Ca1.2d 896 (1948).

90. *Shelley v. Kraemer*, 334 U.S. 1, 21, footnote 26 (1948).

91. Phillip Rea to National Association of Real Estate Boards, August 10, 1948, Part 5, Reel 20, Frame 457, NAACP-MF.

92. Phillip Rea to National Association of Real Estate Boards, August 10, 1948, Part 5, Reel 20, Frame 457, NAACP-MF.

93. Meyer, 95–96.

94. Miller, "A Right Secured," 599.

95. "No Support for Covenants," *The Crisis*, June 1948: 169.

96. *Loving v. Virginia*, 388 U.S. 1, footnote 5 (1967).

97. Dara Orenstein, "Void for Vagueness: Mexicans and the Collapse of Miscegenation Law in California," *Pacific Historical Review*, 74, no. 3 (2005): 367, 368, 372. Throughout this chapter (and book), I refer to the case and case filings as *Perez* (without an accent) in keeping with how it was referenced in the legal documents. In all other instances, I use the accent (Pérez), in keeping with how Andrea Pérez spelled her name.

98. Orenstein, 374.

99. This is how the statute read as of August 1, 1947, when Pérez and Davis filed their marriage license application. The statutory history of Section 60 of the California Civil Code can be traced to 1850 with Section 53 of "An Act Regulating Marriages" which read, "All marriages of white persons with negroes or mulattoes are declared illegal and void" (quoted in Irving G. Tragen, "Comment: Statutory Prohibitions Against Interracial Marriage," *California Law Review* 32 [1944]: footnote 16). The statutory language from 1850 was transferred verbatim to Section 60 of the California Civil Code, adopted in 1872. The California Legislature amended Section 60 in 1901 and 1905 to include "Mongolians." In 1905, Section 60 of the California Civil Code declared, "All marriages of white persons with negroes, Mongolians, or mulattoes are illegal and void" (Statutes of California, 1905, Chapter CDXIV, 554). In 1933, a California appellate court ruled that a Filipino man was "Malay," not "Mongolian," and could therefore marry a white woman, since California law said nothing about "Malays" being prohibited from marrying whites (see *Roldan v. Los Angeles County*, 129 Cal. App. 267 [1933]). In response to *Roldan*, the California legislature amended Section 60 of the California Code in 1933 to read, "All marriages of white persons with negroes, Mongolians, members of the Malay race, or mulattoes are illegal and void" (Statutes of California, 1933, Chapter 104, 561). Section 60 remained like this until 1959, when it was repealed (Statutes of California, 1959, Chapter 146).

100. This is how the statute read as of August 1, 1947, when Pérez and Davis filed their marriage license application (Statutes of California, 1945, Chapter 602, 1132). The first racial reference in Section 69 of the California Civil Code appeared in 1880. It read, "[The county] clerk shall not issue a license authorizing the marriage of a white person with a negro, mulatto, or Mongolian" (California Civil Code, 1887, Section 69). As with Section 60, the state legislature amended Section 69 in 1933 to include "member of the

Malay race" among those to whom the County Clerk could not issue a marriage license with a "white person" (Statutes of California, 1933, Chapter 105). Subsequent amendments to Section 69 left the racial provisions untouched until 1959 when they were removed (Statutes of California, 1959, Chapter 146).

101. Pauli Murray, ed., *States' Laws on Race and Color* (New York: Women's Division of Christian Service of Methodist Church, 1950), 18; Peggy Pascoe, "Race Gender, and Intercultural Relations: The Case of Interracial Marriage," *Frontiers* 13, no. 1 (1991): footnote 20.

102. *Perez v. Sharp*, 32 Cal. 2d 711, 721 (1948).

103. Gunnar Myrdal with the assistance of Richard Sterner and Arnold Rose, *An American Dilemma: The Negro Problem and Modern Democracy* (New York: Harper, 1944), 587.

104. Orenstein, 388.

105. John T. McGreevy, *Parish Boundaries: The Catholic Encounter with Race in the Twentieth-Century Urban North* (Chicago: University of Chicago Press, 1996), 38–47; Ted LeBerthon to Mathew Ahmann, August 10, 1959, Series 10, Box 2, Folder California—Los Angeles: Catholic Human Relations Council Correspondence, 1959–1963, National Catholic Conference for Interracial Justice Collection, Marquette University Department of Special Collections and Archives, Milwaukee, Wisconsin. Special thanks to Michael Engh, Department of History, Loyola Marymount University, for providing me with this document, as well as the documents cited below from the Catholic Interracial Council of Los Angeles

106. Ted LeBerthon to Matthew Ahmann, August 10, 1959. The CIC-LA's initial executive committee consisted of twelve members—six "whites," two "Negroes," one "Chinese," one "Mexican," one "Filipino," and one "Japanese-American." This racial diversity, according to one council leader, made the CIC-LA "unique among interracial groups in America's leading cities. It is not just a white-Negro organization" (Ted LeBerthon, "Council for All Races," *Interracial Review* 18 [October 1945]: 150–152).

107. "Declaration of Principles of The Catholic Interracial Council of Los Angeles," circa 1944, CIC-LA. See also LeBerthon, 150–152.

108. Joseph T. McGucken to Joseph Scott, April 16, 1945, John J. Cantwell Papers, Chancery Archives, Archdiocese of Los Angeles; "First Negro Initiated by California Knights of Columbus," news release, April 4, 1947, CIC-LA; LeBerthon, 151.

109. LeBerthon, 150.

110. Thurgood Marshall to A.L Emery, March 8, 1945, quoted in Peter Wallenstein, *Tell the Court I Love My Wife: Race, Marriage, and Law—An American History* (New York: Palgrave Macmillan, 2002), 177. The JACL was no more enthusiastic about taking on an antimiscegenation case (Orenstein, 392).

111. Milton Konvitz to A.L. Emery, April 17, 1944, quoted in Wallenstein, 177.

112. Statutes of California, 1943, Chapter 349, 1345–1346; Statutes of California, 1945, Chapter 602, 1132–1133. Among other things, the 1943 amendment to Section 69 deleted a paragraph that stipulated a three-day waiting period before receiving a marriage license after filing for one, while the 1945 amendment loosened the restrictions on which county clerk could issue a marriage license.

113. Chapter 349 in 1943 and Chapter 602 in 1945, GCBF.

114. Eugene Noury to Earl Warren, September 11, 1943, File 3655, EW; Verne Scoggins to Eugene Noury, September 15, 1943, File 3655, EW; Iris B. Buaken, "You Can't Marry a Filipino, Not if You Live in California," *Commonweal*, March 16, 1945: 535.

115. Myrdal, 56–57, 606.

116. Thurgood Marshall to Roger Baldwin, quoted in Mark Tushnet, *Making Civil Rights Law: Thurgood Marshall and the Supreme Court, 1936–1961* (New York: Oxford University Press, 1994), 44.

117. Ted LeBerthon to Matthew Ahmann, August 10, 1959.

118. "Interracial Marriage Ban to be Attacked," news release, April 4, 1947, CIC-LA.

119. Dan Marshall to Joseph McGucken, April 23, 1947, Box 17, Folder 29, Rev. John LaFarge, S.J. Papers, Georgetown University Library, Special Collections Division.

120. Joseph McGucken to Dan Marshall, April 26, 1947, Box 17, Folder 29, Rev. John LaFarge, S.J. Papers, Georgetown University Library, Special Collections Division.

121. "Marriage Recorder Uses 'Sixth Sense,'" *Los Angeles Sentinel*, December 23, 1948: 2; "You're Just a Clerk, Miss Rice," *Los Angeles Sentinel*, December 23, 1948: 26.

122. "Petition for Writ of Mandamus," August 8, 1947, Perez.

123. Carey McWilliams, *Nation*, October 16, 1948: 415.

124. "Monthly Report," October 1948, Carton 1, Folder 49, NAACP-WC.

125. Clifford Forster to Dan Marshall, April 16, 1948, Reel 256, Volume 96, ACLU-MF.

126. Matthew O. Tobriner, "Chief Justice Roger Traynor," *Harvard Law Review* 83 (June 1970): 1769; Benjamin Thomas Field, "Justice Roger Traynor and His Case for Judicial Activism" (Ph.D. diss., University of California, Berkeley, 2000).

127. "Petition for Writ of Mandamus," August 8, 1947, Perez.

128. *Perez v. Sharp*, 32 Cal. 2d 711, 716 (1948).

129. *Perez v. Sharp*, 32 Cal. 2d 711, 716, 717, 725 (1948).

130. *Perez v. Sharp*, 32 Cal. 2d 711, 718, 719 (1948).

131. "Oral Argument on Behalf of the Respondent," October 6, 1947, Perez.

132. *Perez v. Sharp*, 32 Cal. 2d 711, 719–724 (1948).

133. *Perez v. Sharp*, 32 Cal. 2d 711, 724, 725, 727 (1948).

134. *Perez v. Sharp*, 32 Cal. 2d 711, 727, 721 (1948).

135. *Perez v. Sharp*, 32 Cal. 2d 711, 718 (1948).

136. Peggy Pascoe, *What Comes Naturally: Miscegenation Law and the Making of Race in America* (New York: Oxford University Press, 2009), 218.

137. "Oral Argument on Behalf of the Respondent," October 6, 1947, Perez.

138. *Perez v. Sharp*, 32 Cal. 2d 711, 729–731 (1948).

139. Miller, "The Power of Restrictive Covenants," 46.

140. "Reporter's Transcript on Appeal," 138, 311–325, 461, 464, 465, 468, *Davis v. Carter*, April 2, 1946, L.A. No. 19696, SACCC.

141. *Perez v. Sharp*, 32 Cal. 2d 711, 741 (1948); "Petitioners' Reply Brief," November 8, 1947, Perez.

142. "Los Angeles County Ready to Challenge High Court Sanction of Mixed Marriages," *Los Angeles Sentinel*, October 14, 1948: 1; "County Re-Opening Intermarriage

Case," *Los Angeles Sentinel*, October 21, 1948: 1; "County Appeals Intermarriage Case to U.S. Supreme Court," *Los Angeles Sentinel*, November 25, 1948: 1; "End of Racial Ban Stands," *New York Times*, November 2, 1948: 32.

143. McWilliams, *Nation*, 415.

144. "The California Marriage Decision," *Interracial Review* 22, no. 1 (1949): 1–2.

145. "Case Note," *California Law Review* 37 (1949): 122.

146. "The Court Rules: Interracial Marriages," *San Jose Mercury News*, November 1, 1948.

147. "Jim Crow Is Dying," *Los Angeles Sentinel*, October 7, 1948: 25.

148. "First Mixed Couple Becomes Married Under New Decree," *Los Angeles Sentinel*, November 18, 1948: 9.

149. "Interracial Wedding Set," *New York Times*, December 14, 1948: 37; "Couple to Wed; Battle for Intermarriage," *Los Angeles Sentinel*, December 16, 1948: 10.

150. Orenstein, 404–405. Eventually Andrea's father came around, after his daughter gave birth to the first of her three children, whom Férmin referred to as "the mulattoes." Andrea and Sylvester settled in Pacoima in the San Fernando Valley on the black side of the line that divided the largely black and Mexican American neighbors from one another. Sylvester spent the rest of his working years at Lockheed, where he became a supervisor, while Andrea became a bilingual teacher's assistant. On September 9, 2000, Andrea died, after fifty-two years of marriage to Sylvester. Though her marriage certificate listed her as "white," her death certificate listed her as "Caucasian" and "Mexican American."

151. Beach Vasey to Earl Warren, June 17, 1949, Chapter 729, GCBF. Another decade would have to pass before California lawmakers would take the symbolic step that remained after *Perez* (California Statutes, 1959, Chapter 146).

152. "Jim Crow Is Dying," *Los Angeles Sentinel*, October 7, 1948: 25.

153. Loren Miller to William Hastie, November 8, 1948, Box 3, folder 5, LM.

154. Carey McWilliams, "Minority Rights on the West Coast," speech, July 1949, Part 1, Reel 12, Frames 717–727, NAACP-MF.

155. Augustus F. Hawkins, Oral History Interview, Conducted 1988 by Carlos Vásquez, UCLA Oral History Program, for the California State Archives State Government Oral History Program, iii; Josh Sides, *L.A. City Limits: African American Los Angeles from the Great Depression to the Present* (Berkeley and Los Angeles: University of California Press, 2003), 33–34; Flamming, 323–325.

156. "Assembly Bill 3," January 9, 1945, Box 16, Folder 1, MR.

157. Augustus Hawkins to Manuel Ruiz, January 18, 1945, Box 5, Folder 9, MR.

158. Louis C. Kesselman, "The Fair Employment Practice Commission Movement in Perspective," *Journal of Negro History*, 31, no. 1 (1946): 30–46.

159. Report to the Board of Directors of the West Coast Regional Office, April 20–May 20, 1945, Carton 1, Folder 46, NAACP-WC.

160. Statewide FEPC Executive Committee, minutes, October 28, 1945, Folder B. Dreyfus Papers, California Fair Employment Practices Act (F.E.P.C.) Initiative, NLG.

161. Beach Vasey to Earl Warren, February 28, 1945, File 8038, EW.

162. Beach Vasey to Earl Warren, March 13, 1945, File 8038, EW.

163. Ed Cray, *Chief Justice: A Biography of Earl Warren* (New York: Simon and Schuster, 1997), 166–167; Michael Charles Tobriner, "The California Fair Employment Practices Commission: Its History, Accomplishments, and Limitations" (M.A. Thesis, Stanford University, 1963), 6–9.

164. Robert Kenny, letter, July 25, 1945, Box 5, Folder 9, MR.

165. "Statewide FEPC Committee Minutes," October 28, 1945, Folder B. Dreyfus Papers, California Fair Employment Practices Act (F.E.P.C.) Initiative, 1943–1946, NLG; "Minutes of FEPC Meeting," October 10, 1945, Folder B. Dreyfus Papers, California Fair Employment Practices Act (F.E.P.C.) Initiative, 1943–1946, NLG; Letter, October 17, 1945, Folder B. Dreyfus Papers, California Fair Employment Practices Act (F.E.P.C.) Initiative, NLG.

166. Noah Griffin, "The Work of the West Coast Region and its Problems," speech, March 1947, Carton 1, Folder 41, NAACP-WC.

167. NAACP West Coast Regional Office, "Annual Report," December 1945, Carton 1, Folder 45, NAACP-WC.

168. "People's Mandate Has Upset 50 Years of Anti-Orientalism in California, Says Masaoka," *Pacific Citizen*, November 9, 1946: 1; Larry Tajiri, "Fighting the Alien Land Law," *Pacific Citizen*, November 2, 1946: 4.

169. For more on Proposition 15, see Chapter 2.

170. Northern California Executive Committee Meeting, minutes, August 2, 1946, Carton 3, Folder Minutes 46–47, CFCU.

171. Fred Ross, "San Diego Report," February 2, 1947, Carton 5, Folder – Incoming Correspondence: R: Ross, Fred, CFCU.

172. Mike Masaoka, "General Report," December 28, 1947, Box 5, Folder 8, MM.

173. "Proposition 15," *Pacific Citizen*, November 9, 1946: 4.

174. "Defeat of FEPC," *Pacific Citizen*, November 9, 1946: 4.

175. Laurence I. Hewes, Jr., "Race Relations on the West Coast," *Nation*, September 21, 1946: 29.

176. "Proposition 15," *Pacific Citizen*, November 9, 1946: 4.

177. "Proposition 15: Validation of Legislative Amendments to the Alien Land Law," 1946. Available online through: http://library.uchastings.edu/library/california-research/ca-ballot-measures.html#ballotprops; Saburo Kido, "Defeat of Proposition 15 Shows Opposition of Voters to Race-Baiting Legislation," *Pacific Citizen*, November 9, 1946: 3.

178. "Proposition 11: Fair Employment Practices Act," 1946. Available online through: http://library.uchastings.edu/library/california-research/ca-ballot-measures. html#ballotprops.

179. John E. Hughes, "To Defend the Legal Right to Picket in Protest of Anti-Negro Discrimination in Employment: Memorandum Concerning the Fight for 'Fair Employment' vs. the Monopoly Chain Store Lucky Stores Inc.," 1947, Carton 89, Folder 14, NAACP-WC.

180. Hughes, "To Defend the Legal Right to Picket in Protest of Anti-Negro Discrimination in Employment."

181. Walter White to Noah Griffin, July 16, 1945, Carton 89, Folder 13, NAACP-WC.

182. "Brief for the Congress of Industrial Organizations as *Amicus Curiae* and Brief for the American Civil Liberties Union, *Amicus Curiae*," October 1949, in *The Hughes Case*, The Bancroft Library, University of California, Berkeley.

183. "Brief of the National Association for Advancement of Colored People as *Amicus Curiae*," October 1949, in *The Hughes Case*, The Bancroft Library, University of California, Berkeley.

184. Noah Griffin to Walter White, et al., September 8, 1944, Part 17, Reel 15, Frame 491, NAACP-MF.

185. Noah Griffin to Gloster Current, November 19, 1947, Carton 89, Folder 14, NAACP-WC

186. NAACP West Coast Regional Conference, minutes, March 1947, Carton 1, Folder 41, NAACP-WC.

187. *Hughes v. Superior Court*, 32 Cal. 2d 850, 856 (1948).

188. *Hughes v. Superior Court*, 339 U.S. 460, 461, 464 (1950).

189. *Hughes v. Superior Court*, 32 Cal. 2d 850, 868–869 (1948).

190. "Report of the West Coast Regional Secretary," 1950, Carton 89, Folder 14, NAACP-WC.

191. McWilliams, "Minority Rights on the West Coast."

192. "Executive Director's Report," December 3, 1949, Carton 3, Folder Board of Directors Material, CFCU.

193. Josephine Duveneck and Ruth Kingman, "Brief Statement Covering Problems Facing California Federation for Civic Unity," February 26, 1948, Carton 3, Folder Board of Directors Meetings, CFCU.

194. "President's Report," December 1949, Carton 3, Folder Board of Directors Meetings, CFCU.

195. Richard Dettering, "The Civic Unity Movement: What? Why? How?" *Blueprint for Action*, June 7, 1949, Carton 4, Folder Race Relations on the West Coast, CM-B.

196. McWilliams, "Minority Rights on the West Coast."

197. "Monthly Report," February 1946, Carton 1, Folder 47, NAACP-WC.

198. "Monthly Report," December 1946, Carton 1, Folder 47, NAACP-WC.

199. Hewes, "Race Relations on the West Coast," 25.

Chapter 5

1. Report, July-September 1950, Carton 1, Folder 51, NAACP-WC. Besides California, the West Coast Region included Arizona, Idaho, Nevada, Oregon, Utah, and Washington. Later, Alaska and Hawaii were added.

2. "Report of the West Coast Regional Council Meeting," February 26,1949, Carton 1, Folder 2, NAACP-WC.

3. The Speakers' Forum of the Boalt Hall Students' Association, announcement of speech by Williams on October 24, 1952, which includes biographical details, Carton 4, Folder 31, NAACP-WC; Report—July-September 1950, Carton 1, Folder 51, NAACP-WC.

4. "First Quarterly Report," 1951, Carton 2, Folder 22, NAACP-WC.

5. "Annual Report," 1953, Box 25, NAACP-WC (previous).

6. Franklin Williams, "Our Unfinished Task," speech, October 11, 1953, Carton 4, Folder 37, NAACP-WC.

7. Williams, "Our Unfinished Task."

8. "Annual Report," 1951, Box 25, NAACP-WC (previous).

9. Franklin Williams, speech, December 1950, Part 25A, Reel 12, NAACP-MF.

10. "Monthly Report," October 1950, Carton 1, Folder 51, NAACP-WC.

11. "Annual Report," 1952, Box 25, NAACP-WC (previous).

12. Williams, speech, December 1950. For more on Williams and the "hegemony that he desired" for his organization "over most civil rights and progressive organizations," see Albert S. Broussard, *Black San Francisco: The Struggle for Racial Equality in the West, 1900–1954* (Lawrence: University of Kansas Press, 1993), 226–229.

13. "Annual Report," 1952, Box 25, NAACP-WC (previous).

14. Williams, "Our Unfinished Task."

15. This issue, according to historian Stephen Pitti, was the CSO's top state legislative priority during the 1950s and into the early 1960s (Stephen Pitti, "Quicksilver Community: Mexican Migrations and Politics in the Santa Clara Valley, 1800–1960" [PhD diss., Stanford University, 1998], 381); "Annual Report," 1953, Box 25, NAACP-WC (previous).

16. Williams, "Our Unfinished Task."

17. *San Francisco Chronicle*, December 3, 1951, in Carton 2, Folder 68, NAACP-WC.

18. Franklin Williams to Walter White, et al., December 3, 1951, Carton 2, Folder 68, NAACP-WC.

19. Franklin Williams to Walter White, et al., December 3, 1951, Carton 2, Folder 68, NAACP-WC.

20. "Annual Report," 1951, Box 25, NAACP-WC (previous); Franklin Williams to Walter White, January 8, 1952, Carton 2, Folder 68, NAACP-WC. For more on the NAACP and anticommunism, see Manfred Berg, "Black Civil Rights and Liberal Anticommunism: The NAACP in the Early Cold War," *Journal of American History* 94, no. 1 (2007): 75–96. Berg views the NAACP's anticommunism as a pragmatic, political calculus of what was required "to keep the cause of black civil rights on the agenda" (77). That agenda, at least in California, remained consistent before and after the NAACP adopted its anticommunist policy in 1947, focusing from the 1940s into the 1960s on fair employment practices and fair housing.

21. Josephine Duveneck to CFCU Board Members, December 4, 1951, Carton 2, Folder 68, NAACP-WC.

22. "Emergency Meeting," minutes, December 7, 1951, Carton 2, Folder 68, NAACP-WC.

23. Walter White to Franklin Williams, December 21, 1951, Carton 2, Folder 68, NAACP-WC.

24. "What's This 'America Plus'?" *San Francisco Chronicle*, December 6, 1951: 26.

25. Pat Brown quoted in "'America Plus': A Mask for Bigotry and Discrimination," pamphlet, March 4, 1952, Carton 2, Folder 68, NAACP-WC.

26. "The Case for Fair Employment Practices Legislation in California," 1953, Carton 70, Folder 38, NAACP-WC.

27. Tarea Hall Pittman, "NAACP Official and Civil Rights Worker," Oral History Interview, Conducted 1974 by Joyce A. Henderson, The Bancroft Library University of California/Berkeley, for the Earl Warren Oral History Project, 88.

28. "NAACP West Coast Regional News," news release, December 20, 1952, Carton 107, Folder 52, NAACP-WC.

29. "NAACP West Coast Regional News," news release, December 30, 1952, Carton 107, Folder 52, NAACP-WC.

30. Franklin Williams to Members of California State Assembly and Senate, January 2, 1953, Box 1, Folder Fair Employment Practices, THP.

31. Tarea Hall Pittman, "The NAACP Campaign for FEPC in California," Carton 104, Folder 28, NAACP-WC.

32. California Poll Release 171, September 2, 1952. Of those polled, forty-five percent supported a federal fair employment practices law.

33. "Regional Advisory Committee Meeting," minutes, January 30, 1953, Carton 1, Folder 5, NAACP-WC.

34. C.L. Dellums, "International President of the Brotherhood of Sleeping Car Porters and Civil Rights Leader," Oral History Interview, Conducted 1973 by Joyce A. Henderson, The Bancroft Library University of California/Berkeley, for the Earl Warren Oral History Project, 119.

35. "FEP Planning Meeting," minutes, January 31, 1953, Carton 104, Folder 3, NAACP-WC.

36. "NAACP West Coast Region Monthly Report," April 22, 1955, Carton 2, Folder 18, NAACP-WC.

37. William Becker, "Working for Civil Rights: With Unions, the Legislature, and Governor Pat Brown" in *The Governor's Office Under Edmund G. Brown, Sr.*, Oral History Interview, Conducted 1979 by Gabrielle Morris, The Bancroft Library University of California/Berkeley, for the Governmental History Documentation Project, Goodwin Knight / Edmund Brown, Sr., Era, 21.

38. Broussard, 197–200.

39. Edward Howden to Tarea Hall Pittman, April 3, 1953, Box 1, Folder Fair Employment Practices, THP.

40. "General Report," December 28, 1947, Box 5, Folder 8, MM.

41. "Organizational Meeting JACL-ADC California Legislative Committee," minutes, September 13, 1951, Box 42, Folder JACL-ADC Calif. Legislative Committee, 1951–1954, JACL.

42. JACL-ADC to California Senate Social Welfare Committee, May 18, 1951, Box 42, folder JACL-ADC Calif. Legislative Committee, 1951–1954, JACL.

43. Toru Ikeda to Earl Warren, July 3, 1951, Folder 14914, EW.

44. Joe Grant Masaoka and June Fujita to Earl Warren, June 25, 1951, Folder 14914, EW.

45. Tats Kushida to Earl Warren, July 28, 1951, Folder 14914, EW.

46. "California Legislative Report," January 19, 1952, Box 42, Folder JACL-ADC Calif. Legislative Committee, 1951–1954, JACL; "NAACP West Coast Regional News," December 20, 1952, Carton 107, Folder 52, NAACP-WC.

47. "Proceedings of Third Annual Convention for Civic Unity," December 1948, Carton 4, Folder Race Relations on the West Coast, CM-B; Fred Ross, "Program of the Industrial Areas Foundation," 1949, Box 5, Folder 11, FR. The CSO eventually became "the most important civil rights organization of its kind in the West," as Stephen J. Pitti described it (Stephen J. Pitti, *The Devil in Silicon Valley: Northern California, Race, and Mexican Americans* [Princeton: Princeton University Press, 2003], 149).

48. Fred Ross, "The First House Meeting," circa 1947, Box 21, Folder 10, FR.

49. Fred Ross, "Community Organizing in Mexican American Colonies: A Progress Report Undertaken in Several Mexican American Communities in Southern California," 1946–1947, Box 20, Folder 19, FR.

50. Fred Ross to Saul Alinsky, September 26, 1947, Box 2, Folder 1, FR.

51. Fred Ross to Saul Alinsky, November 3, 1947, Box 2, Folder 1, FR.

52. "Program of the Industrial Areas Foundation," 1949, Box 5, Folder 11, FR.

53. Katherine Underwood, "Pioneering Minority Representation: Edward Roybal and the Los Angeles City Council, 1949–1962," *Pacific Historical Review* 66, no. 3 (1997): 399–425.

54. Pitti, *The Devil in Silicon Valley*, 150, 165.

55. Fred Ross Ross to Saul Alinsky, circa 1953, Box 3, Folder Outgoing Correspondence, 1953, CFCU.

56. "Proceedings of the Ninth Annual Civic Unity Convention."

57. Fred Ross quoted in Pitti, "Quicksilver Community," 384.

58. "Proceedings of the Ninth Annual Civic Unity Convention."

59. "Proceedings of the Ninth Annual Civic Unity Convention." For Ross's mileage log, see Box 10, Folder 15, FR. The number of unregistered voters comes from Anthony Rios, CSO Third National Convention, March 17–18, 1956, Box 6, Folder 6, FR.

60. Fred Ross to Anthony Rios, May 14, 1953, Box 10, Folder 8, FR.

61. César Chávez, eulogy for Fred Ross, October 17, 1992, Box 38, Folder 759, File 67, JL.

62. Haru Ishimaru to JACL chapter presidents, December 6, 1954, Box 42, Folder JACL-ADC Calif. Legislative Committee, 1951–1954, JACL.

63. "Program of the Industrial Areas Foundation."

64. "Annual Report," 1953, Box 25, NAACP-WC (previous).

65. Herman E. Gallegos, "Equity and Diversity: Hispanics in the Nonprofit World," an oral history, conducted 1988 by Gabrielle Morris, the Regional Oral History Office, the Bancroft Library, University of California, Berkeley, 1989, 33.

66. "Organizational Meeting JACL-ADC California Legislative Committee."

67. "FEP Planning Meeting," minutes, January 31, 1953, Carton 104, Folder 3, NAACP-WC.

68. "The Case for Fair Employment Practices Legislation in California."

69. "Annual Report," 1953, Box 25, NACCP-WC (previous).

70. Becker, "Working for Civil Rights," 23. Years later, during his oral history interview, Gus Hawkins was asked about his work in the 1940s and 1950s, when he was an assemblyman, "Did the black and brown communities not see their interests as being the same?" He replied, "They've never really developed a healthy relationship" (Augustus F. Hawkins, Oral History Interview, Conducted 1988 by Carlos Vásquez, UCLA Oral

History Program, for the California State Archives State Government Oral History Program, 147).

71. Pittman, "The NAACP Campaign for FEPC in California."

72. "Annual Report," 1953, Box 25, NAACP-WC (previous).

73. "A Report on the Working Conference on Civil Rights Legislation for 1955," September 10, 1954, Carton 105, Folder 59, NAACP-WC.

74. "A Report on the Working Conference on Civil Rights Legislation for 1955."

75. "FEP Planning Meeting," November 17, 1954, Carton 36, Folder FEP-List for William Becker, NAACP-WC (previous).

76. "F.E.P.C. for California," December 5, 1954, Carton 104, Folder 28, NAACP-WC.

77. "NAACP West Coast Region Monthly Report," April 22, 1955.

78. Dellums, 128.

79. "Board of Directors Meeting," minutes, February 5, 1955, Carton 3, Folder Oakland, CFCU.

80. Irving Rosenblatt to CFCU affiliates, May 16, 1955, Carton 3, Folder 10, NAACP-WC.

81. "Executive Committee Meeting," minutes, June 28, 1955, Carton 3, Folder Oakland, CFCU.

82. "Board of Directors Meeting," minutes, June 6, 1956, Carton 3, Folder Not Named, CFCU.

83. "Annual Report," 1955, Box 25, NAACP –WC (previous).

84. William Becker, letter, June 6, 1955, Carton 70, Folder 38, NAACP-WC.

85. "Monthly Report," January-February, 1957, Carton 2, Folder 19, NAACP-WC.

86. "Statement by Policy Committee," May 13, 1957, Carton 70, Folder 39, NAACP-WC.

87. Goodwin Knight to Frank Gigliotti, April 1, 1955, Box 61, Folder 4, GK-CA.

88. Franklin Williams and C.L. Dellums to Goodwin Knight, June 23, 1955, Carton 70, Folder 38, NAACP-WC.

89. Memorandum from David Taylor, April 29, 1954, Box 46, Folder 304, GK-S.

90. Goodwin Knight to Franklin Williams, June 27, 1958, Carton 4, Folder 13, NAACP-WC.

91. "Annual Report," 1953, Box 25, NAACP-WC (previous).

92. Loren Miller to Clore Warne, November 2, 1947, Box 7, Folder 11, LM. For more on how African Americans, more so than Asian Americans and Mexican Americans, were the targets of housing discrimination in the 1950s, see Josh Sides, *L.A. City Limits: African American Los Angeles from the Great Depression to the Present* (Berkeley and Los Angeles: University of California Press, 2003), 109–111; Charlotte Brooks, "Sing Sheng vs. Southwood: Residential Integration in Cold War California," *Pacific Historical Review* 73, no. 3 (2004): 490–492; Scott Harvey Tang, "'Pushing at the Golden Gate: Race Relations and Racial Politics in San Francisco, 1940–1955" (PhD diss., University of California, Berkeley, 2002), 294–296.

93. CCFEP meeting, minutes, February 7, 1953, Carton 104, Folder 3, NAACP-WC.

94. "A Report on the Working Conference on Civil Rights Legislation for 1955." On this point, see also Pittman, "NAACP Official and Civil Rights Worker," 93: "There were

those who felt that we needed to include the field of housing. They said they went hand-in-hand. We knew that there was gross discrimination in housing. But we realized that it added to our difficulty in trying to get the legislation on the books because there were delegates to the mobilization who would go off on a tangent and they wouldn't like what was being said about the housing, and would just cause a lot of confusion."

95. NAACP West Coast Region, news release, May 14, 1952, Carton 1, Folder 11, NAACP-WC.

96. "Annual Report," 1954, Box 25, NAACP-WC (previous).

97. Biographical details on Colley drawn from speeches and articles in Box 21, Folder Nathaniel Colley, NAACP-WC; Ronald W. Powell, "Gadfly Battles Racial Bias," *Sacramento Bee*, 26 October 1981: 1; "Nathaniel Colley," *Sacramento Bee*, May 23, 1992: B5; Steve Gibson, "Capital Attorney, Activist Colley Dies," *Sacramento Bee*, May 22, 1992: A1.

98. "Meeting of Legal Committee," minutes, May 17, 1952, Carton 1, Folder 11, NAACP-WC.

99. *Banks v. Housing Authority of the City and County of San Francisco*, Superior Court of the City and County of San Francisco (no. 420534), October 1, 1952, Box 40, Folder 1, NAACP-WC (previous).

100. Resolution contained in "Answer to Respondents," Box 40, Folder 1, NAACP-WC (previous).

101. "Housing Chief Testifies 2 Suing Are Ineligible," *San Francisco Examiner*, October 7, 1952.

102. "Ruling on SF Housing Policy Soon," *San Francisco Chronicle*, September 24, 1952.

103. *Banks v. Housing Authority of the City and County of San Francisco*, Superior Court of the City and County of San Francisco (no. 420534).

104. "Note Threatens Judge for Negro Housing Decision," *San Francisco Chronicle*, October 21, 1952.

105. *Banks v. Housing Authority of the City and County of San Francisco*, 120 Cal. App. 2d 1 (1953).

106. "Annual Report," 1953, Box 25, NAACP-WC (previous).

107. "Meeting of Legal Committee," minutes, May 17, 1952.

108. Franklin Williams to Robert Pitts, September 12, 1952, Box 72, Folder 29, NAACP-WC.

109. *Ming v. Horgan* (No. 97130), Superior Court of California for Sacramento County, June 24, 1958, in Box 10, Folder 3, NAACP-WC (previous).

110. "Annual Report," 1954, Box 25, NAACP-WC (previous).

111. Loren Miller, speech, July 7, 1958, Box 39, Folder 4, NAACP-WC (previous).

112. *Ming v. Horgan.*

113. *Shelley v. Kraemer*, 334 U.S. 1 (1948).

114. Nathaniel Colley as paraphrased by Judge James H. Oakley in *Ming v. Horgan.*

115. *Ming v. Horgan.*

116. *San Francisco Chronicle*, June 24, 1958, in Box 39, Folder Ming v. Horgan Correspondence, NAACP-WC (previous).

117. The account of the Mays incident in this paragraph, as well as the subsequent three paragraphs, draws from numerous newspaper clippings and reports contained within Box 10, Folder Willie Mays, 1957, NAACP-WC (previous).

118. Pitti, *The Devil in Silicon Valley*, 136–140; Ernesto Galarza, *Spiders in the House and Workers in the Field* (Notre Dame: University of Notre Dame Press, 1970), 21–22.

119. Galarza, *Spiders in the House and Workers in the Field*, 14–28.

120. Ernesto Galarza, "The Mexican American: A National Concern—Program for Action," *Common Ground*, 9, no. 4 (1949): 37.

121. Galarza, "The Mexican American: A National Concern—Program for Action," 37.

122. Roger Baldwin to George Sánchez, July 6, 1948, Box 2, Folder 17, GS.

123. H.L. Mitchell to Roger Baldwin, July 19, 1951, Reel 36, STFU.

124. Roger Baldwin to H.L. Mitchell, July 26, 1951, Reel 36, STFU.

125. Roger Baldwin to George Sánchez, December 21, 1950, Box 2, Folder 19, GS.

126. Galarza, *Spiders in the House and Workers in the Field*, 86.

127. Franklin Williams to Ernesto Galarza, October 13, 1951, Carton 3, Folder 52, NAACP-WC.

128. Franklin Williams to Hugh Goodwin, March 4, 1958, Carton 3, Folder 52, NAACP-WC.

129. "Proceedings of Third Annual Convention for Civic Unity."

130. Anthony Rios to Ernesto Galarza, June 24, 1957, Box 13, Folder 7, EG.

131. Ernesto Galarza to Anthony Rios, July 5, 1957, Box 13, Folder 7, EG.

132. National Labor Relations Act 29 U.S.C. §§ 151–169 (1935).

133. News release, September 2, 1958, Box 51, Folder 9, EG; Ernesto Galarza to Thomas Pitts, November 12, 1958, Box 51, Folder 7, EG.

134. George Sánchez to Ernesto Galarza, October 12, 1948, Box 16, Folder 13, GS.

135. Ernesto Galarza quoted in Mae Ngai, *Impossible Subjects: Illegal Aliens and the Making of Modern America* (Princeton: Princeton University Press, 2004), 161.

136. Ellis W. Hawley, "The Politics of the Mexican Labor Issue, 1950–1965," *Agricultural History* 40, no. 3 (1966): 157.

137. George C. Kiser, *The Bracero Program: A Case Study of its Development, Termination, and Political Aftermath* (Ann Arbor: University Microfilms International, 1983), 86–91.

138. Richard B. Craig, *The Bracero Program: Interest Groups and Foreign Policy* (Austin: University of Texas Press, 1971), 45.

139. Hawley, 159–162.

140. Manuel García y Griego, "The Importation of Mexican Contract Laborers to the United States, 1942–1964," in *Between Two Worlds: Mexican Immigrants in the United States,* ed. David G. Gutiérrez, (Wilmington: Scholarly Resources), 49; Hawley, 157.

141. *Seasonal Labor in California Agriculture* (University of California, Berkeley: Division of Agricultural Sciences, 1963), 10–11.

142. *The Bracero Program and its Aftermath: An Historical Summary*, Prepared for the Use of the Assembly Committee on Agriculture (Sacramento, 1965).

143. Ernesto Galarza, "Statement On the Operation and Effects of the International Executive Agreement of 1951 for the Recruitment and Employment of Mexican Nationals in Agriculture in the U.S," circa late 1951 / early 1952, Reel 36, STFU.

144. Ernesto Galarza, "The Present Situation in Imperial Valley," February 1, 1952, Reel 36, STFU; *Migratory Labor in American Agriculture: Report of the President's Commission on Migratory Labor* (Washington, D.C.: 1951), 69.

145. Ernesto Galarza, "Program for Action," *Common Ground* 9, no. 4 (Summer 1949): 36.

146. Lawrence E. Davies, "Farm Union Urges Mexican Deal End," *New York Times*, January 15, 1950: 44. See also "Resolution 1" designating "the Wetback problem as uppermost concern to the NFLU" and opposing "current heavy infiltration in California agriculture," National Farm Labor Union California State Convention, September 15, 1951, Reel 36, STFU.

147. Galarza, "Program for Action," 35.

148. "Mexicans in Jobs on Farms at Issue, *New York Times*, August 18, 1950: 50.

149. Ernesto Galarza, "Report on Imperial Valley," California, March 12, 1951, Reel 35, STFU.

150. Given the benefits that agribusiness reaped from undocumented workers—both as cheap labor and strike breakers—it is perhaps not surprising that they wielded their political clout in the 1940s and 1950s to compel "senators and representatives from the [U.S. / Mexican] border states . . . [to cut] back appropriations for the Border Patrol" in order to keep the undocumented traffic flowing (Galarza quoted in García y Griego, 56–7). As one Immigration and Naturalization Officer explained to President Truman's *Commission on Migratory Labor*: "[The] pressure group is truck farmers and ranchers all over the country that have plenty of money, they are able to make a trip to Washington and to apply that pressure. The man that wants to apply [the immigration law] is the little man. He is the man who gets out there and does the work. He is the one that the wetbacks are taking the job away from. He doesn't have money to go to Washington. . . . On the other hand, your farmer or rancher goes up there, and he can call him by his first name. So I think that is the reason that the pressure group, even though it is a minority group, is so effective" (75).

151. Galarza, "Report on Imperial Valley."

152. Gladwin Hill, "Union Coup Stops Alien-Labor Trek," *New York Times*, March 3, 1951.

153. Ernesto Galarza to H.L. Mitchell, May 26, 1952, Reel 36, STFU.

154. Galarza, "Program for Action," 35.

155. Ernesto Galarza, *Strangers in Our Fields* (Washington, DC: U.S. Section, Joint United States-Mexico Trade Union Committee), 20.

156. Ernesto Galarza, "Interview at UFW Boycott Office," May 7, 1974, Box 3, Folder 6, EG.

157. Ernesto Galarza to H.L. Mitchell, June 16, 1952, Reel 36, STFU.

158. Ernesto Galarza, "Big Farm Strike: A Report on the Labor Dispute at DiGiorgio's," *Commonweal*, June 4, 1948: 179–180.

159. Ernesto Galarza to H.L. Mitchell, June 16, 1952, Reel 36, STFU.

160. On this point, see Ngai, 163: "While sympathetic to the plight of braceros, Galarza ultimately identified with the interest of domestic workers against those of braceros and 'wetbacks.'" See, too, Juan Ramon Garcia, *Operation Wetback: The Mass*

Deportation of Mexican Undocumented Workers in 1954 (Westport: Greenwood Press, 1980), 124.

161. Carey McWilliams, "America's Disadvantaged Minorities: Mexican-Americans," *Journal of Negro Education* 20, no. 3 (Summer 1951): 302–303.

162. Frank L. Noakes, "Foreword" to Galarza, *Strangers in Our Fields*.

163. Ngai, 155.

164. David Gutiérrez, *Walls and Mirrors: Mexican Americans, Mexican Immigrants, and the Politics of Ethnicity* (Berkeley: University of California Press, 1995), 142.

165. Ernesto Galarza quoted in Gutiérrez, *Walls and Mirrors*, 168.

166. García y Griego, 49–50.

167. Galarza, *Strangers in Our Fields*, 20.

168. "Resolution Re: Investigation of the Publication of 'Strangers in our Fields,'" September 17, 1956, Box 10, Folder 11, GK-CA.

169. Ernesto Galarza to Goodwin Knight, September 23, 1957, Box 10, Folder 12, GK-CA.

170. Goodwin Knight to Ernesto Galarza, April 11, 1958, Box 10, Folder 13, GK-CA.

171. Ernesto Galarza to Goodwin Knight, September 23, 1957, Box 10, Folder 12, GK-CA

172. Jacques E. Levy, *Cesar Chavez: Autobiography of La Causa* (New York: W.W. Norton and Company, Inc., 1975), 130–131.

173. Levy, 130–142.

174. Proposition 18: Employer-Employee Relations (1958), available online through: http://library.uchastings.edu/library/california-research/ca-ballot-measures.html#ballotprops.

175. Ernesto Galarza, news release, September 2, 1958, Box 51, Folder 9, EG.

176. Ernesto Galarza to C.J. Haggerty, July 18, 1957, Box 51, Folder 7, EG.

177. Ernesto Galarza to Pat Brown, no date, Box 51, Folder 7, EG.

178. Totton J. Anderson, "The 1958 Election in California," *Western Political Quarterly* 12, no. 1 (1959): 286.

179. Quoted in Anderson, 286.

180. Anderson, 285, 289.

181. Matthew Dallek, *The Right Moment: Ronald Reagan's First Victory and the Decisive Turning Point in American Politics* (New York: Free Press, 2000), 13.

182. Edmund G. Brown, Sr., "Years of Growth, 1939–1966; Law Enforcement, Politics, and the Governor's Office," an oral history conducted 1977–1981 by Malca Chall, Amelia R. Fry, Gabrielle Morris, and James Rowland, Regional Oral History Office, The Bancroft Library, University of California, Berkeley, 1982, 233.

183. Anderson, 276.

184. "Statement on Civil Rights," circa 1958, Box 46, Folder Civil Rights and Equality, PB.

185. Goodwin Knight to Frank Gigliotti, April 1, 1955, Box 61, Folder 4 GK-CA.

186. "Executive Director's Report," December 3, 1949, Carton 3, Folder Board of Directors Material, CFCU.

187. Becker, "Working for Civil Rights," 24.

Chapter 6

1. Lawrence E. Davies, "Democrats Found Leading In Most California Races," *New York Times*, October 23, 1958: 23.

2. Pat Brown, "Statement on Civil Rights," circa 1958, Box 46, Folder Civil Rights and Equality, PB.

3. Frederick Dutton to Loren Miller, January 30,1958, Box 36, Folder 1, LM.

4. Davies, "Democrats Found Leading in Most California Races," 23.

5. William Becker, "Working for Civil Rights: With Unions, the Legislature, and Governor Pat Brown" in *The Governor's Office Under Edmund G. Brown, Sr.* Oral History Interview, Conducted 1979 by Gabrielle Morris, The Bancroft Library University of California/Berkeley, for the Governmental History Documentation Project, Goodwin Knight / Edmund Brown, Sr., Era, 16–32. On Becker's appointment as Assistant to the Governor for Human Rights, see News release, September 10, 1963, Box 602, Folder Ethnic Census, PB.

6. *Californians of Japanese, Chinese, and Filipino Ancestry* (San Francisco: Department of Industrial Relations, Division of Fair Employment Practices, 1965), 17. During the 1950s, the state population increased by half—from 10,586,223 to 15,717,204; the state's Mexican American population increased from 758,000, or 7.2 percent of the overall population, to 1,426,538, or 9.1 percent of the overall population, in 1960; the state's African American population climbed from 462,172, or 4.4 percent of the overall population in 1950, to 883,861 in 1960, or 5.6 percent of the total population.

7. César Chávez to Assemblyman Jerome Waldie, March 25, 1963, Box 18, Folder 385, JL.

8. Brown, "Statement on Civil Rights."

9. Becker, "Working for Civil Rights," 23.

10. "Coast Democrat to Fore," *New York Times*, October 31, 1957: 24.

11. Jonathan Spivak, "California Comer," *Wall Street Journal*, June 9, 1958: 10.

12. "Brown Decides He'll Try for Governor," *Los Angeles Times*, November 1, 1957: B4.

13. Gladwin Hill, "That Dark Horse Named Brown," *New York Times Sunday Magazine*, December 6, 1959: 38.

14. Douglas Flamming, *Bound for Freedom: Black Los Angeles in Jim Crow America* (Berkeley: University of California Press, 2005), 373–374; Matthew W. Dallek, *The Right Moment: Ronald Reagan's First Victory and the Decisive Turning Point in American Politics* (New York: Free Press, 2000), 3. For similar claims about Brown, see Peter Schrag, *Paradise Lost: California's Experience, America's Future* (New York: New Press, 1998), 45, and Bill Boyarsky, *Big Daddy: Jesse Unruh and the Art of Power Politics* (Berkeley: University of California Press, 2008), 108.

15. Pat Brown to Eugene Wyman, June 5, 1963, Box 570, Folder Legis–Civil Rights– May, PB; César Chávez to Assemblyman Jerome Waldie, March 25, 1963, Box 18, Folder 385, JL.

16. Becker, "Working for Civil Rights," 24.

17. Augustus F. Hawkins, Oral History Interview, Conducted 1988 by Carlos Vásquez, UCLA Oral History Program, for the California State Archives State Government Oral History Program, 133–134.

18. C.L. Dellums, "International President of the Brotherhood of Sleeping Car Porters and Civil Rights Leader," Oral History Interview, Conducted 1973 by Joyce A. Henderson, The Bancroft Library University of California/Berkeley, for the Earl Warren Oral History Project, 133–134.

19. "Text of Brown's Inaugural Speech," *Los Angeles Times*, January 6, 1959: 10.

20. According to the NAACP West Coast Region Annual Report for 1958, Rumford was "regional treasurer" for the NAACP and the NAACP asked him to "once again carry and lead the campaign for state-wide FEPC in the 1959 session of the State Legislature" ("Annual Report," 1958, Box 25, NAACP-WC [previous]).

21. "54 Assemblymen Offer Measure for FEPC Law," *Los Angeles Times*, January 8, 1959: 8.

22. "FEPC Bill Due Today in Assembly," *Los Angeles Times*, January 7, 1959: 8.

23. CCFEP, letter to supporters, January 21, 1959, Carton 3, Folder 7, NAACP-WC.

24. Phillip Burton to Franklin Williams, January 14, 1959, Carton 3, Folder 33, NAACP-WC.

25. Edward Gaffney to Franklin Williams, January 21, 1959, Carton 3, Folder 33, NAACP-WC.

26. Meeting of CCFEP officers and co-chairs, minutes, January 6, 1959, Carton 3, Folder 7, NAACP-WC.

27. William Becker to CCFEP officers, January 22, 1959, Carton 3, Folder 7, NAACP-WC.

28. William Becker to CCFEP officers, February 5, 1959, Carton 3, Folder 7, NAACP-WC.

29. Dellums, "International President of the Brotherhood of Sleeping Car Porters and Civil Rights Leader," 128.

30. William Becker, May 8, 1959, Carton 3, Folder 33, NAACP-WC.

31. Chapter 121, Statutes of California, 1959.

32. "FEPC Gets 2 More L.A. Members," *Los Angeles Times*, September 24, 1959: B1.

33. Franklin Williams to Assemblyman Milton Marks, June 17, 1959, Carton 3, Folder 16, NAACP-WC.

34. "Brown 'Proud, Pleased' With Legislature," *Los Angeles Times*, June 21, 1959:1.

35. Chapter 121, Statutes of California, 1959.

36. Fred Ross, "Mexican-Americans on the March," *Catholic Charities*, June 1960, in Box 13, Folder 7, EG.

37. Franklin Williams, "California's New Civil Rights Tool," *Christian Century*, June 15, 1960: 720–721.

38. Before 1959, section 51 of the Civil Code read, "All citizens within the jurisdiction of this State are entitled to the full and equal accommodations, advantages, facilities, and privileges of inns, restaurants, hotels, eating houses, places where ice cream or soft drinks of any kind are sold for consumption on the premises, barber shops, bath houses, theaters, skating rinks, public conveyances, and all other places of public amusement, subject only to the conditions and limitations established by law and applicable alike to all citizens" (*Deering's California Code*, Civil Code Annotated, Section 51).

39. Marvin L. Holen, Oral History Interview, Conducted 1990 by Carlos Vasquez, UCLA Oral History Program, for the California State Archives State Governmental Oral History Program; *Reed v. Hollywood Professional School*, 169 Cal. App. 2d Supp. 887 (1959).

40. Holen, 151.

41. Nathaniel Colley to Franklin Williams, et al., circa early 1959, Box 41, Folder 2, NAACP-WC (previous).

42. Holen, 115, 119.

43. Boyarsky, *Big Daddy*, 83–89.

44. Boyarsky, *Big Daddy*, 83–89.

45. Holen, 124, 173–174.

46. Chapter 1866, Statutes of California, 1959.

47. Chapter 1681, Statutes of California, 1959.

48. Marshall Kaplan, "Discrimination in California Housing: The Need for Additional Legislation," *California Law Review* 50 (1962): 639.

49. Gus Hawkins, testimony, *Hearings Before the United States Commission on Civil Rights, Los Angeles, January 25–26, 1960, and San Francisco, January 27–28, 1960* (Washington, D.C.: GPO, 1960).

50. "Homes Seen Covered by the Law," *Los Angeles Times*, November 15, 1959: 2.

51. Pat Brown, testimony, *Hearings Before the United States Commission on Civil Rights, Los Angeles, January 25–26, 1960, and San Francisco, January 27–28, 1960* (Washington, D.C.: GPO, 1960).

52. Hale Champion, speech, September 27, 1962, Box 10, Folder Department of Industrial Relations, 10/58–8/63, NAACP-WC (previous).

53. Richard Kline, "Governor Brown's Faithful Advisor" in *The Governor's Office Under Edmund G. Brown, Sr.*, Oral History Interview, Conducted 1977 by Eleanor Glaser, The Bancroft Library University of California/Berkeley, for the Governmental History Documentation Project, Goodwin Knight / Edmund Brown, Sr., Era, 22. Similarly, see Edward Howden, "California's Civil Rights Situation," September 14, 1962, Carton 534, Folder FEPC Sept.-Dec., 1962: "Once the Brown Administration had taken office, of course, rapid steps were taken—in the 1959 Legislature—to overcome some of the 14-year lag in civil rights legislation under previous administrations."

54. "Annual Report," 1959, Box 25, NAACP-WC (previous).

55. Stanley Mosk, "Attorney General's Office and Political Campaigns, 1958–1966," (in California's Constitutional Officers), an oral history conducted 1979 by Amelia R. Fry, Regional Oral History Office, The Bancroft Library, University of California, Berkeley, 1980, 26.

56. Franklin Williams to Assemblyman Milton Marks et al., June 17, 1959, Carton 3, Folder 16, NAACP-WC.

57. Fred Dutton to Pat Brown, May 3, 1960, Box 5, Folder 3—Fred Dutton, HC.

58. "Pension for Non Citizens Bill," *CSO Reporter*, circa July 1959, in Box 13, Folder 8, EG.

59. *CSO Reporter*, circa June 1959, in Carton 3, Folder 20, NAACP-WC.

60. "Pension for Non Citizens Bill."

61. "Text of Brown's Inaugural Speech," *Los Angeles Times*, January 6, 1959: 10.

62. "Governor OKs $1 Floor on Farm Wages," *Los Angeles Times*, March 21, 1959: 3.

63. Ethan Rarick, *California Rising: The Life and Times of Pat Brown* (Berkeley: University of California Press, 2005), 130–131.

64. Pat Brown, speech, August 12, 1959, in *Daily Proceedings of the California Labor Federation*, Box 11, Folder 10, AD.

65. "Pension for Non Citizens Bill."

66. "Brown Will Address Latin Organization," *Los Angeles Times*, May 10, 1961: 24.

67. Kenneth C. Burt, *The Search for a Civic Voice: California Latino Politics* (Claremont: Regina Books, 2007), 172, 180–184.

68. "The History of MAPA and the Mexican-American in California," in program for the 4th Annual Convention of MAPA, November 8–10, 1963, Box 7, Folder 2, MR.

69. Edward Howden to Cecile Poole, September 18, 1960, Box 398, Folder FEPC, Sept.-Dec. 1960, PB.

70. FEPC Report, 1960, Box 601, Folder FEPC, September, PB.

71. Ross, "Mexican-Americans on the March."

72. Herman E. Gallegos, "Equity and Diversity: Hispanics in the Nonprofit World," an oral history, conducted 1988 by Gabrielle Morris, the Regional Oral History Office, the Bancroft Library, University of California, Berkeley, 1989, 33.

73. Ross, "Mexican-Americans on the March."

74. See Chapter 5.

75. "NAACP West Coast Region Annual Report Summary," December 8, 1960, Carton 4, Folder 63, NAACP-WC.

76. "The Civil Rights Agenda in the 1961 California State Legislature (A Summary of the California Committee for Fair Practices December 3rd Conference on Civil Rights Legislative Priorities)," December 3, 1960, Carton 70, Folder 19, NAACP-WC.

77. William Becker, report on CCFP meetings in Los Angeles on July 7, 1960 and San Francisco on August 4, 1960, Carton 10, File CCFP—1960-April 1961, NAACP-WC (previous).

78. "The Civil Rights Agenda in the 1961 California State Legislature (A Summary of the California Committee for Fair Practices December 3rd Conference on Civil Rights Legislative Priorities)."

79. CCFP, letter, January 9, 1961, Carton 70, Folder 19, NAACP-WC; Leonard Carter to Ronald Reagan, December 29, 1966, Carton 26, Folder 1, NAACP-WC.

80. Dolores Huerta, "Legislative Report," December 1961, Box 10, Folder 15, FR.

81. John Jacobs, *A Rage for Justice: The Passion and Politics of Phillip Burton* (Berkeley: University of California Press), 76.

82. Jacobs, 78.

83. Huerta, "Legislative Report."

84. Dolores Huerta to CSO Legislative Committee members, January 12, 1961, Box 10, Folder 12, FR.

85. Jacobs, 78–79.

86. J.M. Wedemeyer to Pat Brown, June 23, 1961, MF3:2 (23), GCBF.

87. Alexander Pope to Pat Brown, July 3, 1961, MF3:2 (23), GCBF.

88. Edmund G. Brown, Sr., "Years of Growth, 1939–1966; Law Enforcement, Politics, and the Governor's Office," an oral history conducted 1977–1981 by Malca Chall, Amelia R. Fry, Gabrielle Morris, and James Rowland, Regional Oral History Office, The Bancroft Library, University of California, Berkeley, 1982, 320.

89. "Aged Bill Tribute to CSO," *Los Angeles Times*, July 21, 1961: 8.

90. Huerta, "Legislative Report."

91. Gladwin Hill, "Brown Charting Cautious Course," *New York Times*, January 8, 1961: 51; Rarick, 130–131.

92. "Minimum Wage Bill Under Fire," *Oakland Tribune*, February 8, 1961: 6E.

93. Gladwin Hill, "Brown Charting Cautious Course," *New York Times*, January 8, 1961: 51; "Brown Aims to Mediate Farm Strike," *Los Angeles Times*, March 7, 1961, B1; California Senate Joint Resolution No. 20, Chapter 69, 1961 Regular Session.

94. César Chávez to Fred Ross, July 14, 1961, Box 34, Folder 696, JL.

95. Pat Brown to Sally Ann Fudge, March 6, 1962, Carton 571, Folder Labor 1962, PB.

96. For a summary of the farmers' position, see "Minimum Wage Bill Under Fire," *Oakland Tribune*, February 8, 1961: 6E: "Farmers protest that a California minimum wage bill that left other states with much lower wages would help drive them out of business. They say any minimum wage legislation must be national to prevent inequities to California."

97. "Adequate Labor a Must—Brown," *Stockton Bee*, May 7, 1960 in Box 3, Folder 12, EG.

98. "Brown Aims to Mediate Farm Strike," *Los Angeles Times*, March 7, 1961: B1.

99. "Brown Supports Bracero Renewal," *Oakland Tribune*, June 2, 1961: E11.

100. César Chávez to Dolores Huerta, February 13, 1962, Box 18, Folder 378, JL.

101. Congress of Racial Equality, report, December 1959, RFHAF.

102. Franklin H. Williams, "Keepers of the Wall," *Frontier* (April 1960): 9–11.

103. "California: 1961 Report to the Commission on Civil Rights from the State Advisory Committee," in *The 50 States Report, Submitted to the Commission on Civil Rights by the State Advisory Committees, 1961* (Washington, D.C.: GPO, 1961), 38–49. For further corroboration of this point from the late 1950s and early 1960s, see Midori Nishi and Young Il Kim, "Recent Japanese Settlement changes in the Los Angeles Area," *Yearbook of the Association of Pacific Geographers*, 26 (1964); Wilson Record, *Minority Groups and Intergroup Relations in the San Francisco Bay Area* (Berkeley: Institute for Governmental Studies, 1963); Gladwin Hill, "Negroes on Coast Fight for Housing," *New York Times*, July 9, 1962: 1, 81; John Henning, Director of California Department of Industrial Relations, in *Proceedings of the Governor's Conference on Housing*, June 13–15, 1960, Box 5, Folder Housing, HC; *Hearings Before the United States Commission on Civil Rights, Los Angeles, January 25–26, 1960, and San Francisco, January 27–28, 1960* (Washington, D.C.: GPO, 1960); Midori Nishi, "Japanese Settlement in the Los Angeles Area," *Yearbook of the Association of Pacific Geographers*, 20 (1958).

104. "Minority Problems in Housing," *Proceedings of the Governor's Conference on Housing*, June 13–15, 1960, Box 5, Folder Housing, HC.

105. "In a Nutshell: The Proposed Fair Housing Law," Assembly Bill 801, pamphlet, 1961, RFHAF.

106. Pat Brown, January 3, 1961, quoted in Thomas W. Casstevens, *Politics, Housing and Race Relations: California's Rumford Act and Proposition 14* (Berkeley: Institute of Governmental Studies, June 1967), 11–12.

107. Pat Brown, speech to AB 801 Statewide Conference, April 15, 1961, Box 512, Folder AB 801, PB.

108. Richard Kline to Hale Champion, December 2, 1960, Box 5, Folder Housing, HC.

109. Casstevens, 15.

110. Harvey C. Brown to Pat Brown, February 19, 1961, Box 456, Folder Division of Housing, PB; Chas Johnson to Harvey C. Brown, March 15, 1961, Box 456, Folder Division of Housing, PB.

111. Harold W. Horowitz, "The 1959 California Equal Rights in 'Business Establishments' Statute—A Problem in Statutory Application," *Southern California Law Review* 33 (1960): 262, 286; Franklin Williams, "California's New Civil Rights Tool," *Christian Century*, June 15, 1960: 720–721.

112. "Complaint for Damages and Injunctive Relief," December 31, 1959, BvP.

113. "Appellants' Opening Brief," January 5, 1962, BvP.

114. "Respondents' Brief," January 22, 1962, BvP.

115. "Appellants' Answering Brief," February 1, 1962, BvP.

116. *Burks v. Poppy Construction Company*, 57 Cal. 2d 463 (1962).

117. *Vargas v. Hampson*, 20 Cal. Rptr. 618 (1962).

118. "Reporter's Partial Transcript," Orange County Superior Court, June 30, 1961, VvH.

119. "Appellants' Reply Brief," December 14, 1961, VvH.

120. *Vargas v. Hampson*, 20 Cal. Rptr. 618 (1962). In addition to *Burks* and *Vargas*, the California Supreme Court handed down a third decision on March 26, 1962. In *Lee v. O'Hara*, the Court confronted the question of whether or not the Unruh Act applied to real estate brokers. The Court ruled that it did: "The inclusion in section 51 of the words 'all' and 'of every kind whatsoever,' without any exception and without specification of particular kinds of enterprises, leaves no doubt that the term was used in the broadest sense reasonable . . . The office which a real estate broker is required by law to maintain at a specified location, and from which his business establishment must be transacted, is a business establishment within the meaning of the Unruh Act." The key difference between *Vargas* and *Lee* was just how far the broker's antidiscriminatory responsibility extended. In *Lee* the discrimination was clearly practiced by the brokers—they refused to rent to the black plaintiffs—who were, therefore, in violation of the Unruh Act, whereas in *Vargas* the Court drew the line, holding that the broker could not be held liable for the discrimination of the owner, provided that the broker did not discriminate (*Lee v. O'Hara*, 20 Cal. Rptr. 617 [1962]).

121. Holen, 173.

122. Irving Hill to Pat Brown, May 16, 1962, Box 535, Folder Division of Housing, January-June, PB.

123. Edward Howden to John Henning, September 14, 1962, Box 534, Folder FEPC—September-December, PB.

124. Edward Howden to Pat Brown, July 2, 1962, Box 534, Folder—FEPC, July-August, PB.

125. John Anson Ford to Pat Brown, November 16, 1962, Box 534, Folder FEPC—September-December, PB.

126. Kaplan, 647, footnote 57.

127. Preston Silbaugh and Leo Bromwich to Pat Brown, December 19, 1962, Box 570, Folder Civil Rights—Housing Discrimination, 1962, PB.

128. Pat Brown, speech, September 27, 1962, in *News from FEPC*, October 1, 1962, Box 534, Folder FEPC, September-December, 1962, PB.

129. Edward Howden to Arthur Alarcon, November 19, 1962, Box 641, Folder FEPC—1963, PB.

130. Sherill Luke to Byron Rumford, January 4, 1963, Box 640, Folder Housing Discrimination, 3/29/63, PB.

131. Sherill Luke to Pat Brown, January 11, 1963, Box 640, Folder Housing Discrimination, 3/29/63, PB.

132. CCFP meeting, minutes, December 8, 1962, Box 10, Folder California Committee for Fair Practices, May 1961–1962, NAACP-WC.

133. "Statement of Governor Edmund G. Brown on Human Rights," February 14, 1963, Box 640, Folder Legislation, Civil Rights, January 1—February 28, PB.

134. Loren Miller to Pat Brown, February 26, 1963, Box 12, Folder 3, LM.

135. Michael Harris, "W. Byron Rumford Is Dead at 78," *San Francisco Chronicle*, June 14, 1986; William Byron Rumford, Oral History Interview, Conducted 1973 by Joyce A. Henderson, Amelia Fry, and Edward France, The Bancroft Library University of California/Berkeley, for the Earl Warren Oral History Project; Casstevens, 20–26; Boyarsky, 93.

136. Casstevens, 20–26.

137. Sherill Luke to Margaret Jordan, April 10, 1963, Box 640, Folder Housing Discrimination, April-May, PB.

138. "Statement of Edmund G. Brown on Housing," April 18, 1963, Box 5, Folder Housing, HC.

139. Jud Baker, "JFK to California: Pass Housing Bill," *Los Angeles Herald-Examiner*: A2.

140. Brown, "Years of Growth," 524–525.

141. Dallek, 46.

142. Pat Brown, letter, June 27, 1963, Box 660, Folder Federal Civil Rights, PB. On the influence of Birmingham, Richard Kline recollected, "I think the thing that won it for us was what happened in Selma, Alabama [actually, Birmingham], which occurred right about the time the bill was making its way through the legislature, and Bill [Bull] Connor sic-ing his dogs on people—those kinds of television images probably were really the things that broke that bill though" (Kline, 18).

143. Casstevens, 23.

144. Casstevens, 26–28.

145. Casstevens, 29. NAACP West Region director at the time, Tarea Hall Pittman, remembered Gibson and Burns as "dyed-in-the-wool segregationists" who had earlier opposed FEPC. "They felt that discrimination was not widespread. They felt that [FEPC] should never, never be written into law, that it should be a voluntary thing . . . that it was overstepping the bounds. They felt it was unconstitutional and they were very hostile when you met them, very hostile!" (Tarea Hall Pittman, "NAACP Official and Civil rights Worker." Oral History Interview, Conducted 1974 by Joyce A. Henderson, The Bancroft Library University of California/Berkeley, for the Earl Warren Oral History Project, 100).

146. Tom Bane quoted in James R. Mills, *A Disorderly House: The Brown-Unruh Years in Sacramento* (Berkeley: Heyday Books, 1987), 156. Jesse Unruh made a similar observation: "I thought we were going to get that bill out of that committee without too much trouble before those damned longhairs moved in. . . . You can't blame the senators for getting their backs up. They figure that if they approve the bill now, every bunch of jerks that wants anything out of the Legislature will come up here to camp in the halls till they get it" (Unruh quoted in Mills, 156–157).

147. Rumford, 117.

148. Casstevens, 31

149. *Sacramento Bee*, June 6, 1963, quoted in Casstevens, 33.

150. Casstevens, 33.

151. Brown and Johnson quoted in Dallek, 49.

152. Casstevens, 35.

153. Dallek, 50.

154. Casstevens, 35–37.

155. Brown, "Years of Growth," 493.

156. Rattigan quoted in Dallek, 50.

157. John F. Burby, Oral History Interview, Conducted 1987 by Carlos Vasquez, UCLA Oral History Program, for the California State Archives State Governmental Oral History Program, 110.

158. Rumford, 114.

159. William Byron Rumford, "The Fair Housing Act," circa 1964, in Rumford, 139.

160. Lucien C. Haas, Oral History Interview, Conducted 1989 by Carlos Vasquez, UCLA Oral History Program, for the California State Archives State Governmental Oral History Program, 76.

161. César Chávez to Fred Ross, January 25, 1962, Box 34, Folder 696, JL.

162. César Chávez to Fred Ross, July 14, 1961, Box 34, Folder 696, JL.

163. Jacques E. Levy, *Cesar Chavez: Autobiography of La Causa* (New York: W.W. Norton and Company, Inc., 1975), 147.

164. Dolores Huerta to Fred Ross, April 12, 1962, Box 11, Folder 7, FR.

165. César Chávez to Fred Ross, May 2, 1962 and August 17, 1962, Box 34, Folder 696, JL.

166. César Chávez to Fred Ross, May 10, 1962, June 13, 1962, July 19, 1962, July 11, 1962, and August 7, 1962, Box 34, Folder 696, JL.

167. FWA Convention, minutes, September 30, 1962, Box 19, Folder 410, JL.

168. Constitution of the National Farm Workers Association, circa 1962, Box 34, Folder 696, JL.

169. Jacques Levy, e-mail message to author, December 9, 2002.

170. César Chávez to Fred Ross, August 7, 1962 and May 10, 1962, Box 34, Folder 696, JL.

171. National Farm Workers Association, letter, October 6, 1965, Box 21, Folder 451, JL.

172. César Chávez to Fred Ross, January 7, 1963, Box 34, Folder 696, JL.

173. Farm Workers Association, newsletter, October 18, 1962, Box 19, Folder 410, JL; César Chávez to Dolores Huerta, April 10, 1963, Box 18, Folder 378, JL.

174. Farm Workers Association, newsletter, December 20, 1962 and November 28, 1962, Box 19, Folder 410, JL; César Chávez to Dolores Huerta, March 11, 1963, Box 18, Folder 385, JL; César Chávez to Dolores Huerta, February 13, 1962, Box 18, Folder 378, JL.

175. "Farmers Are Warned of Tough Legislative Fight," *Fresno Bee*, January 25, 1963: 8A.

176. "Brown Balks at Ban on Braceros," *Modesto Bee*, April 10, 1963: 1; "Bracero Farm Help Still Needed," *Los Angeles Times*, April 17, 1963: A4.

177. "Brown Sees Solution to Farm Labor Shortage," *Los Angeles Times*, May 1, 1963: 9.

178. "Farmers Are Warned of Tough Legislative Fight," *Fresno Bee*, January 25, 1963: 8A.

179. News release, July 5, 1963, Carton 18, Folder 1963 Press Releases, PBu.

180. César Chávez to Dolores Huerta, April 10, 1963, Box 18, Folder 378, JL.

181. "Statement of Governor Edmund G. Brown on Human Rights"; César Chávez to Pat Brown, March 25, 1963, Box 18, Folder 385, JL.

182. César Chávez to Assemblyman Jerome Waldie, March 25, 1963, Box 18, Folder 385, JL.

183. Ruben Salazar, "Brown Failed on Promises, Latins Charge," *Los Angeles Times*, February 13, 1963: C14.

184. Julius Castelan quoted in "Job Appointments," *Daily Review* (Hayward, CA), February 13, 1963: 1. On this point, see also Armando Rodriguez, chair of the legislative committee for the American GI Forum, to Julius Castelan, February 14, 1963, Box 14, Folder 9, EG: "As the largest ethnic group in our great state, and as the Governor's strongest supporters and workers, we feel neglected, rejected and victimized."

185. News release, February 13, 1963, Box 603, Folder FEPC, January-June, PB.

186. Ruben Salazar, "Farm Labor Setup Faces Vast Challenge," *Los Angeles Times*, October 20, 1963.

187. César Chávez to Dolores Huerta, April 10, 1963, Box 18, Folder 378, JL.

188. Boyarsky, 98, 100; Jesse Unruh quoted in "Demo Leader Ready to Dump Fair Housing," *California Eagle*, March 7, 1963.

189. Kline, 3–4.

190. Fred Dutton to Pat Brown, May 3, 1960, Box 5, Folder 3—Fred Dutton, HC.

Chapter 7

1. Pat Brown to George Wallace, December 3, 1963, Box 660, Folder Federal Civil Rights, PB.

2. Pat Brown quoted in Bill Boyarsky, "Battle on Rights," *Los Angeles Herald*, January 16, 1964.

3. Martin Luther King, Jr. quoted in "Rev. King Hits Anti-Rumford Initiative," February 19, 1964, Box 52, Folder 4—Anti-Fair Housing Initiative, NAACP-WC (previous).

4. "California—Proposition 14," *Time*, September 25, 1964: 13.

5. Pat Brown, speech, August 25, 1964, Box 673, Folder Civil Rights, August 13–31, PB.

6. William Becker to Pat Brown, July 30, 1965, Box 840, Folder Political—Ethnic Groups, PB.

7. "Statement of Policy," *California Real Estate Magazine*, October 1963: 8.

8. "Gettysburg," *California Real Estate Magazine*, July 1964: 1.

9. Chapter 1853, Statutes of California, 1963.

10. These included: "(1) the sale or rental of the housing accommodation to the aggrieved person, if it is still available; (2) the sale or rental of a like accommodation, if one is available, or the next vacancy in a like accommodation; (3) the payment of damages to the aggrieved person in an amount not to exceed five hundred dollars ($500), if the commission determines that neither of the remedies under (1) and (2) is available" (Chapter 1853, Statutes of California, 1963).

11. Howard W. Lewis, Jr., *An Analysis of Proposition 14: The CREA Amendment* (Mountain View, CA: Aurora Press, 1964), 9, 24. Lewis's analysis drew a distinction between the "housing market" and "housing." "Government sources," he explained, "have estimated that the Rumford Act applies to 'about 60 to 70 percent' of the *housing market*" defined as property for sale or for rent at a given time, a large percentage of which is apartments in buildings covered by the Rumford Act. Lewis did not dispute this figure. He did, however, emphasize that if "all of the *housing* in California were for sale or for rent" at one time, then only about one-third (32%) would be covered by the Rumford Act. "Thus, if Proposition 14 were to pass, it would exempt from the Rumford Act certain people who control about 32% of the housing in California, but the housing concerned consists of about 65% of the properties that are, at any one moment, on the market for sale or for rent" (Lewis, 9).

12. Americans to Outlaw Forced Housing, press release, November 5, 1963, Box 706, Folder Housing Discrimination – Oct, PB.

13. A.C. Morrison to Assemblyman Frank Lanterman, February 2, 1964, RFHAF.

14. "CREA Fights Forced Housing Law, Seeks Initiative on Next Ballot," *California Real Estate Magazine*, October 1963: 7.

15. "Housing Initiative Titled; Petitions Gathering Signatures for Public Voter," *California Real Estate Magazine*, December 1963: 5.

16. "The Forced Housing Issue," *California Real Estate Magazine*, December 1963: 1.

17. "Housing Initiative Titled; Petitions Gathering Signatures for Public Voter."

18. "The Forced Housing Issue."

19. "CORE Initiative Protests Hit," *Los Angeles Herald Examiner*, December 27, 1963, D1.

20. "Petition Drive Meets Public Favor," *California Real Estate Magazine*, January 1964: 4.

21. "The Initiative—Its Purpose and Progress," *California Real Estate Magazine*, April 1964: 5.

22. "Petition Drive Meets Public Favor."

23. Jesse Unruh, speech, December 11, 1963, Box 8, Folder Virna Canson, 1964, NAACP-WC (previous).

24. Robert L. Lewton, Sr., State Chairman of the National States' Rights Party, letter, January 4, 1964, Prop 14 Box 2, PB.

25. "Town Hall Hears Sharp Housing Law Debate," *Los Angeles Times*, February 12, 1964.

26. "Rightists in West Fight Housing Act," *New York Times*, May 10, 1964.

27. Jack Burby to William Becker, February 4, 1964, Box 706, Folder Housing Discrimination, February 1–14, PB; William Becker quoted in "Excerpts from Notes on CCFP Meeting," November 2, 1963, Box 38, Folder 3 Initiative to Repeal AB 1240, NAACP-WC (previous).

28. "Cheers for Realtors," *San Francisco Chronicle*, December 5, 1963: 44.

29. Byron Rumford to Robert A. Wilcox, December 23, 1963, Box 1, Folder January 1963—December 1963, BR.

30. Stanley Mosk quoted in "Rumford Act Repeal Will Fail," *Los Angeles Herald Examiner*, January 13, 1964: B1.

31. Lucien C. Haas, Oral History Interview, Conducted 1989 by Carlos Vasquez, UCLA Oral History Program, for the California State Archives State Governmental Oral History Program, 74.

32. Tarea Hall Pittman quoted in "Excerpts from Notes on CCFP Meeting," November 2, 1963, Box 38, Initiative to Repeal AB 1240, Folder 3, NAACP-WC (previous).

33. Tom Saunders to Pat Brown, April 20, 1964, Box 706, Folder Housing Discrimination, April 15—April 31, PB.

34. Letter from Caspar Weinberger, circa January 1964, Prop 14 Box 2, Folder All Materials, PB.

35. Republicans in Opposition to Proposition 14, statement, October 6, 1964, Prop 14 Box 3, Folder Republicans, PB.

36. Californians Against Proposition 14, press release, October 23, 1964, Box 707, Folder Prop 14 October, PB.

37. Hugh Burns quoted in "Senator Burns Complains of Smear Campaign," *Sacramento Bee*, May 21, 1964.

38. William Becker to Edward Howden, October 3, 1963, Box 601, Folder FEPC, October, PB.

39. Edward Howden, memo, November 8, 1963, Box 602, Folder Housing Discrimination, June, PB.

40. San Francisco Realtors for No on 14, statement, October 1, 1964, Prop 14 Box 2, PB.

41. Earle Vaughn, "Facing the Inevitable Changes," *Apartment Journal*, October 1963.

42. "Developer Says Rumford Repeal Beckons Hate," *Sacramento Bee*, November 11, 1963.

43. Edward Eichler to Pat Brown, June 4, 1964, Box 706, Folder Housing Discrimination, June 1–16, PB.

44. "Coast Drive Focuses on Fair Housing Act," *AFL-CIO News*, July 18, 1964, in Box 40, Folder Proposition 14—NAACP Suit, 1964, NAACP-WC (previous).

45. Thomas Pitts letter to all California Labor Federation affiliates, September 25, 1964, Box 707, Folder Prop 14, October 1–12, PB.

46. "Teamsters Urged to Kill Prop. 14," *San Francisco Chronicle*, September 23, 1964.

47. *Catholic Voice*, December 6, 1963, in Box 1, Folder Fair Housing, June 1963—December 1963, BR.

48. "Reform Rabbis Appeal to State Realtors," *Los Angeles Times*, January 9, 1964.

49. "Statement Adopted by Protestant Clergy Against Proposition 14," October 8, 1964, Prop 14 Box 1, PB.

50. Lu Haas to Pat Brown, July 1, 1964, Prop 14 Box 2, Folder Housing Initiative—Background, PB.

51. Richard Kline, "Governor Brown's Faithful Advisor" in *The Governor's Office Under Edmund G. Brown, Sr.* Oral History Interview, Conducted 1977 by Eleanor Glaser, The Bancroft Library University of California/Berkeley, for the Governmental History Documentation Project, Goodwin Knight / Edmund Brown, Sr. Era, 19.

52. William Becker, "Working for Civil Rights: With Unions, the Legislature, and Governor Pat Brown" in *The Governor's Office Under Edmund G. Brown, Sr.* Oral History Interview, Conducted 1979 by Gabrielle Morris, The Bancroft Library University of California/Berkeley, for the Governmental History Documentation Project, Goodwin Knight / Edmund Brown, Sr. Era, 47.

53. "Report on CAP 14 Campaign Development," July 1964, Prop 14 Box 3, Folder Strategy Organization, PB.

54. Edward Howden, speech, October 1, 1963, Box 601, Folder FEPC-November, PB.

55. "Report on CAP 14 Campaign Development."

56. Jesse Unruh to California legislators, October 15, 1964, Box 1, Folder Fair Housing, April-December, 1964, BR.

57. Carmen Warschaw quoted in "Few Homeowners Affected by Rumford Act," *FEPC News*, August 1964, in Box 706, Folder Housing Discrimination, October, PB.

58. Milton Gordon, speech, November 22, 1963, Box 41, Folder 1 Segregation Initiative—Proposition 14, NAACP-WC (previous).

59. Thomas Lynch, radio statement, September 4, 1964, Prop 14 Box 1, Folder Radio Scripts, PB.

60. "Blueprint for the Anti-Initiative Campaign," January 27, 1964, Box 10, Folder CCFP, June 1963-January 1964, NAACP-WC (previous).

61. Jack McDonald to Lu Haas, July 6, 1964, Prop 14 Box 3, Folder Strategy Organization, PB.

62. Flyer, Prop 14 Box 2, Folder Press, PB.

63. Various fliers, in Box 40, Folder Prop 14 Test Case Contributions, 1964–65, NAACP-WC (previous); Various fliers, in Prop 14 Box 3, Folder Dirty File, PB.

64. Jewish Federation Council of Greater Los Angeles, pamphlet, Prop 14 Box 2, Folder File All Materials, PB.

65. JACL, advertisement, Prop 14 Box 3, Folder Dirty File, PB.

66. MAPA, pamphlet, Prop 14, Box 2, Folder Mexican American, PB.

67. Catholics Against Proposition 14, pamphlet, Prop 14 Box 3, Folder Churches, PB.

68. Howden, speech, October 1, 1963.

69. John Anson Ford to William Becker, December 4, 1963, Box 601, Folder FEPC, December, PB.

70. William Becker to Pat Brown, December 4, 1963, Box 601, Folder FEPC, December, PB.

71. William Becker, speech, August 19, 1964, Prop 14 Carton 3, Folder Labor, PB.

72. Pat Brown to John H. Tolan, Jr., November 15, 1963, Box 601, Folder Civil Rights, November, PB.

73. Pat Brown, speech to California Democratic Council Convention, February 22, 1964, Box 1082, Folder 6, PB.

74. Edmund G. Brown, Sr., "Years of Growth, 1939–1966; Law Enforcement, Politics, and the Governor's Office," an oral history conducted 1977–1981 by Malca Chall, Amelia R. Fry, Gabrielle Morris, and James Rowland, Regional Oral History Office, The Bancroft Library, University of California, Berkeley, 1982, 524–525.

75. Pat Brown, speech to National Council Episcopal Church Center, July 1, 1964, Box 706, Folder Housing Discrimination, July, PB.

76. Brown, speech to California Democratic Council Convention.

77. Brown, speech to National Council Episcopal Church Center; Pat Brown to William Norris, August 18, 1964, Box 708, Folder Prop 14, August 11–18, PB; Pat Brown quoted in "Brown Likens Rumford Act Foes to Nazis," *Los Angeles Times*, August 20, 1964.

78. "Inflammatory Talk on Prop. 14," *Los Angeles Times*, August 31, 1964.

79. "Brown Explains Fear Over Prop. 14 Passage," *Los Angeles Times*, September 5, 1964.

80. Lu Haas to Robert Nelson, September 2, 1964, Box 704, Folder Prop 14, October 22–30, PB.

81. Mrs. Stephen Brieger to Pat Brown, August 30, 1964, Box 707, Folder Prop 14, September 18–30, PB.

82. Jack Burby to Mrs. Stephen Brieger, September 22, 1964, Box 707, Folder Prop 14, September 18–30, PB.

83. Pat Brown, speech to Democratic Women's Forum, October 7, 1964, Prop 14 Box 3, Folder October 1–12, PB.

84. Thomas W. Casstevens, *Politics, Housing and Race Relations: California's Rumford Act and Proposition 14* (Berkeley: Institute of Governmental Studies, June 1967), 68–69.

85. Pat Brown to various clergy members, November 13, 1964, Box 707, Folder Prop 14, November 13–17, PB.

86. Lu Haas to Pat Brown, July 1, 1964, Prop 14 Box 2, Folder Housing Initiative—Background, PB.

87. Becker, 46–47. Similarly, political scientist Thomas Casstevens observed in 1967, "With the exception of the Jews, it is clear that a majority of the Caucasian membership of these organizations did not follow their leaders" (Casstevens, 74).

88. California State Committee Against Prop 14 of the JACL, minutes, Box 17, Folder Japanese Americans Against Prop 14, 1964 (2 of 2), JACL.

89. William Becker to Pat Brown, July 17, 1964, Brown, Prop 14 Box 3, Folder Mexican American, PB.

90. Casstevens, 74.

91. Haas, 135.

92. Pat Brown quoted in *Sacramento Bee*, November 10, 1964, in Box 707, Folder Prop 14, November 19–23, PB.

93. William Becker to Edwin J. Lukes, November 18, 1964, Box 707, Folder Prop 14, November 18, PB.

94. Brown, "Years of Growth, 1939–1966," 526.

95. Becker, 47.

96. John Evans Cudahy to Pat Brown, Box 706, Folder Housing Discrimination, May 1–15, PB; Robert Turner to Pat Brown, March 25, 1964, Box 706, Folder Housing Discrimination, March 25–31, PB; I.M. Woods to Brown, May 11, 1966, Box 848, Folder Proposition 14, May 31, Alpha S-Z, PB; Elerth Erickson to Pat Brown, September 15, 1964, Box 707, Folder Prop 14, September 18–30, PB.

97. Brown, speech to California Democratic Council Convention, February 22, 1964; Letter to Pat Brown, Box 707, Folder Prop 14, September 1–17, PB; James Compton to Pat Brown, September 1964, Box 707, Folder Prop 14, September 18–30, PB; Mrs. Stephen Brieger to Brown, August 30, 1964, Box 707, Folder Prop 14, September 18–30, PB; Mr. and Mrs. Quinton Torrance to Brown, May 27, 1964, Box 706, Folder Housing Discrimination, PB.

98. Mrs. Stephen Brieger to Pat Brown, August 30, 1964, Box 707, Folder Prop 14, September 18–30, PB.

99. For example, in the words of one Bay Area man, "Laws forbidding discrimination of all kinds in public accommodations, etc. are fair and just laws. I am for them 100%. But, when a law such as the Rumford Act is passed which interferes with my property rights to do as I wish with my private property, then I am against that kind of law 100%. . . . I will resist to the last breath the unsolicited efforts of the Legislature to encroach upon my property and private rights. I prefer to think it is still my right to buy, sell, or rent to anyone I choose whether he be white, brown, yellow, black; or whether he be Protestant, Catholic, or Jew" (Clifford Ferner to Pat Brown, February 6, 1964, Box 706, Folder Housing Discrimination, March 25–31, PB).

100. Jack McDonald to Lu Haas, July 6, 1964, Prop 14 Box 3, Folder Strategy Organization, PB.

101. Mark Tushnet, "The Significance of *Brown v. Board of Education*," *Virginia Law Review* 80 (February 1994): 181–182.

102. Robert Alan Goldberg, *Barry Goldwater* (New Haven: Yale University Press, 1995), 174.

103. Cecil Poole, "Executive Clemency and the Chessman Case," in *The Governor's Office Under Edmund G. Brown, Sr.* Oral History Interview, Conducted 1977 by Eleanor Glaser, The Bancroft Library University of California/Berkeley, for the Governmental History Documentation Project, Goodwin Knight / Edmund Brown, Sr., Era, 10.

104. Pat Brown quoted in *Sacramento Bee*, November 10, 1964, in Box 707, Folder Prop 14, November 19–23, PB.

105. Kenneth Bonnell to Pat Brown, September 4, 1964, Prop 14 Box 2, Folder Press, PB.

106. Edward Howden, "Proposition 14: Threat to Human Rights," speech, June 30, 1965, Box 36, Folder 5 FEP Correspondence, NAACP-WC (previous).

107. Jesse Unruh, draft of speech, circa November 1964, File 201, JU.

108. Matthew W. Dallek, *The Right Moment: Ronald Reagan's First Victory and the Decisive Turning Point in American Politics* (New York: Free Press, 2000), 128–149; Ethan Rarick, *California Rising: The Life and Times of Pat Brown* (Berkeley: University of California Press, 2005), 317–338.

109. Miller paraphrased in Howard Jewel to Stanley Mosk, May 29, 1964, Box 29, Folder 9, LM. Miller's warning echoed one that Jewel had given William Becker in April 1964, as he exhorted the Brown administration to improve the FEPC: "I do not mean to suggest that the implementation of a program along these lines will avoid violence. I think the historical forces now in motion augur for some violence no matter what is done. But without such a program the irresponsibles on each side will be encouraged and the possibilities for violence increased" (Howard Jewel to William Becker, April 13, 1964, Box 686, Folder FEPC, PB).

110. Loren Miller, "The Fire This Time," speech, November 19, 1965, Box 29, Folder 9.

111. Edward Howden, speech, November 12, 1965, Box 10, Folder Division of Fair Employment Practices, June 1965 - June 1968, NAACP-WC (previous).

112. Kline, oral history, 8.

113. Pat Brown, speech, September 26, 1964, Box 78, Folder Mexican-American Speeches, PB.

114. William Becker to Fred Ross, March 17, 1964, Box 706, Folder Housing Discrimination, March 17–24, PB.

115. William Becker to Anthony Rios, April 20, 1964, Box 706, Folder Housing Discrimination, April 15–30, PB.

116. "Annual Report," 1964, Box 25, NAACP-WC (previous); "Ruling Due on Initiative," *Los Angeles Herald*, January 13, 1964, in Box 52, Folder 4 Anti-fair housing initiative, 1963–64, NAACP-WC (previous).

117. Nathaniel Colley to C.L. Dellums, December 4, 1963, Box 38, Folder Initiative to Repeal AB 1240, folder 4, NAACP-WC (previous).

118. William Becker to Louis Garcia, May 18, 1964, Box 706, Folder Housing Discrimination, May 16–30, PB.

119. William Becker to Henry Rodriguez, June 24, 1964, Box 708, Folder Prop 14, July 3, PB; Ruben Salazar, "Latin-Negro Unity Move Launched," *Los Angeles Times*, July 5, 1964: B1.

120. William Becker to Pat Brown, July 17 1964, Prop 14 Box 3, Folder Mexican American, PB.

121. Jesus Chavarria and Richard Maullin, "Survey of Mexican American Attitudes Towards Proposition 14," August 19, 1964, in Prop 14 Box 2, Folder Mexican American Community, PB. According to historian Rodolfo F. Acuña, "[M]ost grassroots Mexican Americans knew little about the Rumford Act or Proposition 14. Many believed that it was a Black-white issue" (Rodolfo F. Acuña, *A Community Under Siege: A Chronicle of Chicanos East of the Los Angeles River, 1945–1975* [Los Angeles: Chicano Studies Research Center, 1984], 122). See also Rufus B. Browning, Dale Rogers Marshall, David H. Tabb, *Protest is Not Enough: The Struggle of Blacks and Hispanics for Equality in Urban Politics* (Berkeley: University of California Press, 1984), 37; Phil Ethington, "Segregated Diversity: Race-Ethnicity, Space, and Political Fragmentation in Los Angeles County, 1940–1994," Final Report to the John Randolph Haynes and Dora Haynes Foundation (2000), 41–42.

122. *FEPC Report, January 1, 1963-June 30, 1964* (Sacramento: California Office of State Printing, December 31, 1964), 49.

123. "FEPC Report," 1960, Box 601, Folder FEPC, September, PB.

124. "Mexican-Americans Told FEPC Is For Them, Too," *San Jose Mercury-News*, July 26, 1964, in Box 13, Folder 10, EG. Between July 1, 1963 and June 30, 1964, African Americans filed eighty percent of employment discrimination cases with the FEPC, while "Spanish surnam[ed]" people filed nine percent, Jews two percent, and Asians one percent (*FEPC Report, January 1, 1963-June 30, 1964*, 22).

125. *Californians of Spanish Surname* (San Francisco: Department of Industrial Relations, Division of Fair Employment Practices, May 1964); "Mexican-Americans Told FEPC Is For Them, Too."

126. Carlos Borja, Jr. to John Anson Ford, October 2, 1963, Box 3, Folder 5, EQ.

127. De Van L. Shumway, "FEPC Eyes Mexican-Americans," *San Jose Mercury-News*, August 30, 1964, in Box 13, Folder 10, EG.

128. Ted McHugh to Richard Kline, October 10, 1964, Prop 14 Box 2, Folder Housing Initiative—Background, PB.

129. Eduardo Quevedo to Julius Castelan, October 23, 1964, Box 3, Folder 9, EQ.

130. Brown, "Years of Growth," 531.

131. C.L. Dellums paraphrased in Howden, speech, November 12, 1965.

132. David O. Sears and John B. McConahay, *The Politics of Violence: The New Urban Blacks and the Watts Riot* (Boston: Houghton Mifflin), 164.

133. Carlos Borja Jr. quoted in Ruben Salazar, "Political Integration to be Hit at Meeting," *Los Angeles Times*, June 12, 1964: 28.

134. "Presentation of Mexican-American State Citizens Committee to the Fair Employment Practices Commission," transcript, November 10, 1964, Box 13, Folder 10, EG.

135. Biliana C.S. Ambrecht and Harry P. Pachon, "Ethnic Political Mobilization in a Mexican American Community: An Exploratory Study of East Los Angeles," *Western Political Quarterly* 27, no. 3 (1974): 513–514. This figure would rise to thirty-nine percent in 1972. Though they did not cite such polling data, Ernesto Galarza, Herman Gallegos, and Julian Samora nevertheless commented in 1969, "The historical conditions for

solidarity do not exist," as each group "apprise[s]" their "common lot from different angles, each rooted [their] particular historical experience" (Ernesto Galarza, Herman Gallegos, and Julian Samora, *Mexican-Americans in the Southwest* (Santa Barbara: McNally and Loftin), 64.

136. William Becker to Pat Brown, July 17, 1964, Prop 14 Box 3, Folder Mexican American, PB.

137. "Presentation of Mexican-American State Citizens Committee to the Fair Employment Practices Commission."

138. Minutes, December 7, 1964, Box 3, Folder 8, EQ.

139. News release, December 7, 1964, Box 14, Folder 11, EG.

140. Pat Brown, statement to United States Department of Labor Hearing in San Francisco, December 7, 1964, Box 11, Folder 10, AD.

141. Pat Brown, speech, November 9, 1963, Box 78, Folder Mexican-American speeches, PB.

142. "Perspectives on Department Administration," Interviews with John M. Pierce, Bert W. Levit, Albert B. Tieburg, John Wedemeyer, James Lowry, Albert B. Tieburg, California State Department of Employment, 1945–1966, An Interview Conducted by Gabrielle Morris in 1979, Governmental History Documentation Project, Goodwin Knight/Edmund Brown, Sr., Era, Regional Oral History Office, The Bancroft Library, University of California, Berkeley, 39.

143. William Turner, "No Dice for Braceros," *Ramparts* 4, no. 5 (1965): 26.

144. Louis Garcia quoted in Ruben Salazar, "Brown Crosses Picket Lines to Urge Mexican Farm Labor," *Los Angeles Times*, December 7, 1964: 1.

145. Ernesto Galarza to H.L. Mitchell, November 14, 1964, Reel 50, STFU.

146. Turner, "No Dice for Braceros," 17; "Annual Report," 1964, Box 25, NAACP-WC (Previous).

147. Anne Draper to George Ballis, April 8, 1965, Box 3, Folder 4, AD.

148. "Annual Report," 1964, Box 25, NAACP-WC (Previous).

149. Details of Mexican-American Unity Council Task Force meeting with Pat Brown on January 14, 1965 contained in minutes of MAPA's General Assembly Meeting, July 1965, Box 7, Folder 3, MR; Mexican-American Unity Council Task Force meeting with Pat Brown, minutes, January 14, 1965, Box 6, Folder 4, MR.

150. Resolutions from MAPA Executive Board Meeting, April 25, 1965, Box 3, Folder 11, EQ.

151. Edward Howden to Bert Corona, May 13, 1965, Box 7, Folder 11, MR.

152. "Second Ethnic Survey of Employment and Promotion in State Government," July 1965, Box 6, Folder 14, MR.

153. Pat Brown to Eduardo Quevedo, May 17, 1965, Box 3, Folder 10, EQ.

154. "Resolution on Farm Labor," MAPA Executive Board Meeting, April 25, 1965, Box 3, Folder 11, EQ.

155. Pat Brown, testimony to House Committee on Education and Labor, July 21, 1965, Box 6, Folder 5, MR.

156. Jacques E. Levy, *Cesar Chavez: Autobiography of La Causa* (New York: W.W. Norton and Company, Inc., 1975), 134.

157. Willard Wirtz to Pat Brown, March 7, 1965, Box 21, Folder 466, JL.

158. Willard Wirtz, press conference transcript, March 27, 1965, Box 22, Folder 467, JL.

159. "150 Grape Workers Start 25-Day March in California Strike," *New York Times*, March 18, 1966: 78.

160. National Farm Workers Association, letter, October 6, 1965, Box 21, Folder 451, JL.

161. "Statement of the Mexican American Political Association Regarding the Situation in the Delano Strike and Farm Worker Activities," November 27, 1965, Box 8, Folder 10, MR.

162. Phillip Soto to Pat Brown, November 15, 1965, Box 857, Folder Strikes, PB.

163. William Becker to Phillip Soto, January 28, 1966, Box 857, Folder Strikes, PB.

164. Pat Brown quoted in "Brown Says He May Visit Delano Strike Area," *Fresno Bee*, February 21, 1966: 4.

165. "150 Grape Workers Start 25-Day March in California Strike."

166. Pat Brown, statement, March 14, 1966, Box 77, Folder Governor's Statement, PB

167. Pat Brown to César Chávez, April 13, 1966, Box 19, Folder 404, JL.

168. William Becker to Pat Brown, July 30, 1965, Box 840, Folder Political—Ethnic Groups, PB.

169. Fred Dutton to Pat Brown, May 3, 1960, Box 5, Folder 3—Fred Dutton, HC.

170. Frederick G. Dutton, "Democratic Campaigns and Controversies, 1954–1966," an oral history conducted 1977–1978 by Amelia R. Fry, Regional Oral History Office, The Bancroft Library, University of California, Berkeley, 1981, 141.

171. Lawrence E. Davies, "Grape Strikers Score Gov. Brown as March Ends," *New York Times*, 11 April 1966.

172. William Bennett to Pat Brown, April 1, 1966, Box 857, Folder Strikes-April, PB.

173. "Grape Strike Ends in Sacramento," *Independent* (Pasadena, CA), April 11, 1966: 1.

174. William Becker to Pat Brown, May 19, 1966, Carton 9, Folder Nationality and Racial (Mexican), HC.

175. Richard Bergholz, "Politicians Seek Votes of Mexican-Americans," *Los Angeles Times*, June 23, 1966: 23.

176. Fred Jordan to Winslow Christian, June 20, 1966, Box 921, Folder Ethnic Groups, PB.

177. Reynoso to Winslow Christian, June 22, 1966, Box 921, Folder Ethnic Groups, PB.

178. "Politicians Seek Votes of Mexican-Americans."

179. *Eastside Journal*, June 30, 1966, in Box 4, Folder 2, EQ.

180. Pat Brown, speech to MAPA Statewide Endorsing Convention, June 25, 1966, Box 14, Folder 11, EG.

181. Eduardo Quevedo quoted in *Eastside Journal*, June 30, 1966, in Box 4, Folder 2, EQ.

182. Kenneth C. Burt, *The Search for a Civic Voice: California Latino Politics* (Claremont: Regina Books, 2007), 227.

183. William E. Roberts, "Professional Campaign Management and the Candidate," an oral history conducted 1979 by Sarah Sharp, in "Issues and Innovations in the 1966 Republican Gubernatorial Campaign," in Governmental History Documentation

Project, Goodwin Knight / Edmund Brown Sr., Era, Regional Oral History Office, The Bancroft Library, University of California, Berkeley, 1982, 21.

184. Burt, 231–232.

185. "Ya Basta: Mexican-American Democrats Support Reagan," Box C32, File RR Material (1/4), RR; Harry Shearer, "Brown vs. Reagan: Into the Stretch," *Los Angeles Times*, October 23, 1966.

186. "Reagan Announces He'll Name Two Legislative Liaison Aides," *Los Angeles Times*, November 23, 1966: 3.

187. Richard Bergholz, "Reagan Matches Forces With Brown on East L.A. Tour," *Los Angeles Times*, October 2, 1966.

188. Rowland Evans and Robert Novak, "The Fading Extremist Issue," *Post-Standard*, September 23, 1966: 4.

189. *Mulkey v. Reitman* 64 Cal. 2d 529 (1966).

190. Alfred Pearson to Pat Brown, May 17, 1966, Box 848, Folder Prop 14, May 31, Alpha K-R, PB.

191. Edward Knight to Pat Brown, Box 848, Folder Prop 14, May 31, Alpha K-R, PB.

192. J.H. Williams to Pat Brown, October 2, 1964, Box 706, Folder Housing Discrimination-October, PB.

193. Leo Lewis to Pat Brown, September 25, 1964, Box 707, Folder Prop 14, October 1–12, PB.

194. Estelle Scarbrough to Pat Brown, July 11, 1966, Box 848, Folder Housing Discrimination, PB.

195. Dortha Dunn to Pat Brown, June 17, 1966, Box 848, Folder Prop 14, June 14–30, PB.

196. Ronald Reagan, speech, March 1966, Box C30, Speeches and Statements, Book II, 332–333, RR.

197. Ronald Reagan to Rev. Leland P. Stewart, August 1966, Box C32, File 66 Campaign: RR (3/4), RR.

198. "Majority Favor Testing Constitutionality of Proposition 14 in Higher Court; Oppose Rumford Act," June 28, 1966, Box C32, Folder Campaign Polls (2/3), RR.

199. Tushnet, 181–182.

200. Tony Freyer, *Hugo L. Black and the Dilemma of American Liberalism*, Library of American Biography, ed. Oscar Handlin (Glenview, IL: Scott, Foresman / Little, Brown Higher Education, 1990), 147–148. On this point, see also Howard Ball and Phillip Cooper, *Of Power and Right: Hugo Black, William O. Douglas, and America's Constitutional Revolution* (New York: Oxford University Press, 1992), 167–168.

201. Mrs. George Gluyas to Pat Brown, March 30, 1964, Box 706, Folder Housing Discrimination, March 25–31, PB.

202. Jesse Unruh quoted in James R. Mills, *A Disorderly House: The Brown-Unruh Years in Sacramento* (Berkeley: Heyday Books, 1987), 195.

203. William Becker, draft of speech, August 12, 1966, Box 921, Folder Ethnic Groups Folder, PB.

204. Totton J. Anderson and Eugene C. Lee, "The 1966 Election in California," *Western Political Quarterly* 20, no. 2 (1967): 535–554.

205. Edward Howden, memo, November 2, 1966, Box 10, Folder FEPC, 1957–1966, NAACP-WC (previous).

206. Historian Lisa McGirr, for example, describes the election of 1966 in California "presesag[ing] the rise of a majoritarian conservatism on the national scene" (Lisa McGirr, *Suburban Warriors: The Origins of the New American Right* [Princeton: Princeton University Press], 210). Similarly, Matt Dallek describes it as "*the* [emphasis mine] decisive turning point in America politics." When Brown was defeated so, too, was "the philosophy that he had clung to throughout his adult life" (Dallek, 239–240).

207. Brown, "Years of Growth," 525.

208. John F. Burby, Oral History Interview, Conducted 1987 by Carlos Vasquez, UCLA Oral History Program, for the California State Archives State Governmental Oral History Program.

209. Becker, 57.

210. Haas, "Oral History Interview," 72. On this point, see also Donald L. Bradley, "Managing Democratic Campaigns, 1943–1946," an oral history conducted 1977–1979 by Amelia R. Fry, Regional Oral History Office, The Bancroft Library, University of California, Berkeley, 1982, 157, 175.

211. Richard A. Santillan and Frederico A. Subervi-Vélez, "Latino Participation in Republican Party Politics in California," in *Racial and Ethnic Politics in California*, ed. Bryan O. Jackson and Michael B. Preston (Berkeley: IGS Press, 1994), 294.

212. Roberts, 21.

213. Lou Cannon, *Governor Reagan: His Rise to Power* (New York: Public Affairs, 2003), 160.

214. Dutton, 141.

Chapter 8

1. Virna Canson, "Legislative Newsletter," March 9, 1967, Carton 107, Folder 20, NAACP-WC.

2. CCFP, newsletter, December 29, 1966, Carton 10, Folder CCFP, Apr 1966 – May 1967, NAACP-WC.

3. CCFP, newsletter, March 24, 1967, RFHAF.

4. Letter from Jack Ortega, 1967, Box 14, Folder 10, EG.

5. Vilma Martinez, speech, November 8, 1974, Box 24, Folder 10, MALDEF. In addition, she viewed bilingual education as MALDEF's "central theme" and "noted that many other Chicano organizations . . . have found a similar theme."

6. Ronald Reagan, press conference transcript, April 18, 1967, Box 31, Press Unit, Speeches and Press Conferences, RR-H.

7. *Reitman v. Mulkey*, 387 U.S. 369 (1967). On the Fair Housing Act of 1968, see Stephen Grant Meyer, *As Long as They Don't Move Next Door: Segregation and Racial Conflict in American Neighborhoods* (Lanham: Rowman & Littlefield, 2000), 197–211. Meyer notes that the this "first federal fair-housing law . . . covered nearly 80 percent of dwellings in the United States" (209).

8. "Legislative Report," 1969, Box 41, Folder West Coast Region Legislative Report, 1969, NAACP-WC (previous).

9. Leonard Carter to Virna Canson, June 8, 1971, Box 9, Folder Canson, Virna, June 1971, NAACP-WC (previous).

10. Alan Exelrod, "Chicano Education: In *Swann's* Way," *Inequality in Education*, 9 (1971): 30.

11. "Desegregation and Education Concerns of the Hispanic Community, Conference Report, June 26–28, 1977" (Washington, D.C.: The National Institute of Education, October, 1977), 52.

12. Alan Short to Ronald Reagan, May 18, 1967, Senate Bill 53, Chapter 280, MF3:2(51), GCBF.

13. Max Rafferty to Lynn Nofziger, November 30, 1966, Box 15 (Research Unit), Folder Rafferty-Personalities, RR-H.

14. Gladwin Hill, "Mexicans' Plight Decried on Coast," *New York Times*, August 11, 1963: 61.

15. Ruben Salazar, "Problems of Latins Seen Thing Apart: New Policy for U.S. Spanish-speaking Students Urged," *Los Angeles Times*, September 16, 1963.

16. Carolos Borja, Jr., speech, May 2, 1964, Box 3, Folder 8, EQ.

17. "Presentation of Mexican-American State Citizens Committee to the Fair Employment Practices Commission," transcript, November 10, 1964, Box 13, Folder 10, EG.

18. Phillip Soto to Franklin D. Roosevelt, Jr., May 4, 1967, Box 847, Folder Ethnic Group, May, PB.

19. George Sánchez to Pete Tijerina, February 28, 1967, Box 25, Folder 1, GS.

20. William E. Roberts, "Professional Campaign Management and the Candidate," an oral history conducted 1979 by Sarah Sharp, in "Issues and Innovations in the 1966 Republican Gubernatorial Campaign," in Governmental History Documentation Project, Goodwin Knight / Edmund Brown Sr., Era, Regional Oral History Office, The Bancroft Library, University of California, Berkeley, 1982, 21.

21. Alan Short to Ronald Reagan, May 18, 1967, Senate Bill 53, Chapter 280, MF3:2(51), GCBF.

22. Mexican-American Legislative Conference, announcement, March 1967, Box 8, Folder 4, MR.

23. "Report of the First Annual Nuevas Vista Conference," April 1967, Box 1, Folder 6, MR.

24. News release, May 24, 1967, GO 155, Research File – Education – Bilingual, RR.

25. "Overdue Action on Bilingual Teaching," *Los Angeles Times*, August 16, 1967: A4.

26. "Bilingual Teaching At Last," *Independent Press-Telegram*, June 11, 1967: B2.

27. Ronald Reagan, speech, April 24, 1969, Box P17, File Governor Ronald Reagan, 1967, RR.

28. For more on Nixon's overtures to Latinos through bilingual education, see John David Skrentny, *Minority Rights Revolution* (Cambridge: Harvard University Press, 2002), Chapter 7. For example, Skrentny writes, "Promotion of bilingual education became a favorite strategy to appeal to Latinos in the 1972 election" (211). Similarly, see Gareth Davies, *See Government Grow: Education Politics from Johnson to Reagan* (Lawrence: University of Kansas Press, 2007), 143–147.

29. Richard A. Santillan and Frederico A. Subervi-Vélez, "Latino Participation in Republican Party Politics in California," in *Racial and Ethnic Politics in California*, ed. Bryan O. Jackson and Michael B. Preston (Berkeley: IGS Press, 1994), 293.

30. Kevin P. Phillips, *The Emerging Republican Majority* (New Rochelle, NY: Arlington House, 1969).

31. This latter point will be taken up later in the chapter.

32. Fundraising letter, January 7, 1969, Box 8, Folder Canson, Virna, January 1–14, NAACP-WC (previous).

33. "Legislative Report," 1969.

34. "Annual Report," 1952, Box 25, NAACP-WC (previous).

35. "Freedom's Frontier," 1954, Carton 103, Folder 18, NAACP-WC.

36. "Racial and Ethnic Survey of California Public Schools," 1966, Carton 8, Folder School Deseregation, WB.

37. Wilson Riles, report, November 15, 1969, Box 51 (Research Unit), Folder Education-Busing, 70, RR-H.

38. Max Rafferty to California State Board of Education, February 13, 1969, Box GO 74, Folder Busing – General, 1970 (1/3), RR.

39. "Fixing Imbalance," *Los Angeles Times*, February 16, 1969.

40. "Desegregation of Our Schools," *Los Angeles Times*, February 19, 1969: Part II, 8.

41. On the former, see *Briggs v. Elliot* 132 F. Supp. 776 (1955): "The Constitution . . . does not require integration . . . It merely forbids the use of governmental power to enforce segregation." On the latter, see *United States v. Jefferson County Board of Education* 372 F. 2d 836 (1966): "The only adequate redress for a previously overt system-wide policy of segregation directed against Negroes as a collective is a system-wide policy of integration."

42. *Green v. County School Board of New Kent County, Virginia* 391 U.S. 430 (1968).

43. Alexander M. Bickel, "'Realistic, Sensible' (II)," *New Republic*, August 4 and 11, 1970: 15.

44. *Crawford v. Board of Education of the City of Los Angeles*, "Minute Order of Court's Intended Findings of Fact, Conclusions of Law, Judgment, and for Preemptory Writ of Mandate," February 11, 1970, Box GO 127, RR-H.

45. "L.A. Schools Given Integration Order," *Los Angeles Times*, February 12, 1970.

46. Martin Smith, "New Racial Backlash," *Sacramento Bee*, March 7, 1970.

47. "Press Release #101," February 17, 1970, Box GO 74, Folder Busing – General, 1970 (2/3), RR.

48. "Press Release #441," September 14, 1970, Box 14 (Press Unit), Folder Press Releases, September 1970, RR-H.

49. Leonard Carter, news release, September 15, 1970, Carton 50, Folder 51, NAACP-WC.

50. Nathaniel Colley, speech, March 21, 1966, Box 17, Folder March-May 1966, NAACP-WC (previous).

51. Ronald Reagan, letter, March 3, 1970, Box GO 74, Folder Busing – General, 1970 (2/3), RR.

52. Virna Canson, March 12, 1970, Box 26, Folder Legislative Advocate-Field Director (Virna Canson), Monthly Report, 1970–1971, NAACP-WC (previous).

53. Jan Stevens, Deputy Attorney General, to Ronald Reagan, August 19, 1970, Assembly Bill No. 551, Chapter 1039, MF3:3(2), GCBF.

54. Ronald Reagan, press conference transcript, February 17, 1970, Box GO 155, File Research File – Education – Busing, RR.

55. "Press Release #441."

56. See previous discussion of "Southwest strategy."

57. As Gary Orfield writes, "The Nixon administration decided to enforce bilingual education rights, not desegregation" (Gary Orfield, "Schools More Separate: Consequences of a Decade of Resegregation," *Rethinking Schools*, 16, no. 1 [2001]). This subject will be addressed later in the chapter.

58. Virna Canson to Frank Connor, April 17, 1970, Carton 50, Folder 48, NAACP-WC; Virna Canson to Earl Raines, March 27, 1970, Carton 50, Folder 48, NAACP-WC.

59. Nathaniel Colley, speech, May 13, 1970, Carton 50, NAACP-WC.

60. Mervyn Dymally, press release, February 12, 1970, Box 51 (Research Unit), Folder Education-Busing 70, RR-H.

61. Virna Canson to Roy Wilkins, September 28, 1970, Carton 50, Folder 51, NAACP-WC.

62. Call to Conscience Caucus, minutes, May 13, 1970, Carton 50, NAACP-WC.

63. "MALDEF Newsletter," March 1, 1971, Box 118, Folder 3, MALDEF; "MALDEF Newlsetter," March 1973, Box 118, Folder 4, MALDEF; "Alioto Asks Parents To Sue on Busing," *San Francisco Chronicle*, June 4, 1970.

64. "Demand for Immediate Measures," *San Francisco Chronicle*, June 25, 1970; "Jenkins is 'Sorry' NAACP Filed Suit," *San Francisco Chronicle*, June 25, 1970; "San Francisco NAACP Elects New President," January 26, 1970, in Carton 93, Folder 11, NAACP-WC

65. "Why This Lawsuit," San Francisco NAACP, June 24, 1970, Carton 93, Folder 16, NAACP-WC.

66. "Civil Rights Action For Injunctive Relief," June 24, 1970, Box 657, Folder 6, MALDEF.

67. Ron Moskowitz, "Judge Will Act on S.F. Schools," *San Francisco Chronicle*, April 21, 1970.

68. Leonard Carter, statement, June 7, 1971, Carton 93, Folder 16, NAACP-WC.

69. Robert Gonzales, news release, June 24, 1971, Box 657, Folder 5, MALDEF.

70. Robert Gonzales, statement, July 21, 1971, Box 657, Folder 5, MALDEF.

71. La Raza Caucus, "Position Paper on the April 28, 1971 Order for Integration of the San Francisco Public Schools," June 16, 1971, Box 657, Folder 6, MALDEF.

72. Jim Wood, "Frantic Rush to Integrate S.F. Schools," *San Francisco Chronicle*, May 30, 1971.

73. "Chinatown parents fight school integration plans," *East/West: The Chinese-American Journal*, June 9, 1971.

74. Mario Obledo to Vine Deloria, September 21, 1971, Box 102, Folder 3, MALDEF.

75. "Civil Rights Action For Injunctive Relief (Complaint of Plaintiffs in Intervention)," June 18, 1971, Box 657, Folder 7, MALDEF.

76. "Memorandum of Points and Authorities in Support of Motion to Intervene as Plaintiffs," June 18, 1971, Box 657, Folder 7, MALDEF.

77. Exelrod, 30.

78. "Chinatown Balks at School Busing," *Wall Street Journal*, September 3, 1971.

79. "Memorandum of Points and Authorities in Support of Motion to Intervene as Plaintiffs."

80. *Johnson v. San Francisco Unified School District*, 339 F. Supp. 1315, 1319 (1971). This was reflected in Judge Weigel's definition of racial balance. Drawing on the State Commission on Equal Opportunity's fifteen percent guideline, racial balance meant that the proportion of a group's representation in any given school must not be more or less than fifteen percent of that group's proportion in the school system as a whole. For example, since 28.7 percent of the children in San Francisco's elementary school were black, racial balance at any given school required a black student body of no less than 13.7 percent and no more than 43.7 percent (1331). According to SFUSD figures, the racial and ethnic school composition in 1970–1 was as follows: 35.1 percent white, 28.1 percent African American, 14.8 percent Chinese, 13.6 percent Latino, 4.1 percent Filipino, 1.9 percent other nonwhite, 1.8 percent Japanese, 0.3 percent Korean, and 0.3 percent American Indian (http://www.sfusd.k12.ca.us/Intro/enrlstat.html).

81. *Guey Heung Lee v. Johnson*, 404 U.S. 1215, 1216–1217 (1971).

82. "S.F. Busing to Start Today," *San Francisco Chronicle*, September 13, 1971.

83. *Johnson v. San Francisco Unified School District*, 339 F. Supp. 1315, 1323 (1971)

84. The 25,000 elementary students assigned to new schools requiring busing represented over fifty percent of the expected enrollment in San Francisco Unified School District's elementary schools. Over the summer of 1971, the total elementary school population dropped sixteen percent from approximately 48,000 to approximately 42,000. At the same time, the percentage of white students fell from 34.5 to 30.1, thus undermining SFUSD's quest for racial balance even before the desegregation plan could be put into effect (Doris R. Fine, *When Leadership Fails: Desegregation and Demoralization in the San Francisco Schools* [New Brunswick: Transaction Books], 75).

85. "S.F. Busing to Start Today."

86. "School Scene Smoky Citywide Boycott Set," *East-West: The Chinese American Journal*, September 8, 1971.

87. "Chinese Schools Set to Open," *San Francisco Chronicle*, September 14, 1971.

88. "S.F. School Boycott Statistics," *San Francisco Chronicle*, October 5, 1971.

89. Those four Chinatown schools formed one school system called Telesis, which had been organized in August. Two other school systems containing three schools operated outside of Chinatown with two schools located in Nob Hill and one in North Beach. Ultimately, all three school systems united under one ruling board, primarily for financial reasons. That board, the San Francisco Chinese for Quality Education Committee, included the presidents of the Chinese Chamber of Commerce, the Chinese Six Companies, the Chinese American Citizen's Alliance as well as three representatives from the San Francisco Chinese Parents Committee. Under the new board, the Freedom Schools reported an $18,000 reserve fund on December 1, 1971 (Philip A. Lum, "The Creation and Demise of San Francisco Chinatown Freedom Schools: One

Response to Desegregation," *Amerasia* 5, no. 1 [1978], 64). Within the schools, students attended classes in separate two-and-a-half hour morning and afternoon blocks. The language of instruction was English and the subjects mirrored those of the public school. As James Wong of Chinese Parents for Quality Education explained, children were taught "the basic subjects for a quality education" ("Chinatown 'Freedom School,'" *San Francisco Chronicle*, September 21, 1971).

90. James Wong quoted in "Chinatown 'Freedom School,'" *San Francisco Chronicle*, September 21, 1971.

91. Lum, 62.

92. Nathan Glazer, "Is Busing Necessary," *Commentary* (March 1972): 45.

93. Manuel Ruiz, Jr., news release, April 12, 1970, Box 18, Folder 2, MR.

94. David Sanchez paraphrased in "Board Thwarts Shaheen Plan," *East/West*, April 12, 1972.

95. *Keyes v. School District No.1*, 413 U.S. 189 (1973).

96. *Johnson v. San Francisco Unified School District*, 500 F.2d 349, 351–352 (1974). For more on *Keyes*, the litigation of which included a desegregation / bilingual education conflict similar to *Johnson*, albeit on behalf of Mexican American rather than Chinese American students, see Tom I. Romero, II, "Our Selma is Here: The Political and Legal Struggle for Educational Equality in Denver, Colorado and Multiracial Conundrums in American Jurisprudence," *Seattle Journal of Social Justice* 3 (Fall/Winter 2004): 73–123. As Romero writes, the United States Supreme Court in *Keyes* struggled to reconcile "the unique needs and concerns of Mexican Americans students" for bilingual education in Denver's public schools, on the one hand, with the NAACP's demand for desegregation, on the other hand. Similarly, see Rachel F. Moran, "Courts and the Construction of Racial and Ethnic Identity: Public Law Litigation in Denver Schools," ed. Lawrence M. Friedman and Harry Scheiber, *Legal Culture and the Legal Profession* (Boulder: Westview Press, 1996), 153–179. According to Moran, "Latinos believed that African Americans dominated the *Keyes* case in part because their claims derived from well-established precedents based on the African-American experience with de jure segregation. This bipolar paradigm derived from relations between African Americans and whites did not usefully address many facets of the Latino experience" (165).

97. Fine, 91. In December 1973, the school board reported that thirty-six of the city's ninety-seven elementary schools were still racially imbalanced ("Secondary Schools Racially Unbalanced," *East-West: The Chinese-American Journal*, December 12, 1973).

98. In 1978, the NAACP filed another desegregation suit against SFUSD. Five years later, the parties in the suit reached a consent decree. That decree divided the city's student body into nine racial and ethnic groups (Chinese, Latino, African-American, Other White, Other Nonwhite, Filipino, Korean, Japanese, American Indian). Moreover, it stipulated that to be integrated a school must have students from four of the nine groups represented with no more than forty or forty-five percent (depending upon the type of school) from any one particular group (*San Francisco NAACP v. San Francisco Unified School District* 576 F. Supp. 34 [1983]).

99. Ling-Chi Wang quoted in "Galileo's Crisis Sets Off Row at School Meet," *East-West: The Chinese-American Journal*, March 5, 1969.

100. "A Time Bomb at Marina," *East-West: The Chinese American Journal*, February 18, 1970.

101. Ed Steinman, interview by Mark Brilliant, June 29, 1999.

102. "Civil Rights Action for Injunctive Relief," June 24, 1970, Box 657, Folder 7, MALDEF.

103. "Complaint for Injunction and Declaratory Relief," March 23, 1970, Box 730, Folder 1, MALDEF.

104. Interview with Ed Steinman; *Lau v. Nichols* (United States District Court for the Northern District of California, May 26, 1970).

105. Interview with Ed Steinman.

106. Peter Chacon to Alan Cranston, October 14, 1971, Box 1, Folder September-October, 1971, PC.

107. Bilingual-Bicultural Task Force, report, September 21, 1971, File 3274, BBTF.

108. Peter Chacon to Alan Cranston, October 14, 1971, Box 1, Folder September-October, 1971, PC; Peter Chacon to Tony Gallegos, October 28, 1971, Box 1, Folder September-October, 1971, PC.

109. Ronald Reagan, Press Release #665, December 20, 1972, Box GO 155, Research File - Education – Bilingual, RR.

110. Peter Chacon to Gil Martinez, February 8, 1973, Box 1, Folder January-February 1973, PC.

111. "Enrolled Bill Memorandum to Governor: AB 2284," December 12, 1972, Assembly Bill 2284, Chapter 1258, MF3:3(14), GCBF.

112. Proposition 21: Assignment of Students to Schools (1972). Available online through: http://library.uchastings.edu/library/california-research/ca-ballot-measures.html#ballotprops; Mervyn Dymally, press release, September 15, 1972, Box 99 (Research Unit), Folder November Propositions 11–72, RR-H.

113. *Santa Barbara School District v. Superior Court of Santa Barbara County*, 13 Cal.3d 315 (1975).

114. *Lau v. Nichols*, 483 F.2d 791 (1973).

115. Interview with Ed Steinman.

116. "Brief for the Petitioners in the Supreme Court of the United States," July 25, 1973, Box 728, Folder 4, MALDEF.

117. "Brief of Amici Curiae Chinese Consolidated Benevolent Association, Chinese American Citizens Alliance, Chinese Chamber of Commerce, et al.," July 26, 1973, *U.S. Supreme Court Records and Briefs, 1832–1978*, Gale, Cengage Learning.

118. Sanford Rosen to Alan Exelrod, April 10, 1973, Box 1173, Folder 6, MALDEF.

119. Interview with Ed Steinman.

120. Edward Steinman, "Attorney Representing Kinney Kinmon Lau," in *Revisiting The Lau Decision: 20 Years After – Symposium Proceedings*, November 3–4, 1994 (Oakland: ARC Associates, 1996), 16.

121. "Brief of the Amici Curiae Mexican American Legal Defense and Educational Fund, American G.I. Forum, League of United Latin American Citizens, Association of Mexican American Educators," August 2, 1973, Box 729, Folder 9, MALDEF.

122. "MALDEF Newsletter," May 1970, Box 118, Folder 2, MALDEF. On this point, see also Davies, 146: "Nixon sought to demonstrate his awareness that 'minority' was not synonymous with 'black.'" He was also determined "to address the distinctive problems of Spanish-speaking Americans" with something other than what one campaign strategist called "'warmed over black programs.'"

123. "Memorandum for the United States as Amicus Curiae, October 1973," October 10, 1973, *U.S. Supreme Court Records and Briefs, 1832–1978*, Gale, Cengage Learning. For more on the Nixon administration's role in *Lau*, see Davies, 143–160 and Skrentny, 223.

124. "Brief of Respondents in the Supreme Court of the United States," October 6, 1973, Box 729, Folder 10, MALDEF.

125. For example, Gilbert Martinez, chair of the California's Bilingual-Bicultural Task Force, described *Lau* as the "decision of the century" (Gilbert Martinez to William E. Webster, May 20, 1974, File 3279, BBTF).

126. *Lau v. Nichols*, 414 U.S. 563 (1974).

127. MALDEF meeting agenda, February 21, 1975, Box 104, Folder 14, MALDEF.

128. Tom Wolfe, "Bok Gooi, Hok Gooi and T'ang Jen: or, Why There Is No National Association for the Advancement of Chinese Americans," *New York Magazine*, September 27, 1971: 35.

129. Ling-Chi Wang, "Community Leader for the *Lau* Lawsuit," in *Revisiting The Lau Decision: 20 Years After—Symposium Proceedings*, November 3–4, 1994 (Oakland: ARC Associates, 1996), 14.

130. Matthew Frye Jacobson, *Whiteness of a Different Color: European Immigrants and the Alchemy of Race* (Cambridge: Harvard University Press, 1998), 201.

131. For a similar claim with respect to Latino students, see Raul Yzaguirre of National Council of La Raza to John Buggs of the United States Commission on Civil Rights: "We support our black brothers who define equal educational opportunity in terms of desegregation and we would call for a more lucid analysis of just what that means. This does not necessarily mean that we define equal educational opportunity in the same terms" (Raul Yzaguirre to John Buggs, April 22, 1976, Box 6, Folder 15, MR).

132. Steinman, 16.

133. Interview with Ed Steinman.

134. "Motion for Order Granting Leave to File Amicus," July 8, 1971, Box 657, Folder 7, MALDEF.

135. William Josephson to Mario Obledo, September 15, 1971, Box 5, Folder 2, MALDEF.

136. Vilma Martinez, speech, circa 1975, Box 9, Folder 2, MALDEF.

137. Vilma Martinez, speech, November 8, 1974, Box 24, Folder 10, MALDEF.

138. Carlos M. Alcala, "The Legal Significance of Lau v. Nichols," March 1, 1974, Box 729, Folder 5, MALDEF.

139. "Desegregation and Education Concerns of the Hispanic Community," Conference Report, June 26–28, 1977 (Washington, D.C.: The National Institute of Education, October, 1977), 30.

140. "Desegregation and Education Concerns of the Hispanic Community," 52.

141. Charles Belle quoted in "Chinatown Balks at School Busing," *Wall Street Journal*, September 3, 1971.

142. Virna Canson to Nathaniel Colley, 1976, Box 21, Folder Colley, Nathaniel 1976, NAACP-WC (previous).

143. This tension has endured. See, for example, Edward W. Lew, "Bilingual Education and Resegregation: Reconciling the Apparent Paradox Between Bilingual Education Programs and Desegregation Goals," *UCLA Asian Pacific Law Journal* 7 (Spring 2001), 88–104; Christina M. Rodriguez, "Accommodating Linguistic Difference: Toward a Comprehensive Theory of Language Rights in the United States," *Harvard Civil Rights-Civil Liberties Law Review* 36 (Winter 2001): 133–223. As Rodriguez writes, "Desegregation has repeatedly frustrated efforts to advance bilingual education curricula. The provision of funds for bilingual instruction depends on the existence of a critical mass of non-English speakers and is undermined by the drive to avoid the isolation of racial and ethnic groups" (165–166).

144. Glazer, 45.

Conclusion

1. Carey McWilliams, *Brothers Under the Skin* (Boston: Little, Brown, 1943), 49.

2. *Regents of the University of California v. Bakke*, 438 U.S. 265 (1978).

3. *Regents of the University of California v. Bakke*, 438 U.S. 265, 400, 401 (1978).

4. *Regents of the University of California v. Bakke*, 438 U.S. 265, 274 (1978).

5. Carey McWilliams, "Spectrum of Segregation," *Survey Graphic* 36, no. 1 (1947): 22.

6. On McWilliams and Myrdal, see the Introduction.

7. *Regents of the University of California v. Bakke*, 438 U.S. 265, 297, 295, 309 footnote 45, 295–297, 307, 311, 313, 314 (1978).

8. John D. Skrentny, *The Minority Rights Revolution* (Cambridge: Harvard University Press, 2002), 142.

9. Skrentny, Chapter 4. Elsewhere, Skrentny notes how universities "copied the federal official minorities or took for granted that the same groups were minorities" when it came to developing affirmative action in admissions (165).

10. Evelyn Hu-DeHart, "Ethnic Studies in U.S. Higher Education: History, Development, Goals," in *Handbook of Research on Multicultural Education*, ed. James Banks and Cherry A. McGee Banks (San Francisco: Jossey-Bass, 2004), 870.

11. Michael Omi and Howard Winant, *Racial Formation in the United States: From the 1960s to the 1990s* (New York: Routledge, 1994), 49–50; Ronald Takaki, *A Different Mirror: A History of Multicultural America* (Boston: Little, Brown, and Company, 1993), 4, 10, 6. Elsewhere, Takaki distinguished between "'ethnic' and 'racial' experiences" with the latter being limited to non-whites. He explained, "only blacks were enslaved, only Native Americans were removed to reservations, only Chinese were singled out for exclusion, and only Japanese Americans (not Italian Americans or German Americans) were placed in concentration camps" (Ronald Takaki, ed., *From Different Shores: Perspectives on Race and Ethnicity in America* [New York: Oxford University Press, 1987], 7).

12. McWilliams, *Brothers Under the Skin*, 10.

13. Of course, distinguishing between a singular color line and multiple color lines does not deny the profound differences in the racialized experiences of whites and non-whites in United States history. After all, whites did not suffer slavery, de jure segregation, immigration exclusion, ineligibility to naturalized citizenship, or, in the case of Native Americans, near annihilation. That said, the reality of a singular white/non-white color line at one level need not preclude and ought not obscure the presence of multiple color lines at other levels. Just as conceptualizing race in white/black terms is reductive, so, too, is re-conceptualizing it in more inclusive, but no less dualistic, white/non-white terms, as the history recounted in these pages reveals.

14. Mark Brilliant, "'Intellectual Affirmative Action: How Multiculturalism Became Mandatory and Mainstream in College Curricula," in *Living in the Eighties*, ed. Vincent Cannato and Gil Troy (New York: Oxford University Press, 2009), 98–124.

15. Executive Order 13050, June 13, 1997, in *One America in the 21ˢᵗ Century: Forging a New Future, The President's Initiative on Race, The Advisory Board's Report to the President* (September 1998).

16. "Initiative Announcement: The President's Initiative on Race," June 14, 1997, http://clinton2.nara.gov/Initiatives/OneAmerica/speech.html.

17. *One America in the 21ˢᵗ Century*, 33; Frank Wu, "Not Just Black and White," *Asian Week*, February 5, 1998. See also, Frank H. Wu, "New Paradigms of Civil Rights: A Review Essay," *George Washington Law Review* 66 (March 1998): 699–700; William Powers, "Oh My!" *New Republic*, August 18, 1997: 9; Peter Baker, "A Splinter on the Race Advisory Board," *Washington Post*, July 15, 1997: A4.

18. "What Happened to the National Race Dialogue? An Interview with Angela Oh," *ColorLines*, Spring 1999.

19. *One America in the 21ˢᵗ Century*, 43; *Changing America*, iii, 3.

20. *Changing America*, 35, 65, 20, 22, 32, 53, 47, 36, 37; *One America in the 21ˢᵗ Century*, 113–114.

21. *One America in the 21ˢᵗ Century*, 51; *Changing America*, 10.

22. *One America in the 21ˢᵗ Century*, 77; *Changing America*, 43, 47, 53, 48.

23. *One America in the 21ˢᵗ Century*, 76–77.

24. *Changing America*, 26 (no data provided for Asian Americans).

25. *Changing America*, 28–29 (no data provided for Asian Americans).

26. Edward J.W. Park and John S.W. Park, "A New American Dilemma? Asian Americans and Latinos in Race Theorizing," *Journal of Asian American Studies* 2, no. 3 (1999): 289–309.

27. Manning Marable, "The Problematics of Ethnic Studies," *Black Renaissance/ Renaissance Noire* 3, no. 1 (2000). Historian David Hollinger offers a similar assessment in his critique of what he calls the "one-hate rule" reflected in the Clinton "Initiative on Race"—the "habit of taking the African-American case as a model for understanding and responding to injustices done to other ethnoracially defined minorities." He adds, "publicly accepted 'race talk' in the United States at the turn of the twenty-first century"

posits "that any differences between the particular varieties of 'racial' discrimination and abuse are incidental to what those varieties have in common, and the assumption that the same set of policies can deal with virtually all those varieties of disadvantage" (David Hollinger, "The One Drop Rule and the One Hate Rule," *Daedalus* 134, no. 1 [2005]: 18–28).

28. Claire Jean Kim, "Imagining Race and Nation in Multiculturalist America," *Ethnic and Racial Studies* 27, no. 6 (2004): 339–346.

29. Jennifer Lee and Frank D. Bean, "America's Changing Color Lines: Immigration, Race/Ethnicity, and Multiracial Identity," *Annual Review of Sociology* 30 (2004): 221–242.

30. Kevin R. Johnson, "The End of 'Civil Rights' as We Know It? Immigration and Civil Rights in the New Millennium," *UCLA Law Review* 49 (June 2002): 1482–1511.

31. See, for example, Bill Ong Hing, "Asians Without Blacks and Latinos in San Francisco: Missed Lessons of the Common Good," *Amerasia Journal* 27, no. 2 (2001): 19–27.

32. See, for example, Pew Hispanic Center, *No Consensus on Immigration Problems or Proposed Fixes: America's Immigration Quandary* (March 30, 2006), which reports that 56 percent of black Democrats (and 53 percent of white Democrats) view immigrants as a "burden on the country." The figure for Hispanic Democrats was 36 percent, and no figure was given for Asian Americans (7). The same study reports that 54 percent of blacks (and 55 percent of whites) versus 29 percent of Hispanics say immigrants today "are a burden because they take jobs, housing and health care." Conversely, 38 percent of blacks and whites versus 64 percent of Hispanics say immigrants today "strengthen our country with their hard work and talents" (15).

33. Mike Davis, "In L.A., Burning All Illusions," *Nation*, June 1, 1992. See also Peter Kwong, "The First Multicultural Riots," in *Inside the L.A. Riots*, ed. Don Hazen (New York: Institute for Alternative Journalism, 1992), 88–92.

34. *Newsweek* quoted in Ronald T. Takaki, *Violence in the Black Imagination* (New York: Oxford University Press, 1993), 5.

35. Bernard Weintraub, "Condensing a Riot's Cacophony into the Voice of One Woman," *New York Times*, June 16, 1993: CD15. For University of Southern California sociologist Edward J.W. Park, the "multiple conflicts" on display in the event that Smith dramatized "marked the transition of the United States from a biracial to a multiracial society" (Park quoted in Todd S. Purdum, "Legacy of Los Angeles Riots: Divisions Amid the Renewal," *New York Times*, April 27, 1997: 1).

36. "More than Black and White," *New York Times*, June 20, 2003: A22.

37. Christopher Edley Jr., "Foreword," in *Twenty-First Century Color Lines: Multiracial Change in Contemporary America*, ed. Andrew Grant-Thomas and Gary Orfield (Philadelphia: Temple University Press, 2009), x.

38. Gary Orfield, "Conclusion: Color Lines, the New Society, and the Responsibility of Scholars," in *Twenty-First Century Color Lines*, 302, 293.

39. Orfield, 302, 294.

40. Edley, ix.

Index

Denman, William, 83
desegregation (of schools), 6, 12, 55, 58–88
  and bilingual education, 12, 88, 228–56
"Desegregation and the Education Concerns of the Hispanic Community," 254
Despol, John, 138
Dettering, Richard, 25–26, 123
Donnelly, Hugh P., 38
Donnelly Committee on Japanese Resettlement, 38, 49
Douglas, William, 47, 242, 251, 253
DuBois, W.E.B., 264
Dutton, Fred, 165–67, 189, 217, 226
Duveneck, Josephine, 22–26, 123, 128, 139
Dymally, Mervyn, 238–39, 248

East/West: The Chinese-American Journal, 240, 245
Eastside Journal, 219
Edley, Christopher, Jr., 263
Edmonds, Douglas, 41, 50, 113
Eisenhower, Dwight, 140
El Espectador, 63
El Modena School District, 66, 70, 72–73, 76–77
El Modena Unity League, 77
El Modena's Lincoln School, 70
Emancipation Proclamation, 177
Employment discrimination. *See* fair employment practices
Engle, Clair, 188
Equal Employment Opportunity Commission (EEOC), 231, 258
Evans, Rowland, 220
Executive Order 8802, 115
Executive Order 9066, 33
Executive Order 13050, 259
Exelrod, Alan, 241, 249

Fair Employment Practice Commission Movement, 115

fair employment practices, 5, 10, 11, 18–20, 115–22, 129–31, 136–40, 160, 199
  California Committee for Fair Employment Practices (CCFEP), 130–31, 136–39, 158, 160–61, 166, 168
  Commission (FEPC), 7–8, 116, 161, 165, 167, 172, 177, 180, 192, 198, 209
  CSO and, 132–35, 138, 167
  JACL and, 57, 131–2
fair housing, 140–46, 157–88. *See also* housing discrimination, Proposition 14, Rumford Fair Housing Act
Fair Racial Practice Act, 12, 28
Faragher, John Mack, 14
farm labor. *See* agricultural labor
Farm Placement Bureau, 154
Farm Workers Association (FWA). *See* United Farm Workers
Father's Association, 62
Federal Housing Authority (FHA), 144
Federal Theatre Project troupe, 15
Ferriter, William, 288n124
Fertig, Fred, 102
First Filipino Infantry, 108
Fish and Game Commission, California, 49
Fisk University
  Monthly Summary of Events and Trends in Race Relations, 16
  Social Science Institute, 19
forced busing, 12, 236–38
Ford, John Anson, 177, 201
Fordham University, 125
Forster, Clifford, 103
Fortune magazine, 18
Fourteenth Amendment, 94, 97, 104, 194, 220, 222, 248, 257, 258
  Equal Protection Clause, 81, 105, 249–51
Frankfurter, Felix, 121–22, 235, 289n140
Franklin, John Hope, 259, 260
"Freedom of Choice" initiative, 127–29

Steinman, Ed, 245–53
Stephens, Albert Lee, 81
Stilwell, Joseph, 42
Sugar Hill cases, 95, 97
Sugrue, Thomas J., 13, 274–75*n*44, 277*n*51
Swing, Joseph, 152

Tajiri, Larry, 28, 30, 38, 54, 92, 102
Takaki, Ronald, 259, 347*n*11
Taketa, Henry, 23–24
Tanabe, Eiji, 102
Tang, Scott, 275*n*49, 315*n*92
*Tarao Takahashi v. Fish and Game
    Commission*, 49–52, 55, 102,
    106–107, 114, 117, 124. *See also*
    commercial fishing licenses in
    ocean waters for aliens ineligible for
    citizenship
Taylor, Quintard, 277*n*52
Tenney, Jack, 42, 118, 128–29
Texas Office of the Attorney General, 77
Theoharis, Jeanne, 274–75*n*44
Thomas, Prentice, 90
Tieburg, Albert, 212–14
Tijerina, Pete, 231
Time Magazine, 190
Traynor, Roger, 41, 50, 110–12, 122
Truman, Harry, 149
    Commission on Migratory Labor,
    318*n*150
Tushnet, Mark, 270*n*23

UCLA, 162
Ulibarri, Horatio, 232
unemployment insurance for agricultural
    labor, 11, 158, 167–69, 185–87
United Farm Workers Organizing
    Committee. *See* United Farm Workers
United Farm Workers, 127, 184–86
United Republicans of California, 195, 200
United States Commission on Civil
    Rights, 164–65, 172, 244
Unity Leagues, 58–59, 64, 86, 117
University of California Regents v. Bakke,
    6, 257–59

University of California, 74, 95, 100, 110,
    179, 257–59
    Davis medical school, 6, 257–59
University of New Mexico, 232
University of Redlands, 18
Unruh, Jesse Marvin, 162, 176, 182,
    188–89, 195, 206, 327*n*146
Unruh Civil Rights Act, 162–64, 173,
    174–76, 204, 223

Vargas, Alex, 175, 176
Vargas, Zaragosa, 272*n*24
Vargas v. Hampson, 325*n*120
Varzally, Allison, 276*n*50
Vasey, Beach, 83, 84, 116
Veteran's Authority (VA) financing, 144
Vidaurri, Soledad, 62
Vinson, Fred, 46
"Viva Reagan" clubs, 225

Wang, Ling-chi, 245, 252
Wakefield, Floyd, 237, 248
WALK, 243
Wall Street Journal, 158, 241
Wallace, George, 190
Ward v. Flood, 294*n*39
Warren, Earl, 17, 18, 20–21, 36, 39, 42, 60,
    83, 85, 105, 107, 114, 116, 132, 140, 179
Warschaw, Carmen, 200
Washington Post, 48
Ways and Means Committee (of the
    California Assembly), 163
Webb, Ulysses S., 34, 65
Wedemeyer, J.M., 169
Weigel, Stanley, 239–40, 242, 244, 343*n*80
Weinberger, Caspar, 196
West, Elliott, 13
Western Association of Reform Rabbis, 197
*Westminster School District of Orange
    County v. Mendez. See Mendez
    v. Westminster School District of
    Orange County*
wetbacks, 149–53
White, Richard, 13
White, Walter, 96, 120, 128